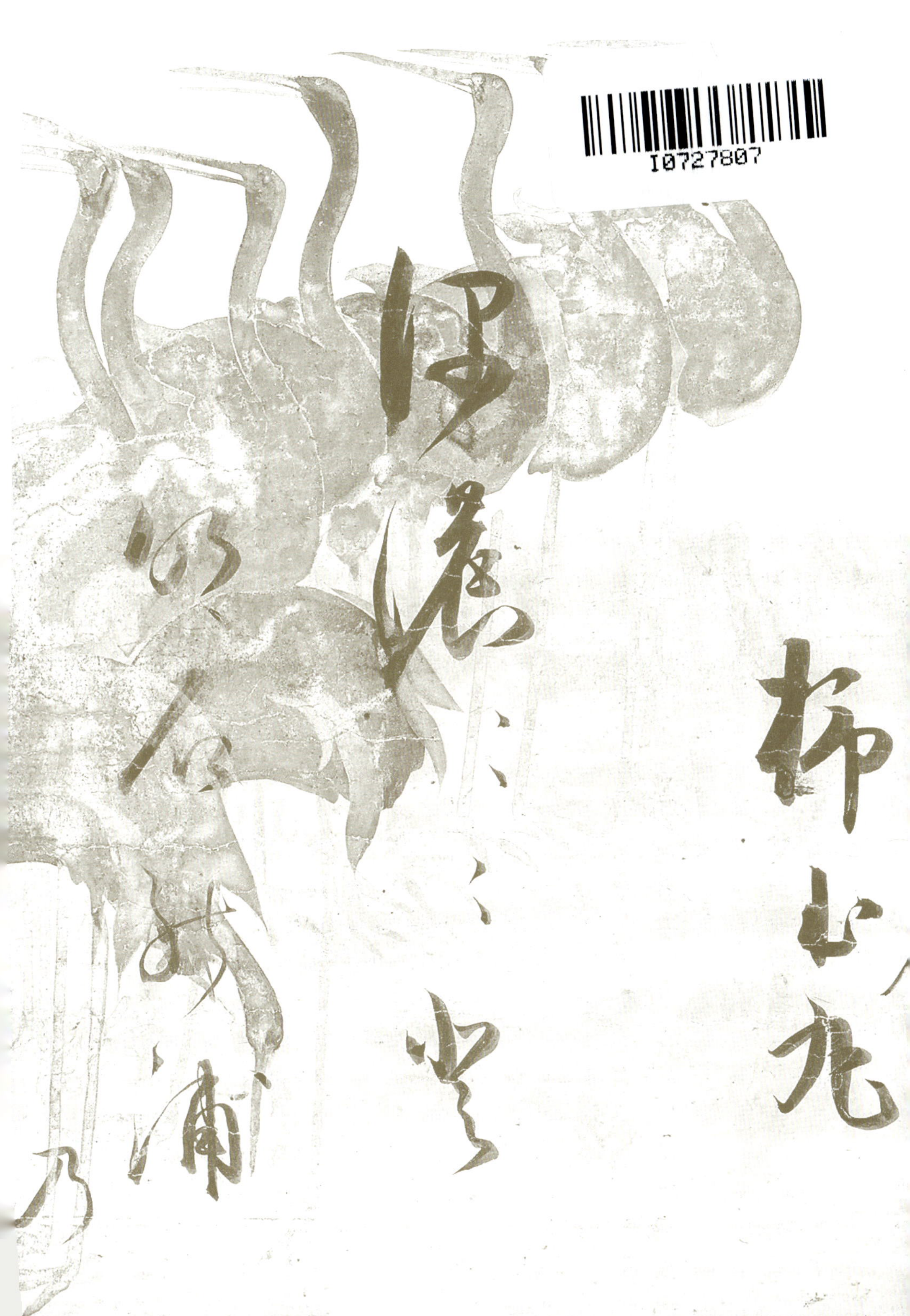
柿山伏

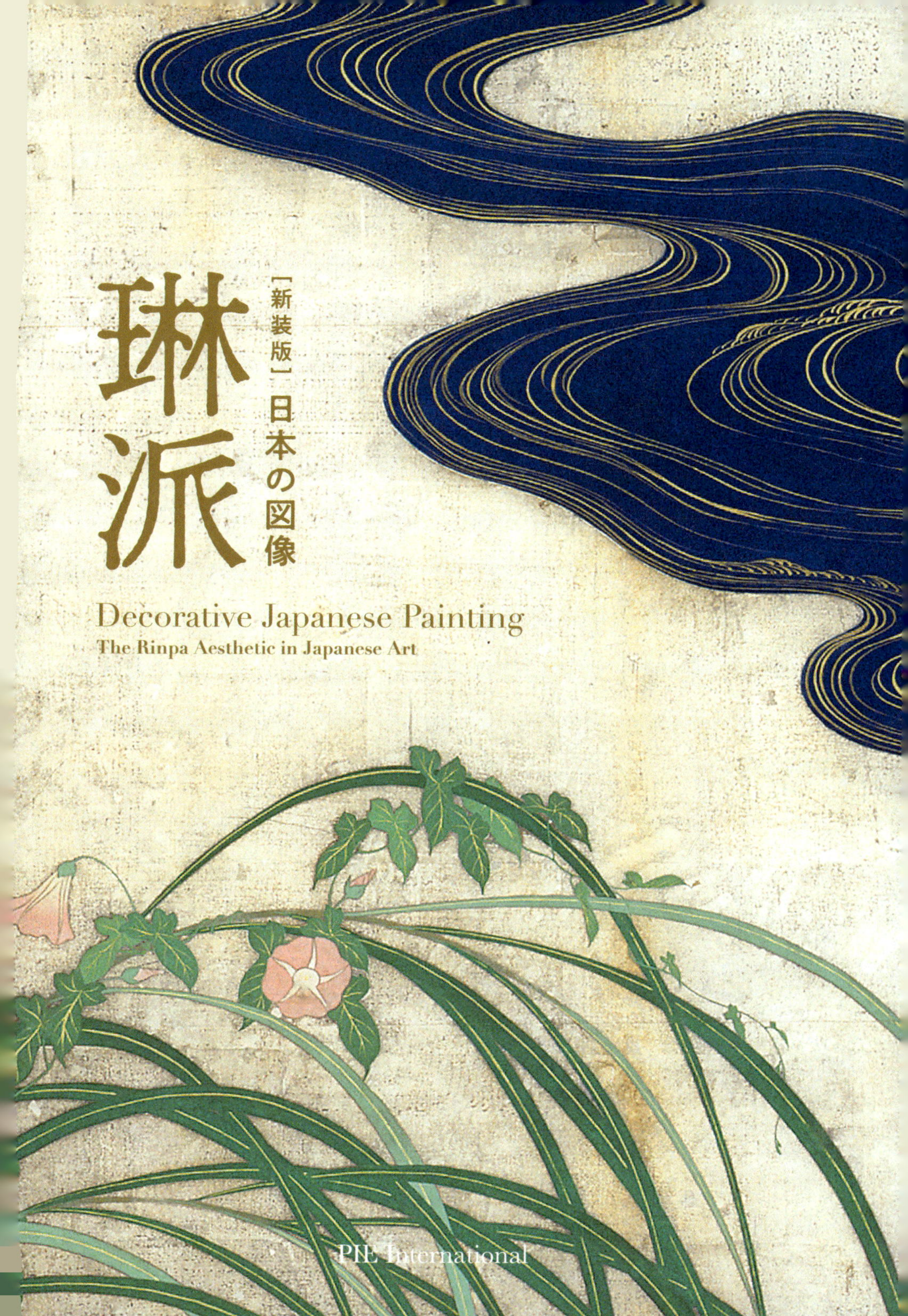

琳派

Decorative Japanese Painting
The Rinpa Aesthetic in Japanese Art

PIE International

目次 *Table of Contents*

はじめに

　琳派は尾形光琳の「琳」をとって名づけられた呼称で、京都を中心に、桃山時代末期の本阿弥光悦、俵屋宗達に始まり、江戸時代中期に活躍した尾形光琳、乾山の兄弟に受け継がれ、江戸時代末期の酒井抱一にいたる系譜である。

　まさにその時代は徳川幕府の草創期でもあり、政治や経済の中心が江戸に移り、江戸文化という新たな潮流が渦巻き始めようとしていた。

　そして京都ではこの武家政権に対して、後水尾天皇を中心とする宮廷文化人や、王朝文化の復興をめざし伝統文化を守る京都の裕福な町衆が琳派芸術の創造の舞台を生み出した時期であると考えられる。

　慶長年間から安政年間（17世紀初期から19世紀中頃まで）のおおよそ350年に渡る琳派の系譜は、光悦、宗達から光琳までが約百年をへだて、さらに光琳から抱一までの間に百余年の時が流れている。それでは何故このような隔世の師を求めながら琳派という芸術様式の継承がなされたのであろうか。

　それは高尚な和風趣味を通して創作された琳派が、日本人の心の根底に流れている純粋な芸術表現だったからであろう。そして最近では海外においても評価が高まっていることは、琳派こそ日本的な優美さと豪華さを美の世界に昇華させた最たるものであると認識されたからである。

　琳派は絵画のみならず、陶芸、漆工、染織などの幅広い工芸の分野にも自由な装飾的造形を展開し、新たな意匠の世界を創造した。光悦は「寛永の三筆」といわれたほど書家として優れ、また陶芸家としても格調の高い楽茶碗をつくった。光琳は蒔絵硯箱などの漆芸の世界にも才を現し、弟の乾山と共に陶芸にも携わった。

　このような琳派の画家たちの工芸への進出はこれ以降も琳派の体質として受け継がれていき、その後の酒井抱一や、近代琳派の神坂雪佳、洋画家の浅井忠の作品の中にも琳派の本質が息づいている。

　本書では琳派の誕生からその後の展開、開花、そして近代における転生までを、主要な作家たちの代表的な作品を通して紹介する。

　琳派芸術の大胆にして繊細な画面構成、そして軽快でリズミカルな意匠デザインが優しく眼に写るだろう。そしてこの感覚が日本人の最も好む美的感覚であることに間違いはない。

Introduction

While the name Rinpa derives from the "rin" in Ogata Korin, the style originated in the late Momoyama period with Hon'ami Kōetsu and Tawaraya Sotatsu. Originally a Kyoto movement, it was continued in the mid Edo period by Ogata Korin and his brother Kenzan and in late Edo by Sakai Hōitsu.

The rise of the Rinpa style thus overlaps closely with the inauguration of the Tokugawa bakufu, with the transfer of political and economic power to Edo and the efflorescence of a new culture there.

In Kyoto, in response to the establishment of a warrior government in Edo, the Emperor Go-Mizuno was the center of an effort by courtiers, literati, and wealthy townsmen to revive and preserve the traditional court culture that had flourished during the Heian period. That drive set the stage for the creation of the Rinpa style.

The Rinpa lineage spans about 350 years, from the early sixteenth to the mid nineteenth centuries. The transmission from Kōetsu and Sotatsu to Korin covers about a century. More than another century passed between the time of Korin and Hōitsu. For some reason, the transmission of the Rinpa style always seems to skip a generation, yet continue unwaveringly.

Its resilience may be derived from its roots in the Japanese soul. Rinpa is the quintessential Japanese style--but not exclusively Japanese, for it has won great acclaim abroad as well. Indeed, Rinpa is recognized as the most sublime expression of a very Japanese aesthetic of gorgeous elegance.

Rinpa is not a style confined to painting. It has created a world of innovative design in ceramics, lacquerware, textiles, and other craft arts. Kōetsu himself was a calligrapher—in fact, was regarded as one of the three great calligraphers of his age—and also created superb Raku tea bowls. Korin lent his talents to the craft of lacquerware and also collaborated with his brother Kenzan in creating ceramics.

That involvement by Rinpa painters in the craft arts lived on as an essential aspect of the Rinpa school over the centuries, as the achievements of Sakai Hōitsu, Kamisaka Sekka, the star of modern Rinpa, and the Rinpa-influenced Western-style artist Asai Chu all demonstrate.

This book explores the history of the Rinpa style through masterworks created by its leading exemplars, from the birth of the style through its subsequent development and rebirth in modern times. The bold yet delicate compositions of Rinpa paintings and their deft, rhythmic designs delight the eye and nourish the soul; we invite you to share that very Japanese experience.

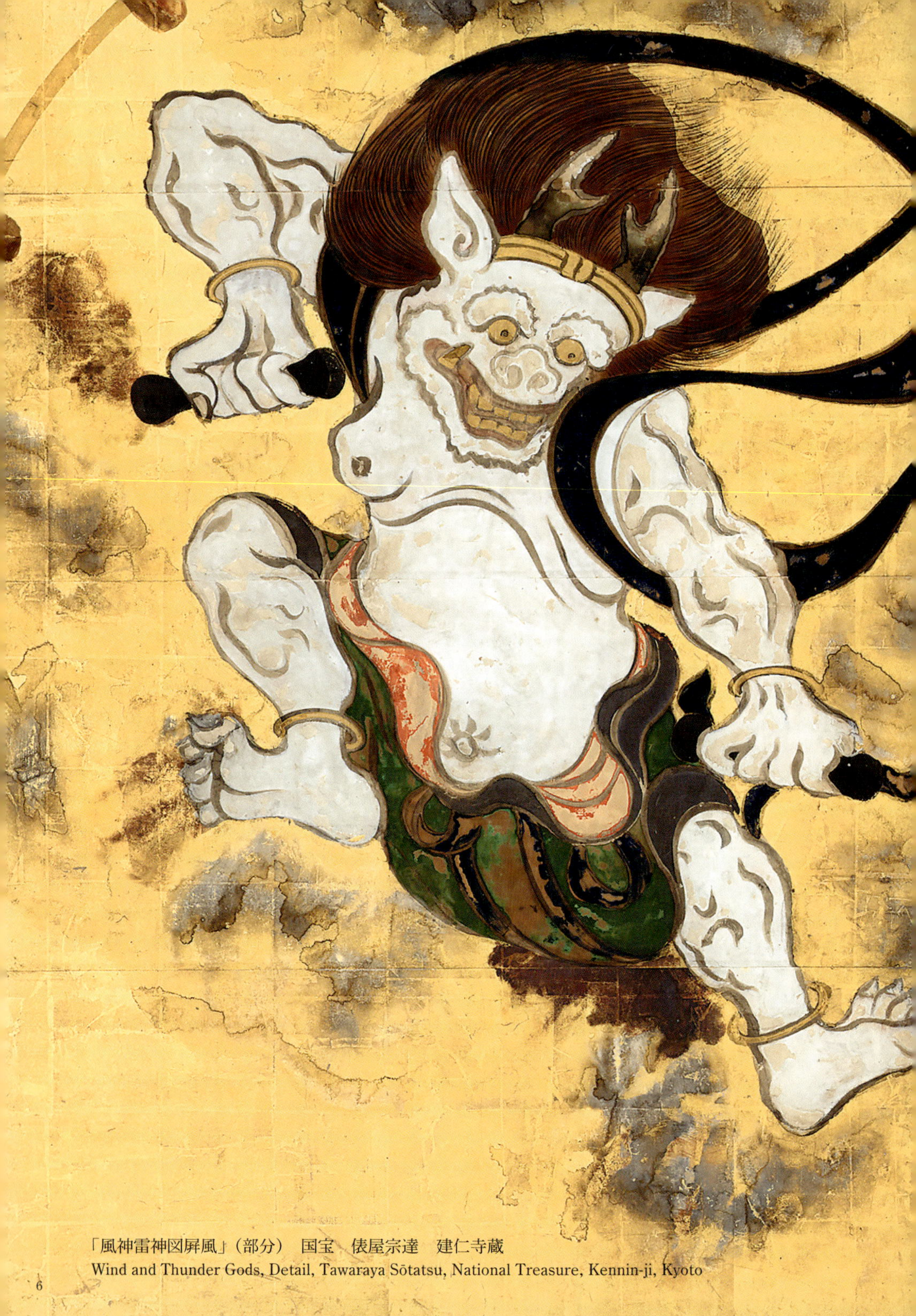

「風神雷神図屏風」（部分）　国宝　俵屋宗達　建仁寺蔵
Wind and Thunder Gods, Detail, Tawaraya Sōtatsu, National Treasure, Kennin-ji, Kyoto

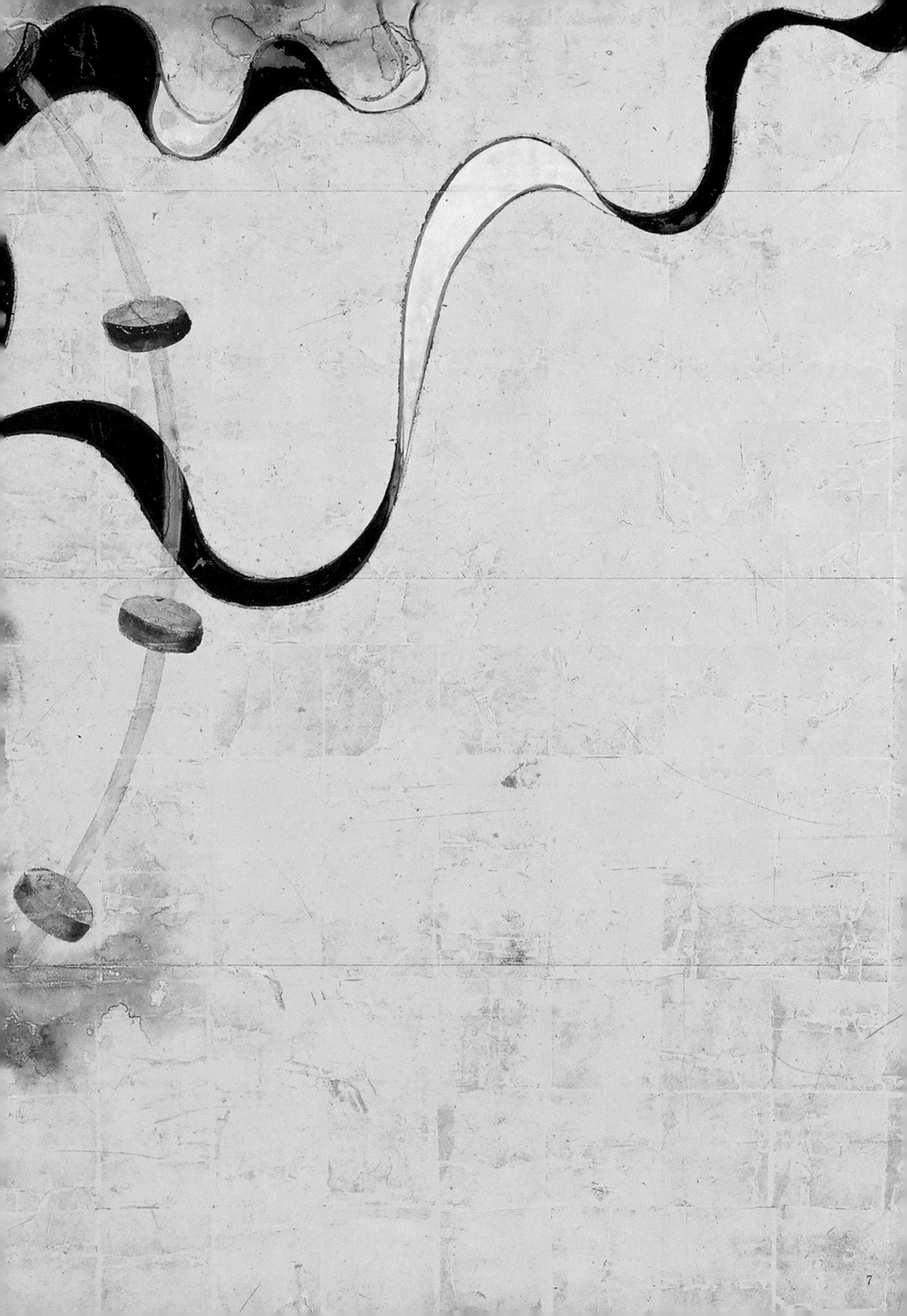

琳派――装飾への感性を刺激し続けるもの

安村 敏信（北斎館館長）

　日本人の装飾に対する好みは、平安朝の長い鎖国の間に熟成され、金銀や雲母による料紙装飾や、つくり絵と呼ばれる色彩豊かなやまと絵などに代表される優美な王朝文化として結実した。その伝統は中世を通じて継承され、桃山時代にはその装飾感覚が豪壮な城郭建築の空間に開放され、金碧障屏画を舞台として、この世に弥勒の浄土を出現させた。

　この桃山の余光を受け、京都の富裕な町衆たちは王朝貴族の文化の復興を図った。その造形面での中心となったのが本阿弥光悦（1588〜1637）である。光悦は刀剣の目利を家業とするかたわら、能書家として活躍し、角倉素庵と企てた典雅な装幀の嵯峨本に光悦流の書を提供したり、流麗な金銀泥下絵の料紙に和歌をしたためたりして、王朝の芳潤な香を書芸術の中に復興した。

　また、元和元年（1615）、徳川家康より洛北鷹峰に拝領した土地に、法華長者や職人を集めて光悦村というべきものを作り上げ、作陶に専念したり、工芸品にアイデアを提供するなどして、芸術三昧の日々を送った。

　先の嵯峨本や光悦和歌などに豪華で美しい下絵を提供したのが、京都で俵屋という絵屋工房を主宰する俵屋宗達（生没年不祥）であった。宗達は、慶長7年（1602）、平家納経の修理に携わり、表紙や見返しに金銀泥のすぐれたデザイン感覚による装飾画を描いた。

　その後、光悦の書と金銀泥下絵の競演を繰り返して、色紙や扇面に極彩色の物語絵などを描いていたが、元和7年（1621）再建の養源院の襖絵と杉戸絵を描くことになった。下絵画工から本格的な画家への転身である。これは、金碧の襖にやまと絵の巨大な松と岩を描いた襖絵で、桃山期に流行した狩野派らの漢画による金碧障壁画に対し、やまと絵で対抗した意欲作だ。とりわけ、杉戸に彫塗り技法（線の周辺を彩色する手法）で描かれた唐獅子や白象は、宗達の大らかな造形感覚にあふれた傑作となっている。

　これらの障壁画に落款はないが、宗達作品の中でもう一つ落款のない代表作がある。「風神雷神図屏風」（建仁寺）である。二曲一双の色紙に似た正方形に近い金碧屏風に描かれた本図は、養源院杉戸絵同様彫塗り技法で風雷神が描かれている。しかも、白象図が画面からはみ出さんばかりの膨張性をもち、大らかな気分であるのと同様、風雷神も各々画面の端からはみ出しており、大らかな空間性を持っている。

この作品の制作期は、養源院以後法橋叙任以前に置くべきだろう。従来の説では最高傑作は最晩年に描かれたとして、晩年に位置づけている。また大正期の伝聞によって、この屏風が妙光寺にあったとし、同寺再興の打它公軌が注文したという推論も提出されているが、全く確証がない。

　この宗達は遅くとも寛永7年（1630）までには法橋に叙任されている。それ以後の「松島図屏風」「雲龍図屏風」などの大らかな気分の六曲一双屏風には法橋宗達の落款を晴れがましく入れている。ところが寛永8年に制作された「関屋澪標図屏風」になると、景物や人物の配置に構成的要素が強くなる。二曲一双の「舞楽図屏風」に至っては、もはや「風神雷神図屏風」の天空を駆けぬけるような大らかさを失い、左右の端を火焔太鼓と松で堰止め、あいた空間に舞人を配し、舞人の形と色を理知的に構成してゆく。寛永期の幾可学的構図様式の流行に敏感に呼応した宗達晩年の冷く堅い造形感覚がうかがえる。

　一方、水墨画の世界においても宗達は画期的な画風を作りあげた。「蓮池水禽図」に代表される没骨描を主体とし、たらし込みという薄い墨が乾く前に濃墨をたらし、墨のにじみむらをつくる技法を用いて、面的な広がりを持ちながらボリューム感を出す独特の水墨画である。これは水墨画から線の要素を取り除き、和風化された墨絵に仕上げたものといってよい。この水墨画の和様化と、彩色画におけるやまと絵の復興こそ、宗達の果した重要な役割であり、その際にあみ出したたらし込み技法が、後の琳派の画家達に受け継がれてゆく重要な技法であった。

　宗達の俵屋工房は、「蔦の細道図屏風」を描いた斬新なデザイン感覚を持つ画工も抱えていたが、この工房を継いだのは俵屋宗雪であった。宗雪は草花を金地に並列的に美しく配置する手法で人気を得、同時代の喜多川相説も草花図を得意とし、俵屋工房の装飾的草花図が一世を風靡した感がある。この俵屋工房には国春という女性画家や「鬼との首引き」を描くのどかな画家も出て、江戸中期まで続いたようだ。

　京都の裕福な呉服商雁金屋の次男に、尾形光琳（1658〜1716）が生まれた。京都町衆の掉尾を飾る雁金屋の次男は、若くして能や遊蕩にふけったが、30代終わりの頃、とうとう遺産も使い果たし、画家として身を立てる決心をする。当初手ほどきを受けていた狩野派では独立することはむずかしく、俵屋工房で流行していた草花図の路線を引き継ぐことを決めた。まずは法橋位をもらうため、二条家へ出入り

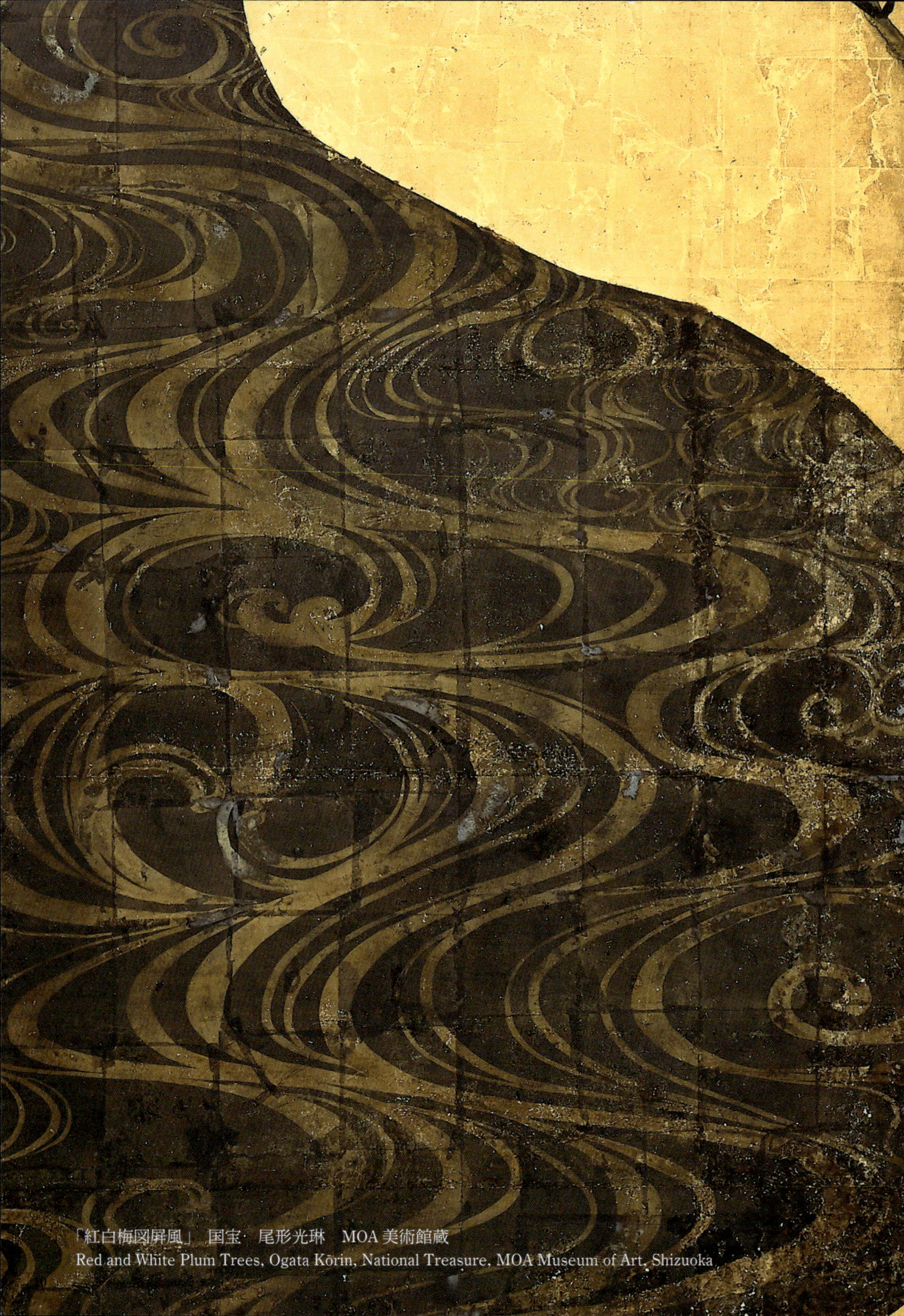

「紅白梅図屏風」　国宝・尾形光琳　MOA 美術館蔵
Red and White Plum Trees, Ogata Kōrin, National Treasure, MOA Museum of Art, Shizuoka

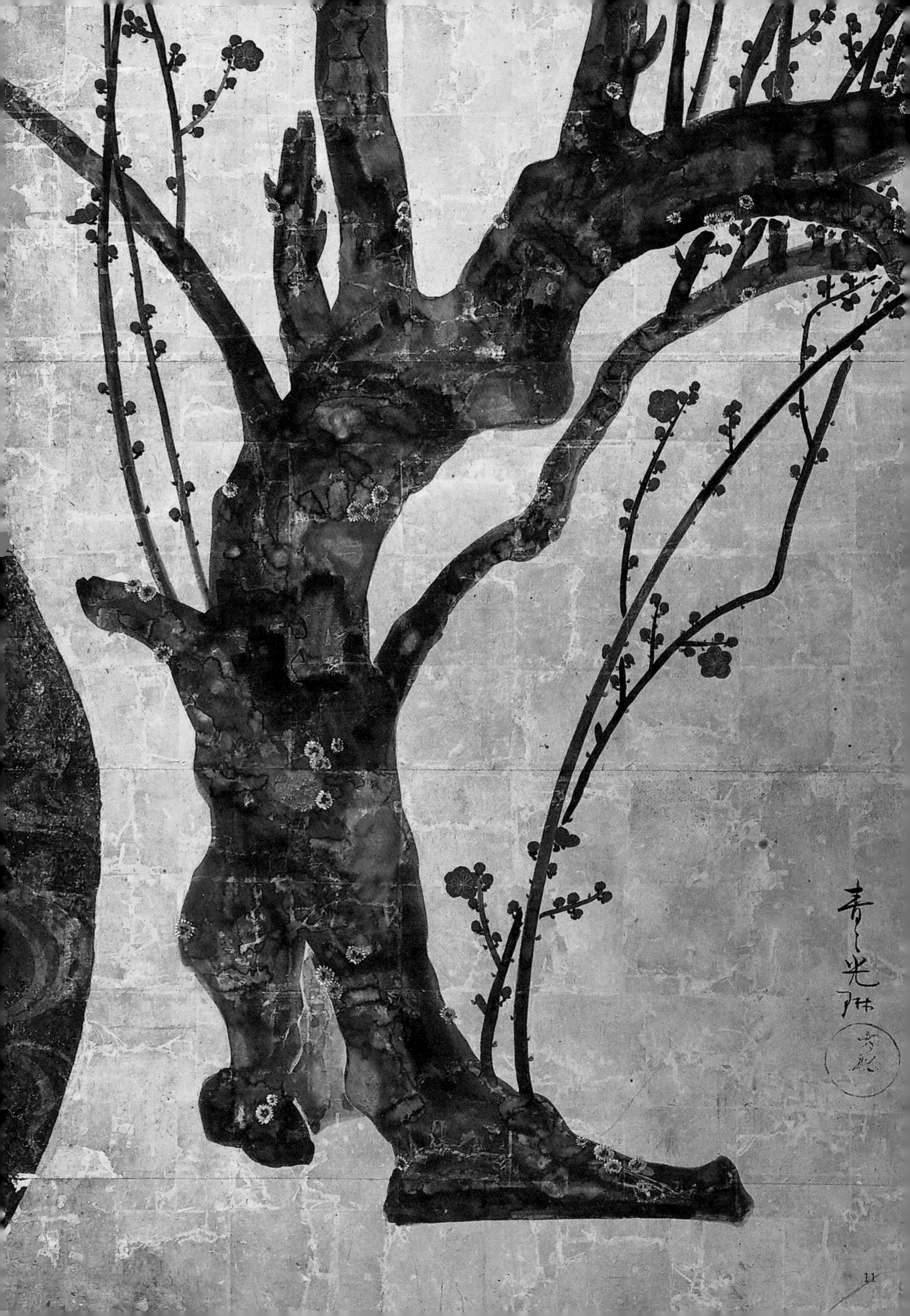

し、元禄 14 年（1701）44 歳で法橋に叙任された。その後間もなく、俵屋工房とは全く異なる草花図「燕子花図屏風」を描き法橋光琳の名を入れた。これは型紙を使って燕子花の群生を繰り返すことにより、金地にリズミカルな空間を生み出そうとしたデザイン屏風の力作であった。しかし、京都の教養豊かな町衆たちには単なるデザインの奇抜さだけでは受け入れられなかったとみえる。

その後光琳はたらし込み技法を取り入れ、中国の古典に取材した「太公望図屏風」や「白楽天図屏風」を描き、燕子花に八橋を加えて『伊勢物語』の世界を明快に表現した「八橋図屏風」を描いて、教養豊かな町衆の需要にこたえた。しかし、町衆の衰退を受け、新たなパトロンを求めて 47 歳から 5 年ほど江戸に下った。江戸では材木商冬木家の知遇を得、また姫路藩のお抱え絵師ともなったが、宮仕えや江戸の生活になじめず、52 歳で帰京した。

この江戸では、雪舟画や雪村画の模写を通して、輪郭線重視の水墨画様式に磨きをかけた。光琳の水墨画は「竹梅図屏風」や「維摩図」に代表されるように線に頼ったもので、宗達が達成した水墨画の和様化など眼中にない。

光琳はまた、「波濤図屏風」のように波という単一の景物を描きながらも、そそり立つ波や襲いかかる大波を対比させて群青を刷くことにより、ほの暗い鬱屈した心象風景を覗き見させる作品も描いており、楽天的な宗達とは明確な違いを見せている。

光琳が宗達との違いを自覚したのは宗達の「風神雷神図屏風」「松島図屏風」「槇楓図屏風」の模写的作品を依頼されたことによる。三作とも正確な模写を頼まれたのではなく、宗達を超える変形を求められたようだが、どうも自身の体質と合わず、あまり成功したとはいえない。

こうした作風変遷を経て、光琳が最後に到達したのが「紅白梅図屏風」の世界である。その水流には銀箔が酸化したかに見えるだましの手法が使われており、水の荒い流れに自らの暗い情念が込められている。またデザイン化された水流は後の光琳模様を生み出す。工芸的手法を用いながら、絵画の世界に高めたこの傑作は光琳のデザイン屏風の窮極の成果であった。

光琳は一方で蒔絵や陶器にもデザインを提供し、それらの紋様は後に光琳の知らぬところで「光琳模様」の名を冠せられて大流行してゆく。

　光琳の弟乾山（1663～1743）は、陶芸の世界に没頭し、光琳の絵付をもらう一方で、オランダ写しのモダンな模様を試みたりしたが、基本的には文人趣味的な詩書画の世界を陶芸に展開した。

　京都で生まれ大坂に住んだ文人画家中村芳中（？～1819）は、木村蒹葭堂と親しく、また青木木米や池玉瀾とも交友し、指頭画を得意とした。この人がいつの頃からか、光琳に刺激され、たらし込みを多用した絵を描くようになった。芳中は寛政11年（1799）から3・4年江戸に滞在し、享和2年（1802）『光琳画譜』を江戸で出版した。書名に光琳と銘打ったものの、図は全く芳中風の丸味のあるのんびりとした造形で占められている。

　江戸に琳派を移植したのは酒井抱一（1761～1828）である。抱一は姫路藩主となる兄忠以の下に生まれ、酒井家嫡流から外されて俳諧や絵の世界に没頭していった。狩野派や南蘋派の手ほどきを受けながらも、自らは浮世絵師歌川豊春に私淑し、豊春風の美人図を描いていた。寛政後半頃から没骨法やたらし込み技法を使った草花図を描くようになり、四条派の影響も強く受けた。文化4年（1807）頃から光琳に関心を持ち始め、文化12年（1825）6月2日、遂に光琳百年忌を営み、光琳遺墨展を開催し、『光琳百図』『尾形流略印譜』を刊行した。この2年後に抱一は自らの画風を広めるために、『鶯村画譜』を刊行している。そこに見られる抱一画風は、光琳画の装飾性に刺激されながらも、俳諧的な軽みや、四条派風の平明さを加味した独自のものである。たらし込みも節度を保って使用される。

　文政4・5年（1821・22）頃の制作と判明した「夏秋草図屛風」は、抱一の代表作にふさわしい叙情性にあふれており、驟雨に首をたれる夏草や、野分に吹き飛ぶ紅葉した葉の「あはれ」を見事に表現している。

　抱一の弟子には鈴木其一、池田孤邨らの俊英が出た。とりわけ鈴木其一（1796～1858）は抱一の浮世絵風を受け継いだが、抱一の叙情性を排し、「椿に薄図屛風」（フリーア美術館）に代表される鋭敏な造形と近代的な視覚をもつ作品を作り出した。「夏秋渓流図屛風」などは視覚中枢を直接刺激して異様な感覚を見る者に与える作品だ。

　この其一の作品は近代に入ってから、菱田春草や速水御舟らに直接的な刺激を与え、琳派作品が近代日本画に強い影響を与えたことを物語っている。

　また、洋画家の浅井忠（1856～1907）はパリ滞在中に琳派を再発見し、帰国後、京都で工芸家たちに琳派風の図案を提供していった。

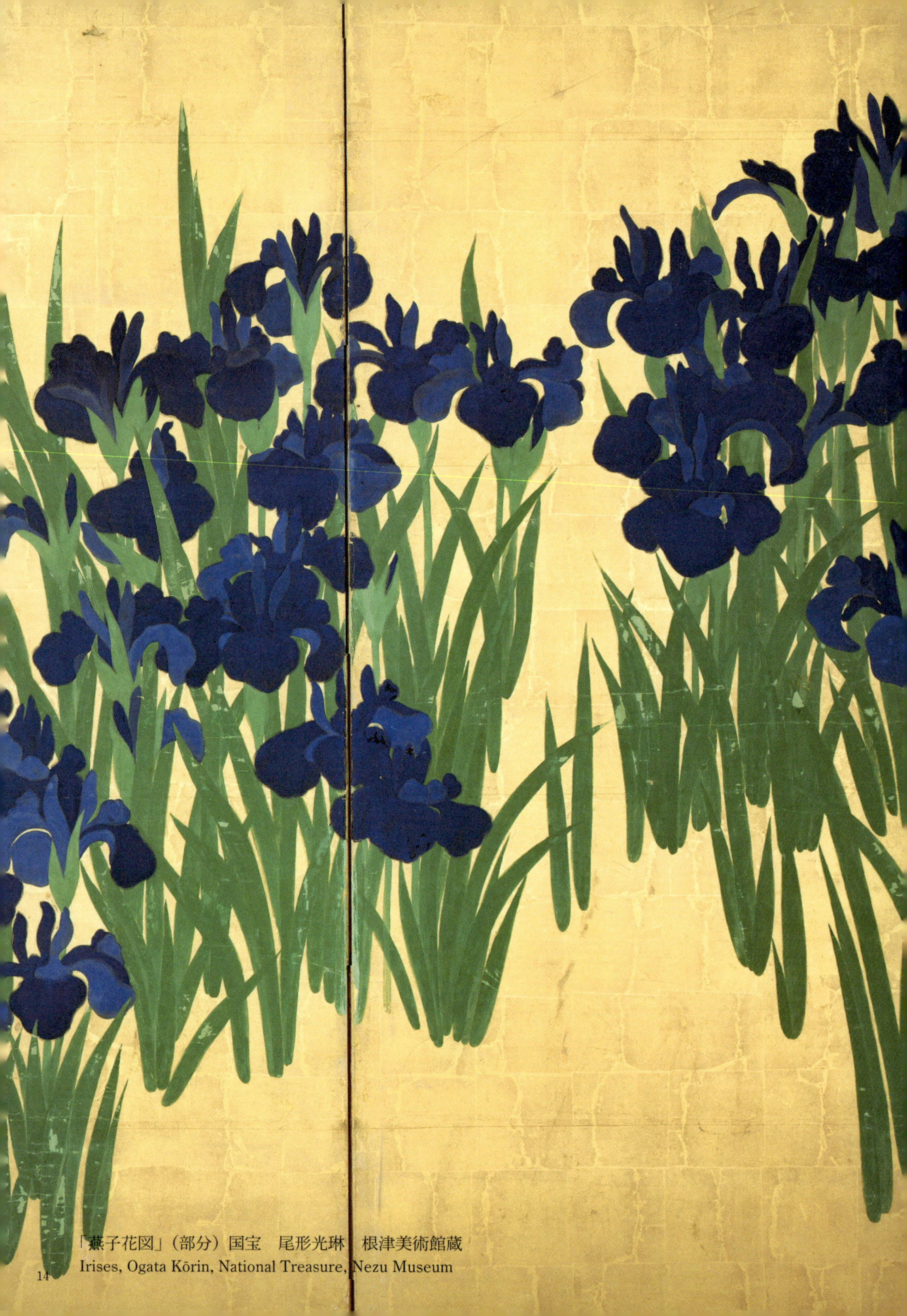

「燕子花図」（部分）国宝　尾形光琳　根津美術館蔵
Irises, Ogata Kōrin, National Treasure, Nezu Museum

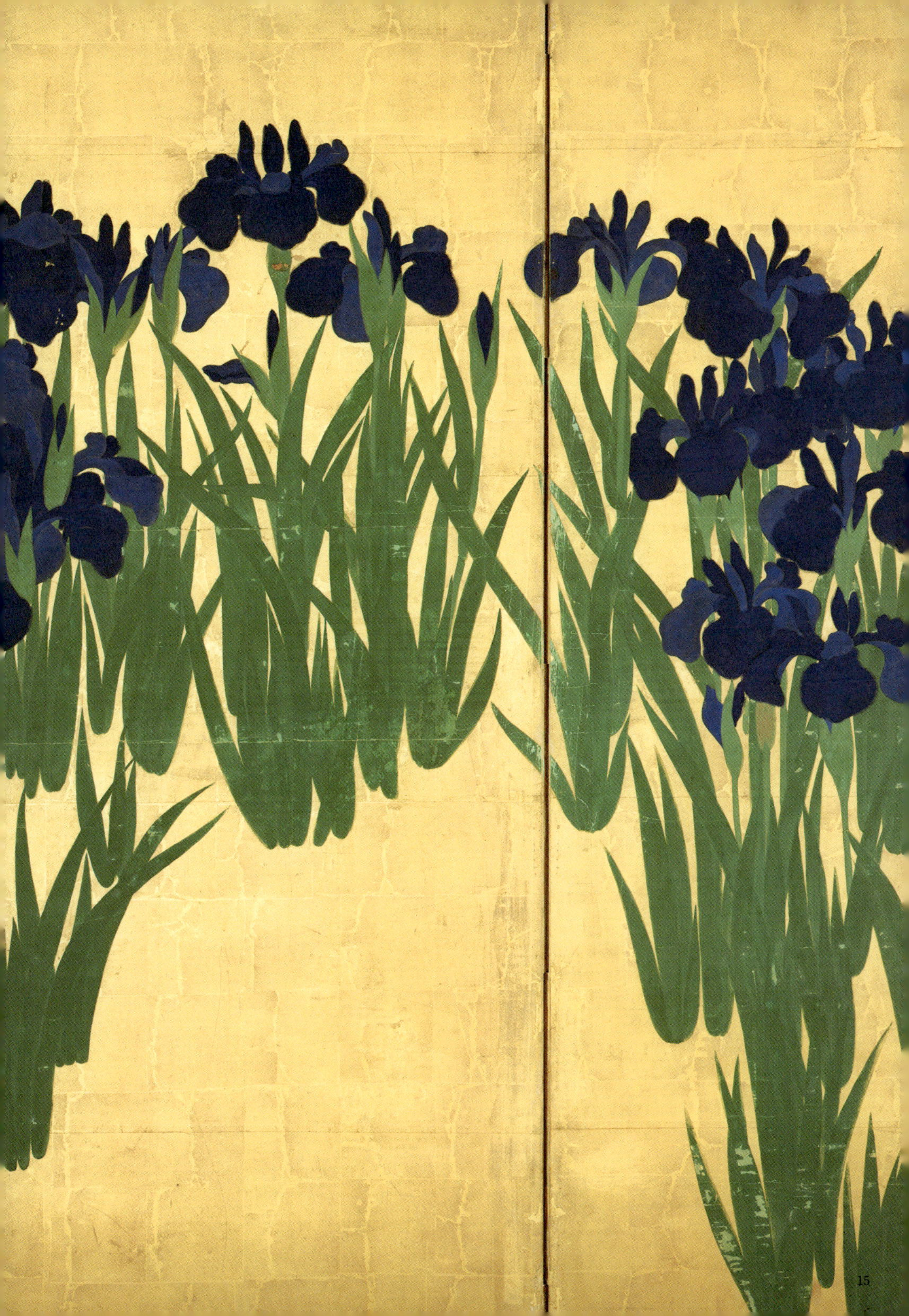

漆工家杉林古香に図案を与えて制作された「朝顔蒔絵手箱」などは、光悦や光琳の蒔絵手箱を近代に復興したものだ。

京都では神坂雪佳（1866〜1942）が出て、琳派の図案を大胆に翻案し、近代工芸に甦らせた。木版摺図案集『百々世草』は大胆なデフォルメによる形態の意匠化と色面構成の見事さで雪佳の最高傑作となっている。

昭和に入ってからも琳派は生き続け、様々な画家に影響を与えている。日本画家加山又造（1927〜2004）は「千羽鶴」（昭和45年）で波の線、鶴の群れの形、金銀の加飾すべてにおいて俵屋宗達への熱いオマージュを捧げているし、「雪月花」「春秋波濤」などの一連の装飾屏風は、琳派からの強い影響を受けて描かれている。

琳派の影響を受けたのは画家だけではない。戦後を代表するグラフィックデザイナーの田中一光（1930〜2002）は「JAPAN」において宗達による『平家納経』の願文見返しにある「鹿図」を現代のポスターデザインの中に甦らせた。

こうしたデザイン界への琳派の影響は国境を越え、ヨーロッパにも強い刺激を与えた。20世紀初頭のアール・ヌーヴォーに刺激を与えたことはよく知られているが、現代においても2001年、フランス・エルメス発行のブランドＰＲ誌「ル・モンド・エルメス」の表紙に、雪佳の『百々世草』の「八つ橋」が採用されて話題を呼んだ。

まさに、琳派の装飾感覚は、日本人のみならず、世界の装飾芸術に携わる人々の視神経を強烈に刺激し続けているのである。まさに琳派の感覚こそ、日本人が本質的に持つ装飾感覚のエッセンスを集約したものといえるだろう。

安村 敏信　やすむら・としのぶ
1953年富山県生まれ。東北大学大学院修士課程（日本美術史）修了。1979年より板橋区立美術館に勤務、2005〜13年まで同館館長を務める。現在、北斎館館長。江戸期を中心に、日本美術の魅力を伝えるユニークな企画展を多数開催している。『琳派美術館3　抱一と江戸琳派』（集英社）、『狩野探幽』（新潮社）、『日本の幽霊名画集』（人類文化社）、『美術館商売　美術なんて…と思う前に』（勉誠出版）、『すぐわかる画家別近世日本絵画の見かた』『もっと知りたい狩野派　探幽と江戸狩野派』『ワイドで楽しむ奇想の屏風』（以上東京美術）、『河鍋暁斎』『柴田是真』（以上平凡社「別冊太陽」／監修・共著）ほか著書多数。

Rinpa: Still Stimulating Our Decorative Senses

Yasumura Toshinobu Director, Hokusai Museum

The Japanese taste for the decorative, ripening during a long period of national introspection during the Heian period (806-1183), came to fruition in an elegant court culture exemplified by such riches as papers decorated in gold, silver, and mica, and colorful yamato-e paintings. That tradition, carried on through Japan's medieval period, was set free in the magnificent spaces of Momoyama period (1573-1615) castles. There paradises were created through wall, sliding door, and screen paintings, often on gold leaf backgrounds.

Inspired by the flowering of Momoyama culture, affluent Kyoto townspeople worked to revive the culture of the court and the aristocracy. A central figure in that effort was Hon'ami Kōetsu (1588-1637). While carrying on the family business as an appraiser of swords, Kōetsu was also a talented calligrapher who contributed calligraphy in the style that has been given his name to the sagabon, a series of literary classics, many set in moveable type, that he co-produced with Suminokura Soan. He also wrote waka poems on papers elegantly decorated in gold and silver pigments.

In 1615, Kōetsu founded an artists' community, gathering artists and craftsmen together on land in Takamine, in northern Kyoto, that Tokugawa Ieyasu had granted him. There he dedicated himself to the arts, creating pottery and providing ideas for other objects.

Tawaraya Sotatsu, who headed a painting studio, the Tawaraya, provided lavishly beautiful decorated papers for the sagabon and for Kōetsu's poems. In 1602, Sotatsu was engaged in the restoration of the Heike Nokyō, sutras that the Taira family had dedicated to Itsukushima Shrine. His paintings for the sutras' covers and endpapers, in gold and silver pigment, revealed a brilliant design sense.

Sotatsu subsequently collaborated extensively with Kōetsu, creating the papers for his calligraphy as well as richly colored narrative paintings on shikishi, squares of heavy paper used for writing poems, and fan papers. In time, he shifted from providing the materials for others' work to becoming a serious painter in his own right. The turning point was the large sliding door paintings (fusuma-e and sugido-e) he created for the Yogen'in temple, which was rebuilt in 1621. The fusuma-e in which he painted a huge pine and crag on a gold background on a fusuma in the yamato-e manner was an ambitious work that rivaled the Chinese-influenced, Kano-style wall, screen, and sliding door paintings on gold backgrounds popular during the Momoyama period. The lion and white elephant he depicted on the cedar sugido using the horinuri line and color wash technique are regarded as masterpieces.

The paintings for the Yogen'in are unsigned, as are another of Sotatsu's masterworks, the Wind God, Thunder God folding screens he created for the Kenninji temple. Each of this pair of double-fold screens is almost square, resembling shikishi poem papers, with gold backgrounds. The paintings of these gods use the same horinuri technique as in the Yogen'in cedar panels.

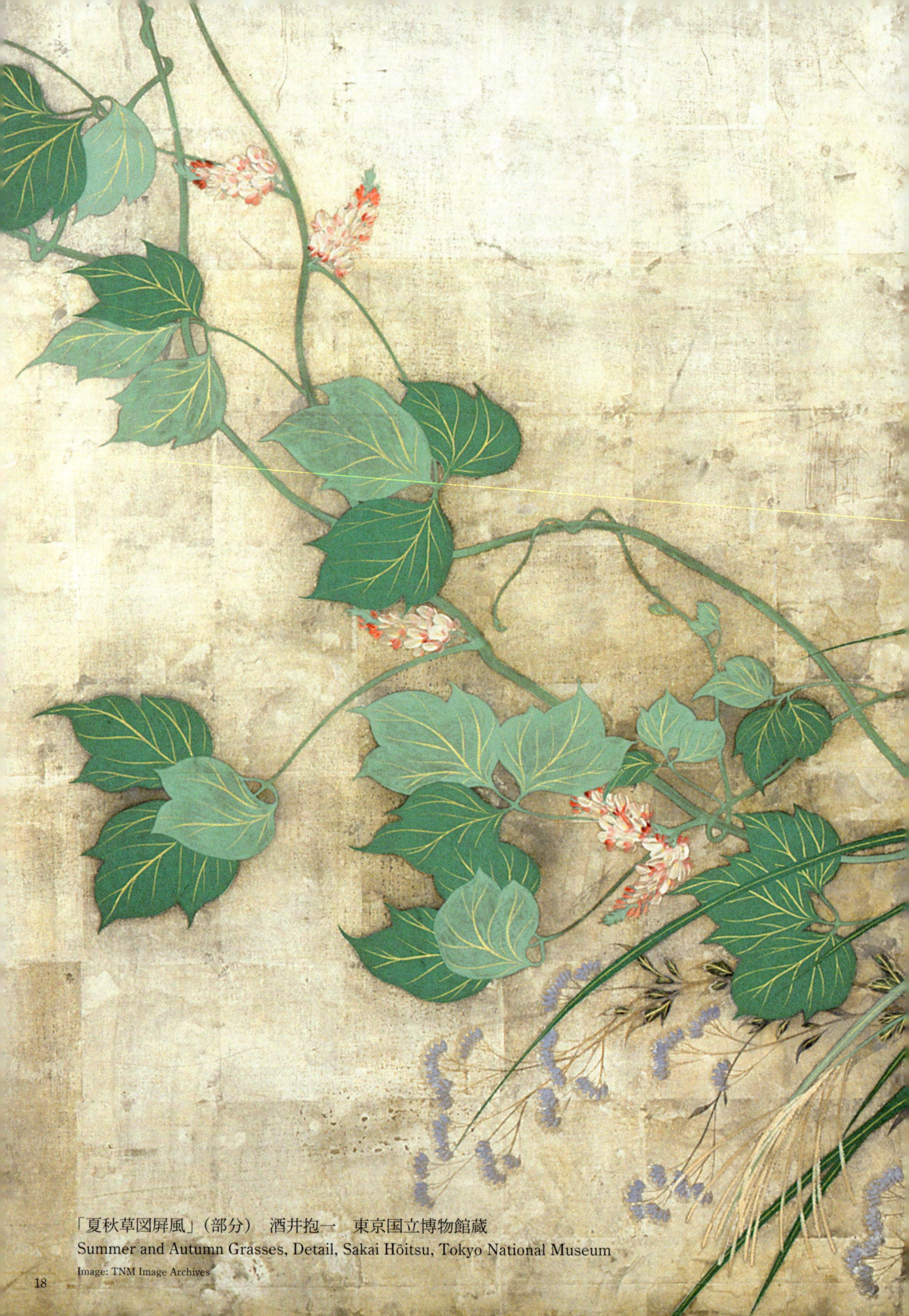

「夏秋草図屏風」（部分）　酒井抱一　東京国立博物館蔵
Summer and Autumn Grasses, Detail, Sakai Hōitsu, Tokyo National Museum

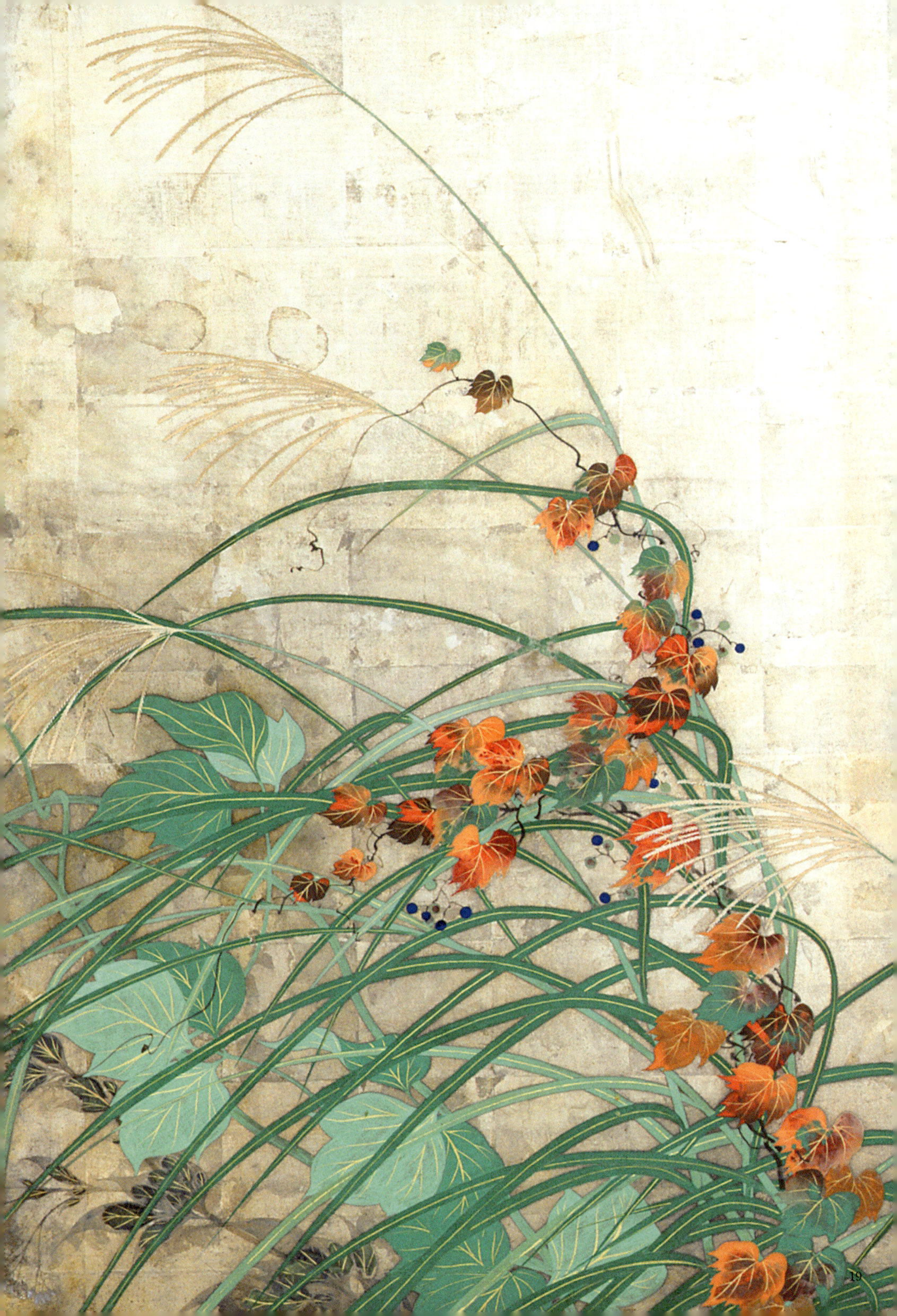

Moreover, just as the painting of the elephant seems almost to expand out of the picture plane, with a placid, generous feel, the wind and thunder gods both extend over the edges of their picture planes, creating a generous sense of space. This work probably dates from after the Yogen'in paintings but before Sotatsu was awarded the honorary artistic rank of hokkyō. (Since the conventional view is that he created his greatest work late in life, these screens had been positioned as from his late period.) A Taisho-era tale that the screens had been in Myokoji temple suggested that they might have been were ordered by Uda Kinnori when the temple was revived. That is, however, utterly unsubstantiated.

Sotatsu was granted hokkyō status by 1630 at the latest. Later work such as the Matsushima screens and the Cloud and Dragon screens, two pairs of imposing six-fold screens, are formally signed "Hokkyō Sōtatsu." In his 1631 Sekiya and Miotsukushi folding screens, on themes from the Tale of Genji, the compositional elements, the placement of the human figures and objects, has grown stronger. In the Bugaku Dancers pair of two-fold screens, however, the expansiveness of the Wind God, Thunder God folding screens, which seemed ready to leap into the sky, is gone; a flame drum (kaendaiko) and pine tree nail down the left and right ends of the pair of screens and the dancers are placed in the empty space available, their forms and coloring developed rather mechanically. Here we see the cold, rigid design sense of Sotatsu in his late period, swayed by the Kan'ei era fashion for geometric compositions.

Sotatsu also created a landmark style in the domain of ink painting. Using mokkotsu (depiction of objects without outlines) and tarashikomi (application of dark ink before pale ink has dried) technique that create diffusion and subtle gradations in the ink, he produced distinctive ink paintings that give a dense of volume while expanding in a planar fashion. By removing linear elements from ink painting, he achieved a distinctively Japanese style. Sotatsu thus played an important role in the domestication of ink painting and the revival of yamato-e style in paintings using pigments. The tarashikomi technique he devised is an important one that later Rinpa school painters continued to use.

Sotatsu's Tawaraya painting studio included talented painters with a fresh design sense, such as the creator of the Tsuta-no-hosomichi (Ivy lane) folding screens. It was, however, Tawaraya Sosetsu, who inherited the studio. Sosetsu became popular for his technique of painting grasses and flowers, arranged beautifully in rows, on a gold ground. Kitagawa Sosetsu, his contemporary, also excelled at paintings of grasses and flowers, and decorative Tawaraya studio paintings in that genre dominated their age. The studio continued in operation until the mid Edo period; its painters included Kuniharu, a noted woman artist, and the artist who painted the Oni-no-kubihiki (Demon tug of war) screen.

Ogata Kōrin (1658 – 1716) was born into a prosperous Kyoto textile merchant family who operated the Karigeneya. As the second son of one of the most successful of the Kyoto townsmen families, Kōrin spent his youth engaging in Noh and other pleasures, but in his late 30s, having finally used up his inheritance, he made a decision to establish himself as a painter. Since it would be difficult to become independent within the Kano school of painting, in which he had initially been trained, he decided to carry on the line of paintings of grasses and flowers that were then so popular at the Tawaraya studio. First, in order to acquire the honorary artistic rank of hokkyō, he cultivated the Nijō family; in 1701, at the age of 44, he was duly named hokkyō. Soon after, he created his Irises folding screens, a painting of grasses and flowers utterly unlike those that the Tawaraya studio was producing. By using a pattern to repeat the clumps of irises, he created a forceful work in which design seems to emerge rhythmically across the gold ground. The highly educated townsmen of Kyoto, however, were not receptive to merely unconventional design.

Thereafter Kōrin incorporated the tarashikomi method in painting his Taigong Wang and Bai Letian folding screens, which take their subjects from the Chinese classics, followed by his Eight-planked Bridge screens, in which he adds an eight-planked bridge to the irises in a clear reference to the world of the Tales of Ise. Those paintings satisfied the demands of cultivated Kyoto townsmen. With such townsmen in decline, however, he was forced to find a new patron, a project on which he spent about five years in Edo. There he was taken under the wing of the Fuyuki family of lumber merchants and then became employed as a painter by the Himeji domain. Unable to adjust to serving the Himeji daimyo and to life in Edo, he returned to Kyoto at the age of 52.

In Edo, by copying paintings by Sesshu and Sesson, he polished his skills in ink painting, in which outlines play a significant role. Kōrin's ink paintings, exemplified by his Bamboo and Plum folding screens and his painting of Yuima (Vimalakirti), relied on line and showed no sign of the Japanese transformation of ink painting that Sōtatsu had achieved.

As in his Waves folding screen, Kōrin also made effective of the blue gunjō pigment to create, in a scene on the single subject of waves, a contrast between towering waves and the even greater wave about to pass over them. He also created works that seem like glimpses into a melancholy internal landscape; there, too, he showed a clear difference from the optimistic Sotatsu.

Kōrin's s versions of Sotatsu's Wind God, Thunder God, Matsushima, and Black Pine and Maple Trees folding screens demonstrate the differences between Kōrin and Sotatsu. None are precise copies. Kōrin went beyond Sotatsu in altering forms, yet these versions did not seem to suit him and were not very successful.

Working through these changes in style, where Kōrin finally arrived was the world of his Red and White Plum Trees folding screens. He creates the illusion that the silver foil in the stream has been oxidized, pouring his own dark emotions into the rough flow of the stream. That stylized stream also led to one of the Kōrin Motifs popularized later. This masterpiece was Kōrin's ultimate success in screen painting, in which he used craft techniques but elevated the result to the world of fine art.

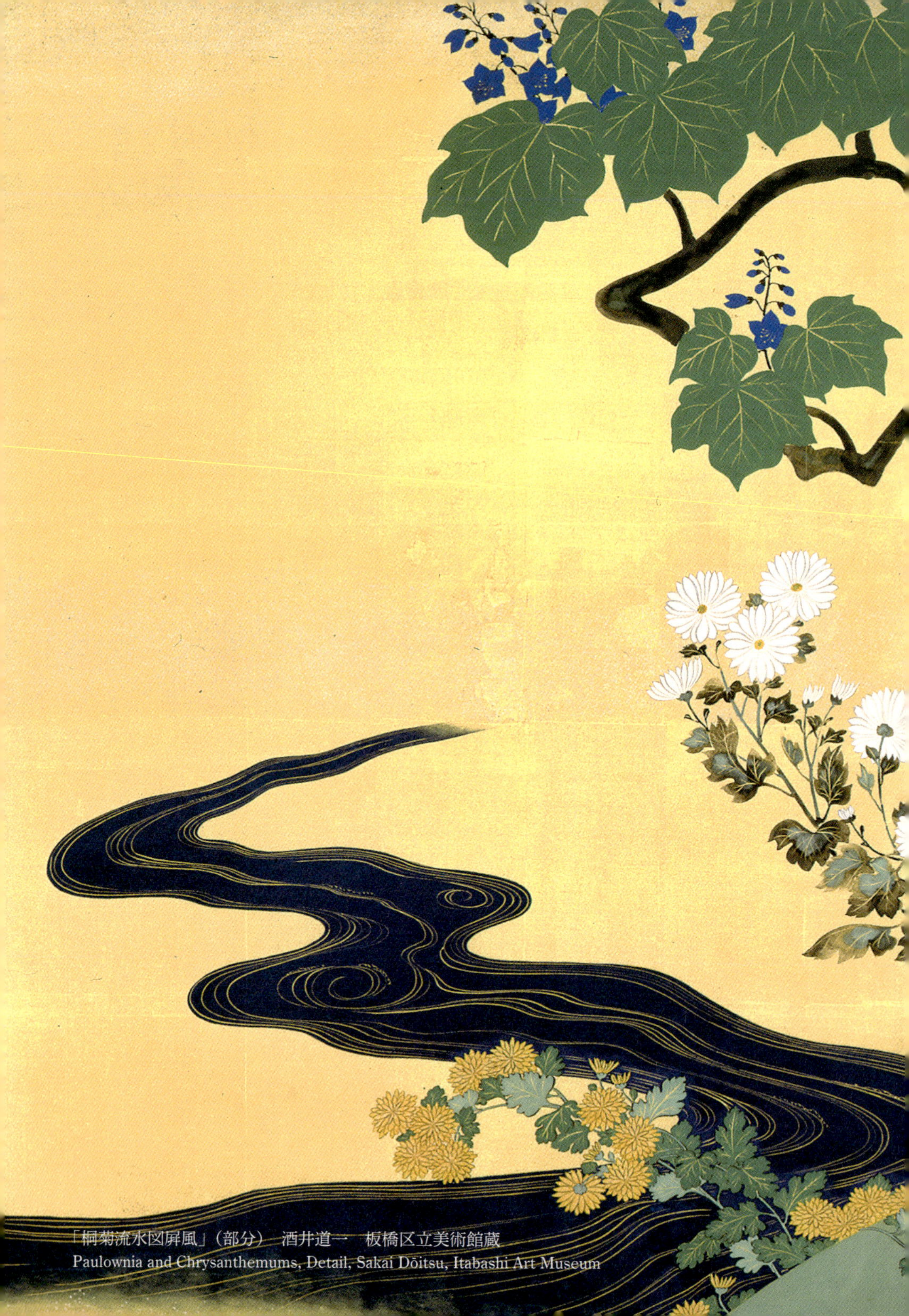

「桐菊流水図屏風」（部分）　酒井道一　板橋区立美術館蔵
Paulownia and Chrysanthemums, Detail, Sakai Dōitsu, Itabashi Art Museum

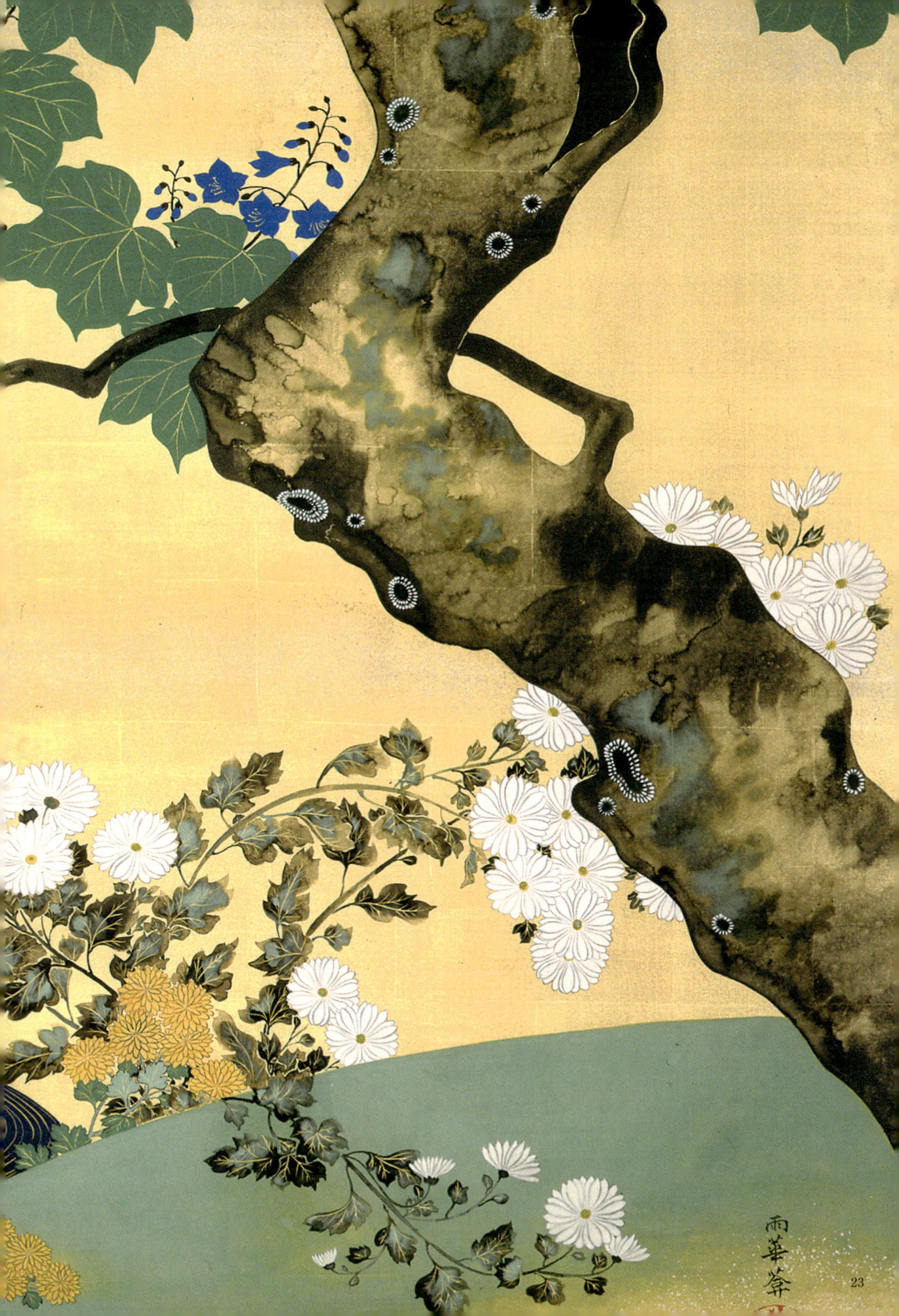

Kōrin also designed maki-e lacquerware and ceramics. The motifs he used later were named the Kōrin Motifs and became vastly popular.

Kōrin's younger brother, Kenzan (1663 – 1743) dedicated himself to pottery. He had Kōrin decorate some of his and also experimented with modern motifs copied from objects from the Netherlands, basically incorporating the literati world of poetry, calligraphy, and painting into the ceramic arts.

Nakamura Hochu, a literati painter who was born in Kyoto and resided in Osaka (– 1819) was on close terms with the literati painter Kimura Kenkadō and also acquainted with the potter Aoki Mokubei and the nanga painter Ikena Gyokuran. He is said to have excelled at ink painting with his fingertips. At some point, stimulated by Kōrin, he began producing paintings that made extensive use of the tarashikomi technique. Hochu spent three to four years in Edo, starting in 1799, and in 1802 published the Kōrin Gafu, an album of designs in the style of Kōrin, there. While the title proclaims these as Kōrin's work, the designs are entirely in Hocho's rounded, placid style.

It was Sakai Hōitsu (1761 – 1828) who transplanted the Rinpa style to Edo. Hōitsu, whose elder brother Sakai Tadazane was lord of the Himeji domain, was excluded from the Sakai line of succession and devoted himself to haikai poetry and painting. He received training in the Kano and Nanpin schools of painting but was himself fascinated by the work of the ukiyo-e master Utagawa Toyoharu and painted portraits of beautiful women in the style of Toyoharu. Towards 1800 he began using the mokkotsu and tarashikomi techniques in plant and flower paintings and was also strongly influenced by the Shijō school. From about 1807, he became interested in Kōrin. In 1815, for the centenary of Kōrin's death, he held an exhibition of Kōrin's paintings and published the Kōrin Hyakuzu and Ogata-ryu Ryaku Impu on Kōrin and the Kōrin school. To publicize his own style, Hōitsu also published the Oson Gafu (Album of paintings by Oson) two years later. Hōitsu's style, as we see it in that album, is very much his own, though flavored with a haikai-like nimbleness and the simplicity of the Nijo style. He also made restrained use of tarashikomi.

Hōitsu's richly lyrical Summer and Autumn Flowers folding screen, which is now judged to date from 1821 or 1822, is justly regarded as one of his masterpieces. The summer plants bending under a rain shower, the red leaves of autumn being blown off into the fields brilliantly express the evanescence of things.

Hōitsu's students included many talented artists such as Suzuki Kiitsu and Ikeda Koson. In particular, Suzuki Kiitsu (1796 – 1858) carried on Hōitsu's ukiyo-e style but rejected Hōitsu's lyricism. He created works with a sensitive style and modern sensibility, as in his Camellias and Silver Grass folding screen (Freer Gallery). His Summer and Autumn Streams folding screens and other works directly stimulate the visual cortex so strongly that viewers often feel something strange is occurring within them.

In the modern era, Hoitsiu directly influenced such artists as Hishida Shunso and Hayami Gyoshu. Rinpa works thus had a strong impact on modern

Nihonga. The Western-style artist Asai Chū (1856 – 1907) also rediscovered Rinpa painting while in Paris. After returning to Japan, he provided Rinpa-style designs to craftsmen in Kyoto. The Cowherd and Flowers Maki-e Box by lacquerworker Sugibayashi Kokō and other works achieved a modern revival of the world of Kōetsu's and Kōrin's maki-e boxes.

In Kyoto, Kamisaka Sekka (1866 – 1942) boldly reinterpreted Rinpa designs in helping to revive modern craft arts. The greatest of his masterpieces, Momoyogusa (A world of things), three albums of woodblock prints, made brilliant use of stylization through radical use of deformé and color field composition.

The Rinpa style lived on into the twentieth century, influencing a variety of artists. The Nihonga artist Kayama Matazo (1927 - 2004), for example, paid warm homage to Tawaraya Sotatsu in every aspect of his A Thousand Cranes—the lines of the waves, the form of the flock of cranes, the decoration with gold and silver. His series of decorative folding screens, including Snow, Moon, Flower and Spring and Autumn Waves, were created under strong Rinpa influence.

Painters were not alone in being influenced by the Rinpa style. Tanaka Ikko (1930 – 2002), Japan's leading postwar graphic designer, used the painting of a deer from Sotatsu's endpapers for the restored Heike Nokyo in contemporary poster design in his JAPAN.

Rinpa's influence on design transcends borders to have a strong impact in Europe as well. The connection with Art Nouveau in the early twentieth century is well known, and it continues: in 2001, the cover of Le Monde d'Hermes, a PR magazine published by the French fashion house Hermes, aroused much comment by featuring the Eight-planked Bridge from Sekka's Momoyogusa. The Rinpa decorative sense thus continues to stimulate the vision of people involved in the decorative arts throughout the world. Rinpa, the concentrated essence of the Japanese decorative sense, is an enduring source of inspiration.

Yasumura Toshinobu

Born in Toyama Prefecture in 1953, he earned a master's degree in Japanese art history at Tohoku University. From 1979, he worked at the Itabashi Art Museum, where he was the director from 2005 to 2013. Currently he directs the Hokusai Museum. He has curated many unique exhibitions on Japanese art, particularly in the Edo period. His many publications (all in Japanese) include Rinpa Art Museum 3: Hōitsu and Edo Rinpa (Shueisha), Kano Tanyu (Shinchosha), A Collection of Japanese Ghost Paintings (Jlnrui Bunkasha), The Art Museum Business: Before Wondering What Art Is (Bensey Publishing), Early Modern Japanese Painting, Easily Understood, Kano School Arts of Note: Tanyu and the Edo Kano School, and Amazing Folding Screens (all from Tokyo Bijutsu), and Kawanabe Kyosai and Shibata Zehin (both from Heibonsha).

本阿弥光悦

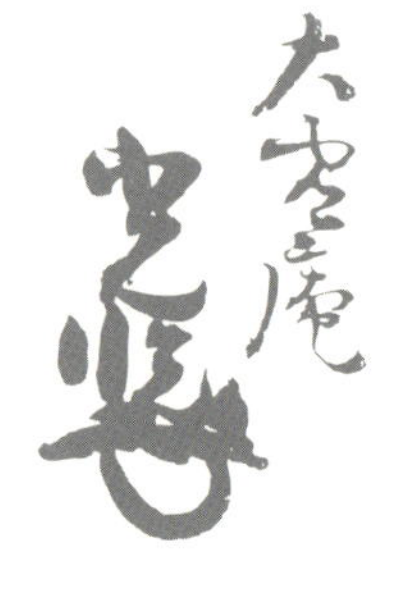
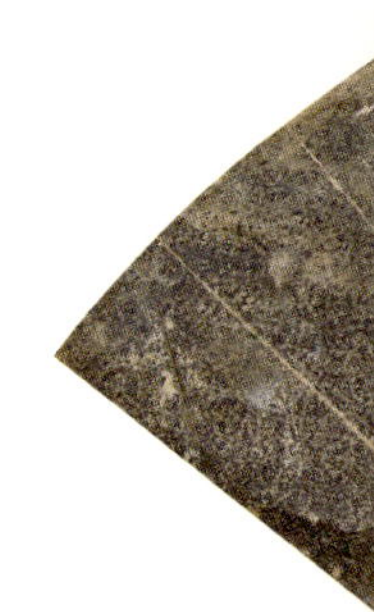

ほんあみ こうえつ

永禄元年〜寛永 14 年（1558‑1637）

刀の鑑定や研磨を家業とし、足利将軍家にも仕えた本阿弥家に生まれる。特に書は近衛信尹（のぶただ）、松花堂昭乗と共に「寛永の三筆」に数えられ、その書風は光悦流と呼ばれる様式をつくりあげた。また蒔絵や陶芸にも斬新なデザインとフォルムを取り入れ、茶道や築庭にも才能を発揮した。特に宗達とは金銀泥下絵の色紙、和歌巻の共作を通して親しく交わっていたと思われる。

Hon'ami Kōetsu （1558‑1637）

Kōetsu was born in the Hon'ami family, sword experts who had served the Ashikaga shoguns. One of the three great calligraphers of the Kan'ei era, he founded the Kōetsu style of calligraphy. He designed maki-e lacquerware, gardens, and ceramics, including tea bowls, and collaborated with Sōtatsu in creating paintings and handscrolls.

「和歌扇面画賛」　本阿弥光悦
石川県立美術館蔵
Poem Anthology *Kokinshū* Over Painting of Plum Tree, Hon'ami Kōetsu, Ishikawa Prefectural Museum of Art

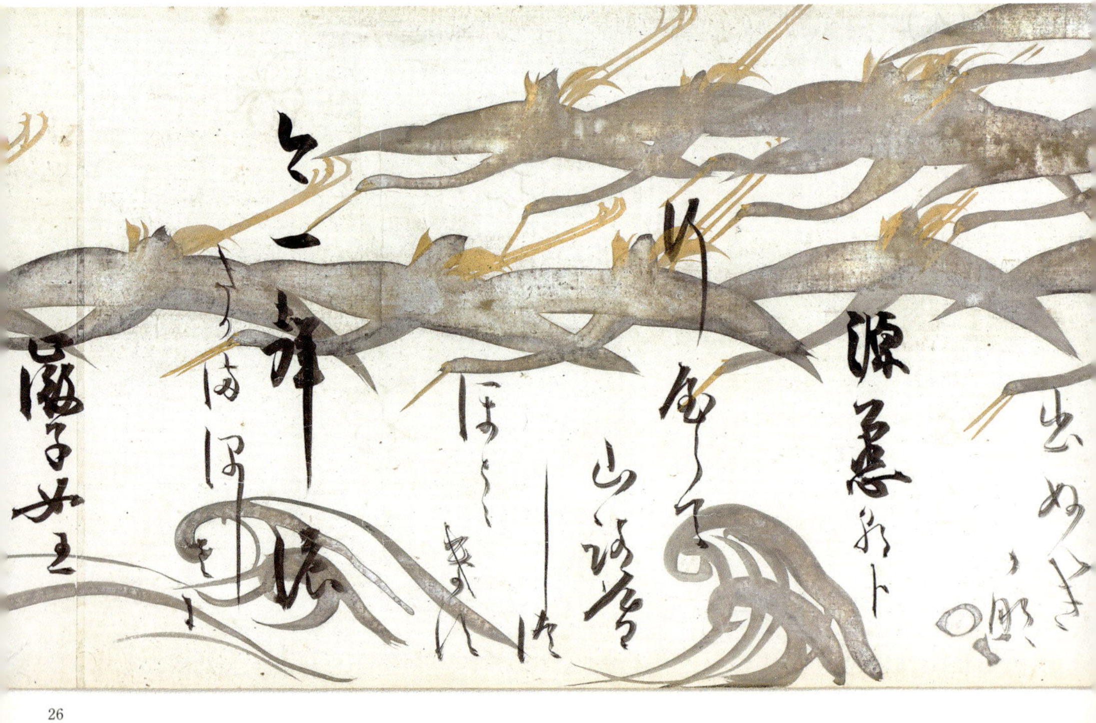

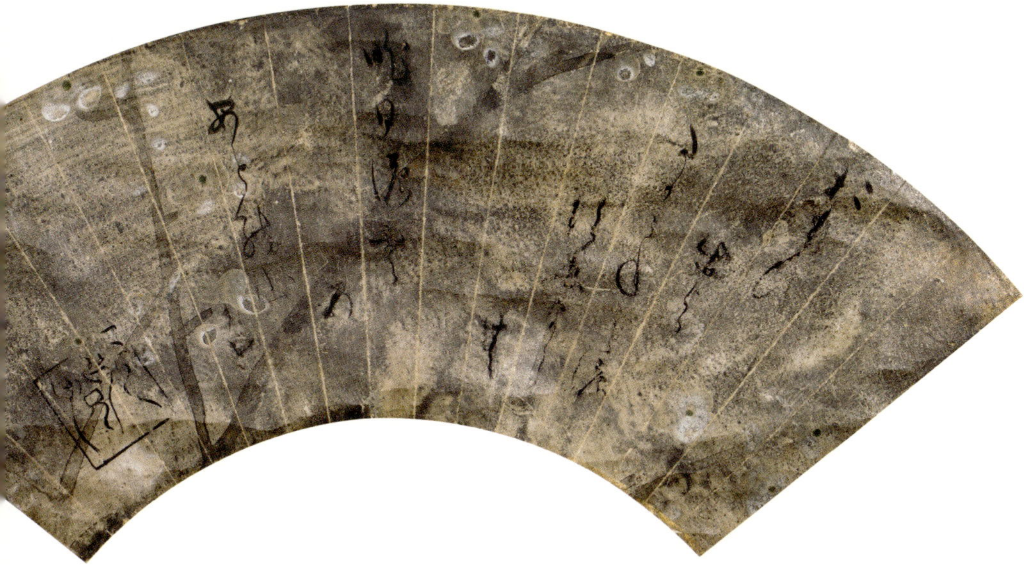

「鶴図下絵和歌巻」（部分）　重文　本阿弥光悦・書　俵屋宗達・下絵　京都国立博物館蔵
Poem Scroll with Under Painting of Cranes, Detail, Painting by Tawaraya Sōtatsu,
Calligraphy by Hon'ami Kōetsu, Important Cultural Property, Kyoto National Museum

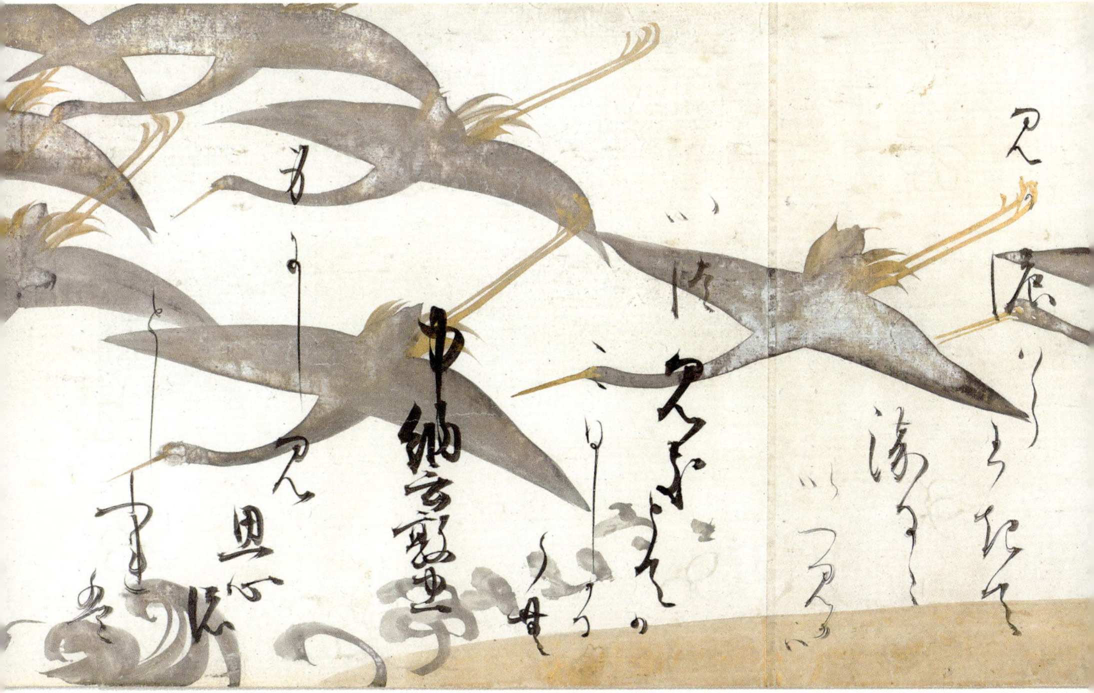

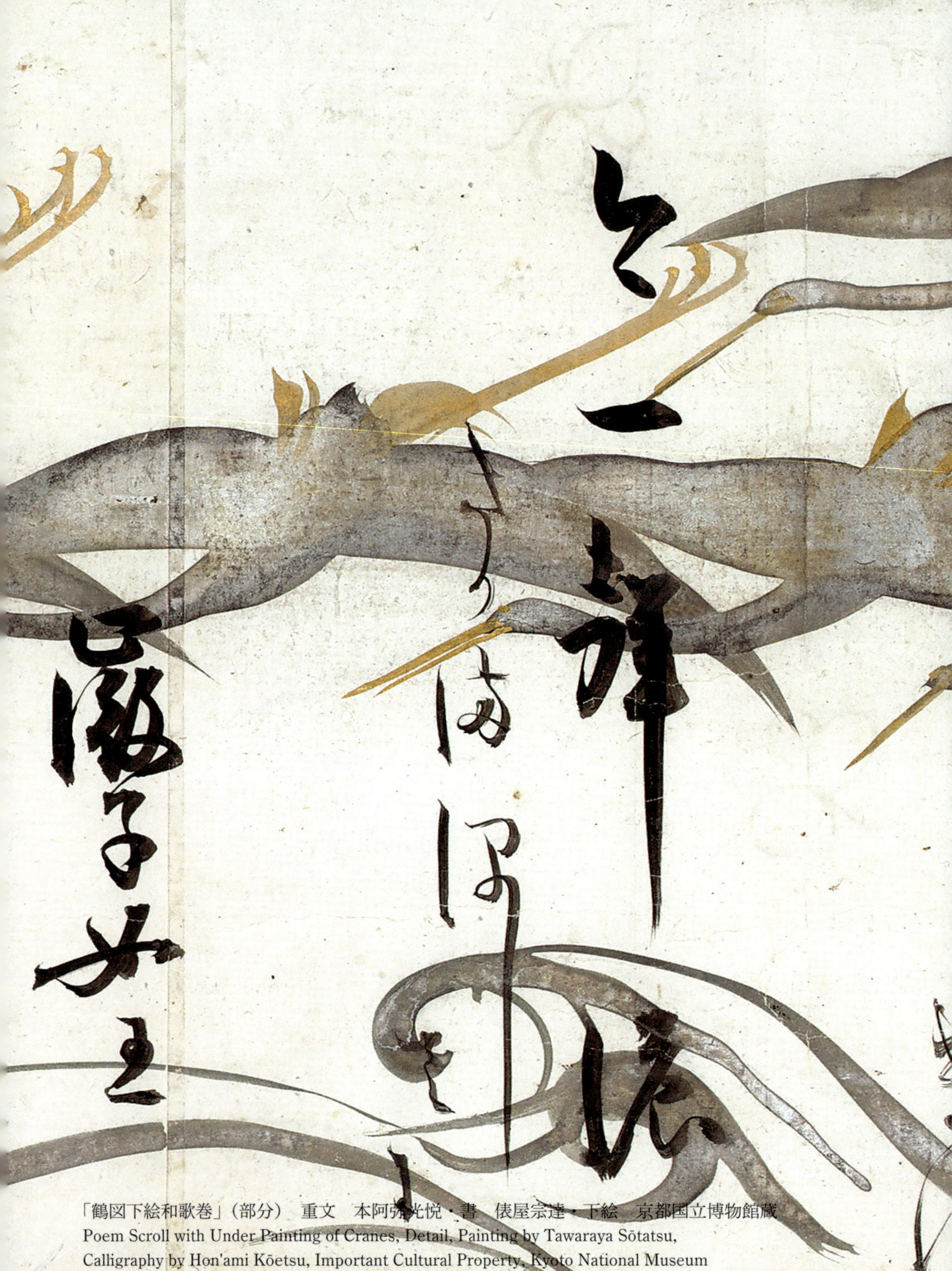

「鶴図下絵和歌巻」（部分）　重文　本阿弥光悦・書　俵屋宗達・下絵　京都国立博物館蔵
Poem Scroll with Under Painting of Cranes, Detail, Painting by Tawaraya Sōtatsu,
Calligraphy by Hon'ami Kōetsu, Important Cultural Property, Kyoto National Museum

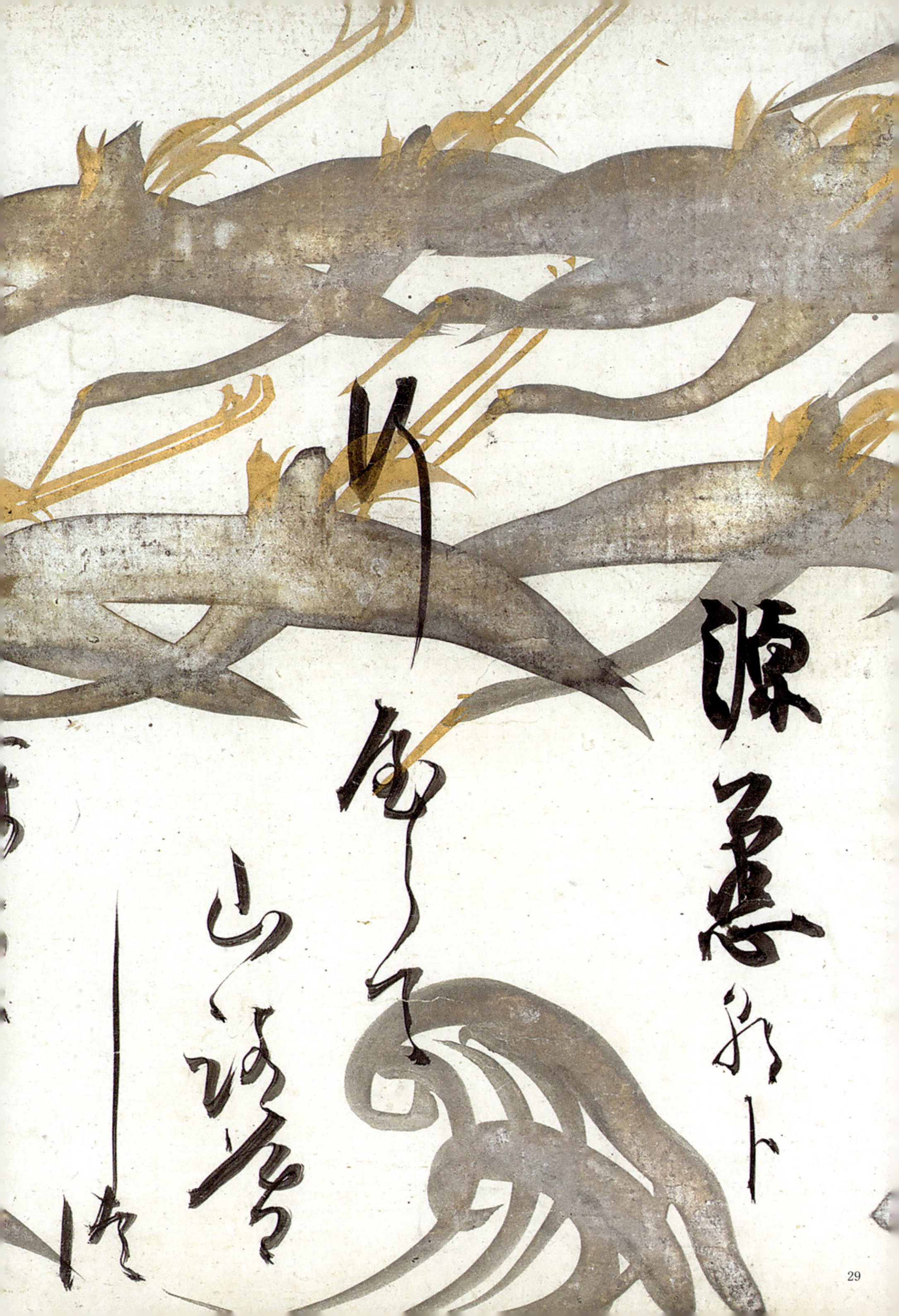

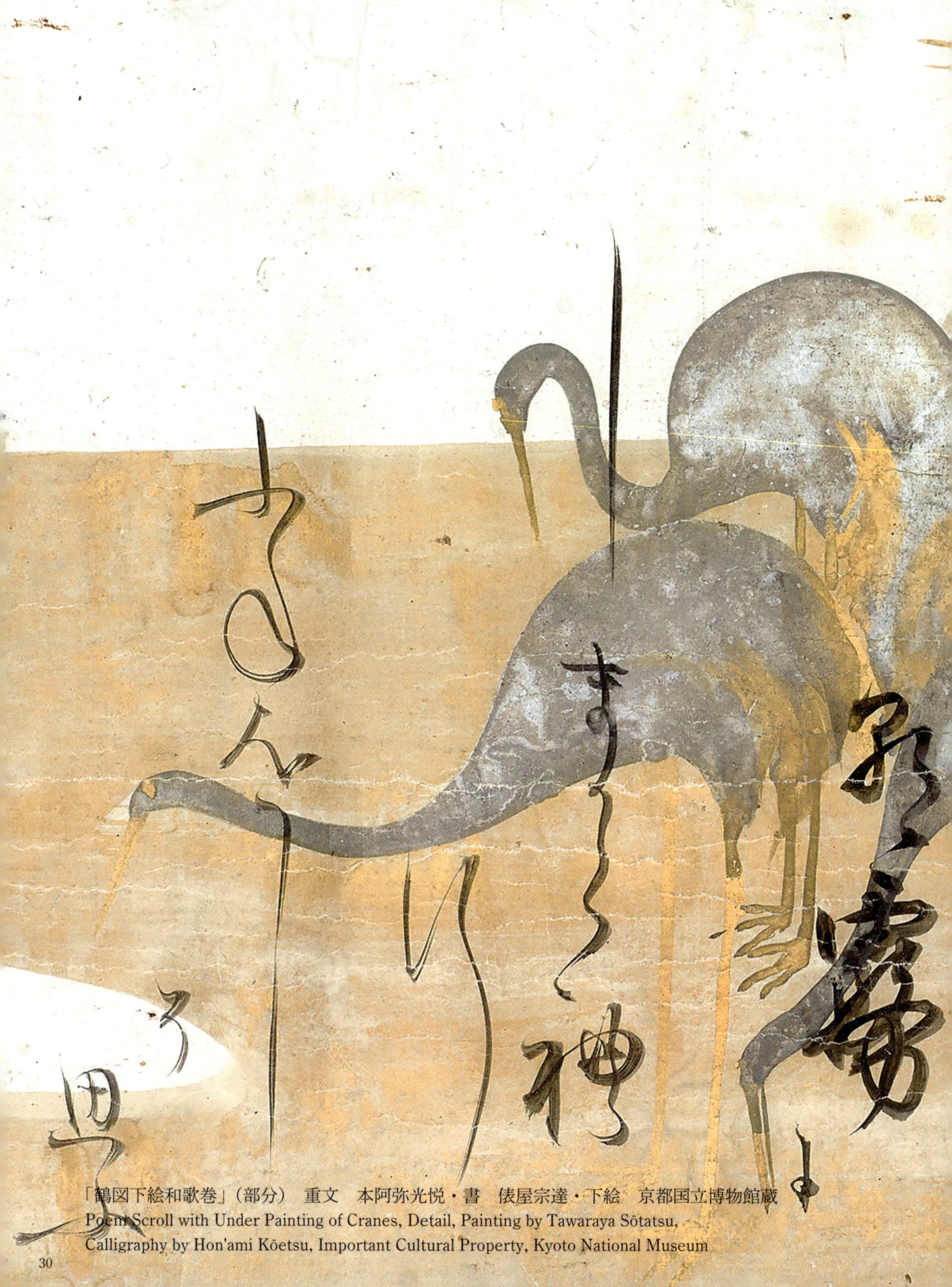

「鶴図下絵和歌巻」（部分）　重文　本阿弥光悦・書　俵屋宗達・下絵　京都国立博物館蔵
Poem Scroll with Under Painting of Cranes, Detail, Painting by Tawaraya Sōtatsu,
Calligraphy by Hon'ami Kōetsu, Important Cultural Property, Kyoto National Museum

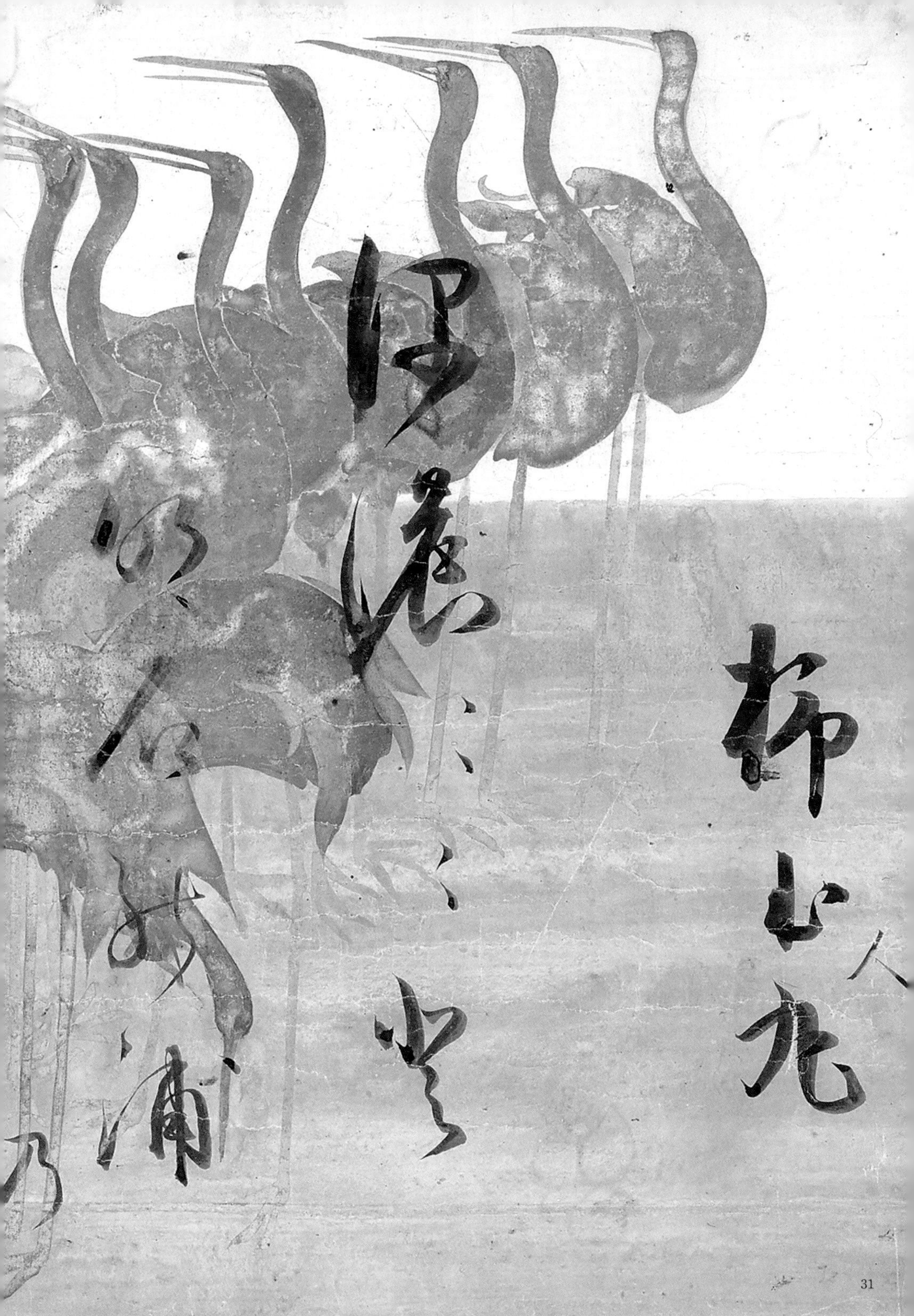

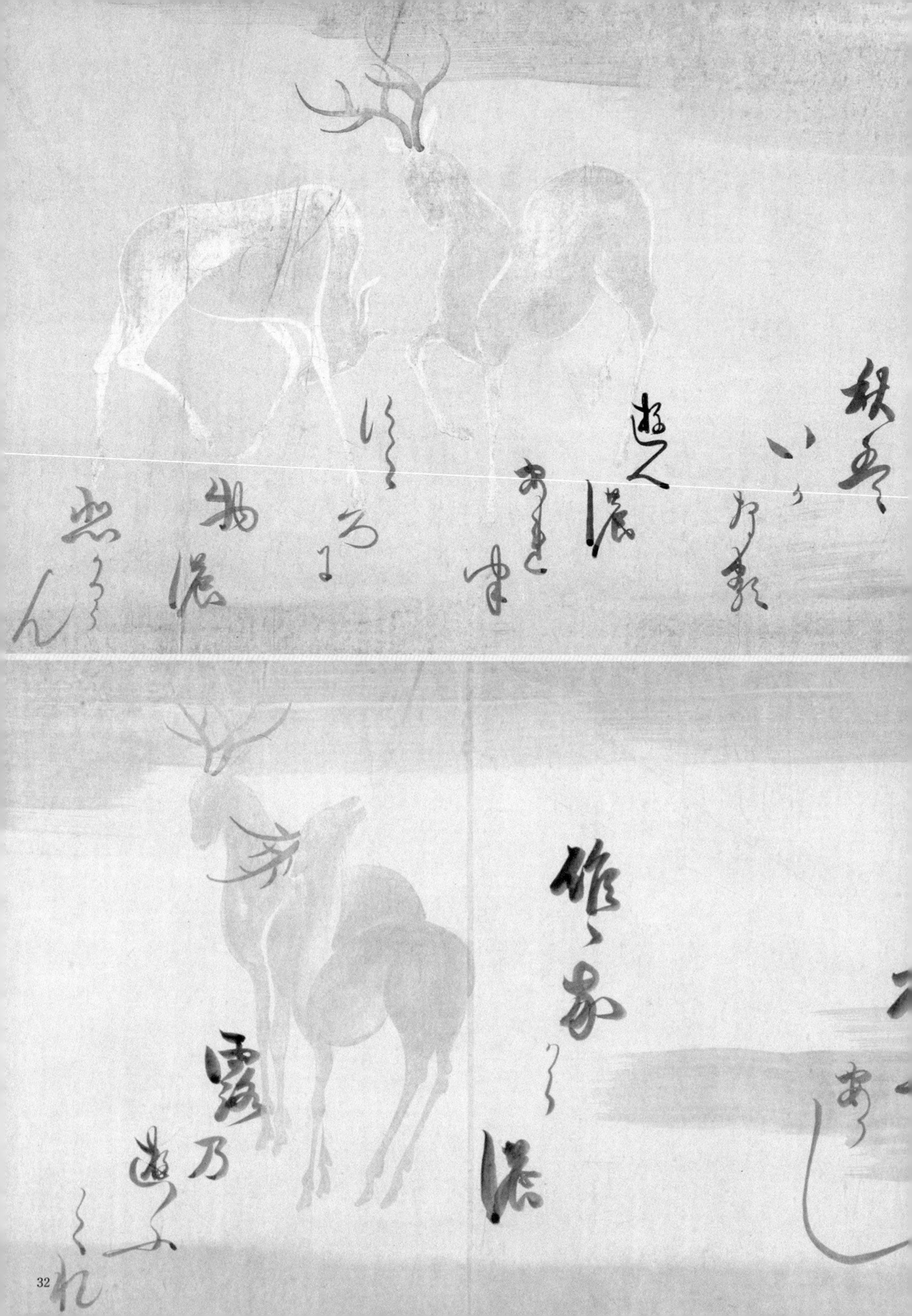

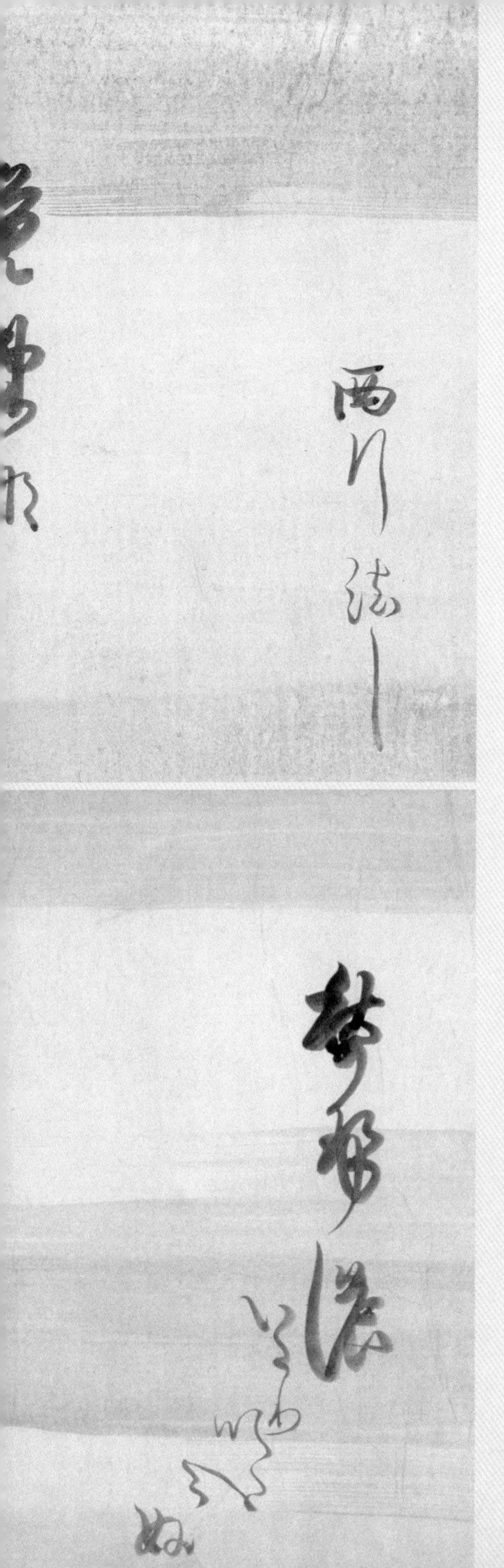

「鹿下絵和歌」（新古今和歌集）
本阿弥光悦　石川県立美術館蔵
Poem Scroll with Under Painting of Deer,
Shinkokinwaka-shū Anthology, Hon'ami Kōetsu,
Ishikawa Prefectural Museum of Art

俵屋宗達

たわらや そうたつ　生没年不詳

宗達の伝記の詳細は不明で、おそらく扇面や色紙、短冊、巻子など、様々な形式の料紙装飾を手掛ける工房「俵屋」を主宰し、王朝美を新しい感性で復興させた。金銀泥を用いた雅で大胆な構図の金地屏風や華麗な料紙装飾に新しい画境を獲得し、生命感あふれる様式を生み出した。また没骨、たらし込みの技法や斬新な意匠で水墨画にも比類ない傑作を残した。

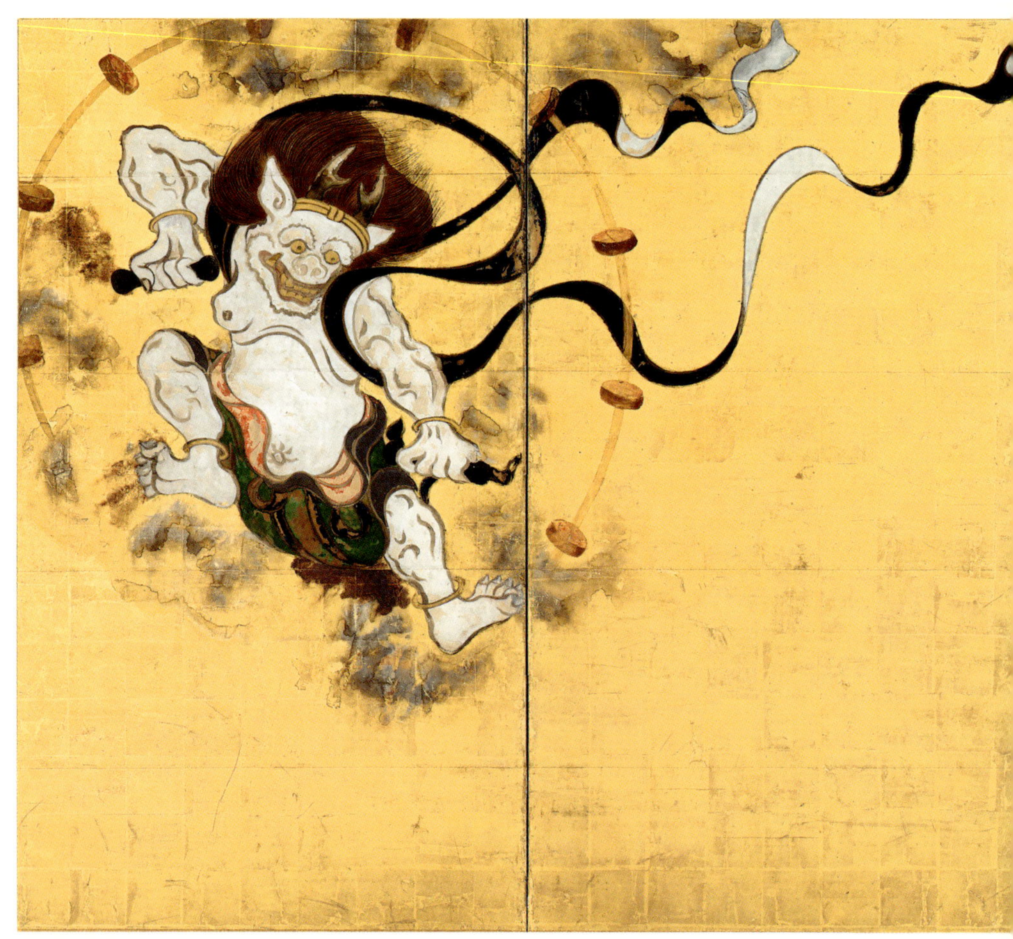

「風神雷神図屏風」　国宝　俵屋宗達　建仁寺蔵
Wind and Thunder Gods, Tawaraya Sōtatsu, National Treasure, Kennin-ji, Kyoto

Sōtatsu ran the Tawaraya painting studio, which produced decorative papers for fans and picture scrolls. He revitalized the court aesthetic with bold compositions for folding screens and the use of gold and silver pigments. In ink painting, his masterpieces use the mokkotsu (depiction of objects without outlines) and tarashikomi (application of ink to ink that is still wet) techniques.

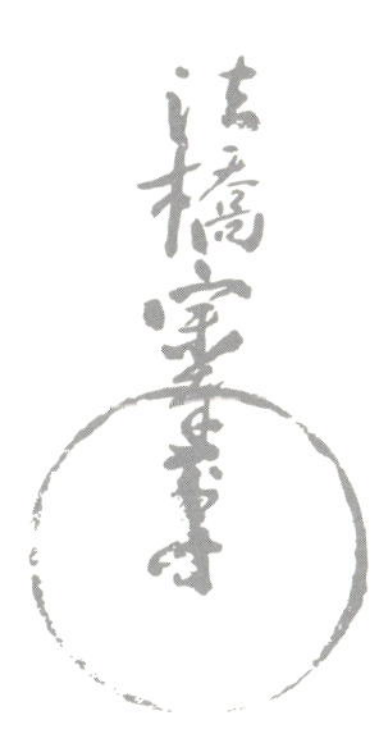

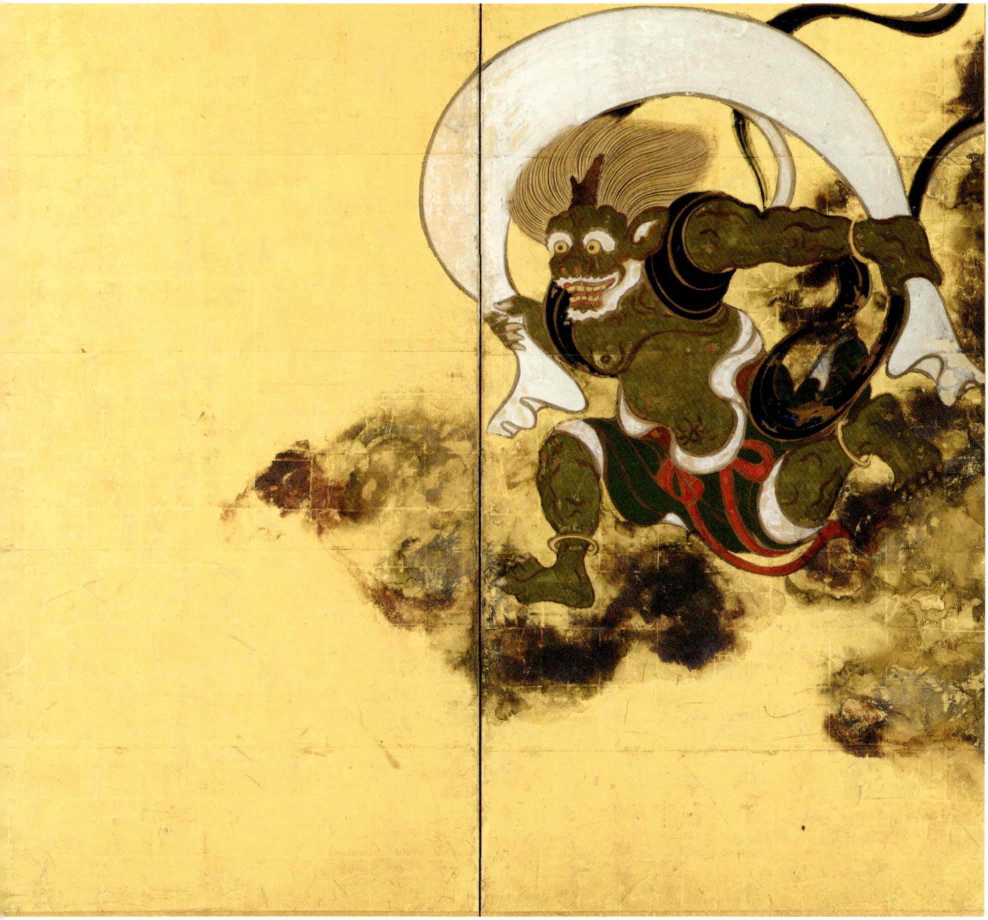

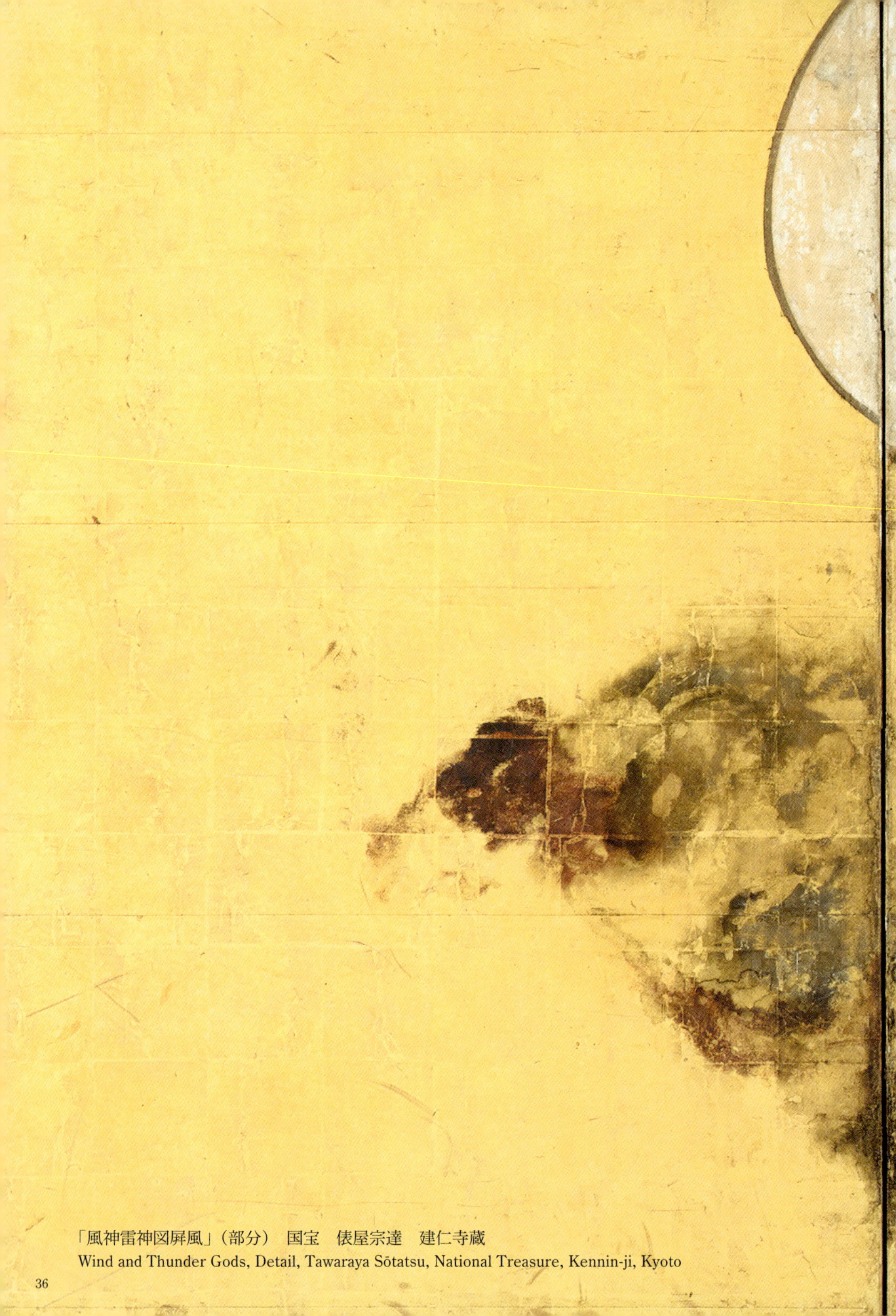

「風神雷神図屏風」（部分）　国宝　俵屋宗達　建仁寺蔵
Wind and Thunder Gods, Detail, Tawaraya Sōtatsu, National Treasure, Kennin-ji, Kyoto

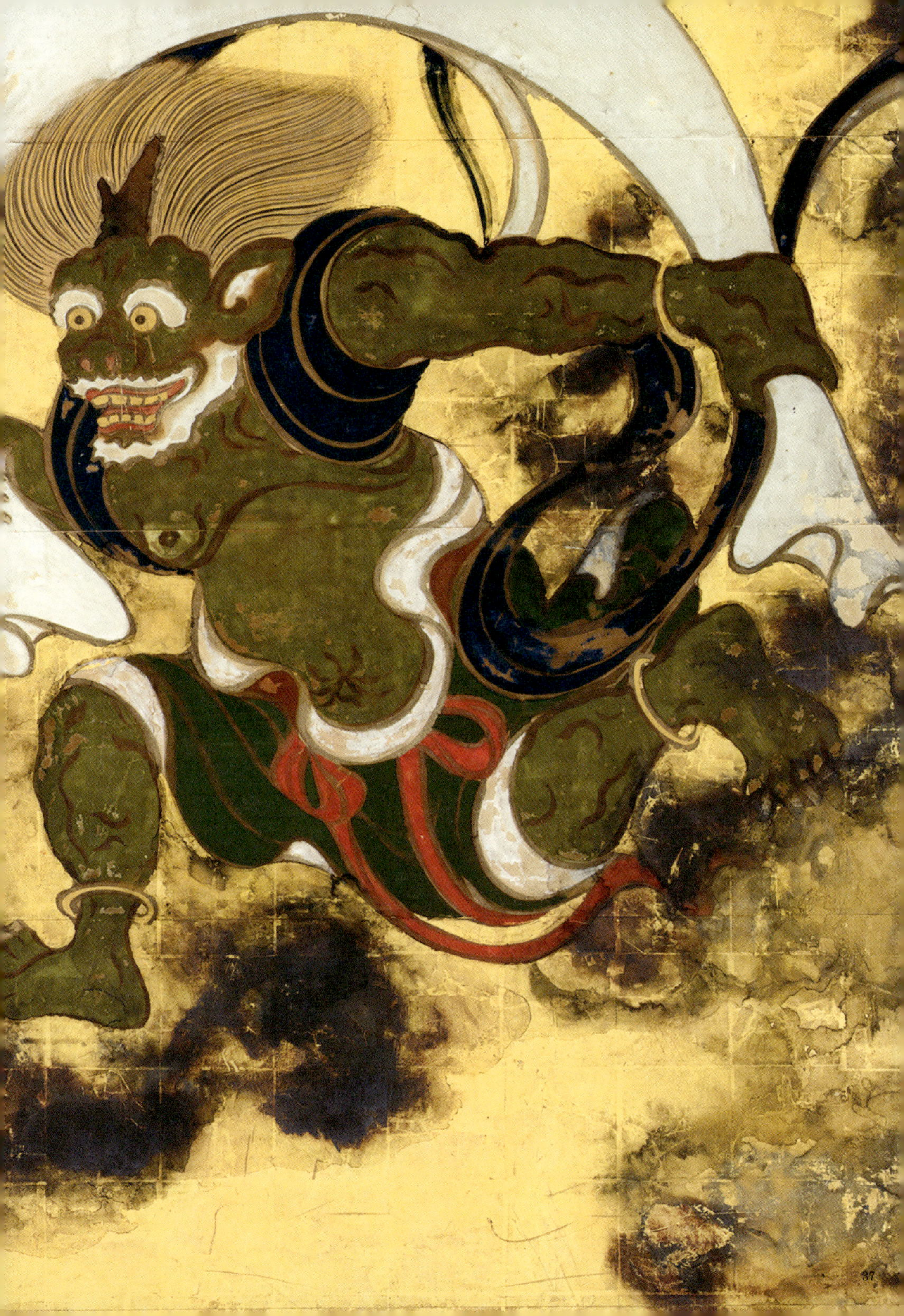

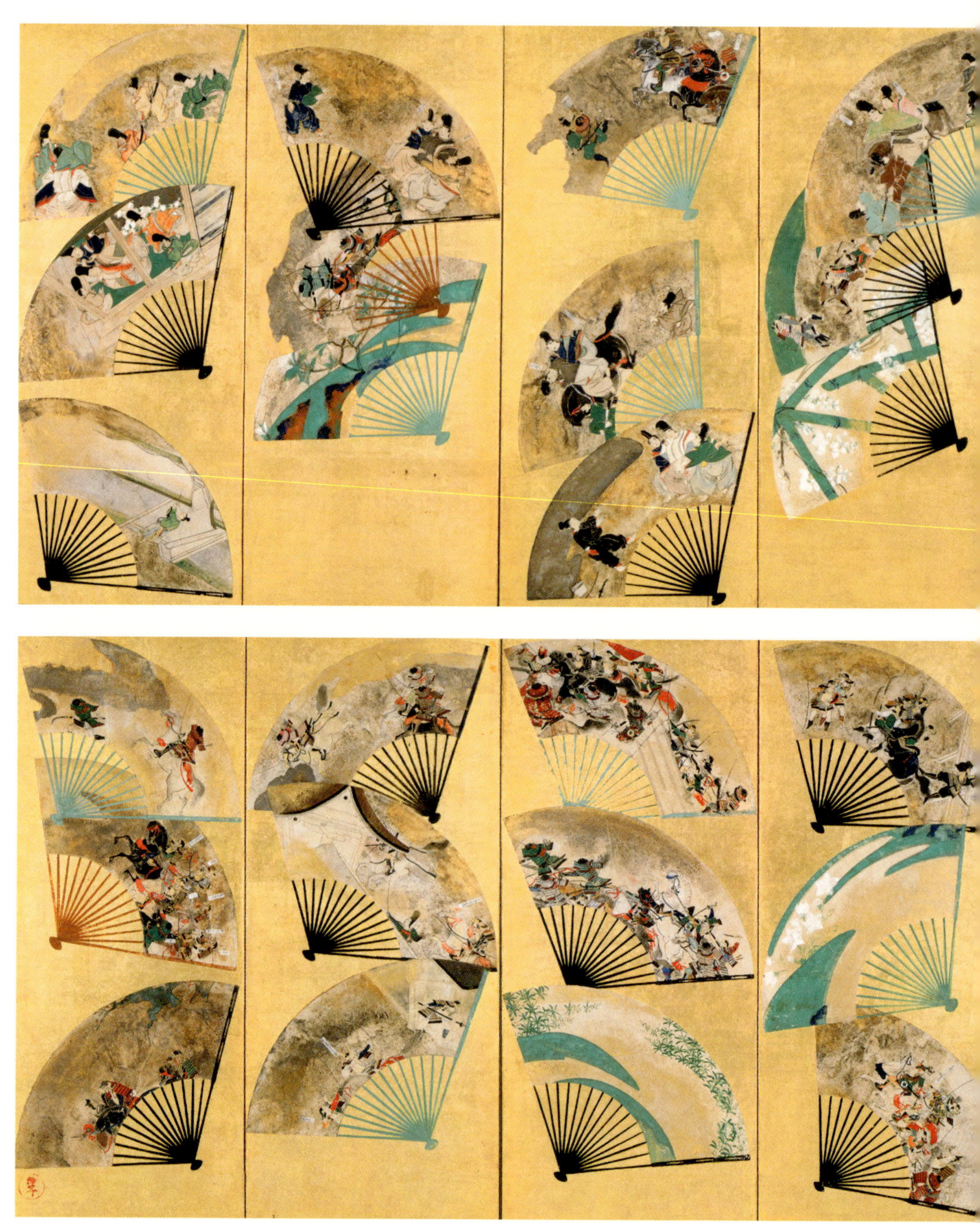

「扇面散屏風」　俵屋宗達　宮内庁三の丸尚蔵館蔵
Scattered Fans, Tawaraya Sōtatsu, Sannomaru Shozokan（The Museum of the Imperial Collections）

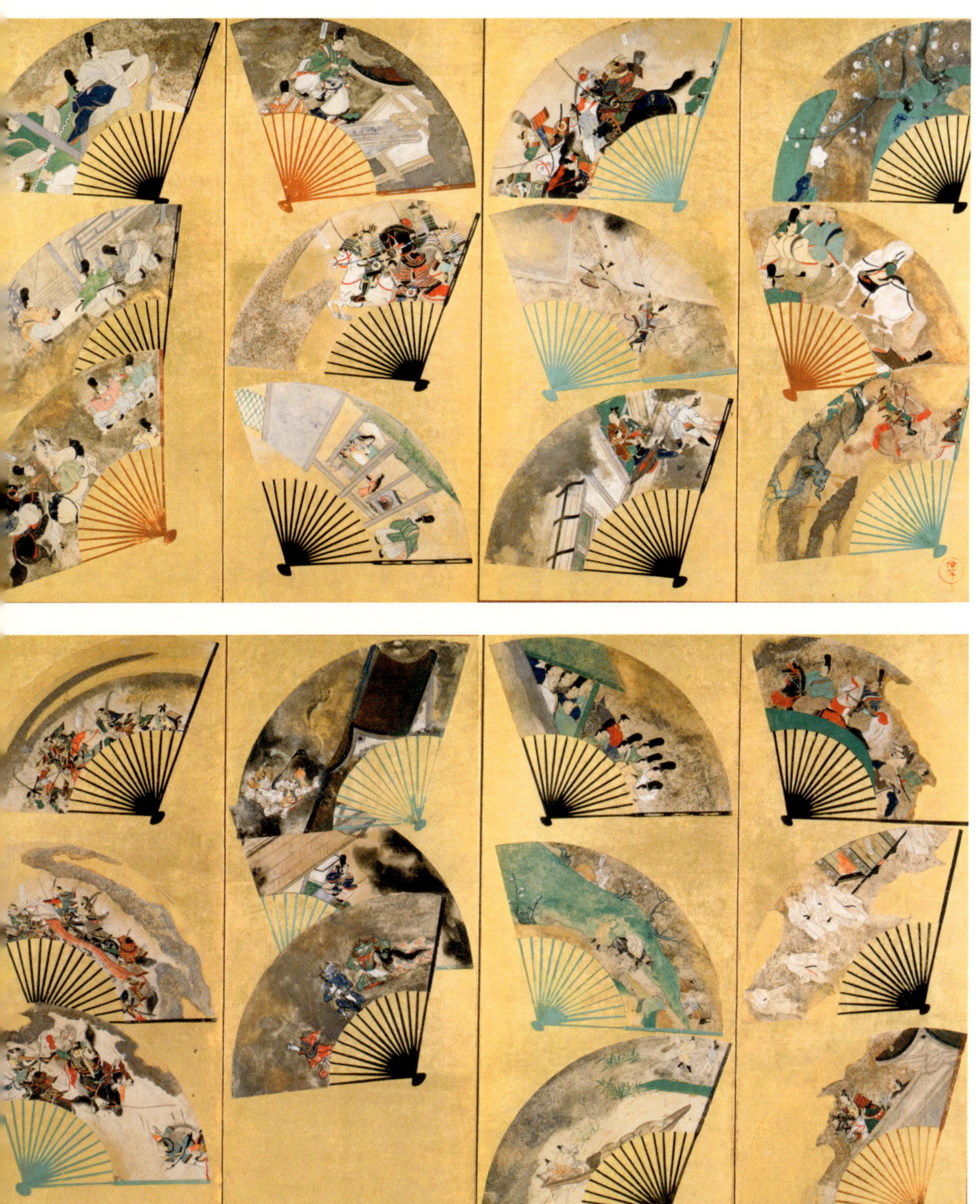

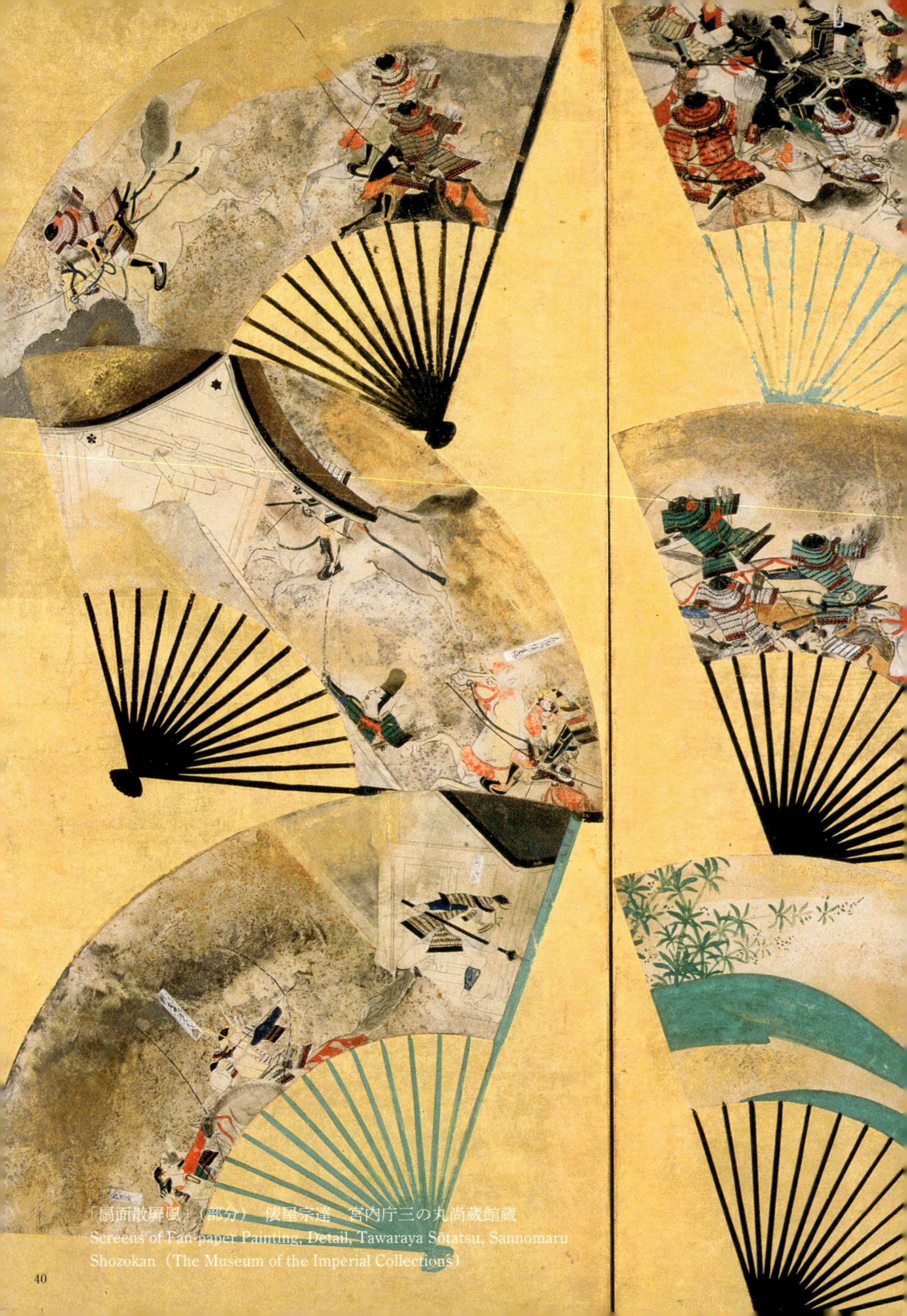

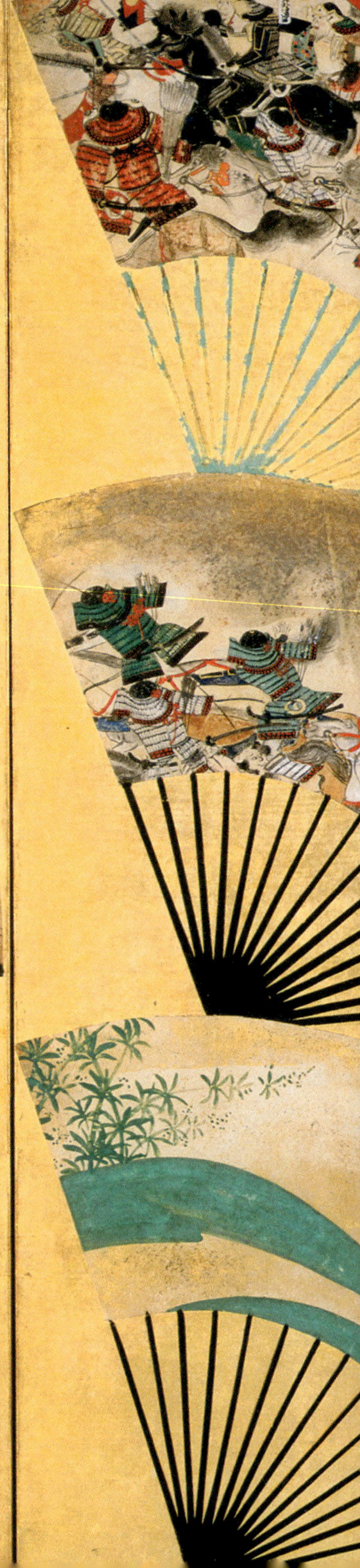

「扇面散屏風」（部分）　俵屋宗達　宮内庁三の丸尚蔵館蔵
Screens of Fan-paper Painting, Detail, Tawaraya Sōtatsu, Sannomaru
Shozokan（The Museum of the Imperial Collections）

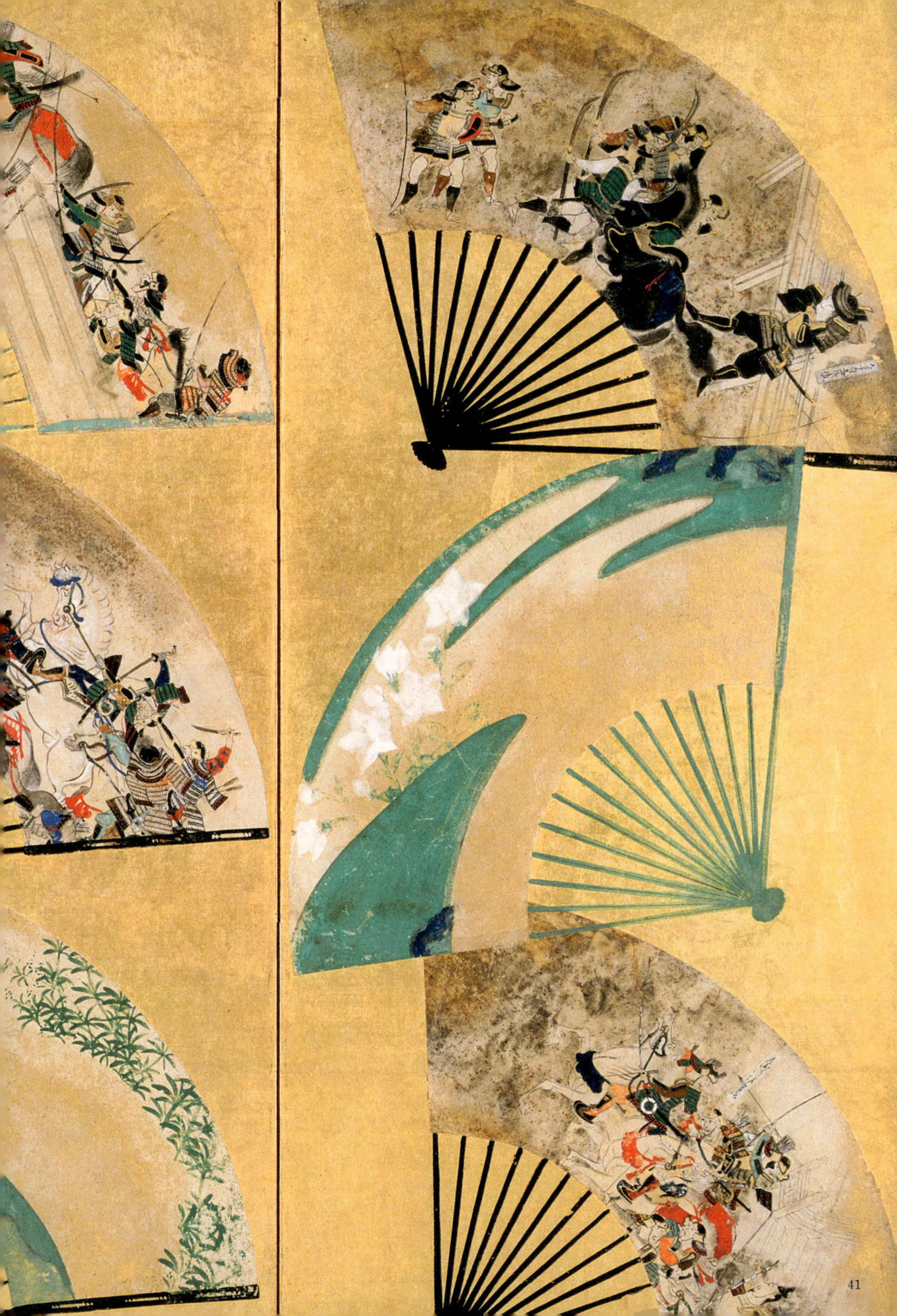

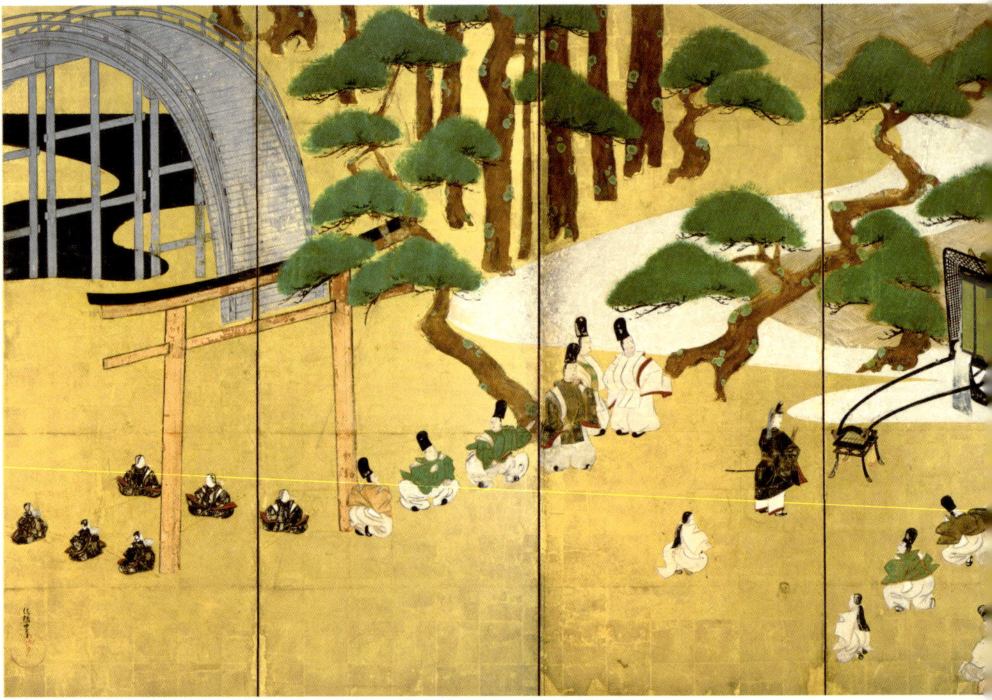

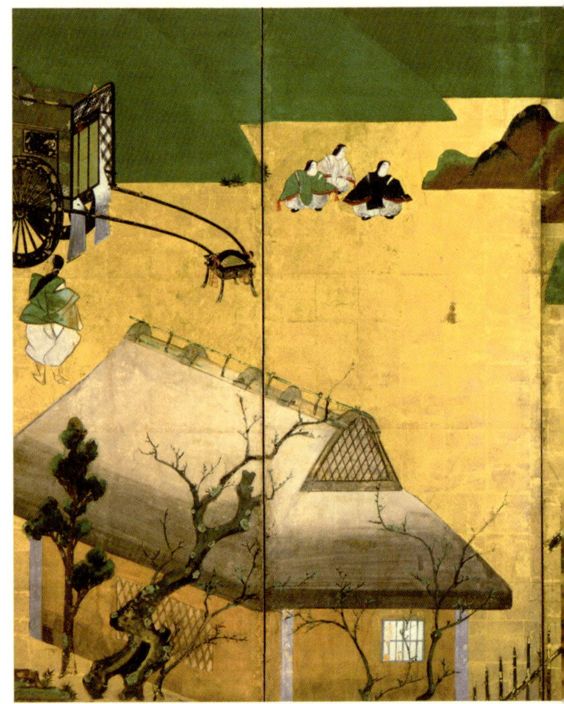

「源氏物語関屋・澪標図屛風」
国宝　俵屋宗達　静嘉堂文庫美術館蔵
Scenes from the Barrier Gate ("*Sekiya*") and
Channel Buoys ("*Miotsukushi*") Chapters of
the Tale of *Genji*, Tawaraya Sōtatsu, National
Treasure, Seikado Bunko Art Museum
画像提供：静嘉堂文庫イメージアーカイブ / DNPartcom

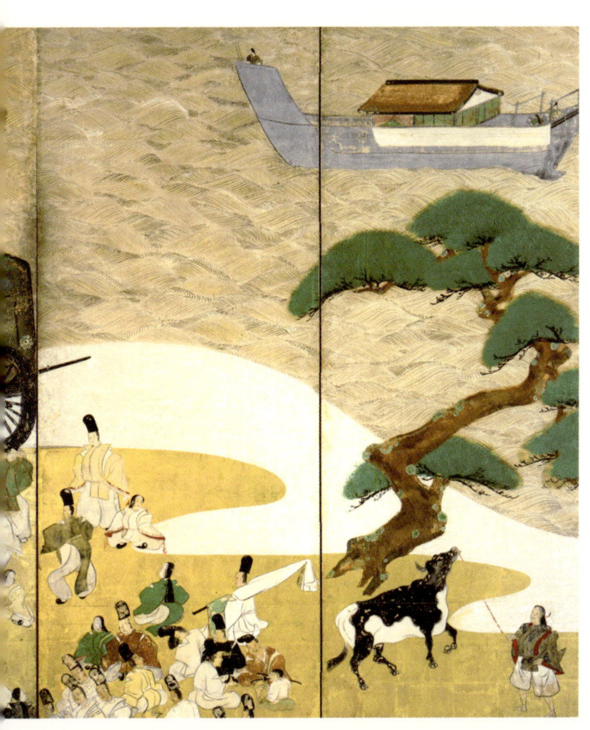

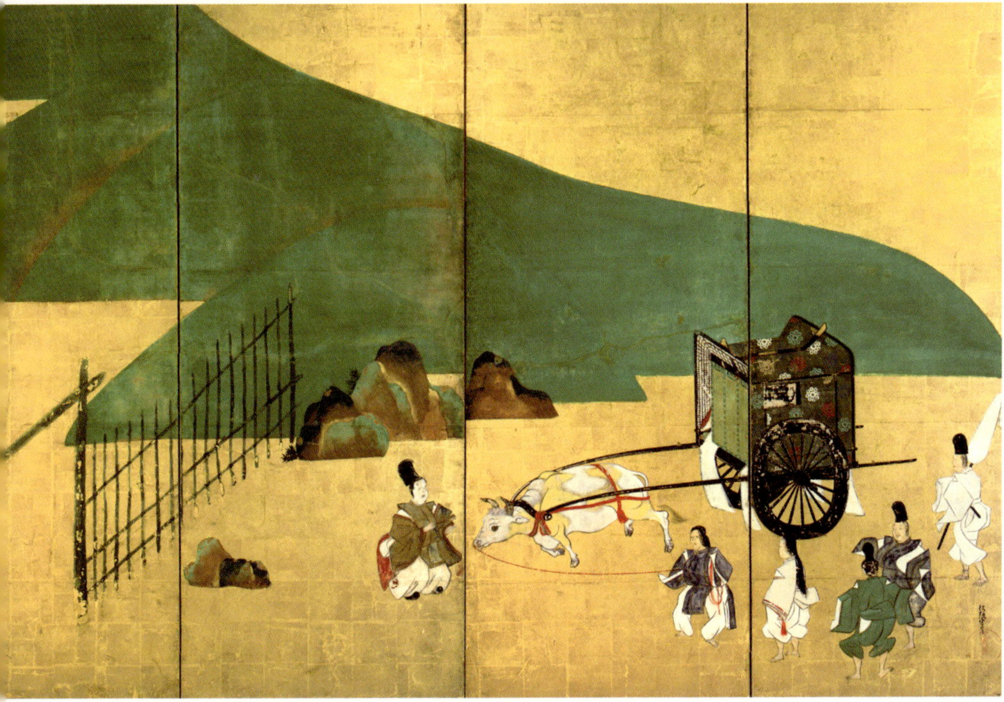

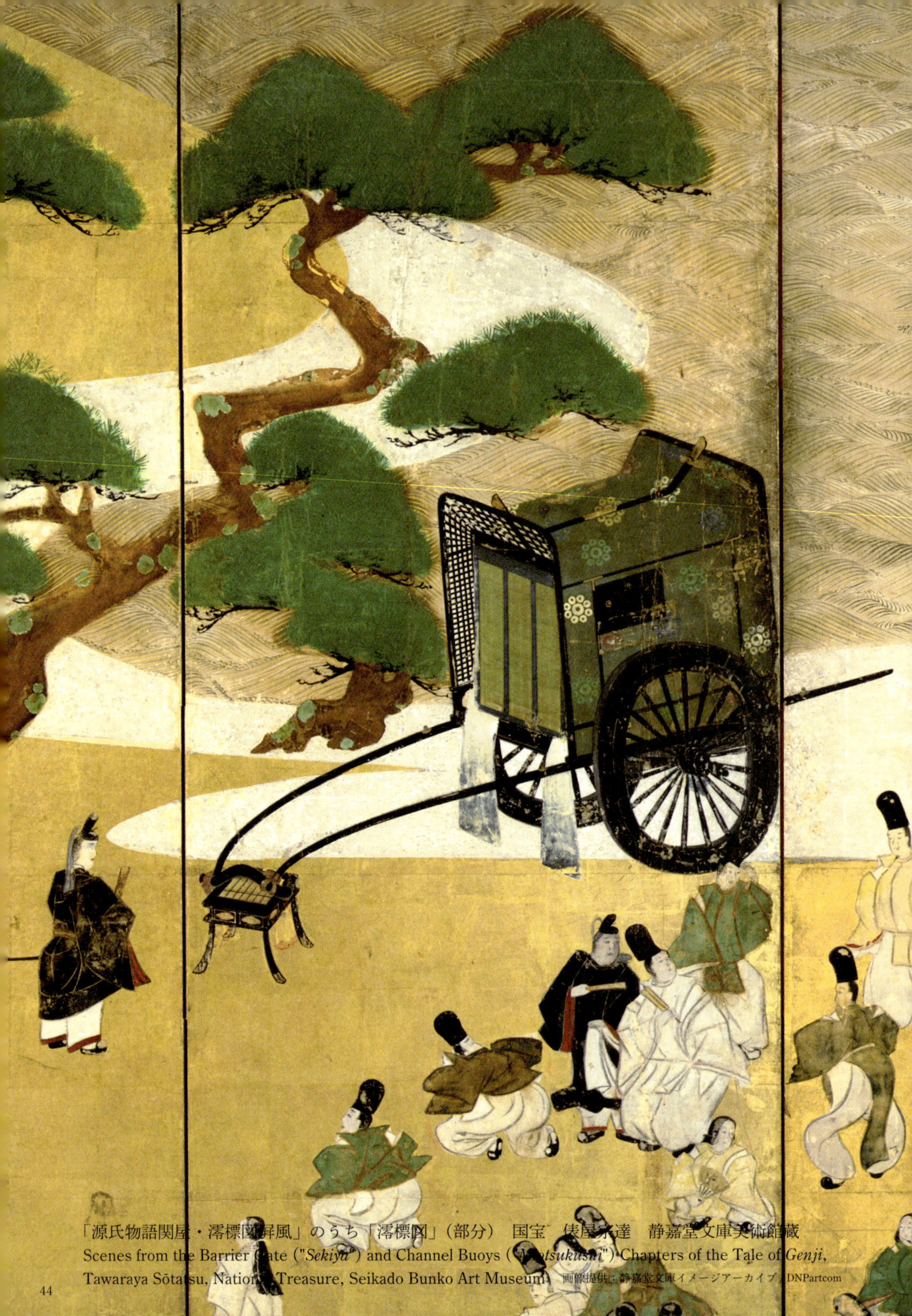

「源氏物語関屋・澪標図屏風」のうち「澪標図」（部分）　国宝　俵屋宗達　静嘉堂文庫美術館蔵
Scenes from the Barrier Gate ("*Sekiya*") and Channel Buoys ("*Miotsukushi*") Chapters of the Tale of *Genji*,
Tawaraya Sōtatsu, National Treasure, Seikado Bunko Art Museum　

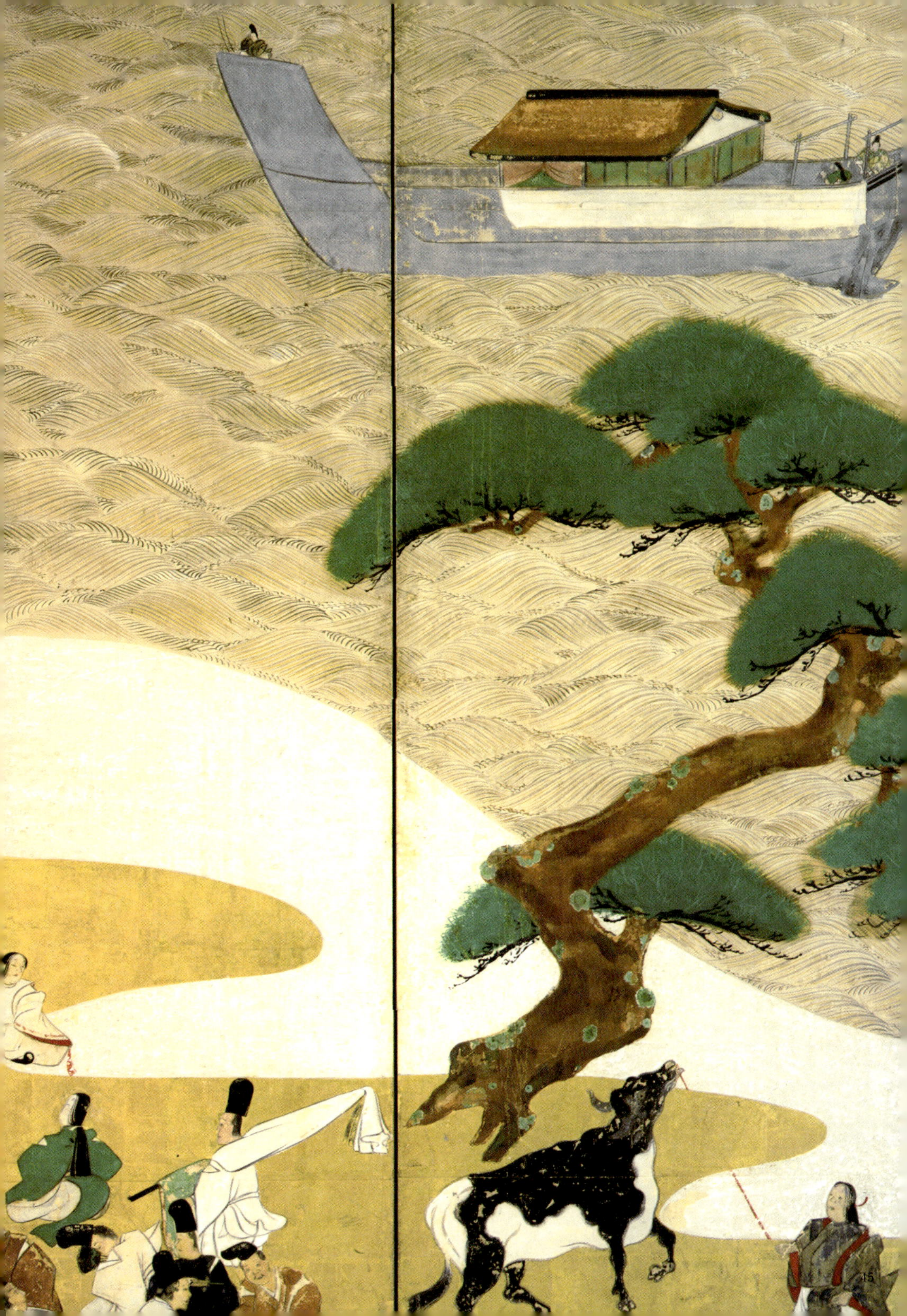

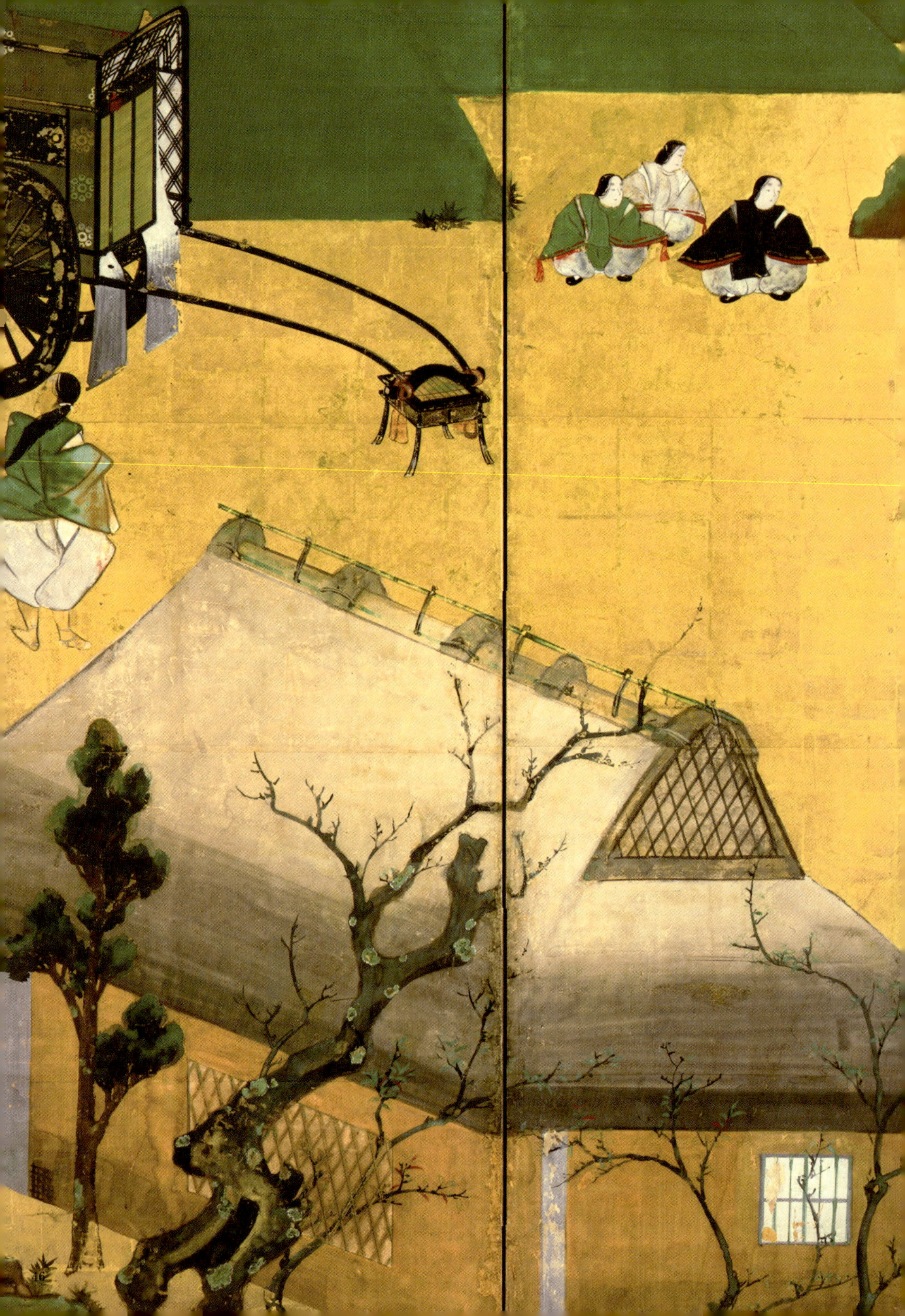

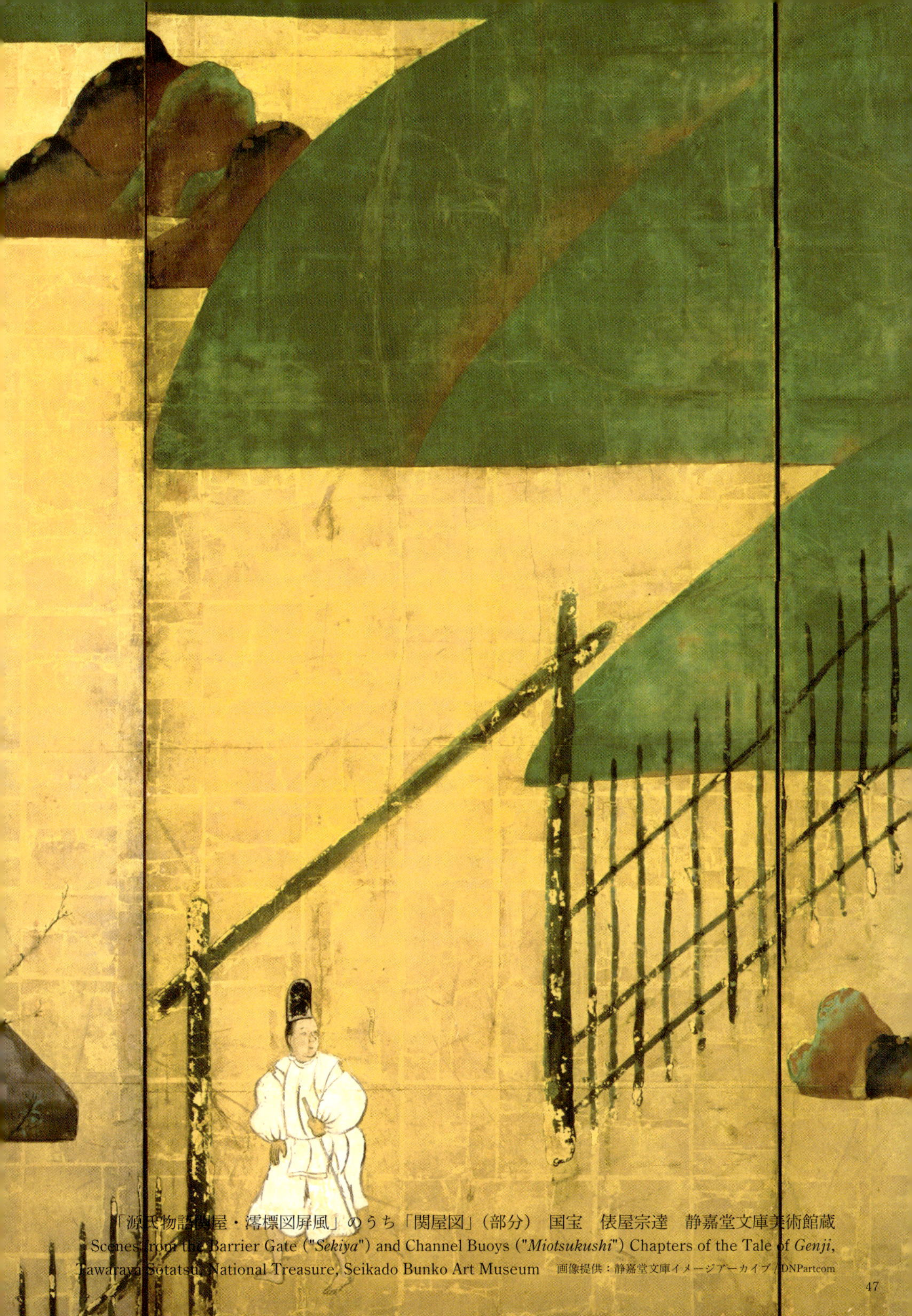

「源氏物語関屋・澪標図屏風」のうち「関屋図」（部分）　国宝　俵屋宗達　静嘉堂文庫美術館蔵
Scenes from the Barrier Gate ("*Sekiya*") and Channel Buoys ("*Miotsukushi*") Chapters of the Tale of *Genji*,
Tawaraya Sotatsu, National Treasure, Seikado Bunko Art Museum　画像提供：静嘉堂文庫イメージアーカイブ/DNPartcom

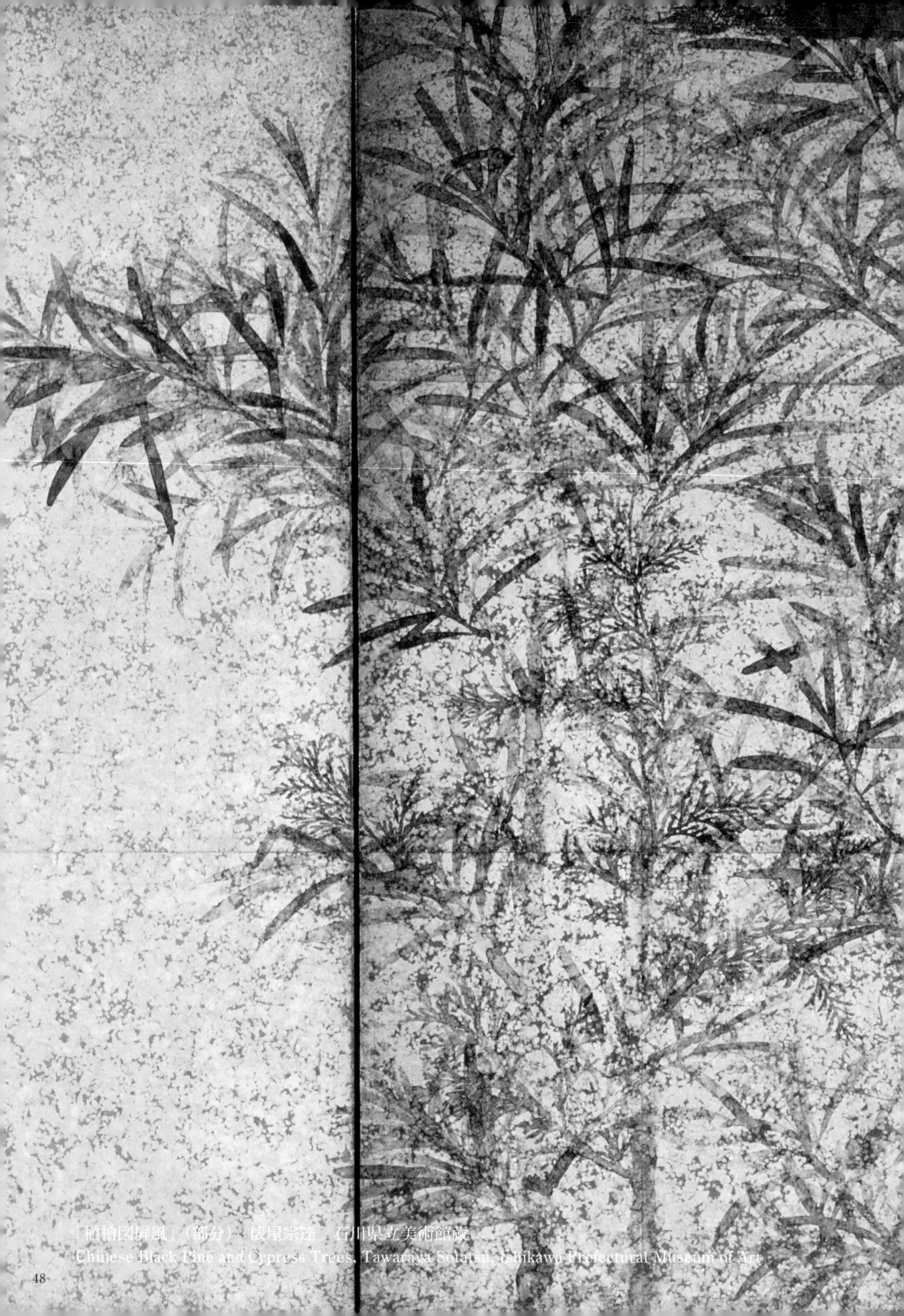

「楢楢図屏風」（部分）　俵屋宗達　石川県立美術館蔵
Chinese Black Pine and Cypress Trees, Tawaraya Sotatsu, Ishikawa Prefectural Museum of Art

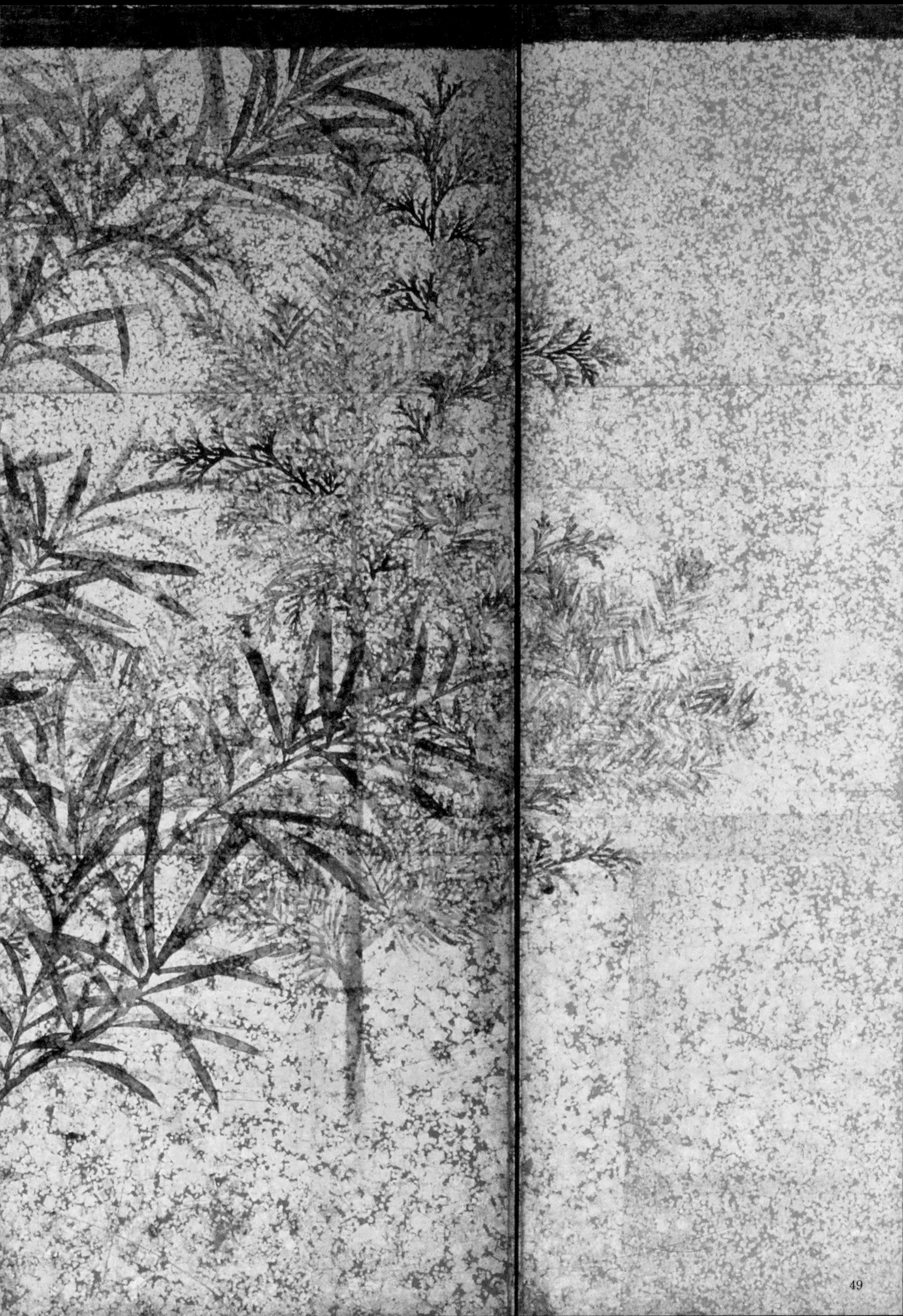

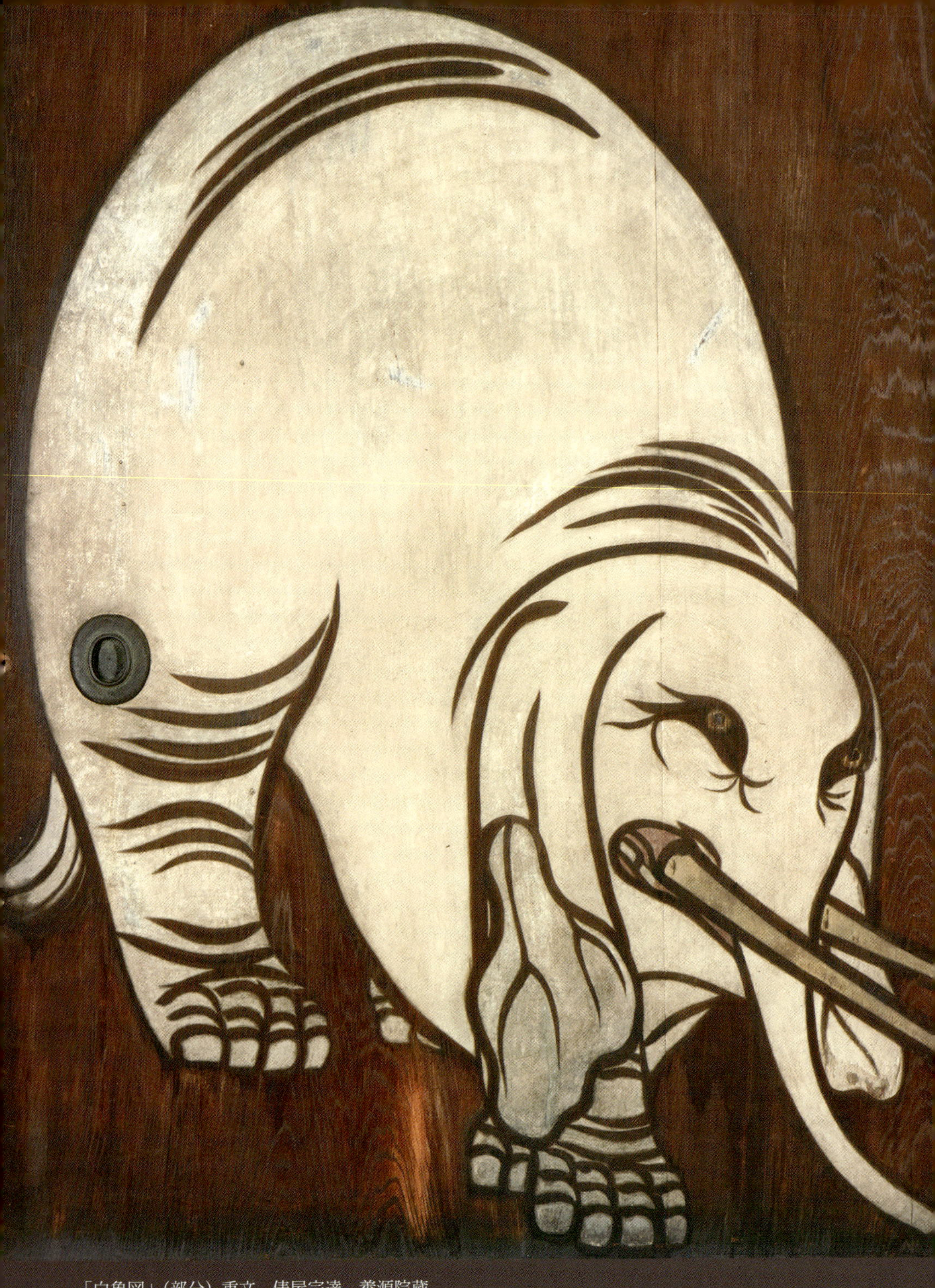

「白象図」（部分）重文　俵屋宗達　養源院蔵
Cedar Doors with White Elephant, Tawaraya Sōtatsu, Important Cultural Property, Yōgen-in, Kyoto

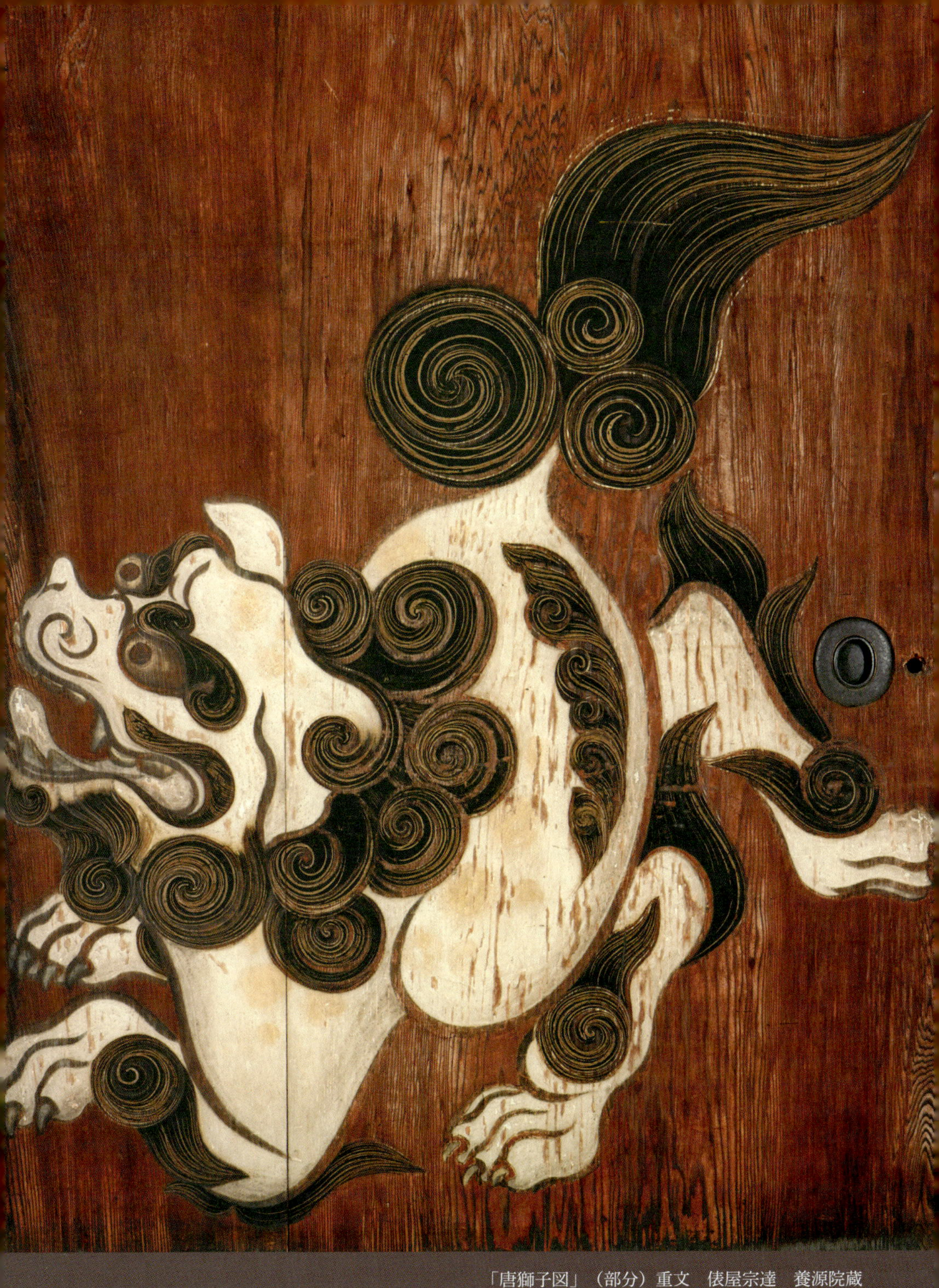

「唐獅子図」（部分）重文　俵屋宗達　養源院蔵
Cedar Doors with Chinese Lion, Tawaraya Sōtatsu, Important Cultural Property Yōgen-in, Kyoto

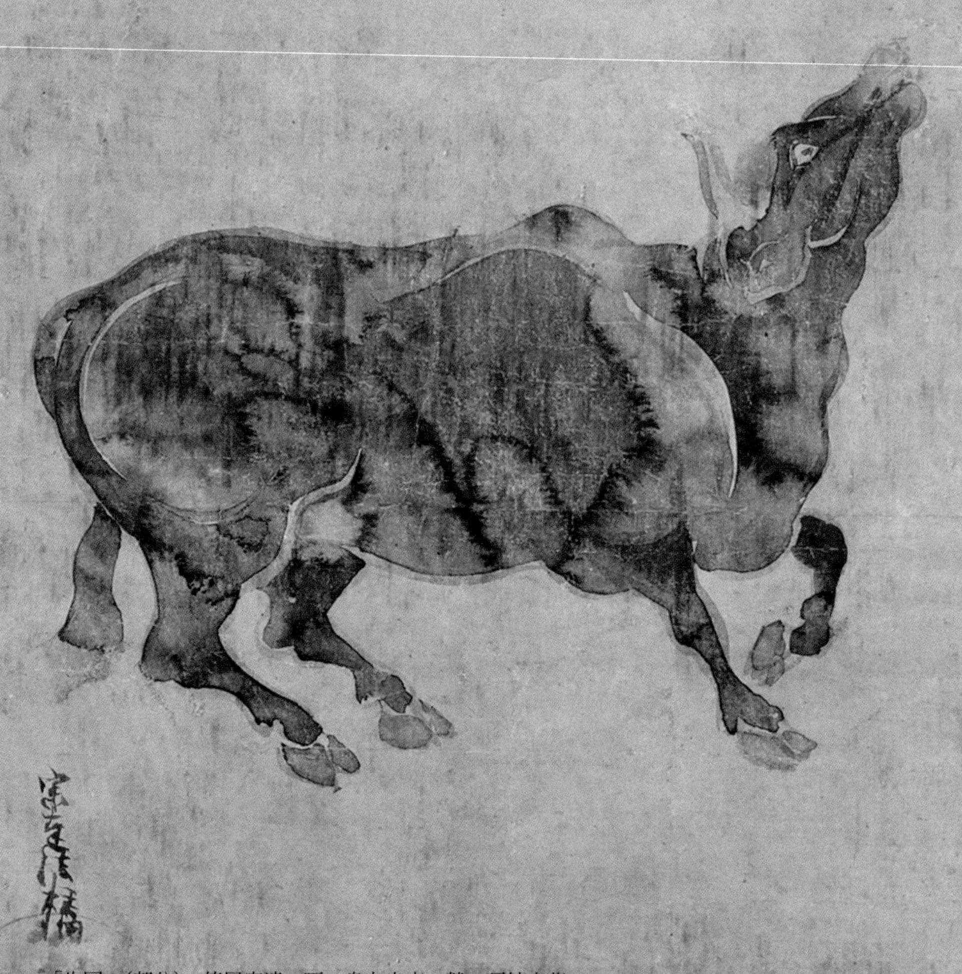

「牛図」（部分）　俵屋宗達・画　烏丸光広・賛　頂妙寺蔵
Oxen, Tawaraya Sōtatsu, Inscription by Karasumaru Mitsuhiro, Chōmyō-ji, Kyoto

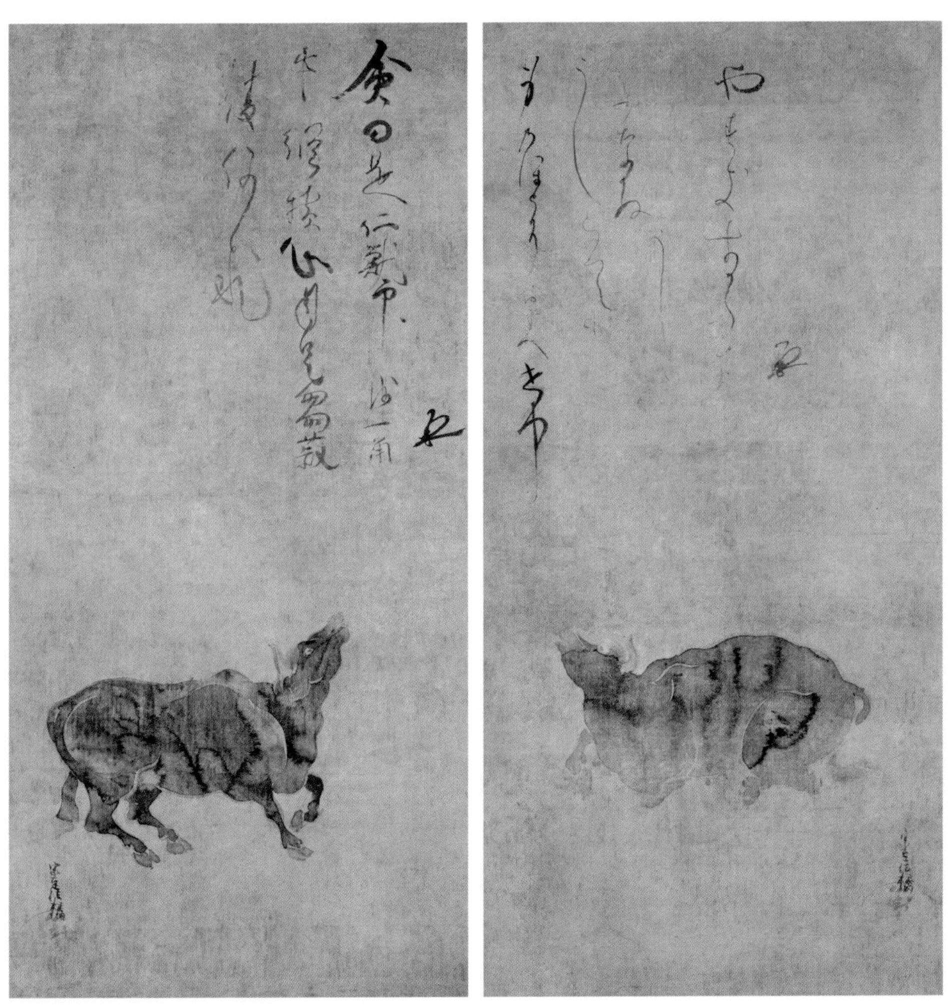

「牛図」　俵屋宗達・画　烏丸光広・賛　頂妙寺蔵
Oxen, Tawaraya Sōtatsu, Inscription by Karasumaru Mitsuhiro, Chōmyō-ji, Kyoto

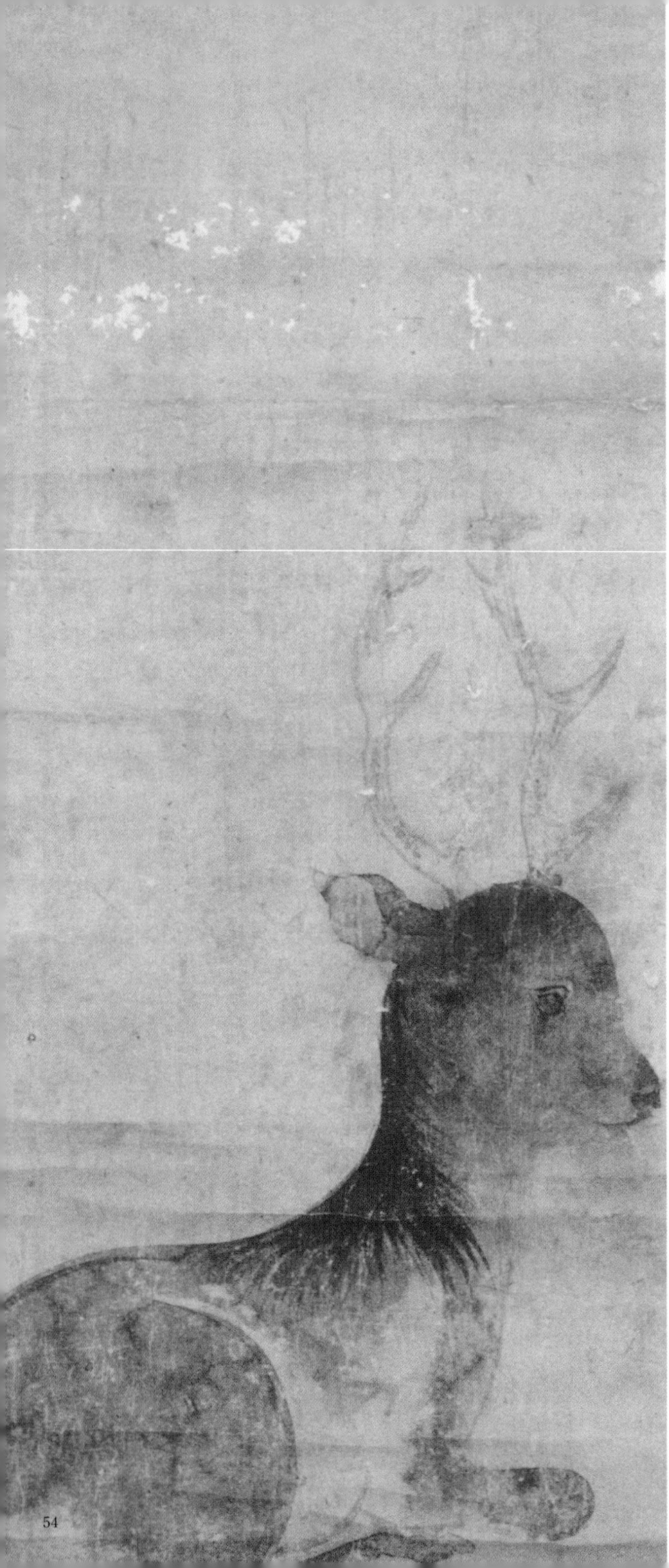

「鹿図」　俵屋宗達
宮内庁京都事務所
Deer, Tawaraya Sōtatsu,
Imperial Household Agency
Kyoto Office

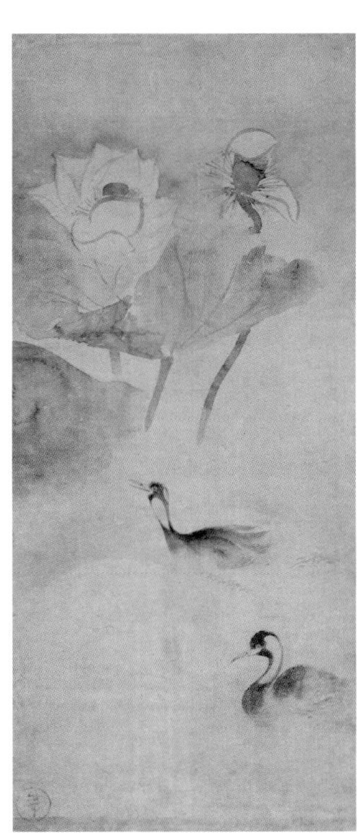

「蓮池水禽図」　国宝　俵屋宗達
京都国立博物館蔵
Water Birds in Lotus Pond,
Tawaraya Sōtatsu, National
Treasure, Kyoto National Museum

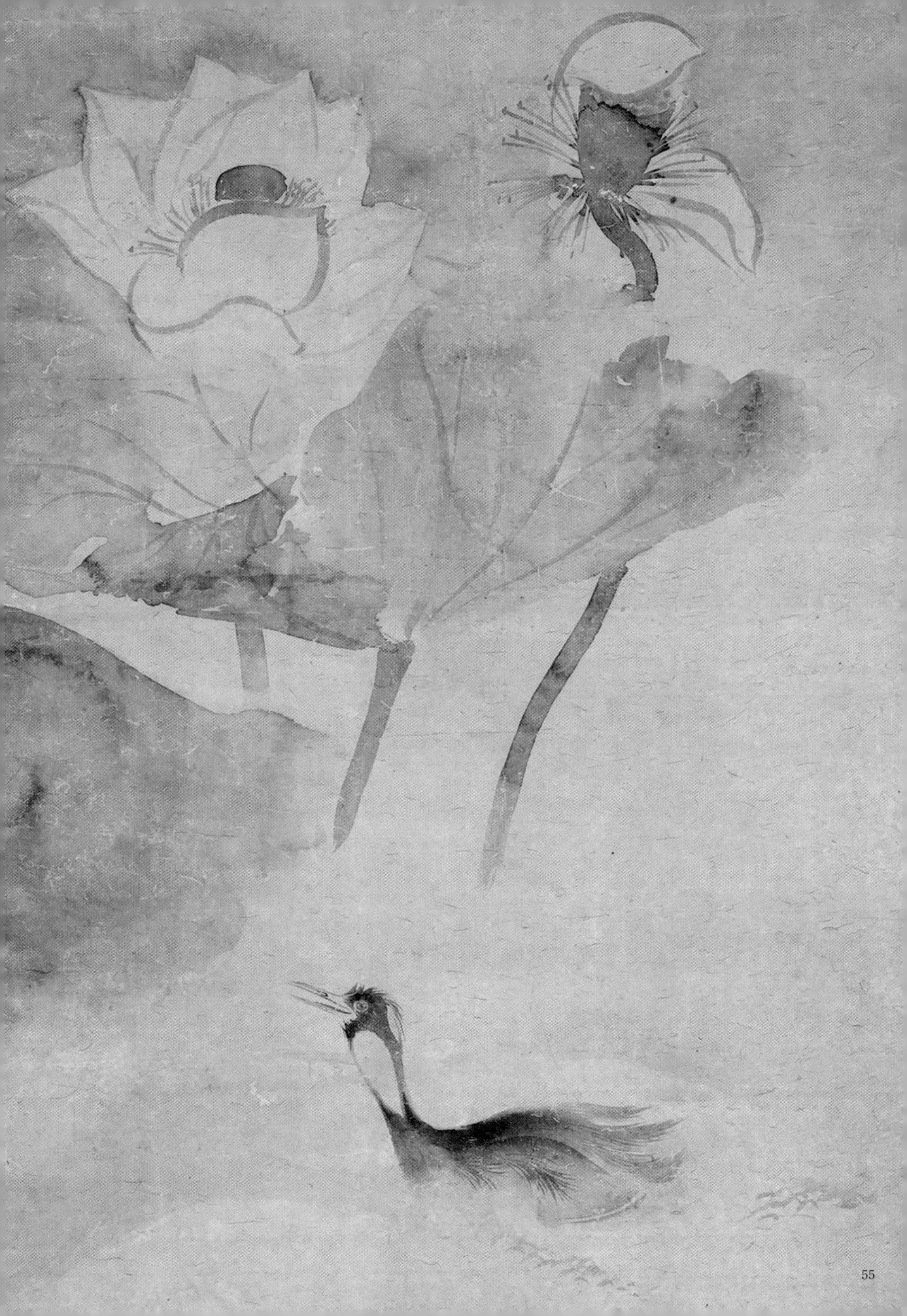

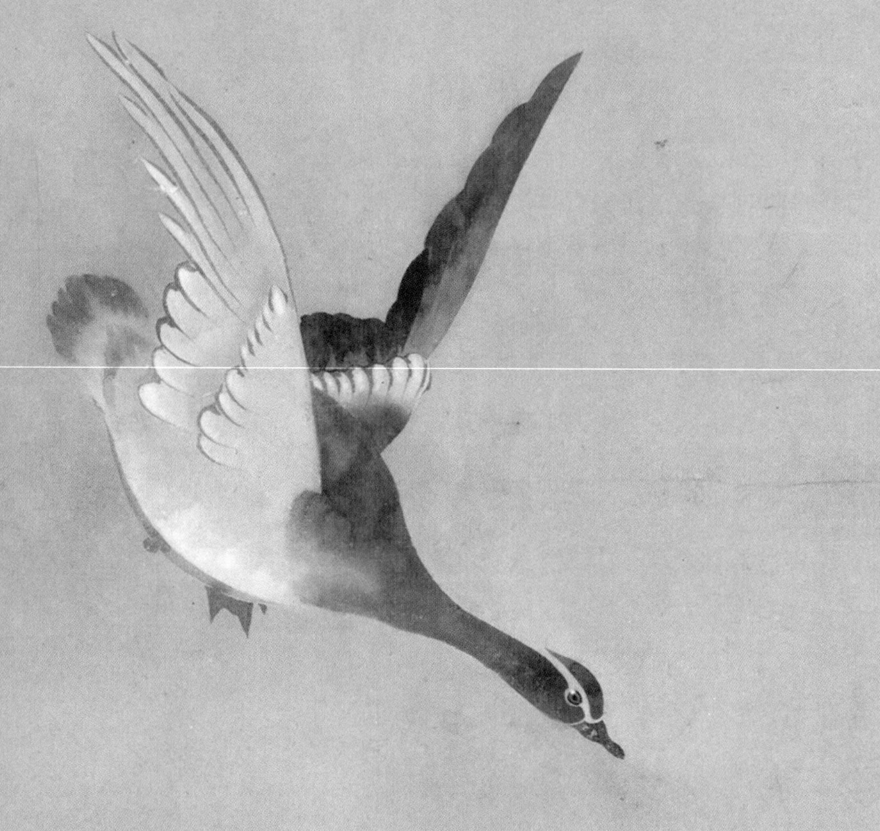

「鴨図　山田近之助旧蔵」伝俵屋宗達　京都国立博物館蔵
Wild Ducks, formerly belonged to Yamada Chikanosuke, Attributed to Tawaraya Sōtatsu, Kyoto National Museum

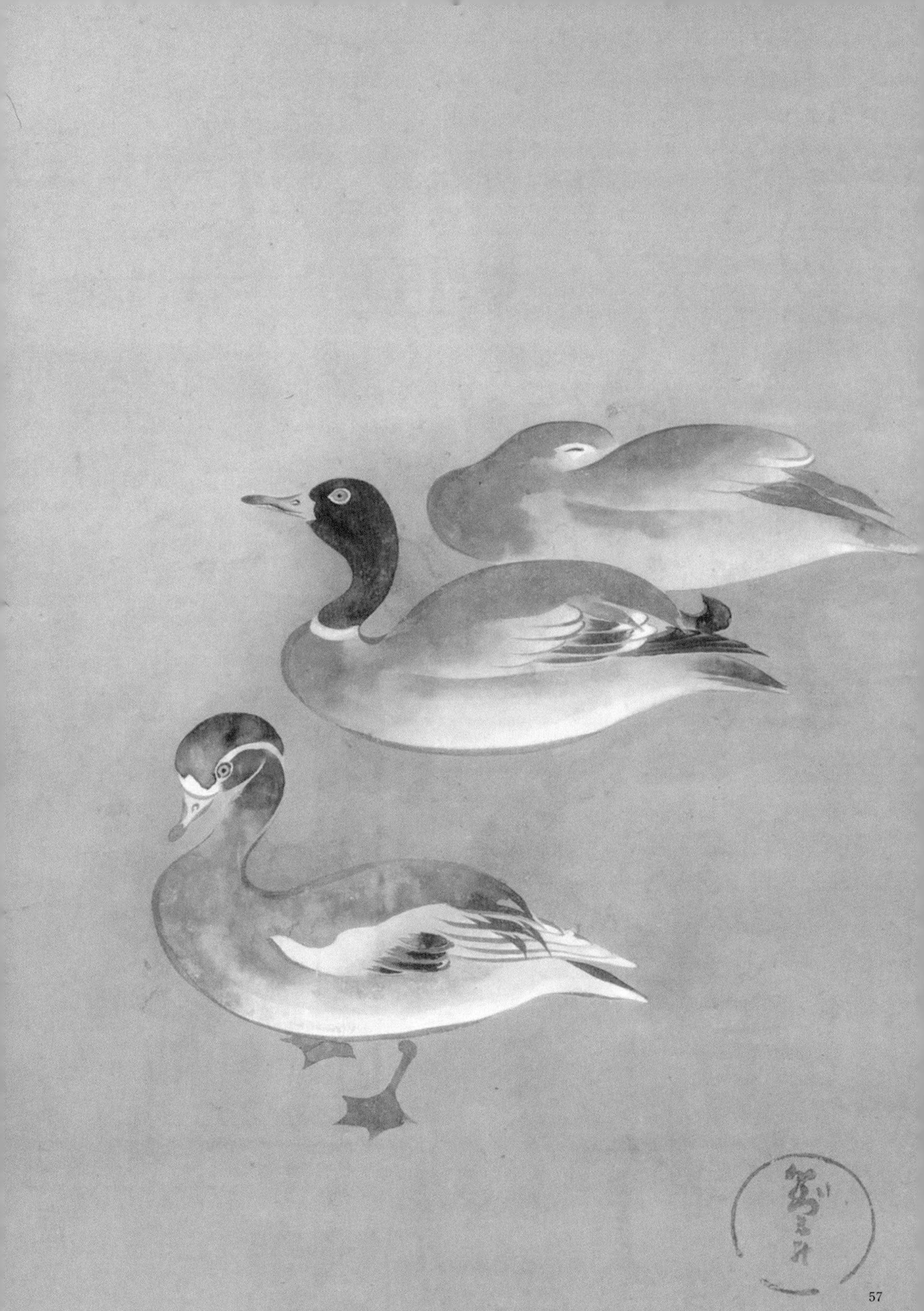

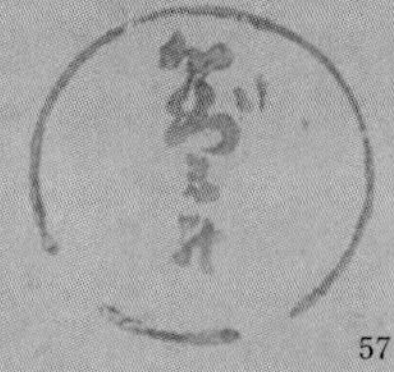

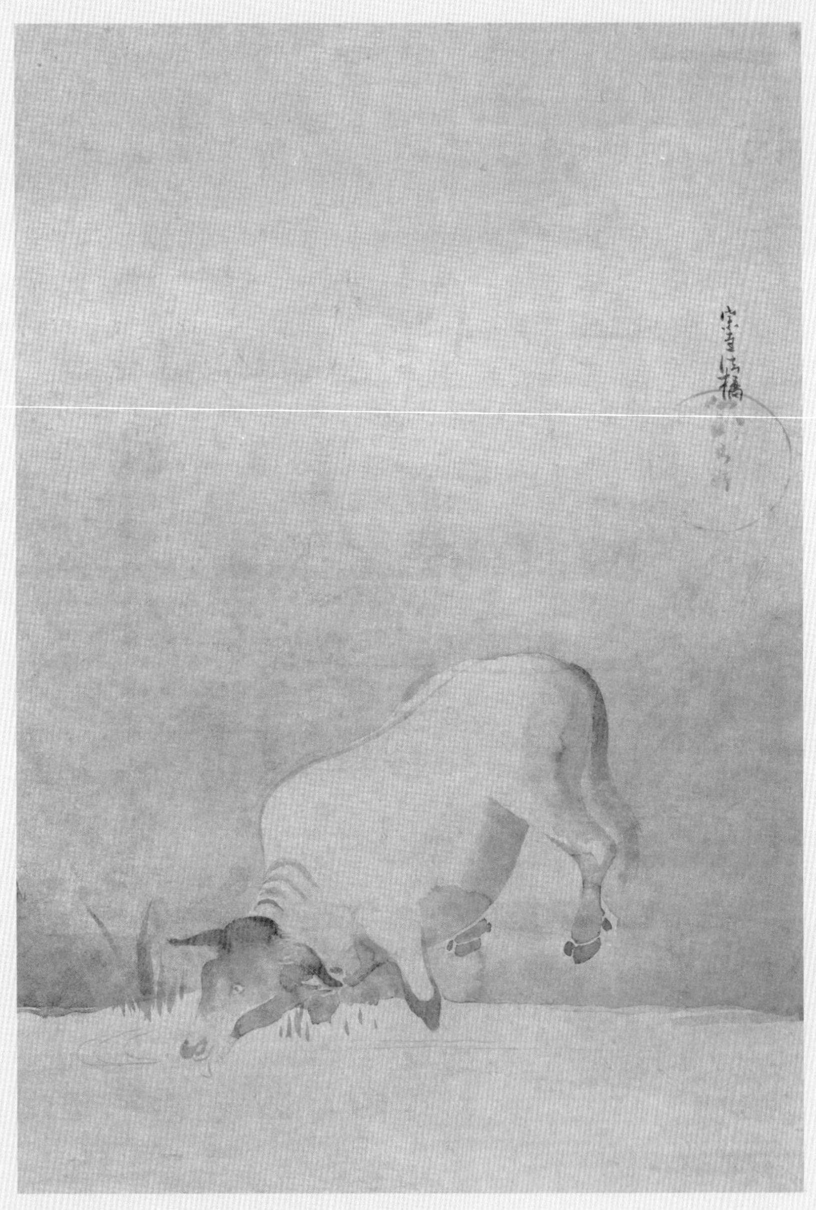

左）「牛図」　俵屋宗達　東京藝術大学大学美術館蔵
Ox, Tawaraya Sōtatsu, The University Art Museum-Tokyo University of the Arts

右）「童子の図」（部分）　伝俵屋宗達　石川県立美術館蔵
A Child, Detail, Attributed to Tawaraya Sōtatsu, Ishikawa Prefectural Museum of Art

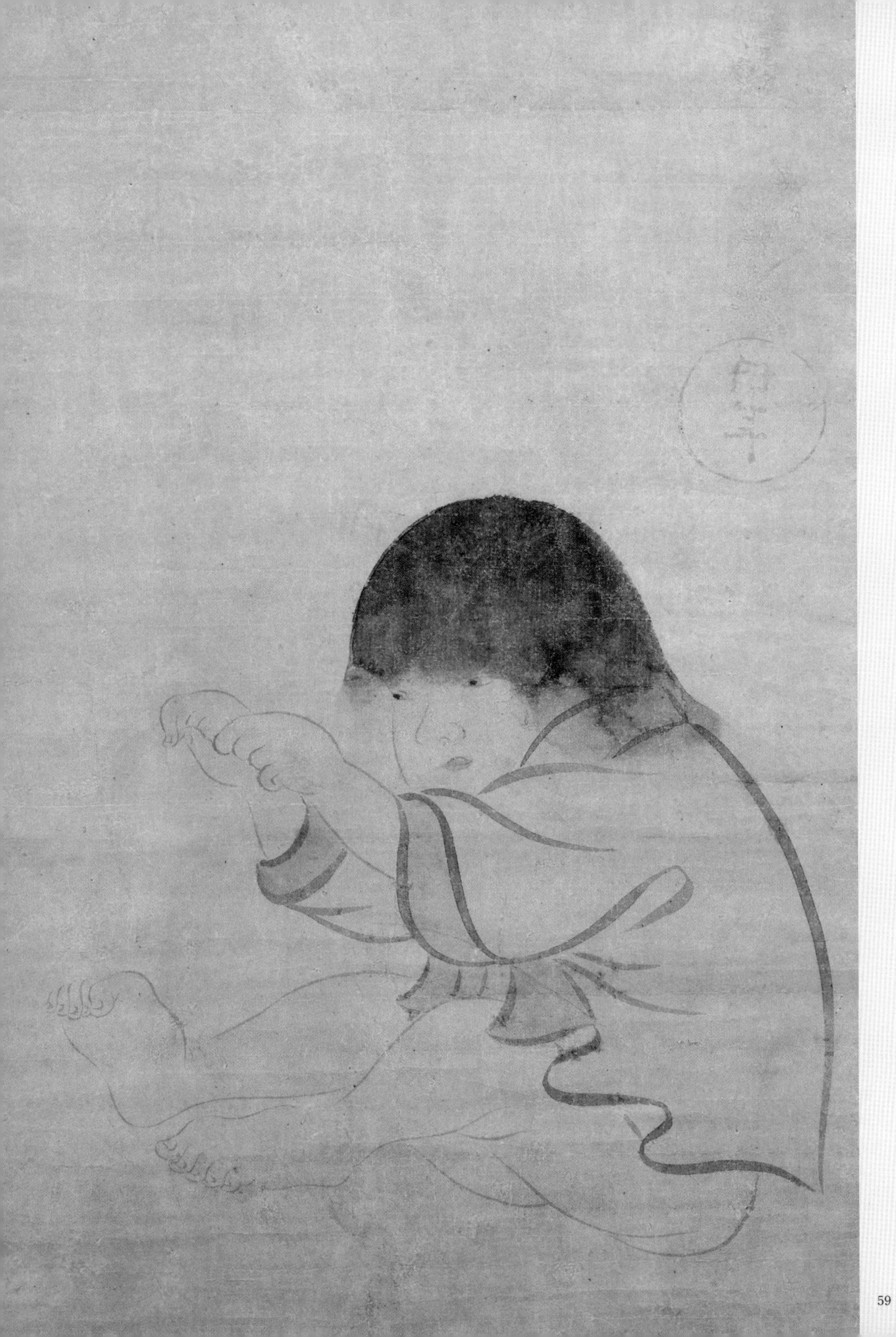

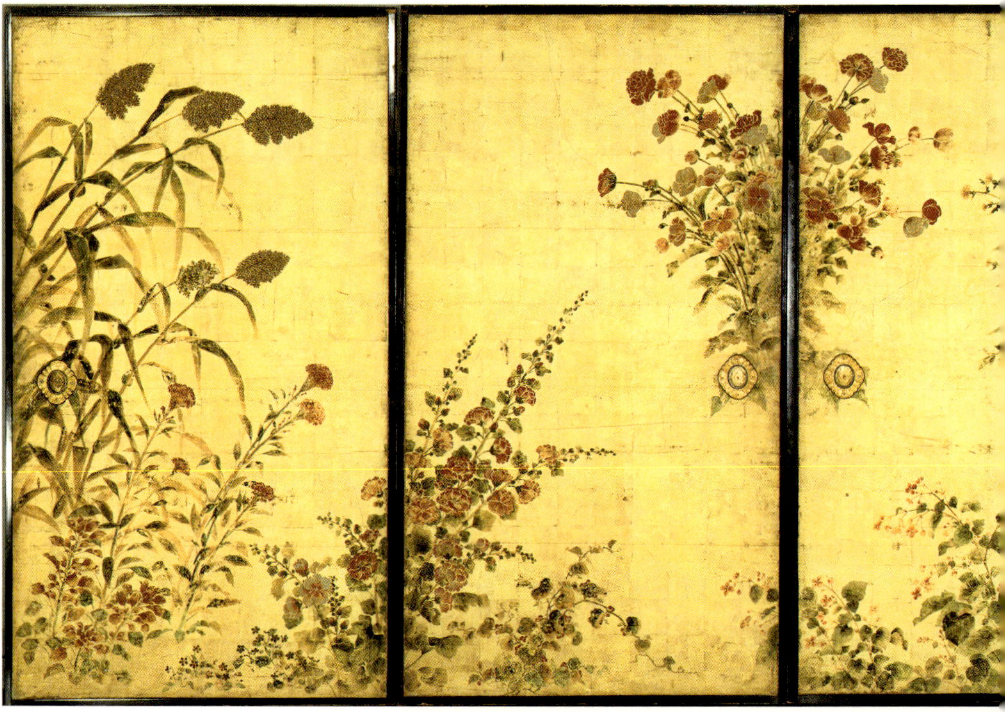

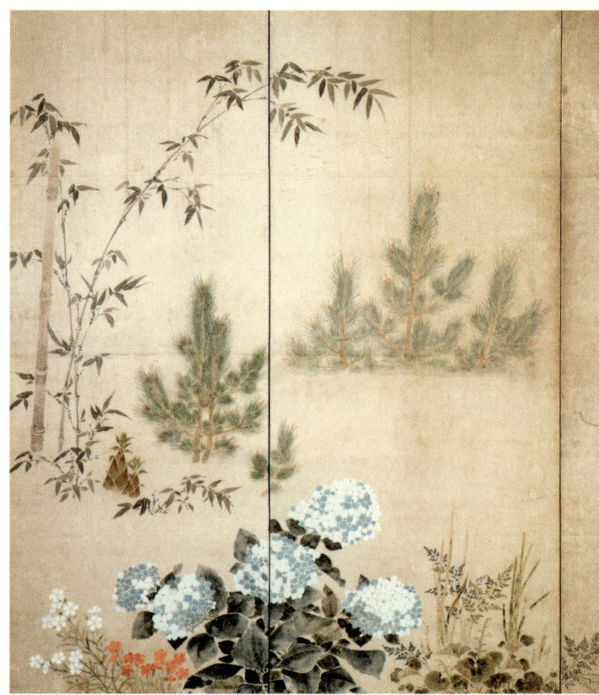

「四季草花図屏風」　伊年印
石川県立美術館蔵
Flowers and Grasses of the Four
Seasons, Seal of Inen, Ishikawa
Prefectural Museum of Art

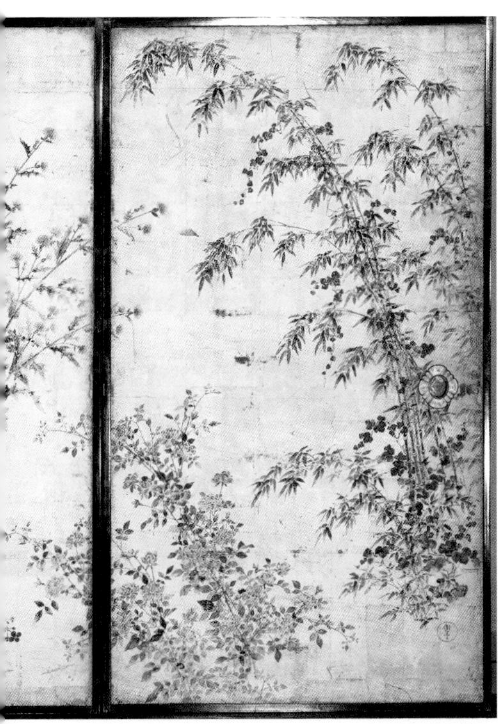

「草花図」　伊年印
京都国立博物館蔵
Flowering Plants, Seal of Inen,
Kyoto National Museum

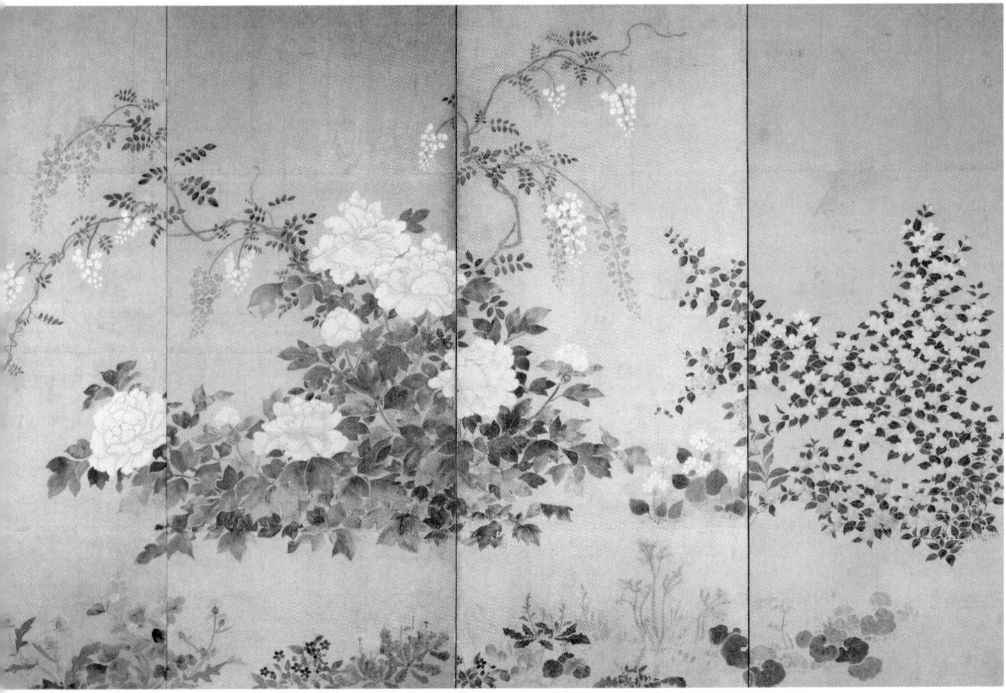

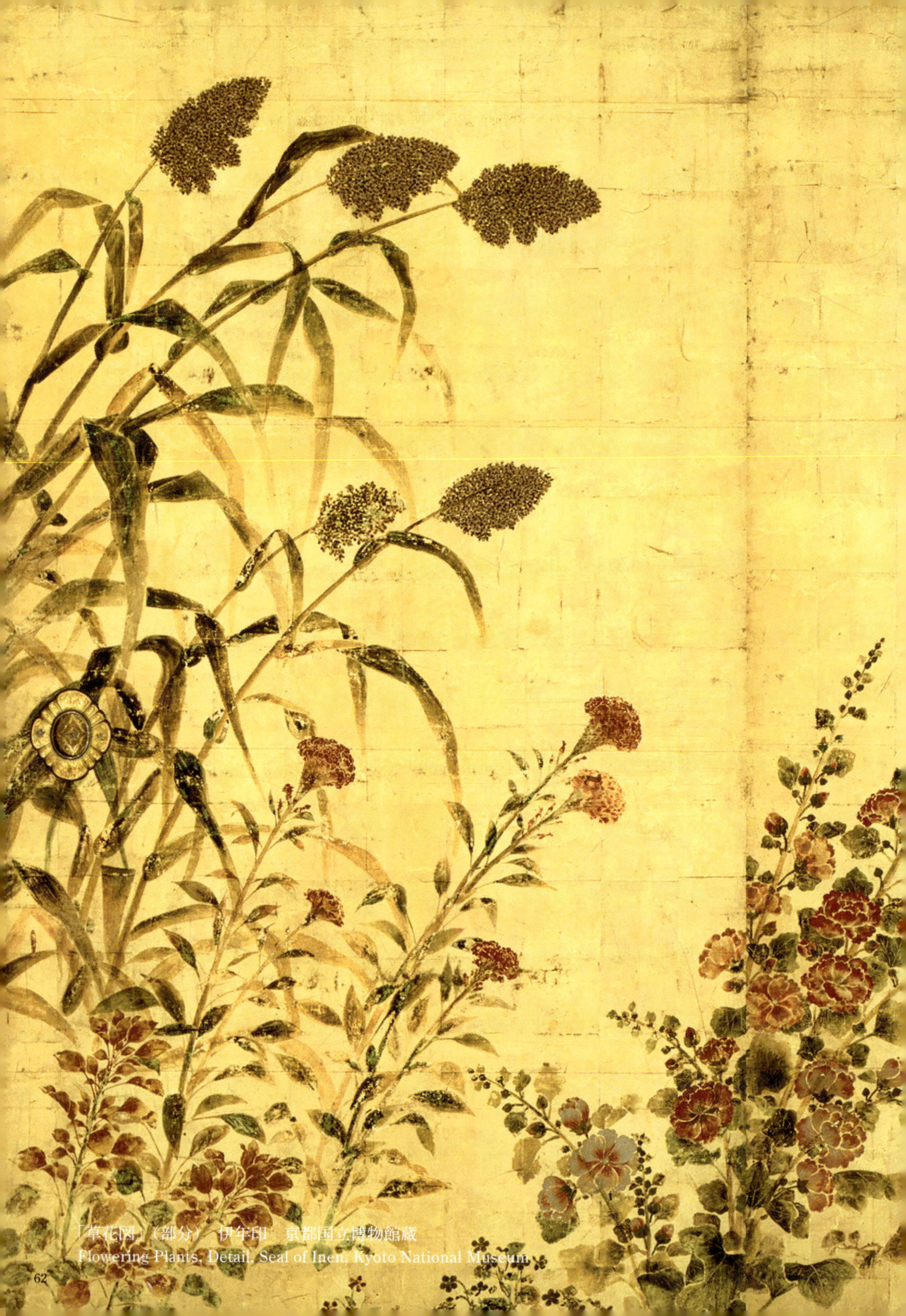

「草花図」（部分）　伊年印　京都国立博物館蔵
Flowering Plants, Detail, Seal of Inen, Kyoto National Museum

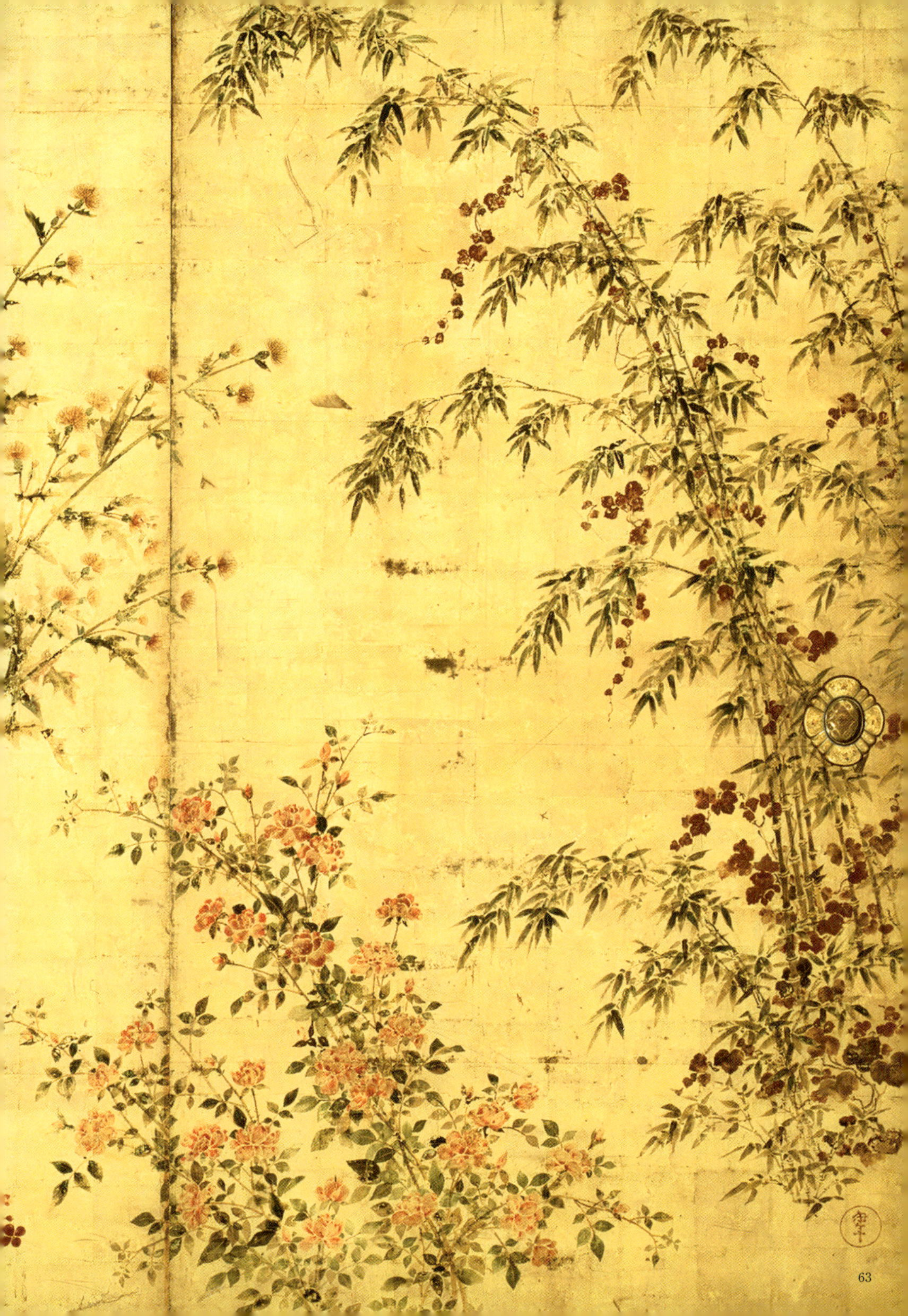

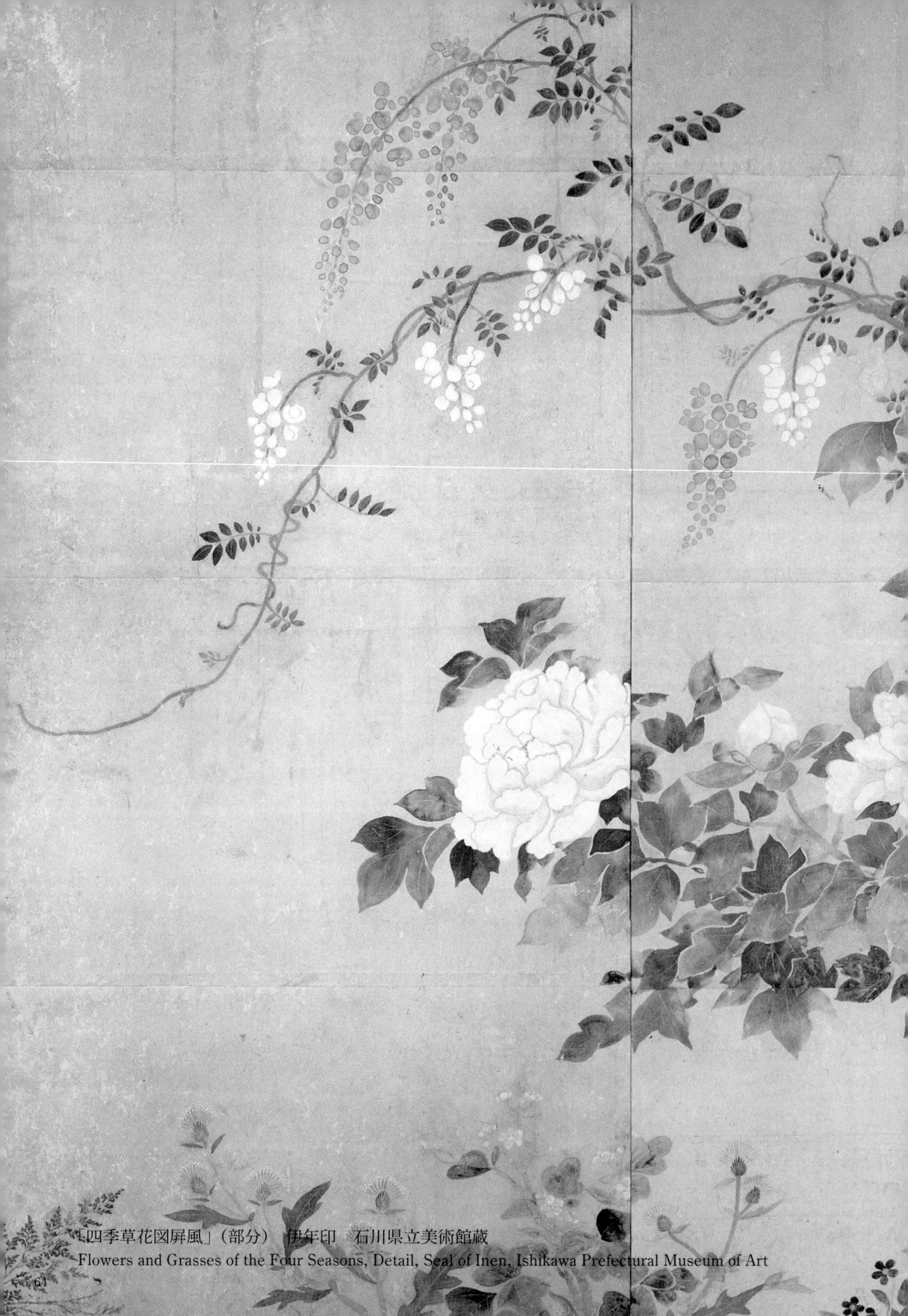

「四季草花図屏風」（部分）　伊年印　石川県立美術館蔵
Flowers and Grasses of the Four Seasons, Detail, Seal of Inen, Ishikawa Prefectural Museum of Art

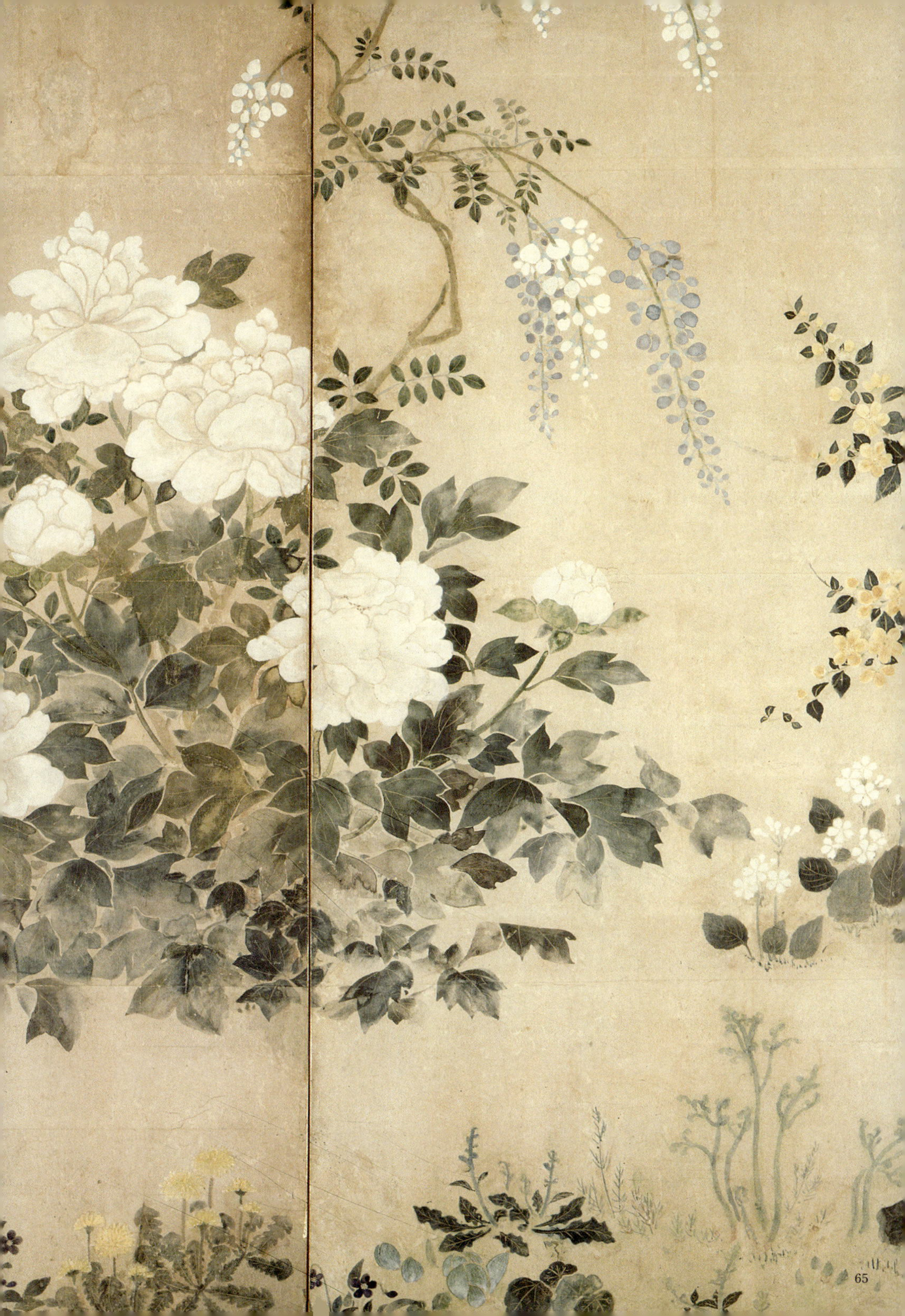

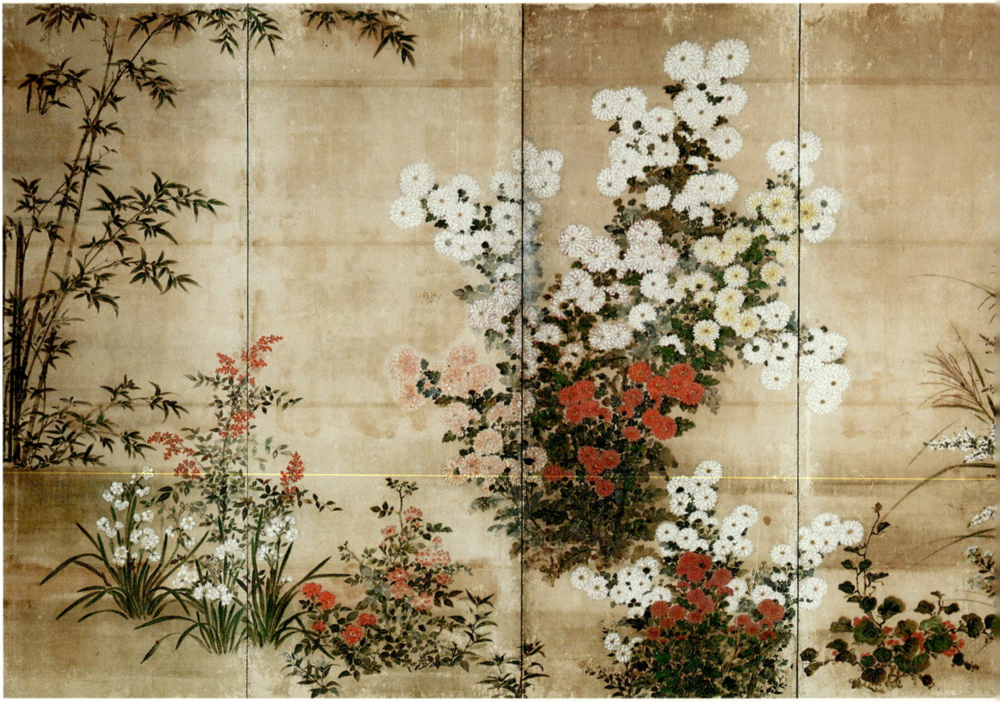

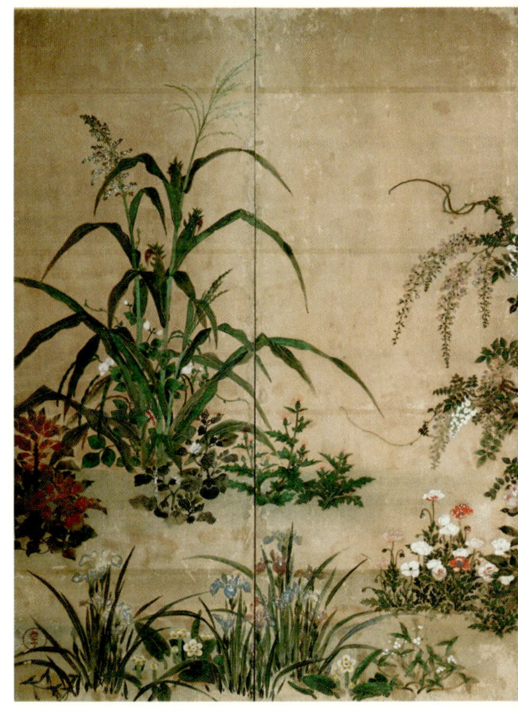

「四季草花図屏風」　伊年印　黒部市美術館蔵
Flowers and Grasses of the Four Seasons, Seal of
Inen, Kurobe City Art Museum

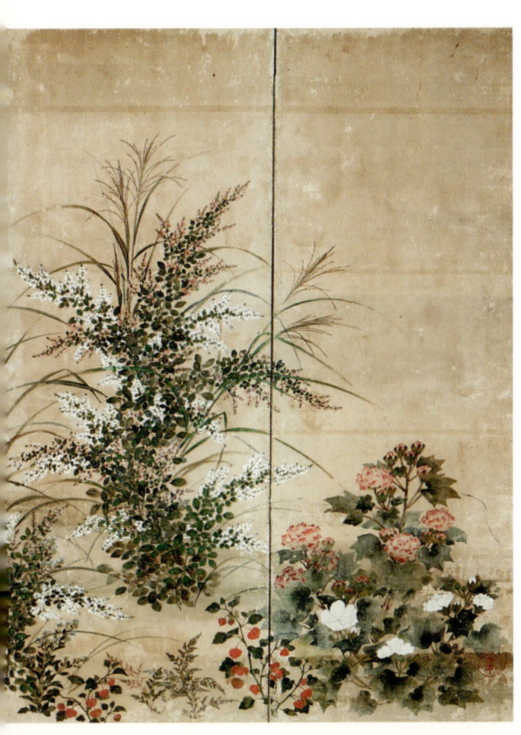

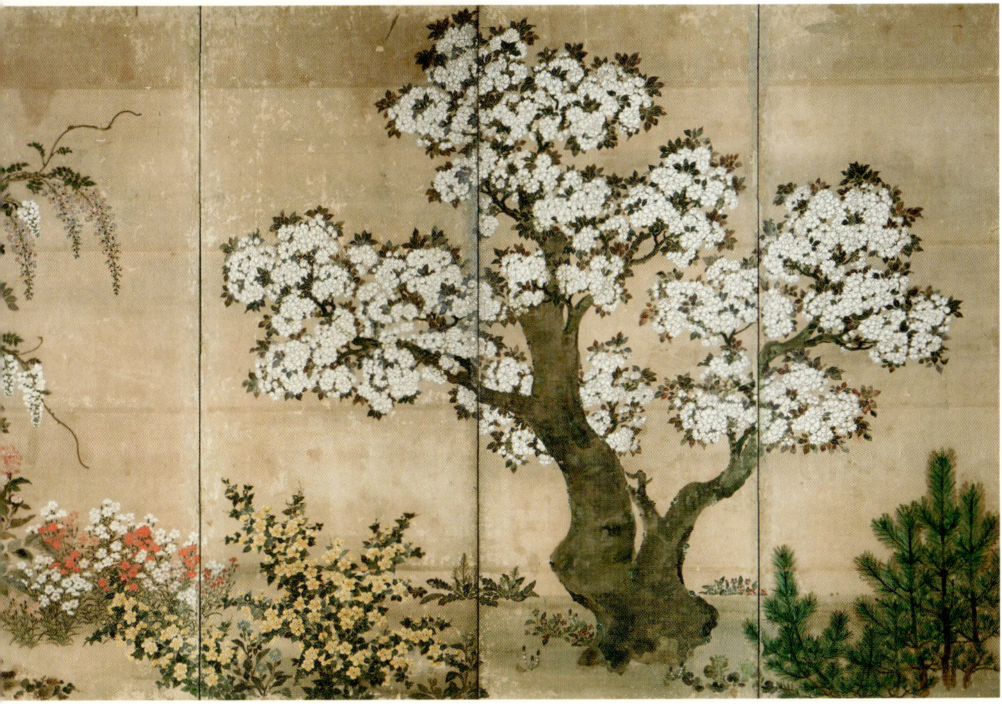

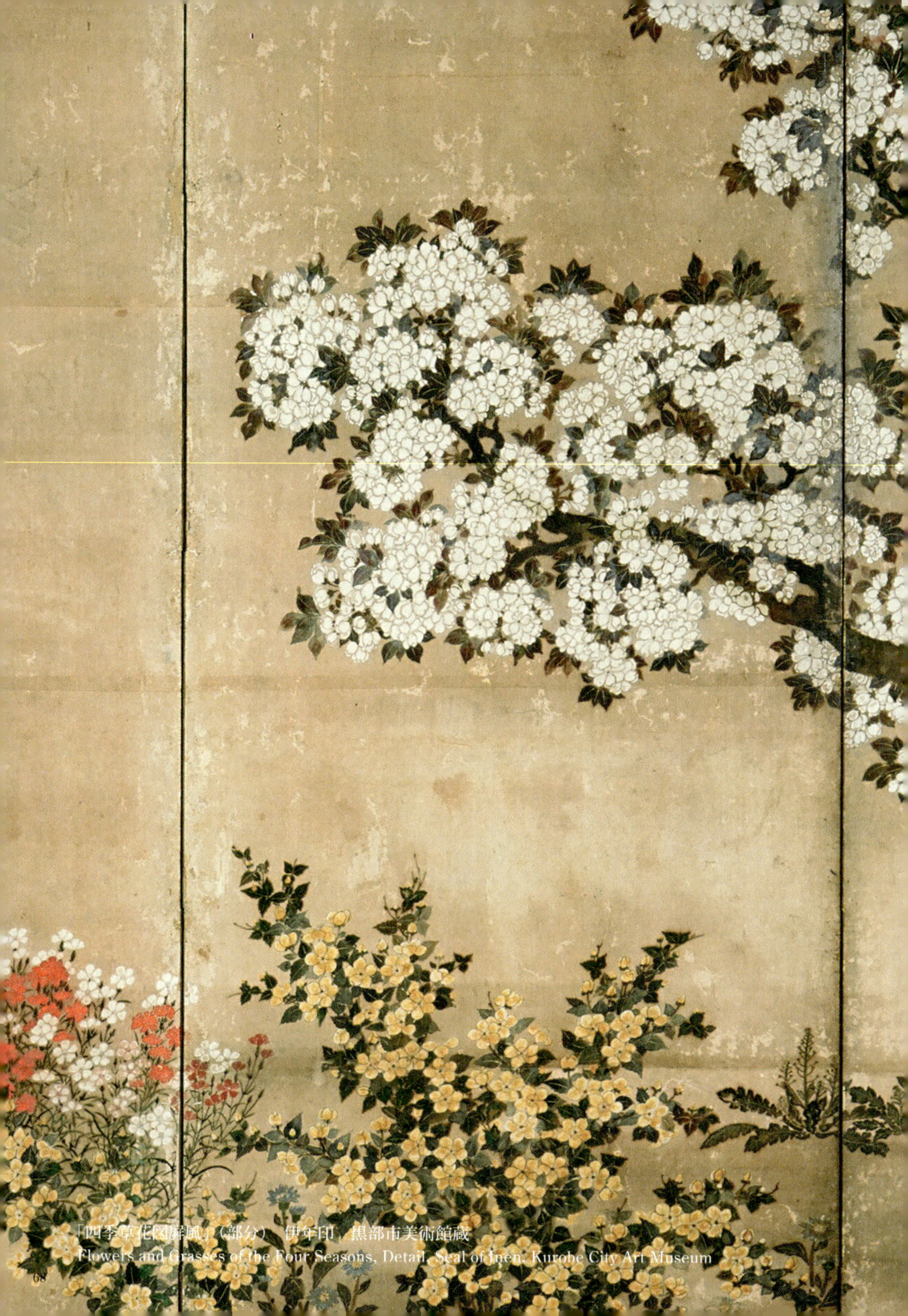

「四季草花図屏風」（部分）　伊年印　黒部市美術館蔵
Flowers and Grasses of the Four Seasons, Detail, Seal of Inen, Kurobe City Art Museum

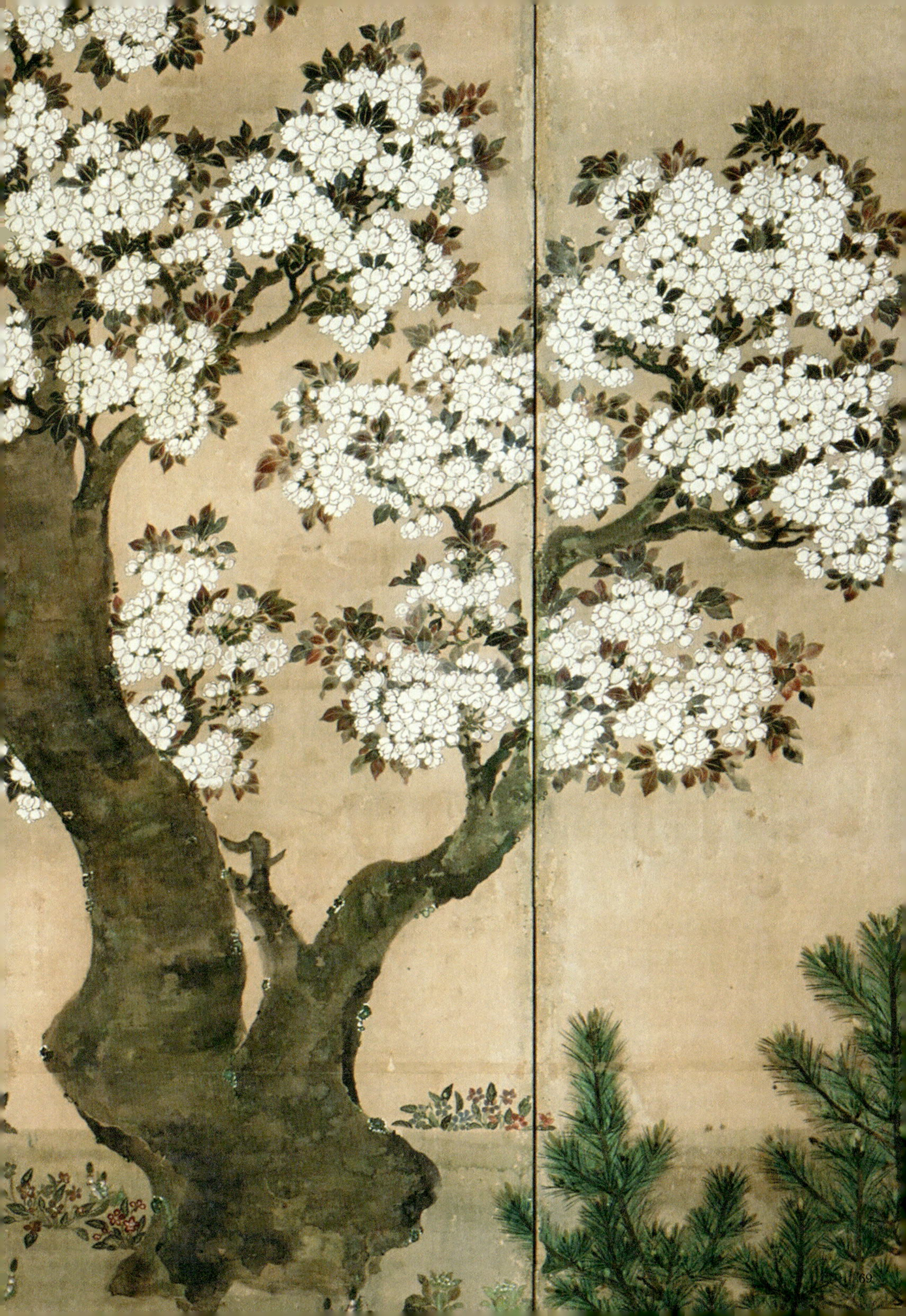

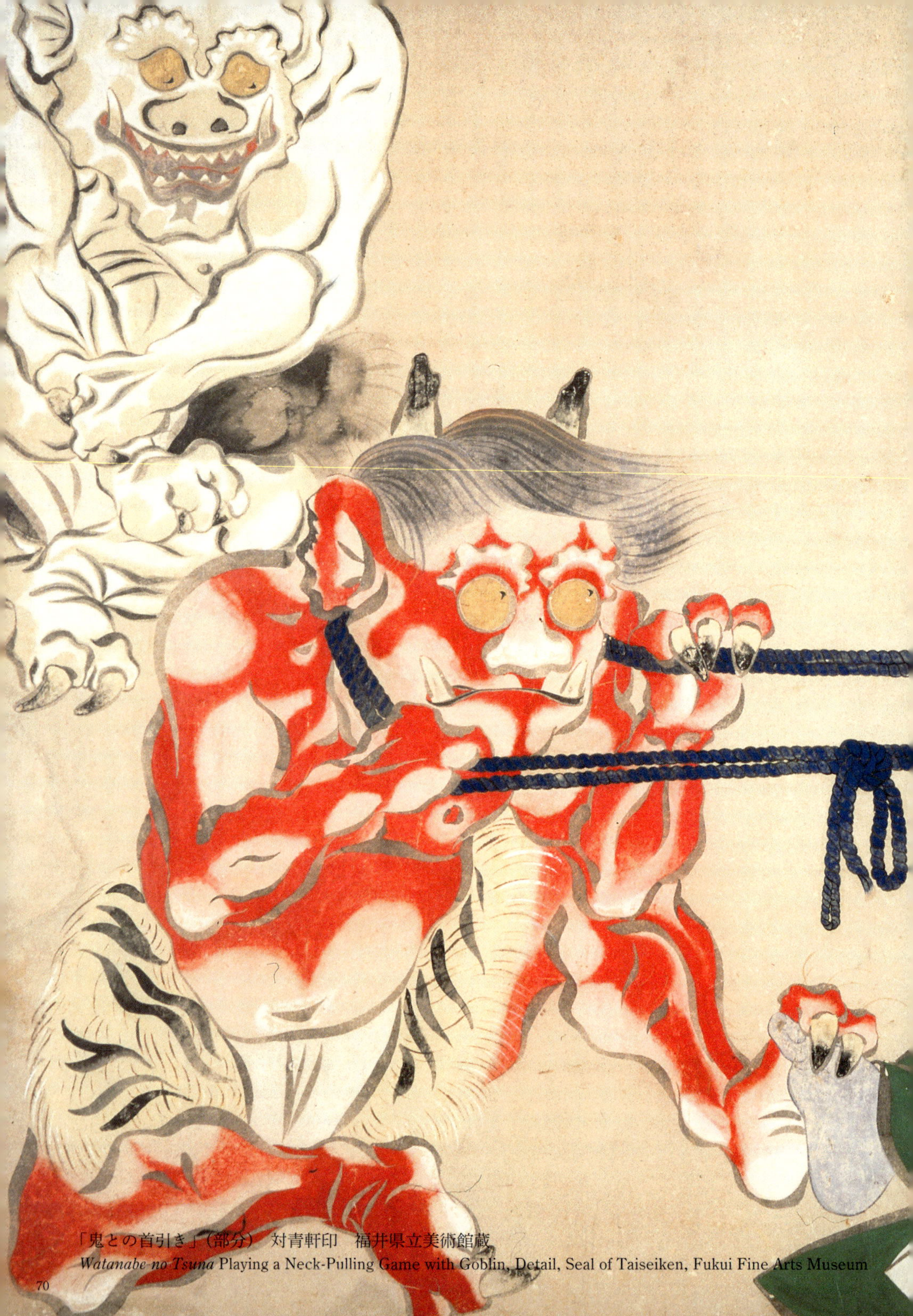

「鬼との首引き」（部分）　対青軒印　福井県立美術館蔵
Watanabe no Tsuna Playing a Neck-Pulling Game with Goblin, Detail, Seal of Taiseiken, Fukui Fine Arts Museum

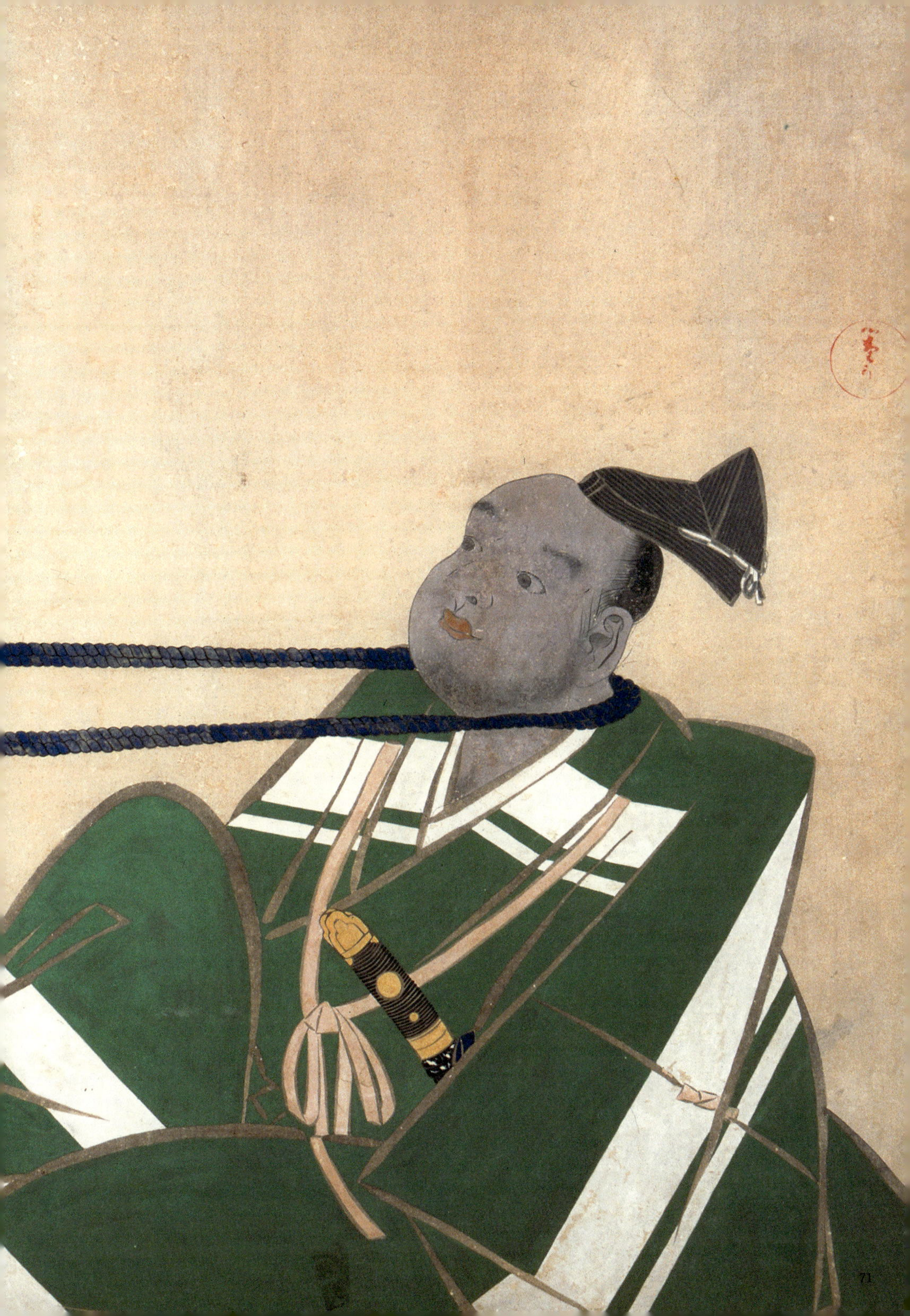

俵屋宗雪

たわらや そうせつ　生没年不詳

俵屋宗達の子とも、あるいは弟、弟子とも伝えられるが、いずれにしても宗達の工房にいた画人で、宗達の死後その工房を継承している。1642年（寛永19）には法橋の位にあり、同年、加賀金沢藩前田家の御用絵師になった。前田利常の息女が八条宮家に輿入れする際、宮家の新築の御殿に襖絵を描いたことが知られる。

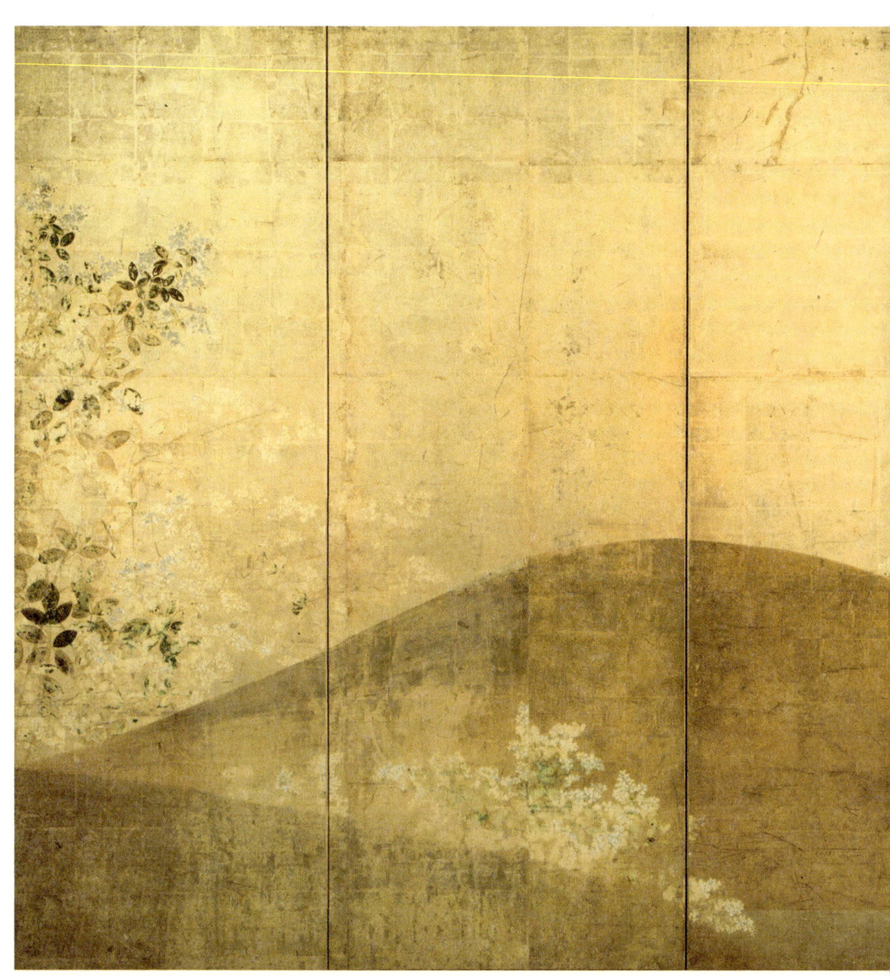

「萩に兎図」　俵屋宗雪　石川県立美術館蔵
Bush Clover and Rabbits, Tawaraya Sōsetsu, Ishikawa Prefectural Museum of Art

Tawaraya Sōsetsu (dates uncertain)
Tawaraya Sōtatsu's son, younger brother, or pupil, Sōsetsu inherited Sōtatsu's studio. He received the artistic rank of hokkyō by 1642, the year he became official painter to the Maeda family, rulers of Kaga. When Maeda Toshitsune's daughter married into the Hachijō-no-miya branch of the imperial family, Sōsetsu created the sliding door paintings for the prince's new residence.

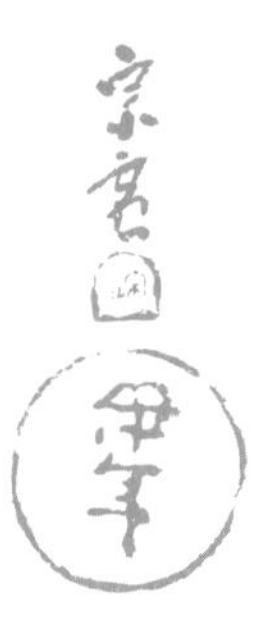

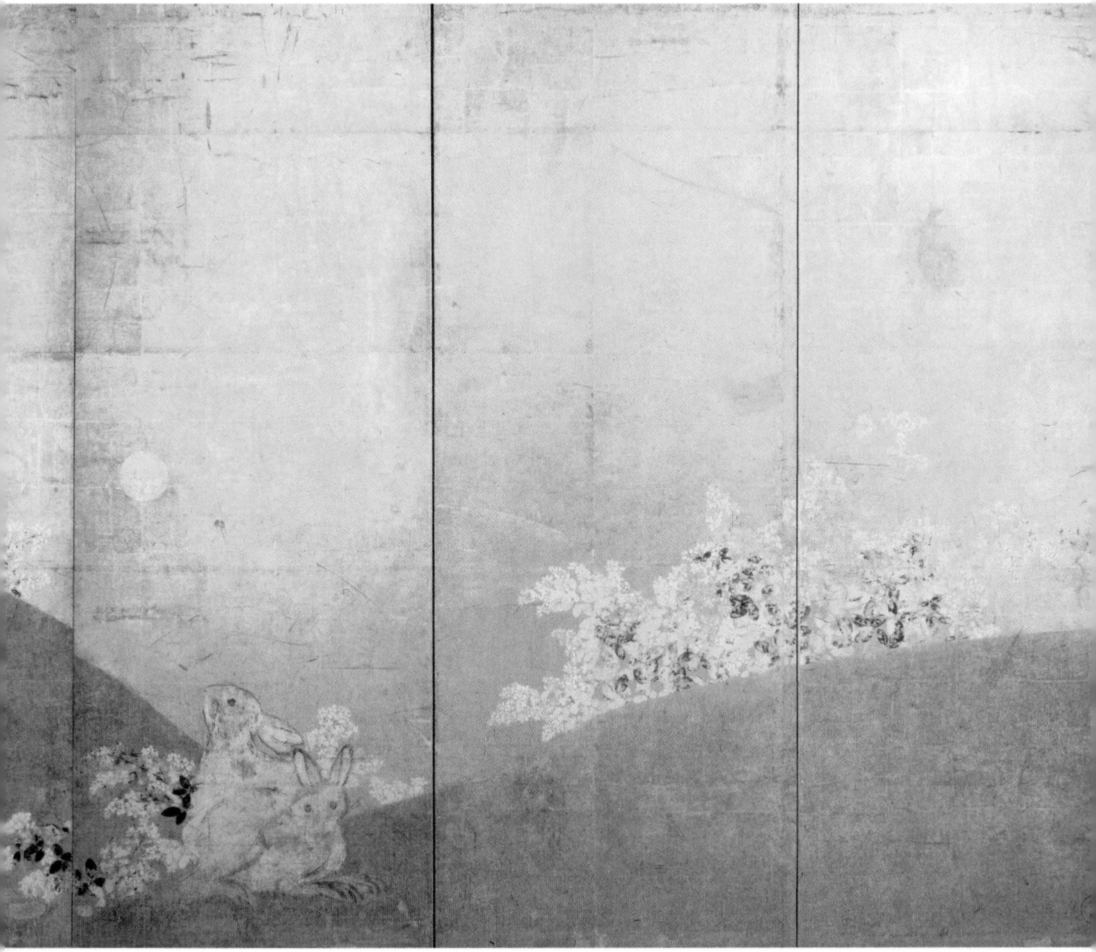

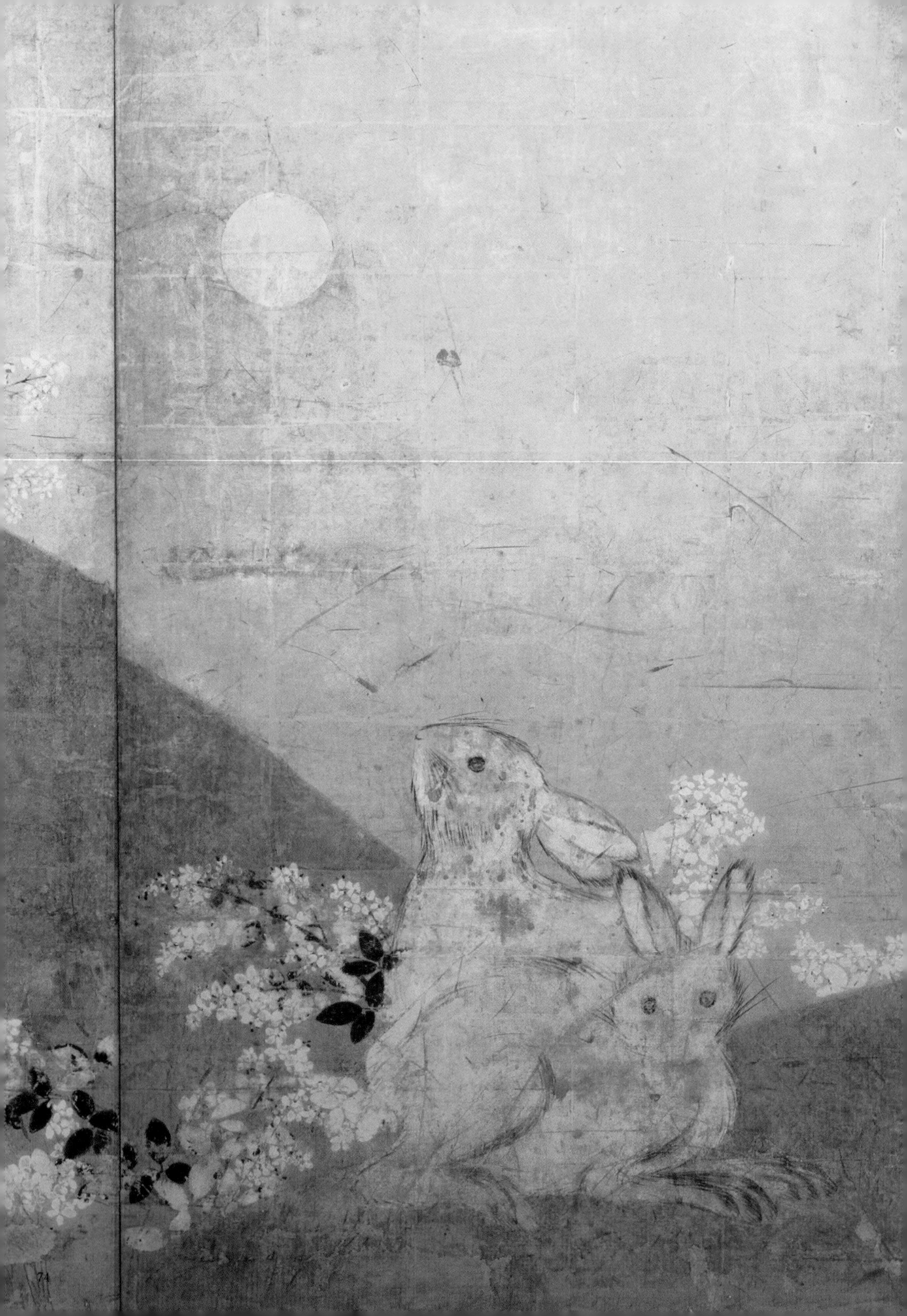

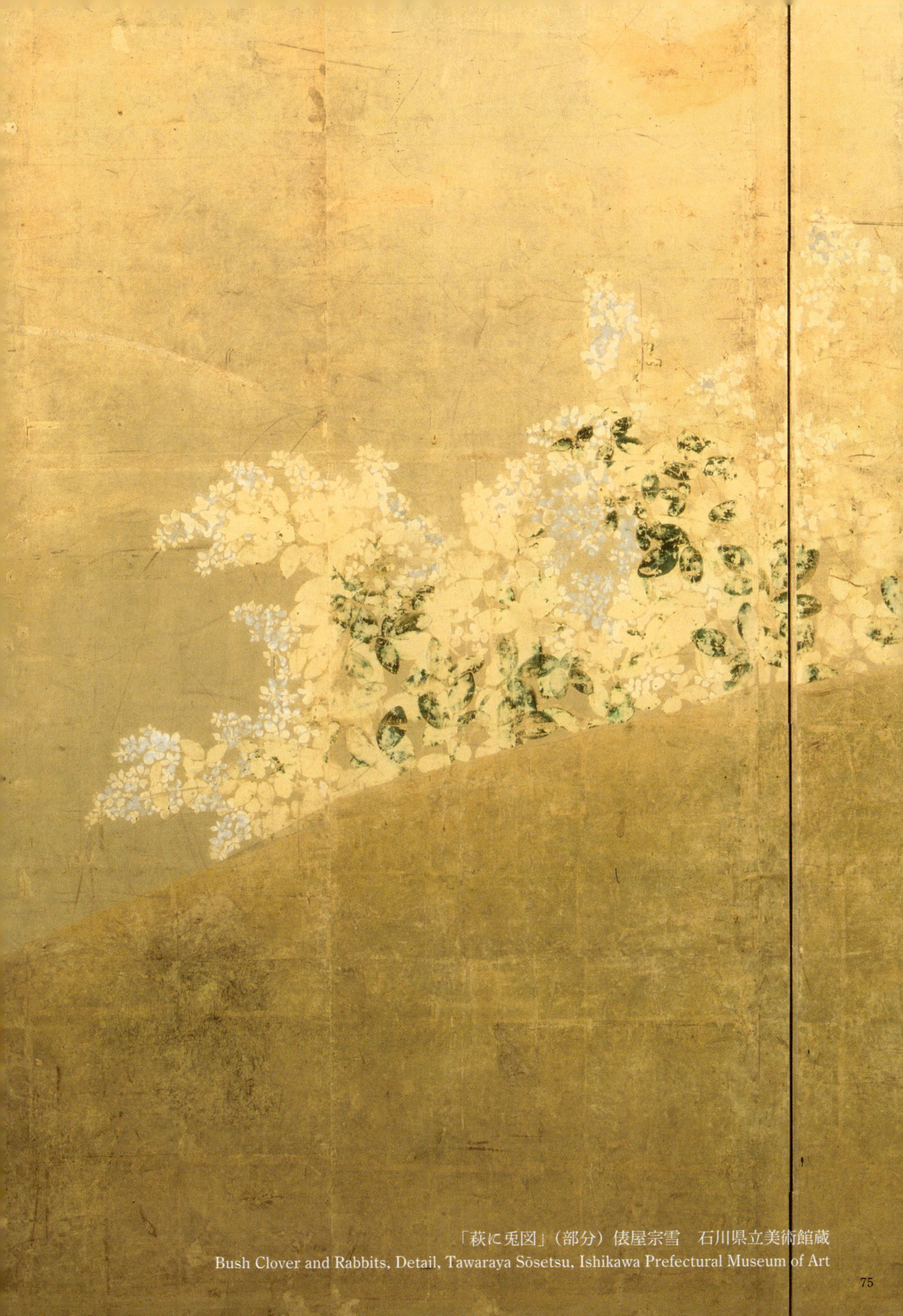

「萩に兎図」（部分）俵屋宗雪　石川県立美術館蔵
Bush Clover and Rabbits, Detail, Tawaraya Sōsetsu, Ishikawa Prefectural Museum of Art

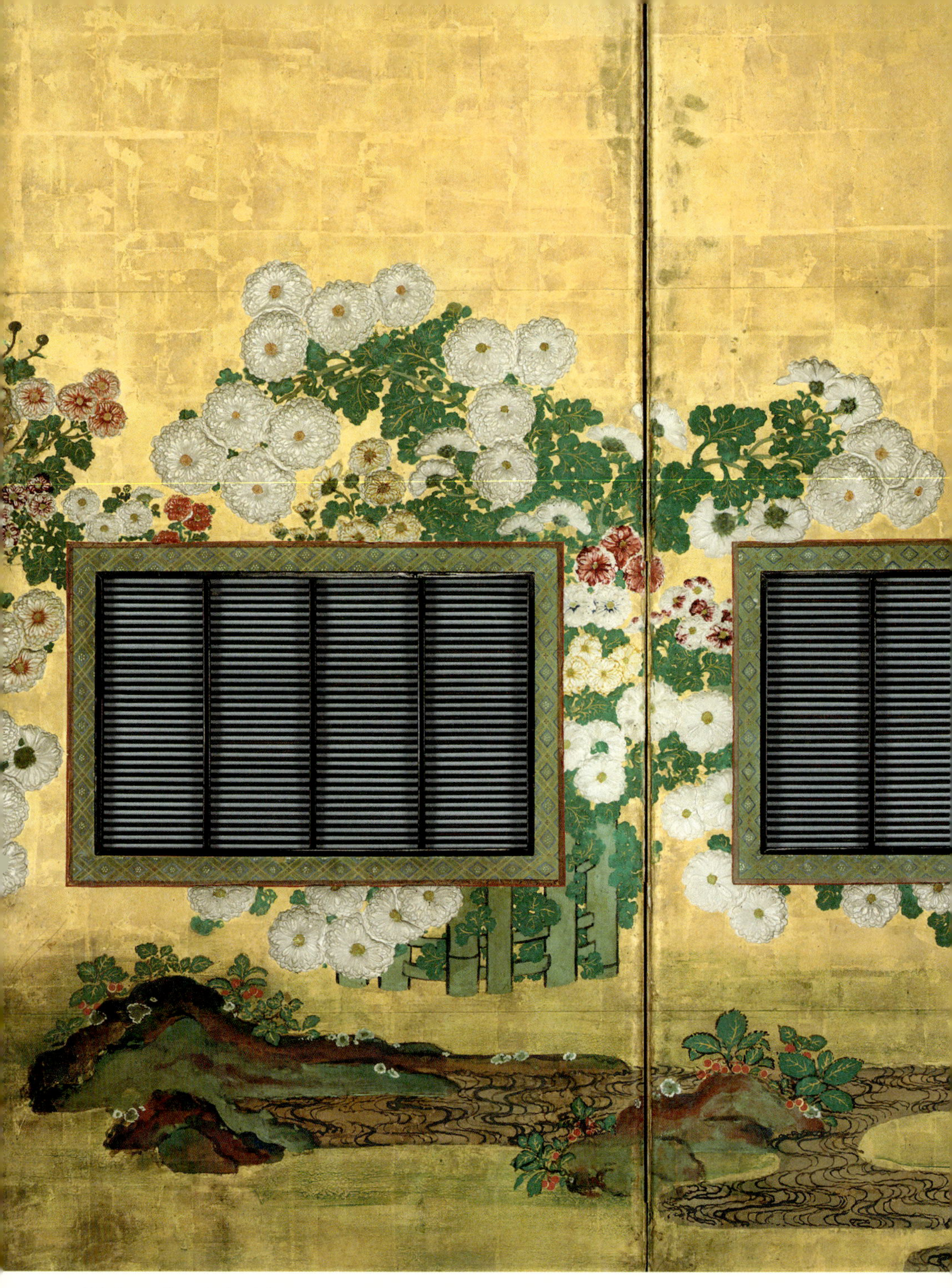

「籬菊図」俵屋宗雪　京都国立博物館蔵
Chrysanthemums and Fences, Detail, Tawaraya Sōsetsu, Kyoto National Museum

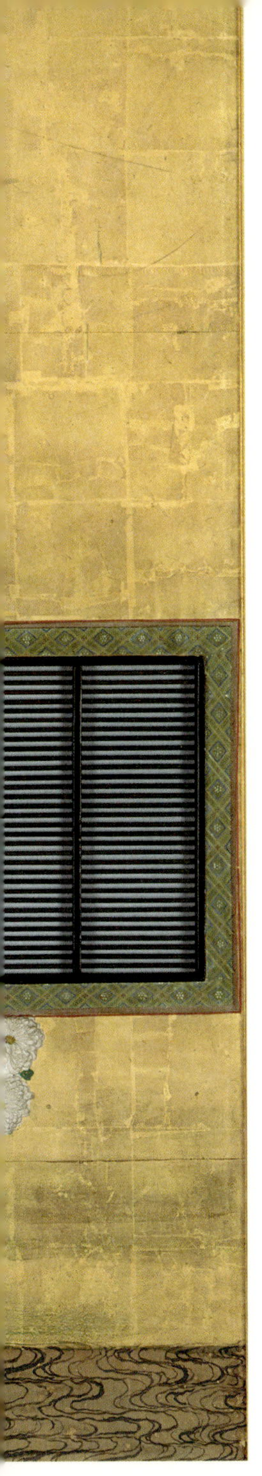

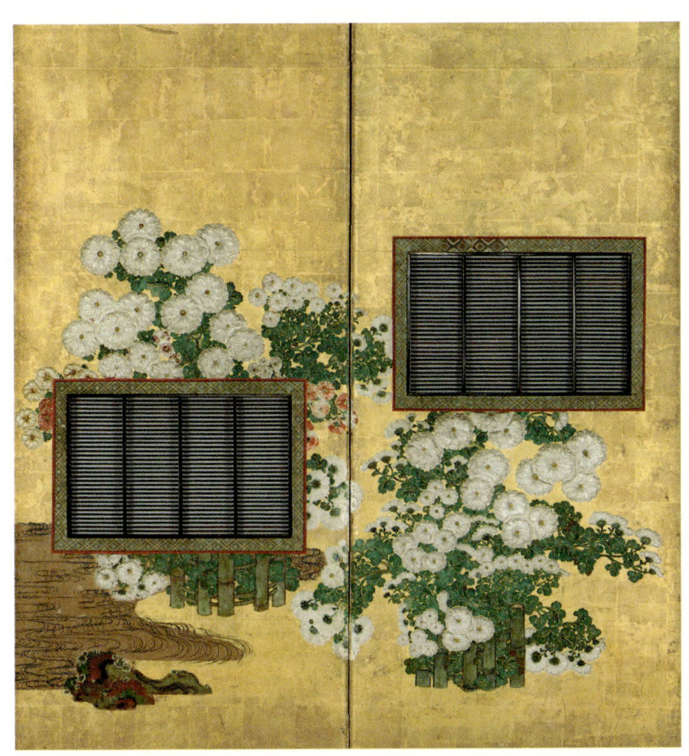

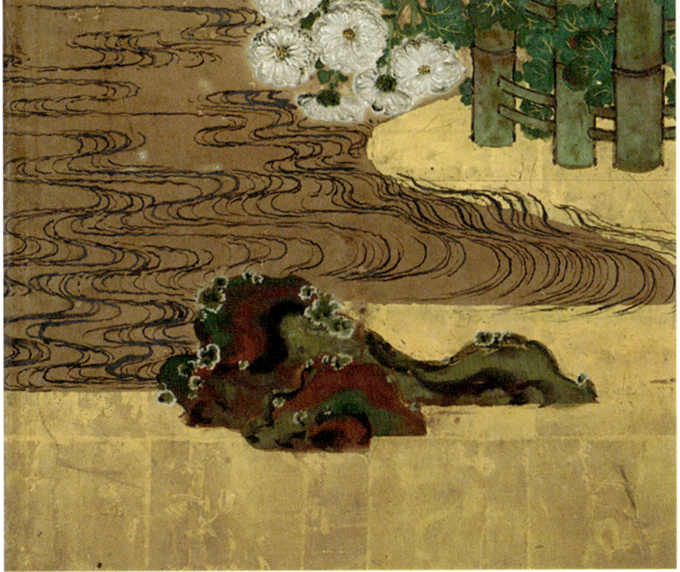

きたがわ　そうせつ　生没年不詳

俵屋宗達、俵屋宗雪と同じ「伊年」印を用い、宗達の後継者と伝えられ、宗雪の没後、工房の指導にあたったと思われる。草花図を得意とし、薄墨と淡彩を用いて繊細に描かれた押絵貼の屏風が多く残されている。17世紀後半、金沢地方で活躍したと思われる。

喜多川相説

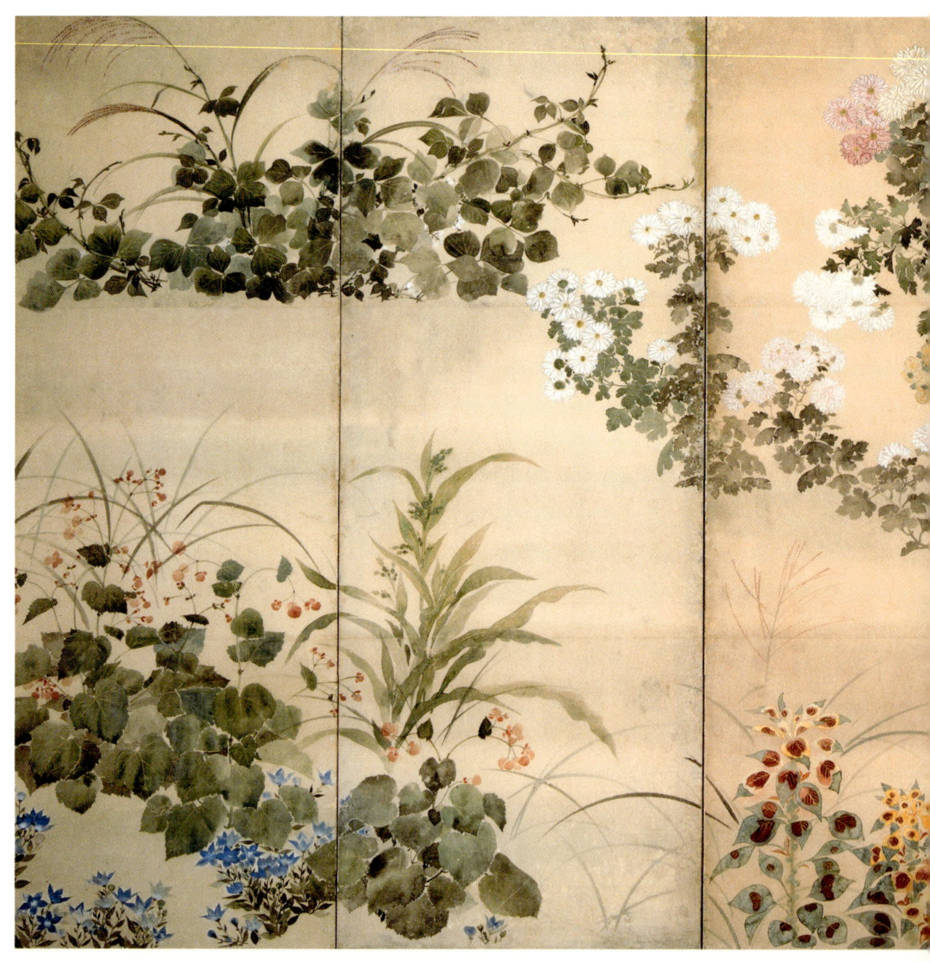

「秋草図」　喜多川相説　石川県立美術館蔵
Flowering Plants of Autumn, Kitagawa Sōsetsu, Ishikawa Prefectural Museum of Art

Kitagawa Sōsetsu (dates uncertain)
Used the same "Inen" seal as Tawaraya Sōtatsu and Sōsetsu
and may have headed the Tawaraya studio after Sōsetsu's
death. Specialized in paintings of flowers and grasses; left many
delicately painted appliqué folding screens in pale ink and wash.
Is thought to have been active in the Kanazawa region in the
latter half of the 17th century.

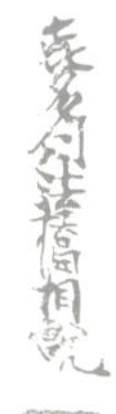

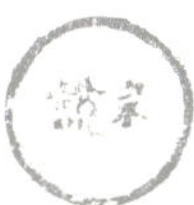

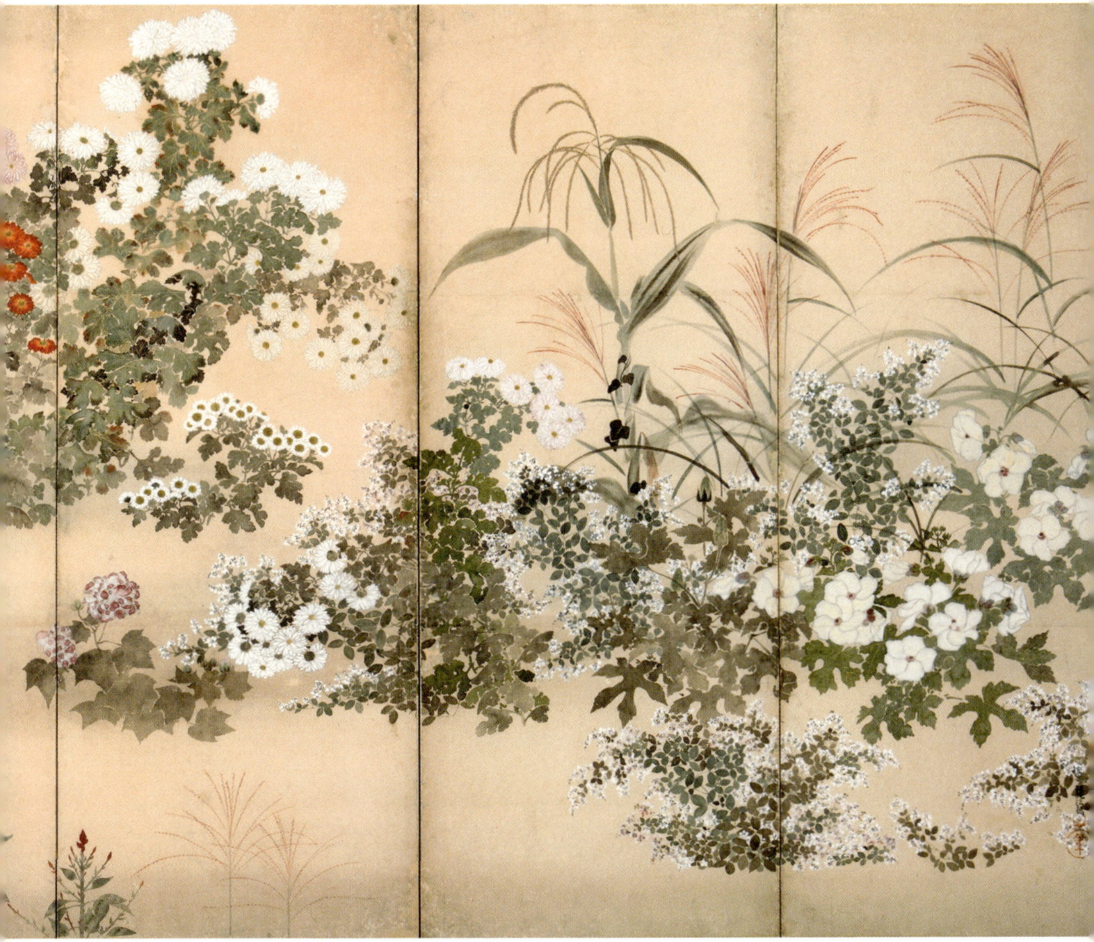

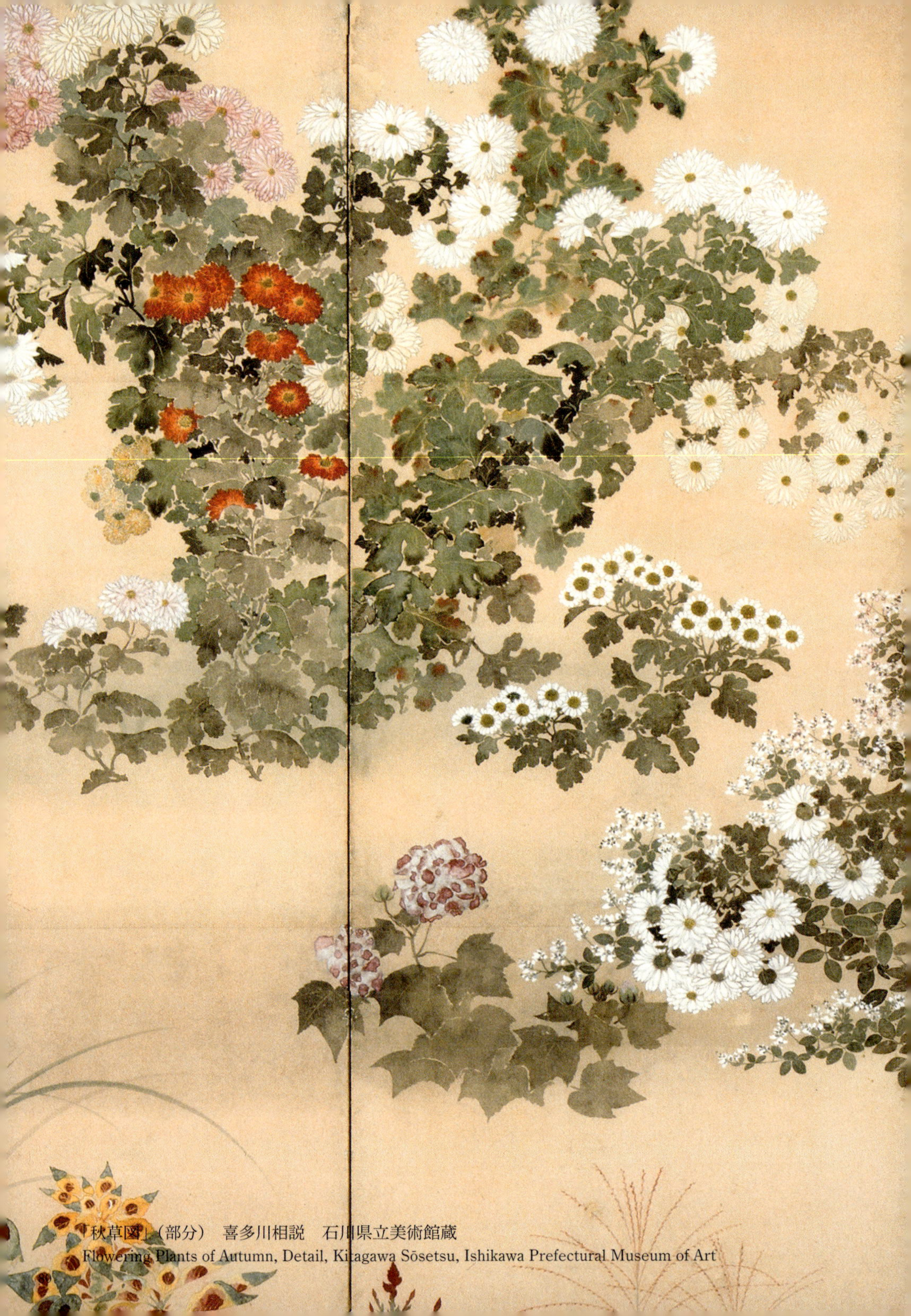

「秋草図」（部分）　喜多川相説　石川県立美術館蔵
Flowering Plants of Autumn, Detail, Kitagawa Sōsetsu, Ishikawa Prefectural Museum of Art

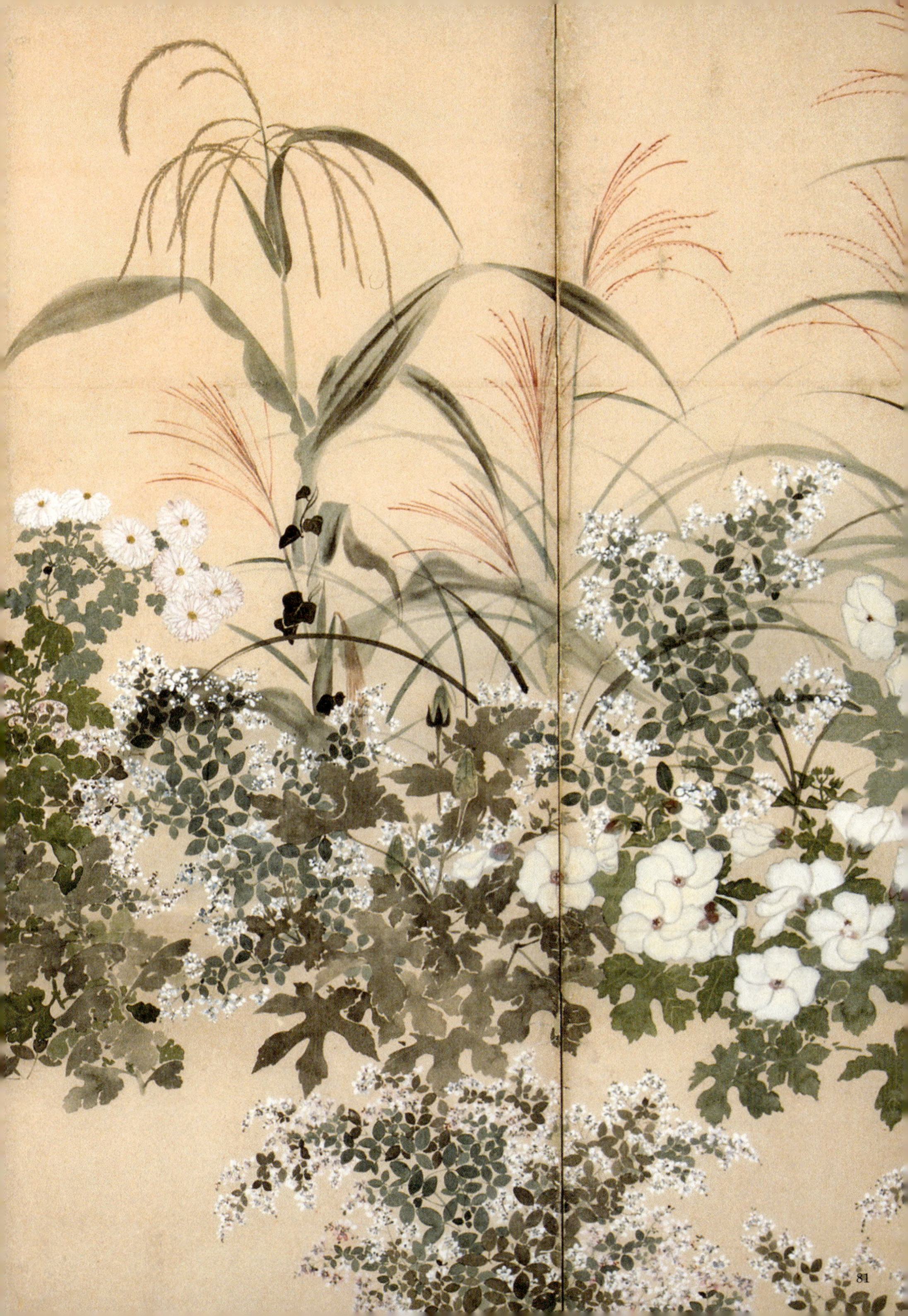

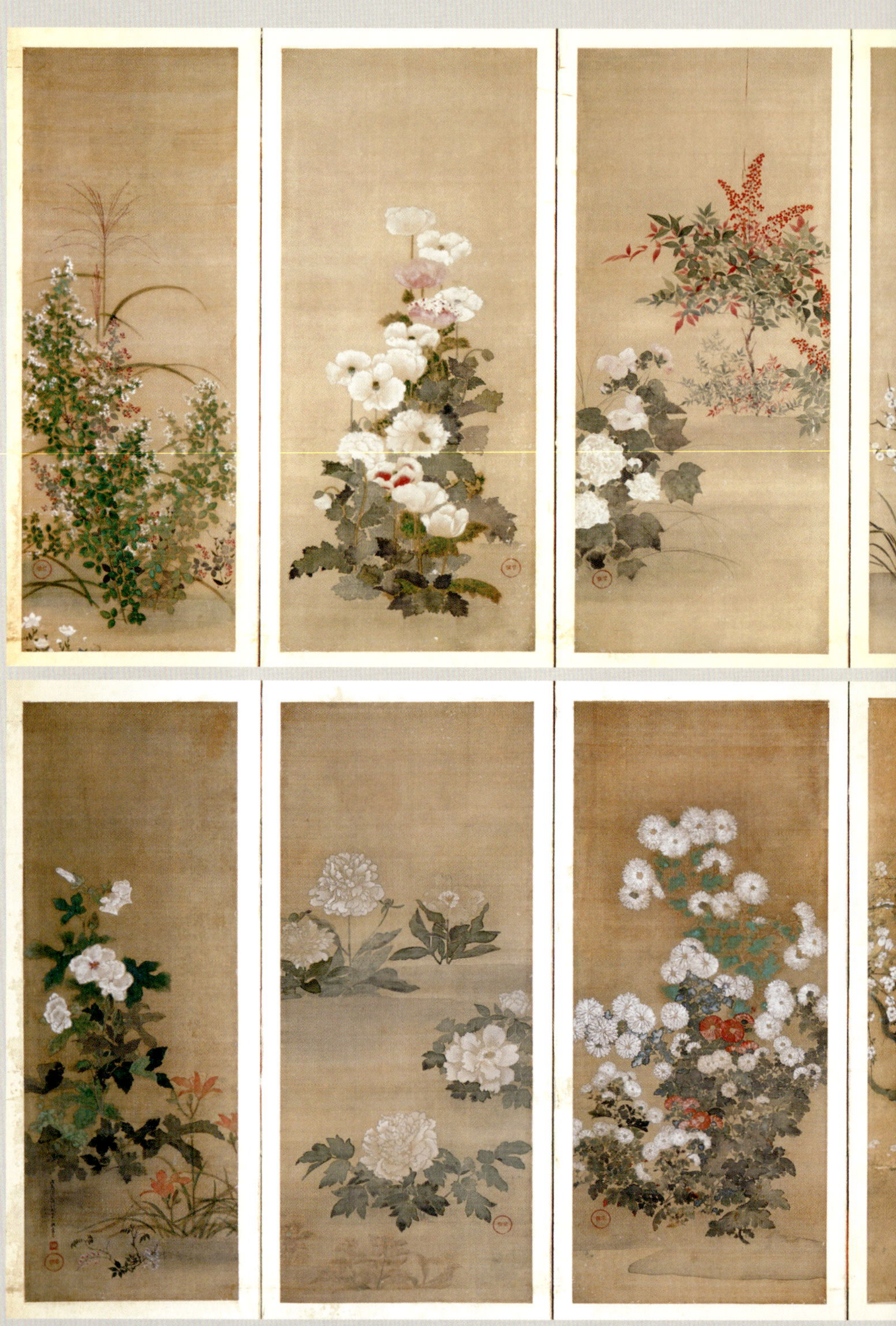

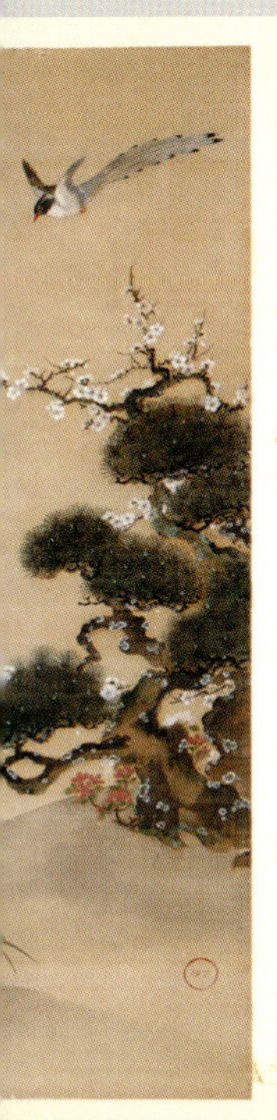
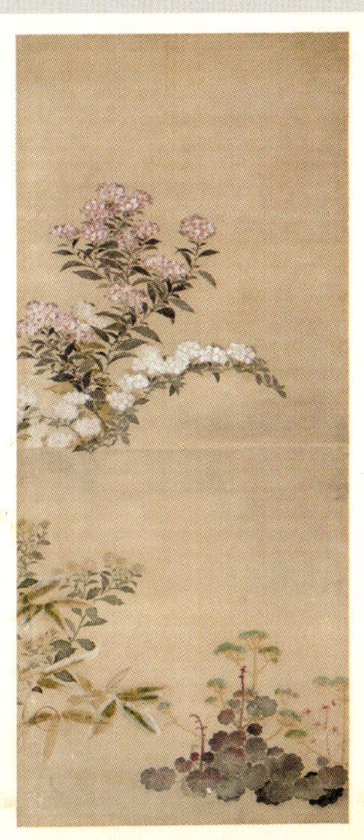
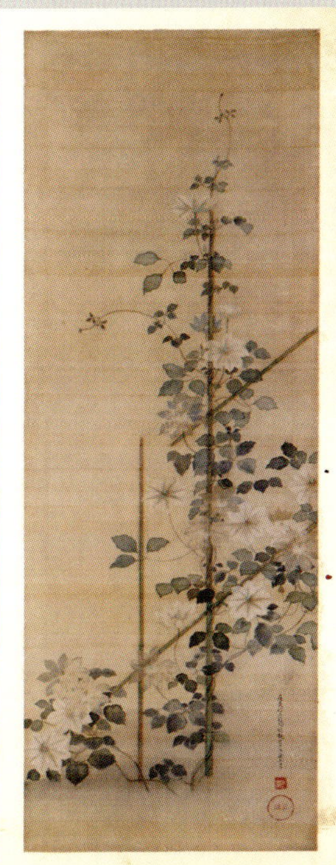
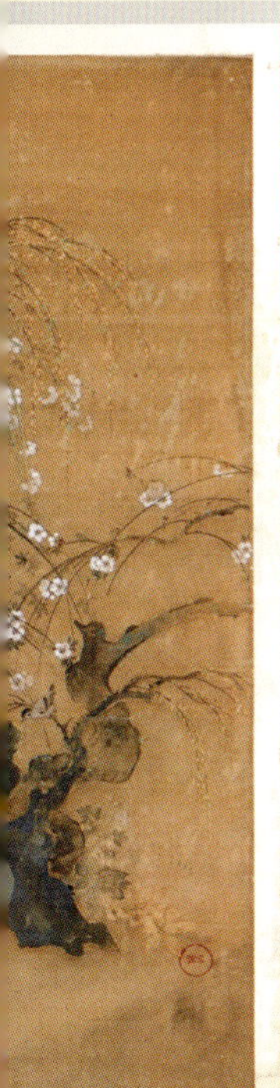
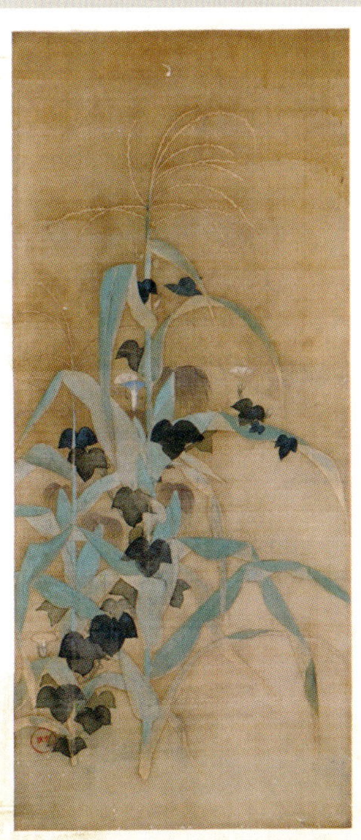
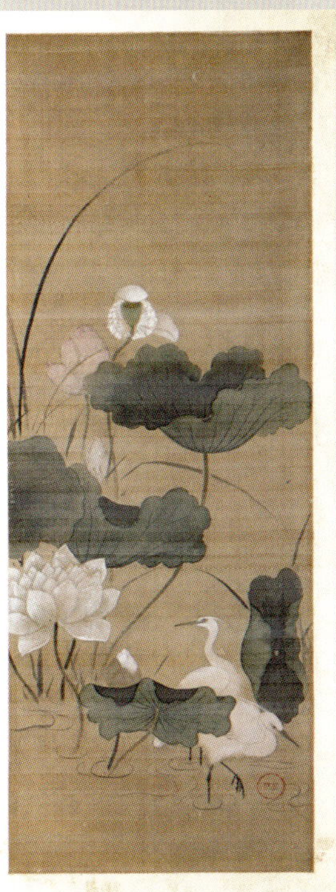

「四季草花図押絵貼
屏風」 喜多川相説
黒部市美術館蔵
Flowering Plants of
the Four Seasons,
Kitagawa Sōsetsu,
Kurobe City Art
Museum

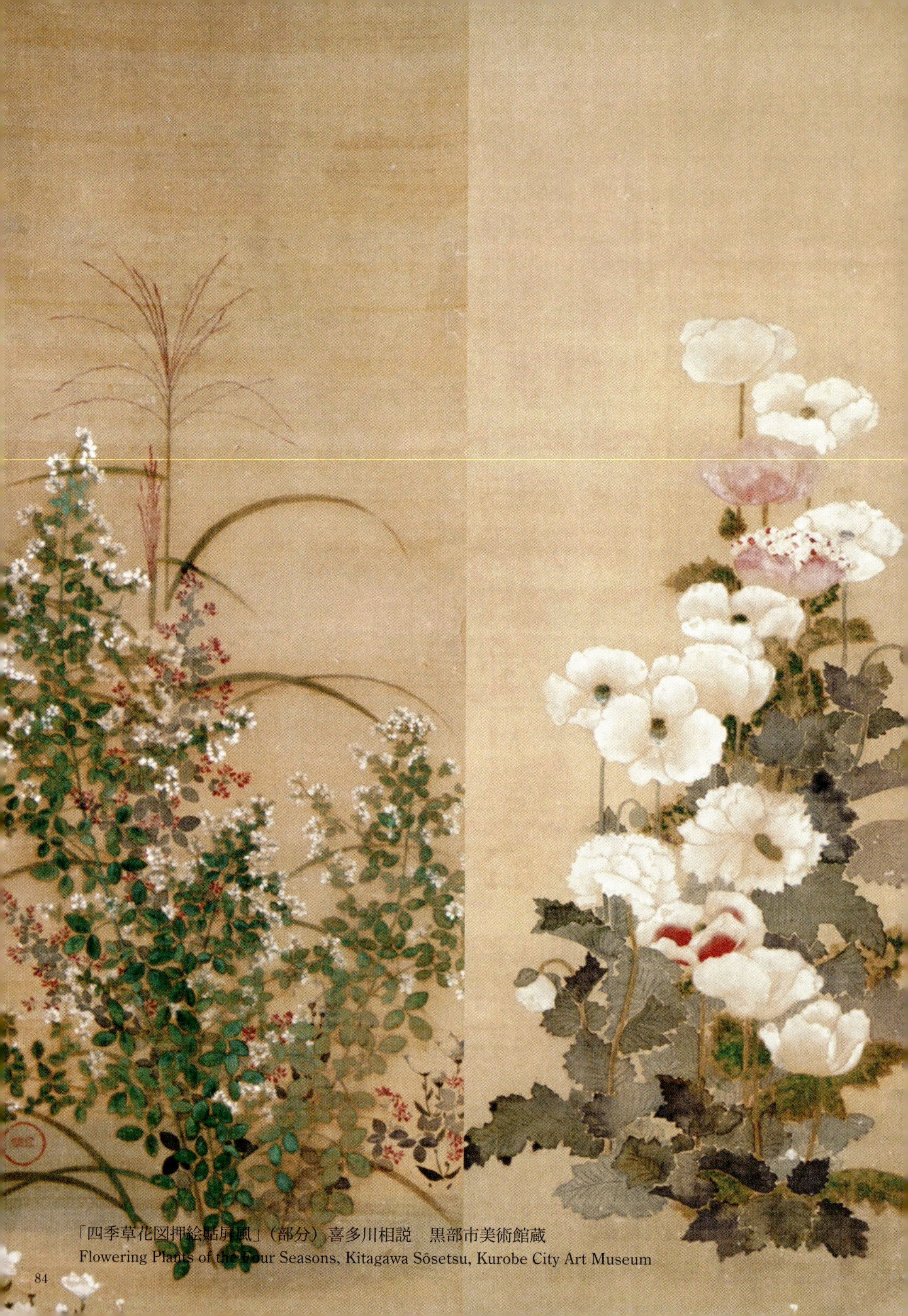

「四季草花図押絵貼屏風」（部分）喜多川相説　黒部市美術館蔵
Flowering Plants of the Four Seasons, Kitagawa Sōsetsu, Kurobe City Art Museum

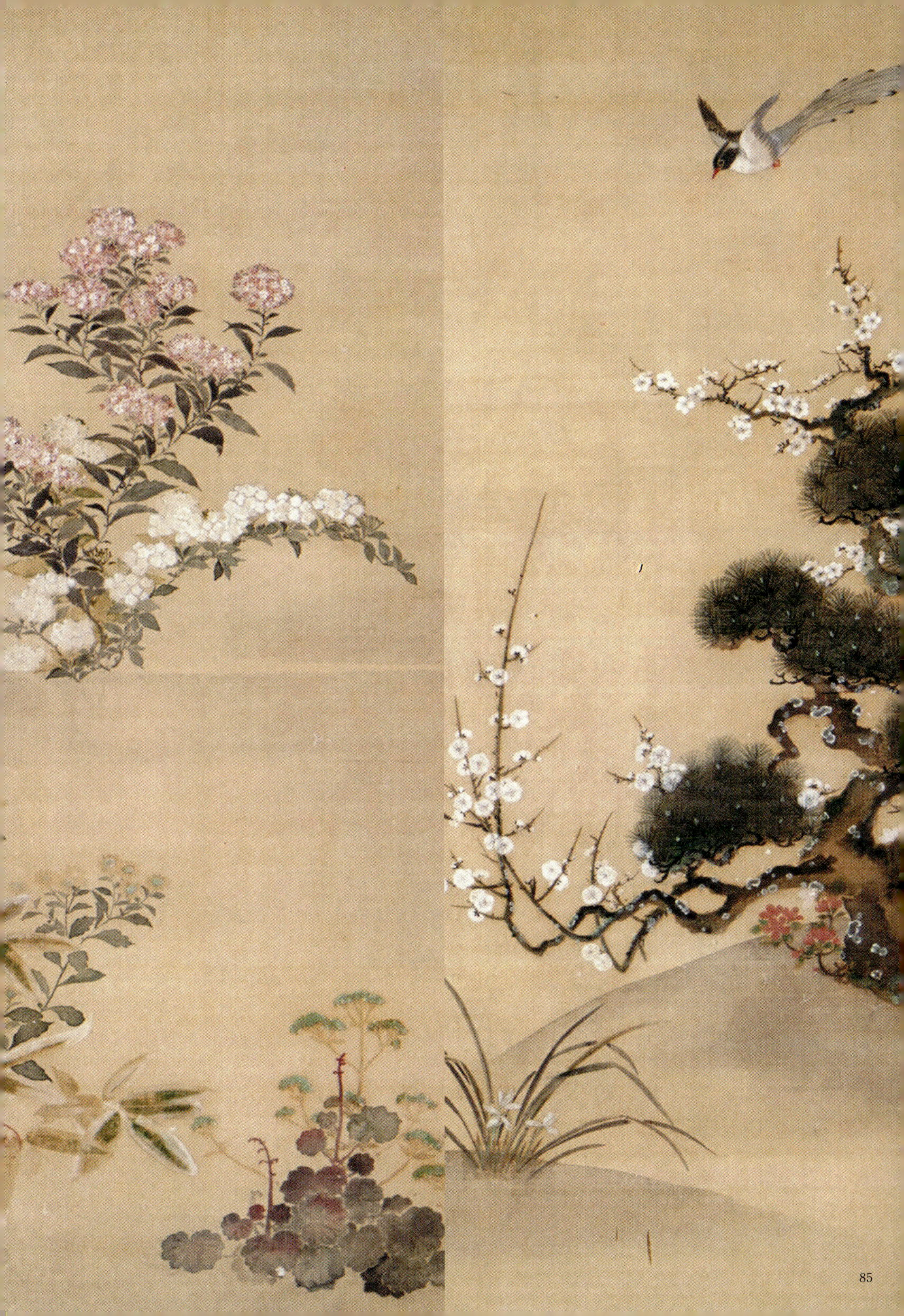

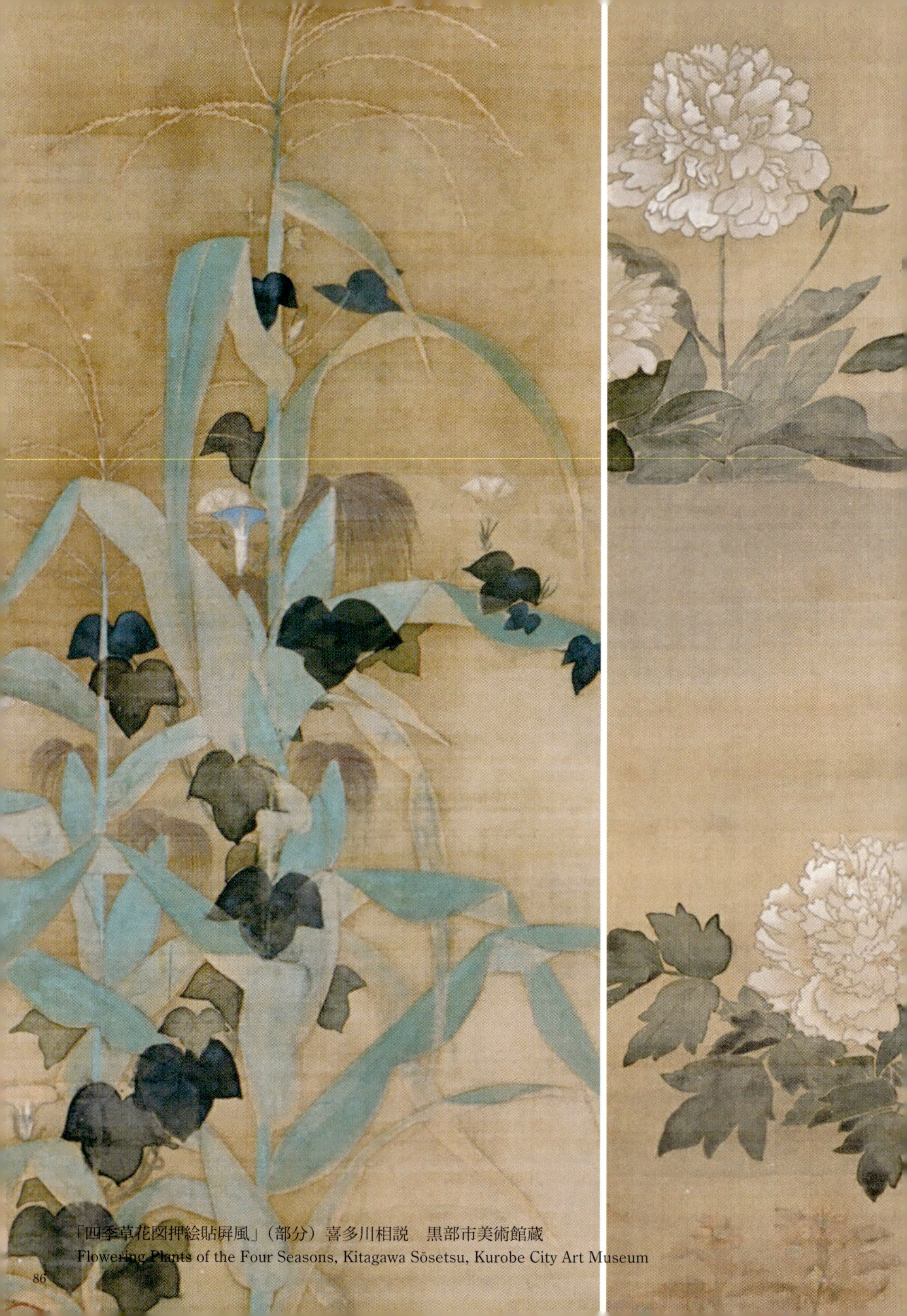

「四季草花図押絵貼屏風」（部分）喜多川相説　黒部市美術館蔵
Flowering Plants of the Four Seasons, Kitagawa Sōsetsu, Kurobe City Art Museum

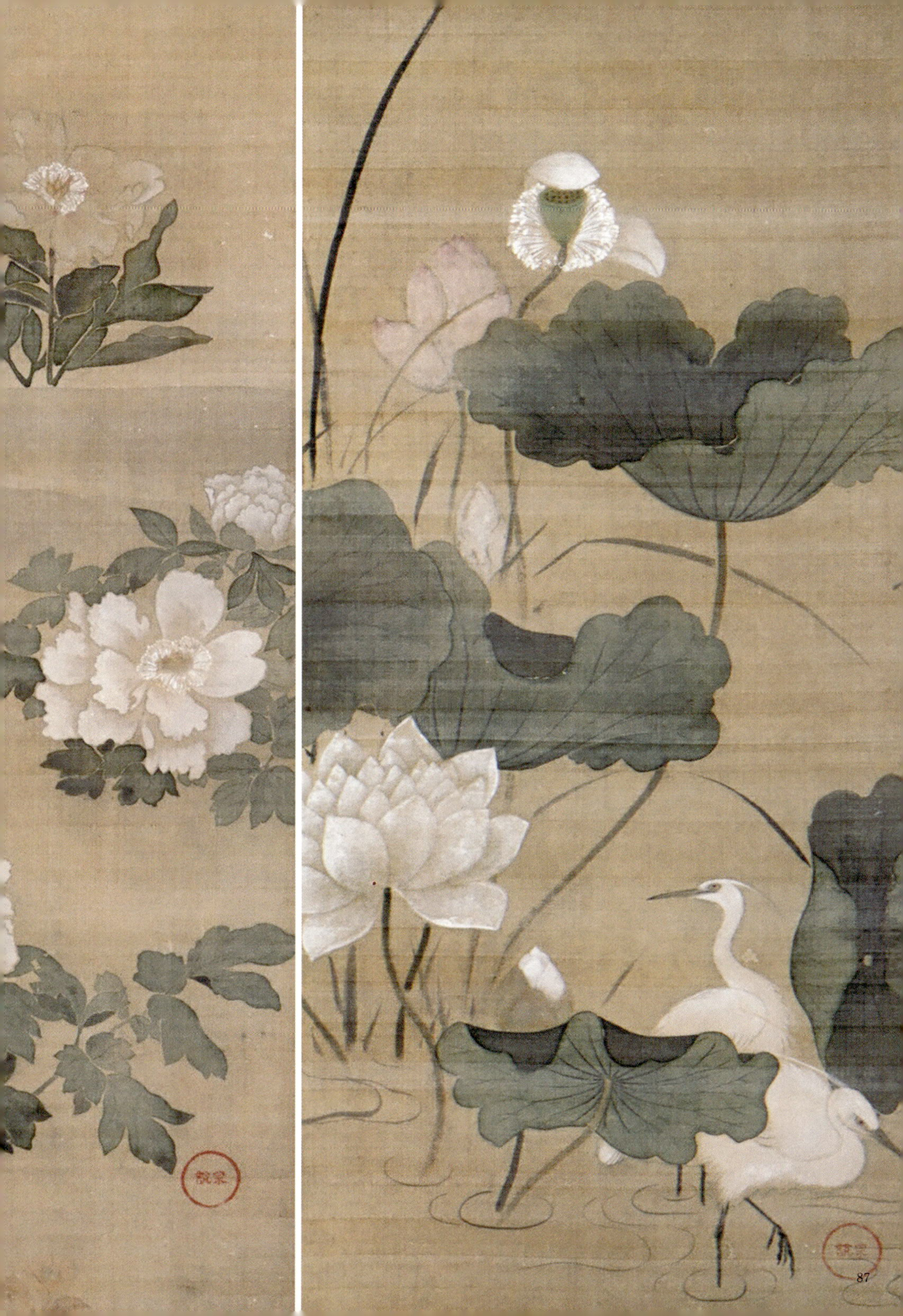

尾形光琳

おがた こうりん　万治元年〜享保元年（1658-1716）

京都有数の呉服商雁金屋に生まれ、幼少より能や絵に造詣の深かった父宗謙の影響を受けた。初め山本素軒に狩野派を、のち生家に伝わる俵屋宗達画の美に出合いその画風を学んだ。光琳模様と呼ばれる独自の装飾性に富むやまと絵画風を確立し、のちに琳派と呼ばれた。晩年は弟尾形乾山の陶器の絵付、蒔絵、小袖の下絵など、工芸意匠にも優れた作品を残した。

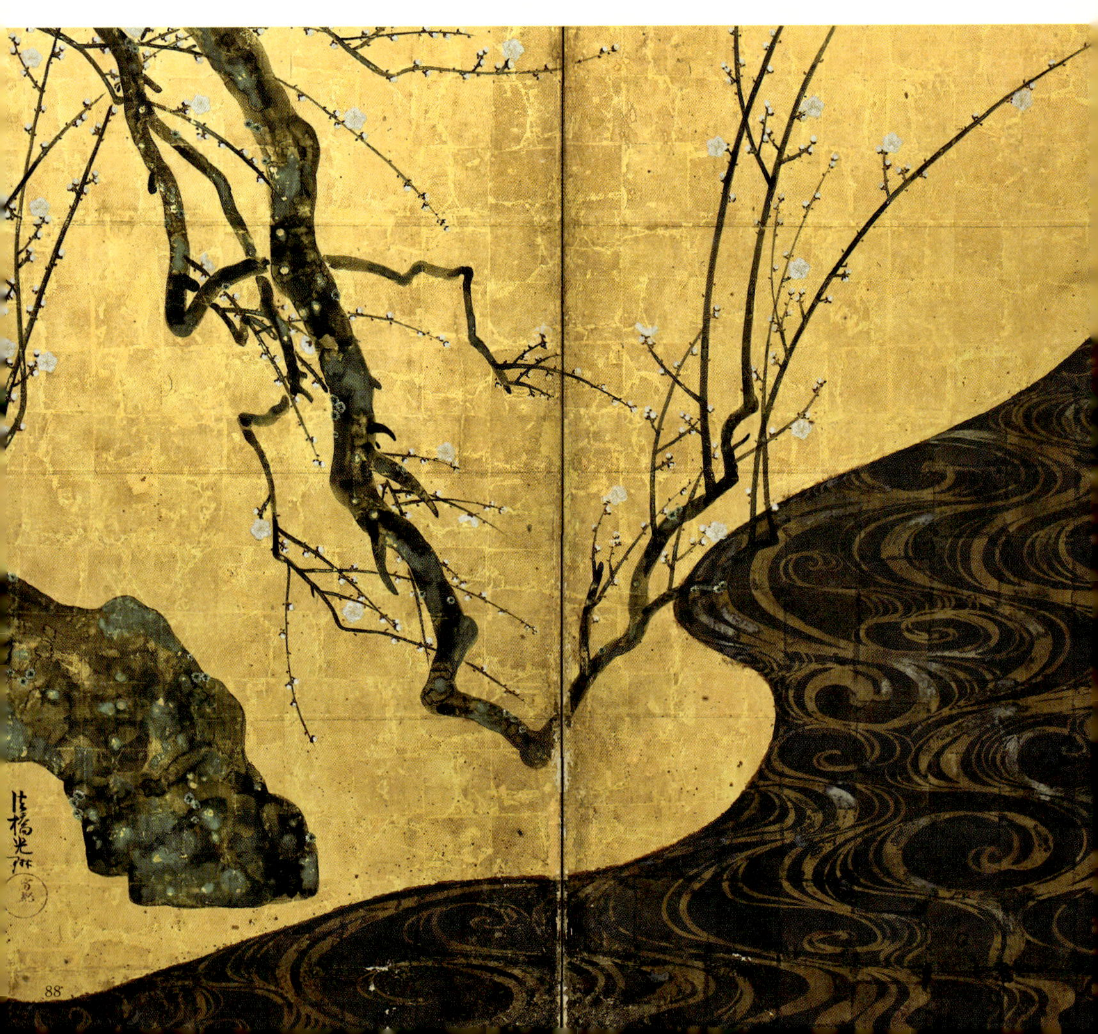

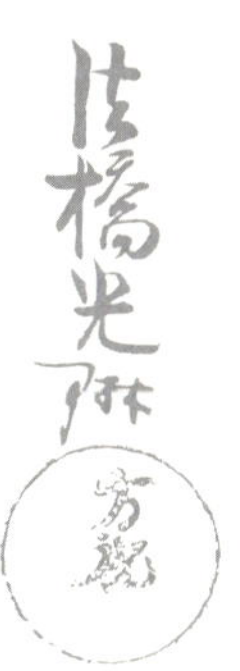

Ogata Kōrin (1658 – 1716)
Born into a prosperous Kyoto merchant family, Kōrin was
influenced by his father Sōken, who was well versed in Noh and
painting. He studied Kanō-school painting with Yamamoto Sōken,
then, attracted by paintings by Tawaraya Sōtatsu, studied Sōtatsu'
s style, producing the richly decorative yamato-e paintings that
define the Rinpa school. Kōrin decorated his brother Ogata
Kenzan's ceramics and created brilliant designs for craft objects,
including sketches for textile designs and maki-e lacquerwares.

「紅白梅図屏風」　国宝　尾形光琳　MOA 美術館蔵
Red and White Plum Trees, Ogata Kōrin, National Treasure, MOA Museum of Art, Shizuoka

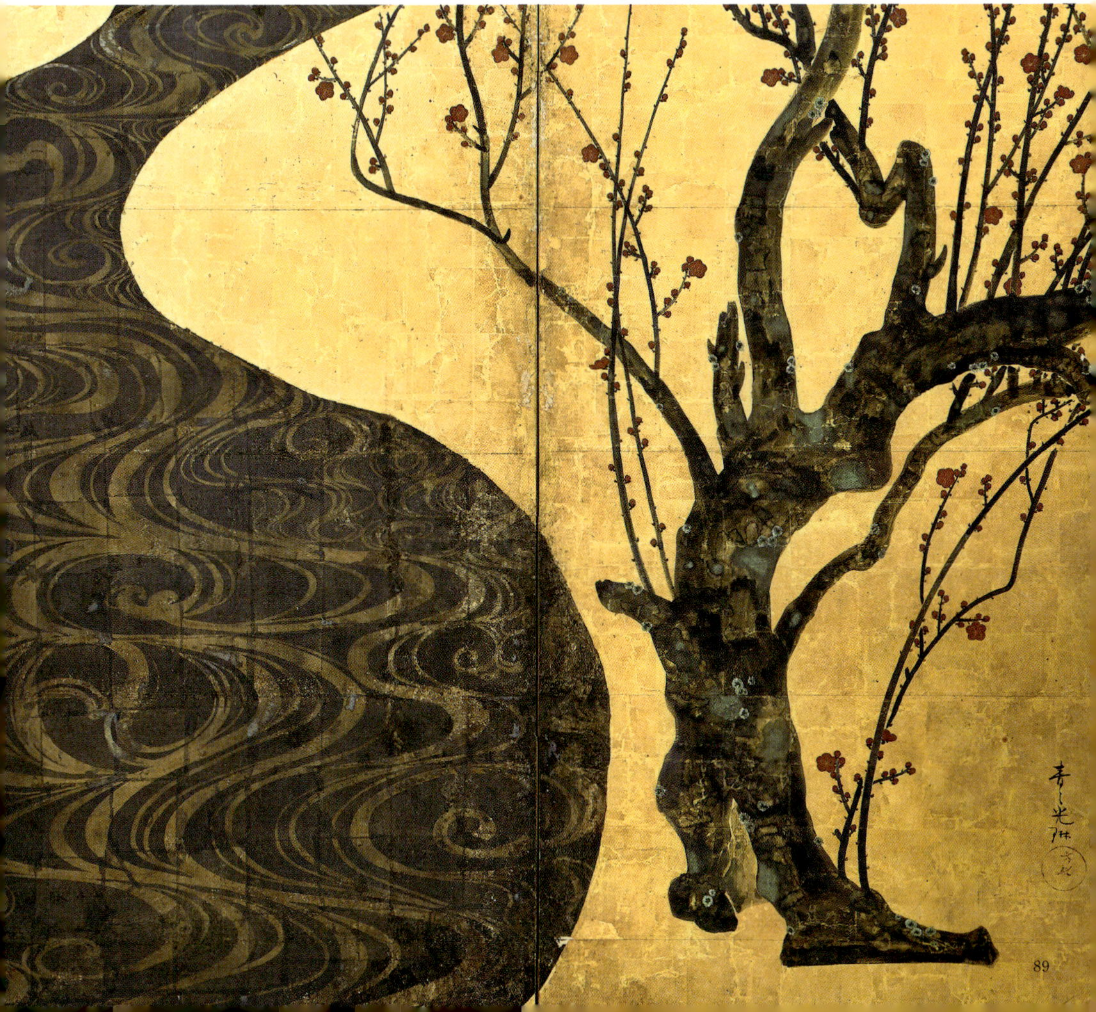

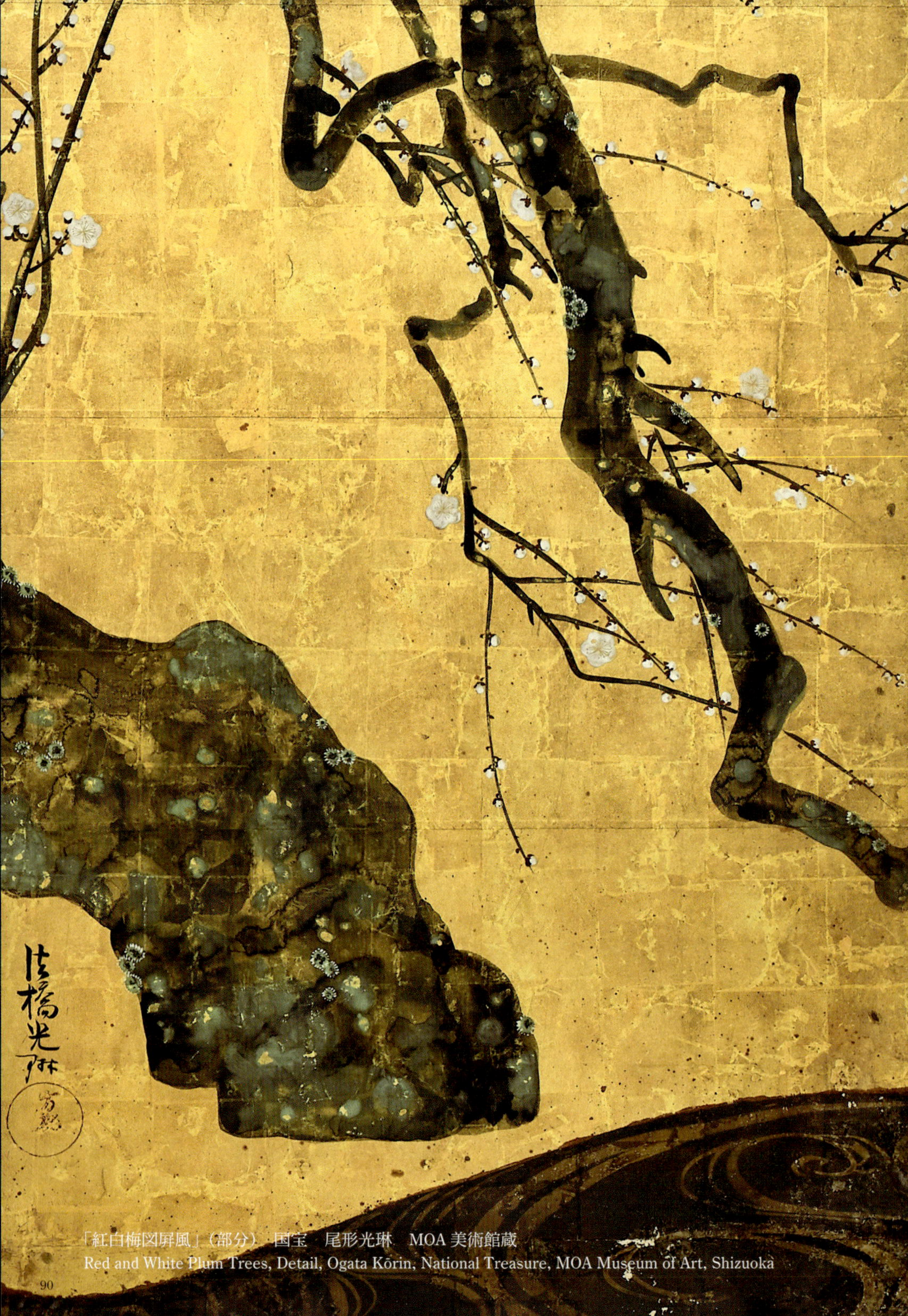

「紅白梅図屏風」〔部分〕 国宝 尾形光琳 MOA 美術館蔵
Red and White Plum Trees, Detail, Ogata Kōrin, National Treasure, MOA Museum of Art, Shizuoka

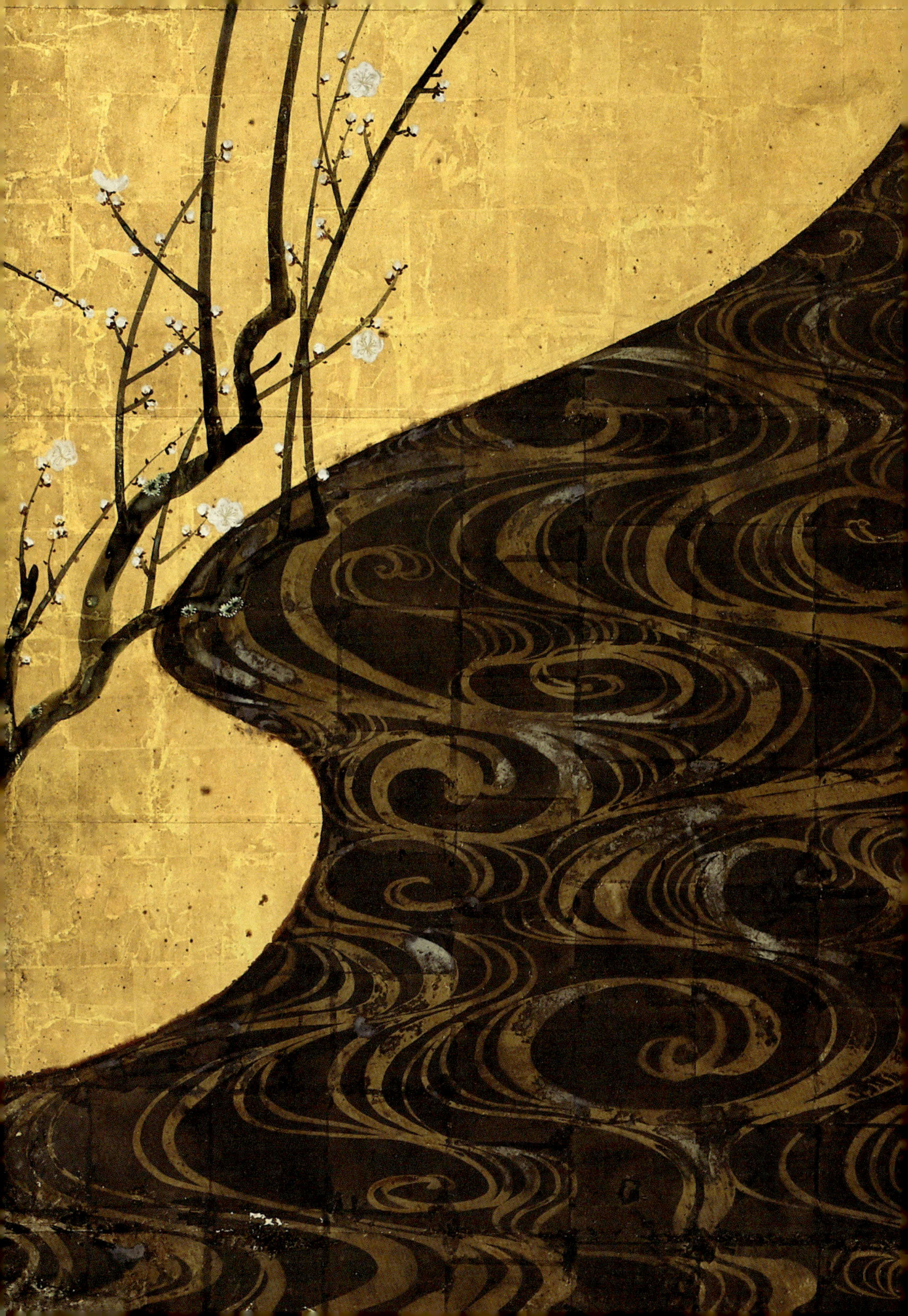

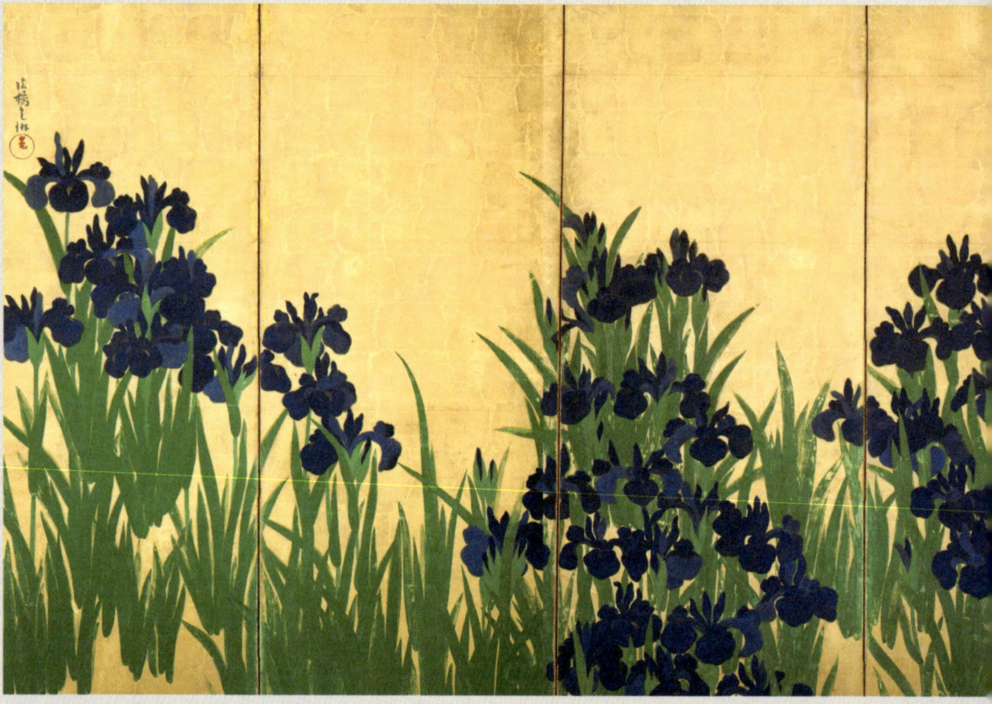

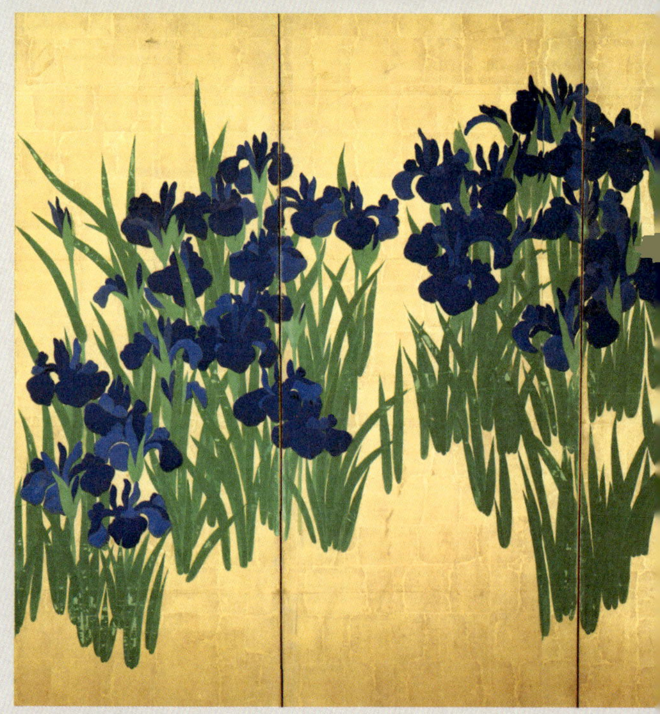

「燕子花図」国宝　尾形光琳
根津美術館蔵
Irises, Ogata Kōrin, National
Treasure, Nezu Museum

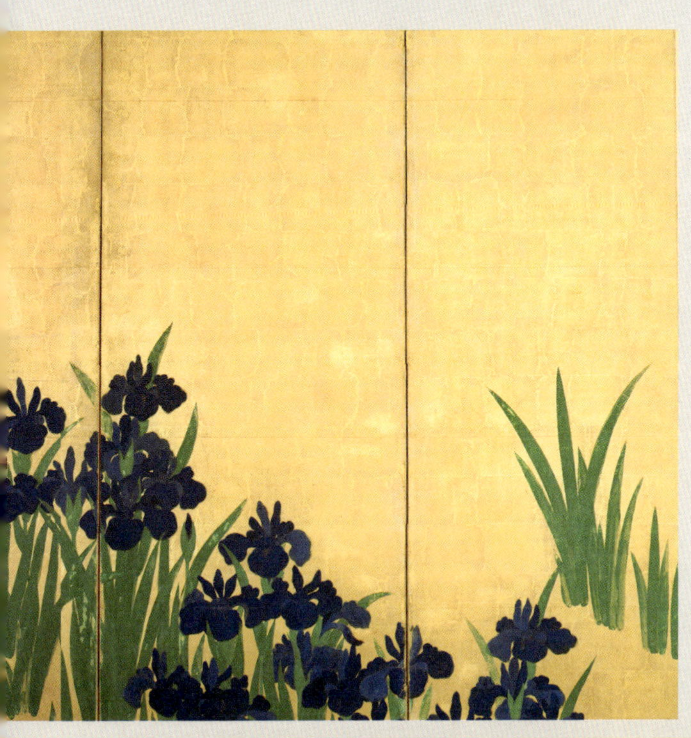

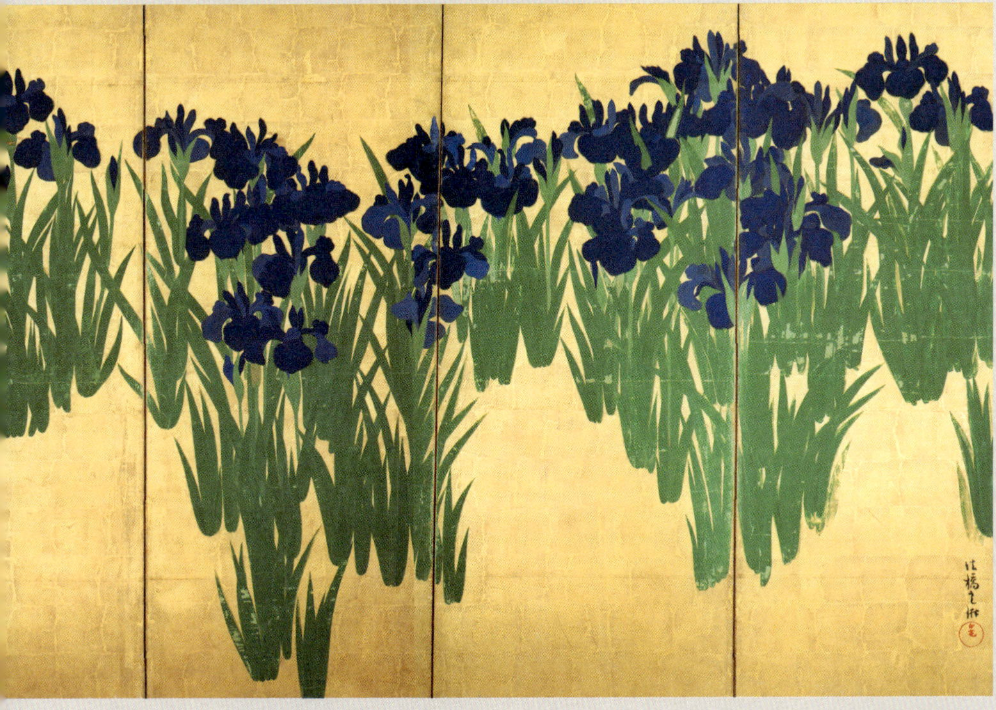

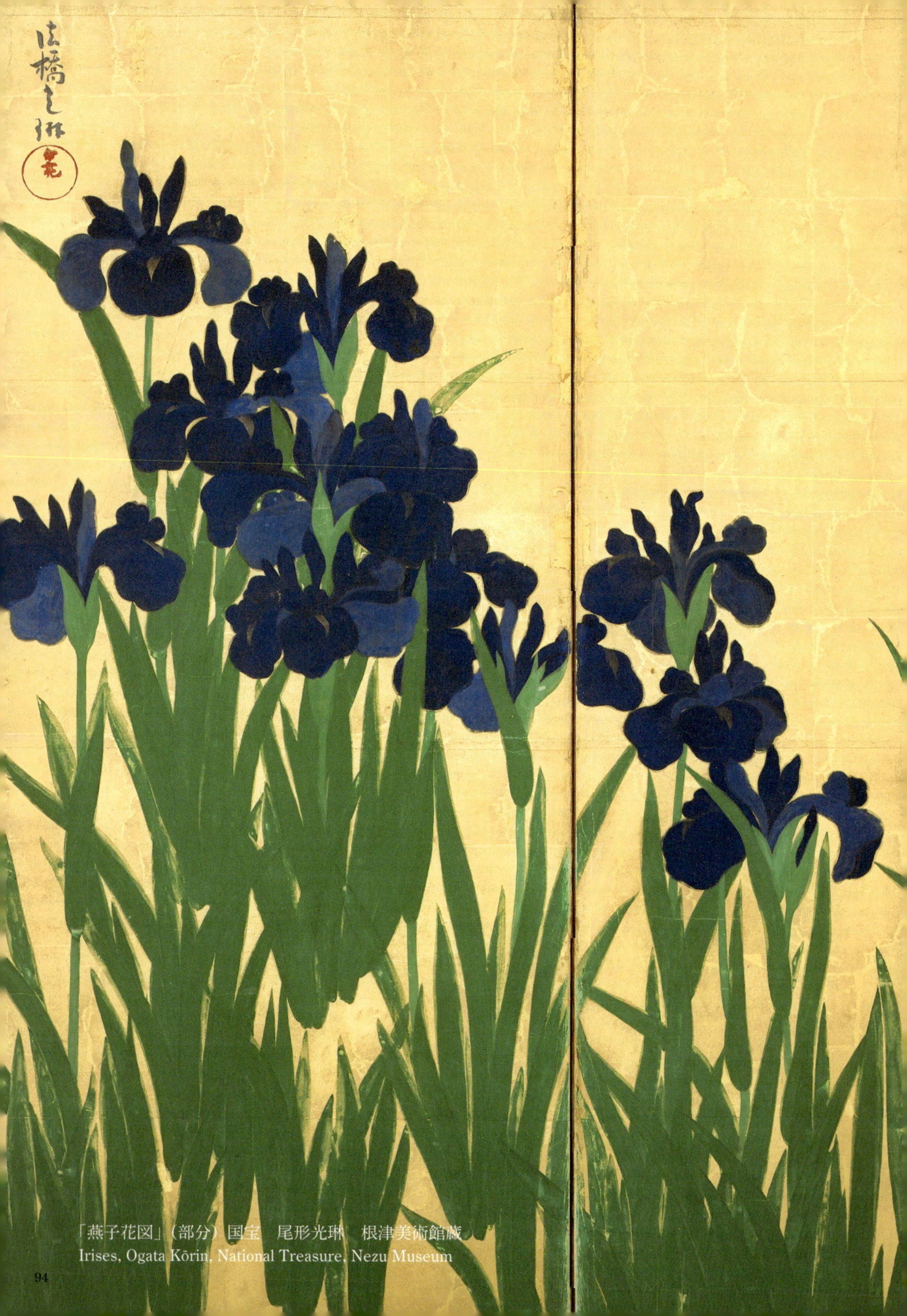

「燕子花図」（部分）国宝　尾形光琳　根津美術館蔵
Irises, Ogata Kōrin, National Treasure, Nezu Museum

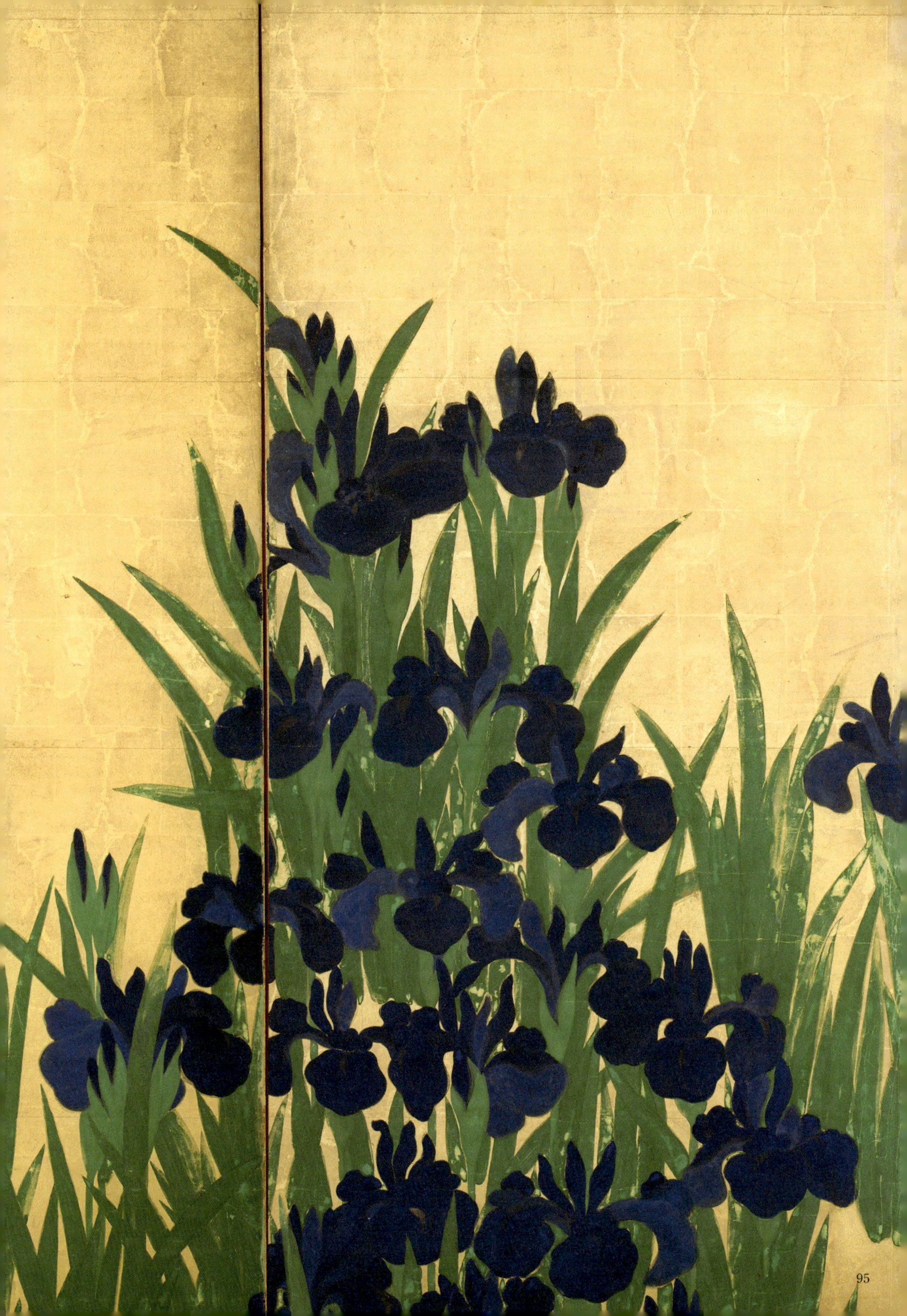

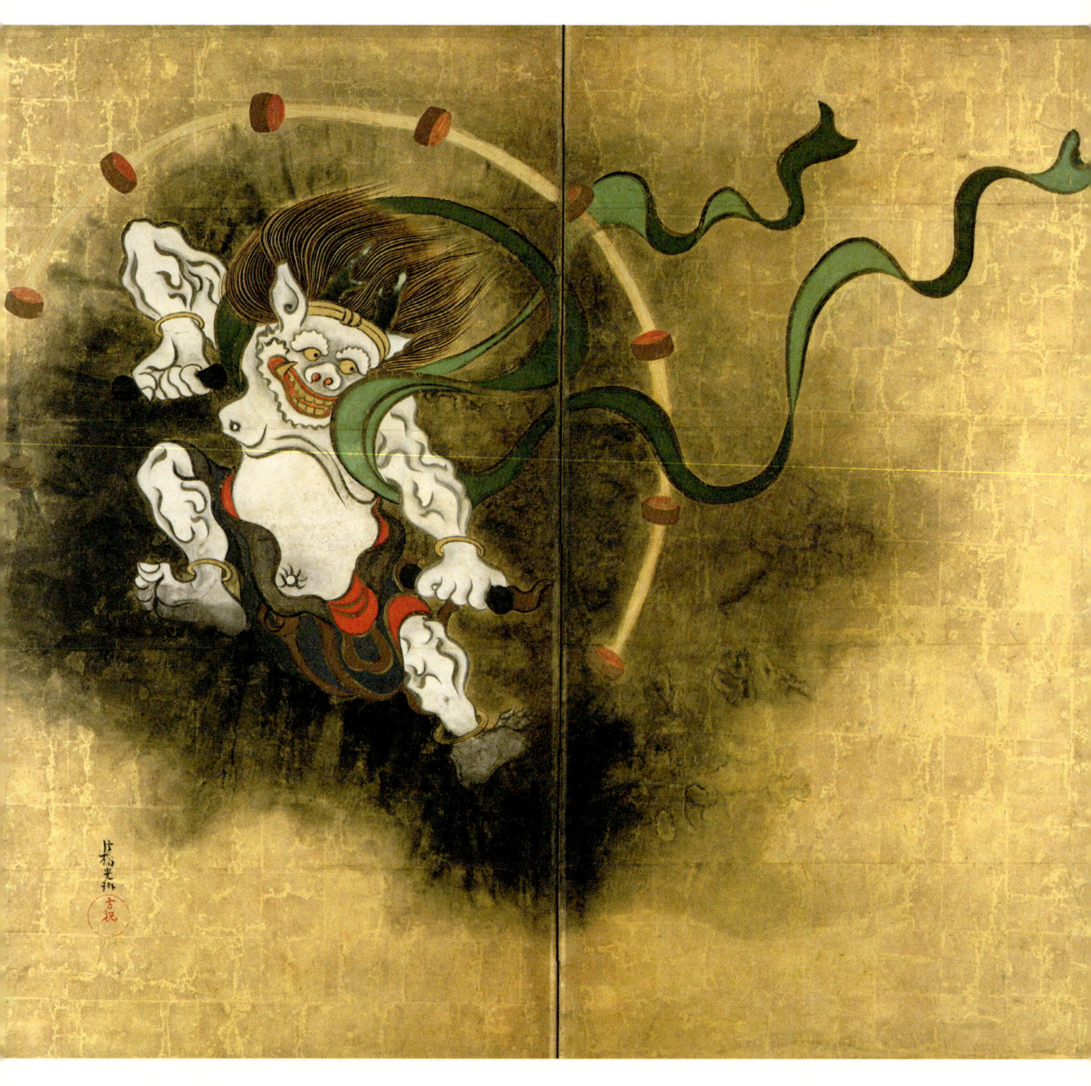

「風神雷神図屏風」　重文　尾形光琳　東京国立博物館蔵
Wind and Thunder Gods, Ogata Kōrin, Important Cultural Property, Tokyo National Museum
Image: TNM Image Archives

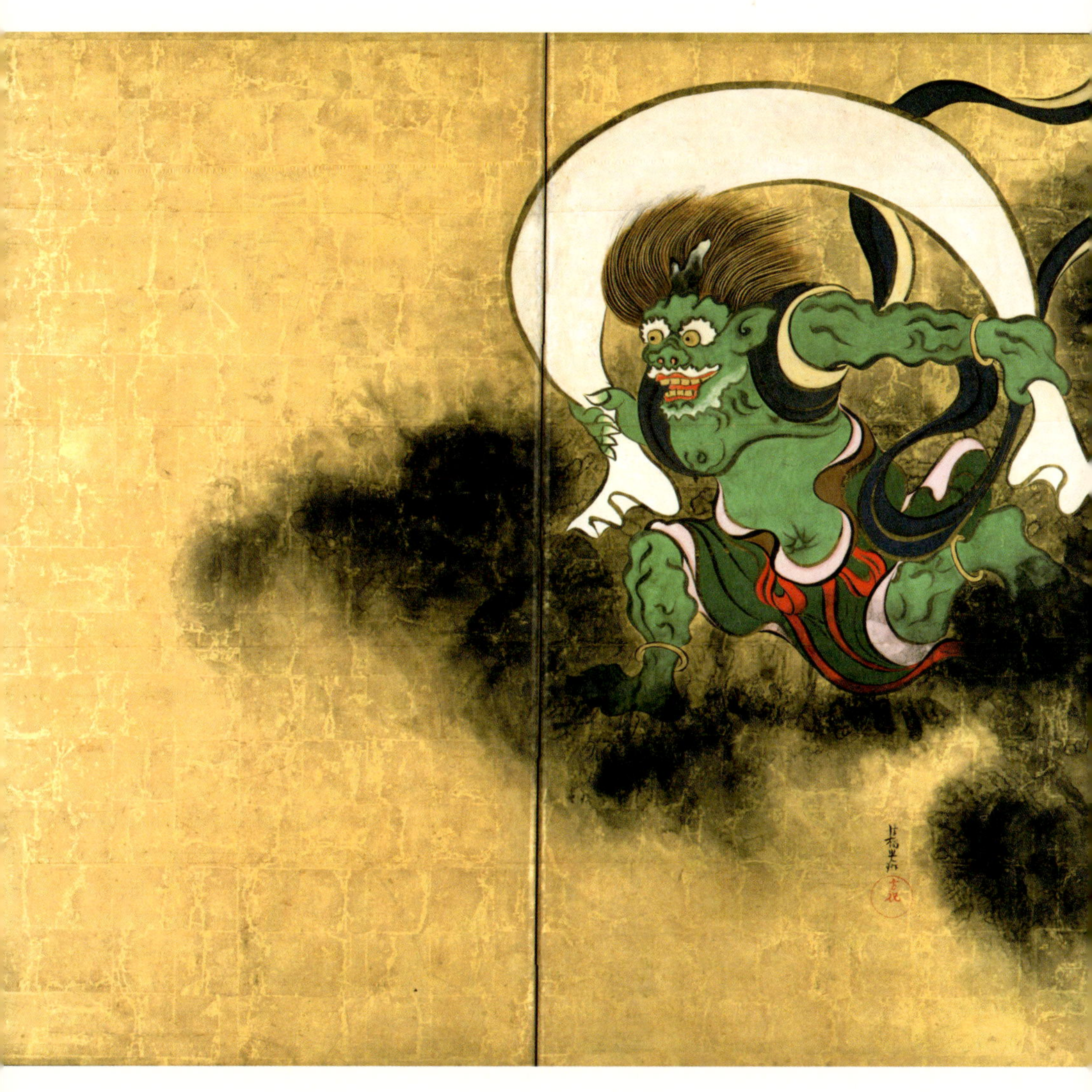

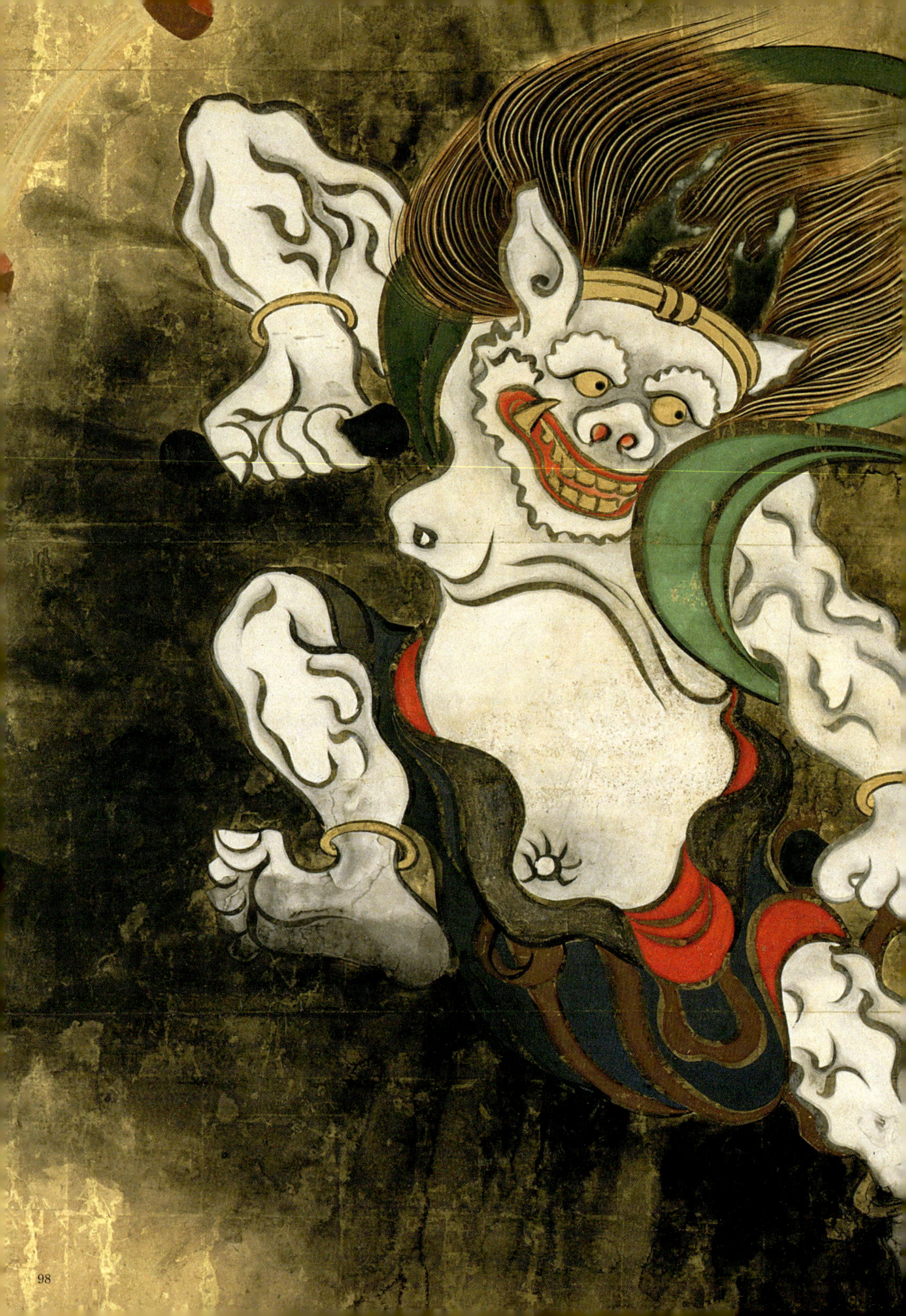

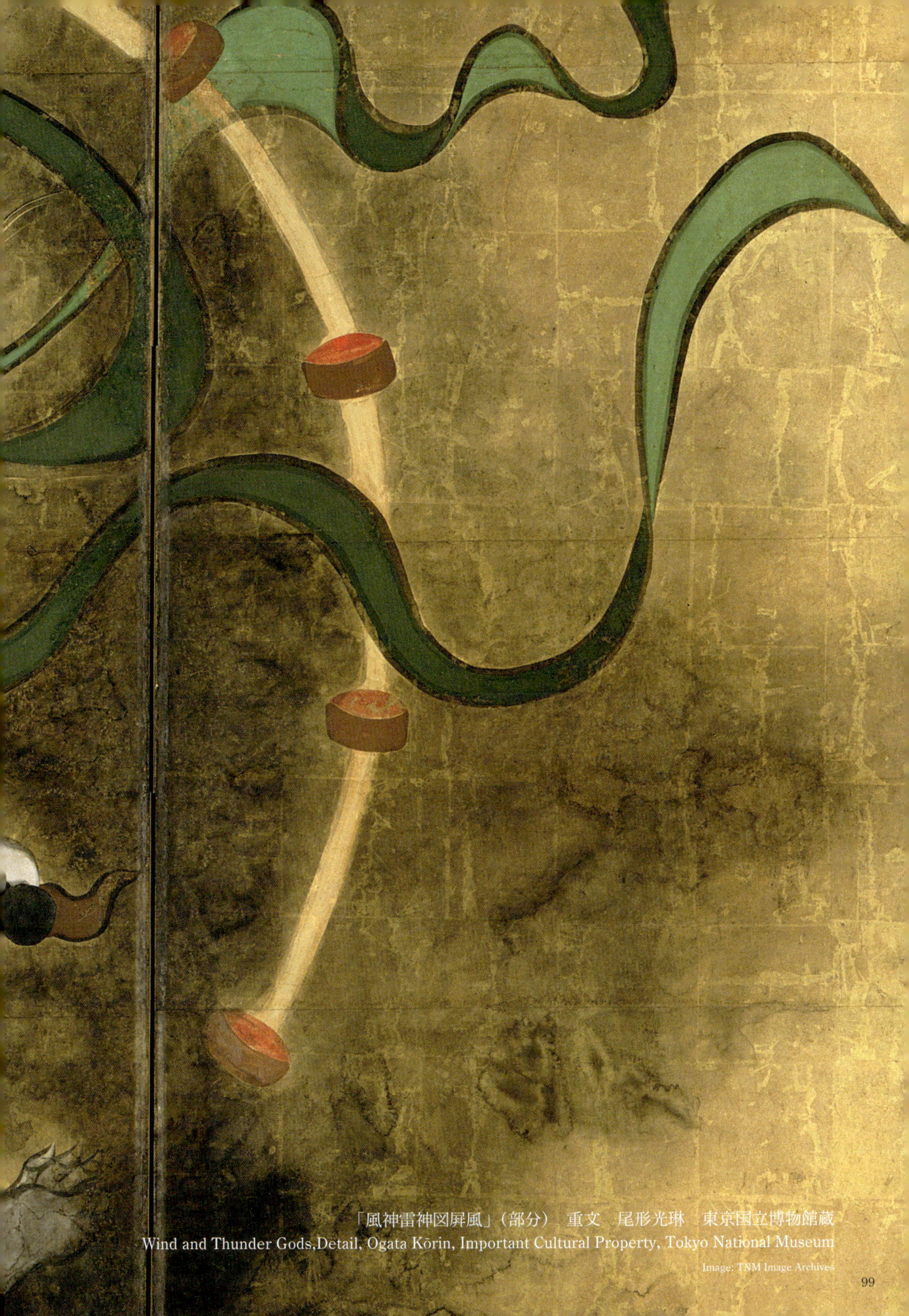

「風神雷神図屏風」（部分）　重文　尾形光琳　東京国立博物館蔵
Wind and Thunder Gods, Detail, Ogata Kōrin, Important Cultural Property, Tokyo National Museum

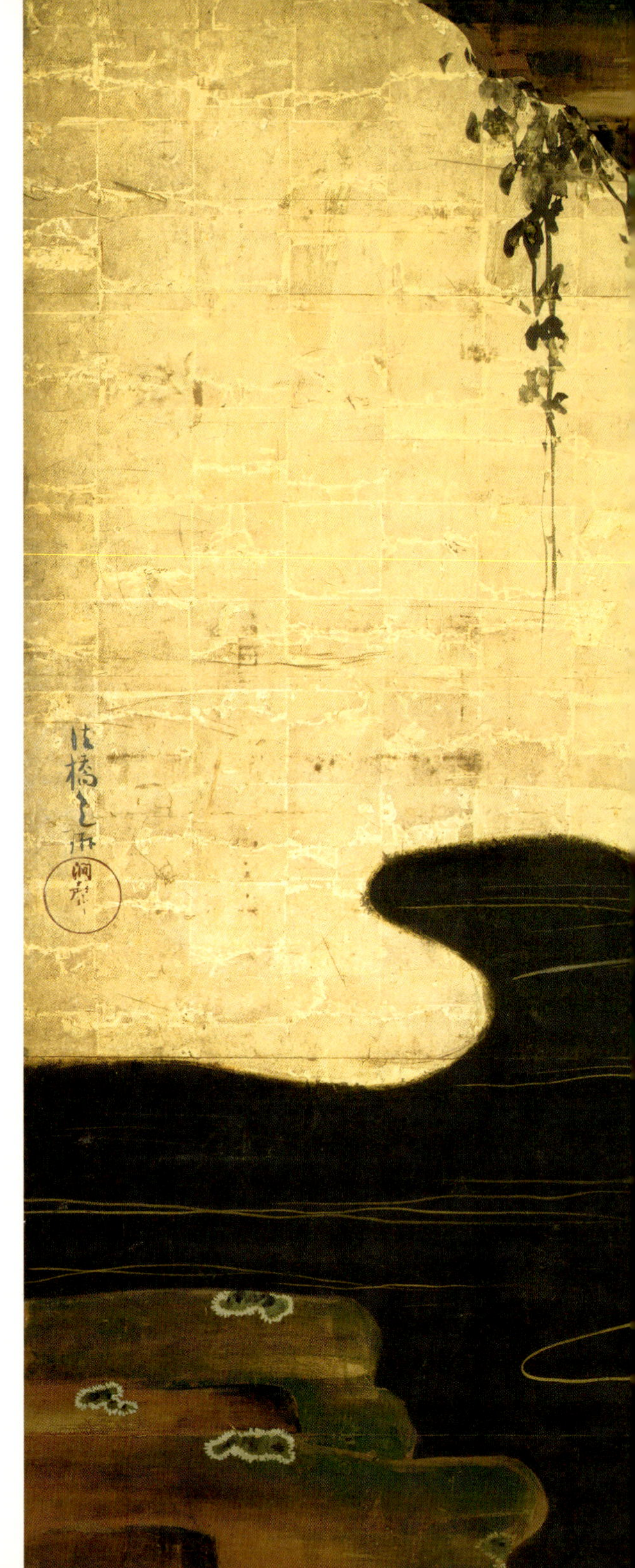

「太公望図屏風」　重文　尾形光琳
京都国立博物館蔵
General *Tai Gong Wang*, Ogata Kōrin,
Important Cultural Property, Kyoto
National Museum

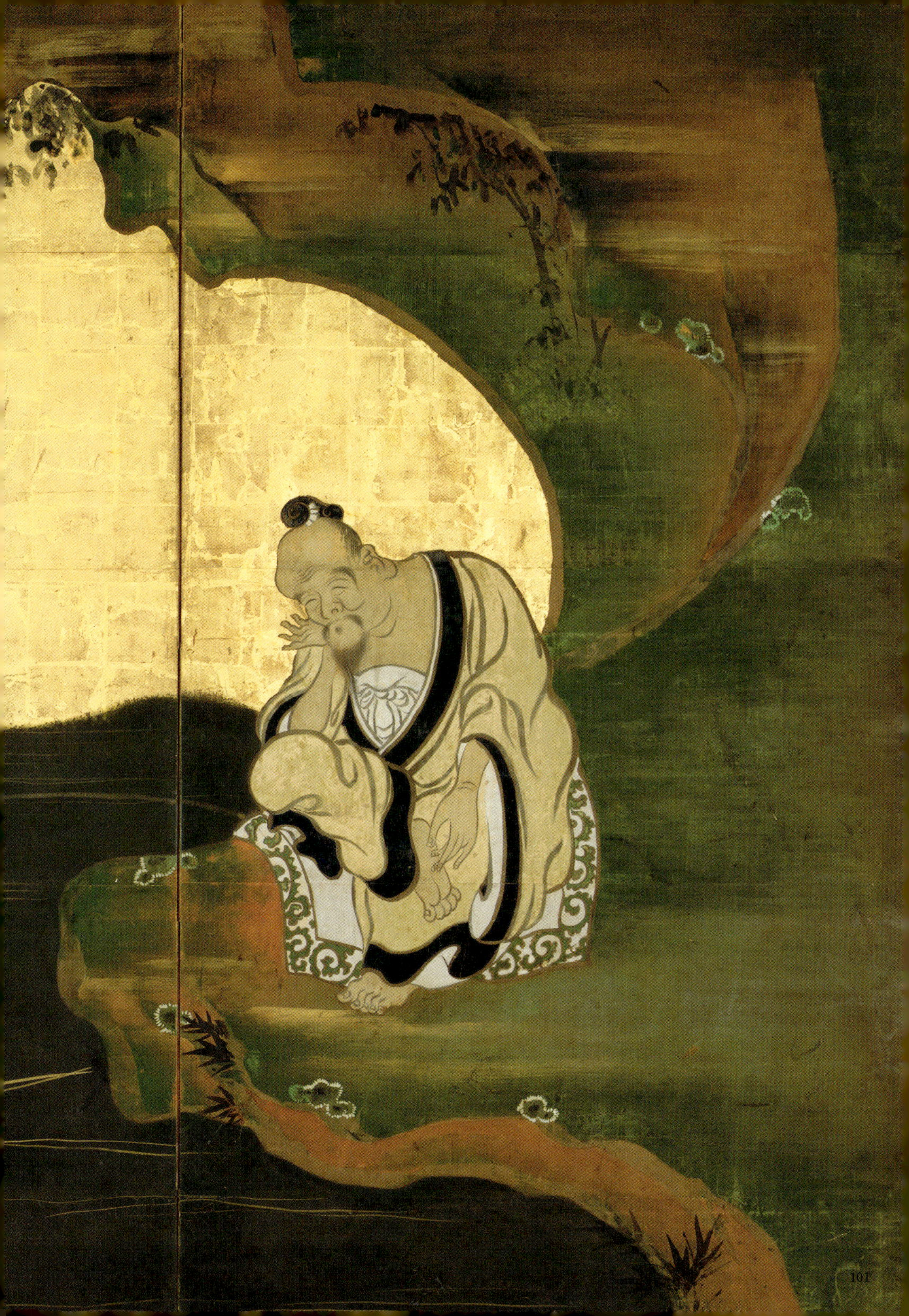

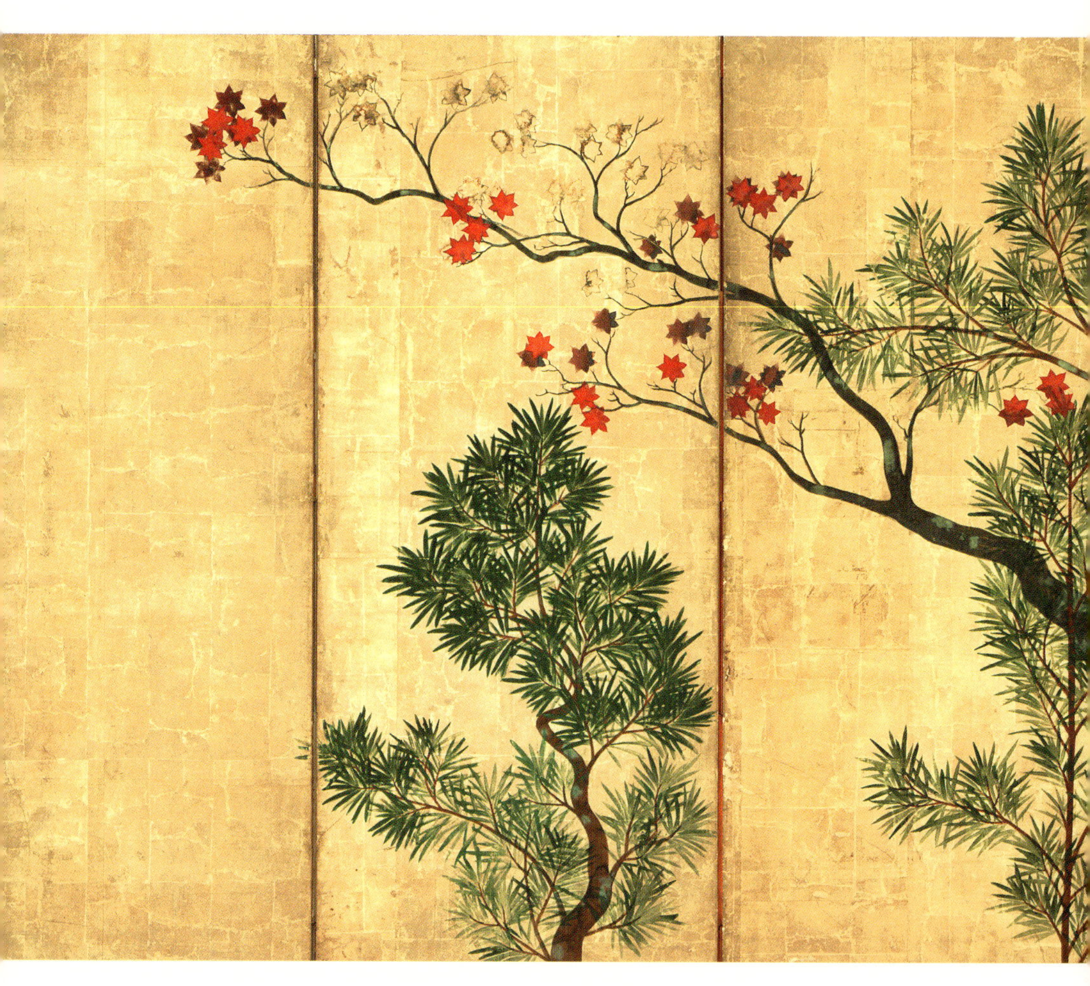

「槇楓図屛風」　重文　尾形光琳　東京藝術大学大学美術館蔵
Black Pine and Maple Tree, Ogata Kōrin, Important Cultural Property,
The University Art Museum-Tokyo University of the Arts

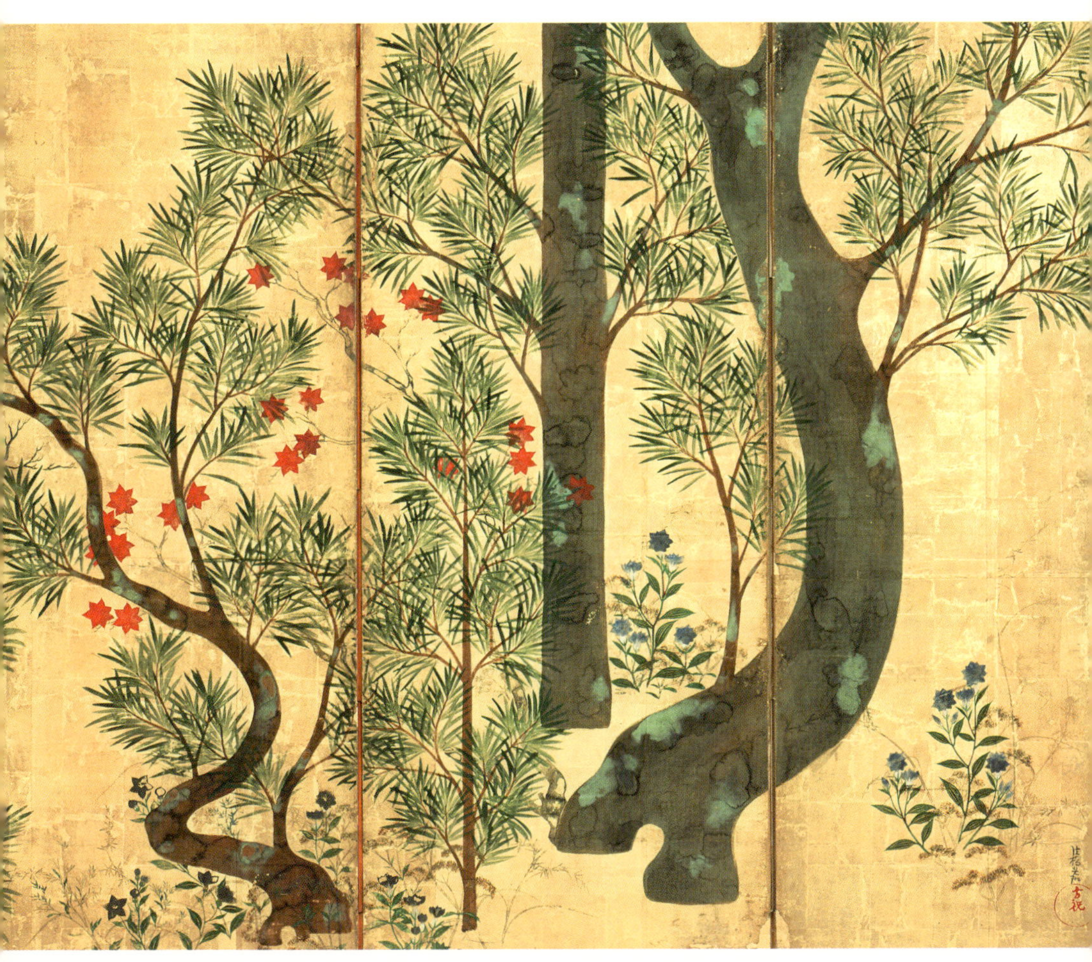

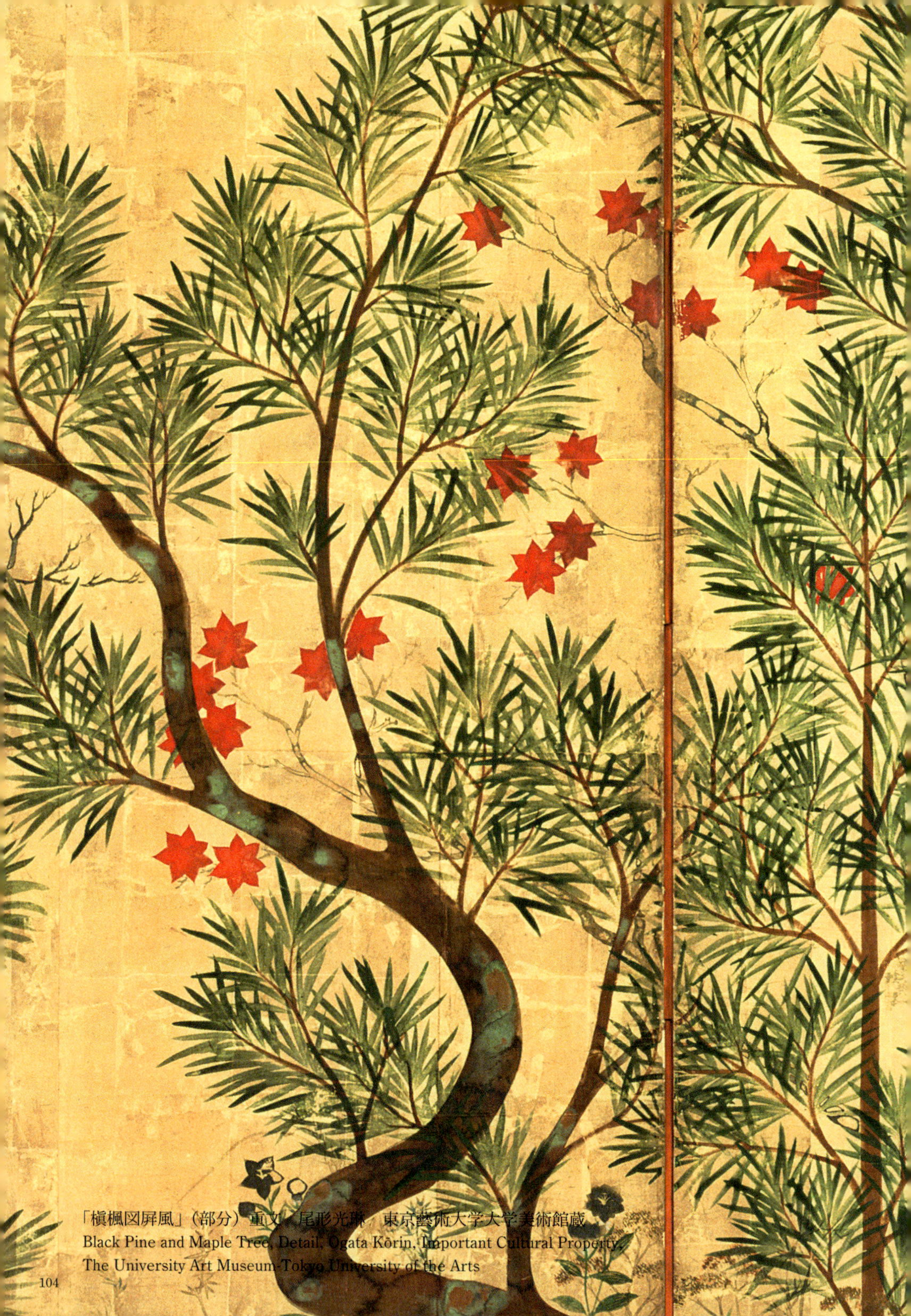

「槇楓図屏風」（部分）重文　尾形光琳　東京藝術大学大学美術館蔵
Black Pine and Maple Tree, Detail, Ogata Kōrin, Important Cultural Property,
The University Art Museum-Tokyo University of the Arts

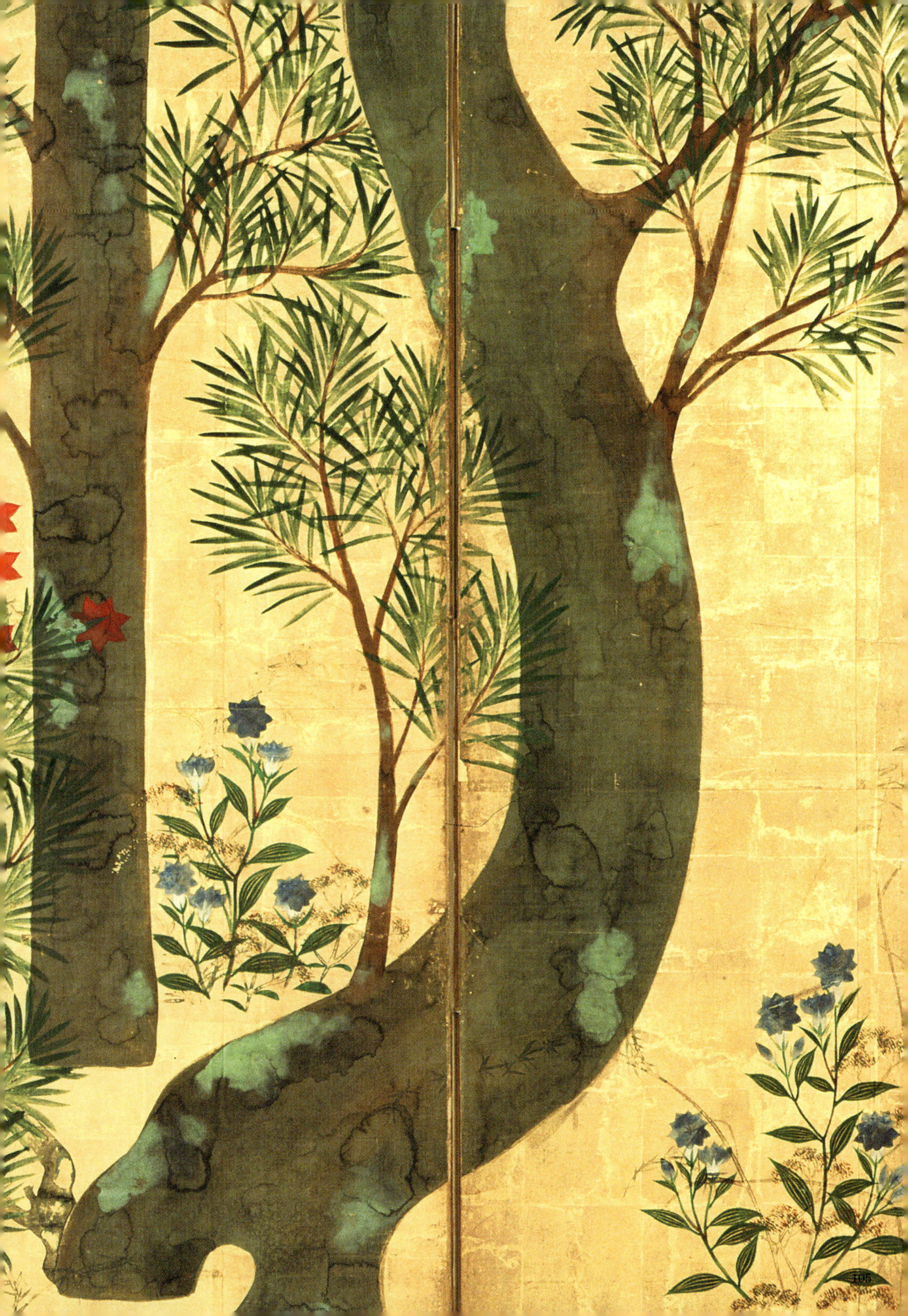

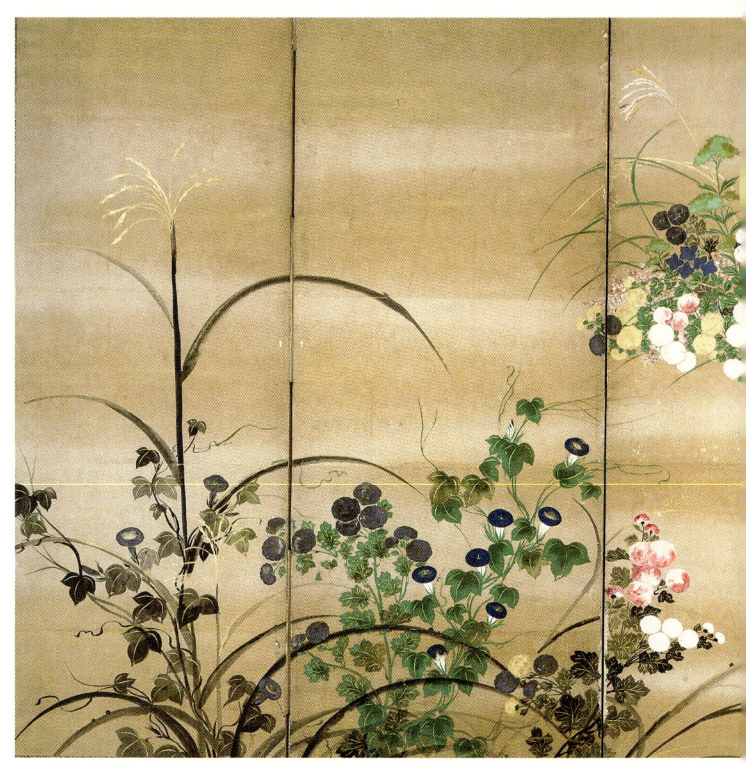

「秋草図屏風」　尾形光琳
東京藝術大学大学美術館蔵
Flowering Plants of Autumn,
Ogata Kōrin, The University
Art Museum-Tokyo
University of the Arts

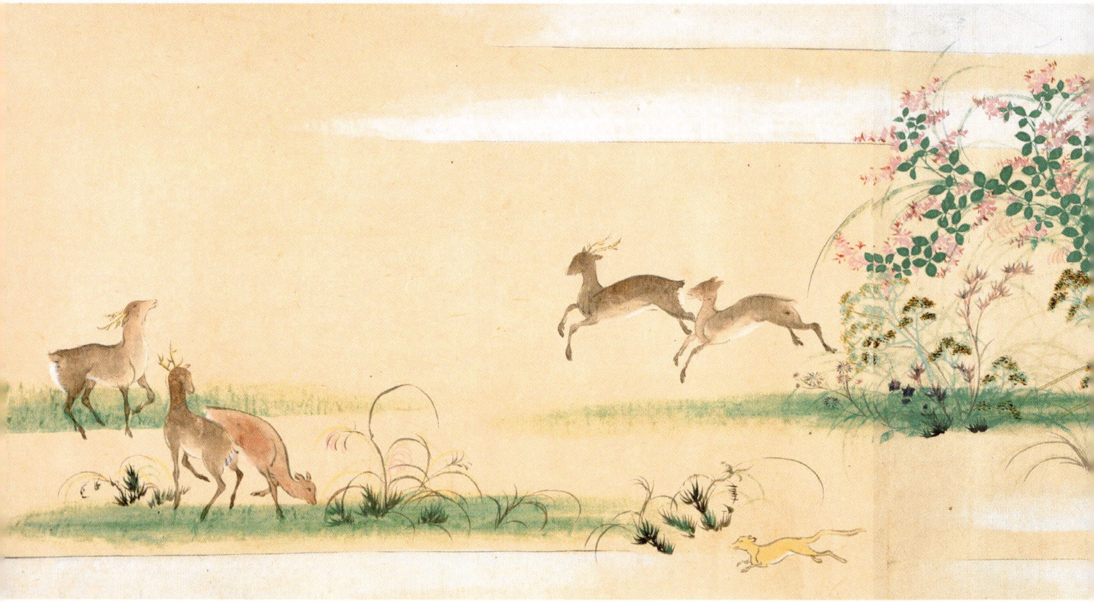

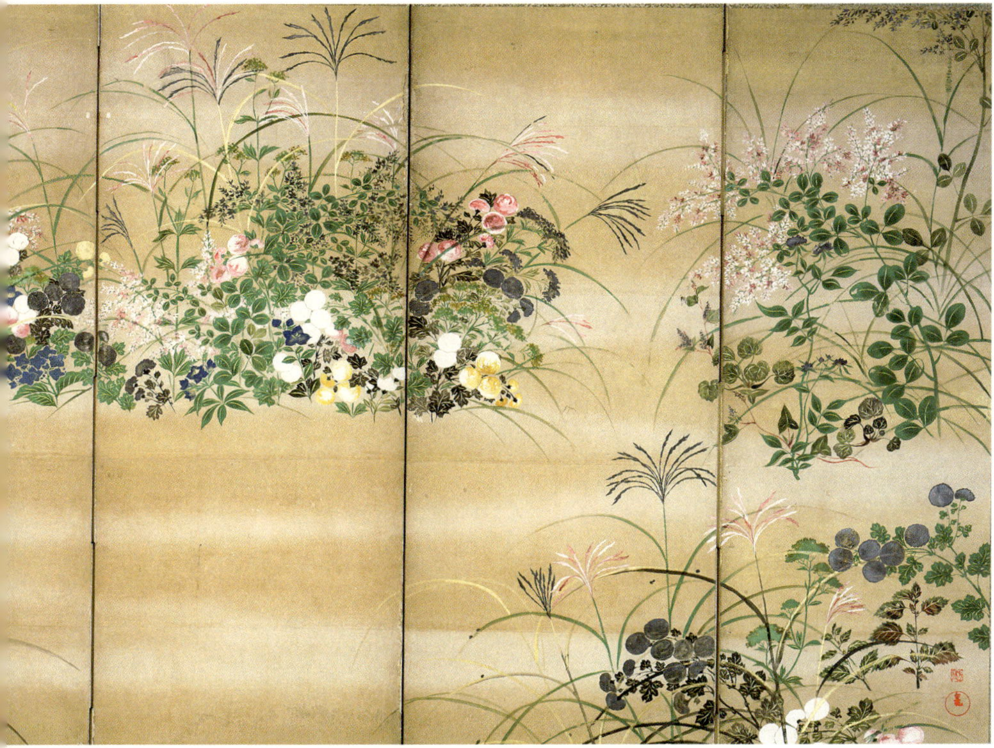

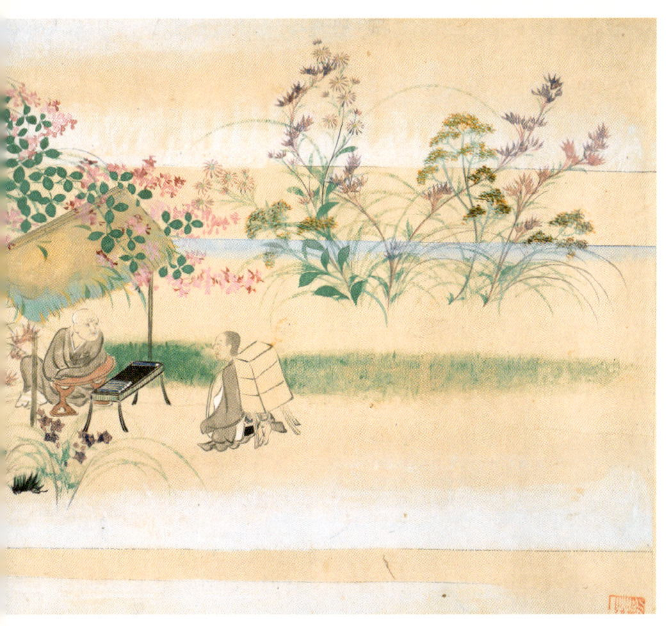

「西行物語絵巻　巻四第九段」
尾形光琳　宮内庁三の丸尚蔵館蔵
Illustrated Scrolls of the Life of
Priest *Saigyō*, Scroll 4, Chapter 9,
Ogata Kōrin, Sannomaru Shozokan
(The Museum of the Imperial
Collections)

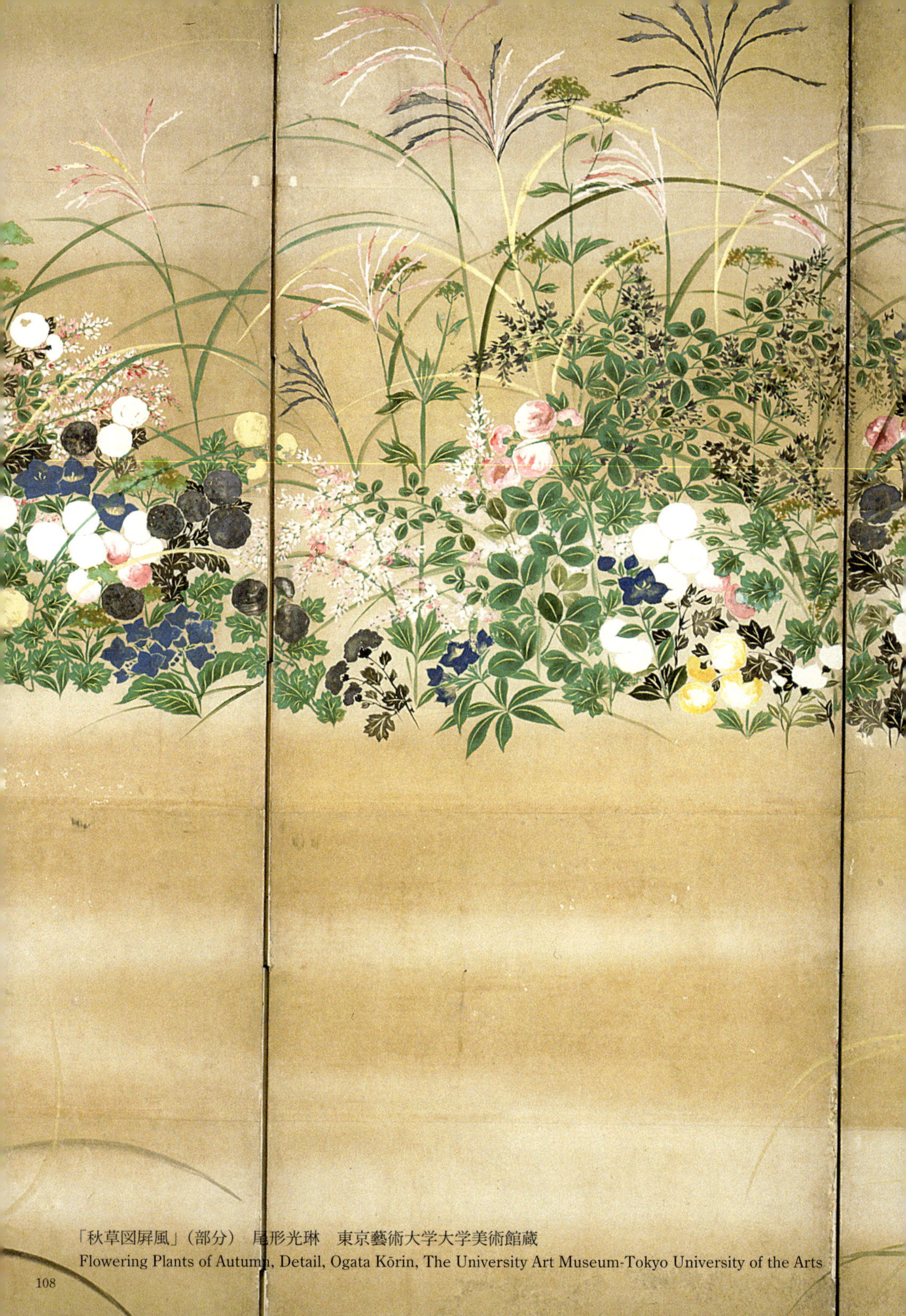

「秋草図屏風」（部分）　尾形光琳　東京藝術大学大学美術館蔵
Flowering Plants of Autumn, Detail, Ogata Kōrin, The University Art Museum-Tokyo University of the Arts

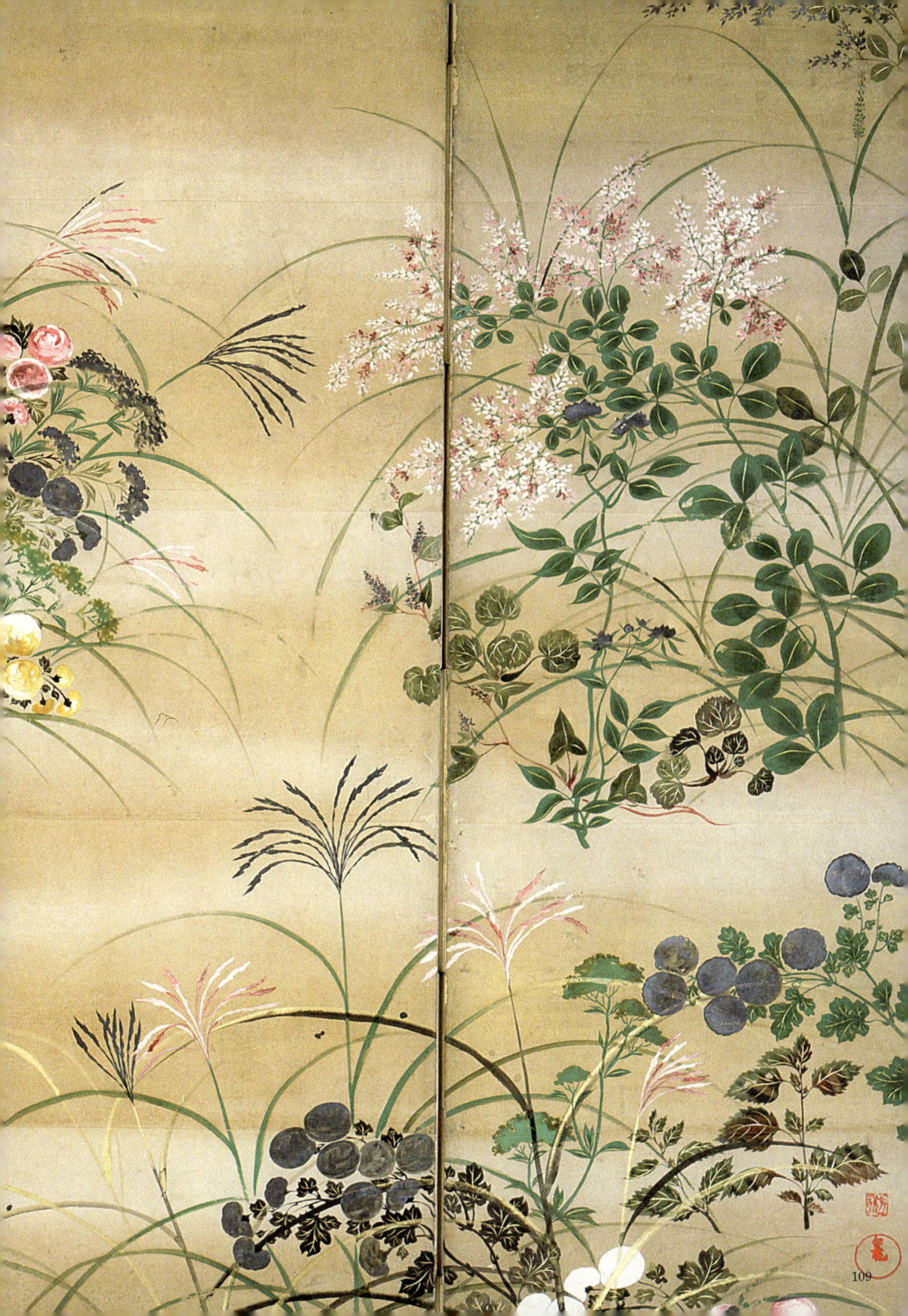

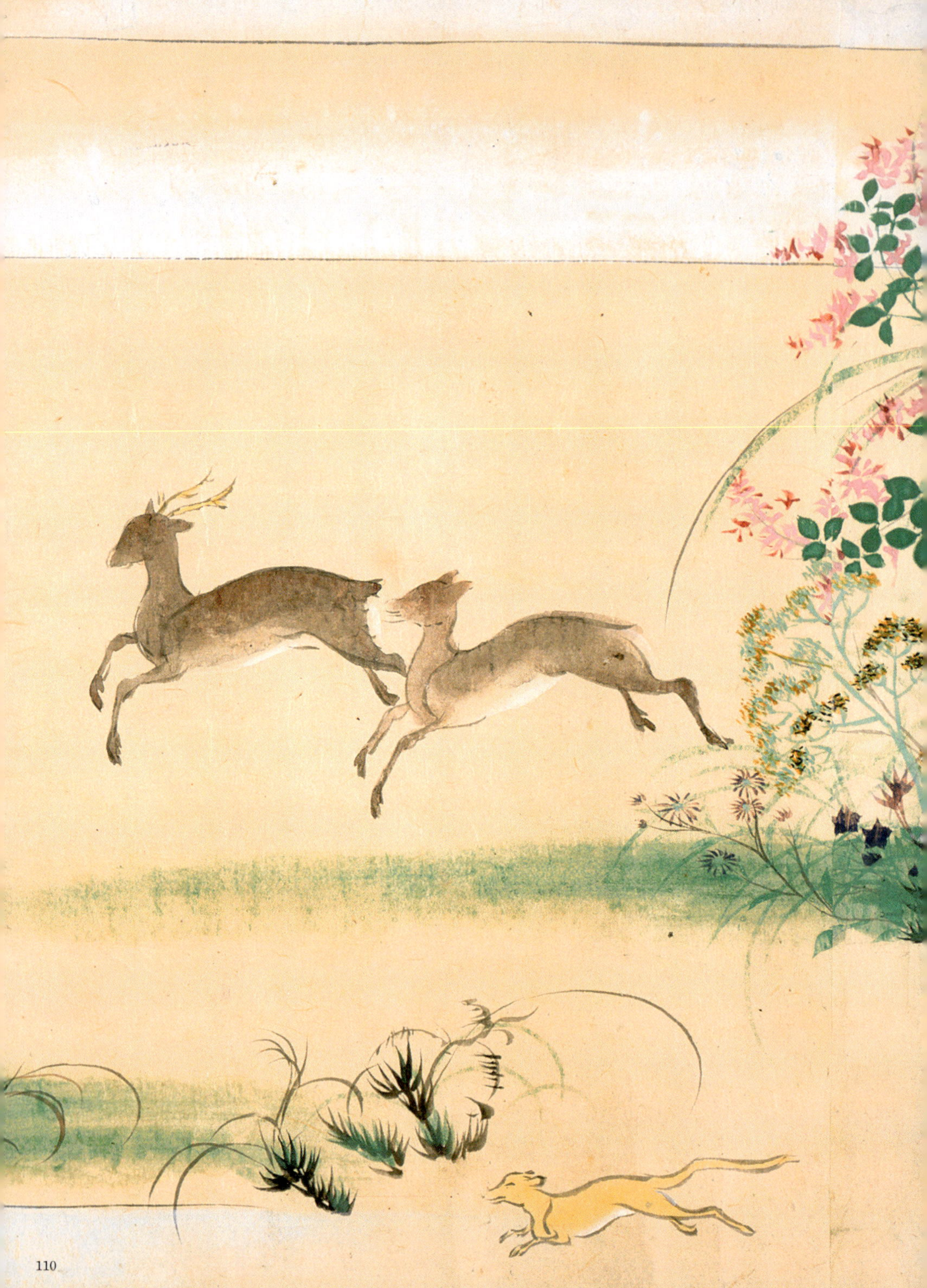

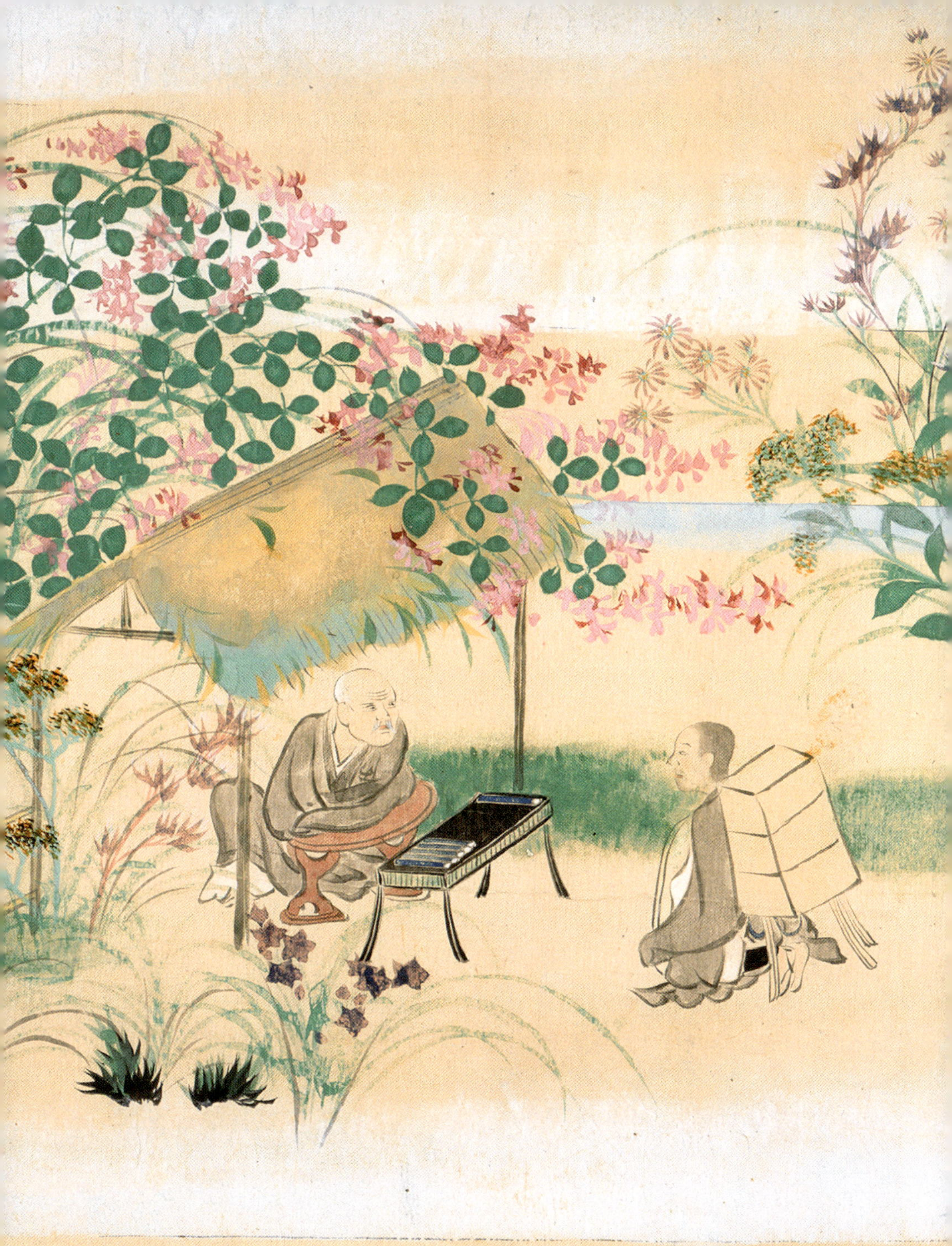

Illustrated Scrolls of the Life of Priest *Saigyō*, Scroll 4, Chapter 9, Detail, Ogata Kōrin,
Sannomaru Shozokan（The Museum of the Imperial Collections）

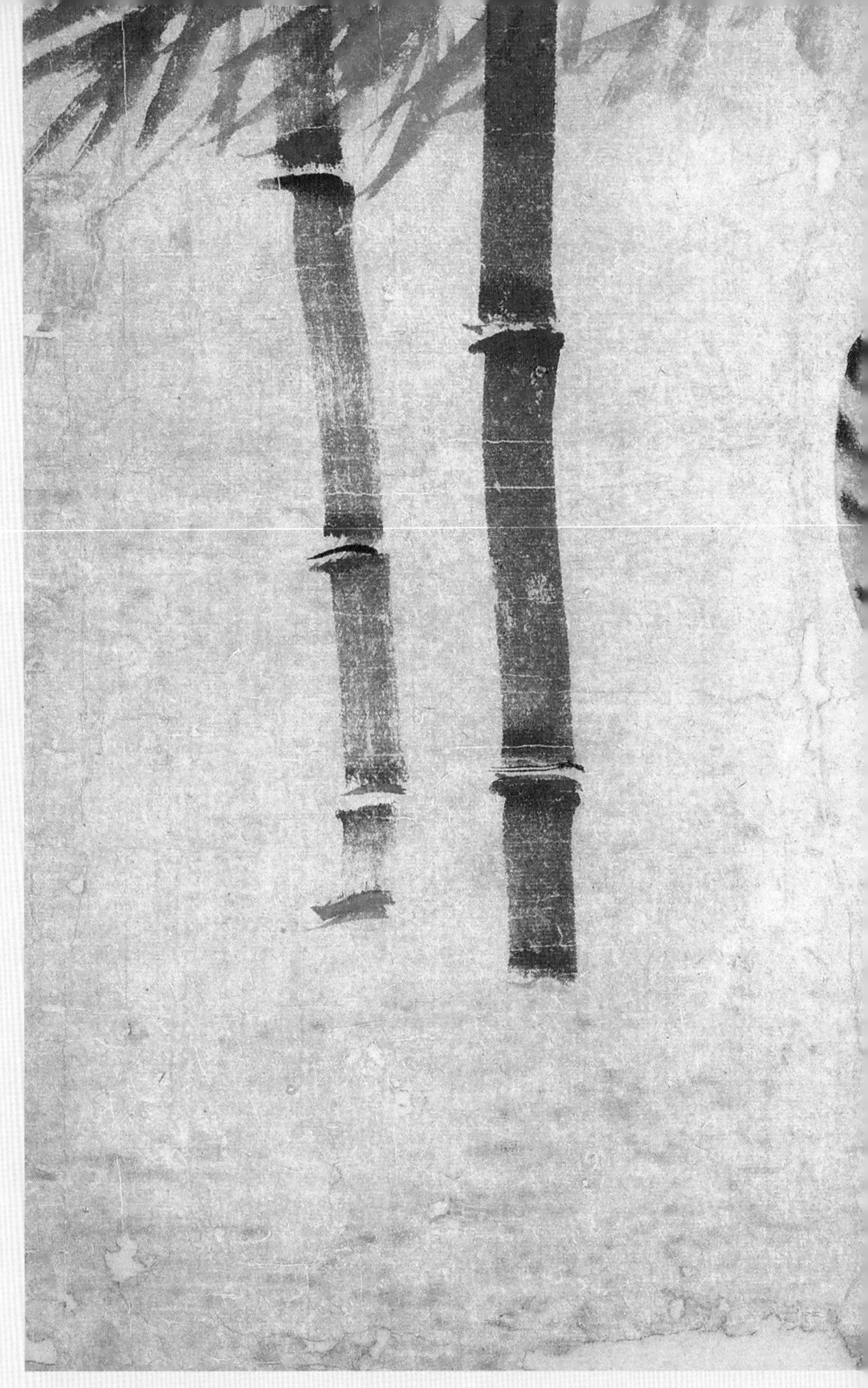

「竹虎図」　重文　尾形光琳　京都国立博物館蔵
Bamboos and Tiger, Ogata Kōrin, Important Cultural Property,
Kyoto National Museum

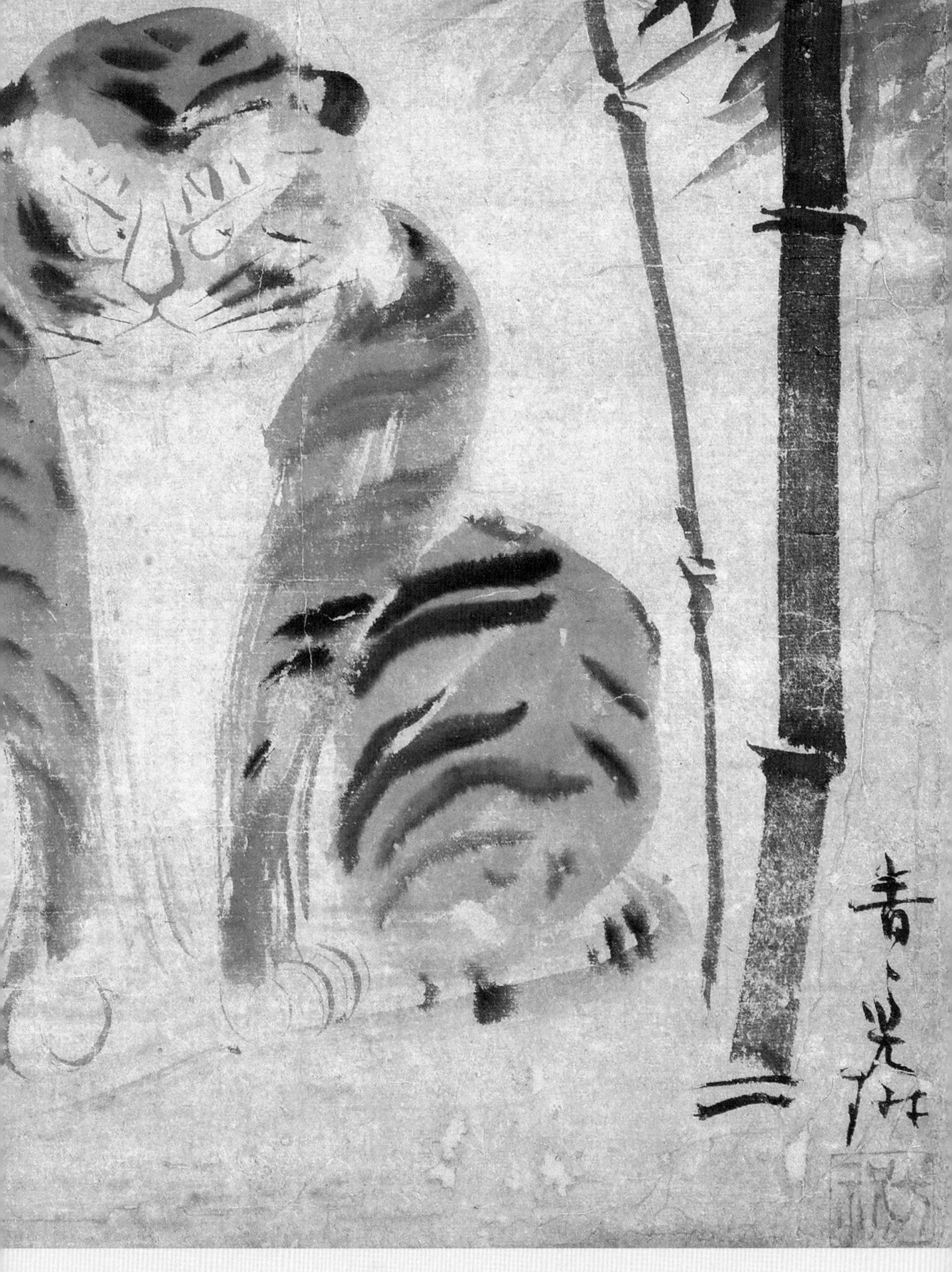
青光斉

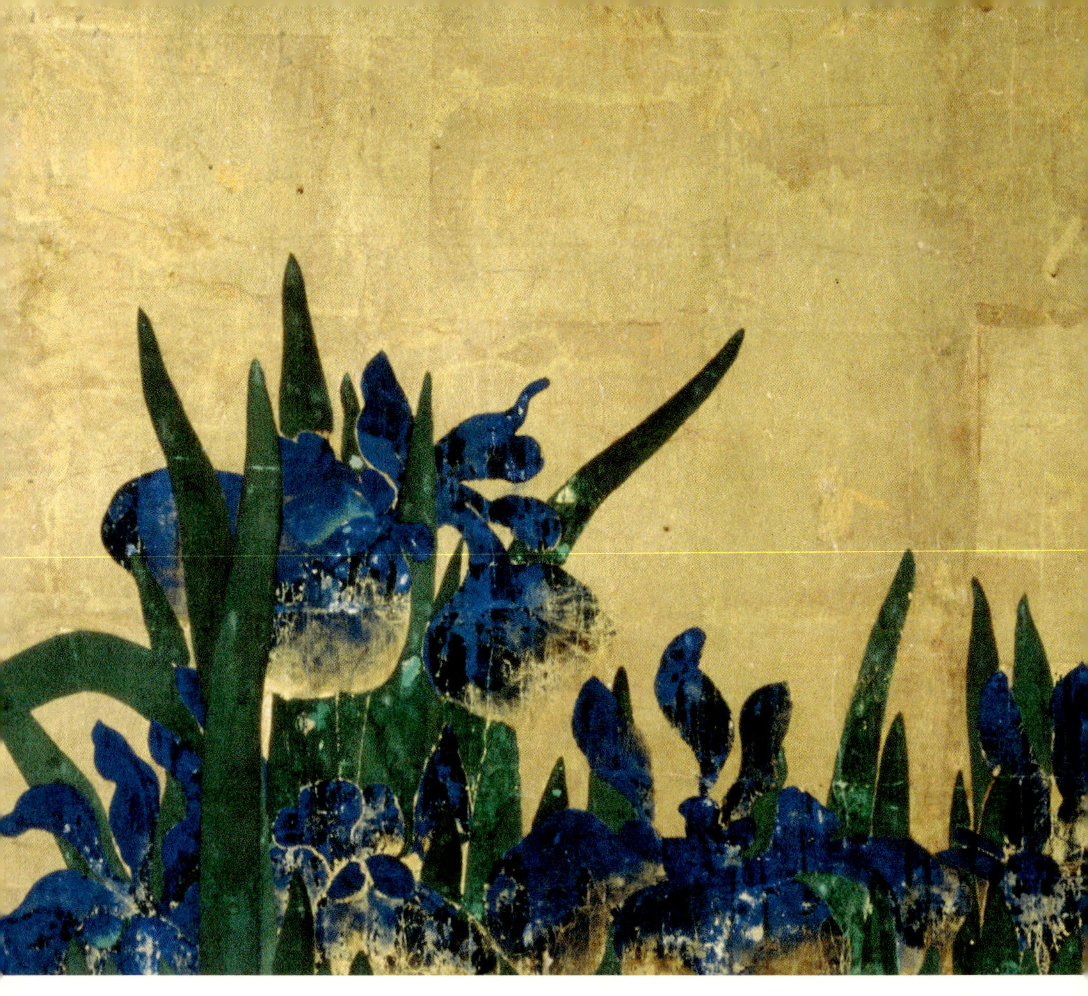

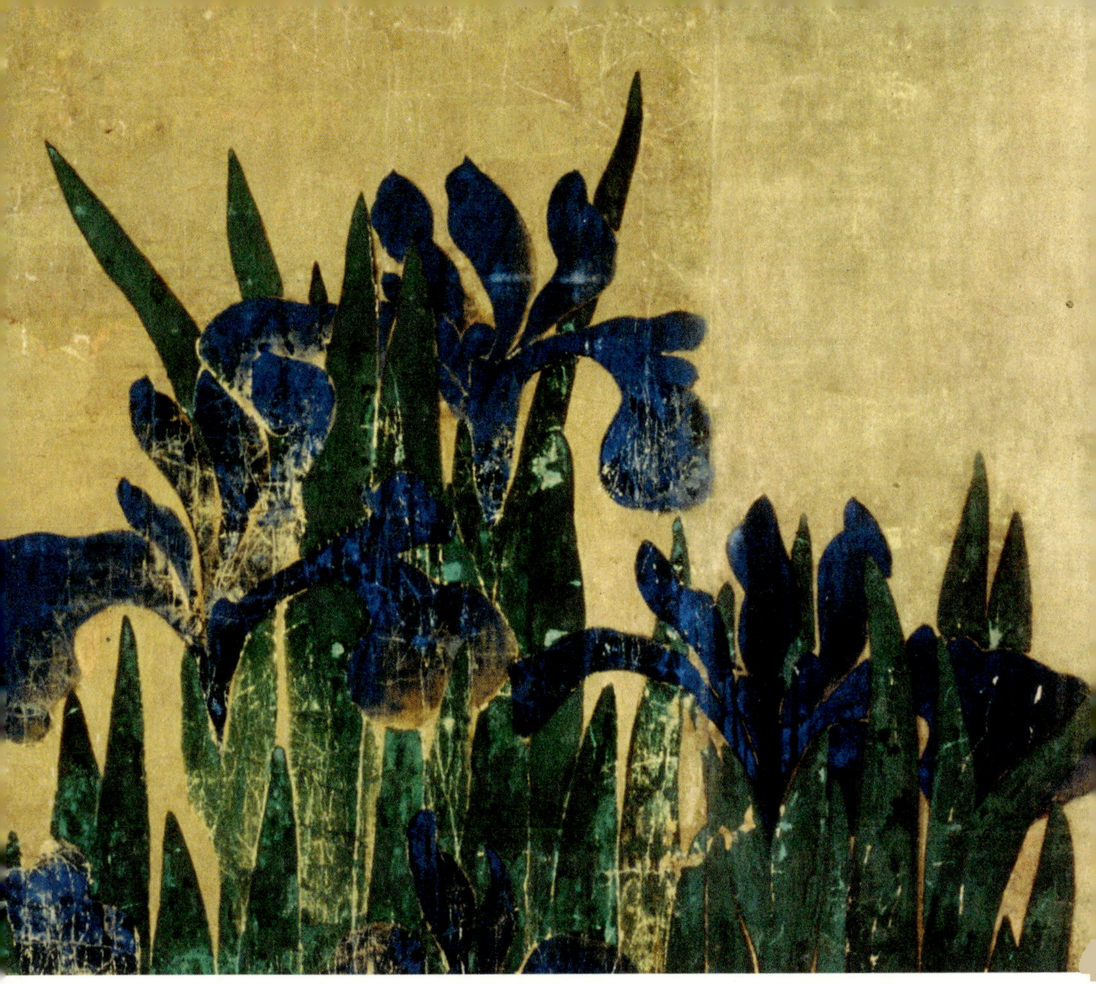

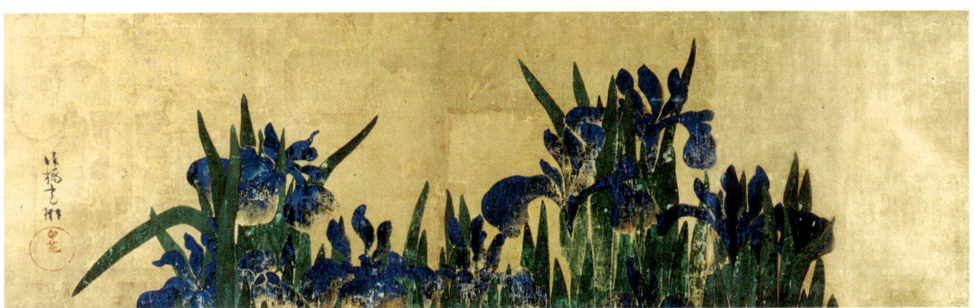

「燕子花図」　尾形光琳　大阪市立美術館蔵
Irises, Ogata Kōrin, Osaka City Museum of Fine Arts

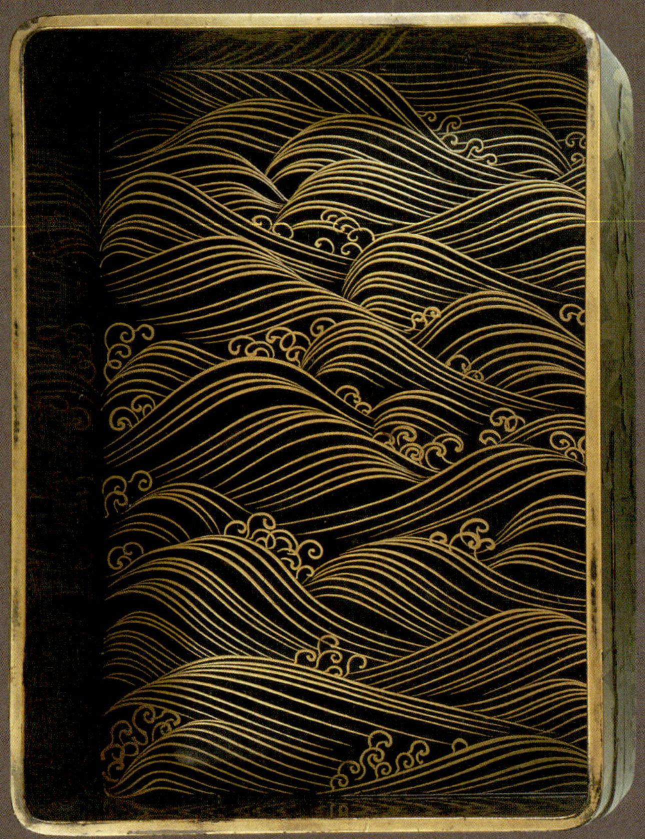

「八橋蒔絵螺鈿硯箱」　国宝　尾形光琳　東京国立博物館蔵
Lacquered Writing Box, *Maki-e* design of *Yatsu-hashi* Bridge and Irises, Ogata Kōrin, National Treasure,
Tokyo National Museum　Image: TNM Image Archives

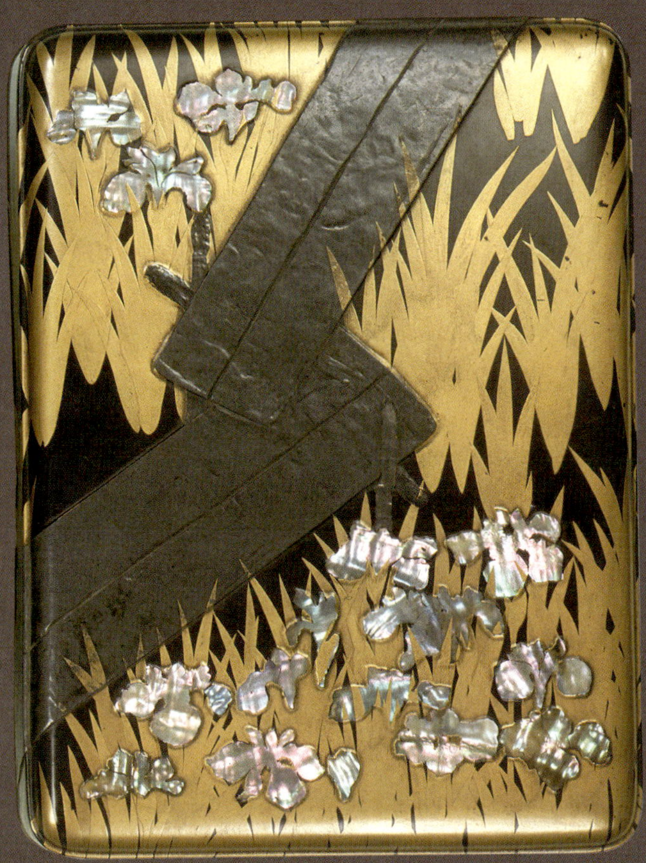

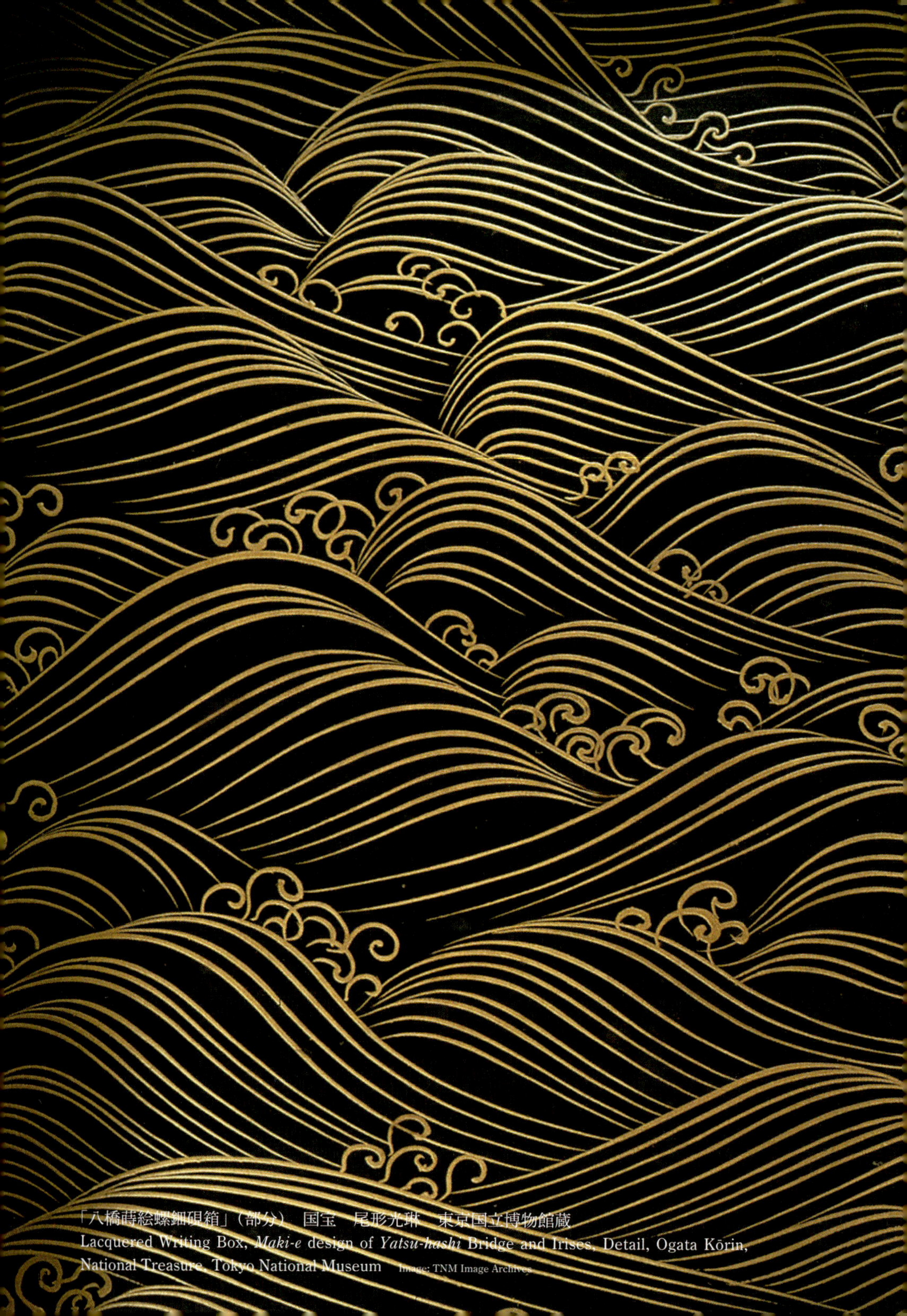

「八橋蒔絵螺鈿硯箱」（部分）　国宝　尾形光琳　東京国立博物館蔵
Lacquered Writing Box, *Maki-e* design of *Yatsu-hashi* Bridge and Irises, Detail, Ogata Kōrin, National Treasure, Tokyo National Museum　Image: TNM Image Archives

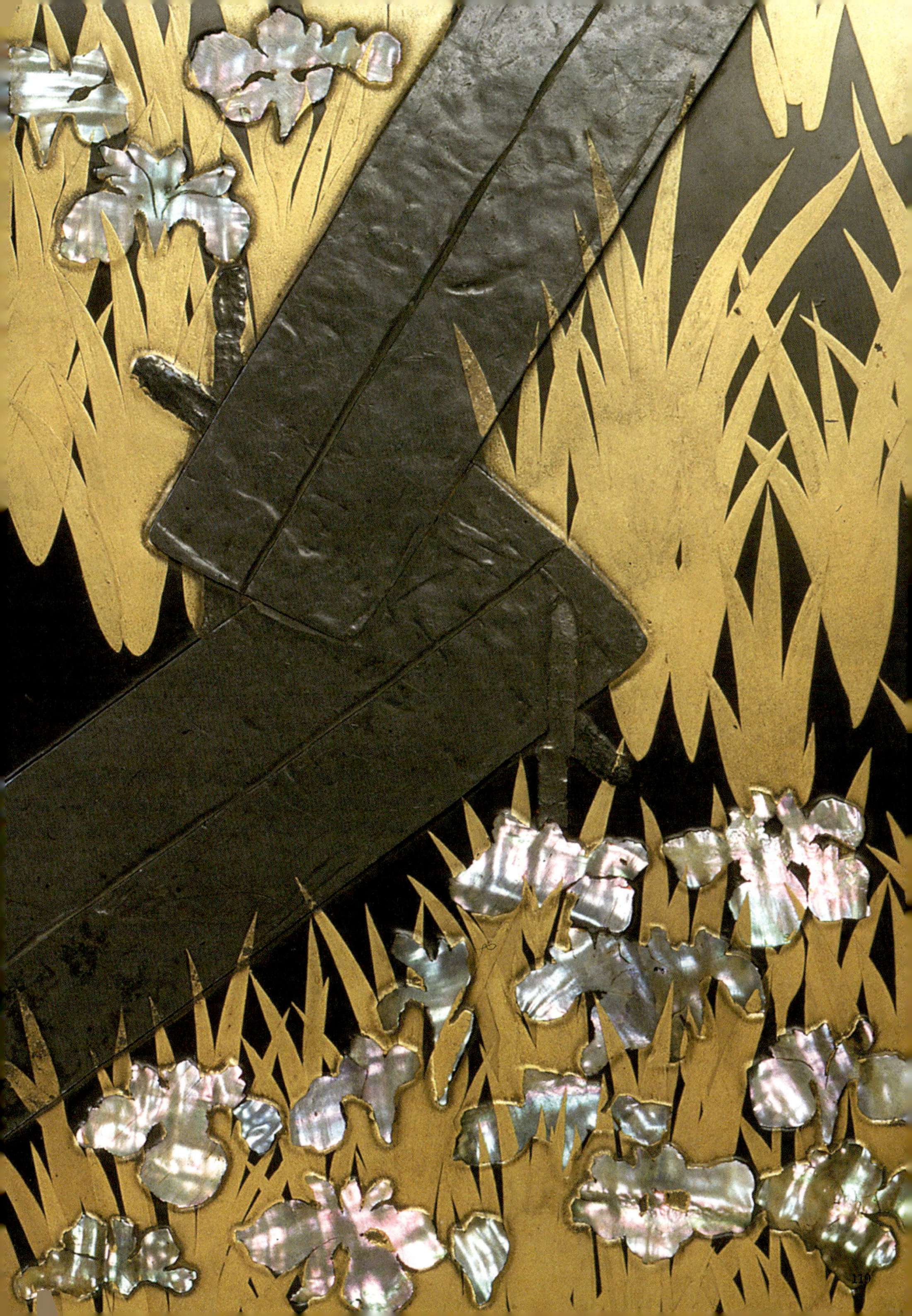

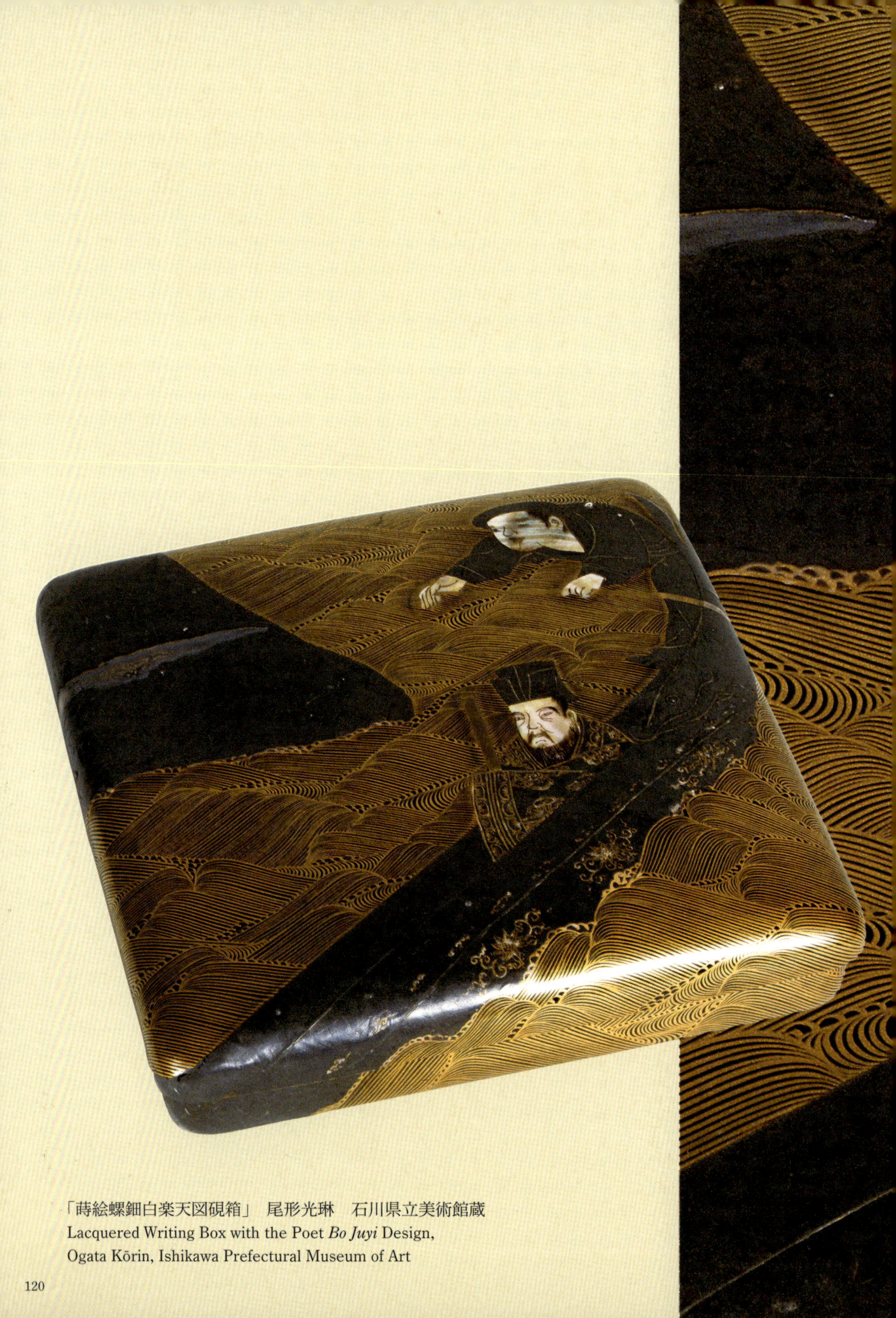

「蒔絵螺鈿白楽天図硯箱」　尾形光琳　石川県立美術館蔵
Lacquered Writing Box with the Poet *Bo Juyi* Design,
Ogata Kōrin, Ishikawa Prefectural Museum of Art

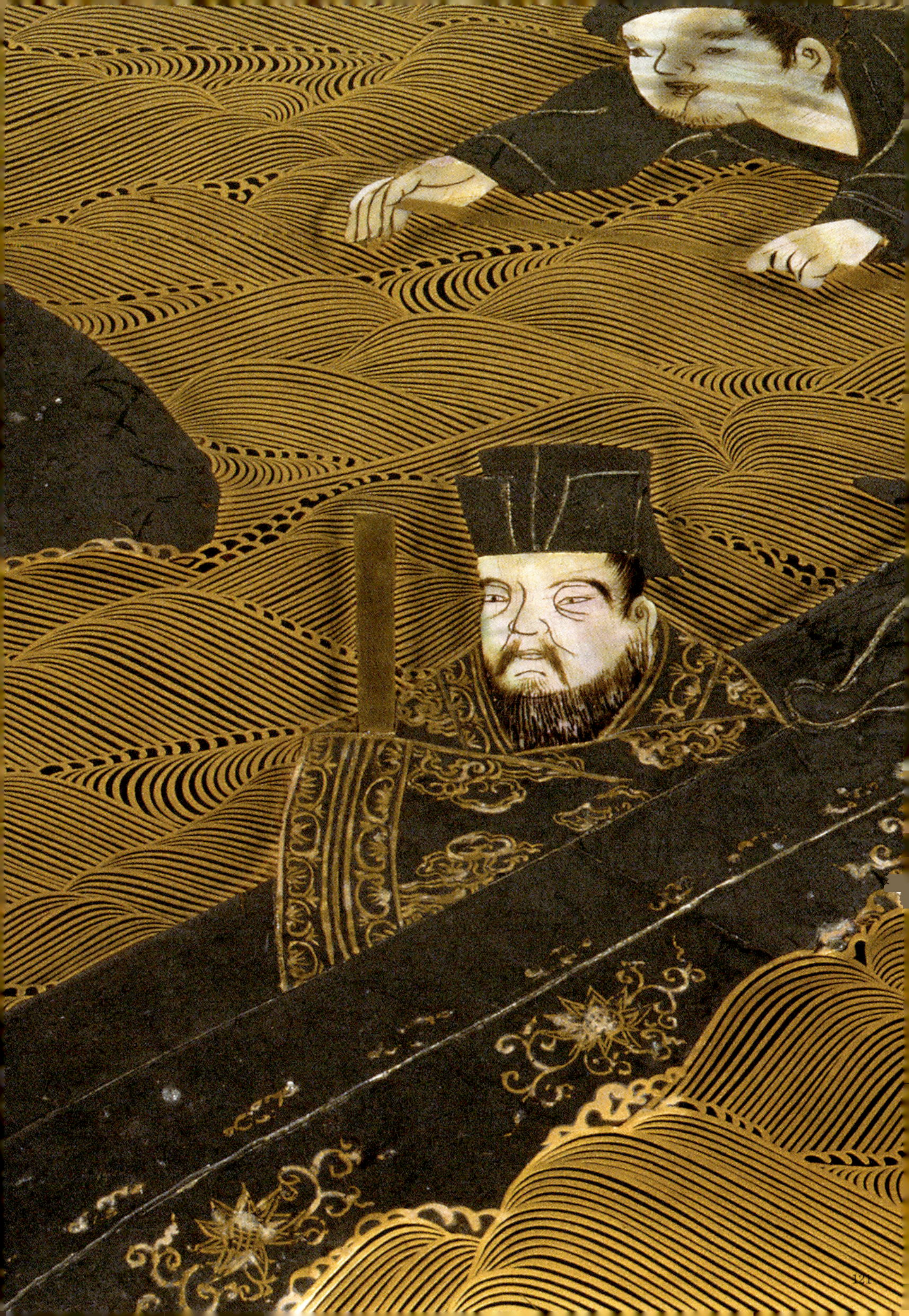

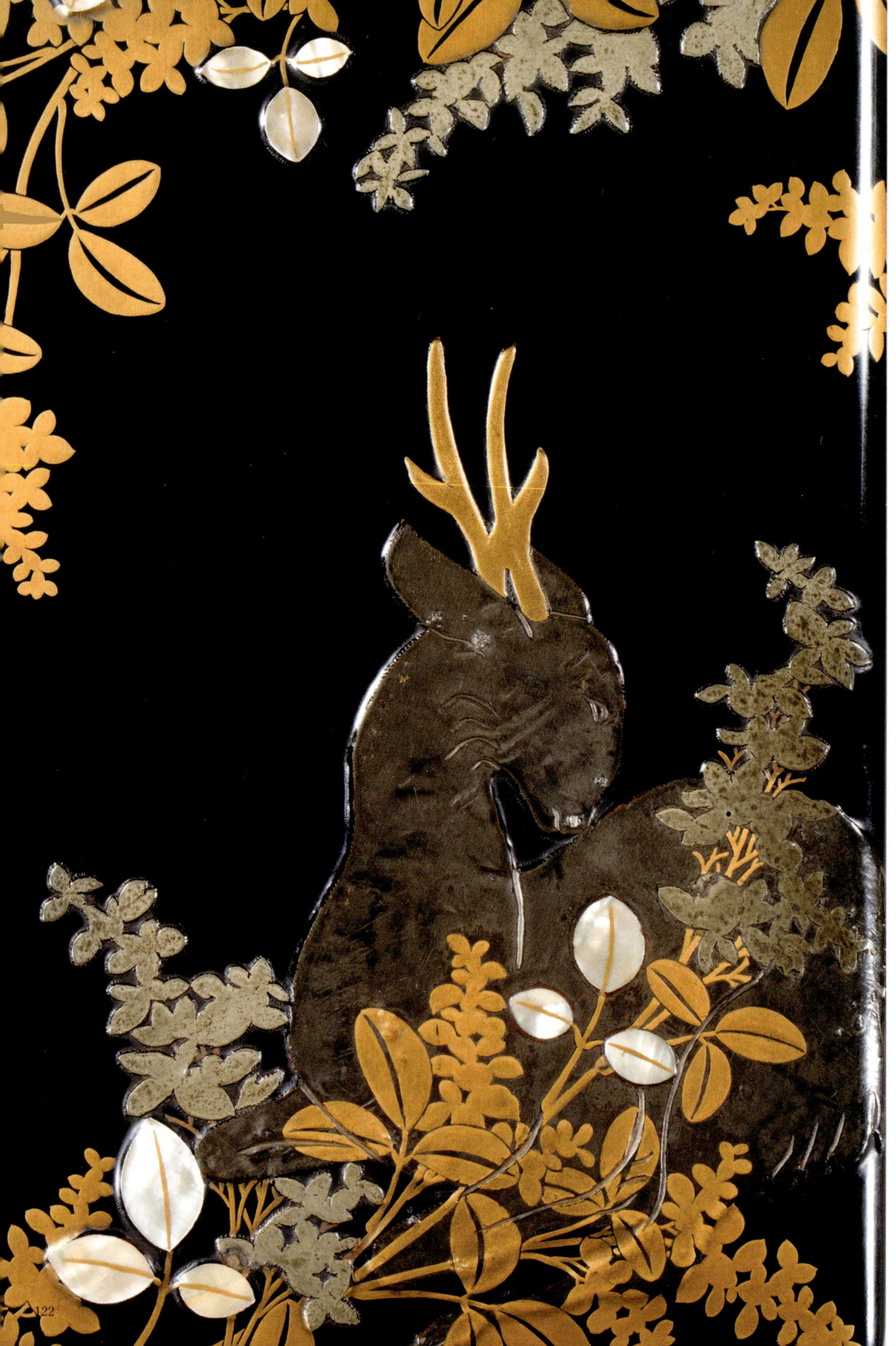

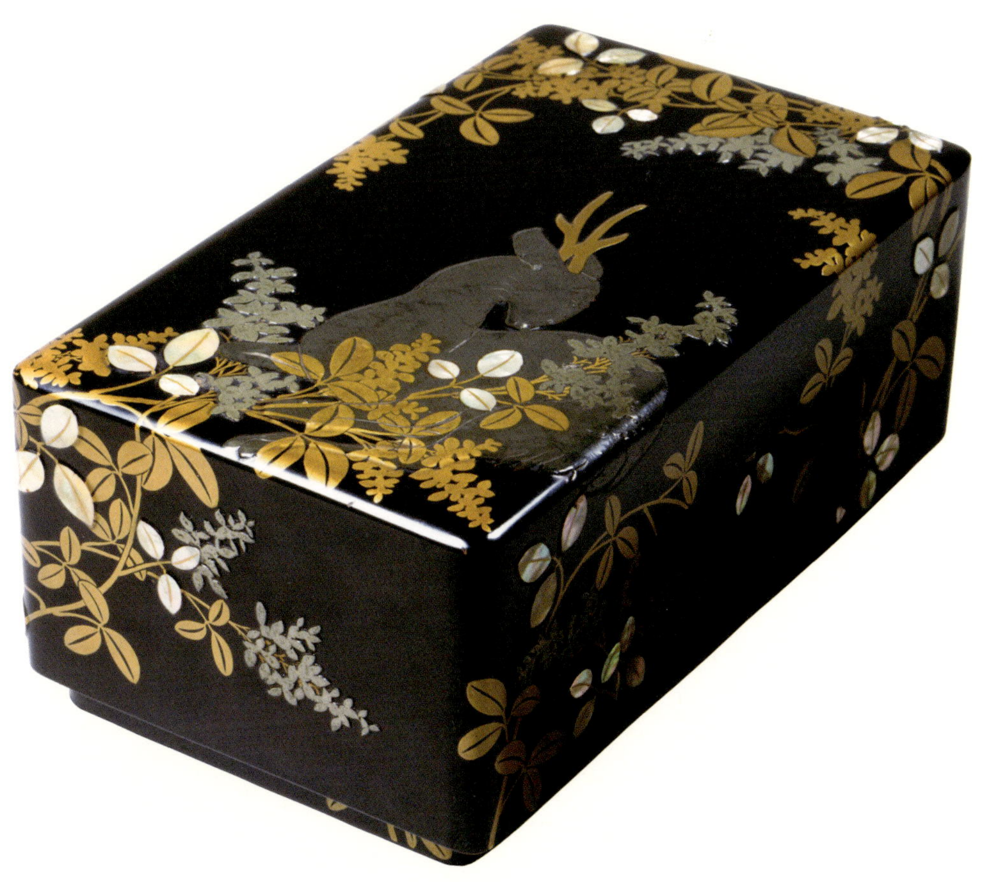

「蒔絵鹿に萩図硯箱」　尾形光琳　石川県立美術館蔵
Lacquered Writing Box with the Bush Clover and Deer Design,
Ogata Kōrin, Ishikawa Prefectural Museum of Art

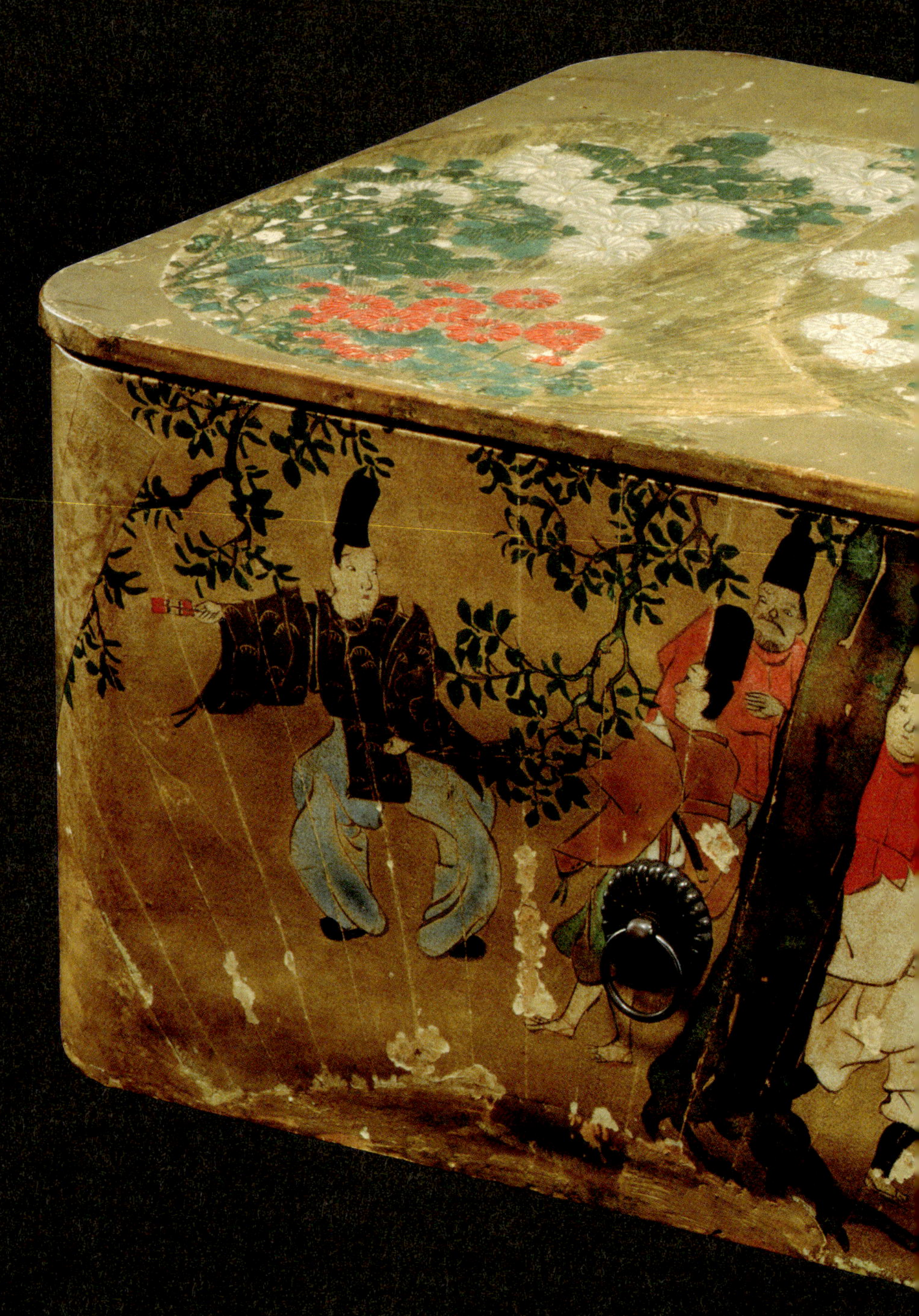

「扇面貼交手筥」　重文　尾形光琳　大和文華館蔵
Cosmetic Box with Fan-shaped Painting, Ogata Kōrin, Important Cultural Property,
The Museum Yamato Bunkakan, Nara

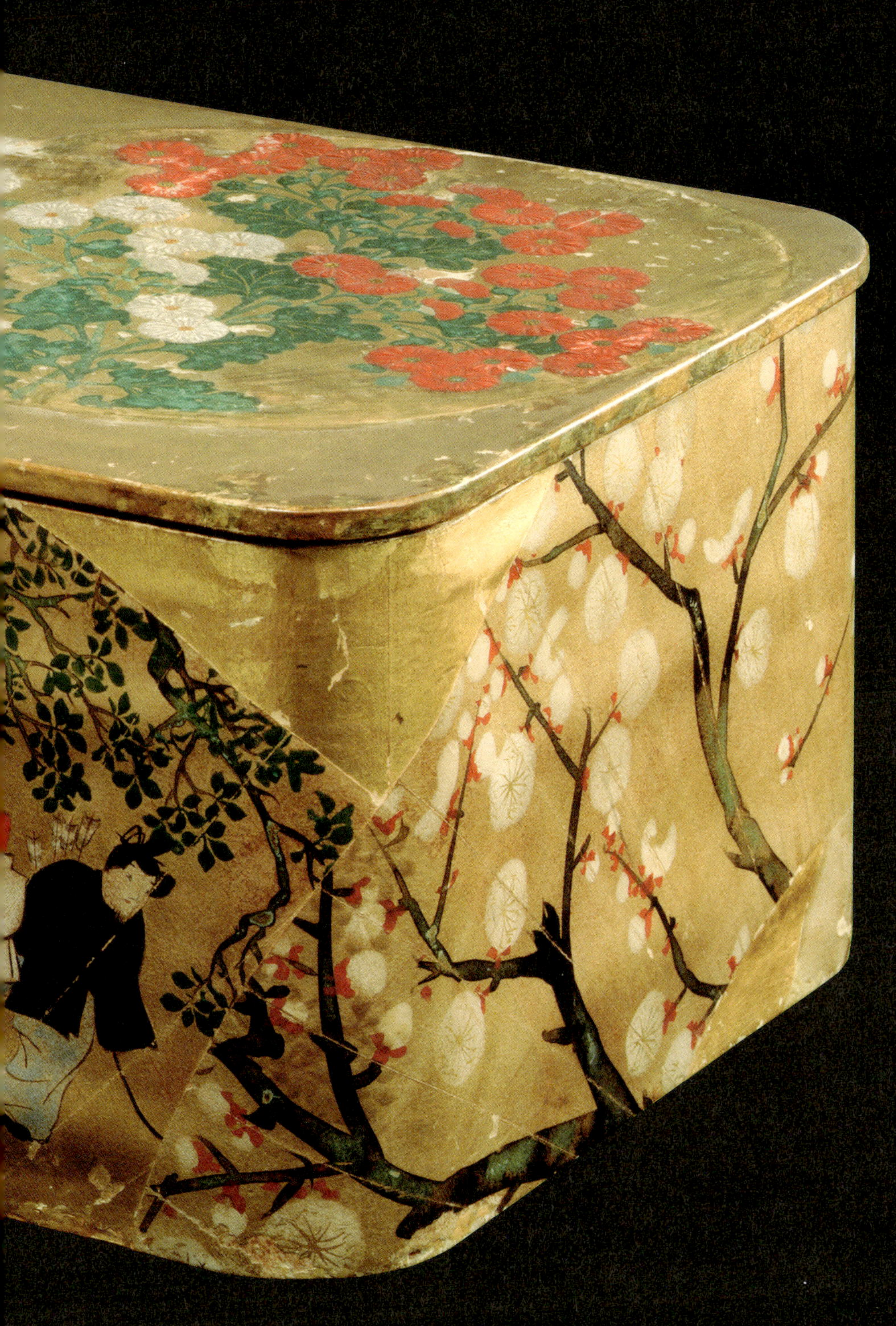

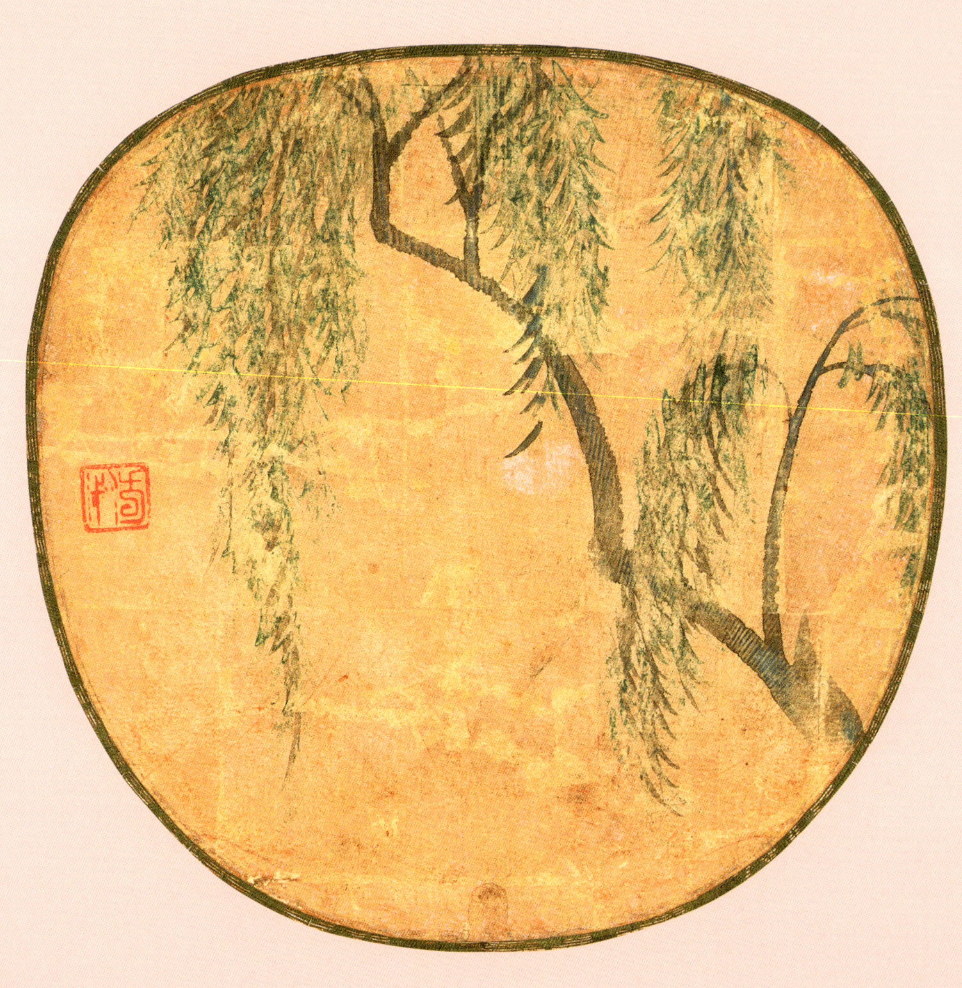

「柳図団扇」　方淑印　大阪市立美術館蔵
Willows, Seal of Hōshuku, Osaka City Museum of Fine Arts

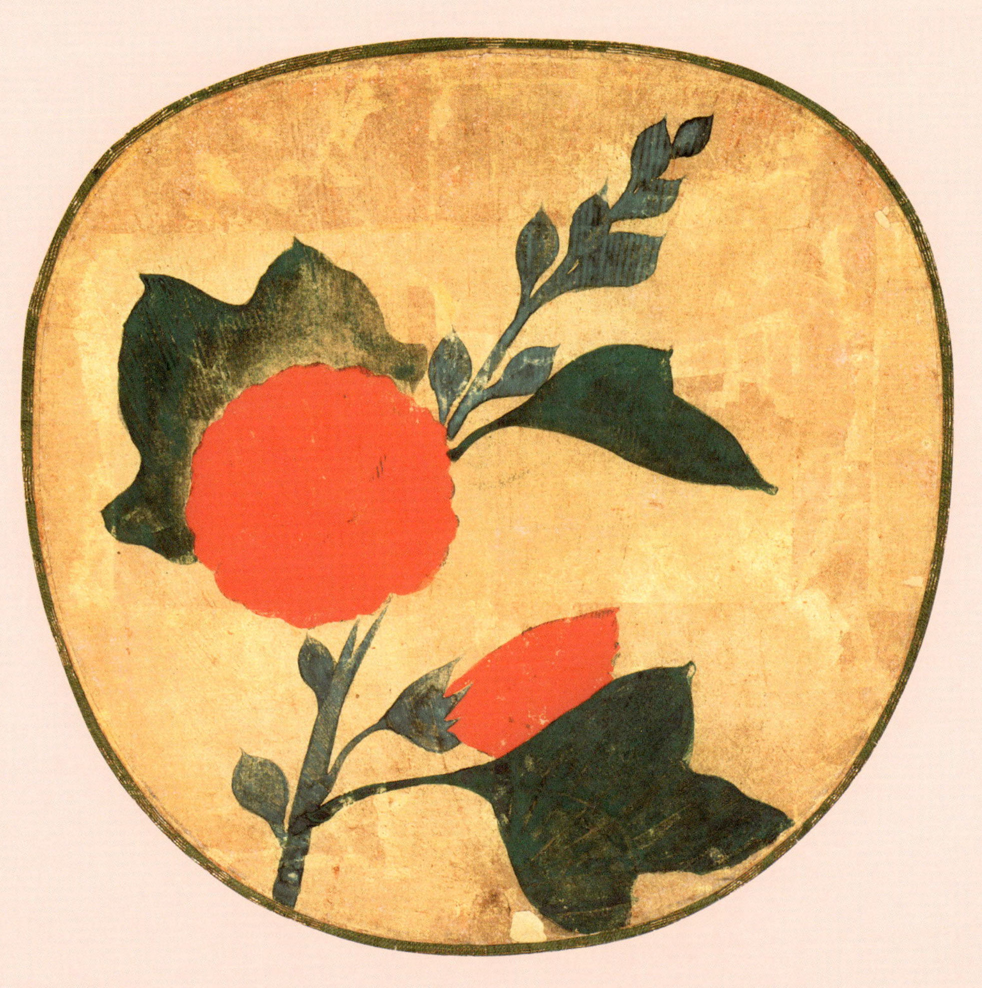

「立葵図団扇」　方淑印　大阪市立美術館蔵
Hollyhock, Seal of Hōshuku, Osaka City Museum of Fine Arts

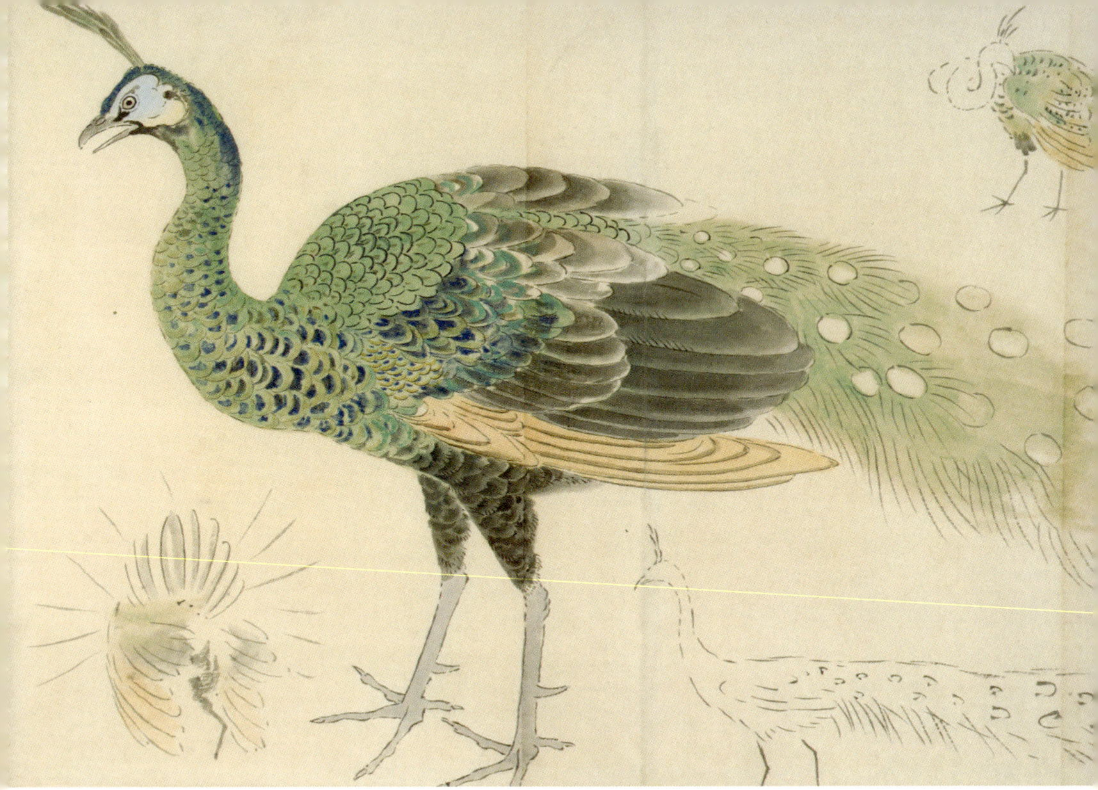

「鳥獣写生図巻」（上巻）　重文　尾形光琳　京都国立博物館蔵
Birds and Animals Sketches, Ogata Kôrin, Important Cultural Property, Kyoto National Museum

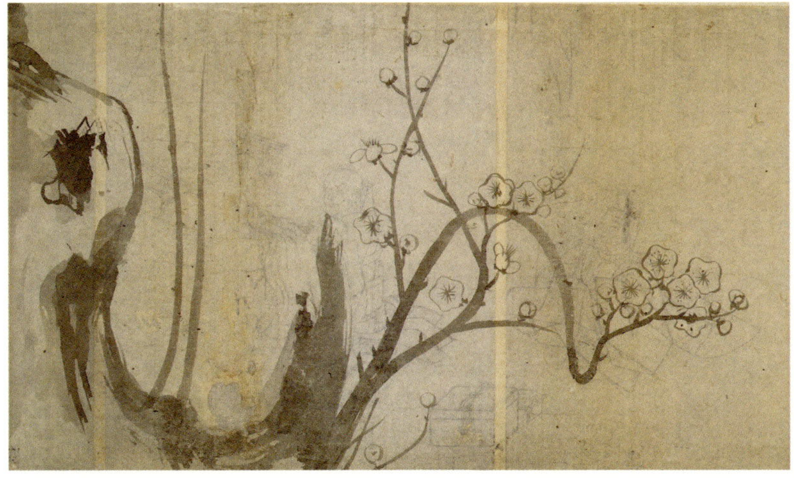

「梅花図画稿」　重文　尾形光琳　大阪市立美術館蔵
Sketch of a Plum Tree, Ogata Kōrin, Important Cultural Property,
Osaka City Museum of Fine Arts

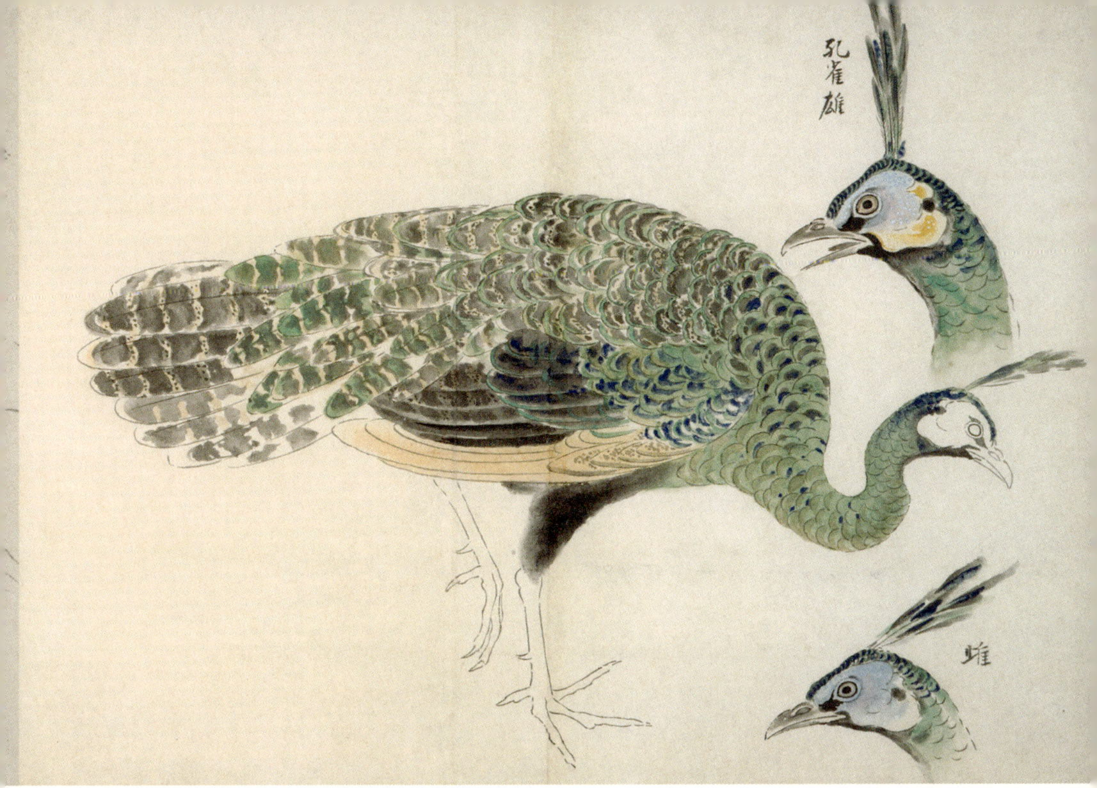

孔雀雄
雌

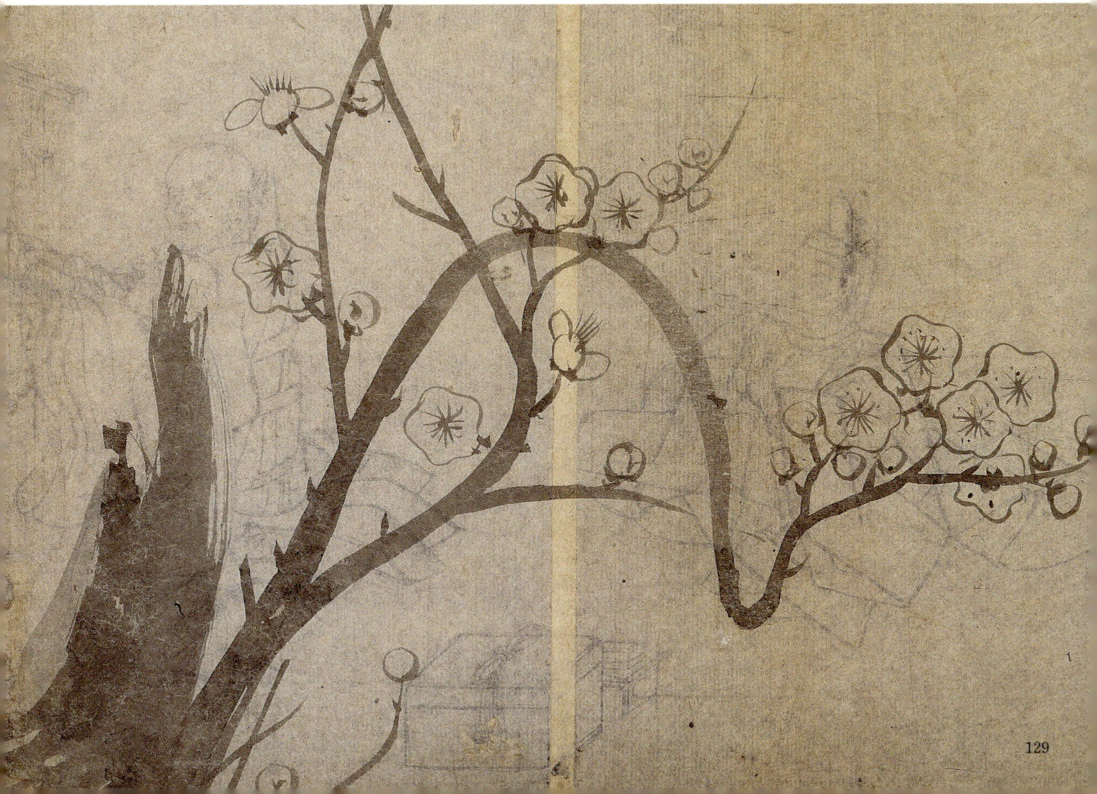

尾形乾山

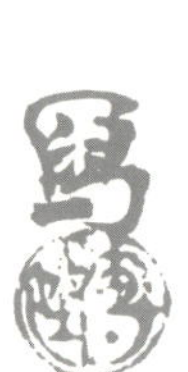
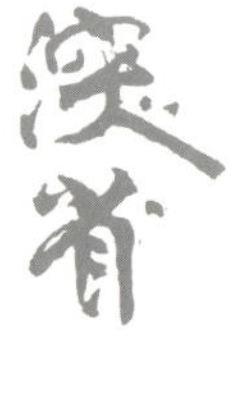

おがた けんざん
寛文3年〜寛保3年（1663-1743）

尾形光琳の弟で宗謙の三男に生ま
れ、学問、茶事を藤村庸軒に、絵
を狩野安信に学んだといわれる。
本阿弥光悦の影響を受け、野々村
仁清から本格的に作陶を学び修業
する。兄光琳との合作による絵付、
光琳風の素朴な意匠、また乾山得
意の詩賛を記した詩画一体の雅陶
を制作した。また晩年は江戸で絵
画制作も始め、光琳風を受け継ぎ
ながらも技巧を嫌った朴訥で味わ
い深い作品を描いた。

Ogata Kenzan (1663 – 1743)
Ogata Kōrin's younger brother,
Kenzan studied poetry and the tea
ceremony with Fujimura Yōken,
painting with Kanō Yasunobu, and
pottery with Nonomura Ninsei. He
and his brother collaborated on
pieces that integrate his poetry and
Kōrin's painting. Kenzan was later
active as a painter in Edo, creating
lyrical works that, while continuing
Kōrin's style, have a rugged honesty
that eschews displays of technique.

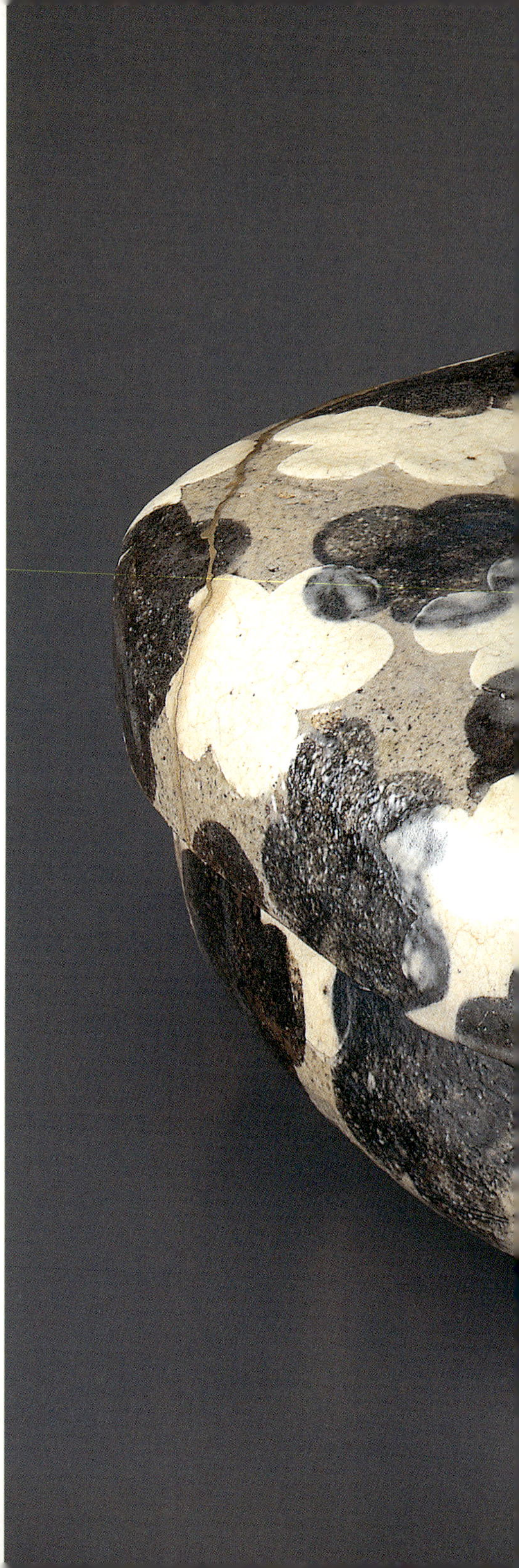

「銹絵染付梅波文蓋物」
尾形乾山　MIHO MUSEUM 蔵
Lidded dish with Design of Plum Blossoms
and Waves in Iron Brown Underglaze,
Ogata Kenzan, Miho Museum, Shiga

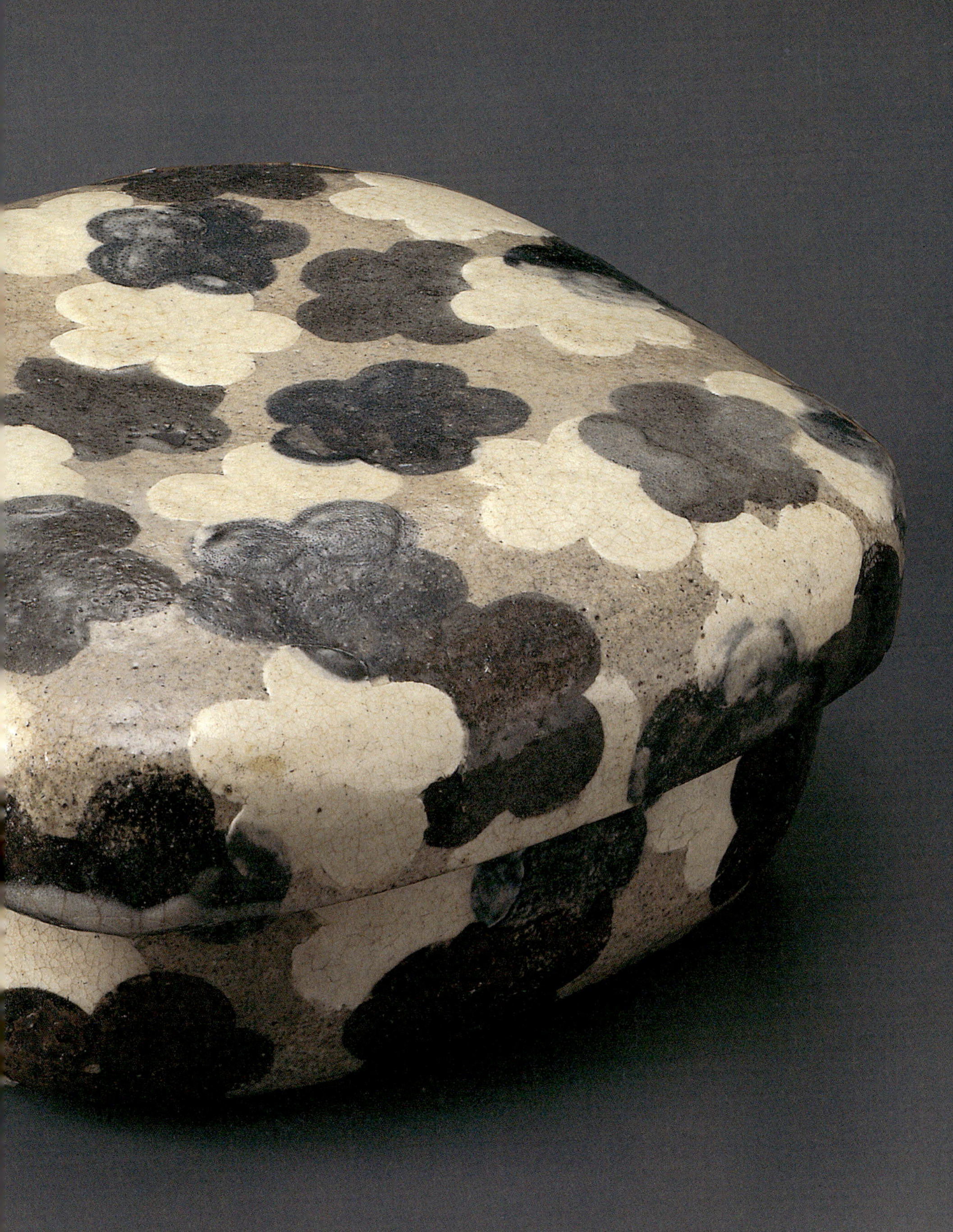

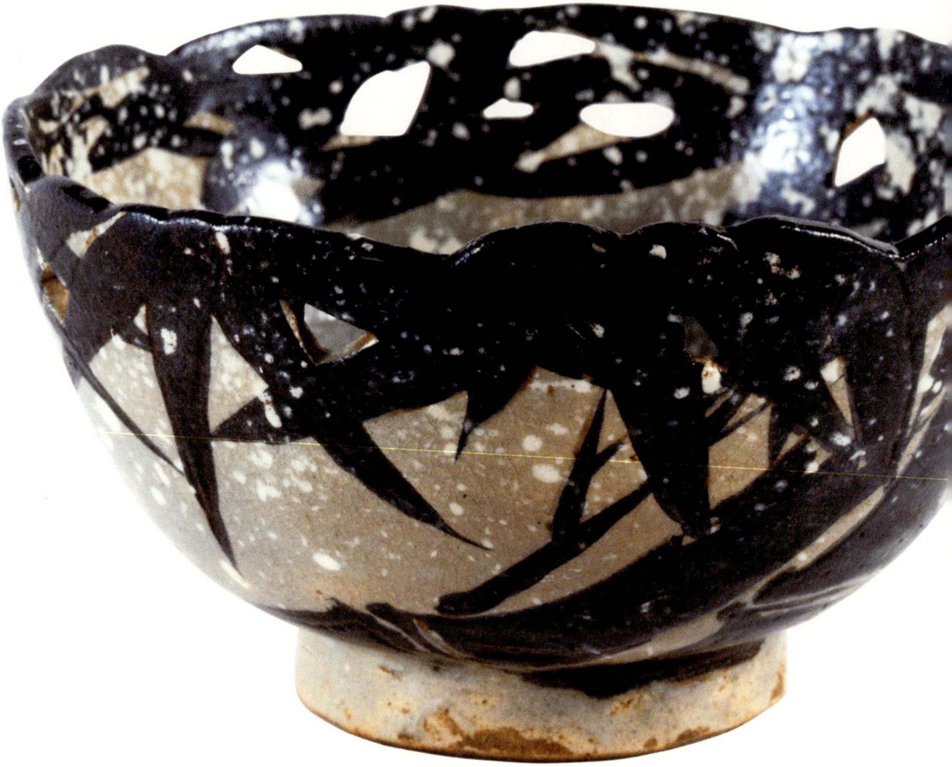

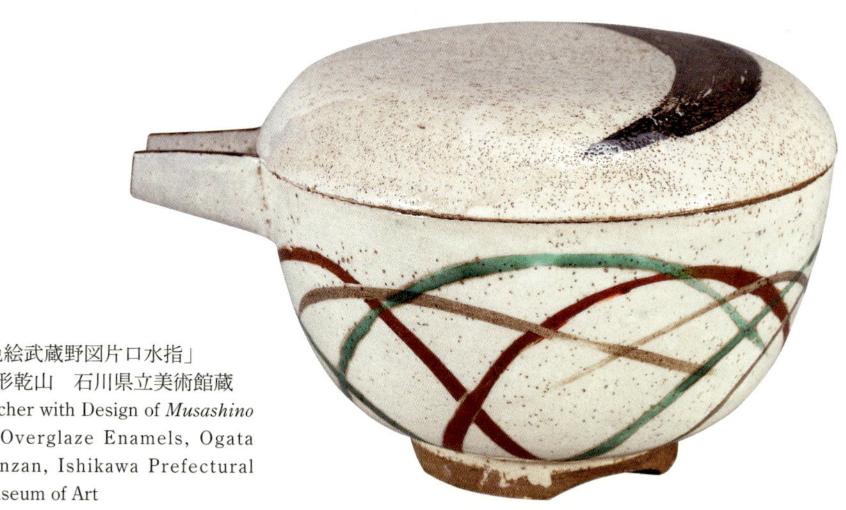

「色絵武蔵野図片口水指」
尾形乾山　石川県立美術館蔵
Pitcher with Design of *Musashino*
in Overglaze Enamels, Ogata
Kenzan, Ishikawa Prefectural
Museum of Art

「銹絵雪笹図鉢」　尾形乾山
石川県立美術館蔵
Bowl with Design of Snow-
covered Bamboo in Iron Brown
Underglaze,Ogata Kenzan, Ishikawa
Prefectural Museum of Art

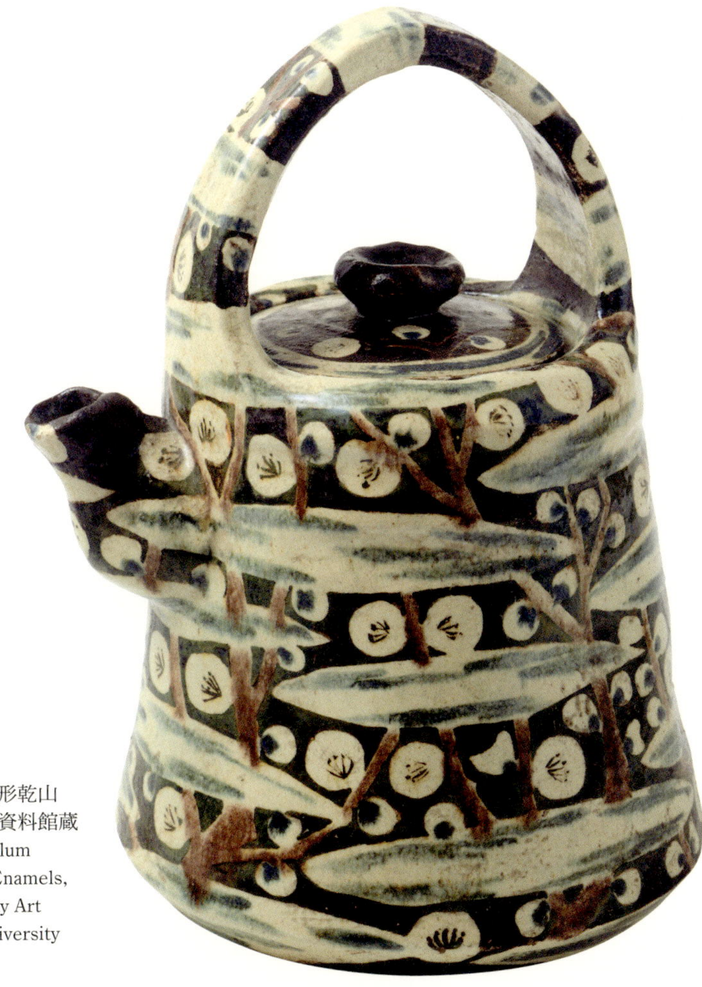

「色絵槍梅文水指」　尾形乾山
京都市立芸術大学芸術資料館蔵
Pitcher with Design of Plum
Blossoms in Overglaze Enamels,
Ogata Kenzan, University Art
Museum, Kyoto City University
of Arts

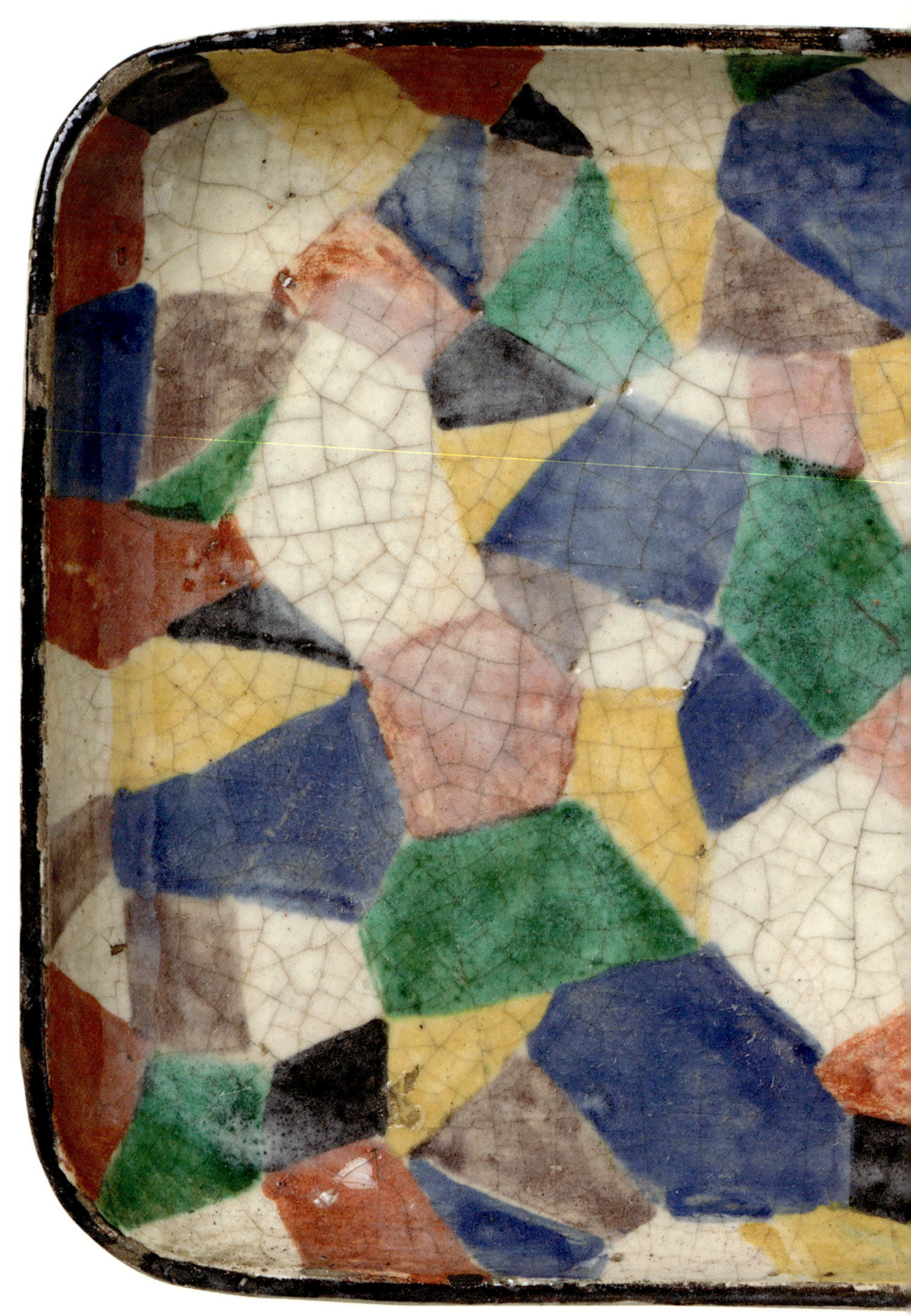

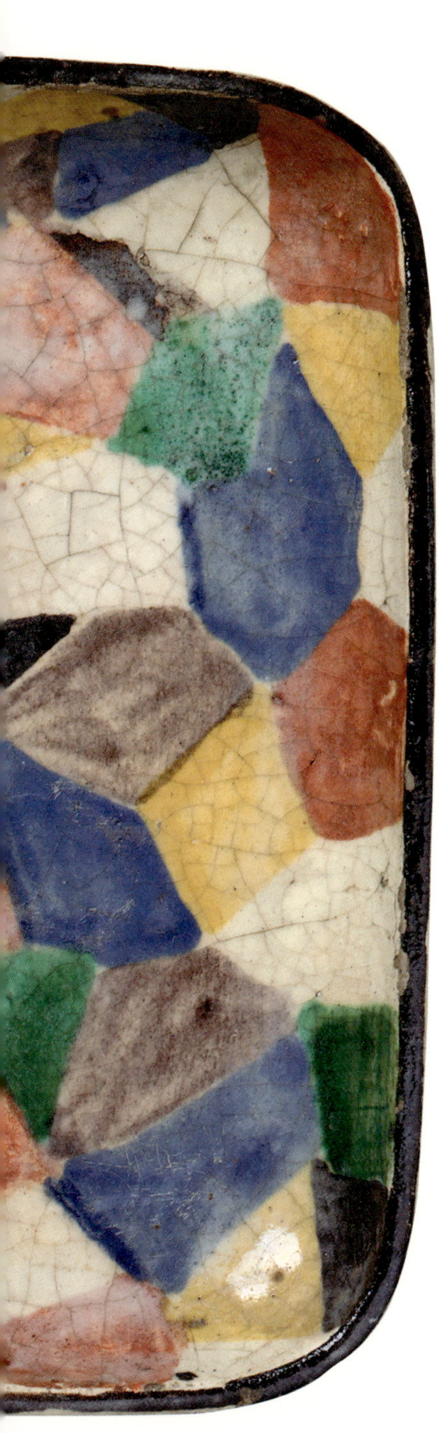

「色絵石垣文角皿」　尾形乾山　京都国立博物館蔵
Square Dish with Design of Stone Wall in Overglaze Enamels,
Ogata Kenzan, Kyoto National Museum

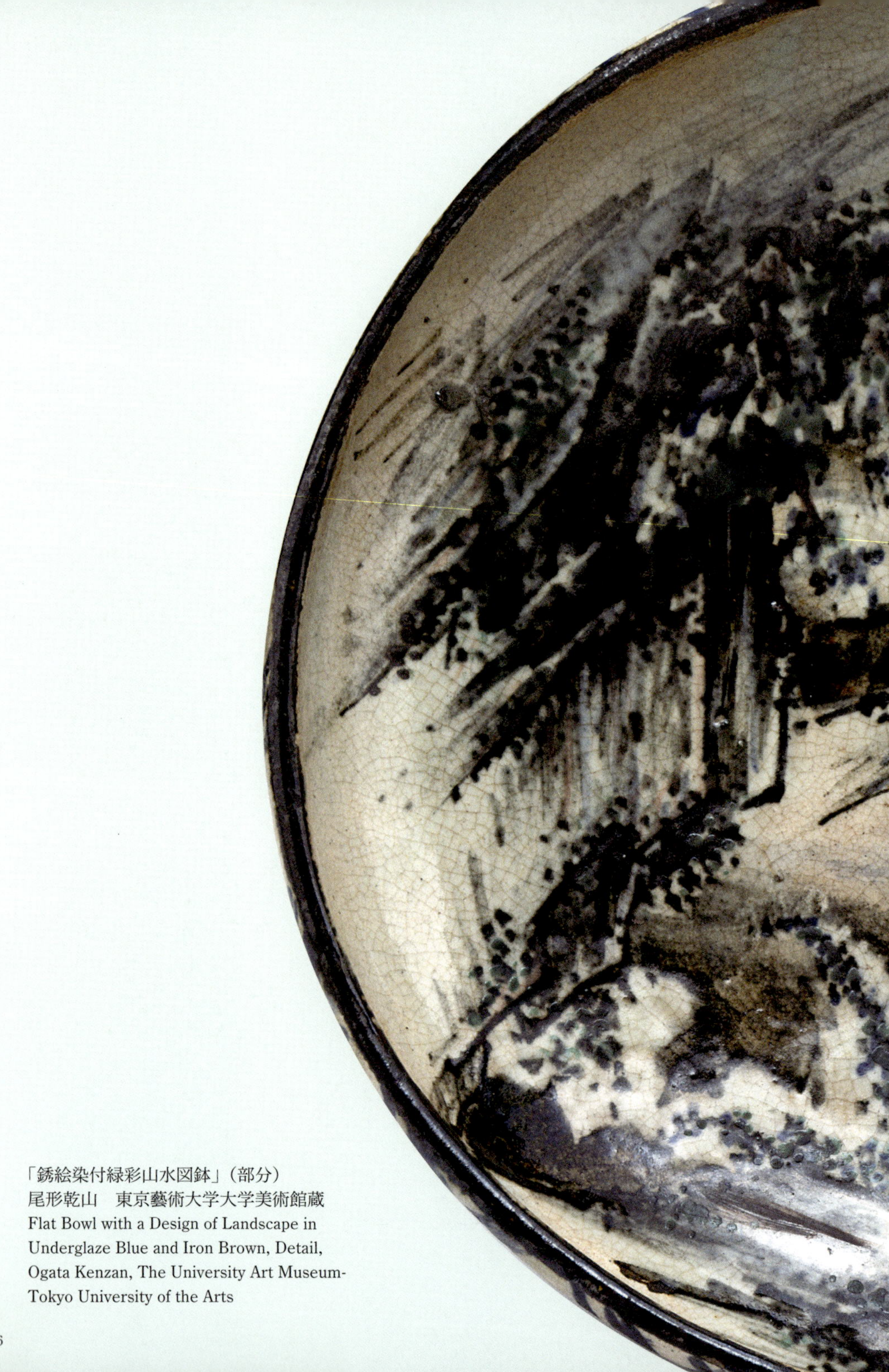

「銹絵染付緑彩山水図鉢」（部分）
尾形乾山　東京藝術大学大学美術館蔵
Flat Bowl with a Design of Landscape in
Underglaze Blue and Iron Brown, Detail,
Ogata Kenzan, The University Art Museum-
Tokyo University of the Arts

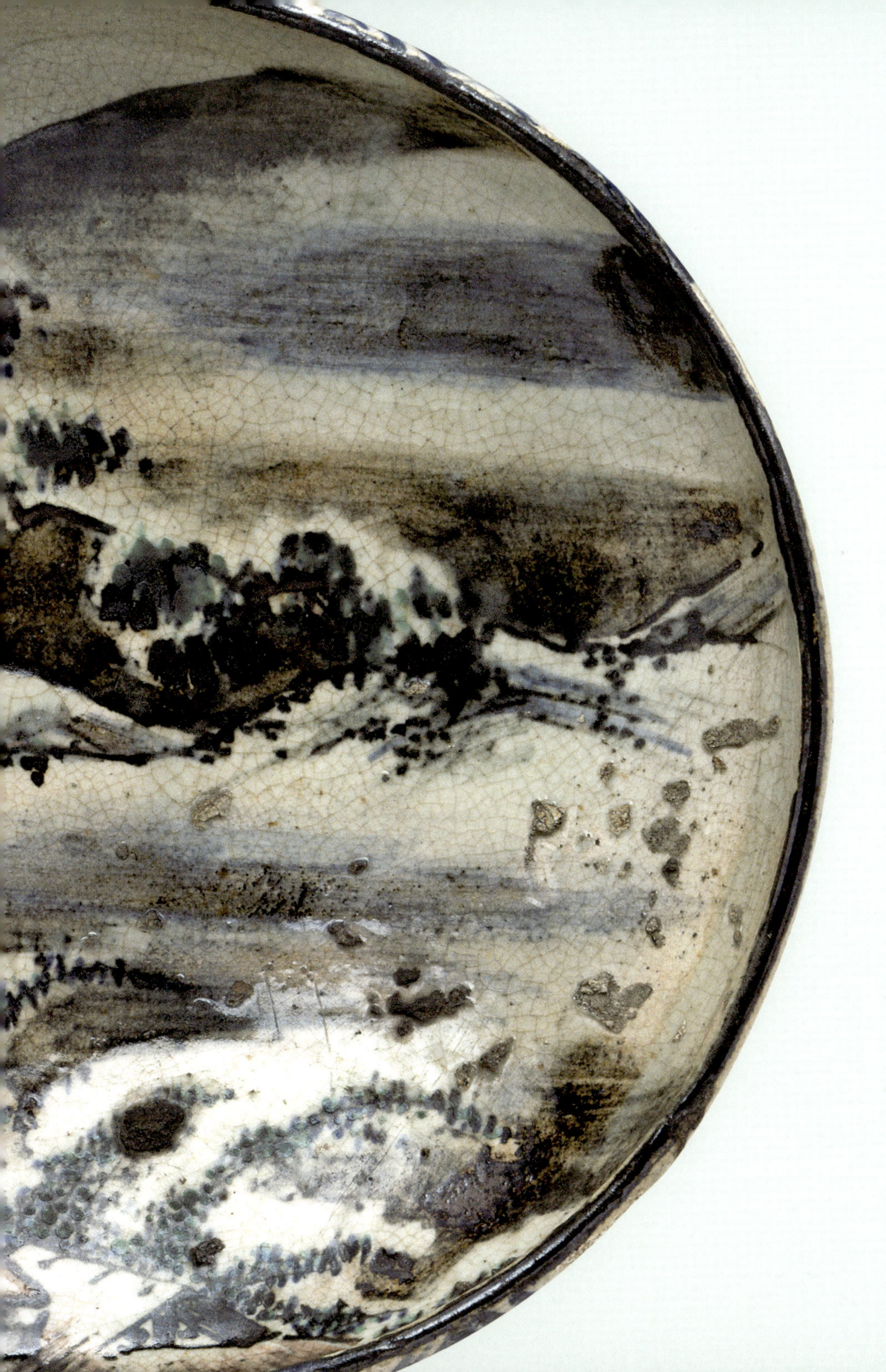

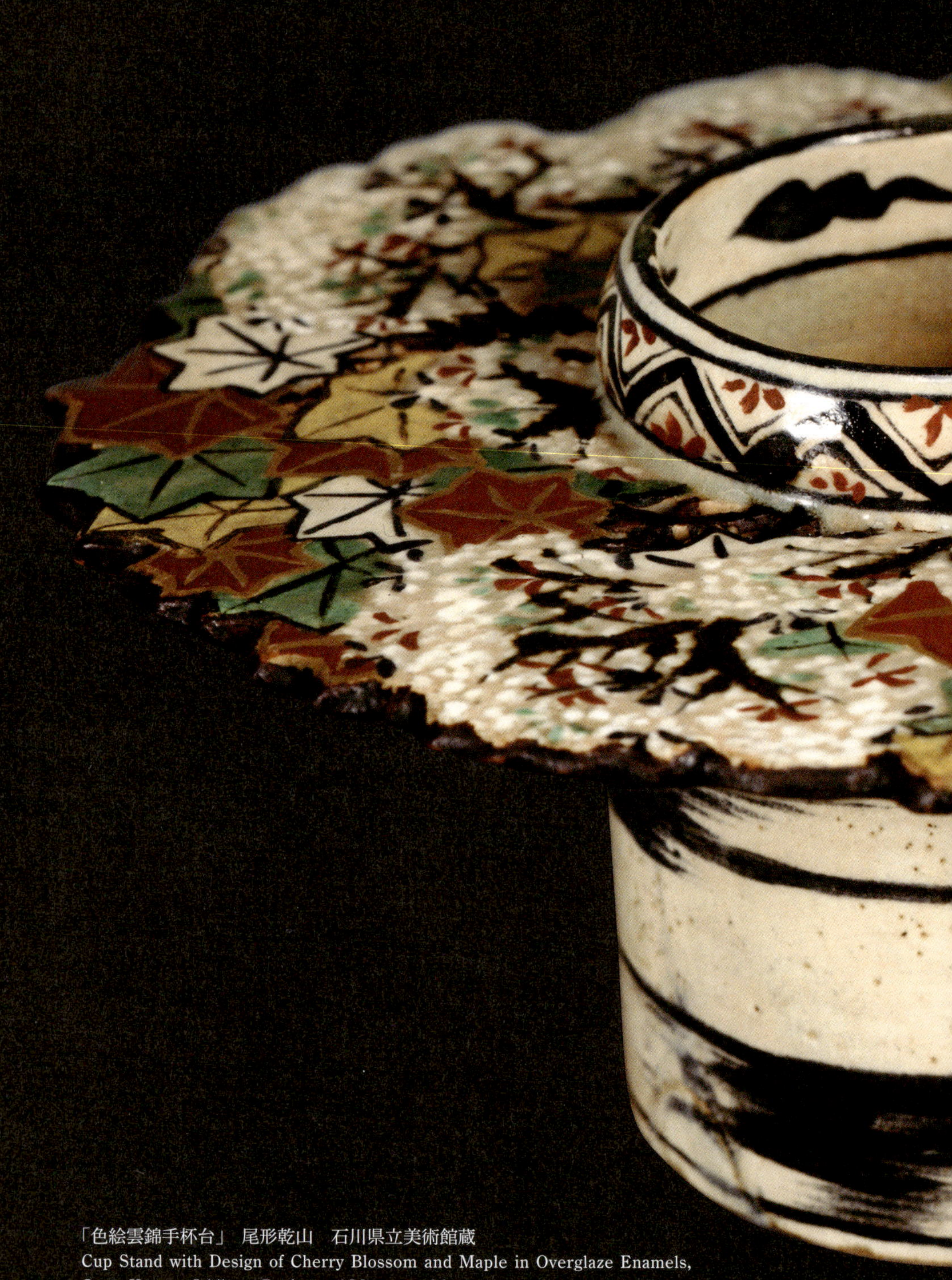

「色絵雲錦手杯台」　尾形乾山　石川県立美術館蔵
Cup Stand with Design of Cherry Blossom and Maple in Overglaze Enamels,
Ogata Kenzan, Ishikawa Prefectural Museum of Art

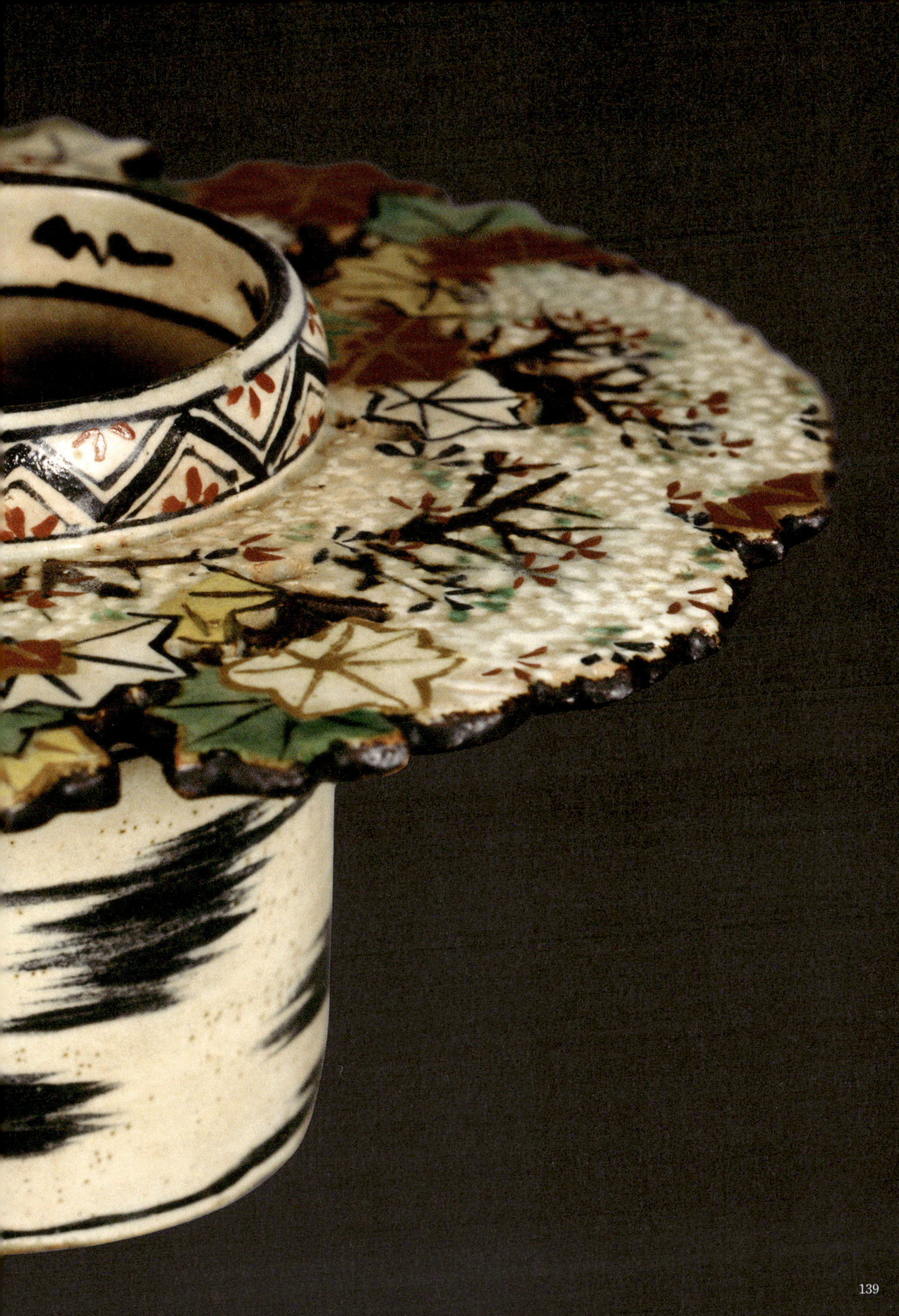

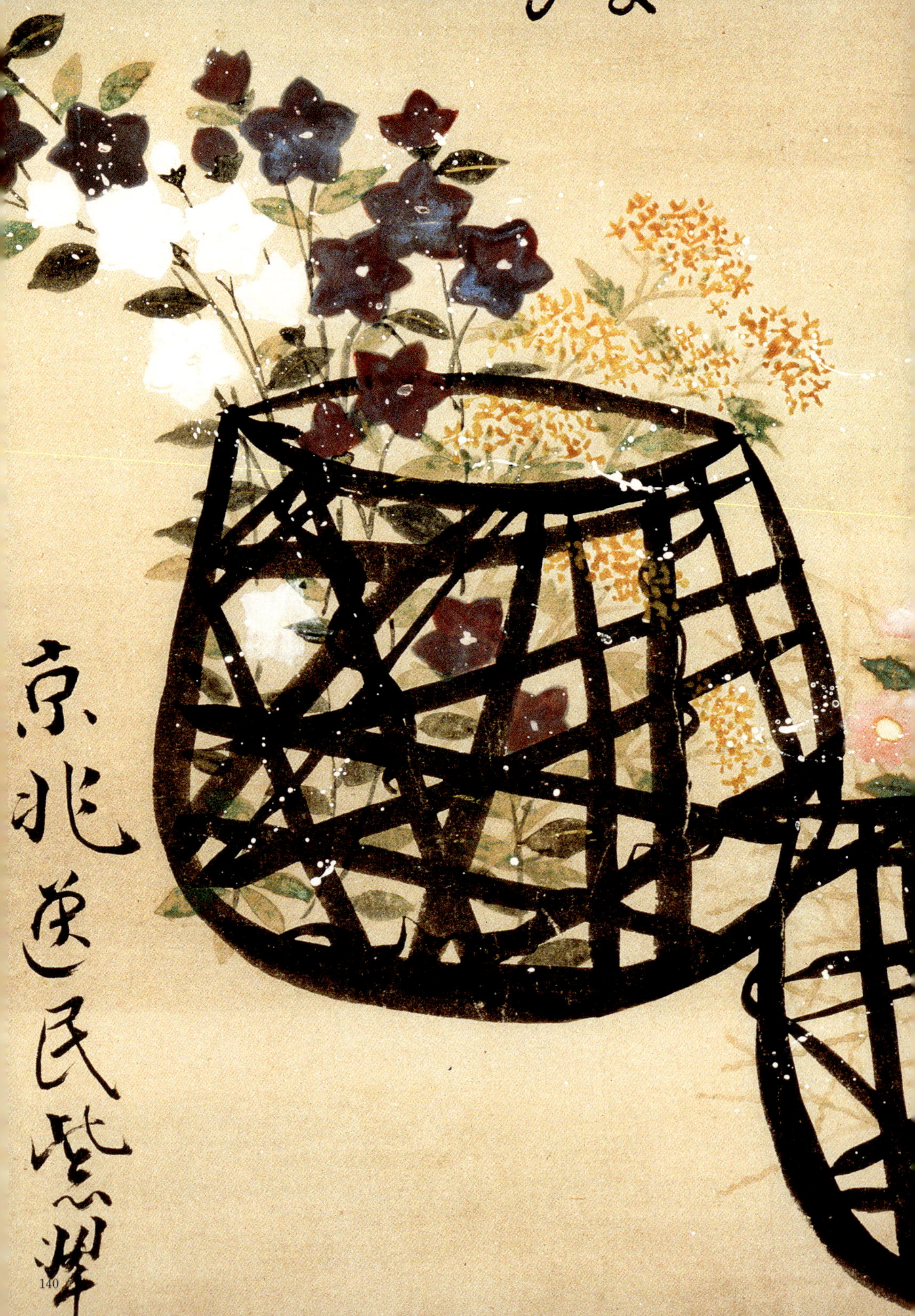

京兆逸民逸翠

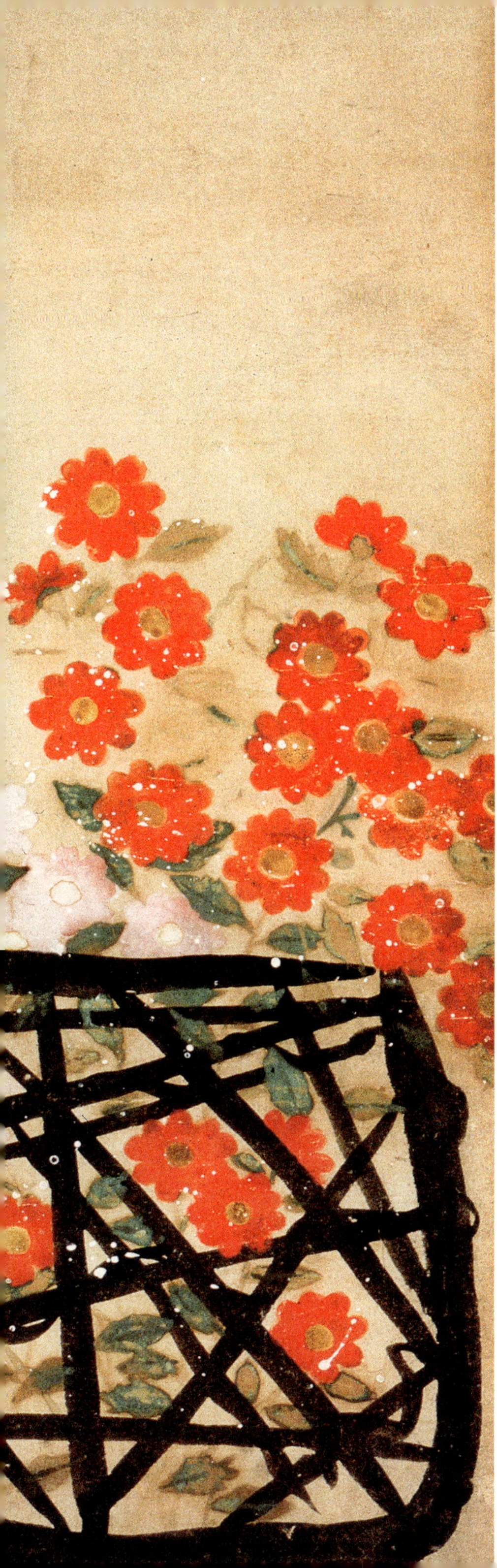

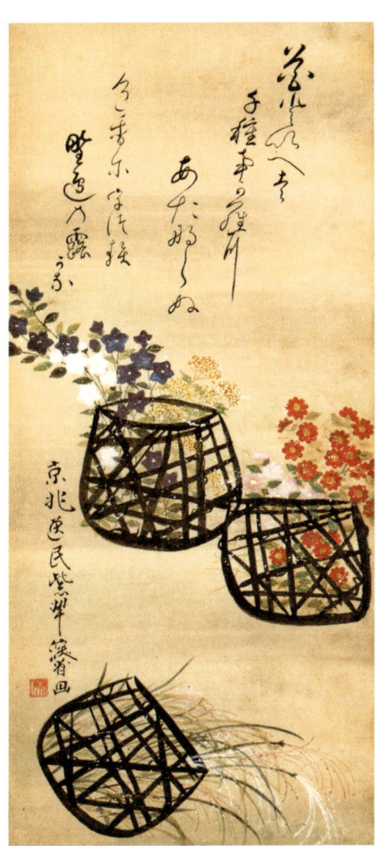

「花籠図」重文　尾形乾山
福岡市美術館蔵
Flowers in Baskets, Ogata Kenzan, Important
Cultural Property, Fukuoka Art Museum
画像提供：福岡市美術館／DNPartcom

渡辺始興

京都に生まれ、25歳頃から近衛家熙に仕える。また東宮御所や光琳にゆかりの深い二条家にも出入りしていた。初め山本素軒や鶴沢探山といった狩野派に学ぶが、のちに光琳の影響を受けて琳派様式の作品を描いた。また『春日権現霊験記絵巻』を模写するなどしてやまと絵も学んでいる。18世紀前半の京都にあって、特定の画派や様式にとらわれず、様々な画風を巧みにこなして一家をなした。

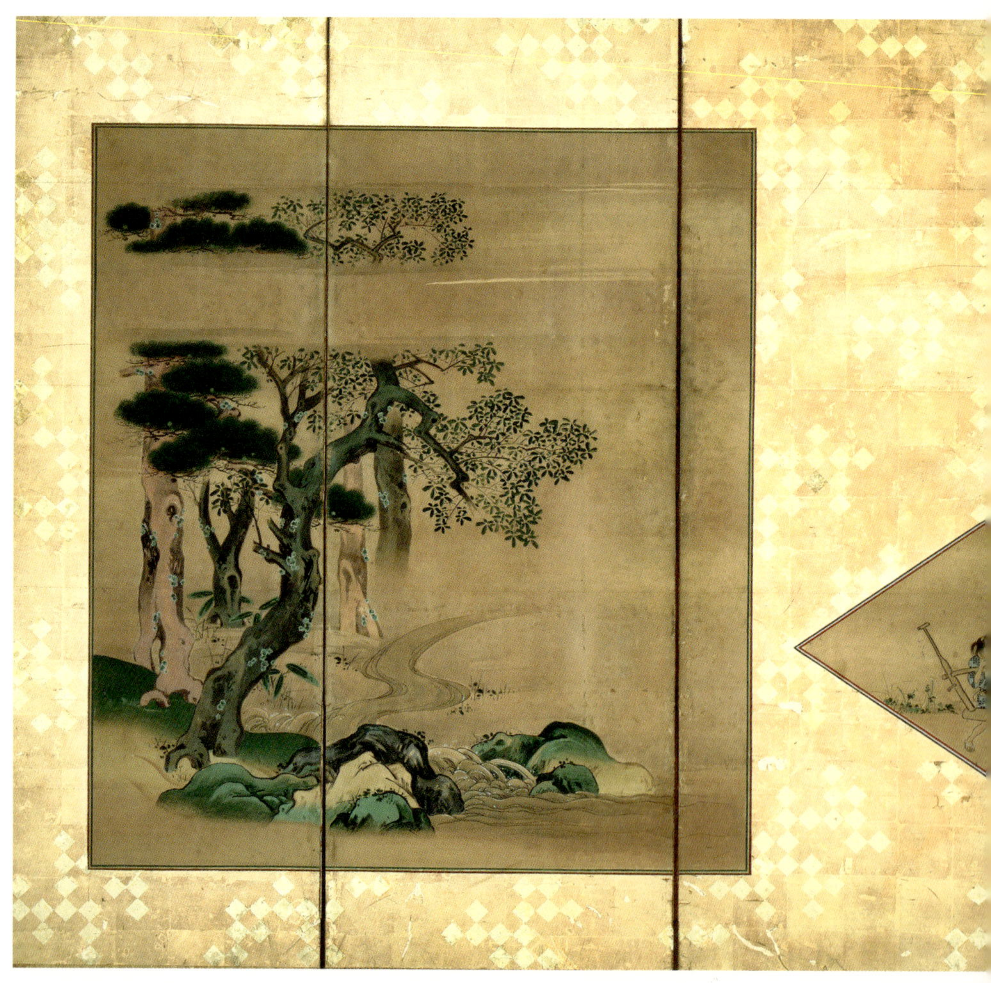

Watanabe Shikō (1683 – 1755)

Born in Kyoto, Shikō served Konoe Iehiro from about the age of
25 and was also connected with the Nijō family, which had deep
ties to both the imperial family and Kōrin. He studied with the
Kanō-school painters Yamamoto Soken and Tsurusawa Tanzan,
then, influenced by Kōrin, began painting in the Rinpa style. He
also studied yamato-e painting, making a copy of the Kasuga
Gongen Reigen-ki picture scroll. He made a name for himself in
Kyoto for his mastery of a variety of styles of painting.

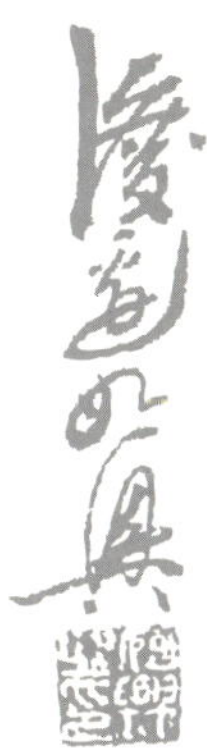

「四季図屏風」右隻　渡辺始興　宮内庁三の丸尚蔵館蔵
Landscapes of the Four Seasons, Right, Watanabe Shikō,
Sannomaru Shozokan（The Museum of the Imperial Collections）

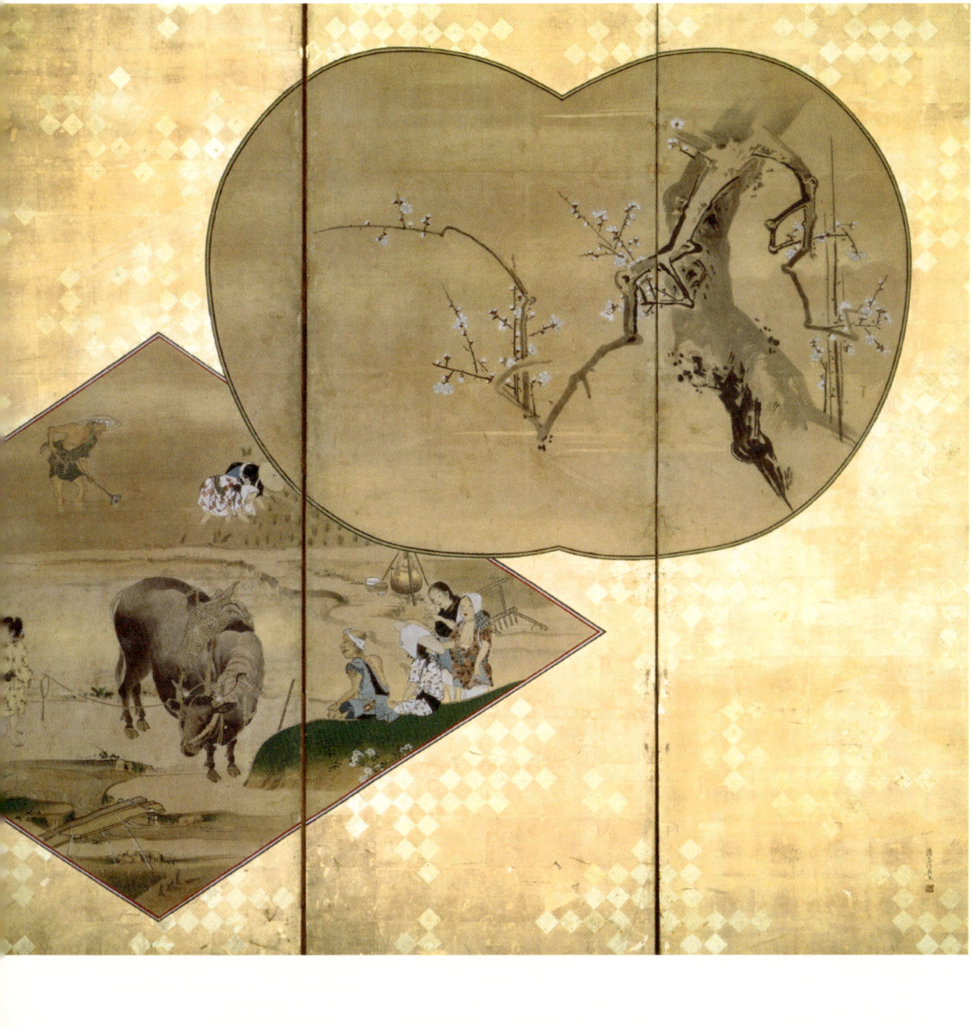

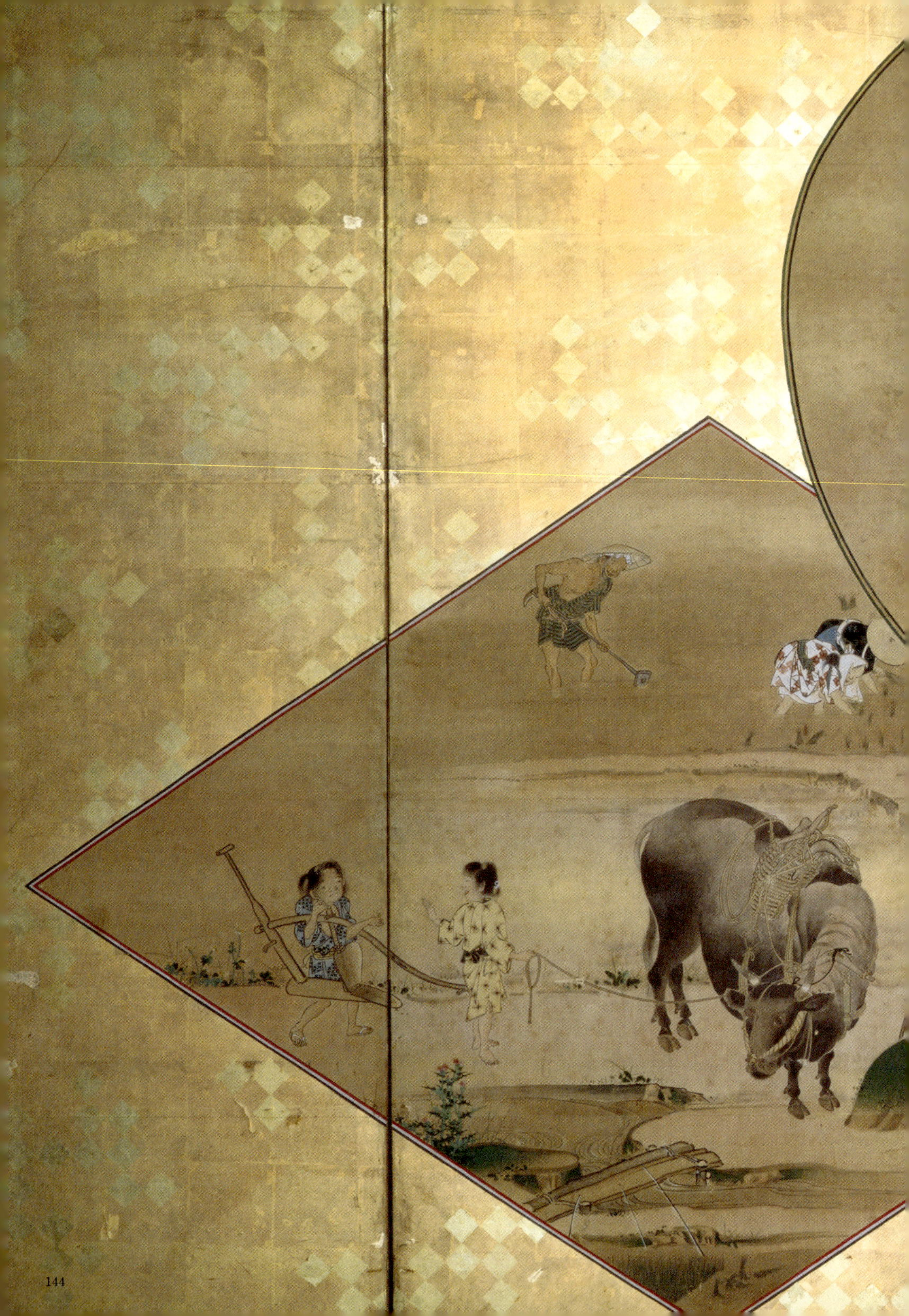

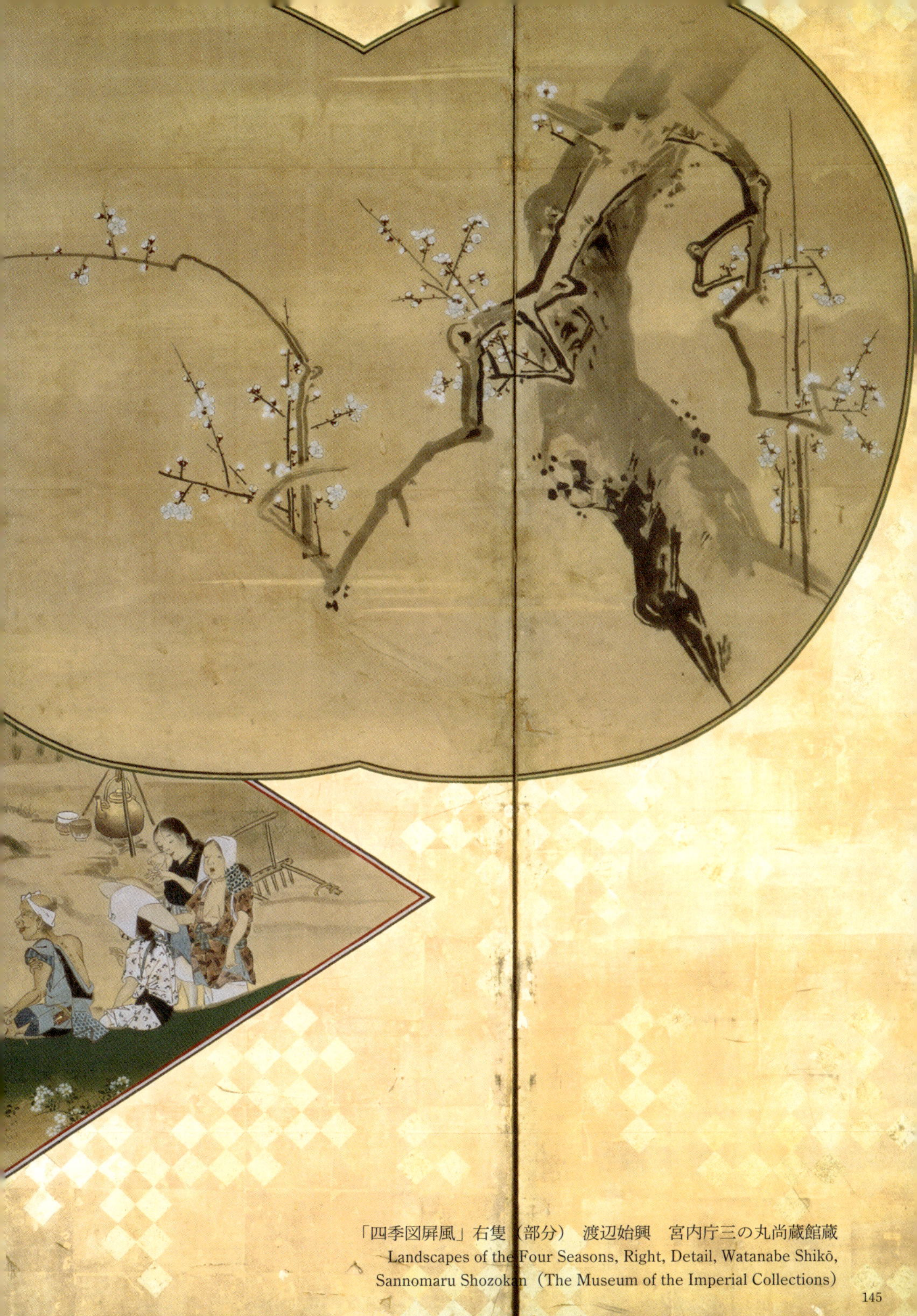

「四季図屏風」右隻（部分）　渡辺始興　宮内庁三の丸尚蔵館蔵
Landscapes of the Four Seasons, Right, Detail, Watanabe Shikō,
Sannomaru Shozokan（The Museum of the Imperial Collections）

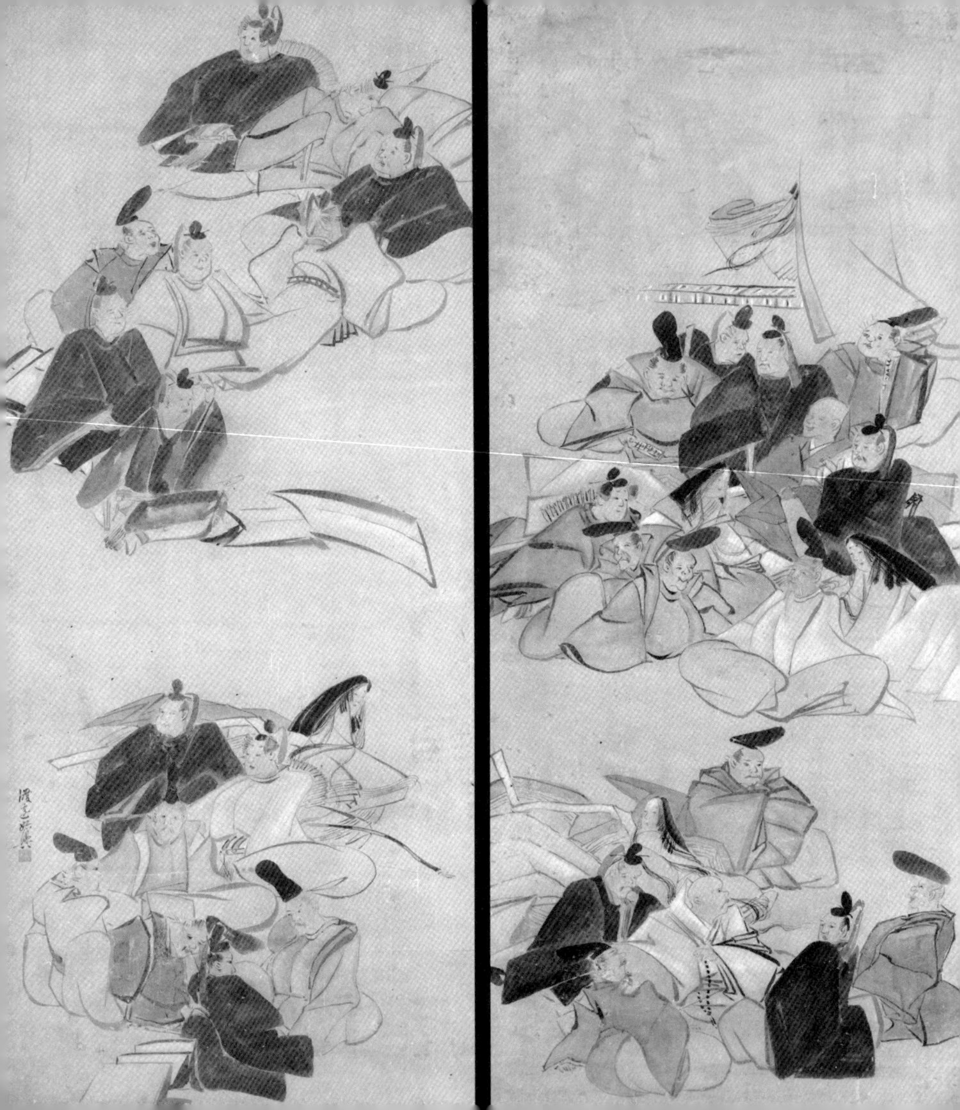

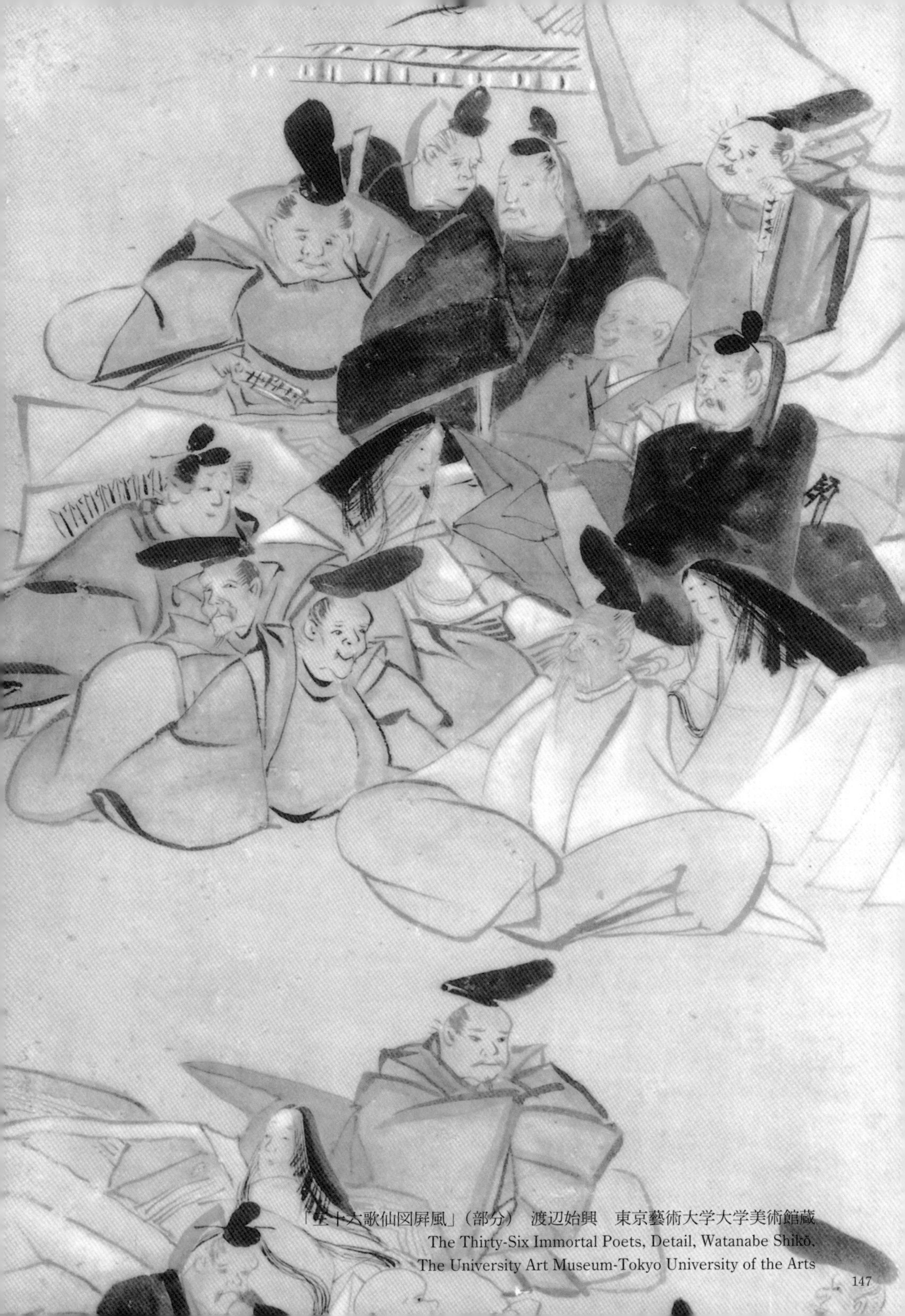

「三十六歌仙図屛風」（部分）　渡辺始興　東京藝術大学大学美術館蔵
The Thirty-Six Immortal Poets, Detail, Watanabe Shikō,
The University Art Museum-Tokyo University of the Arts

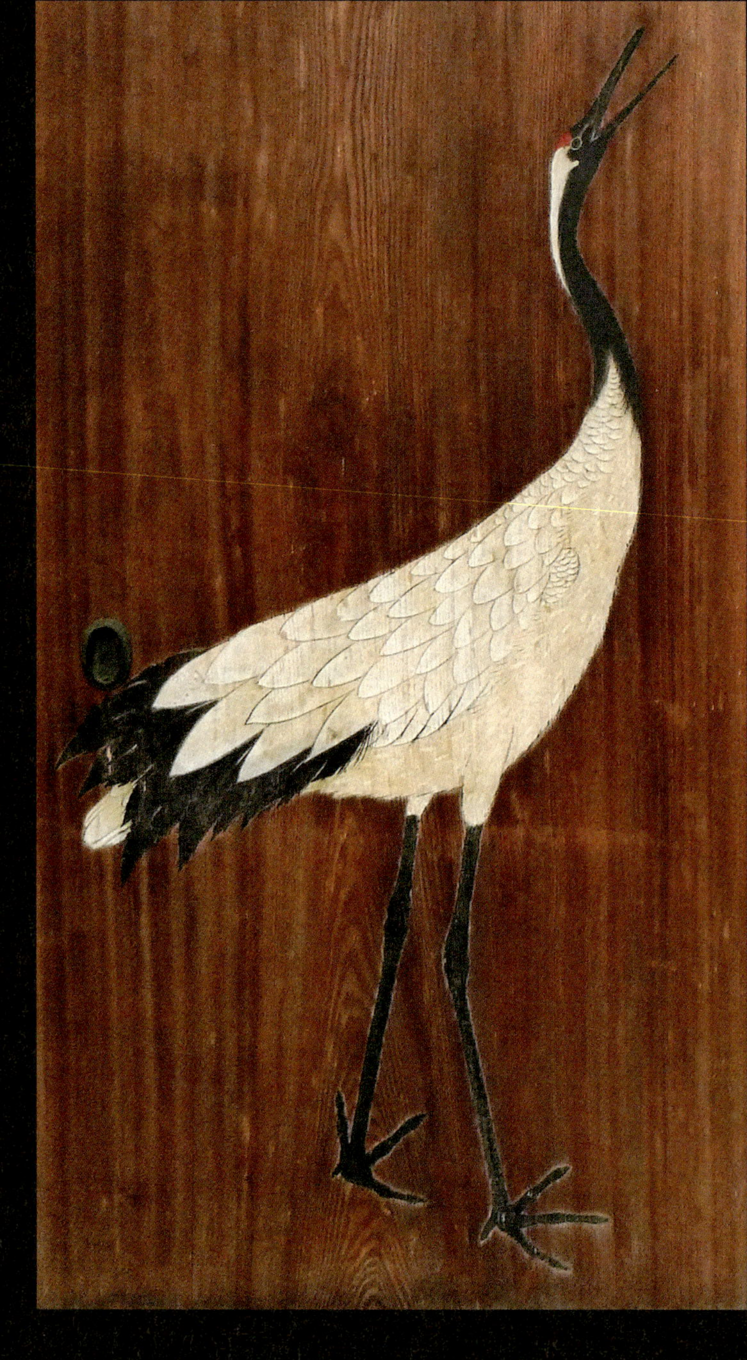

「鶴図杉戸」　重文　渡辺始興　大覚寺蔵
Cranes, Watanabe Shikō, Important Cultural Property, Daikaku-ji, Kyoto

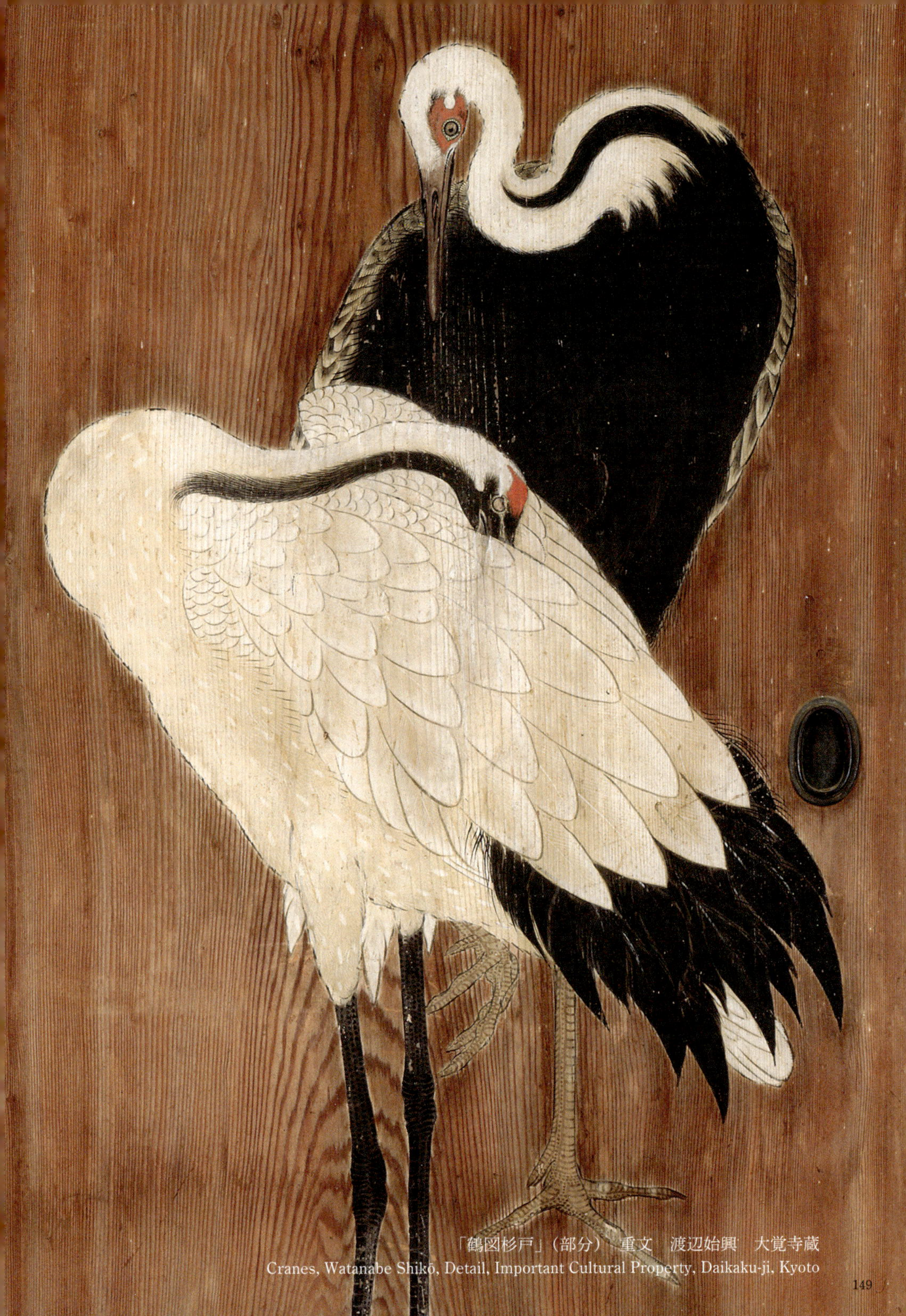

「鶴図杉戸」（部分）　重文　渡辺始興　大覚寺蔵
Cranes, Watanabe Shikō, Detail, Important Cultural Property, Daikaku-ji, Kyoto

149

深江蘆舟

銀座方役人、深江庄左衛門の長男として京都に生まれる。恵まれた幼年期を送ったが、正徳 4 年（1714）、16 歳のとき父が銀座事件に連座して流罪に処され、蘆舟自身も追放の身となった。その後、父が尾形光琳のパトロン中村内蔵助の同僚であったところから、晩年の光琳に絵を学んだと思われる。のびやかな線描やたらし込みの筆致など光琳に直接師事した様子がうかがわれる。

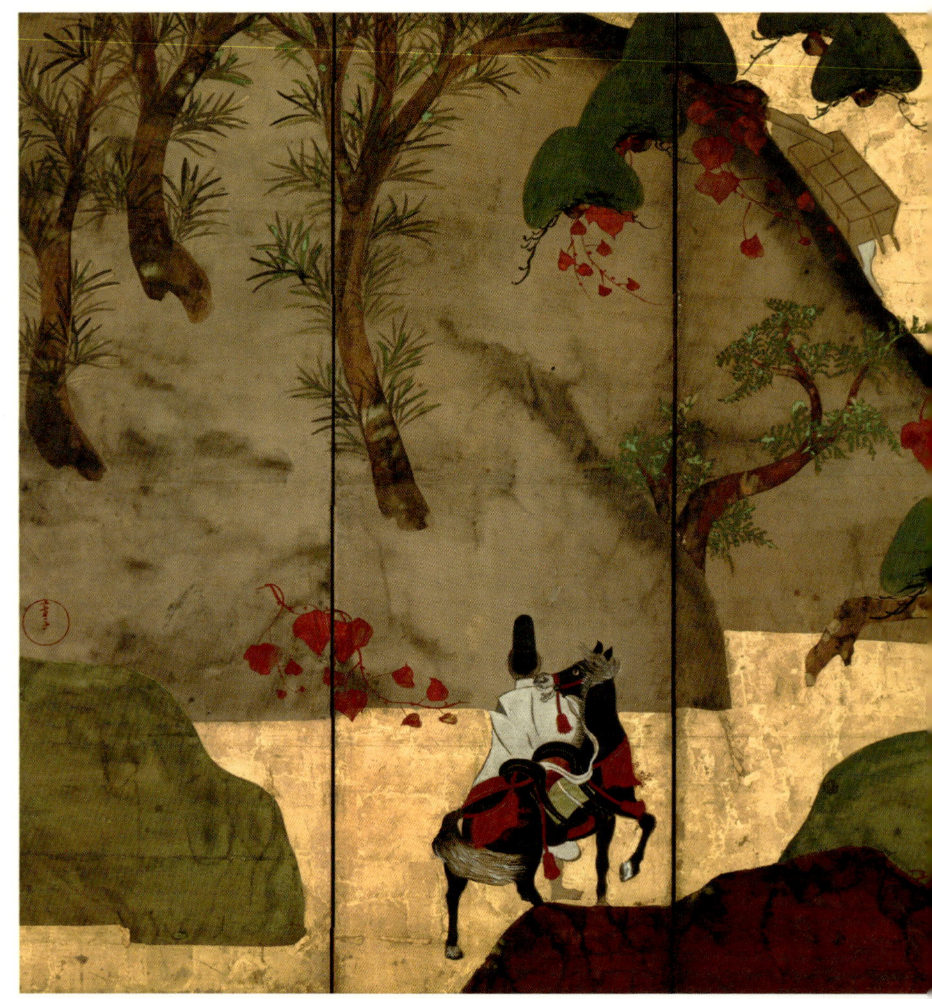

Fukae Roshū (1699 – 1757)

As the eldest son of Fukae Shōzaemon, an official associated
with the government mint, Roshū grew up in comfortable
circumstances in Kyoto until the age of 16. Then, when his father
was implicated in a scandal, Roshū followed him into exile. Later,
because his father was a colleague of Kōrin's patron, Nakamura
Kuranosuke, he is thought to have studied with Kōrin late in that
artist's life, as Roshū's brushwork, with its flowing line and use of
tarashikomi, suggests.

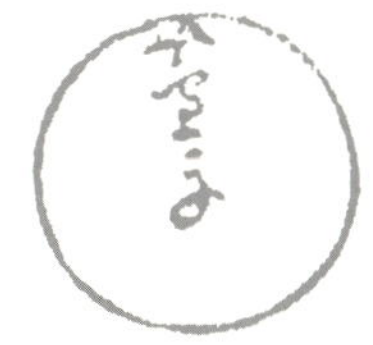

「蔦の細道図屏風」　重文　深江蘆舟　東京国立博物館蔵
The Ivy Lane from the Tales of *Ise*, Fukae Roshū, Important Cultural Property,
Tokyo National Museum　Image: TNM Image Archives

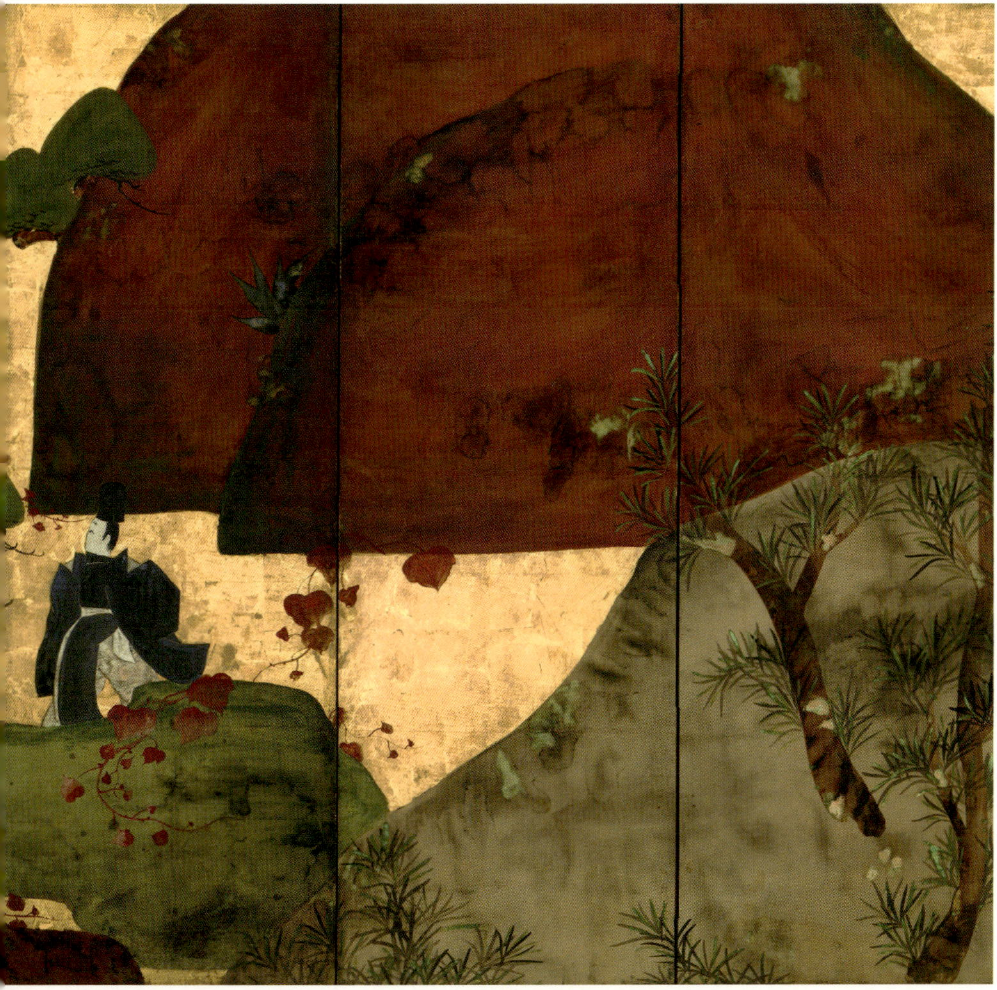

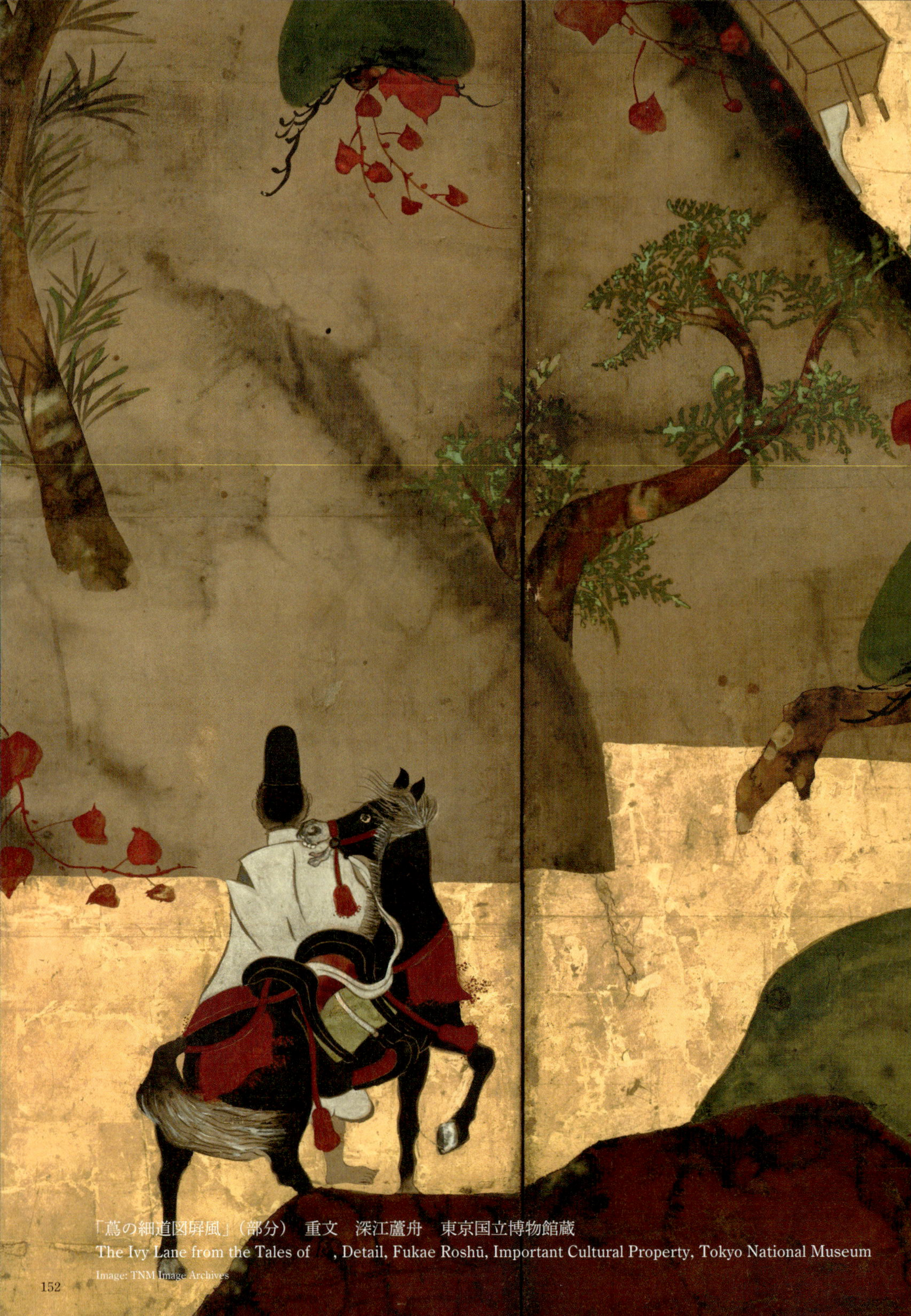

「蔦の細道図屏風」（部分）　重文　深江蘆舟　東京国立博物館蔵
The Ivy Lane from the Tales of   , Detail, Fukae Roshū, Important Cultural Property, Tokyo National Museum

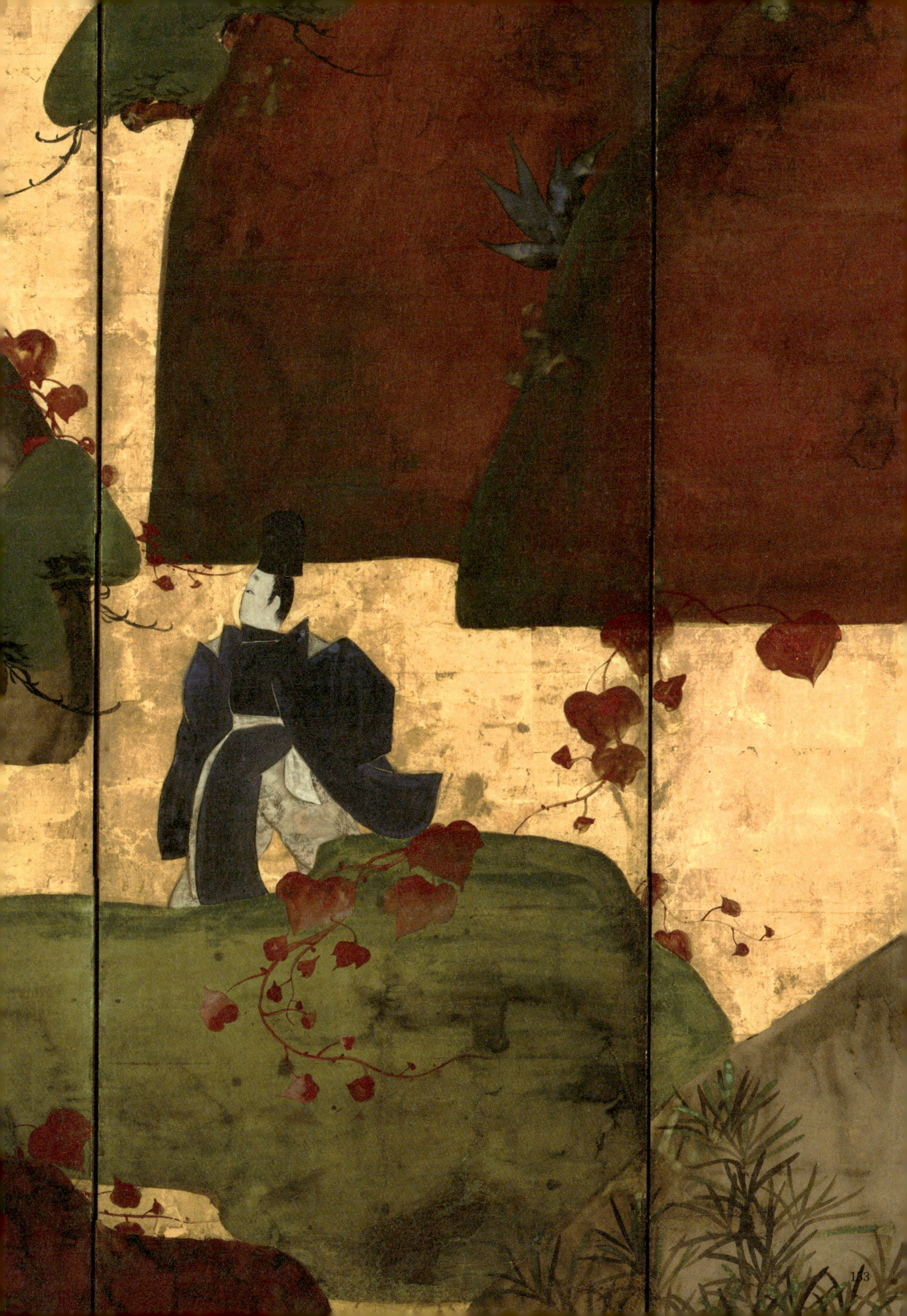

立林何帠

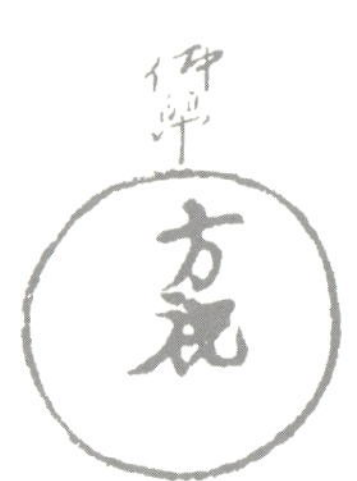

たてばやし かげい　　生没年不詳

加賀前田家の侍医を務めたといわれ
ており、のち江戸に出て白井宗謙と
称したといわれる。江戸に移ってい
た尾形乾山に師事し、尾形光琳の「宗
達写扇面画」を与えられ、光琳画風の
直系を託されたといわれる。また光琳
の「方祝」印の使用も許され、光琳
三世としてその画風の継承に努めた。
酒井抱一、谷文晁ら江戸の文人の間
でも、宗達・光琳・乾山の後継者と
して知られていた。

Tatebayashi Kagei (dates uncertain)
Kagei served as physician to the Maeda
family, rulers of Kaga, then moved to
Edo, where he used the name Shirai
Sōken. There he studied with Ogata
Kenzan and was given a fan painting
that was Kōrin's copy of one by
Sōtatsu, signifying his status as Kōrin's
successor. He was later permitted to use
Kōrin's "Masatoki" seal and, as Kōrin
III, continued his style. Among such
Edo literati as Sakai Hōitsu and Tani
Bunchō, he was known as the successor
to Sōtatsu, Kōrin, and Kenzan.

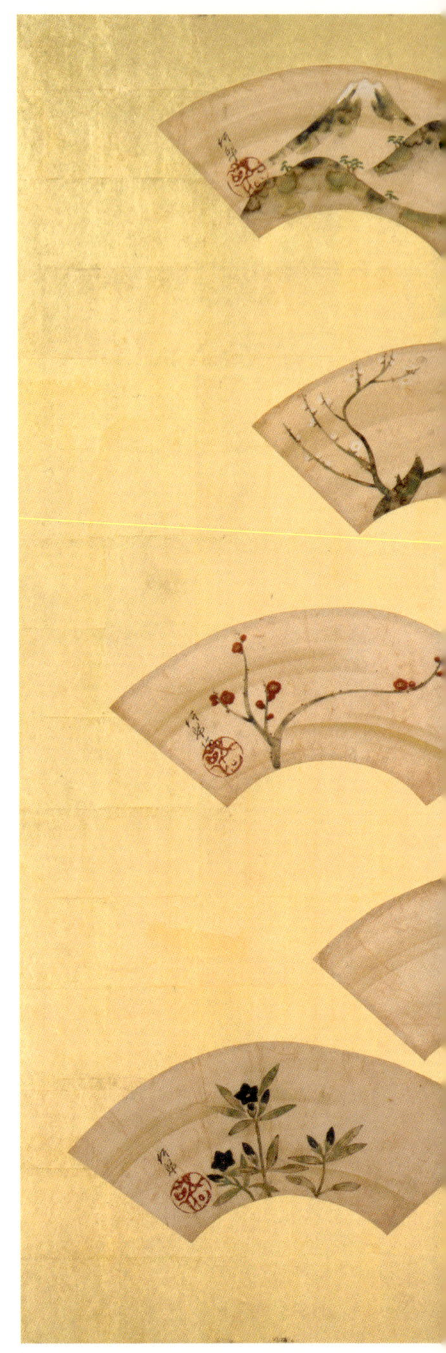

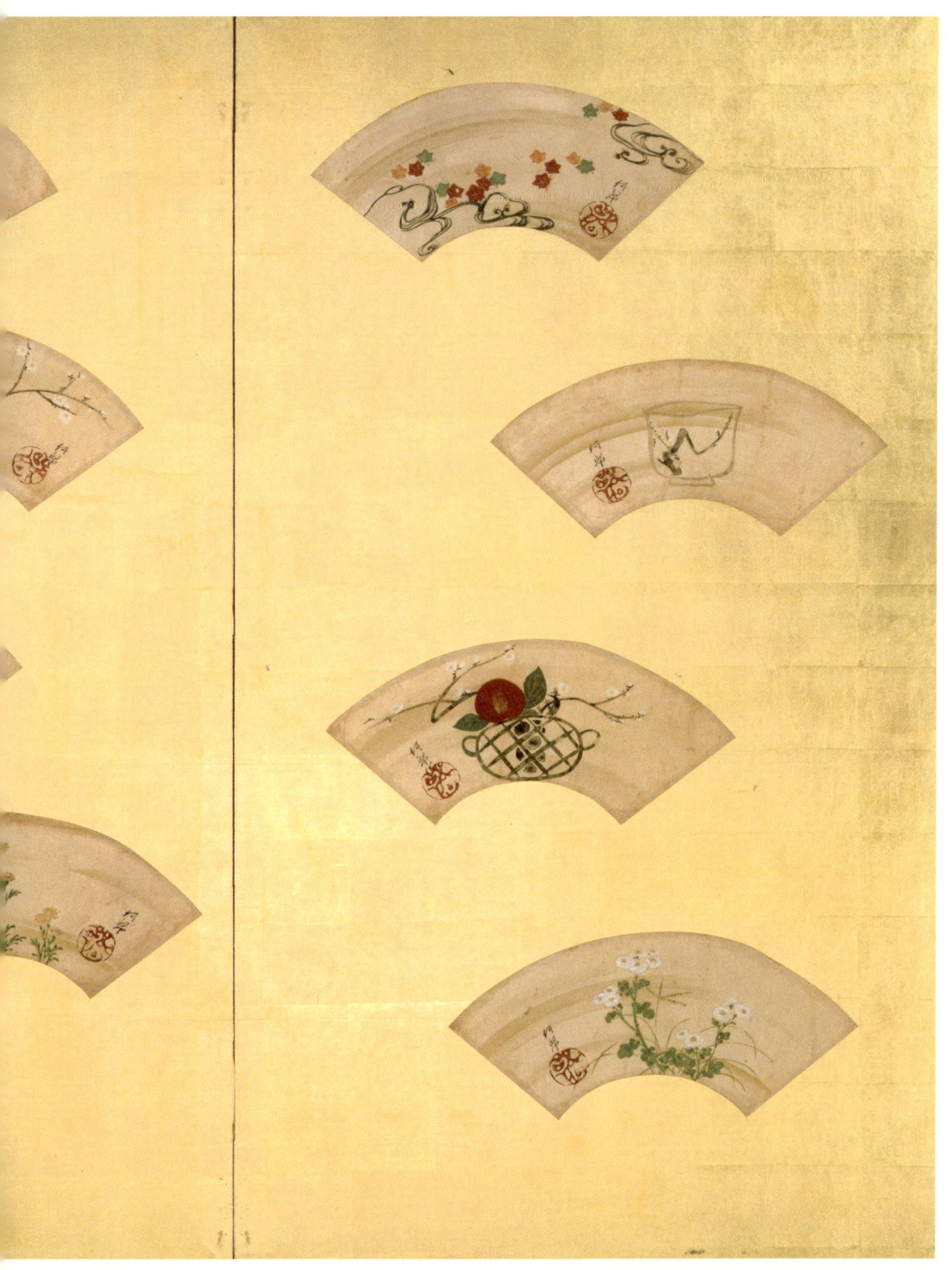

「扇面貼交屏風」　立林何帠　千葉市美術館蔵
Screens with Fan-shaped Paintings, Tatebayashi Kagei, Chiba City Museum of Art

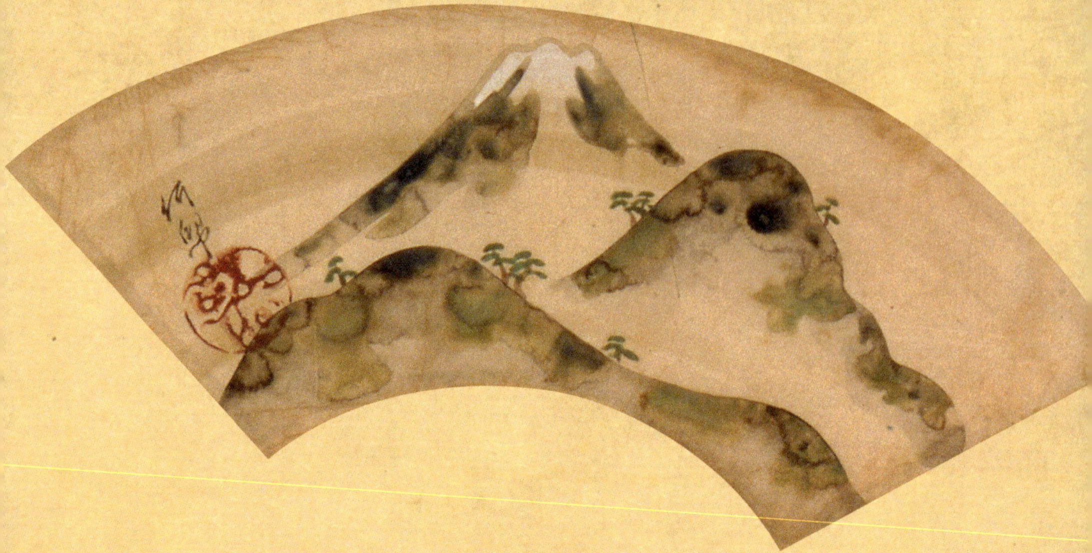

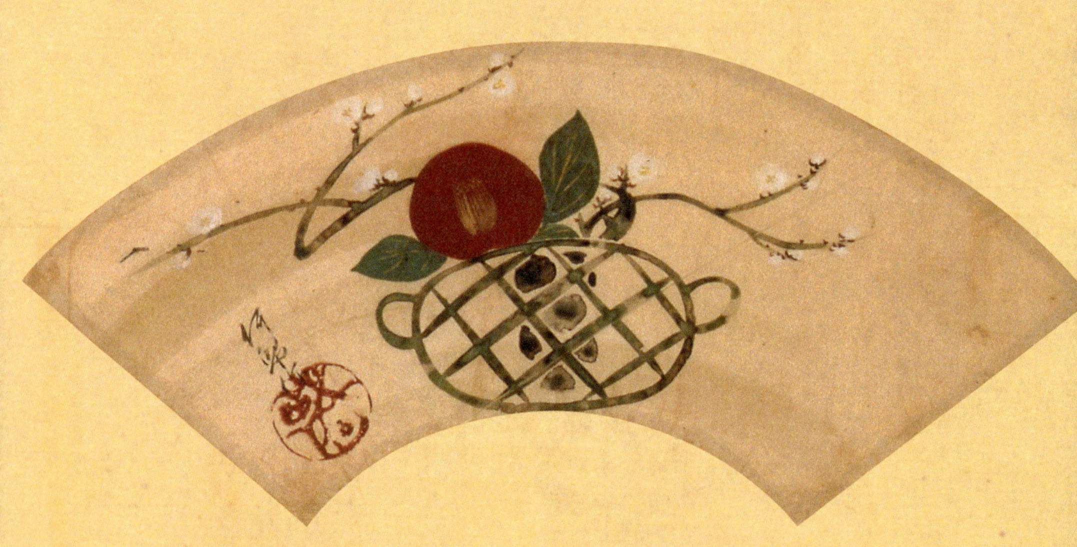

「扇面貼交屏風」（部分）　立林何帠　千葉市美術館蔵
Screens with Fan-shaped Paintings, Detail, Tatebayashi Kagei, Chiba City Museum of Art

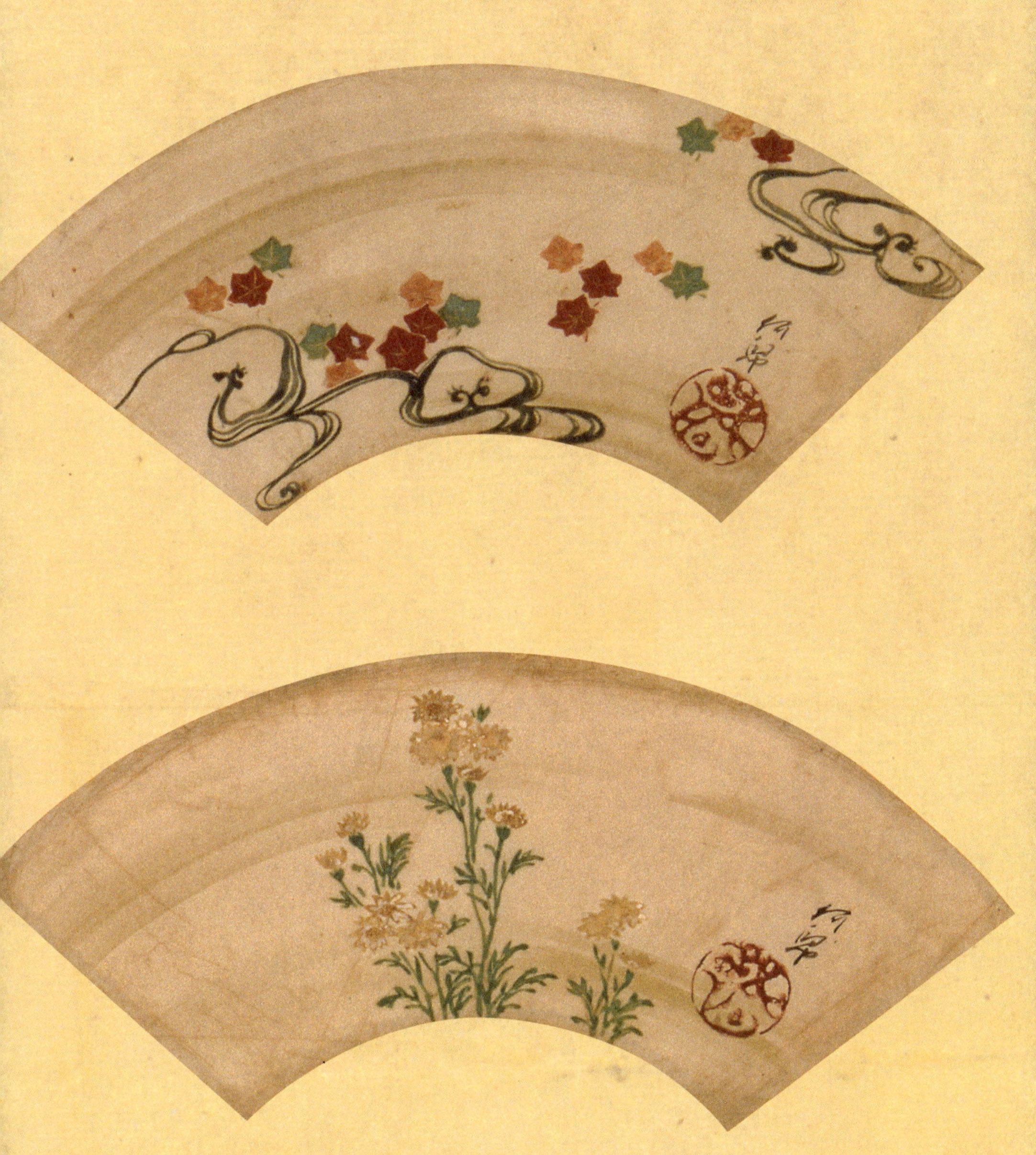

酒井抱一

さかい ほういつ　宝暦 11 年〜文政 11 年（1761 -1828）

播磨姫路藩主、酒井忠以の弟として江戸に生まれる。37 歳の時に出家し、のち下根岸に庵を結ぶ。若年より書、和歌、俳諧、能などに親しみ、絵は狩野派、円山四条派、土佐派、浮世絵など諸派を学んだが、とりわけ光琳の画風に傾倒し、これを江戸に広めた。文化 12 年（1815）には光琳の百回忌を営み、『光琳百図』、『尾形流略印譜』を刊行し、積極的に江戸での光琳・乾山の顕彰活動に努めた。

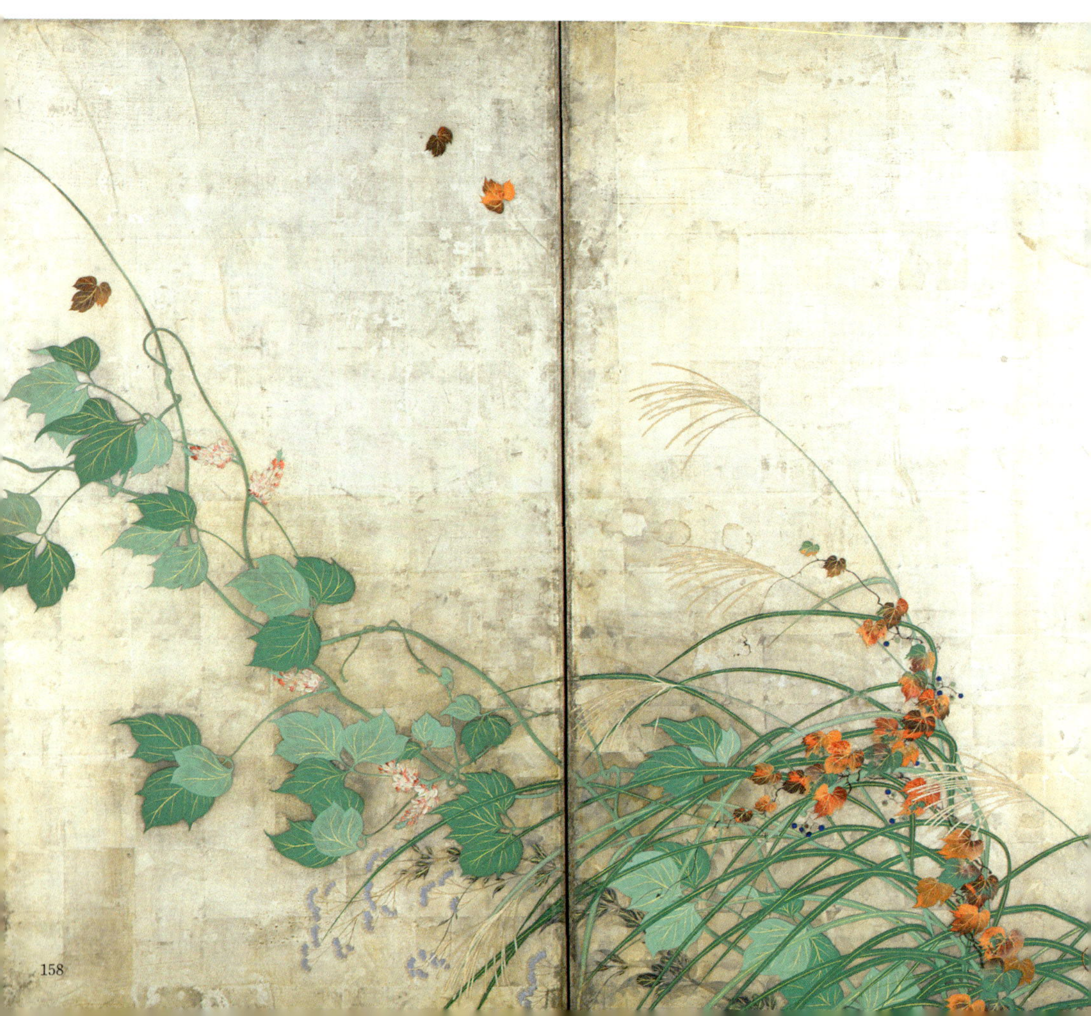

Sakai Hōitsu (1761 – 1828)

Hōitsu, born in Edo as the younger brother of Sakai Tadazane, lord of Himeji, became a Buddhist priest at the age of 37. Well versed in calligraphy, poetry, and Noh, Hōitsu studied the Kanō, Maruyama Shijō, Tosa, and ukiyo-e styles of painting and was drawn to Kōrin's work. In 1815, for the centenary of Kōrin's death, he published Kōrin Hyakuzu and Ōgata-ryū Ryaku Impu and promoted appreciation of Kōrin and Kenzan in Edo.

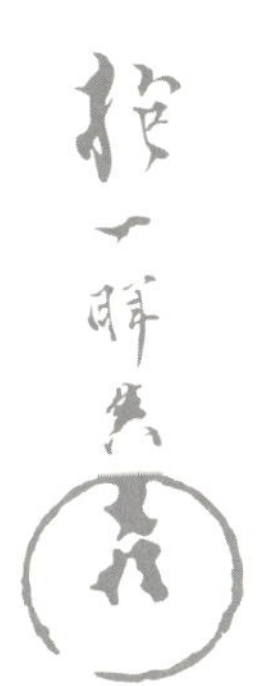

「夏秋草図屏風」　酒井抱一　東京国立博物館蔵
Summary and Autumn Grasses, Sakai Hōitsu, Tokyo National Museum　Image: TNM Image Archives

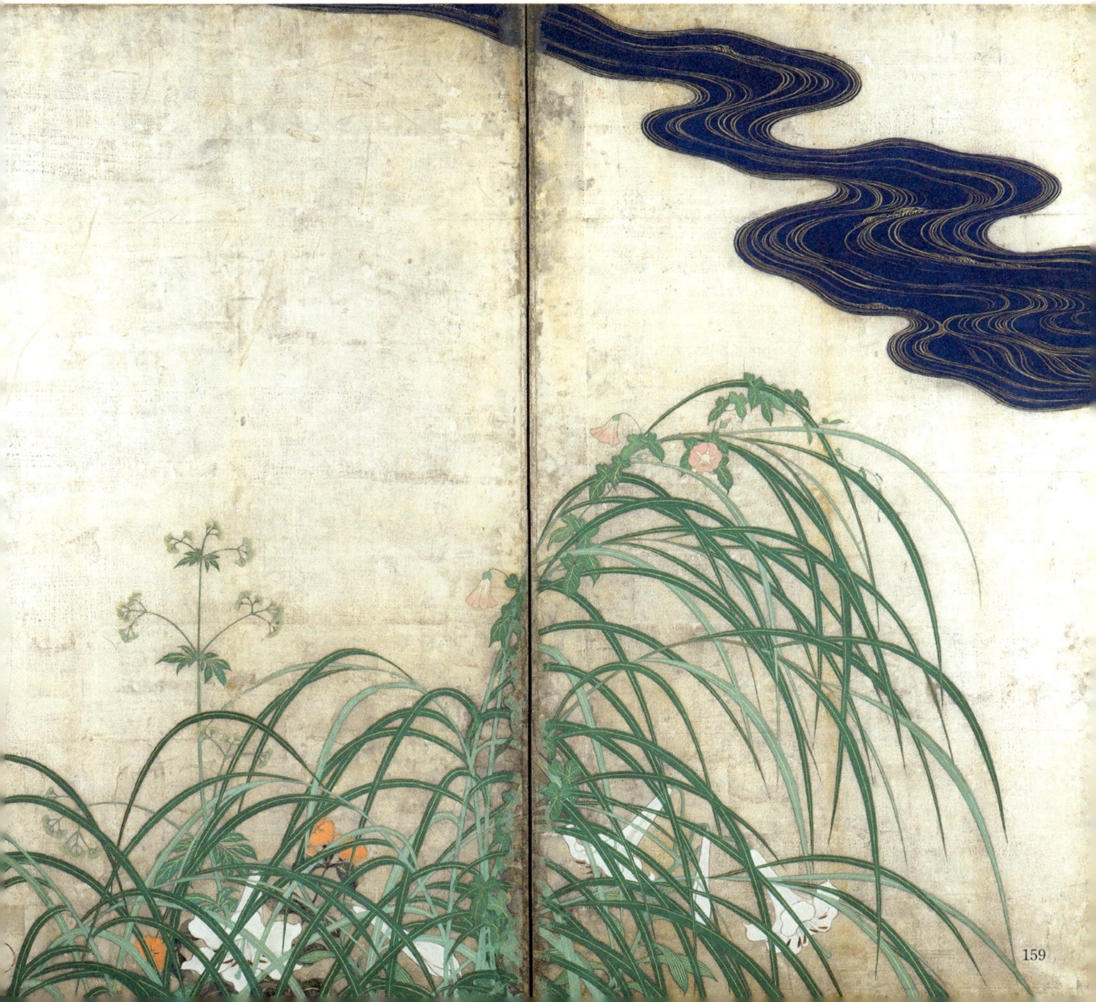

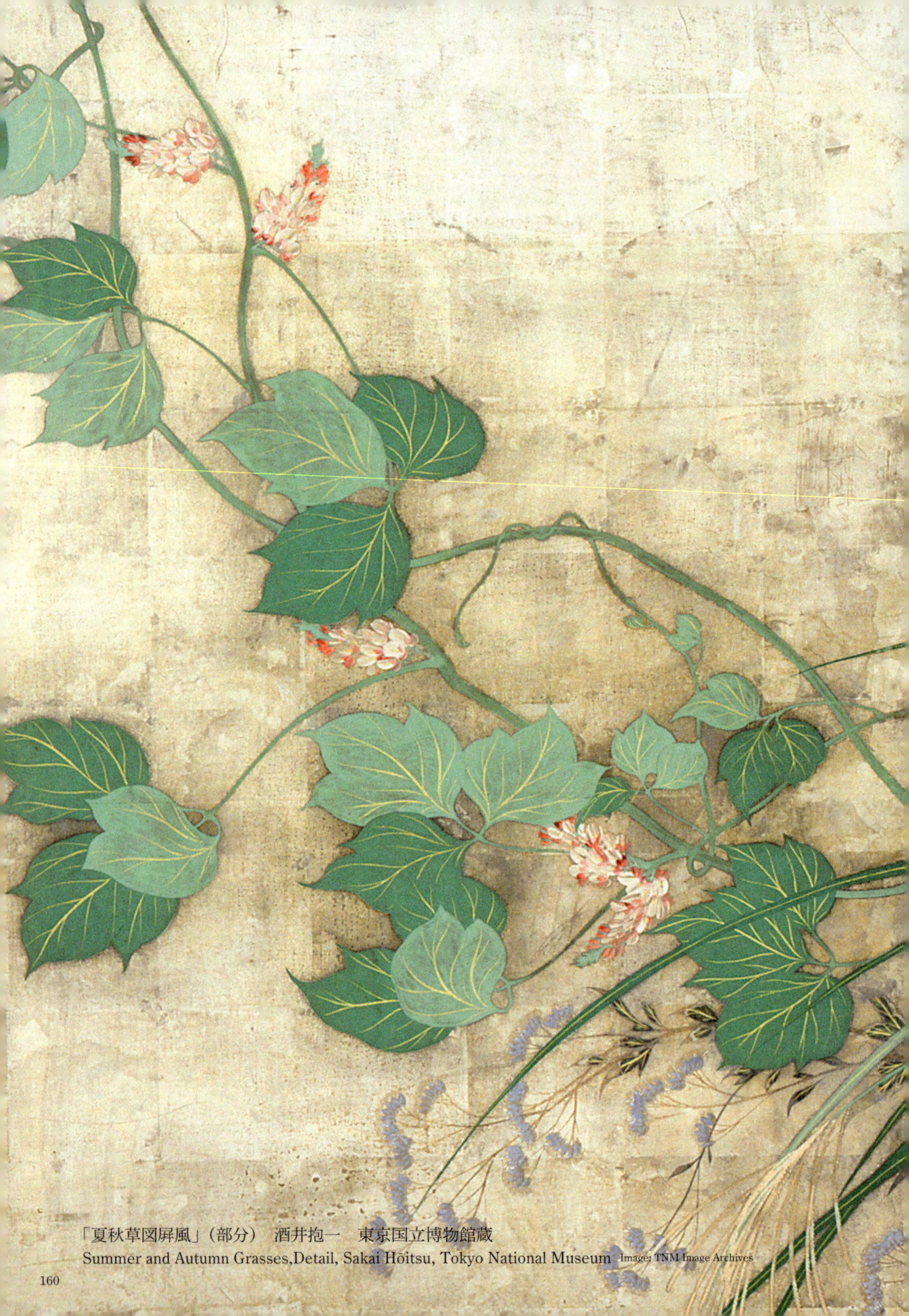

「夏秋草図屏風」（部分）　酒井抱一　東京国立博物館蔵
Summer and Autumn Grasses,Detail, Sakai Hōitsu, Tokyo National Museum

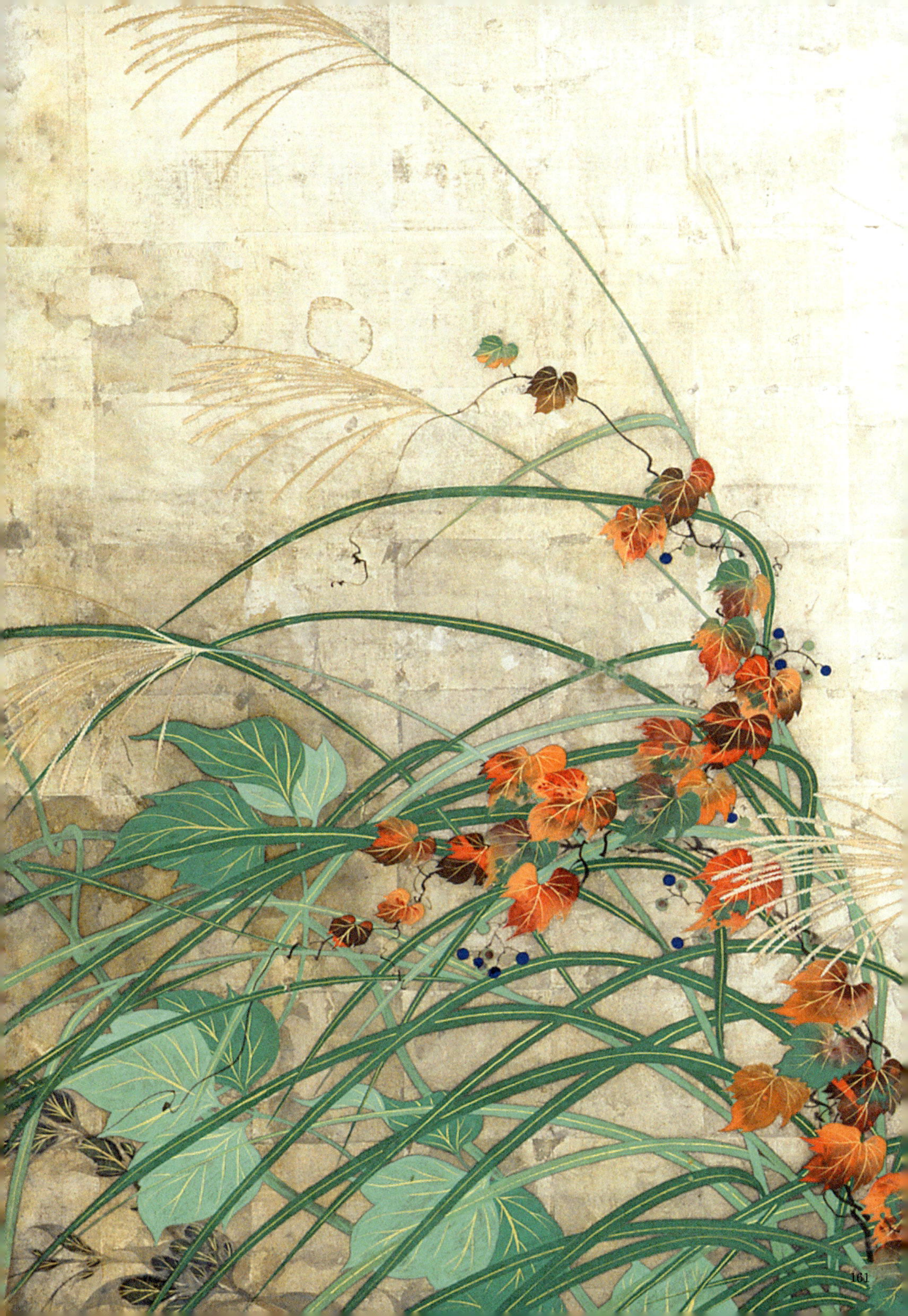

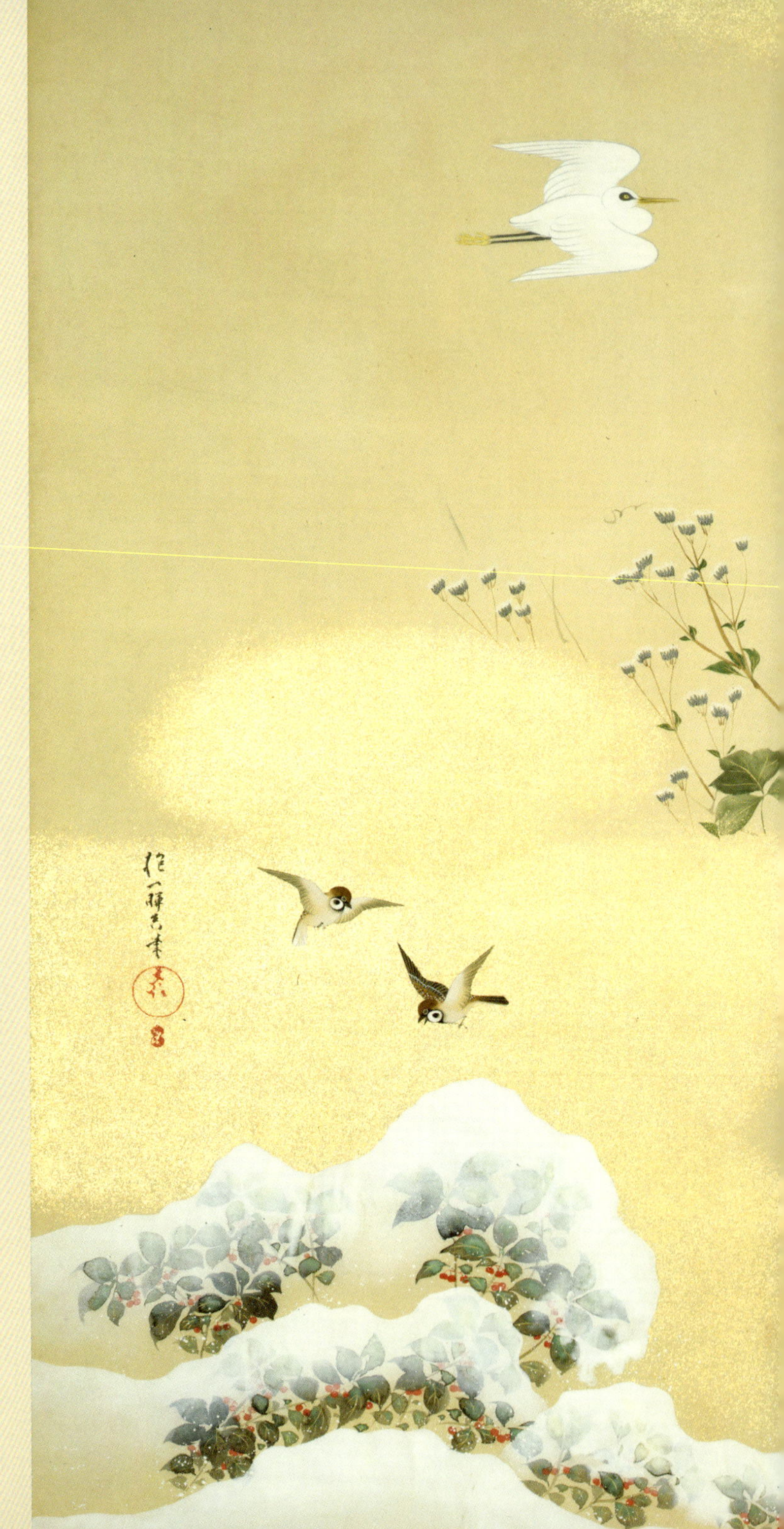

「四季花鳥図屏風」
左隻　酒井抱一
京都国立博物館蔵
Birds and Flowers of
the Four Seasons, Left,
Sakai Hōitsu, Kyoto
National Museum

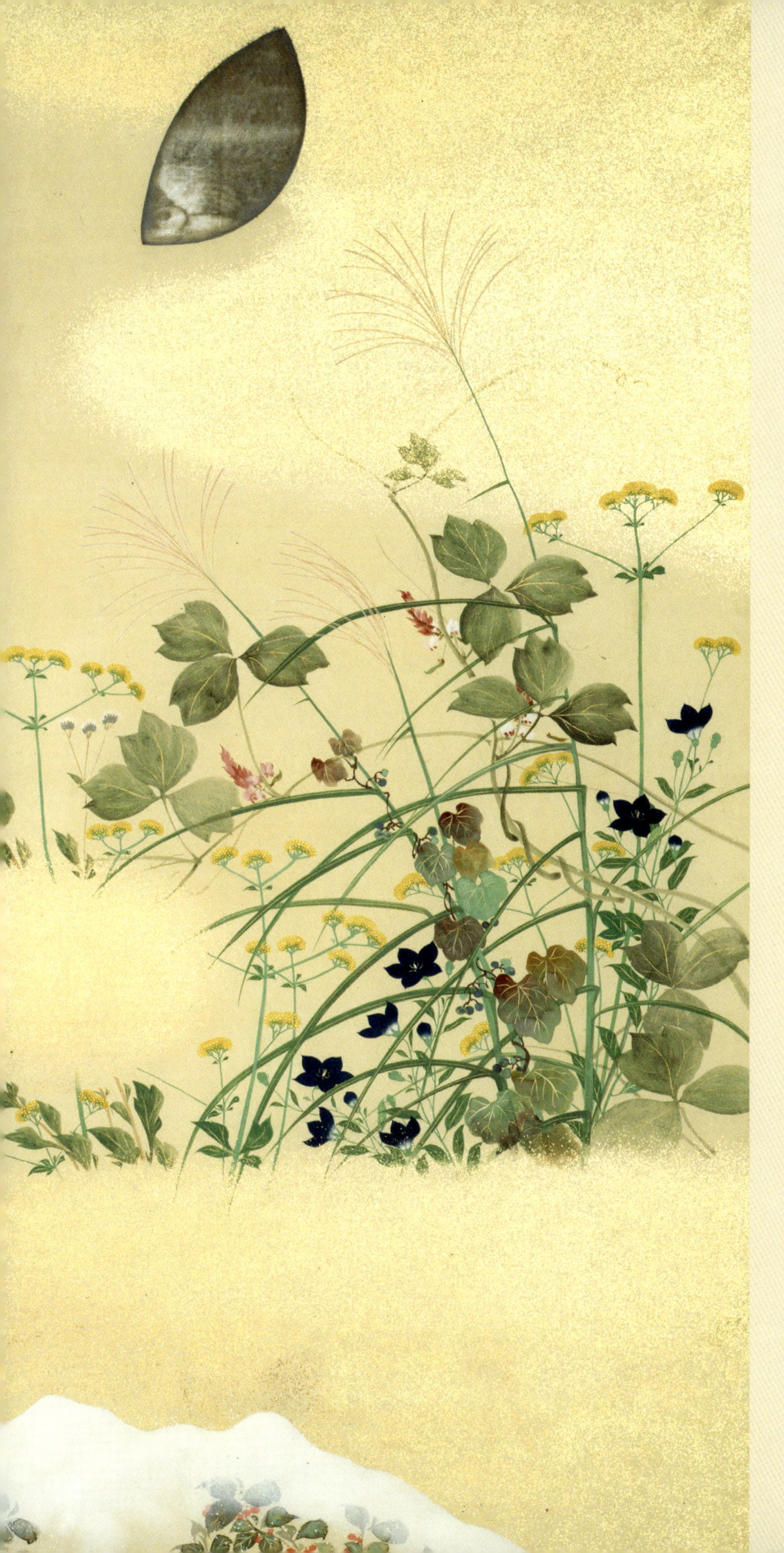

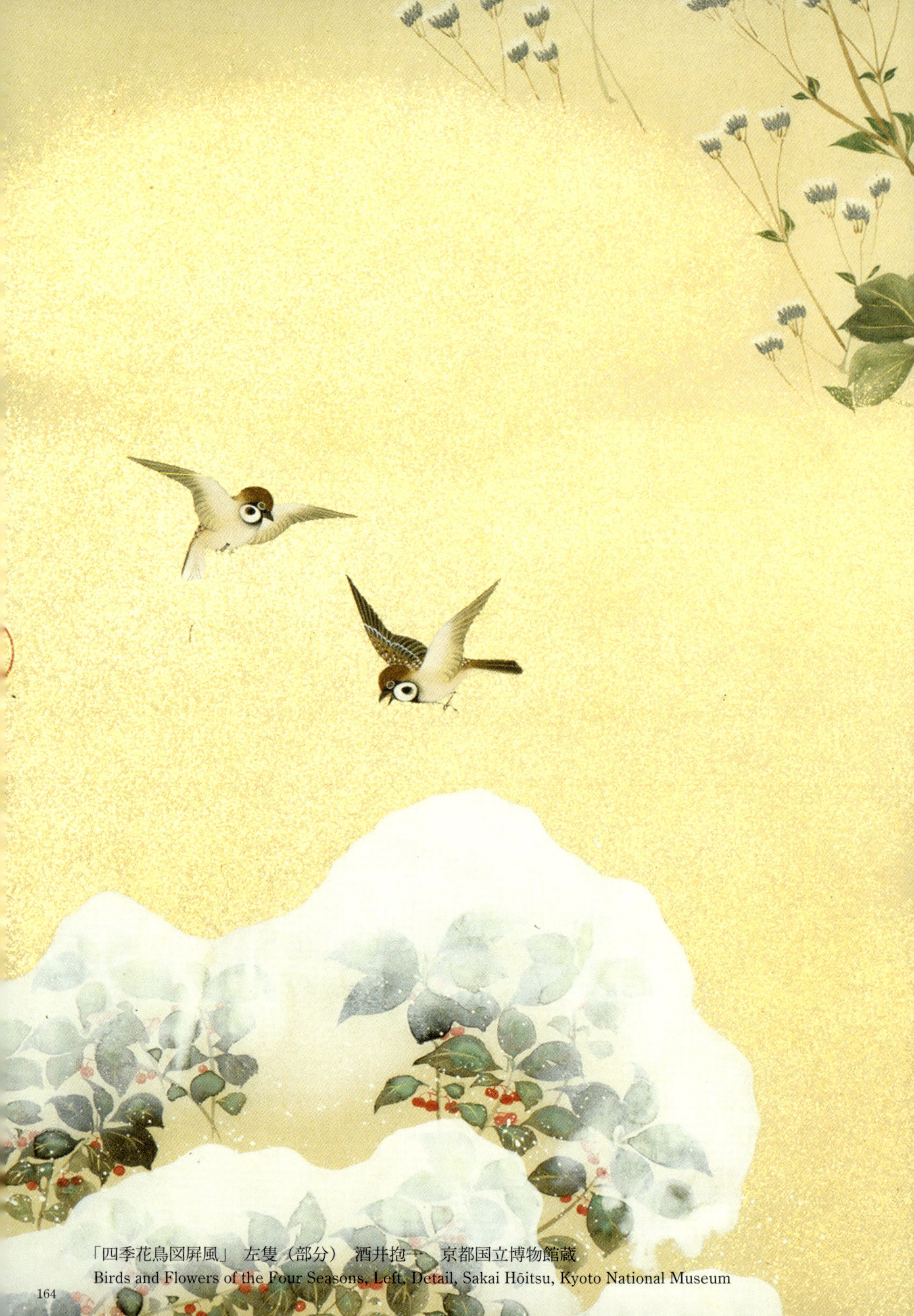

「四季花鳥図屏風」　左隻（部分）　酒井抱一　京都国立博物館蔵
Birds and Flowers of the Four Seasons, Left, Detail, Sakai Hōitsu, Kyoto National Museum

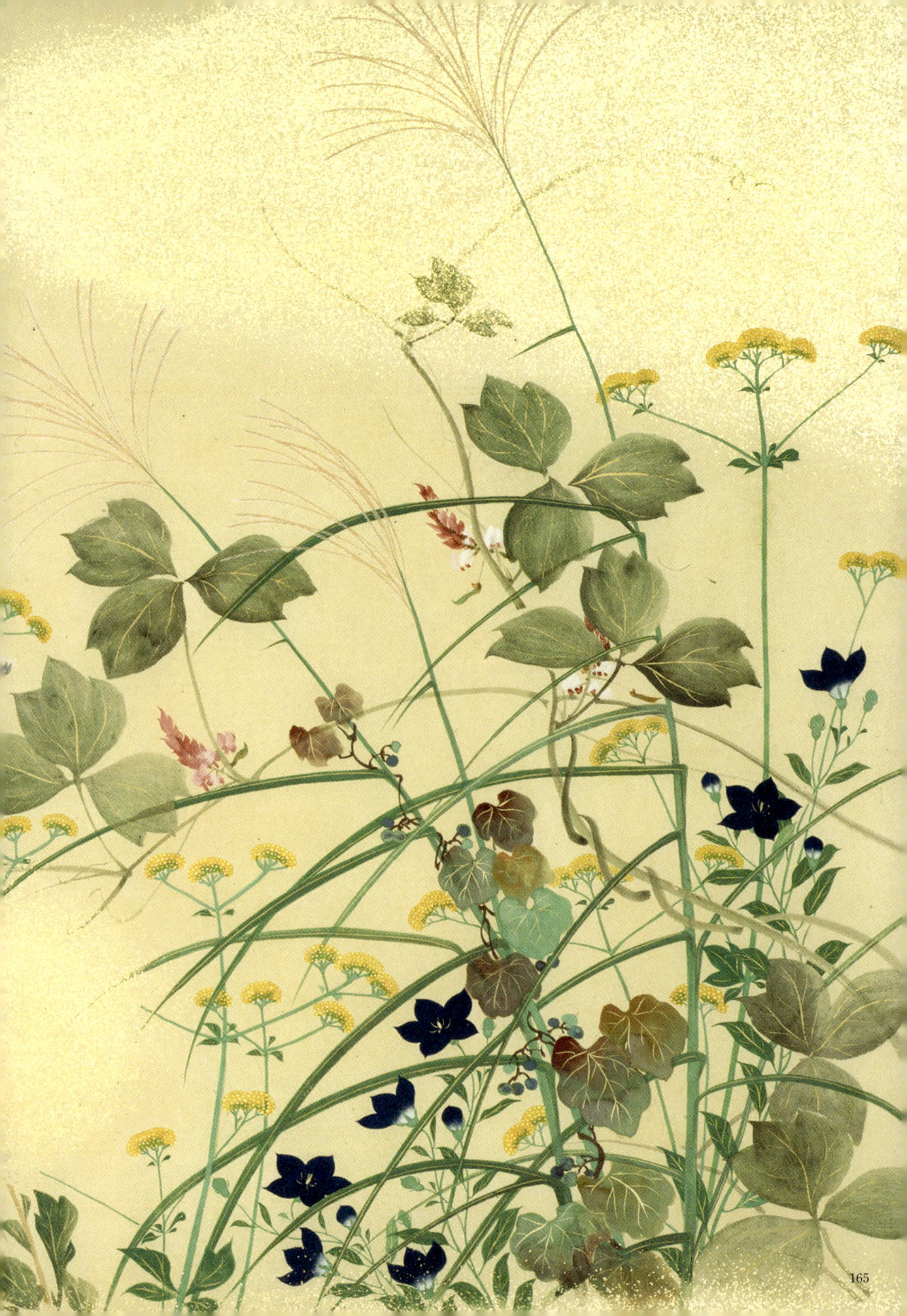

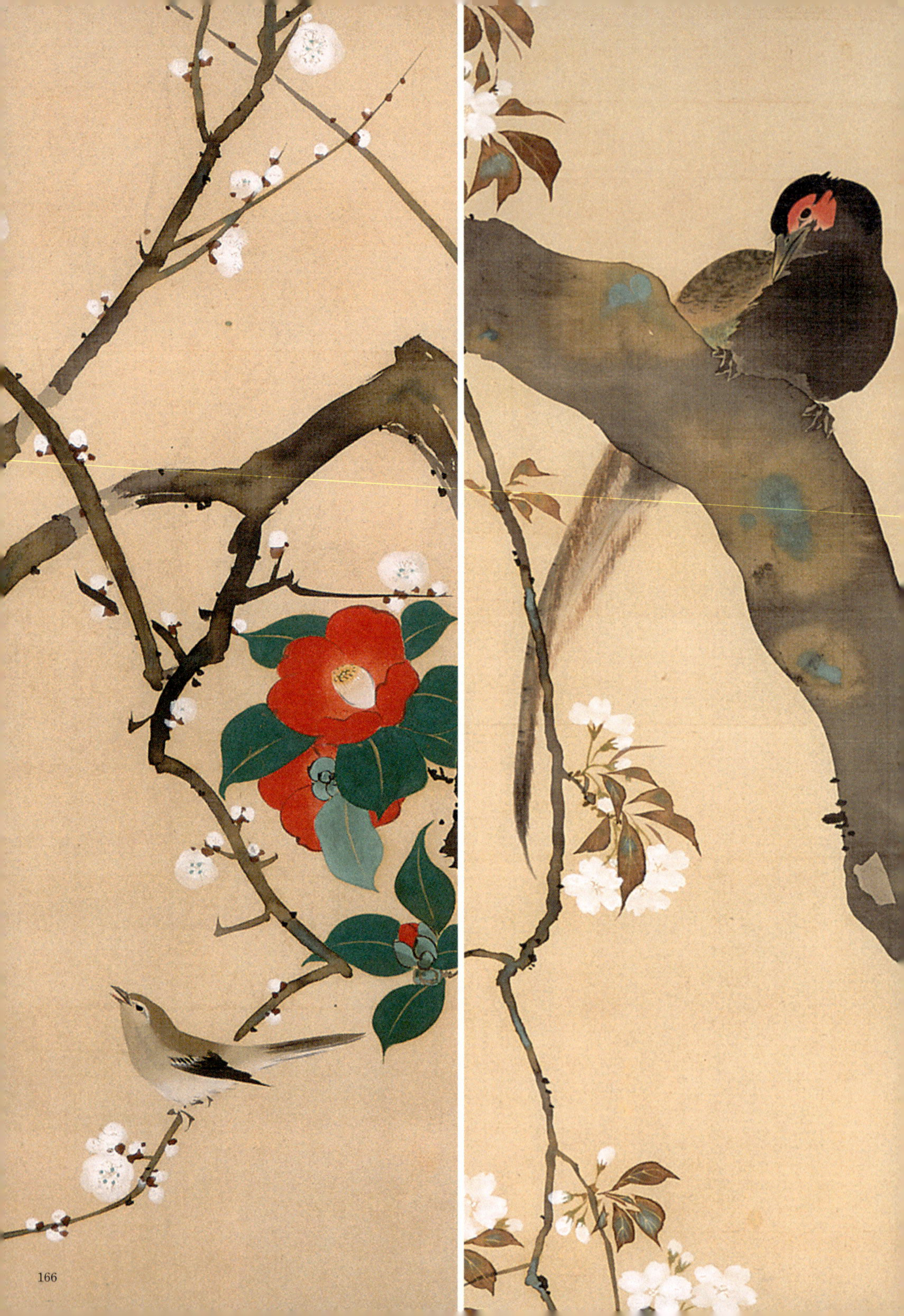

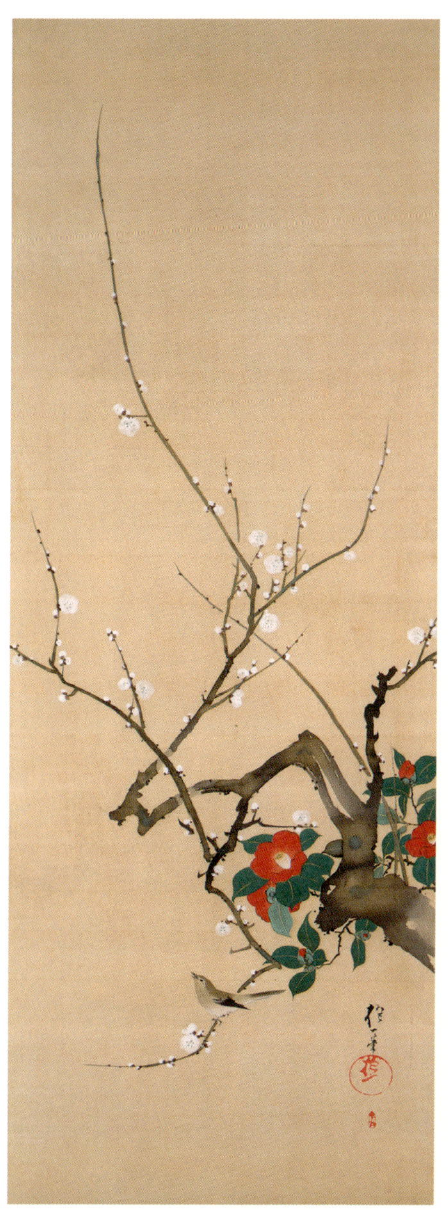

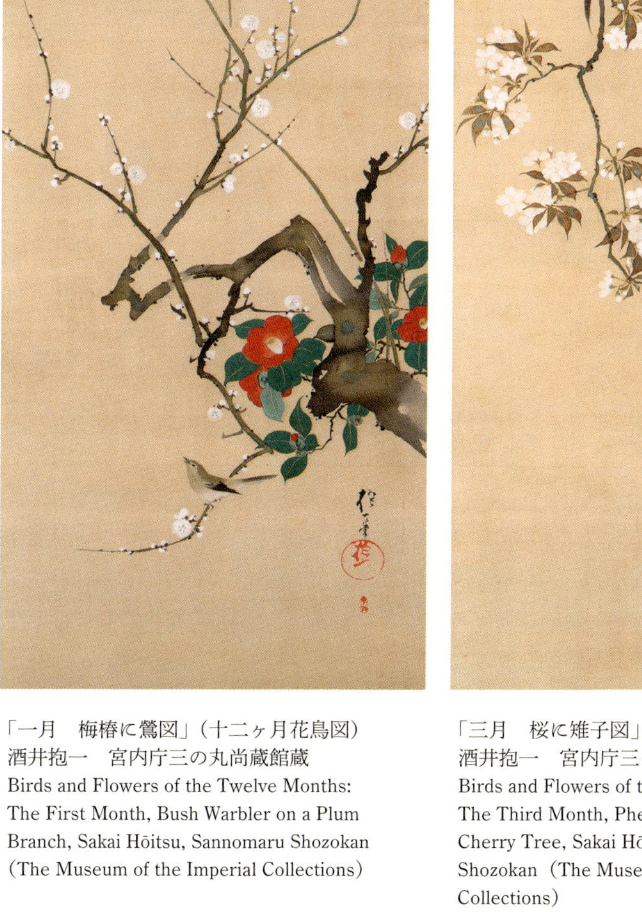

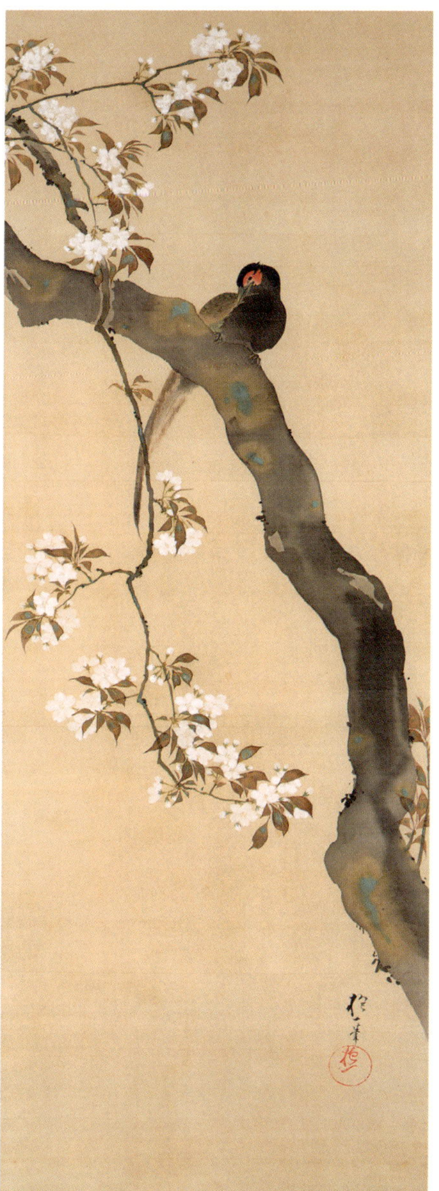

「一月　梅椿に鴬図」（十二ヶ月花鳥図）
酒井抱一　宮内庁三の丸尚蔵館蔵
Birds and Flowers of the Twelve Months:
The First Month, Bush Warbler on a Plum
Branch, Sakai Hōitsu, Sannomaru Shozokan
(The Museum of the Imperial Collections)

「三月　桜に雉子図」（十二ヶ月花鳥図）
酒井抱一　宮内庁三の丸尚蔵館蔵
Birds and Flowers of the Twelve Months:
The Third Month, Pheasant on a Blooming
Cherry Tree, Sakai Hōitsu, Sannomaru
Shozokan（The Museum of the Imperial
Collections）

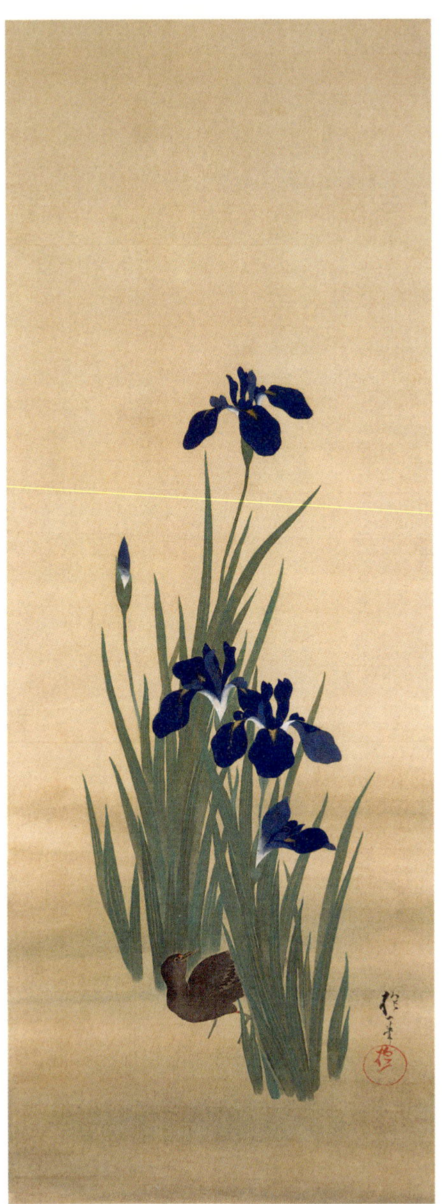

「五月　燕子花に鶍図」（十二ヶ月花鳥図）
酒井抱一　宮内庁三の丸尚蔵館蔵
Birds and Flowers of the Twelve Months: The
Fifth Month, Rail amid Sweet Flags, Sakai
Hōitsu, Sannomaru Shozokan（The Museum
of the Imperial Collections）

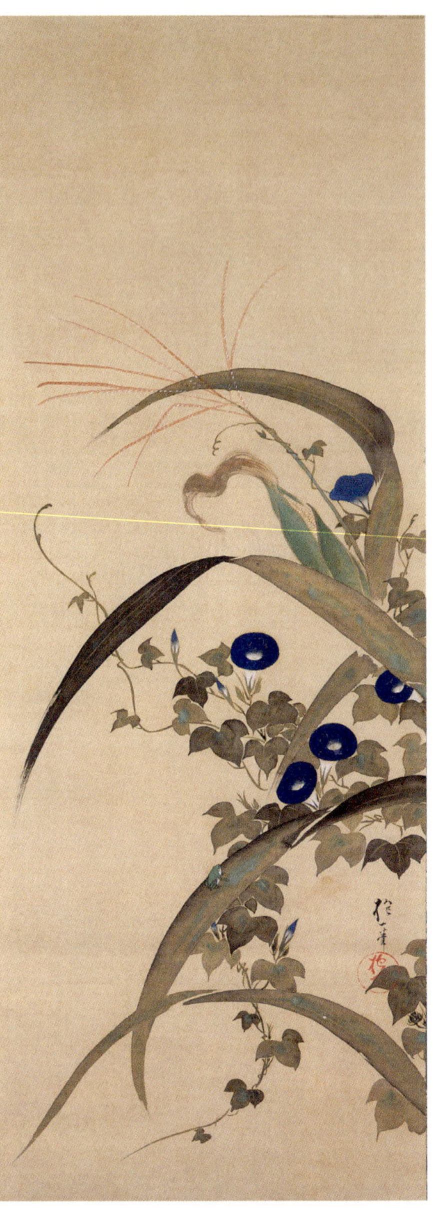

「七月　玉蜀黍朝顔に青蛙図」（十二ヶ月花
鳥図）　酒井抱一　宮内庁三の丸尚蔵館蔵
Birds and Flowers of the Twelve Months: The
Seventh Month, Flog with Maize and Morning
Glories, Sakai Hōitsu, Sannomaru Shozokan
（The Museum of the Imperial Collections）

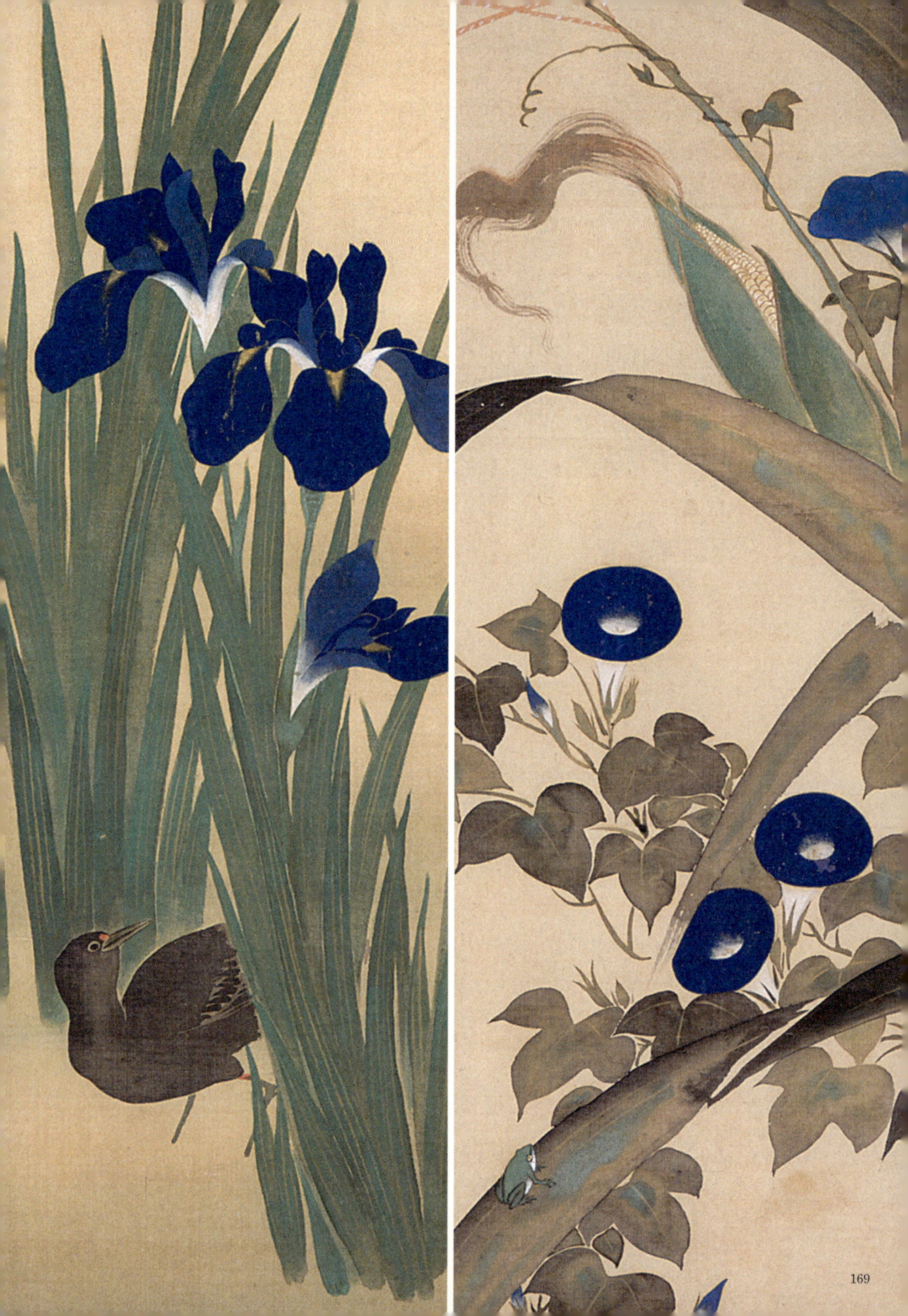

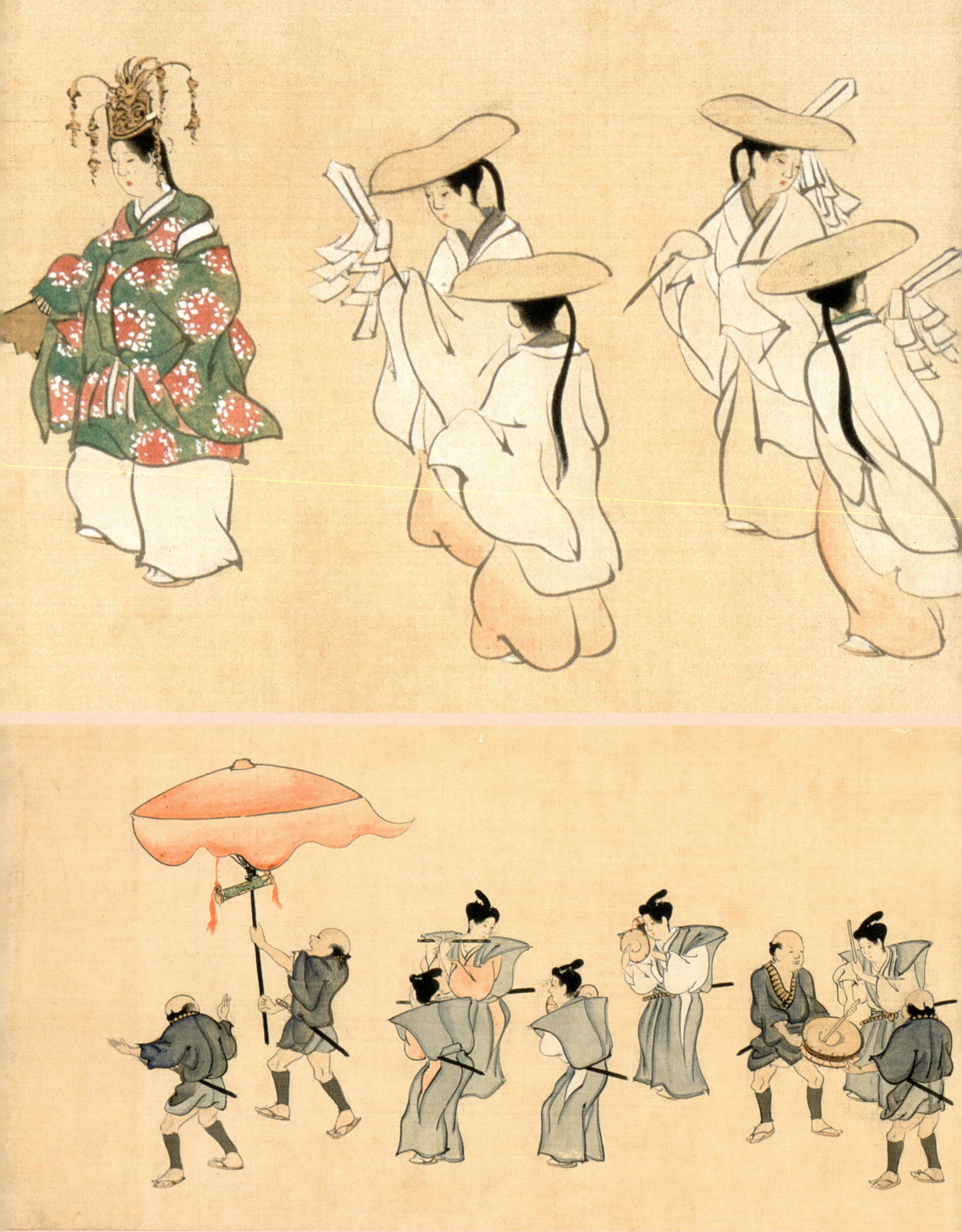

「播州室明神神事　棹歌之遊女行列図」　酒井抱一　姫路市立美術館蔵
Parade of Muromyojin Shrine in Banshu Area, Sakai Hōitsu, Himeji City Museum of Art

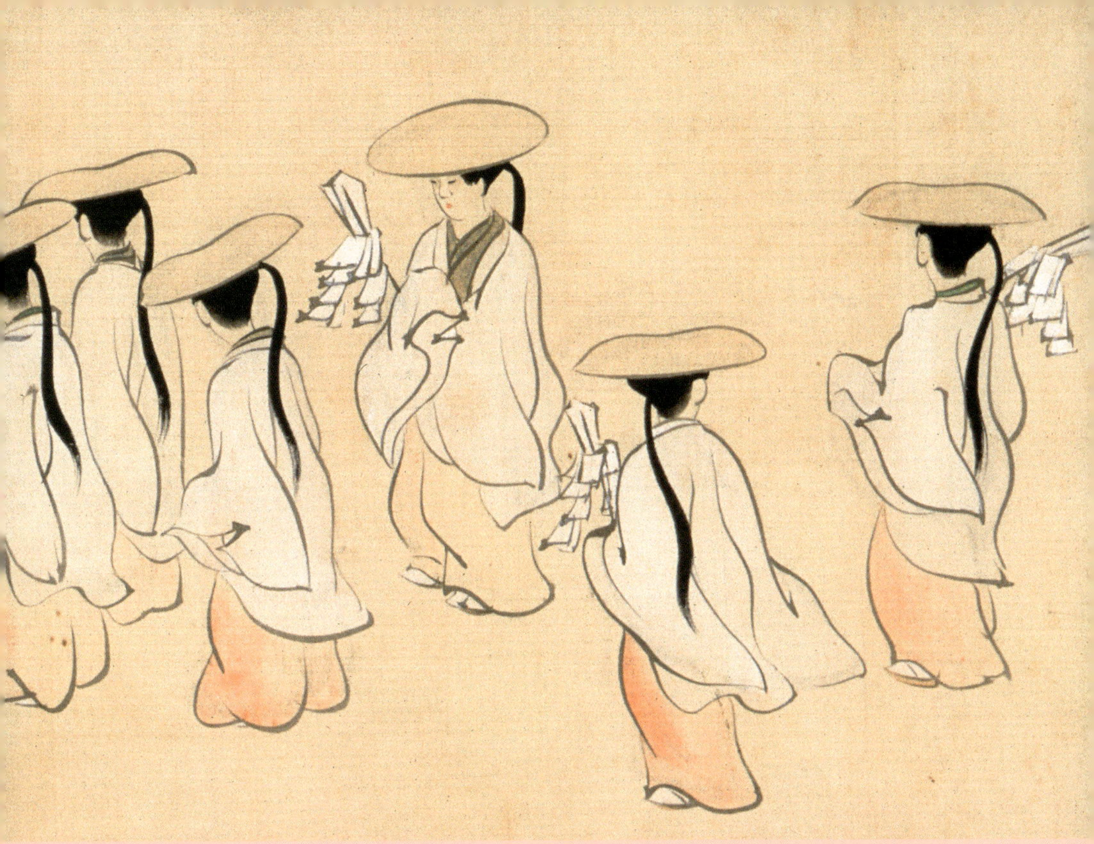

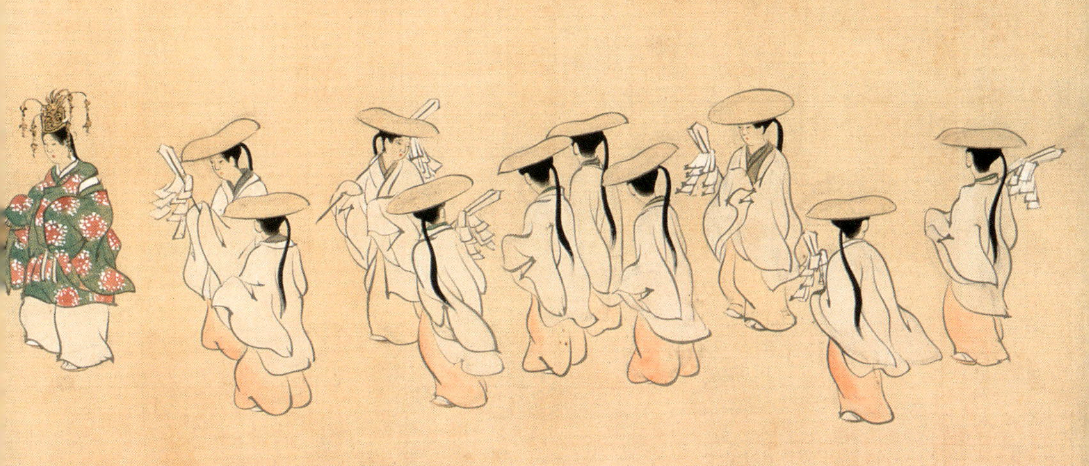

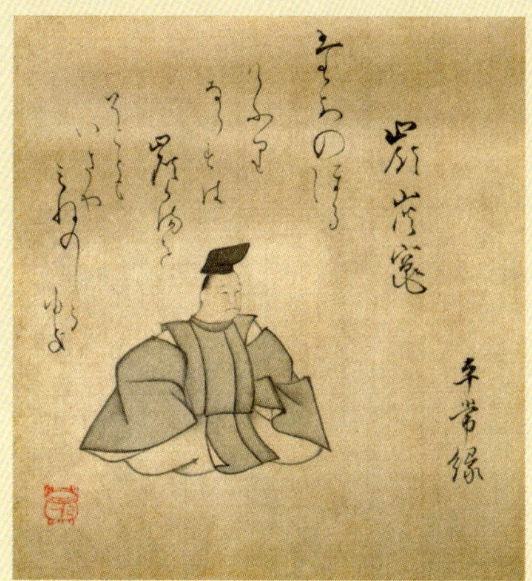 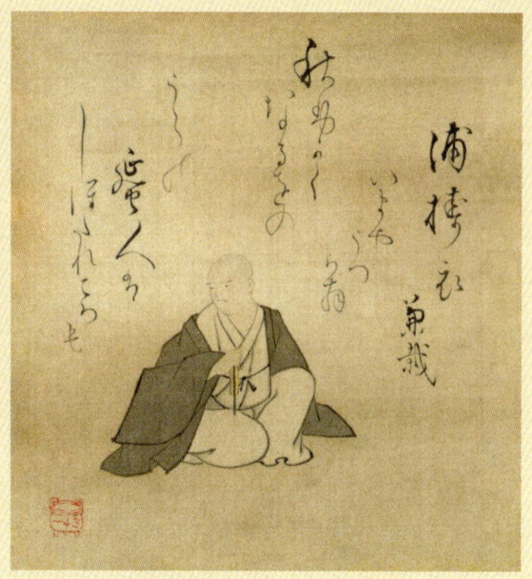

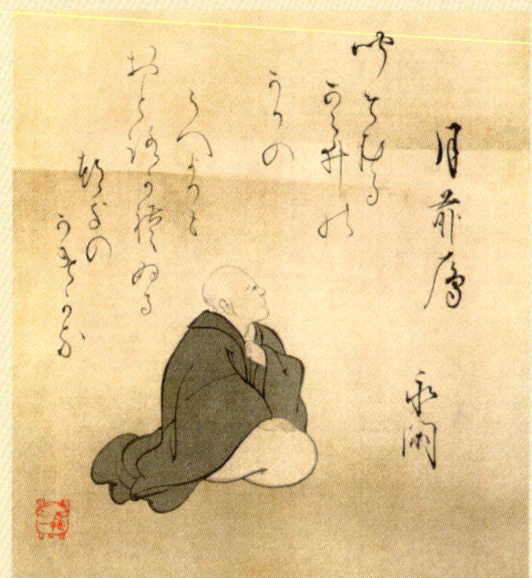 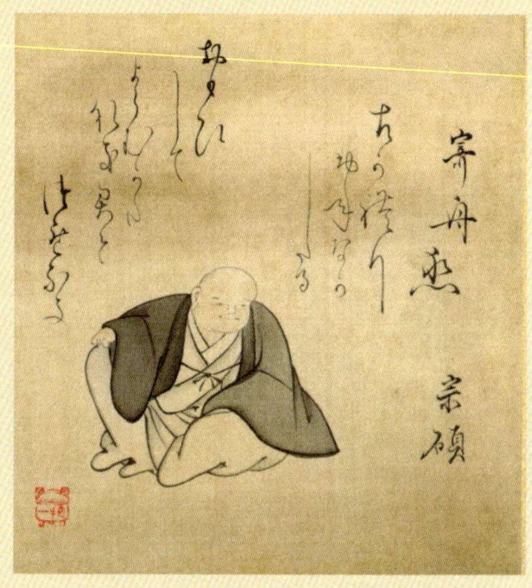

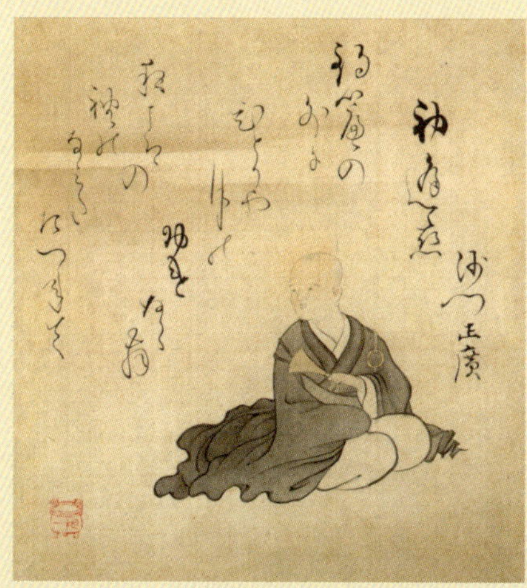 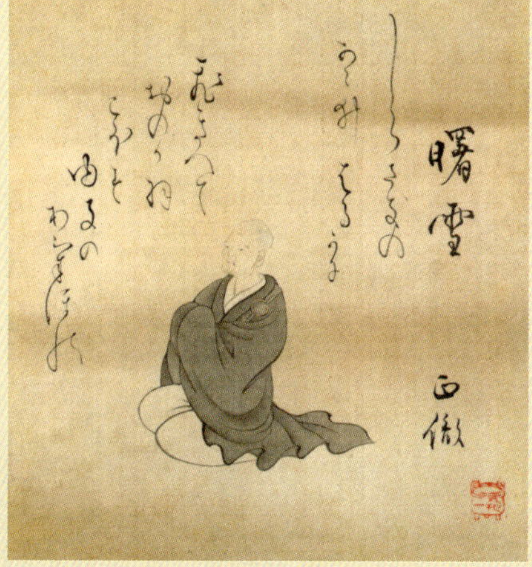

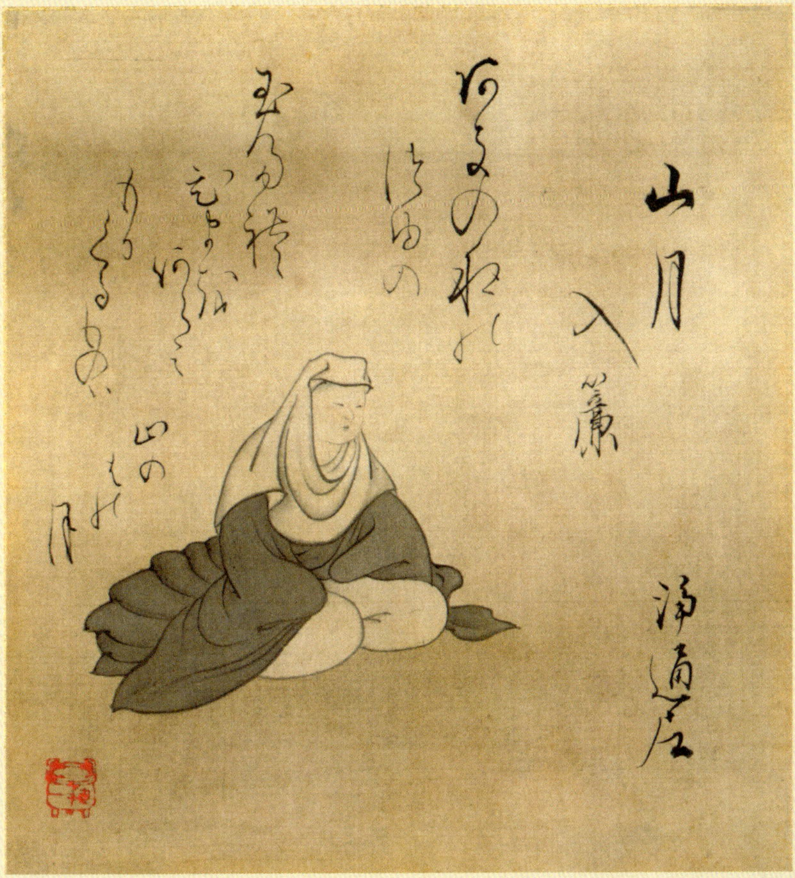

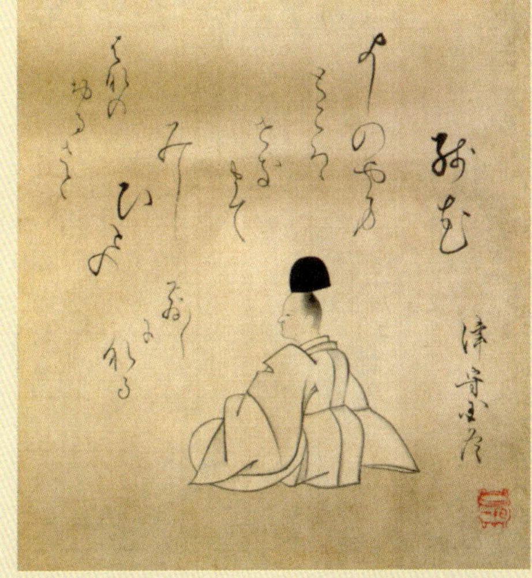

「集外三十六歌仙」　酒井抱一
姫路市立美術館蔵
Honorable Mention of 36 Master Poets,
Sakai Hōitsu, Himeji City Museum of Art

酒井鶯蒲

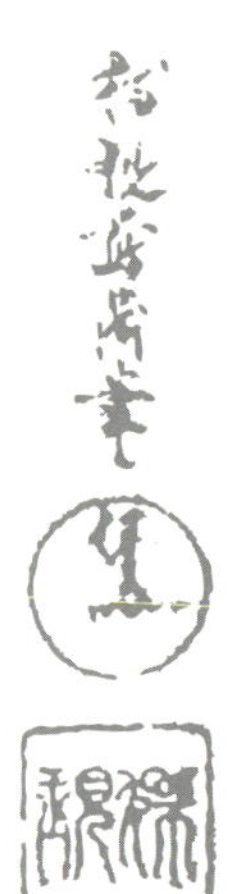

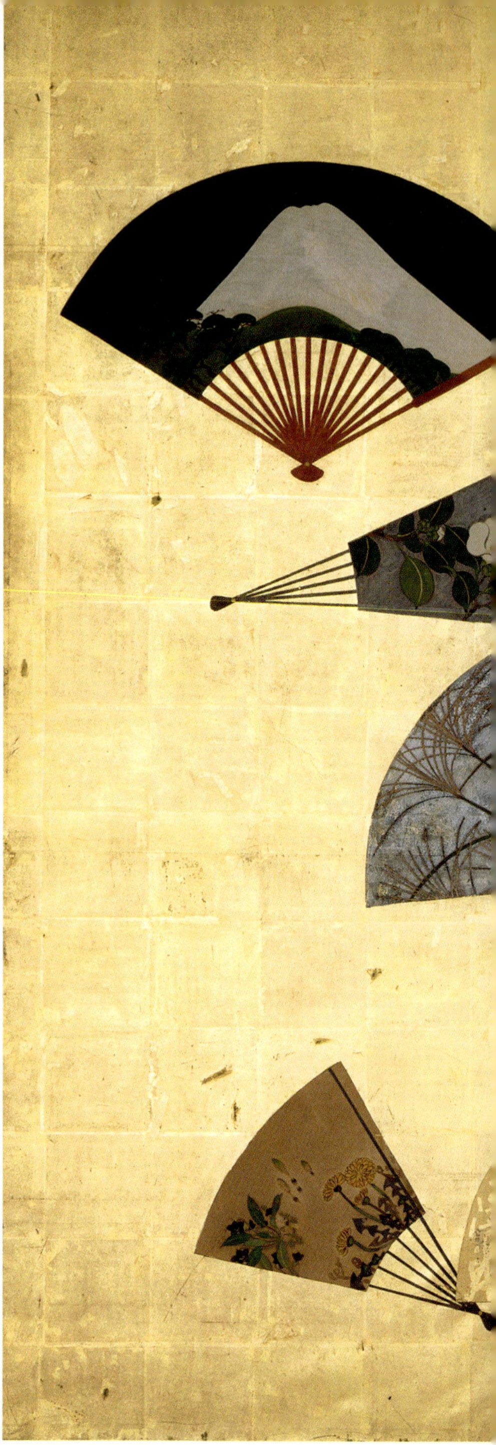

さかい おうほ

文化 5 年〜天保 12 年（1808 - 41）

築地本願寺の末寺にあたる市ヶ谷浄栄寺の住職香阪雪仙の次男に生まれる。12 歳の時、酒井抱一が吉原大文字楼から身請けして身の回りの世話をさせていた妙華（みょうげ）の願いで迎えられ養子となり、抱一の門に学んだ。書物を学ぶことが苦手であったが茶事を好んだといわれる。

Sakai Ōho (1808 – 1841)

Born in Edo as a son of a Buddhist priest, Ōho was adopted by Sakai Hōitsu at the request of Myōge, whom Hōitsu had redeemed from a Yoshiwara brothel. Ōho, who studied with Hōitsu, is said to have been a poor scholar but fond of the tea ceremony.

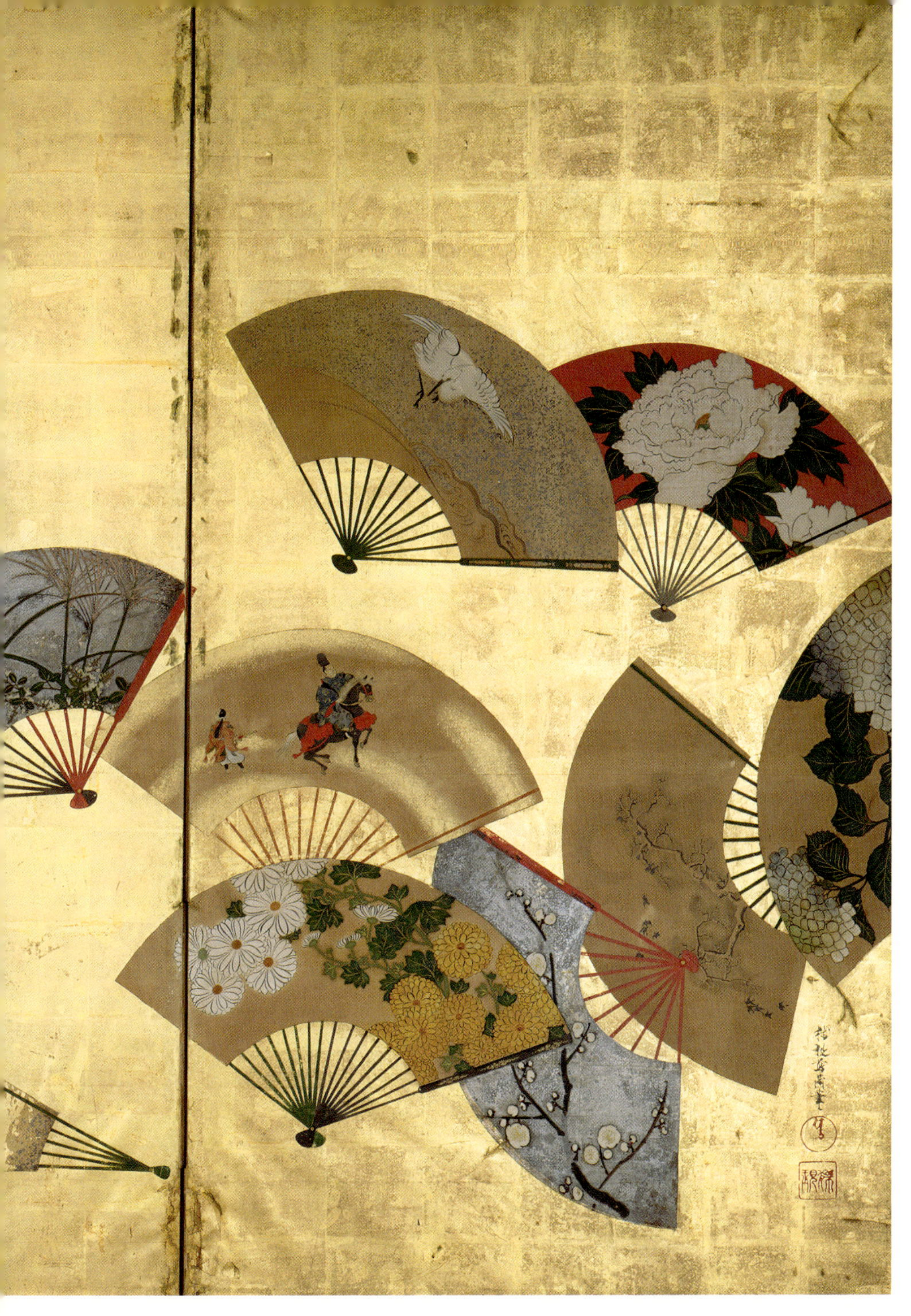

「扇面散図屏風」 酒井鶯蒲 他　東京国立博物館蔵
Scattered Fans, Sakai Ōho and others, Tokyo National Museum Image: TNM Image Archives

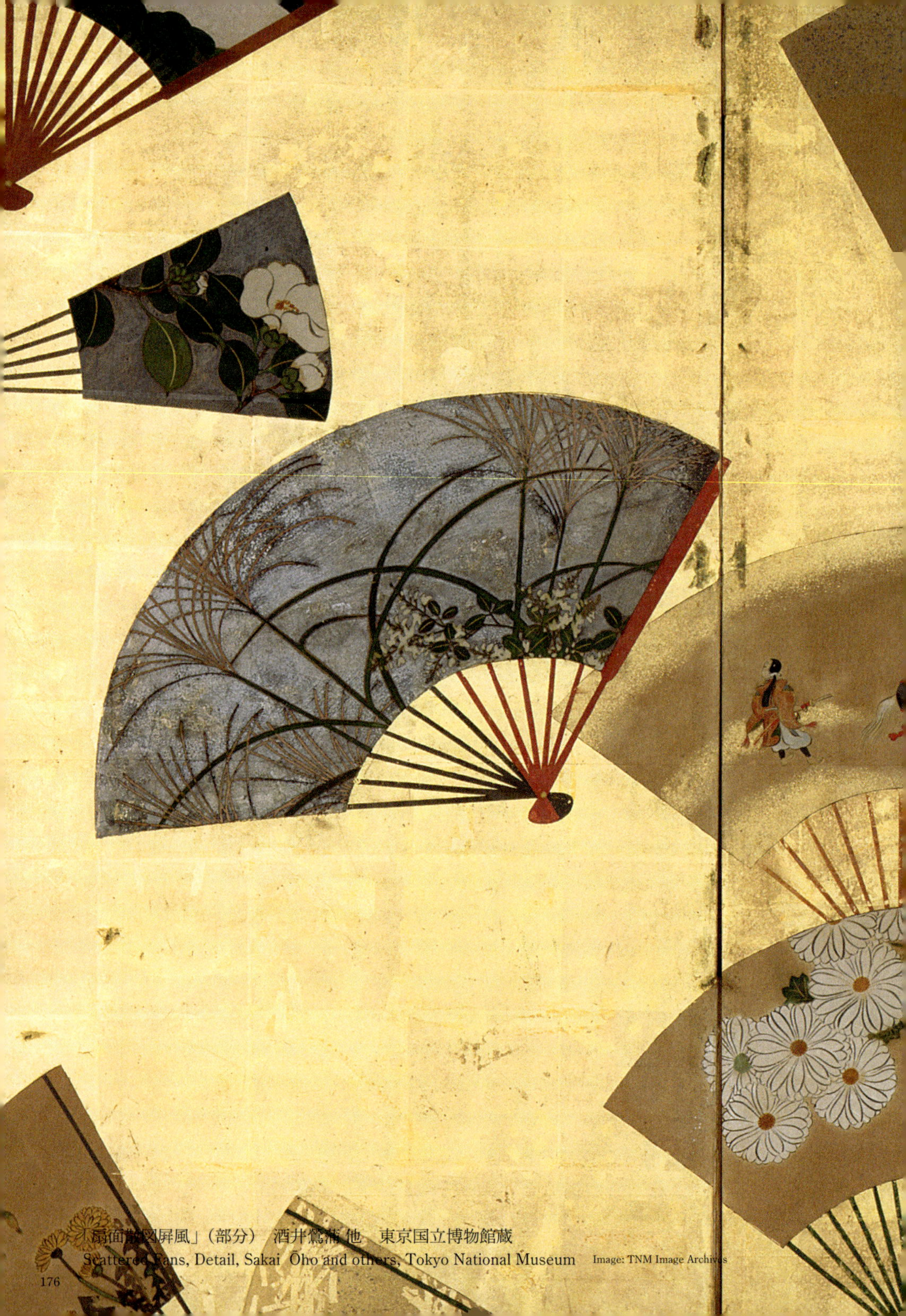

「扇面散図屏風」（部分）　酒井鷺浦 他　東京国立博物館蔵
Scattered Fans, Detail, Sakai Ōho and others, Tokyo National Museum　Image: TNM Image Archives

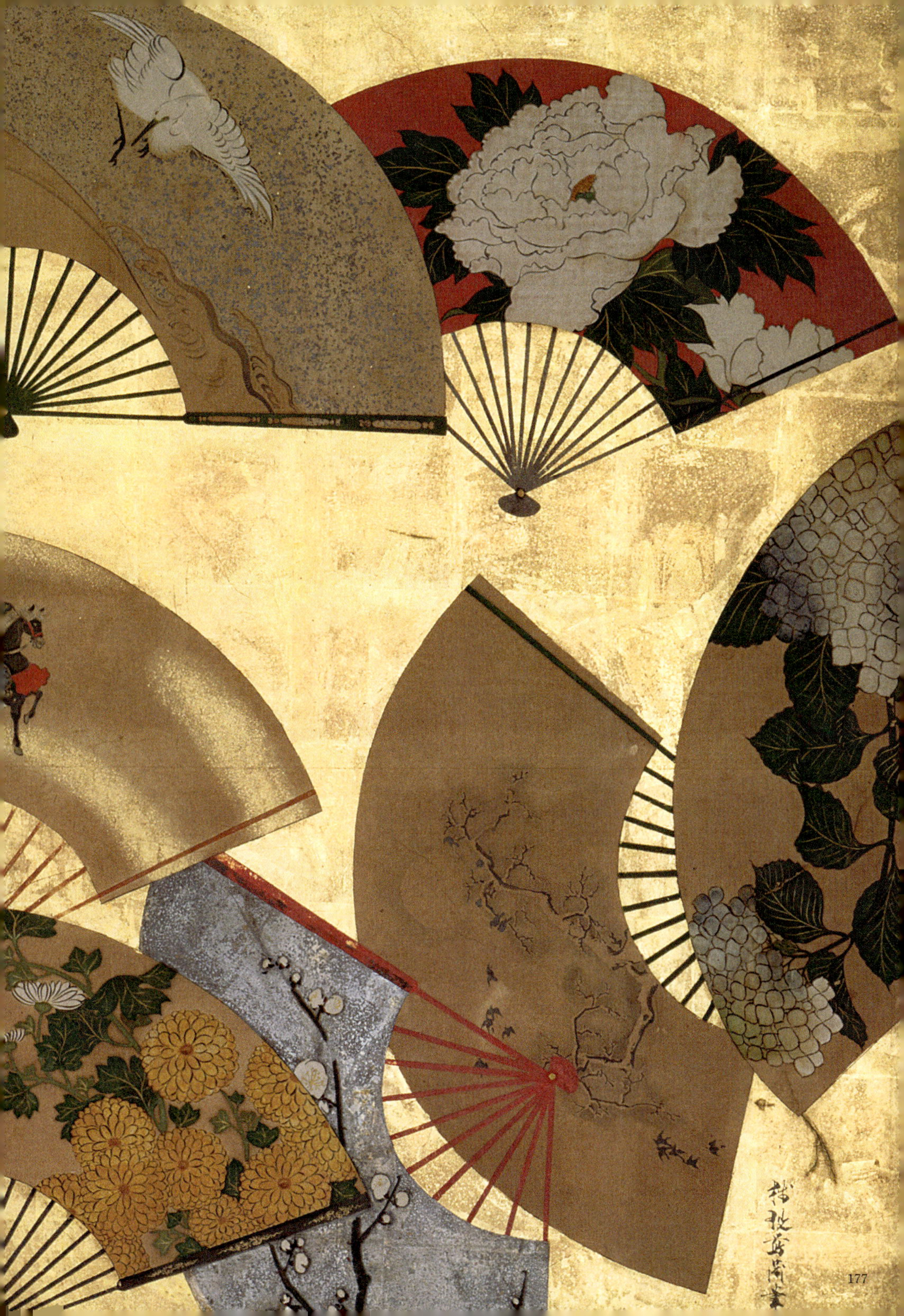

鈴木其一

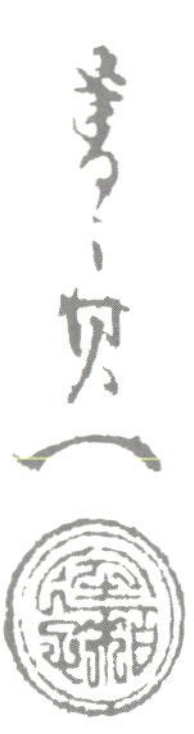

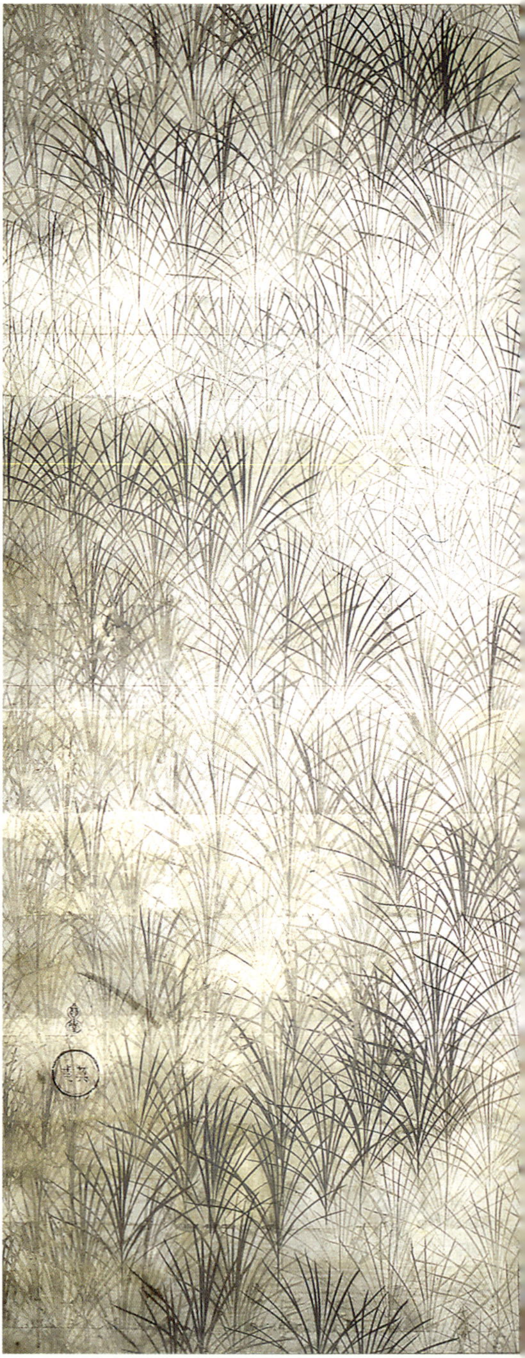

すずき きいつ

寛政 8 年〜安政 5 年（1796 – 1858）

1813 年（文化 10）、18 歳の時、酒
井抱一の内弟子となり、のちに同門
の鈴木蠣潭の養子となって酒井家に
仕えた。抱一が没するまで師の画風
を継承しつつ、やがて新たな近代感
覚を盛り込んだ独自の画風を築きあ
げた。そして晩年は伝統的な琳派絵
画を描いた。

Suzuki Kiitsu (1796 – 1858)

In 1813, at 18, Kiitsu became Sakai
Hōitsu's live-in apprentice. He later
was adopted by Suzuki Reitan, a
samurai pupil of Hōitsu, and served
the Sakai clan. He continued his
master's style until Hōitsu's death,
gradually building his own style with
a new, modern feel. In later years,
he produced traditional Rinpa style
paintings.

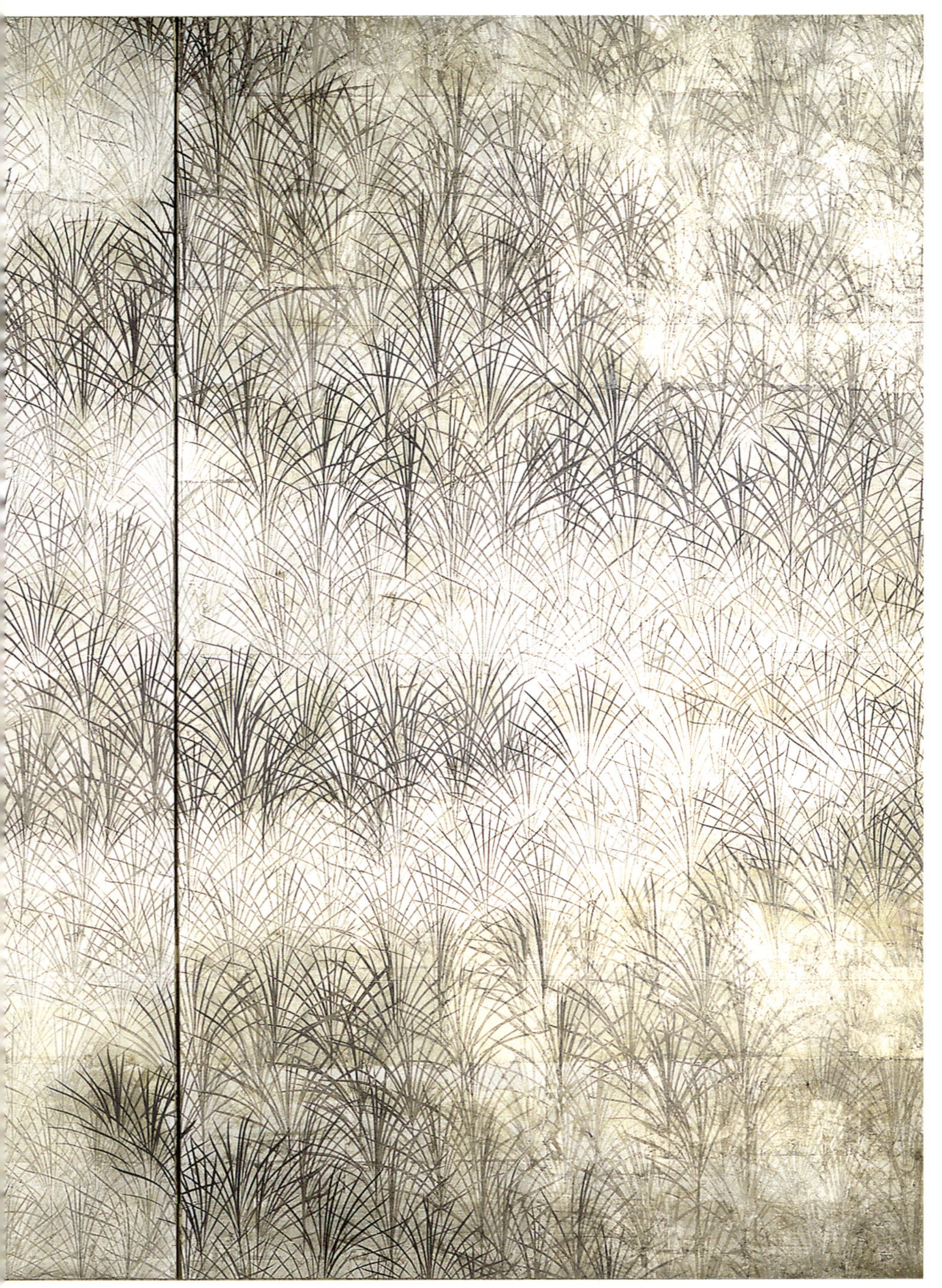

「芒図」　鈴木其一　千葉市美術館蔵
Field of Pampas Grass, Suzuki Kiitsu, Chiba City Museum of Art

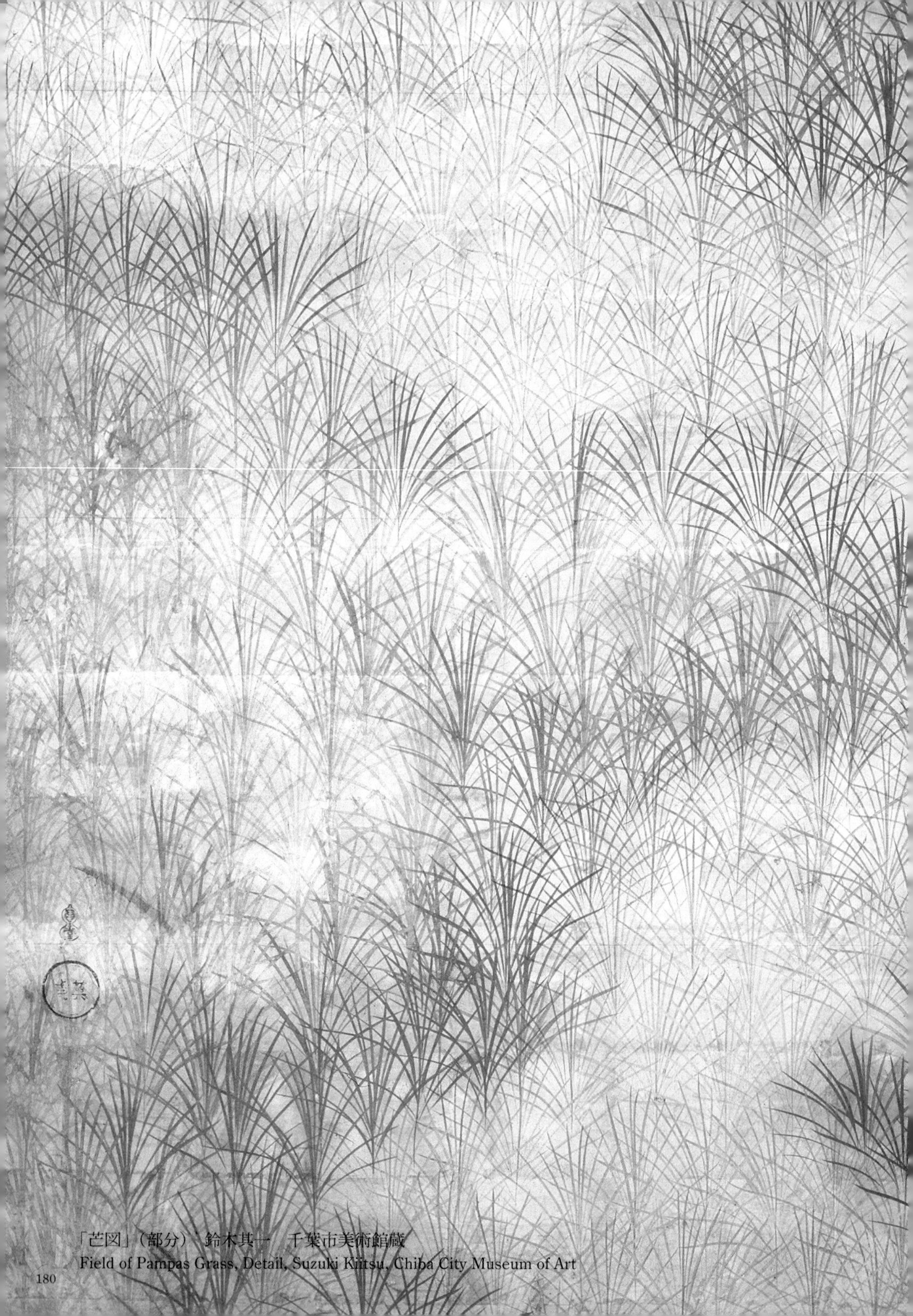

「芒図」（部分）　鈴木其一　千葉市美術館蔵
Field of Pampas Grass, Detail, Suzuki Kiitsu, Chiba City Museum of Art

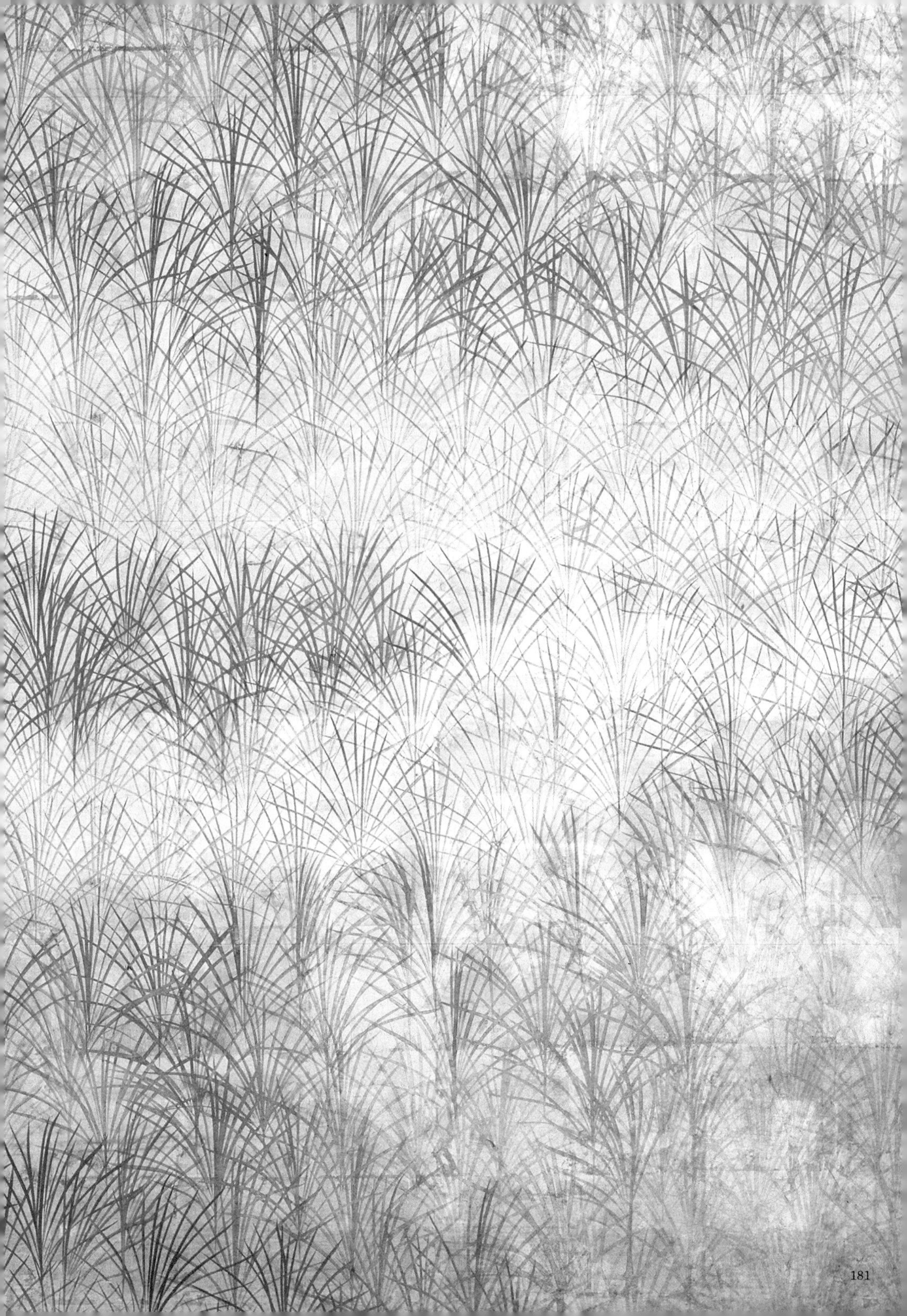

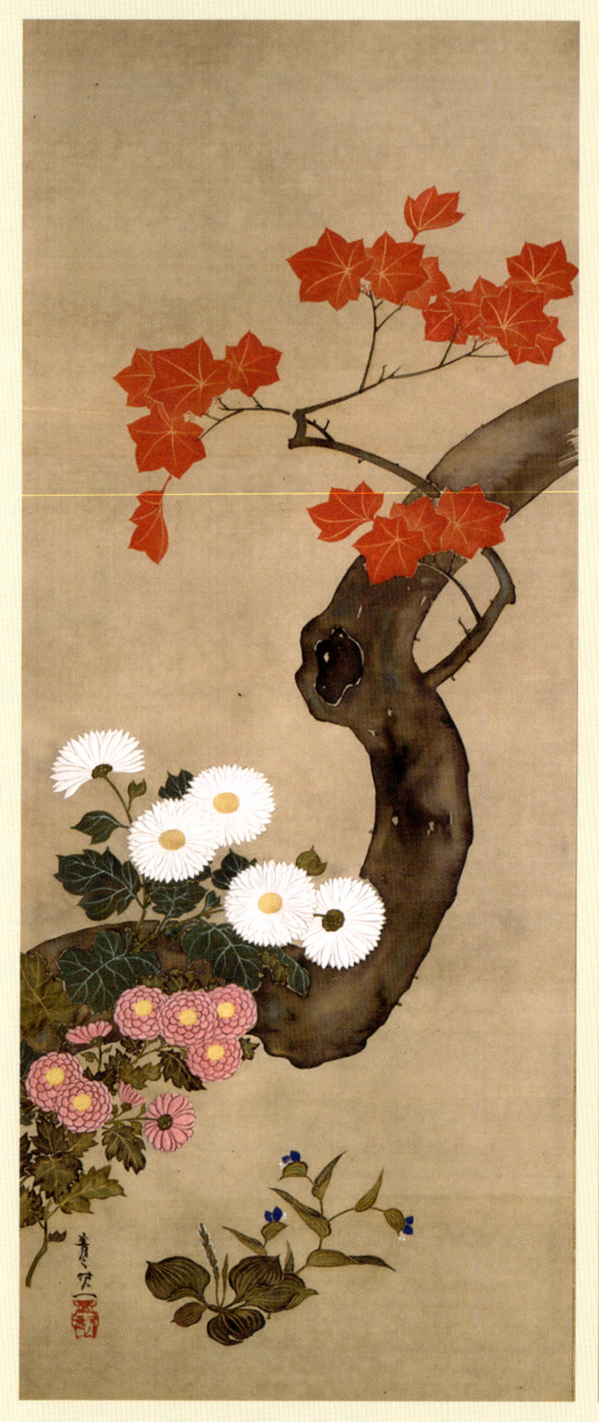

「双鶴春秋花卉図」
鈴木其一　板橋区立美術館蔵
Cranes, Flowers of Spring and
Autumn, Suzuki Kiitsu, Itabashi
Art Museum

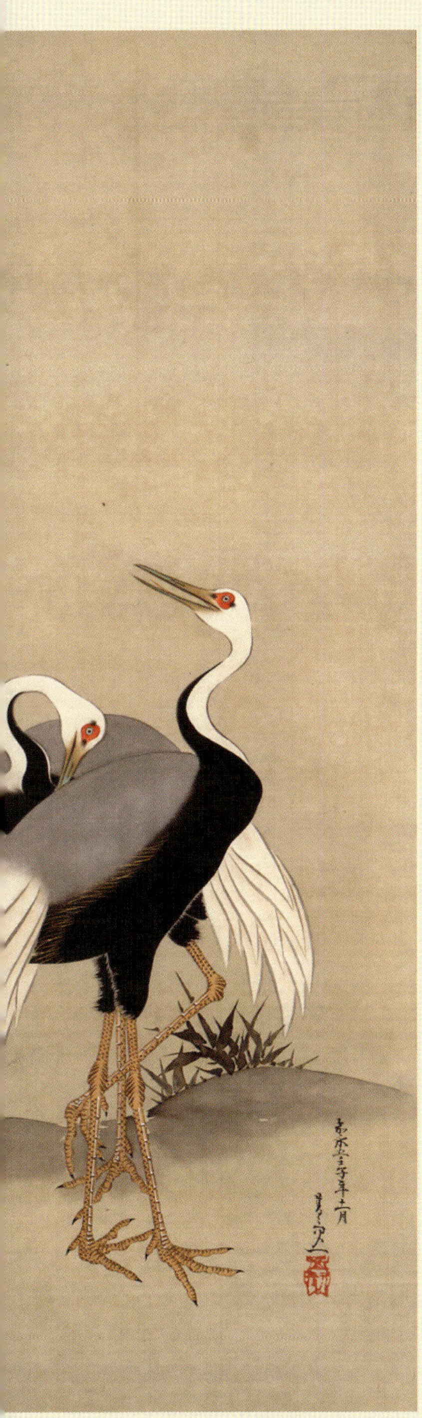

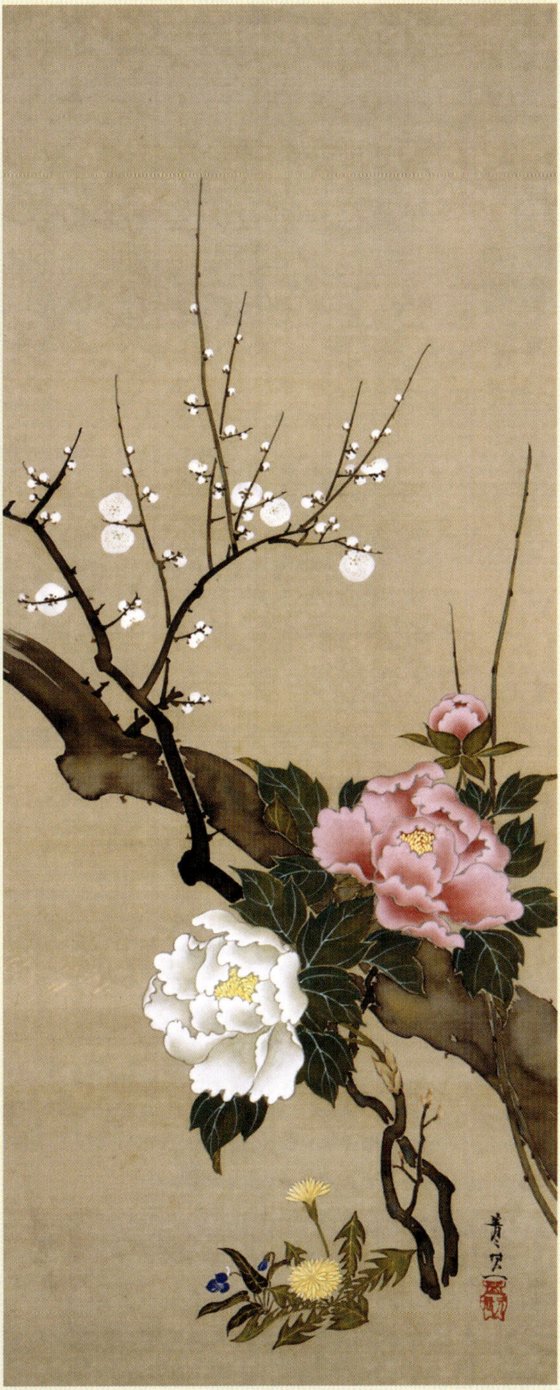

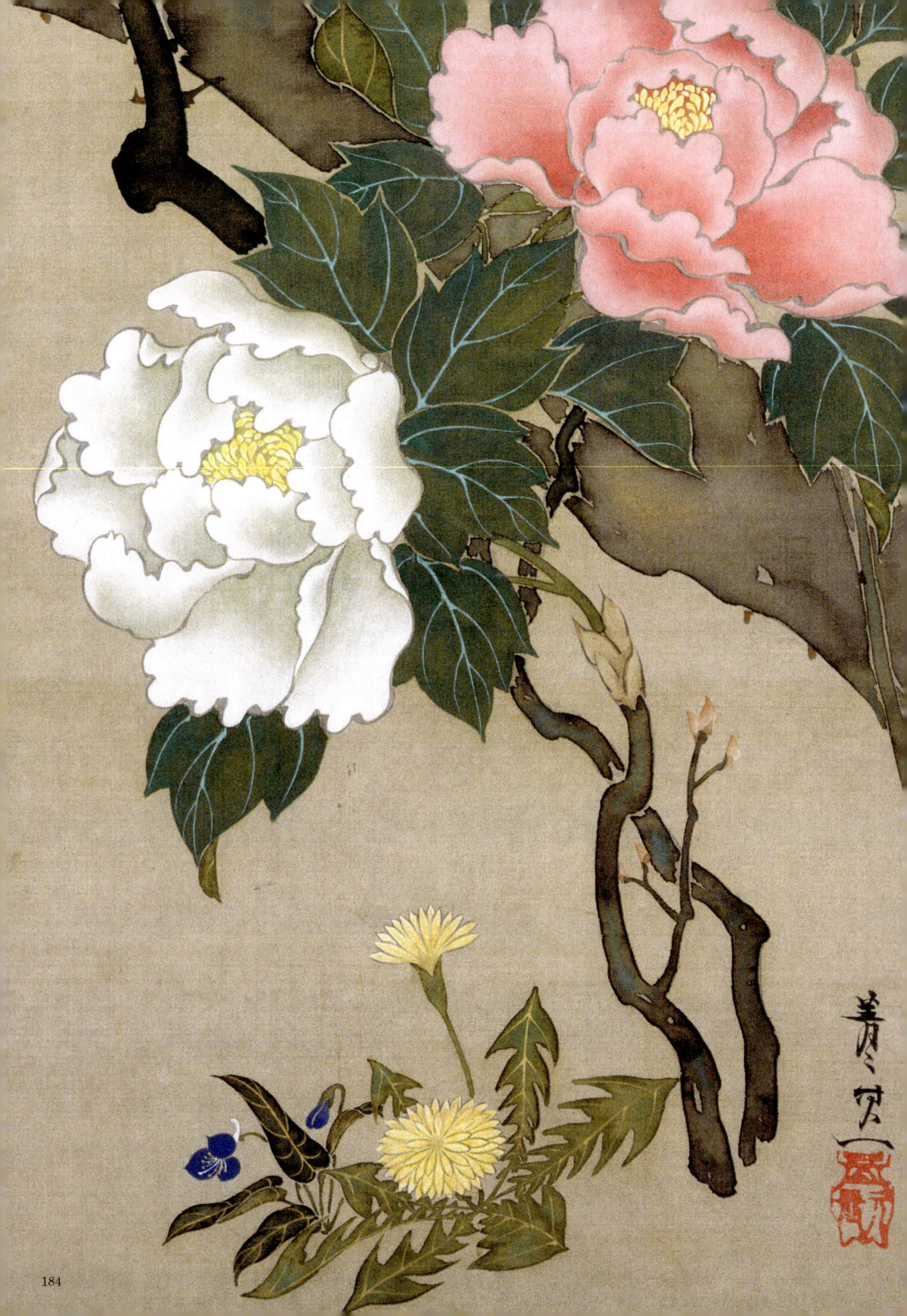

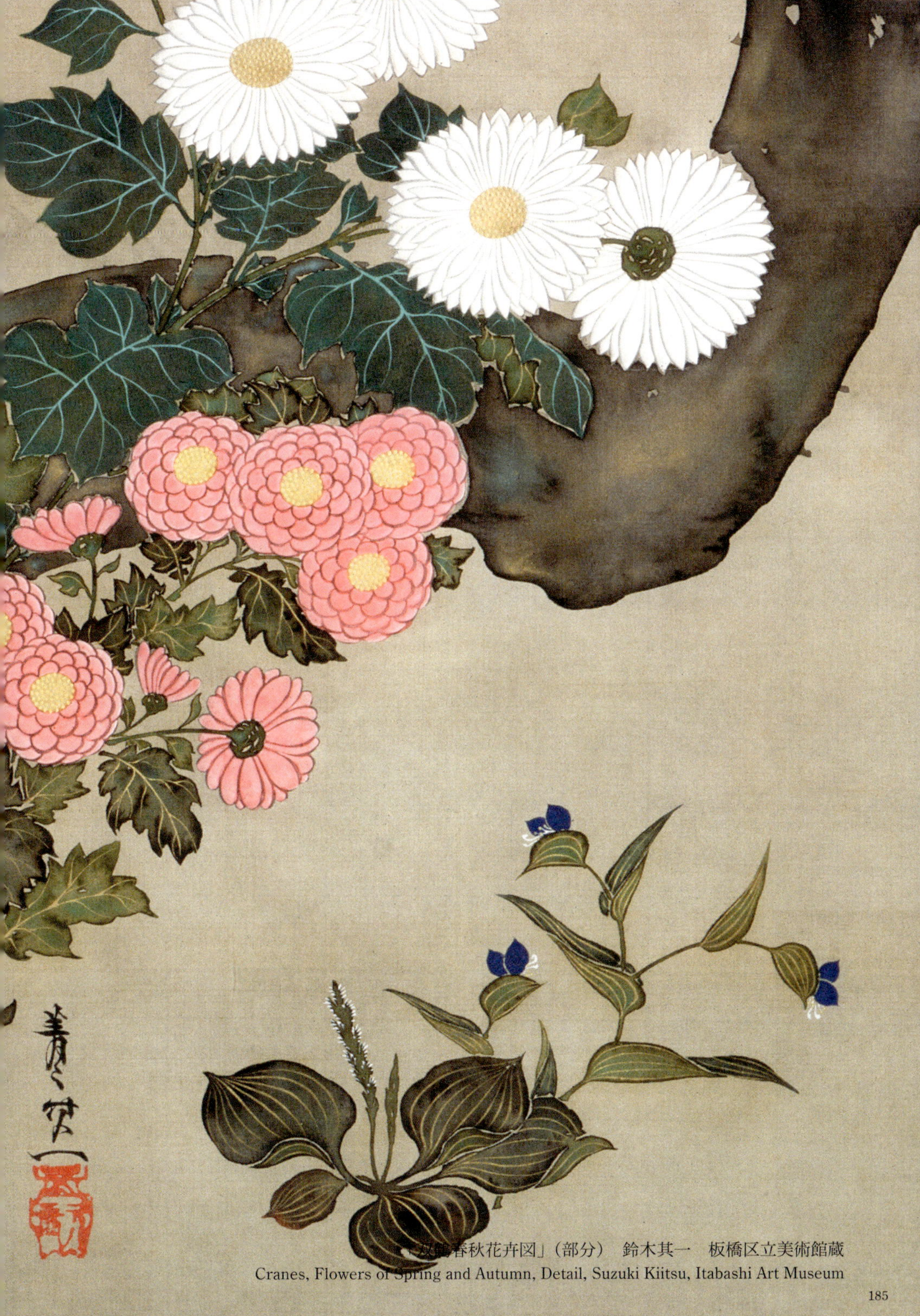

「双鶴春秋花卉図」（部分）　鈴木其一　板橋区立美術館蔵
Cranes, Flowers of Spring and Autumn, Detail, Suzuki Kiitsu, Itabashi Art Museum

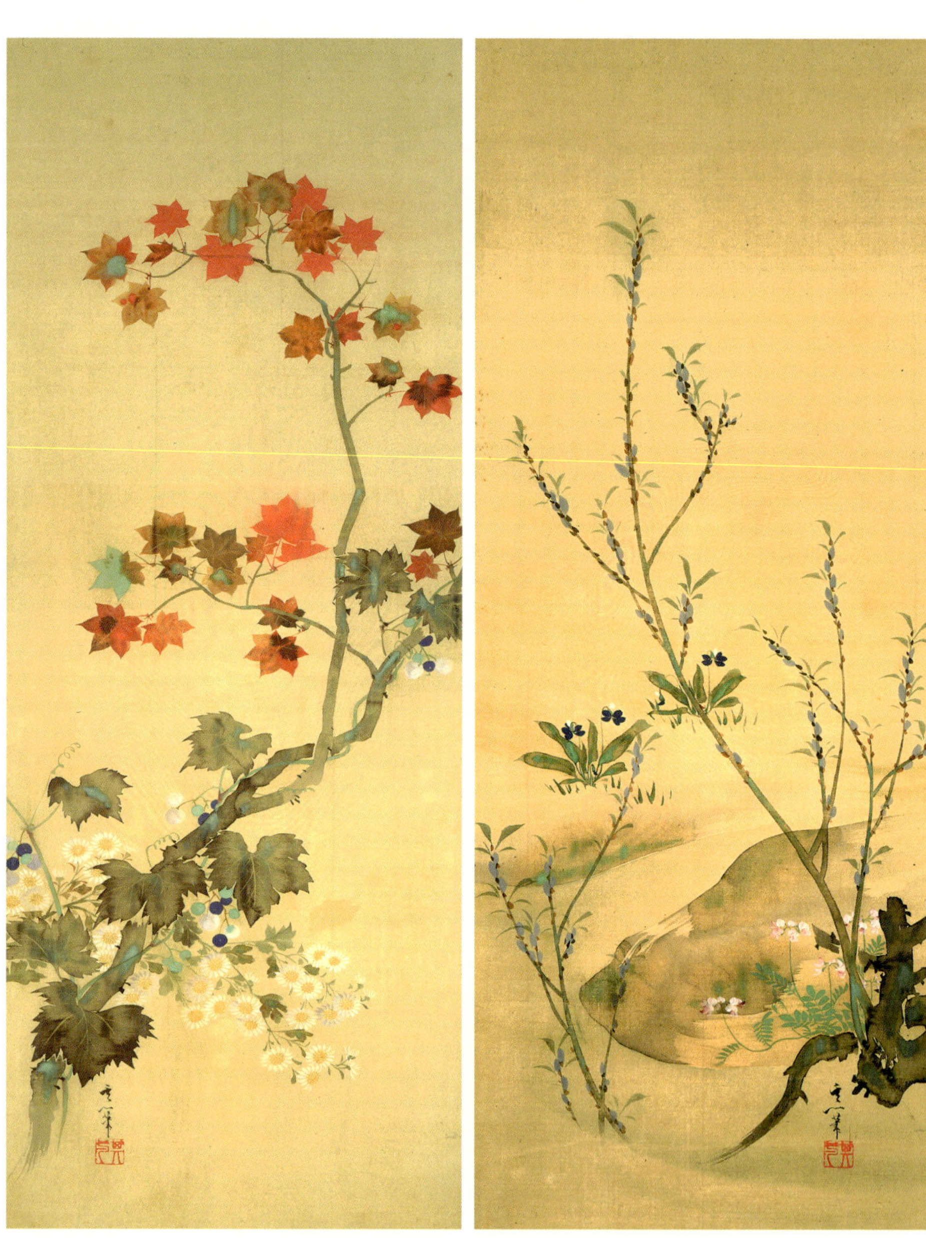

「猫柳図・楓図」　鈴木其一　群馬県立近代美術館蔵
Pussy Willow and Maple, Suzuki Kiitsu, The Museum of Modern Art, Gunma

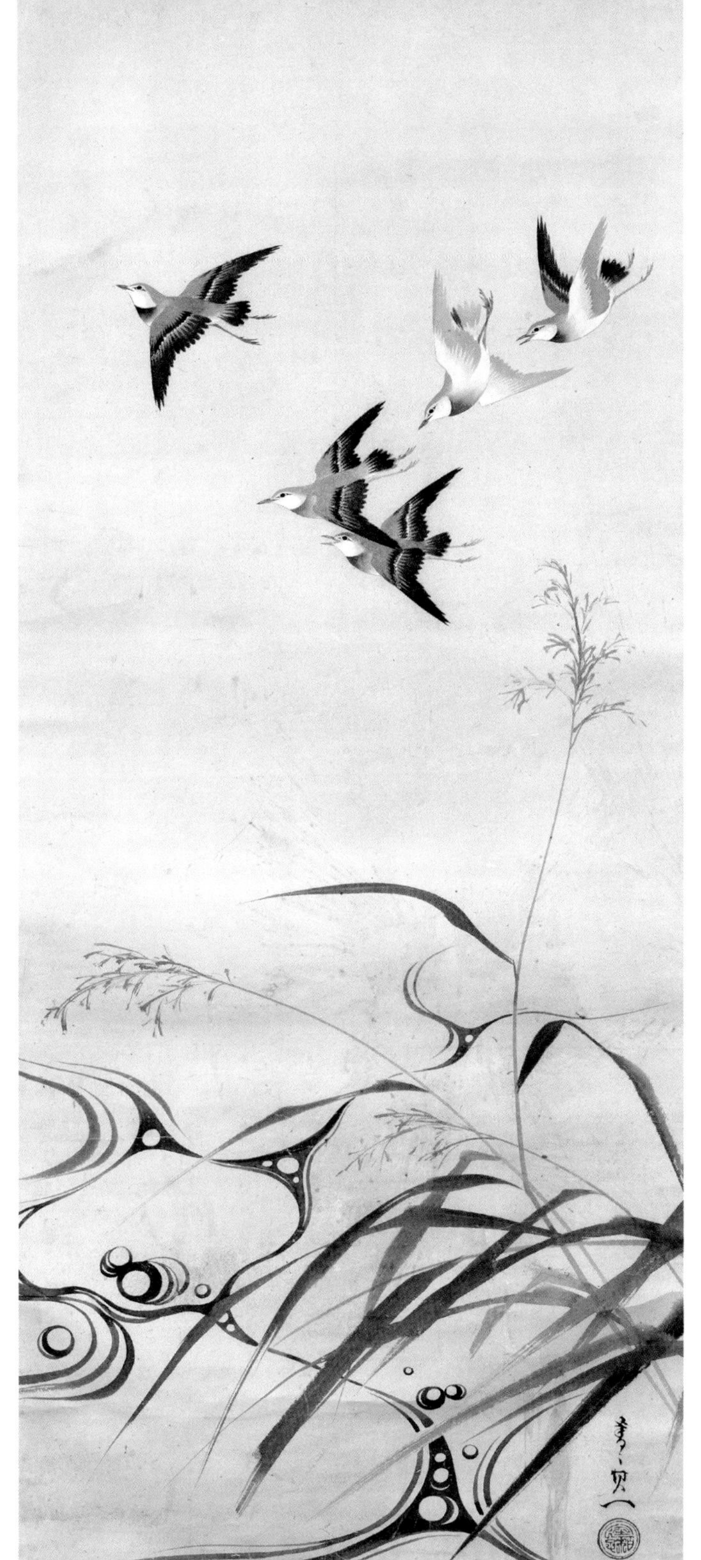

「流水に千鳥図」鈴木其一
島根県立美術館蔵
Flowing Stream and Plovers,
Suzuki Kiitsu, Shimane Art
Museum

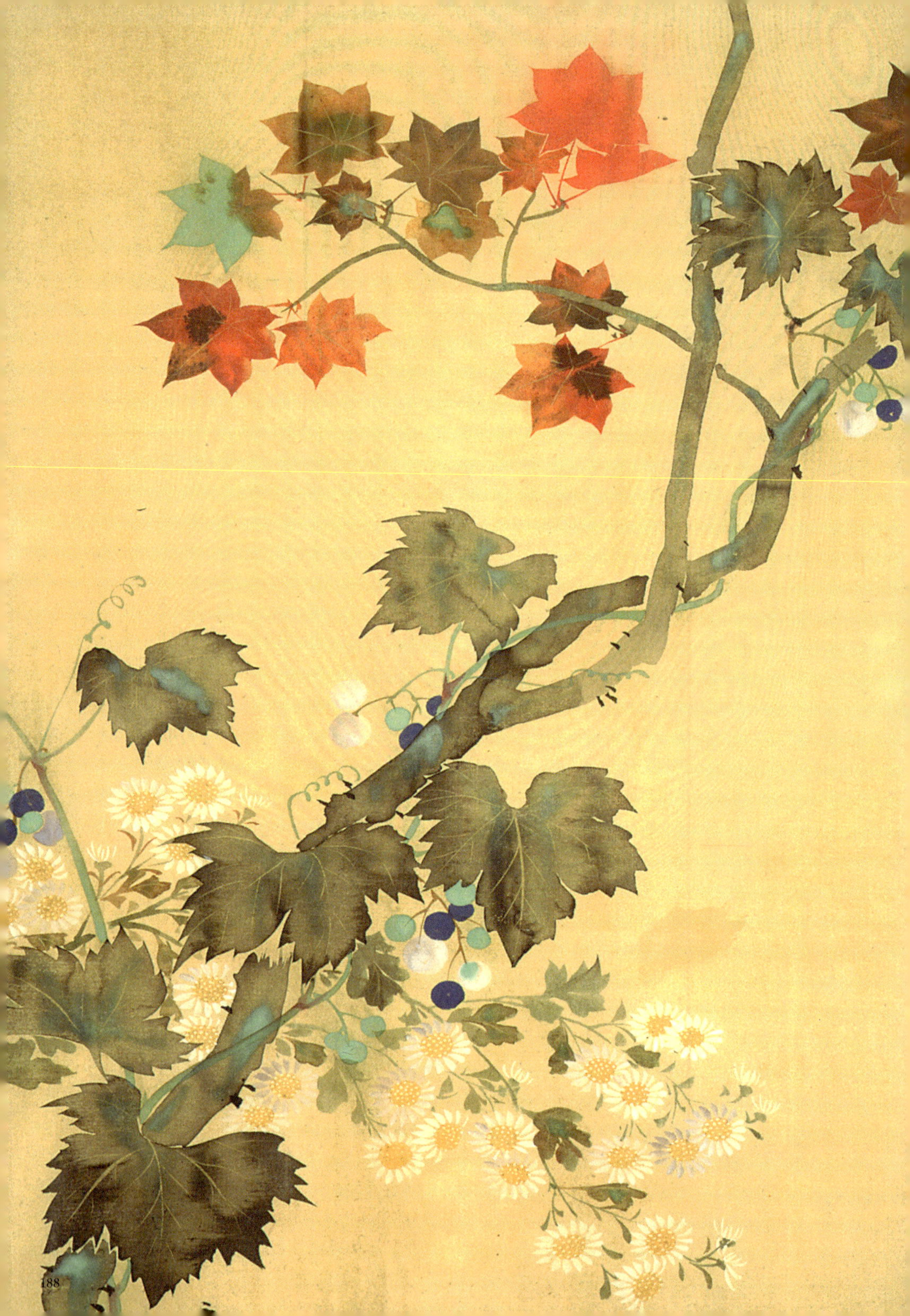

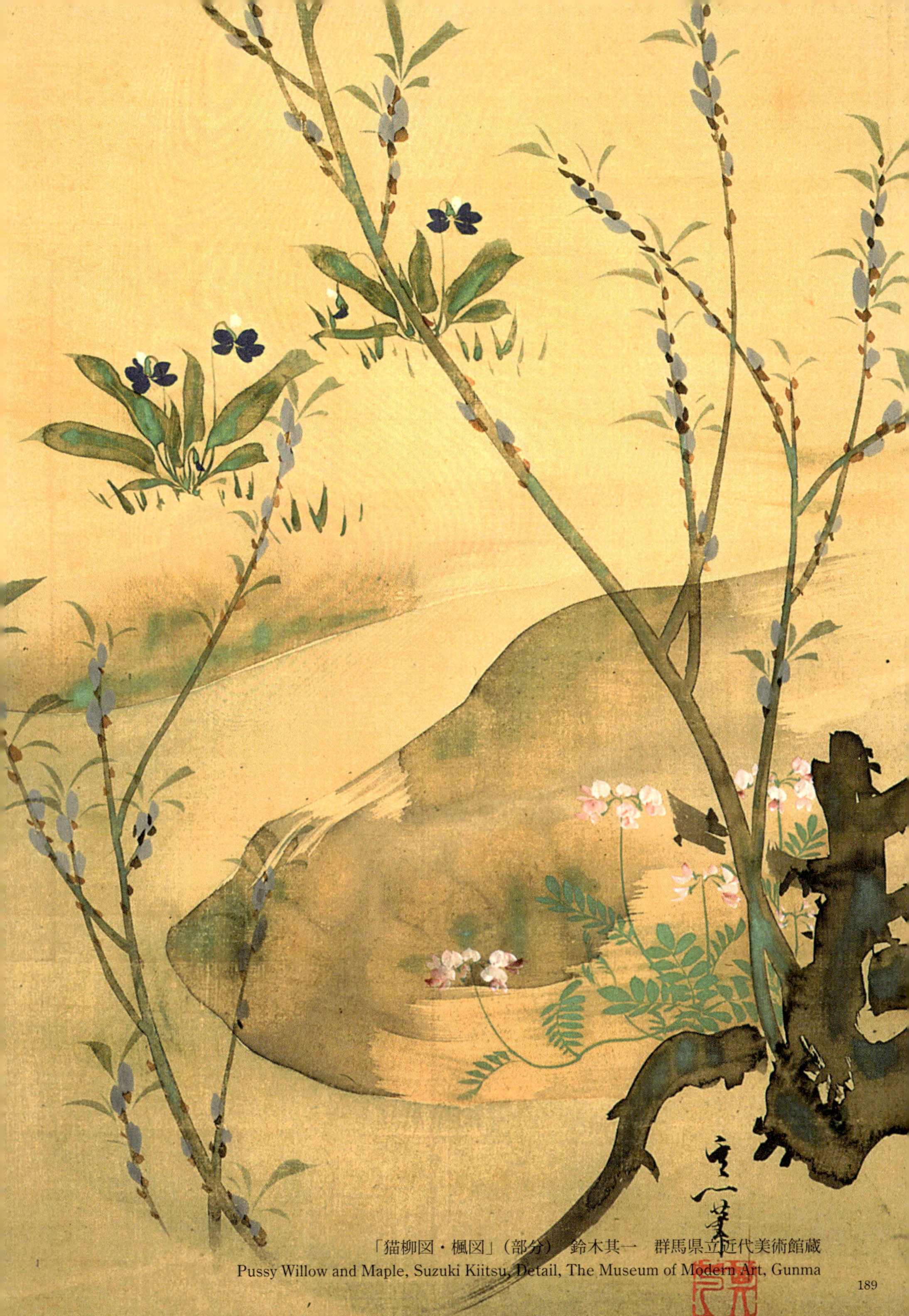

「猫柳図・楓図」（部分）　鈴木其一　群馬県立近代美術館蔵
Pussy Willow and Maple, Suzuki Kiitsu, Detail, The Museum of Modern Art, Gunma

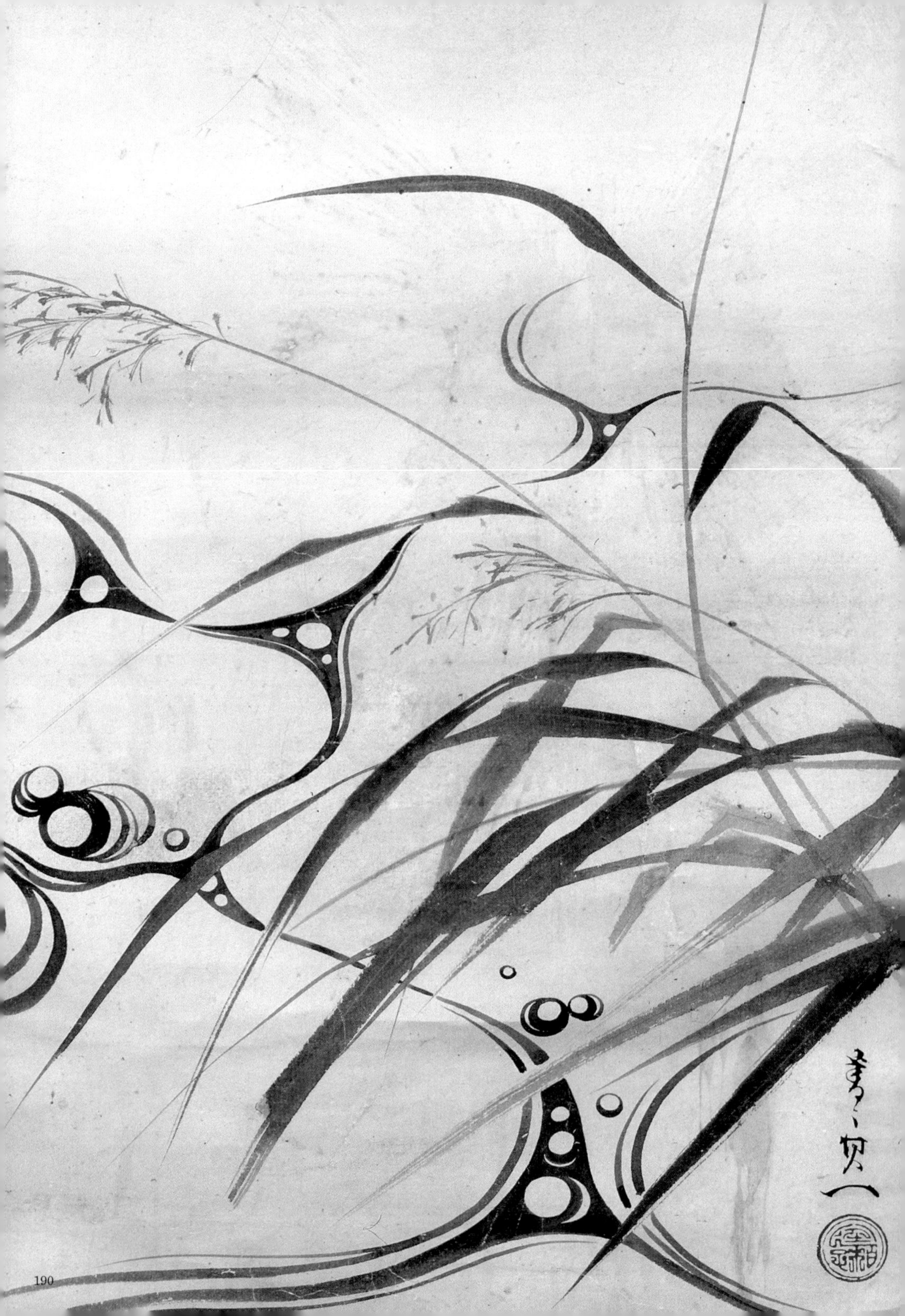

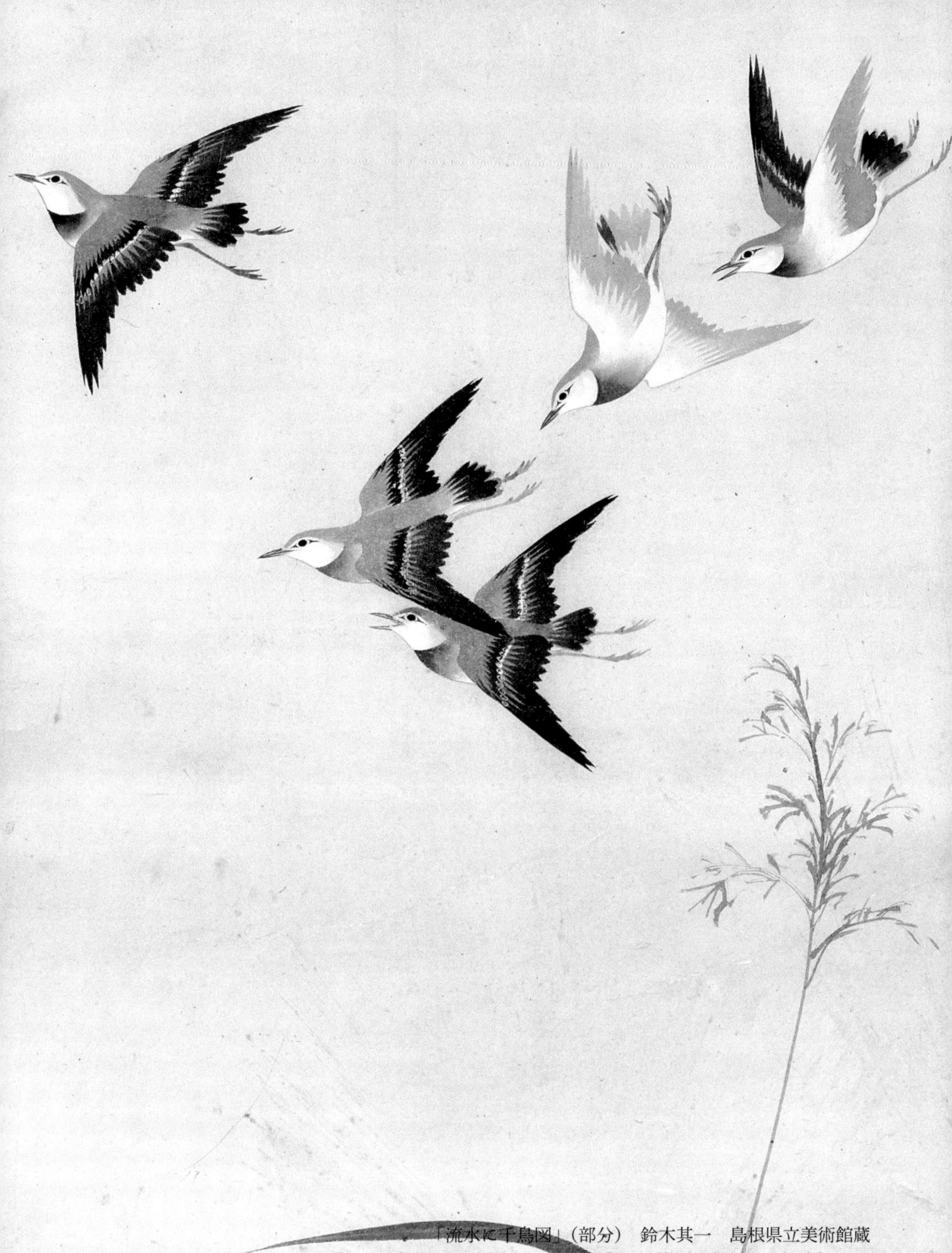

「流水に千鳥図」（部分）　鈴木其一　島根県立美術館蔵
Flowing Stream and Plovers, Detail, Suzuki Kiitsu, Shimane Art Museum

中村芳中

なかむら ほうちゅう　生年不詳〜文政 2 年（? - 1819）

京都に生まれ、のちに大坂に移住し活躍した。尾形光琳に私淑し、たらし込みの技法を用いたユーモラスでほのぼのとした装飾的画風が特徴である。また草花を描いた琳派風作品も多く、特に扇面画を数多く制作している。1799 年（寛政 11）から享和初めにかけて江戸に下り、『光琳画譜』（1802 年）を出版した。多くの狂歌本に挿絵を描き、俳諧も好んだと伝えられる。

Nakamura Hōchū (? - 1819)

Born in Kyoto, Hōchū lived in Osaka. Greatly influenced by Kōrin, he worked in a humorous, decorative style with skillful use of the tarashikomi technique, producing many paintings of flowers and grasses, particularly fan paintings, in the Rinpa style. In Edo in the early 1800s, he published the Kōrin Gafu, in 1802. He illustrated many books of humorous poems and was fond of haikai linked verse.

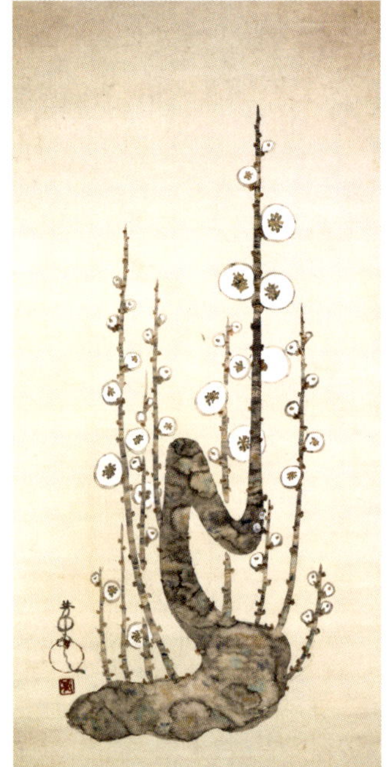

「白梅図」中村芳中
千葉市美術館蔵
White Plum Tree,
Nakamura Hōchū, Chiba
City Museum of Art

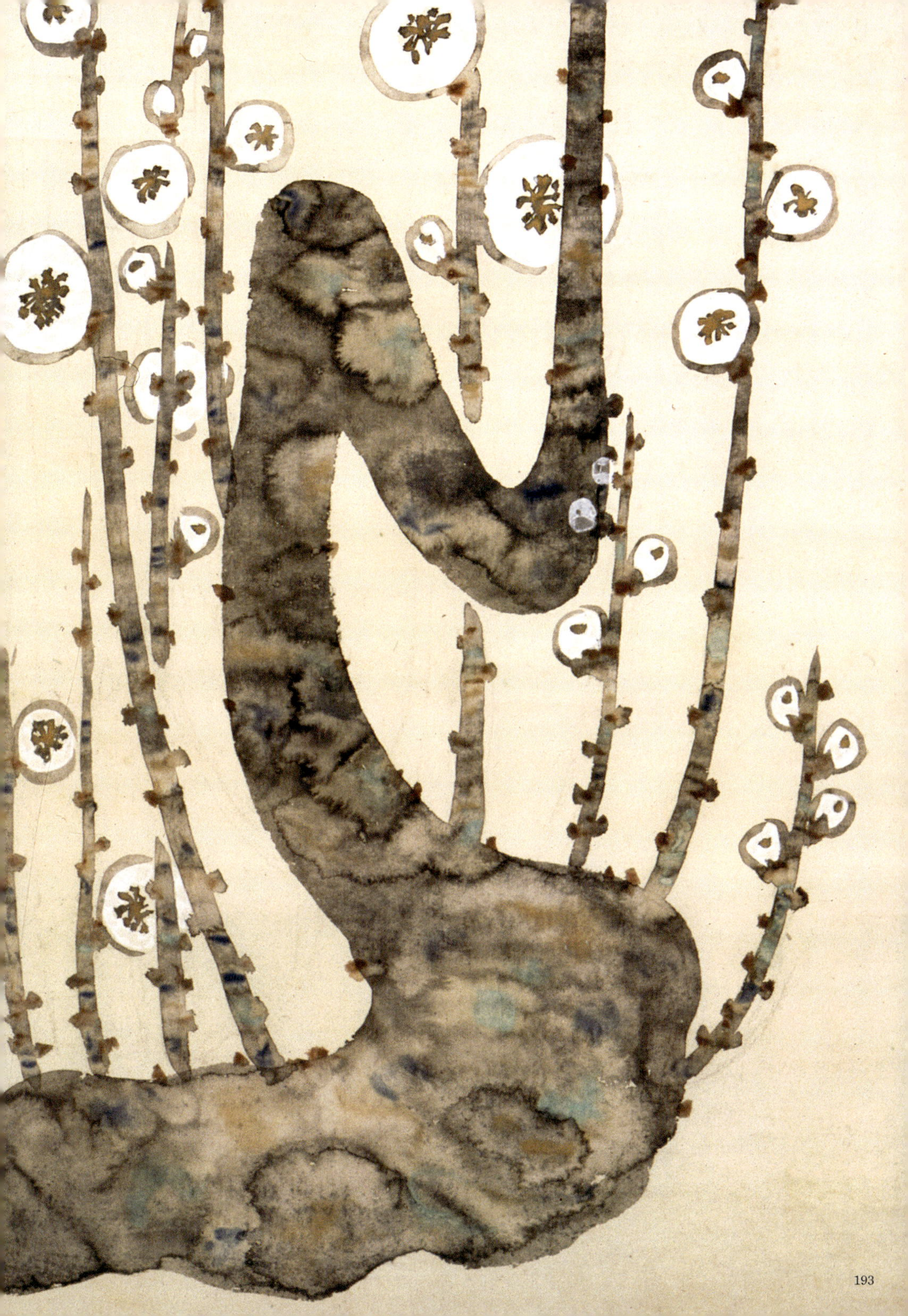

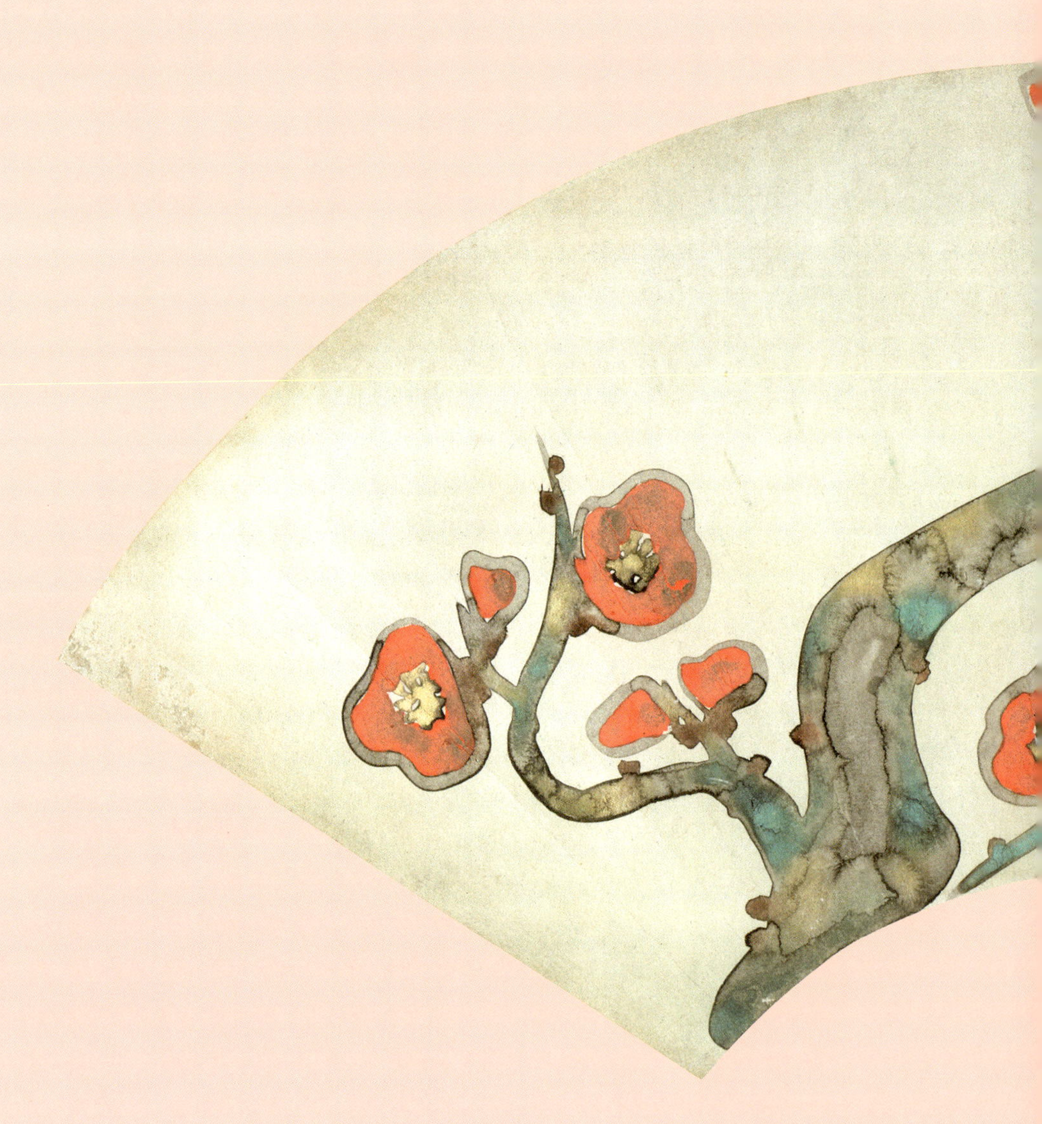

「梅図」 中村芳中 群馬県立近代美術館蔵
Plums, Nakamura Hōchū, The Museum of Modern Art, Gunma

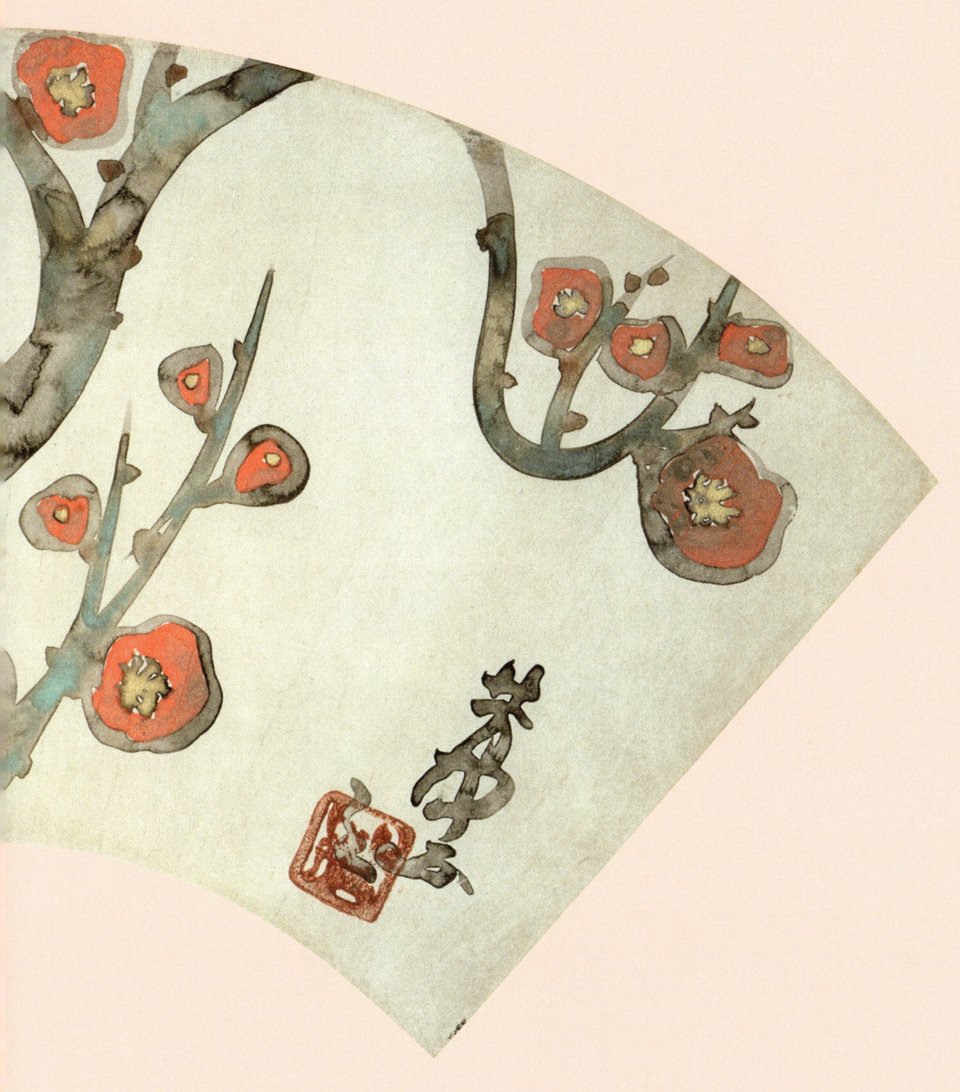

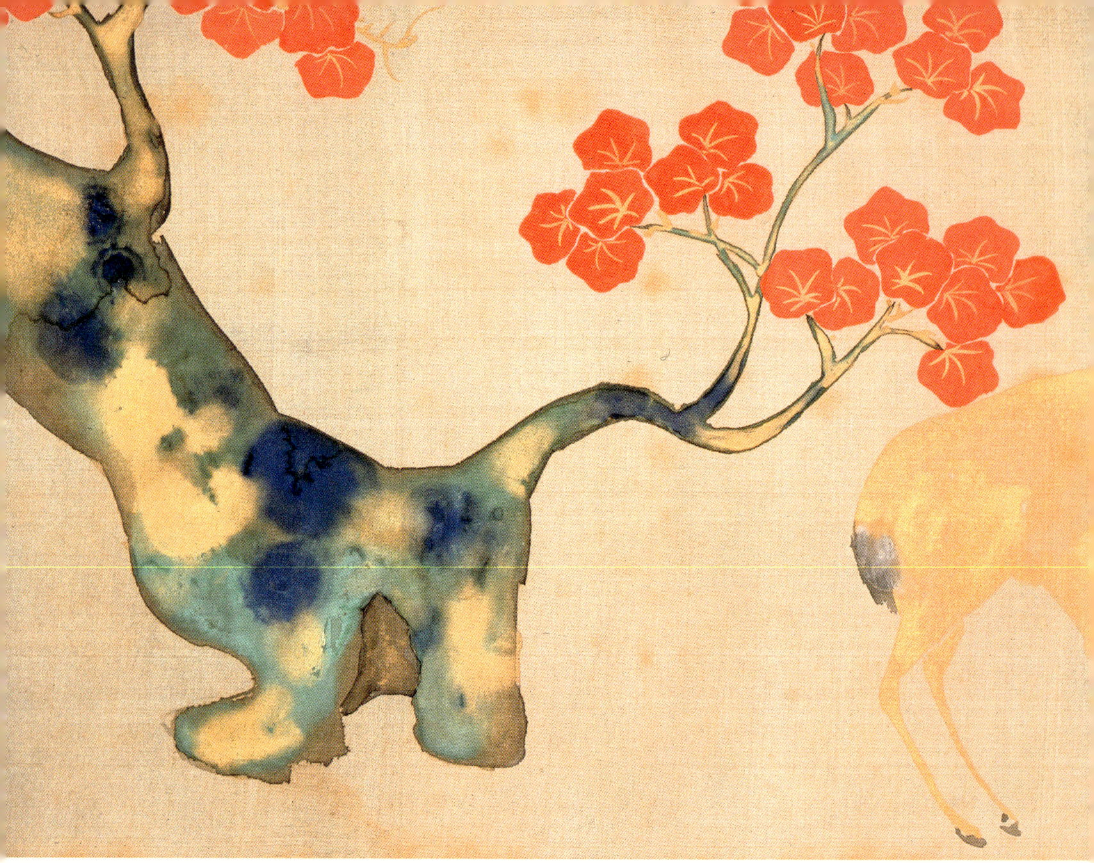

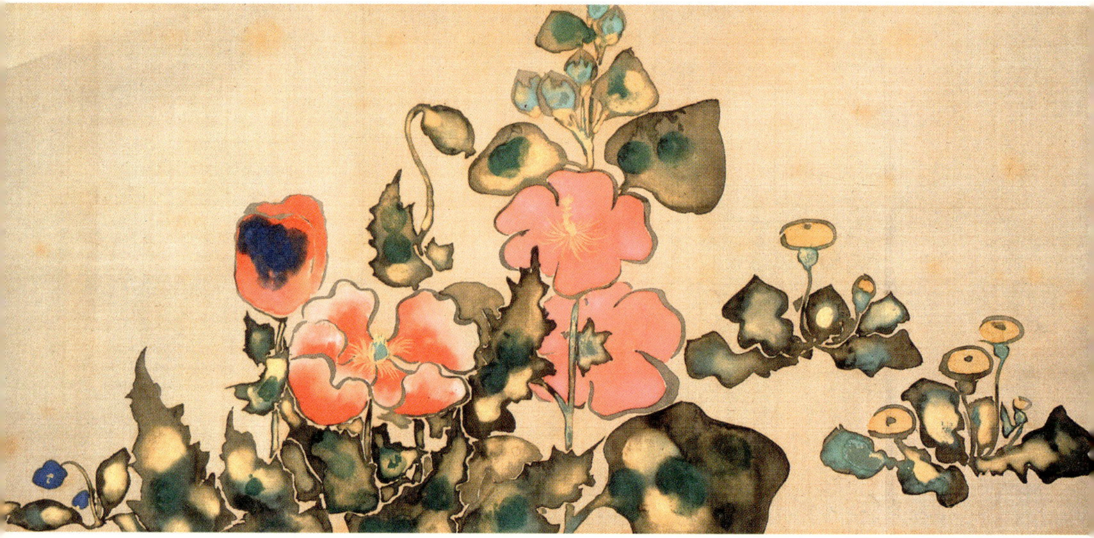

「人物花鳥図巻」　中村芳中　真田宝物館蔵
Scroll of Portrait, Flowers and Birds Pictures, Nakamura Hōchū, The Sanada Treasures Museum, Nagano

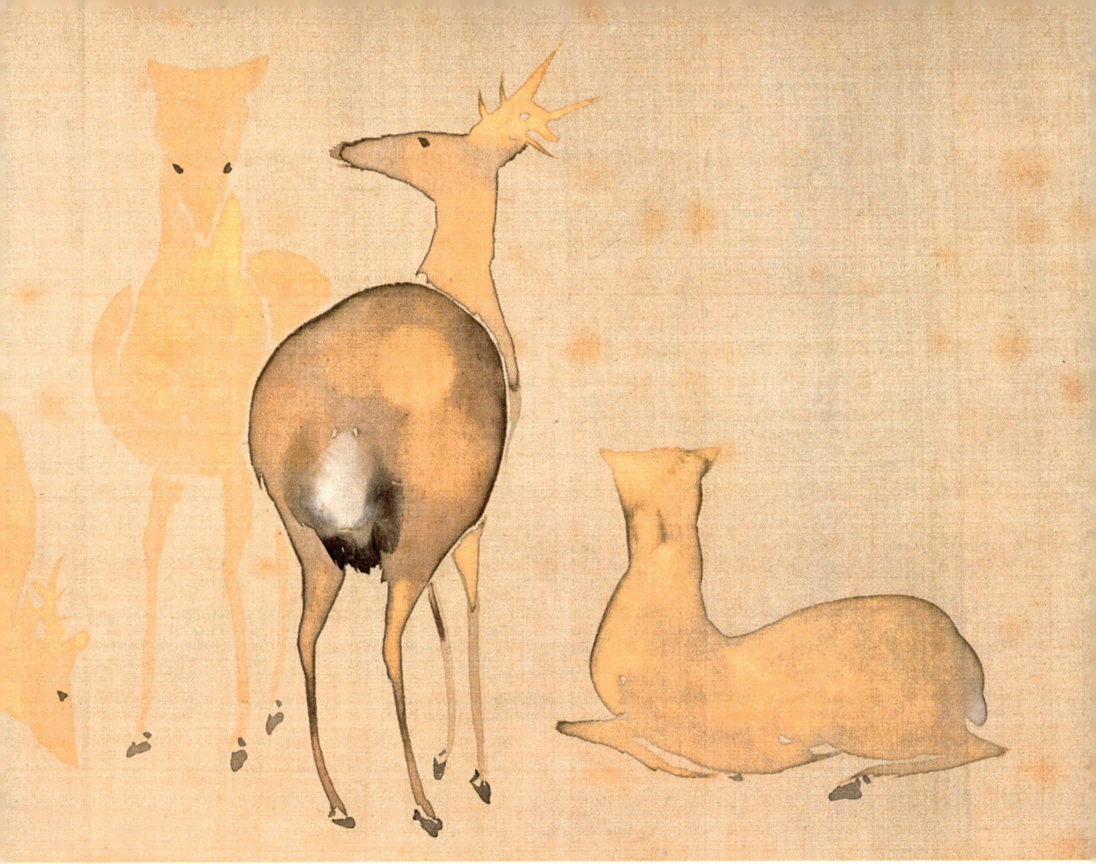

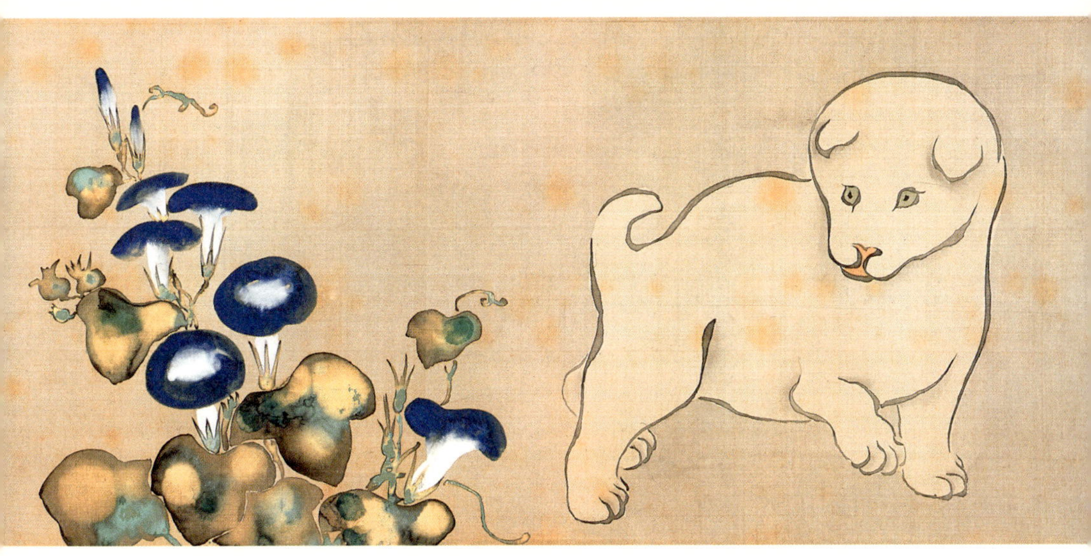

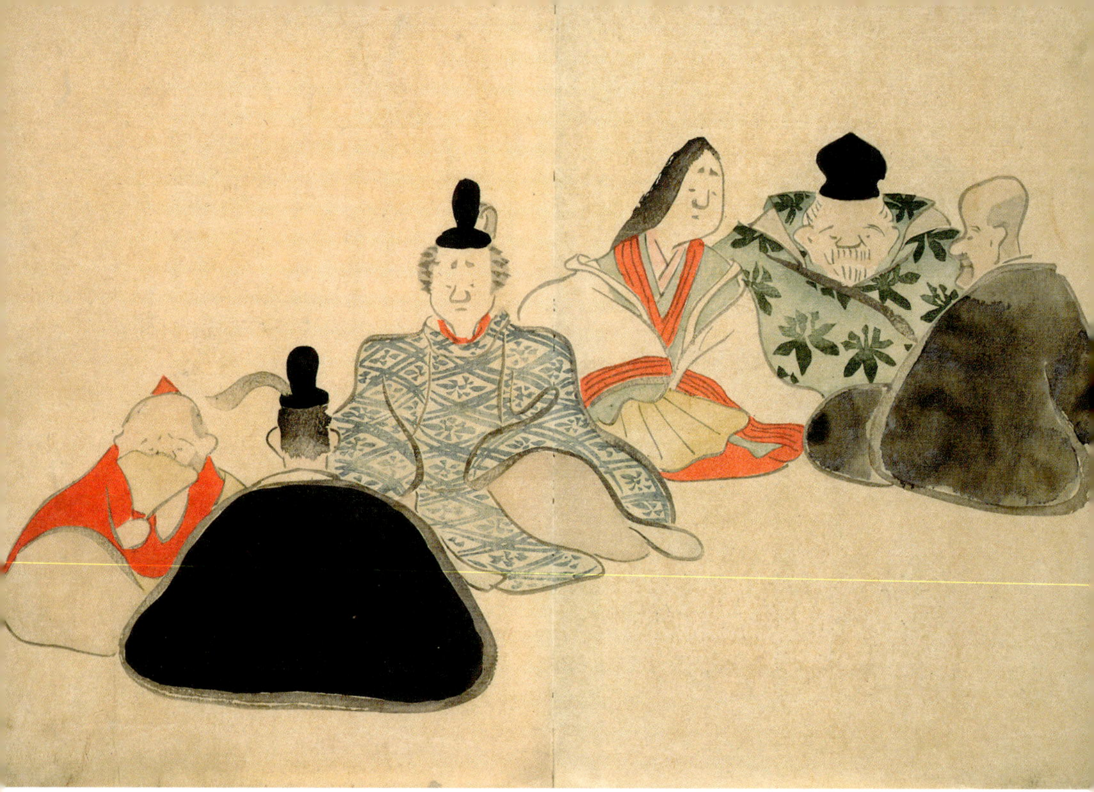

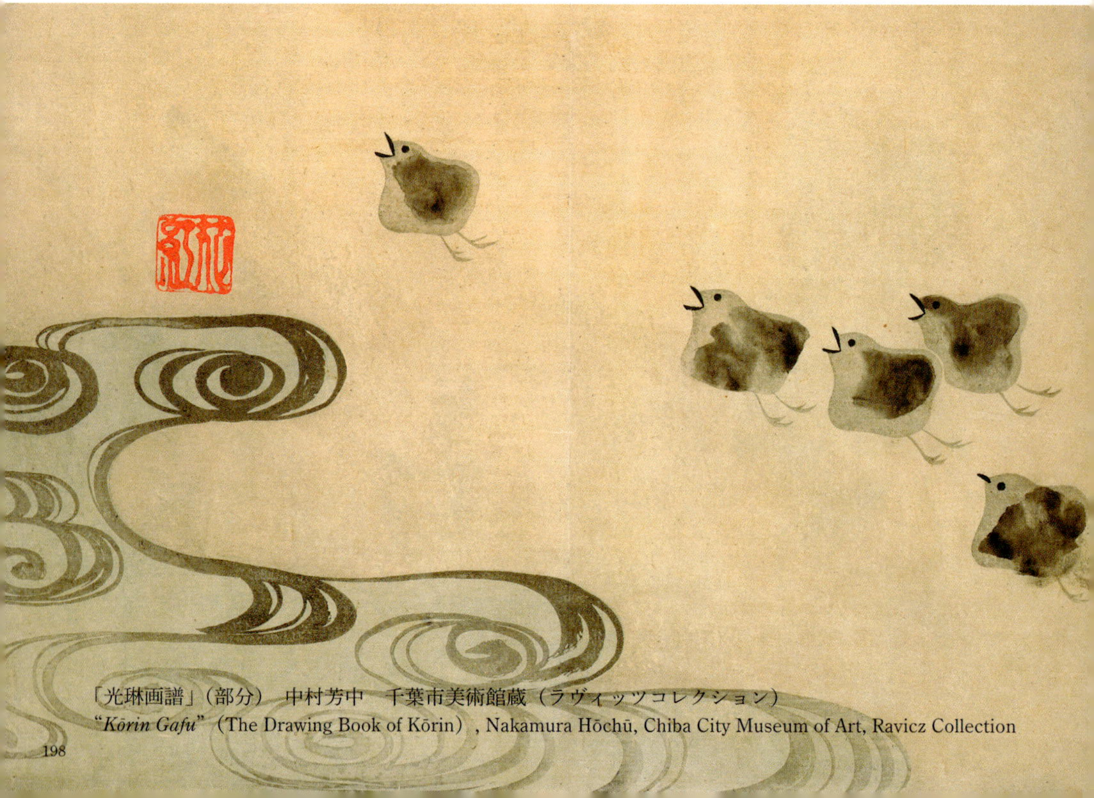

「光琳画譜」（部分）　中村芳中　千葉市美術館蔵（ラヴィッツコレクション）
Kōrin Gafu (The Drawing Book of Kōrin), Nakamura Hōchū, Chiba City Museum of Art, Ravicz Collection

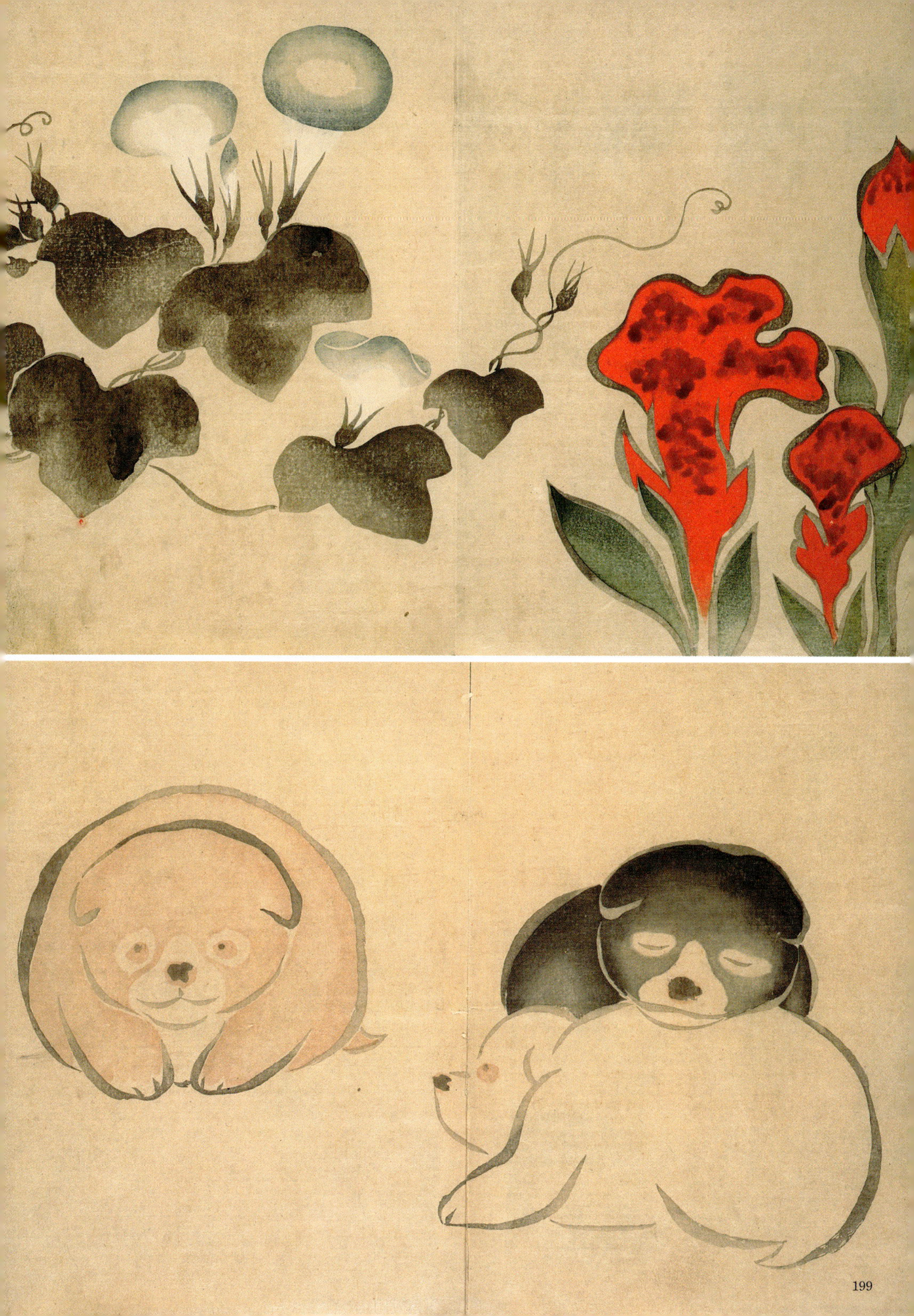

池田孤邨　いけだ こそん

享和元年〜慶応２年（1801 - 66）

越後の出身で、若い時に江戸に出て酒井抱一に師事し琳派様式を学ぶ。抱一工房では鈴木其一と共に中核をなした一人である。書画の鑑定に優れ、茶や和歌も好んだと伝えられる

俵屋宗理　たわらや そうり

生没年不詳

幕府御用絵師の住吉広守に学んだが、のち宗達、光琳の画風に私淑して俵屋宗理を名乗る。作風は光琳風であるが、19世紀になって開花する江戸琳派の先駆け的な画風も見せている。

市川其融　いちかわ きゆう

生没年不詳

鈴木其一門下の古河藩士で、安政年間（1854-60）に活躍した。鮮明な色彩と明確な構図には、其融のこざっぱりした性格がうかがえる。

酒井道一　さかい どういつ

弘化２年〜大正２年（1845 -1913）

酒井抱一の弟子である山本素堂の次男で、絵を父および鈴木其一に学んだ。明治の新しい気運に触れ、博覧会にも出品し活躍、琳派の画風を明治の画壇に伝えた。

田中抱二　たなか ほうじ

文化９年〜明治17年（1812 -84）

江戸両替町の生まれで、酒井抱一に師事した。幕府の御用絵師となり、晩年は向島で隠遁生活を送った。

山本光一　やまもと こういつ

天保４年〜明治36年（1833 -1903）

酒井抱一の弟子である山本素堂の長男で、酒井道一の兄。酒井鶯一の門下で名を信敬といい、靖々、皎々、露聲、木石閑人などと号した。

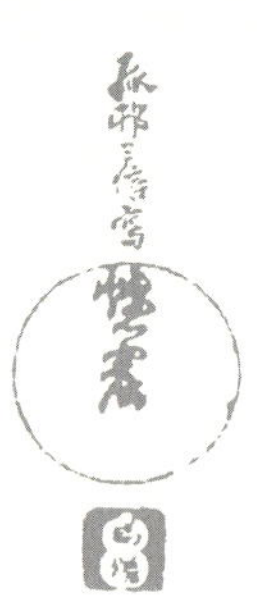
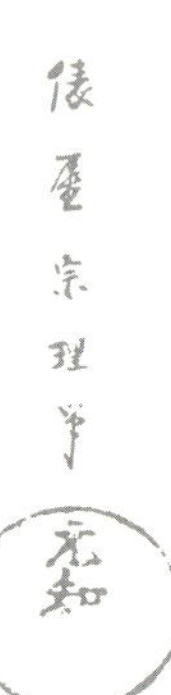

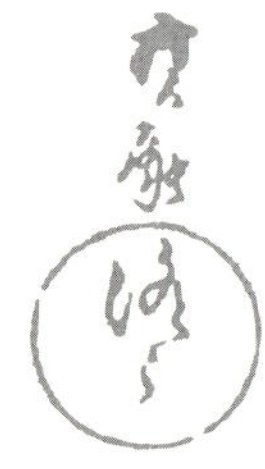
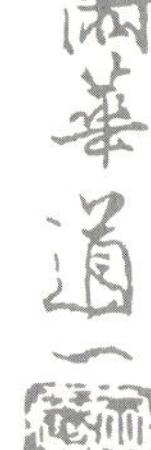

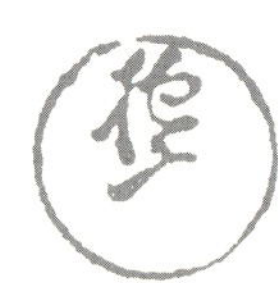
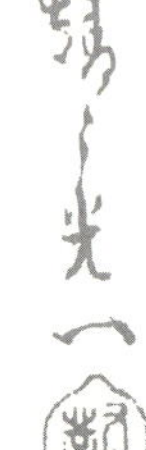

「四季草花図」　池田孤邨
東京藝術大学大学美術館蔵
Flowers and Grasses of the
Four Seasons, Ikeda Koson, The
University Art Museum-Tokyo
University of the Arts

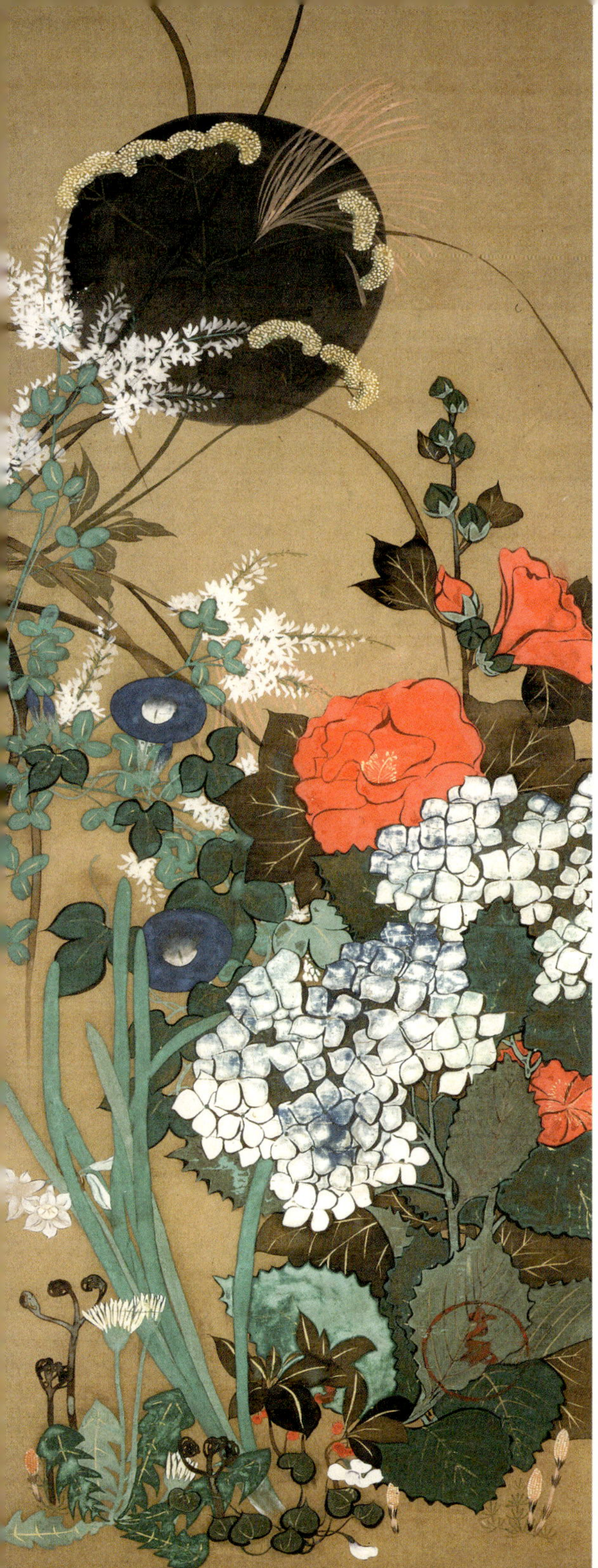

Ikeda Koson (1801 – 1866)
A native of Echigo, Koson moved to Edo and studied the Rinpa style with Sakai Hōitsu, becoming, with Suzuki Kiitsu, core members of the Hōitsu studio. A connoisseur of calligraphy and painting, he enjoyed the tea ceremony and waka poetry.

Tawaraya Sōri (dates uncertain)
Sōri studied with Sumiyoshi Hiromori, official painter to the shogunate, then, influenced by Sōtatsu and Kōrin's work, changed his name to Tawaraya Sōri. His work, while in the style of Kōrin, was a harbinger of the 19th century Edo Rinpa style.

Ichikawa Kiyū (dates uncertain)
A samurai of the Koga domain and student of Suzuki Kiitsu, Kiyū was active around 1854-60. Fresh colors and crisp compositions suggest Kiyū's dapper character.

Sakai Dōitsu (1845 – 1913)
Son of Yamamoto Sodō, a student of Sakai Hōitsu, he studied painting with his father and with Suzuki Kiitsu. In the new world of Meiji, he submitted work to expositions and introduced the Rinpa style to Meiji art circles.

Tanaka Hōji (1812 – 84)
Born in Edo, Hōji studied with Sakai Hōitsu, becoming an official painter to the Tokugawa bakufu. He spent the latter part of his life in seclusion in Mukōjima.

Yamamoto Kōitsu (1833 – 1903)
Elder brother of Sakai Dōitsu and son of Yamamoto Sodō, who studied with Sakai Hōitsu, Kōitsu also used the names Nobutaka, Seisei, Kōkō, Rosei, and Bokuseki Kanjin.

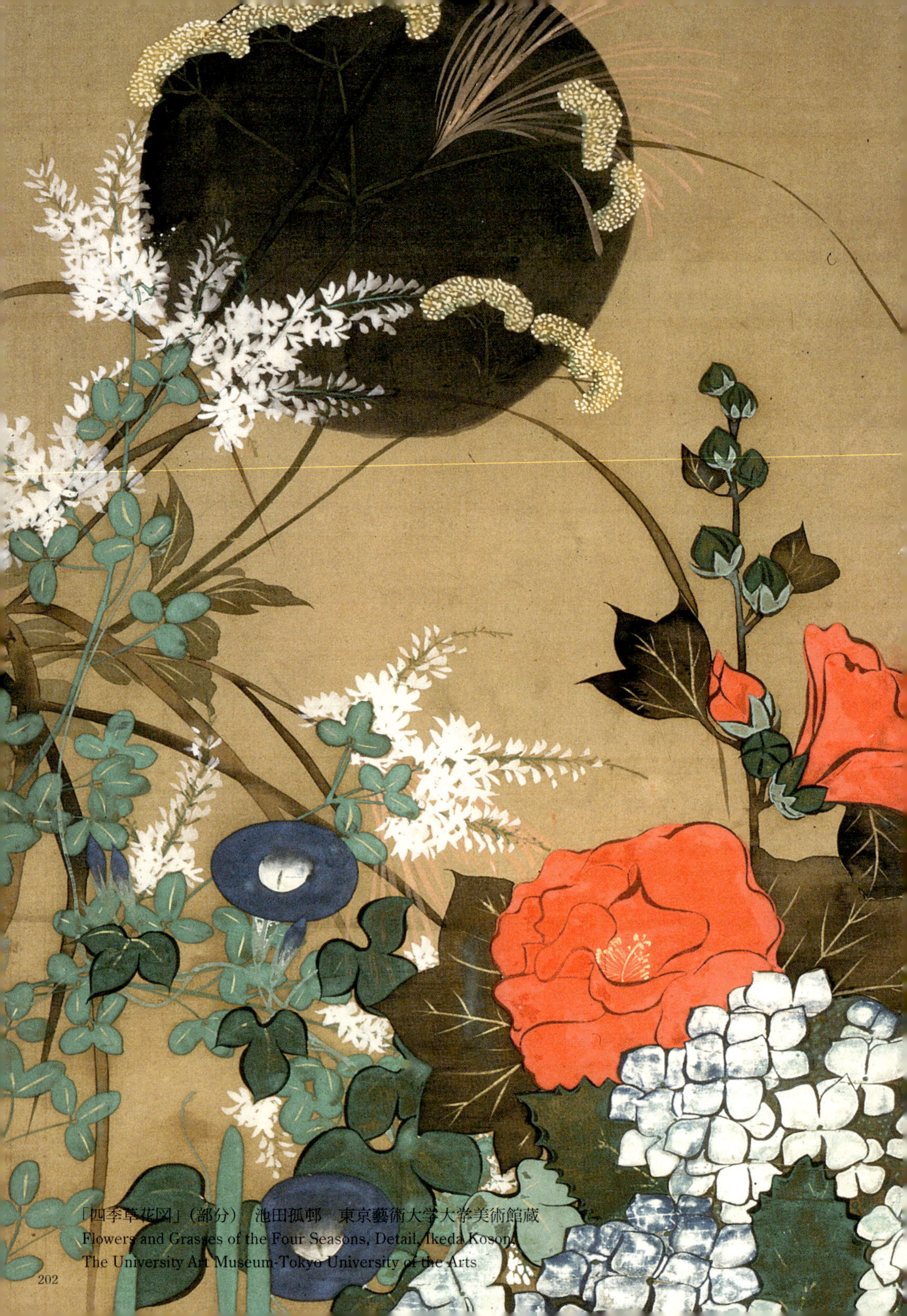

「四季草花図」（部分）　池田孤邨　東京藝術大学大学美術館蔵
Flowers and Grasses of the Four Seasons, Detail, Ikeda Koson
The University Art Museum-Tokyo University of the Arts

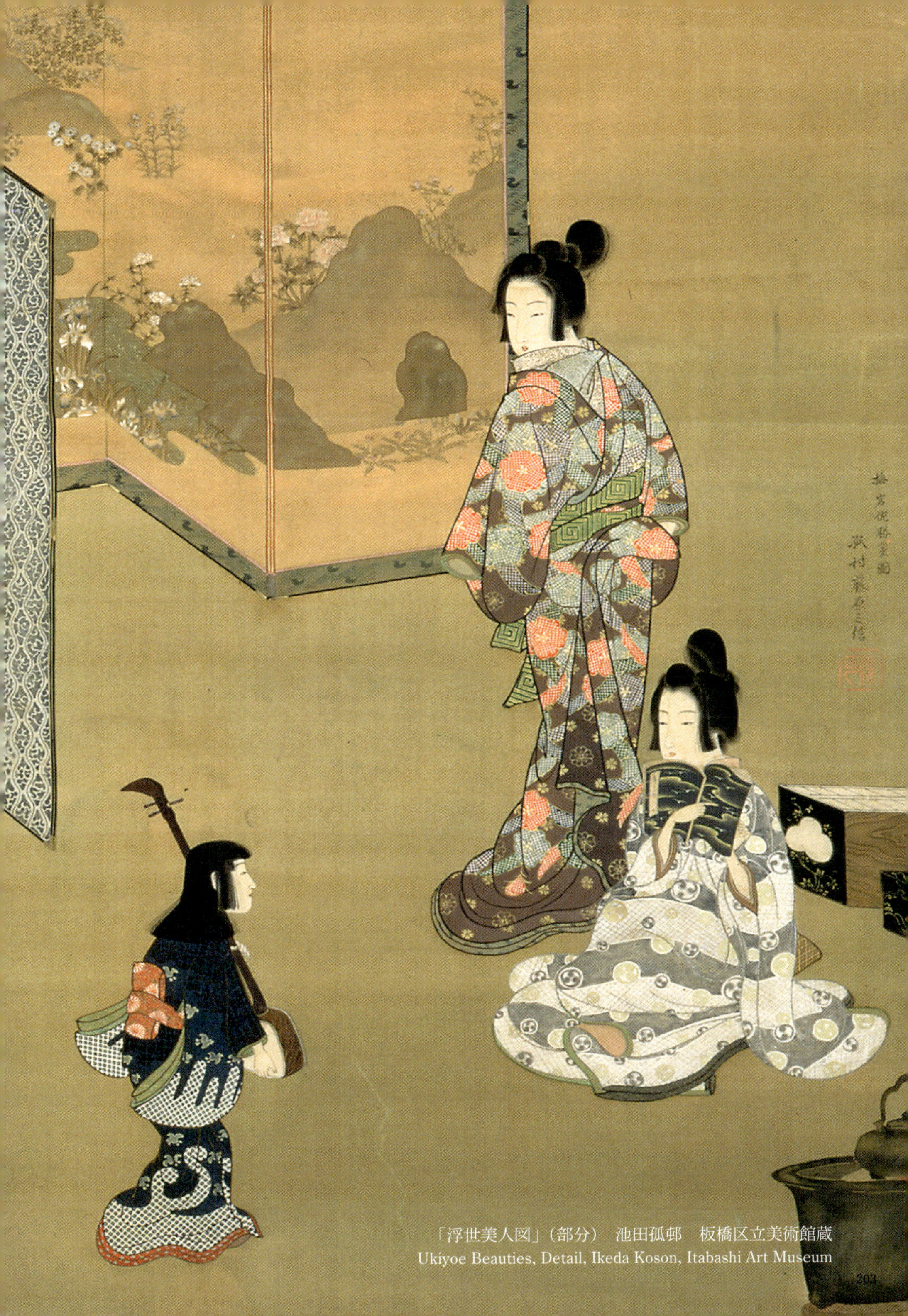

「浮世美人図」（部分）　池田孤邨　板橋区立美術館蔵
Ukiyoe Beauties, Detail, Ikeda Koson, Itabashi Art Museum

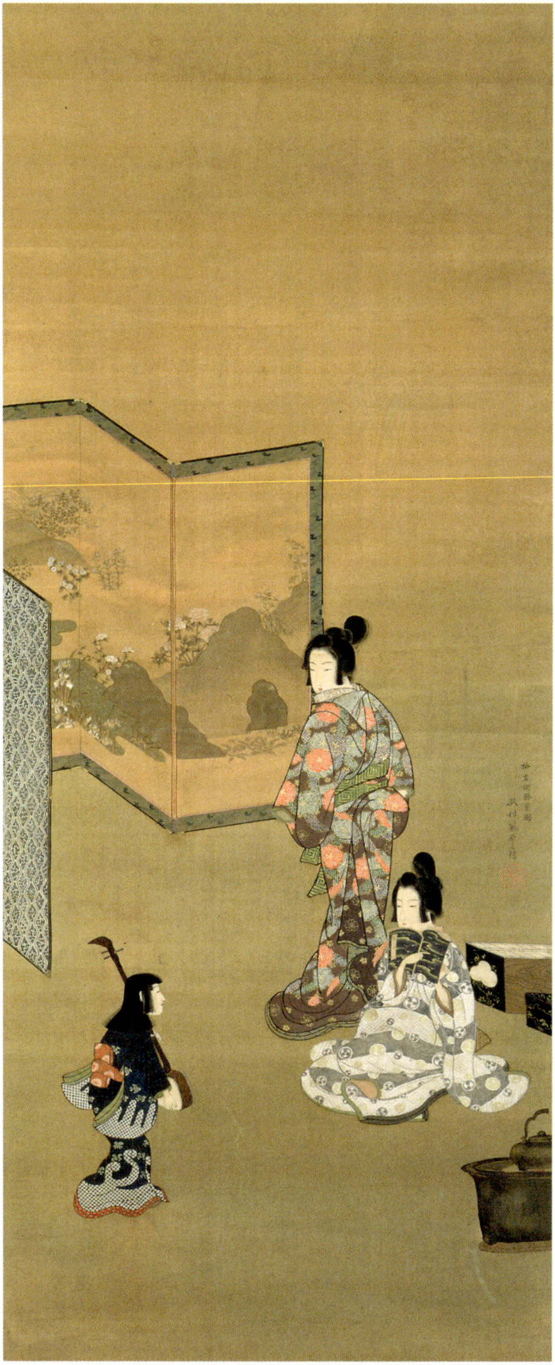

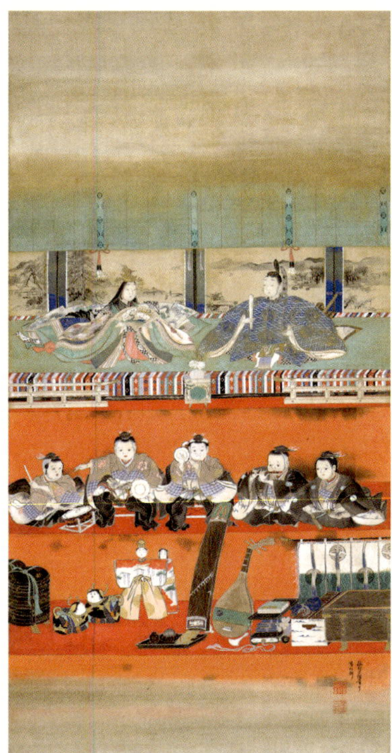

「雛祭図」　池田孤邨
板橋区立美術館蔵
The Doll's Festival, Ikeda
Koson, Itabashi Art
Museum

「浮世美人図」　池田孤邨
板橋区立美術館蔵
Ukiyoe Beauties, Detail, Ikeda
Koson, Itabashi Art Museum

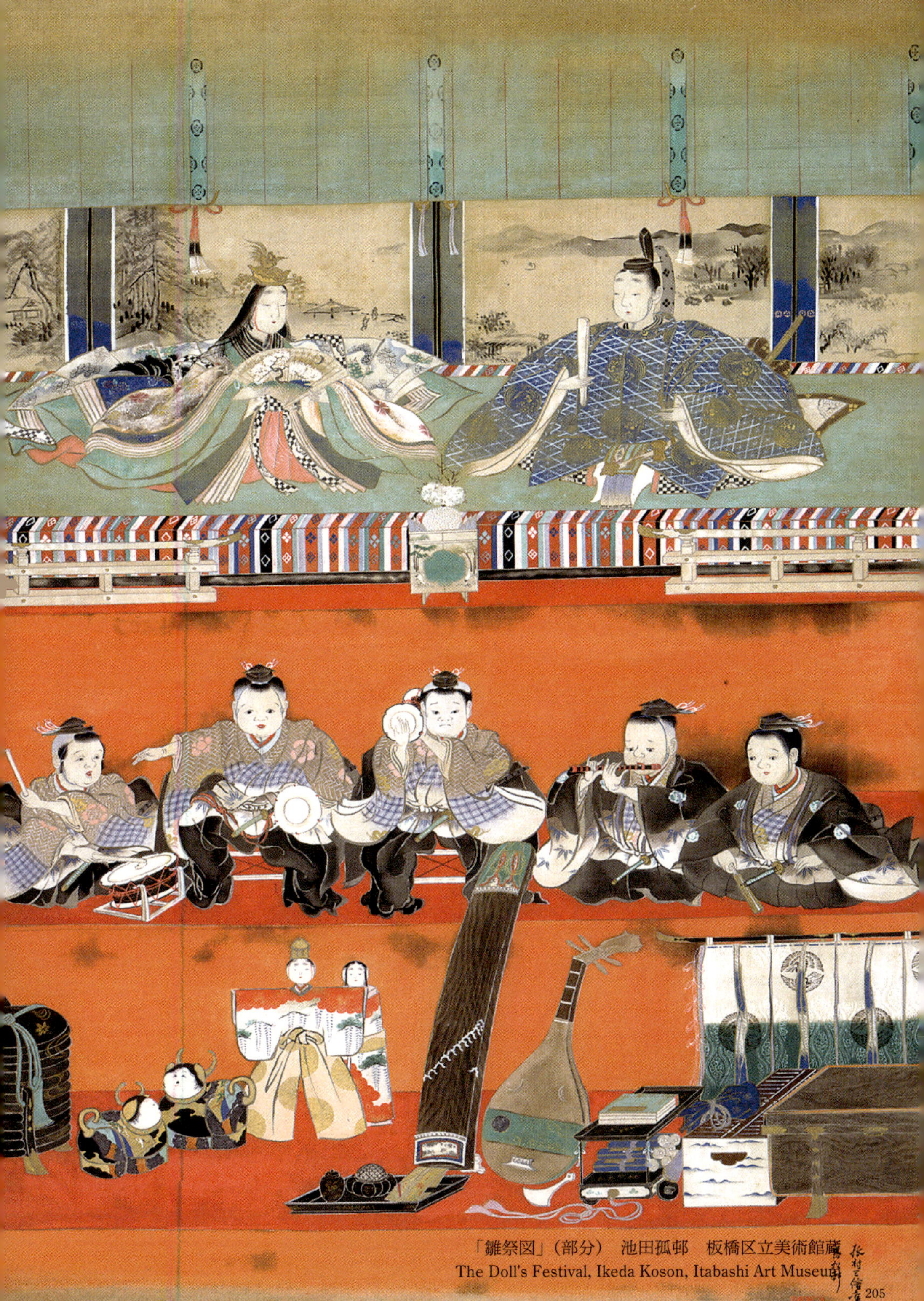

「雛祭図」（部分）　池田孤邨　板橋区立美術館蔵
The Doll's Festival, Ikeda Koson, Itabashi Art Museum

205

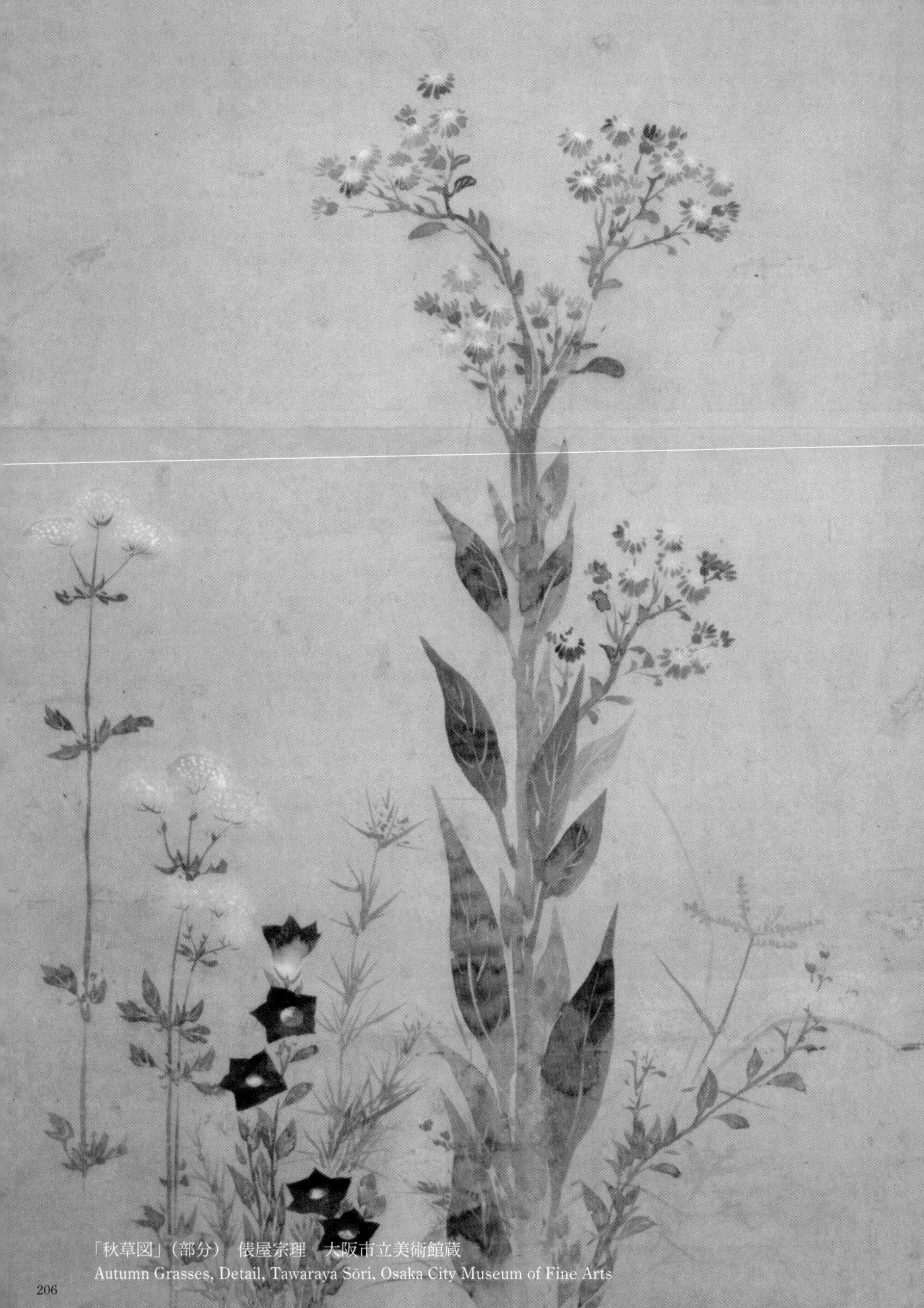

「秋草図」（部分）　俵屋宗理　大阪市立美術館蔵
Autumn Grasses, Detail, Tawaraya Sōri, Osaka City Museum of Fine Arts

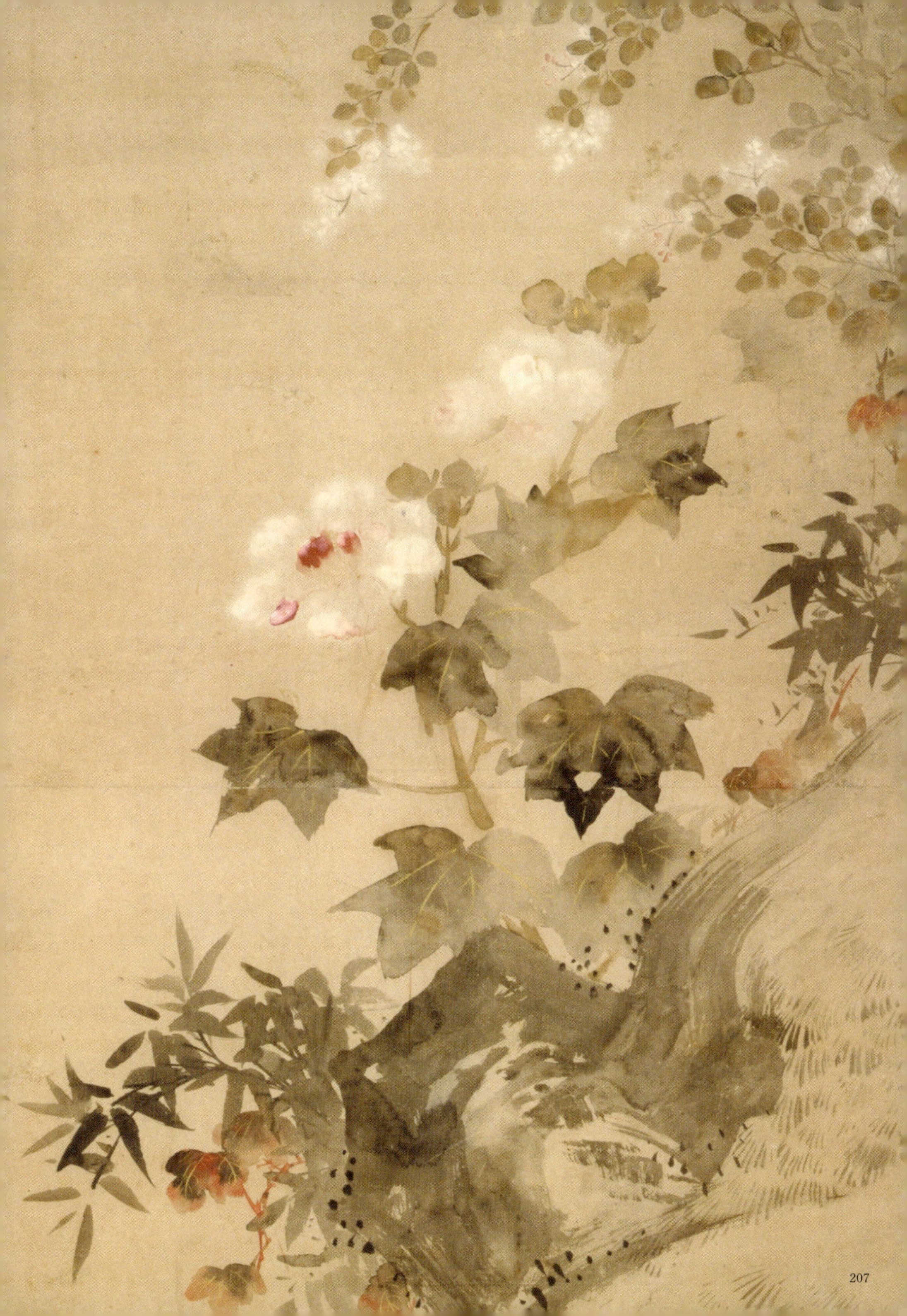

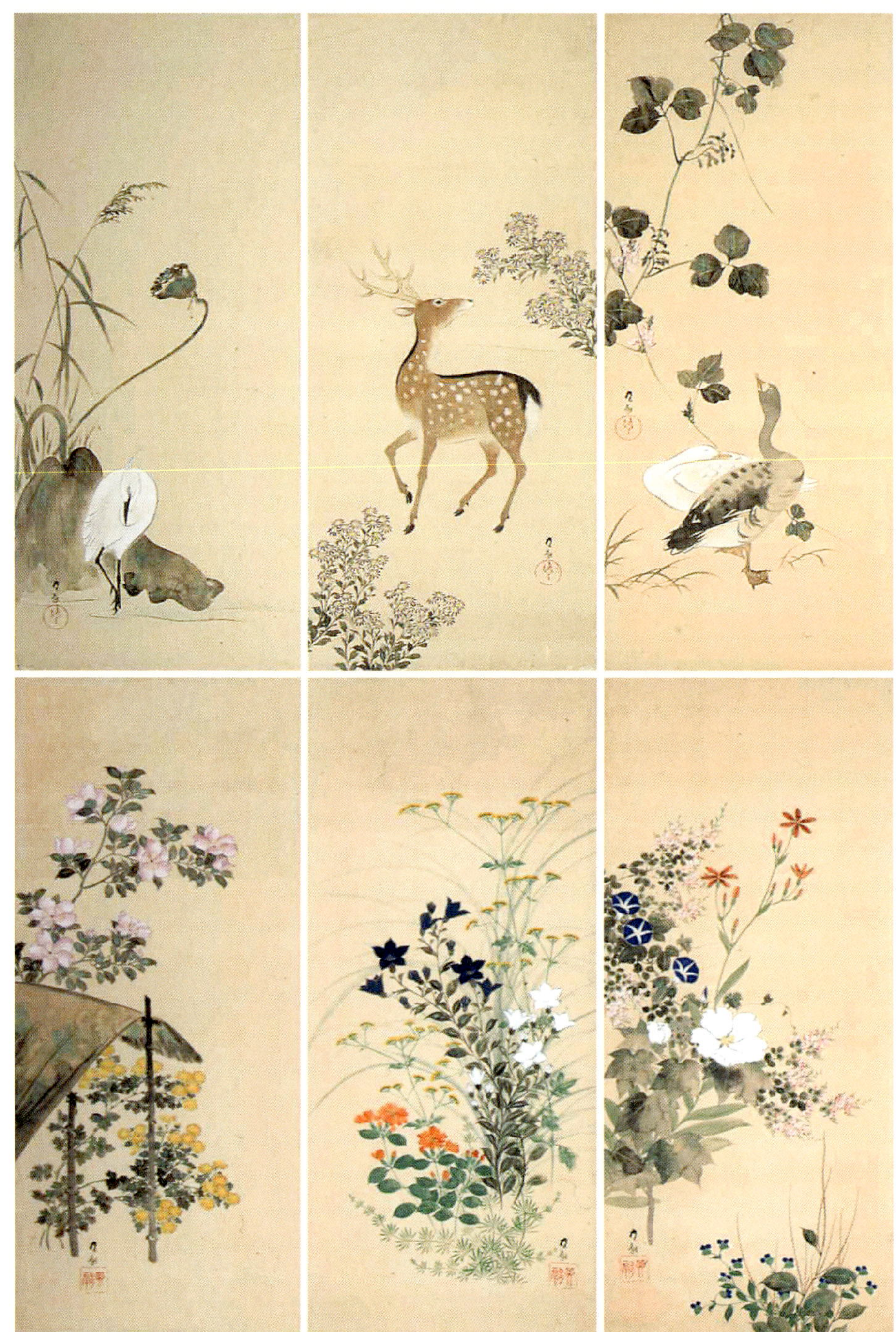

「四季草花鳥獣図押絵貼屏風」　市川其融　茨城県立歴史館蔵
Flowers, Birds and Animals of the Four Seasons, Ichikawa Kiyū, Ibaraki Prefectural Archives and Museum

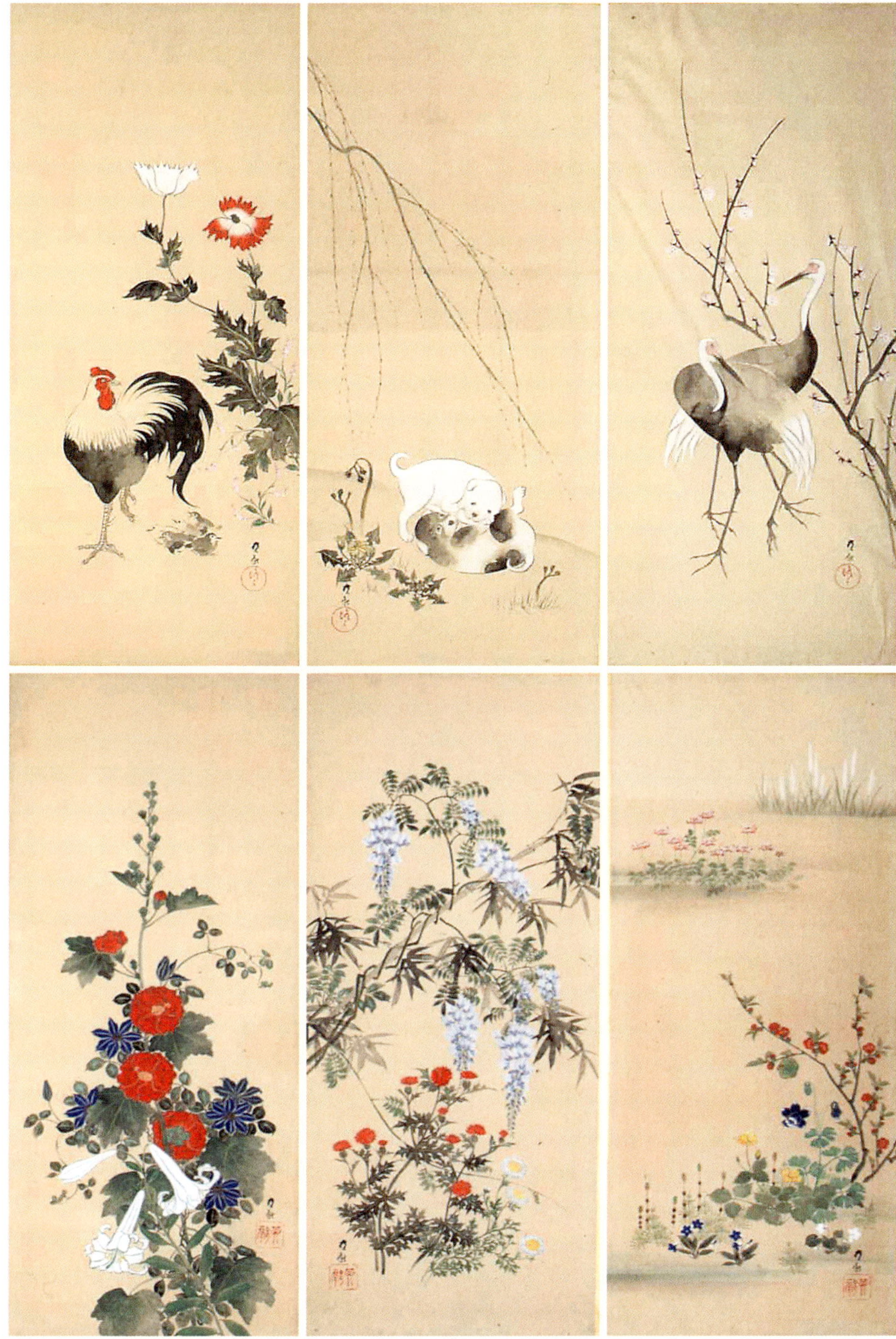

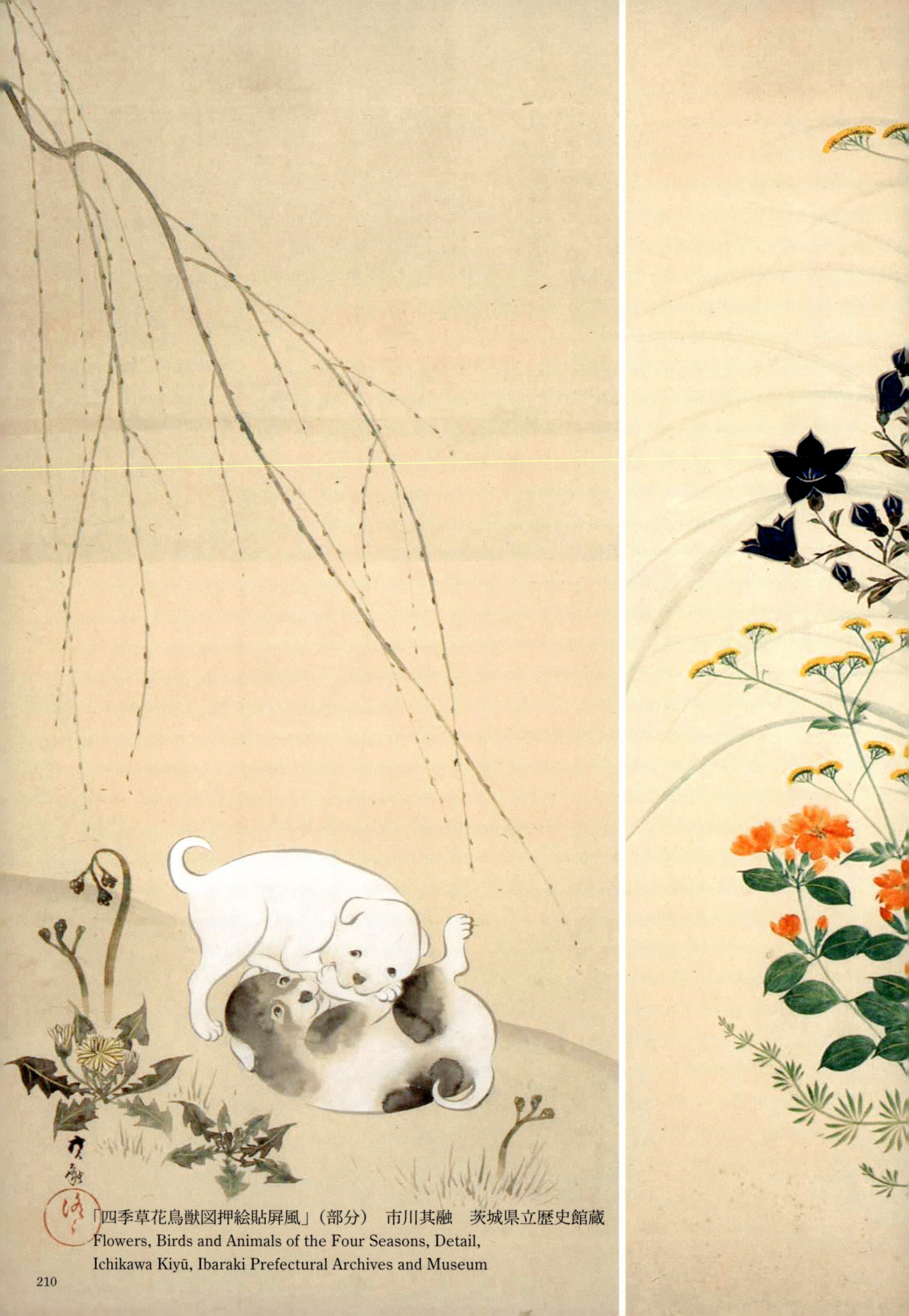

「四季草花鳥獣図押絵貼屏風」（部分）　市川其融　茨城県立歴史館蔵
Flowers, Birds and Animals of the Four Seasons, Detail,
Ichikawa Kiyū, Ibaraki Prefectural Archives and Museum

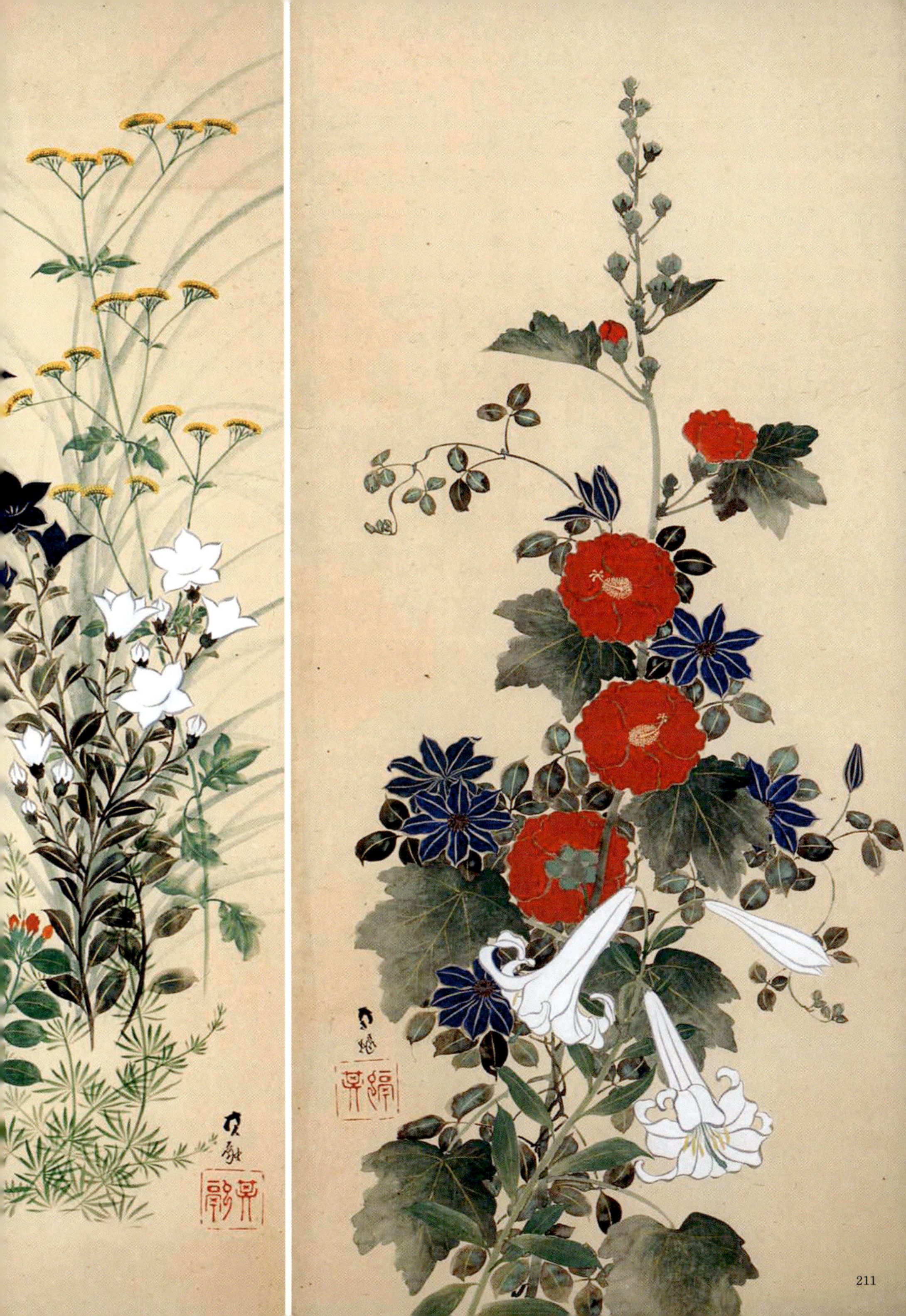

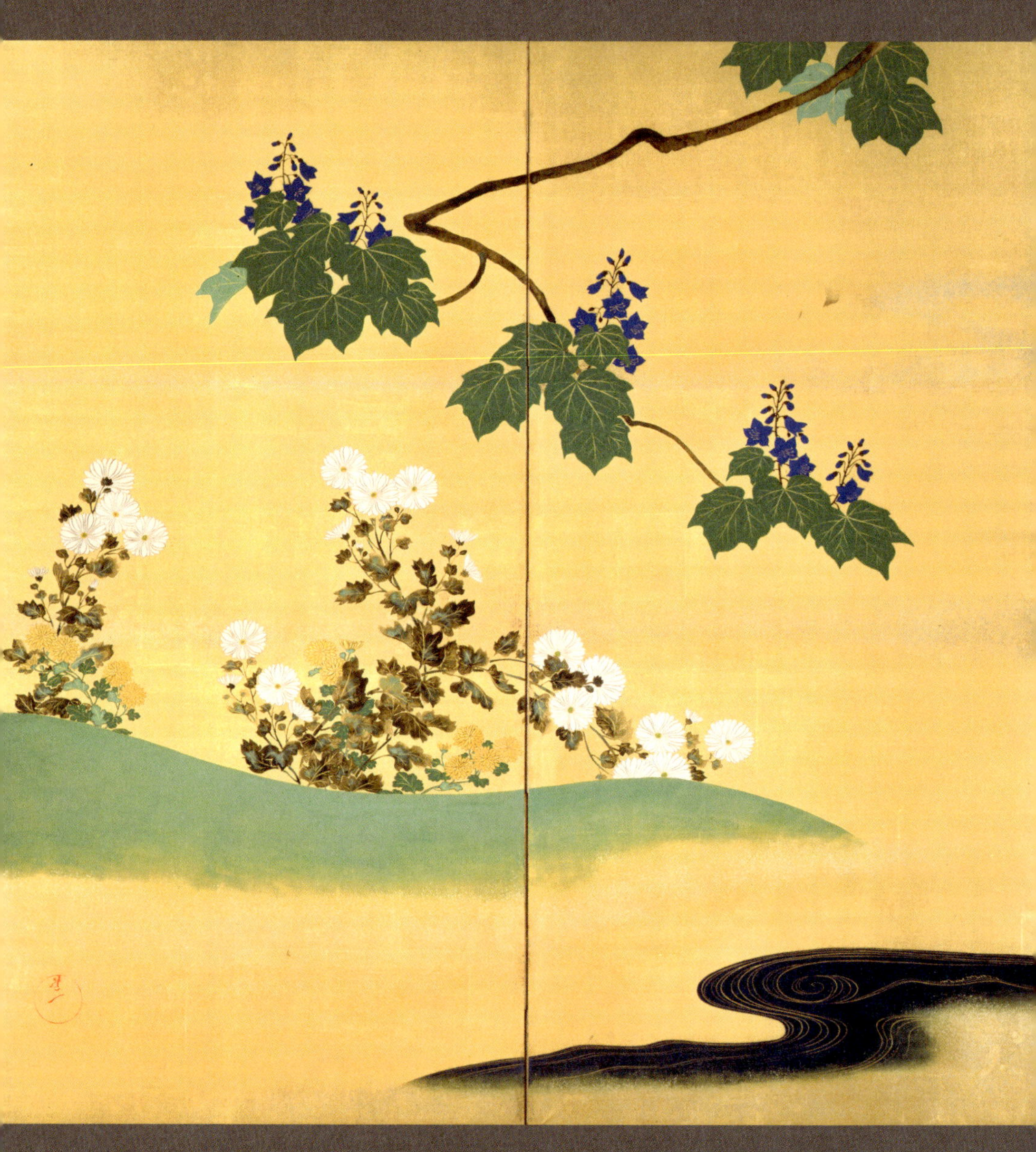

「桐菊流水図屏風」 酒井道一　板橋区立美術館蔵
Paulownia and Chrysanthemums, Sakai Dōitsu, Itabashi Art Museum

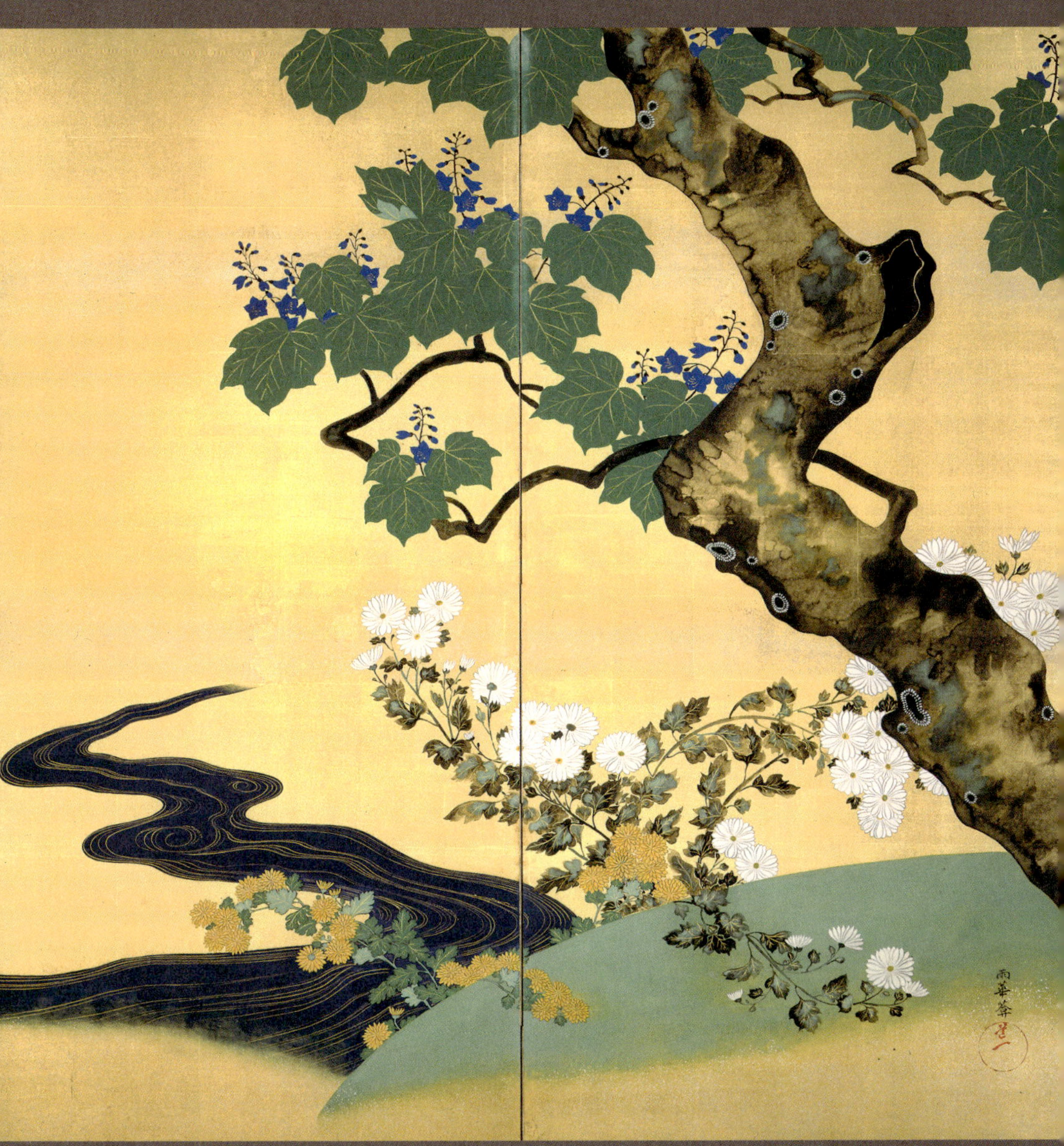

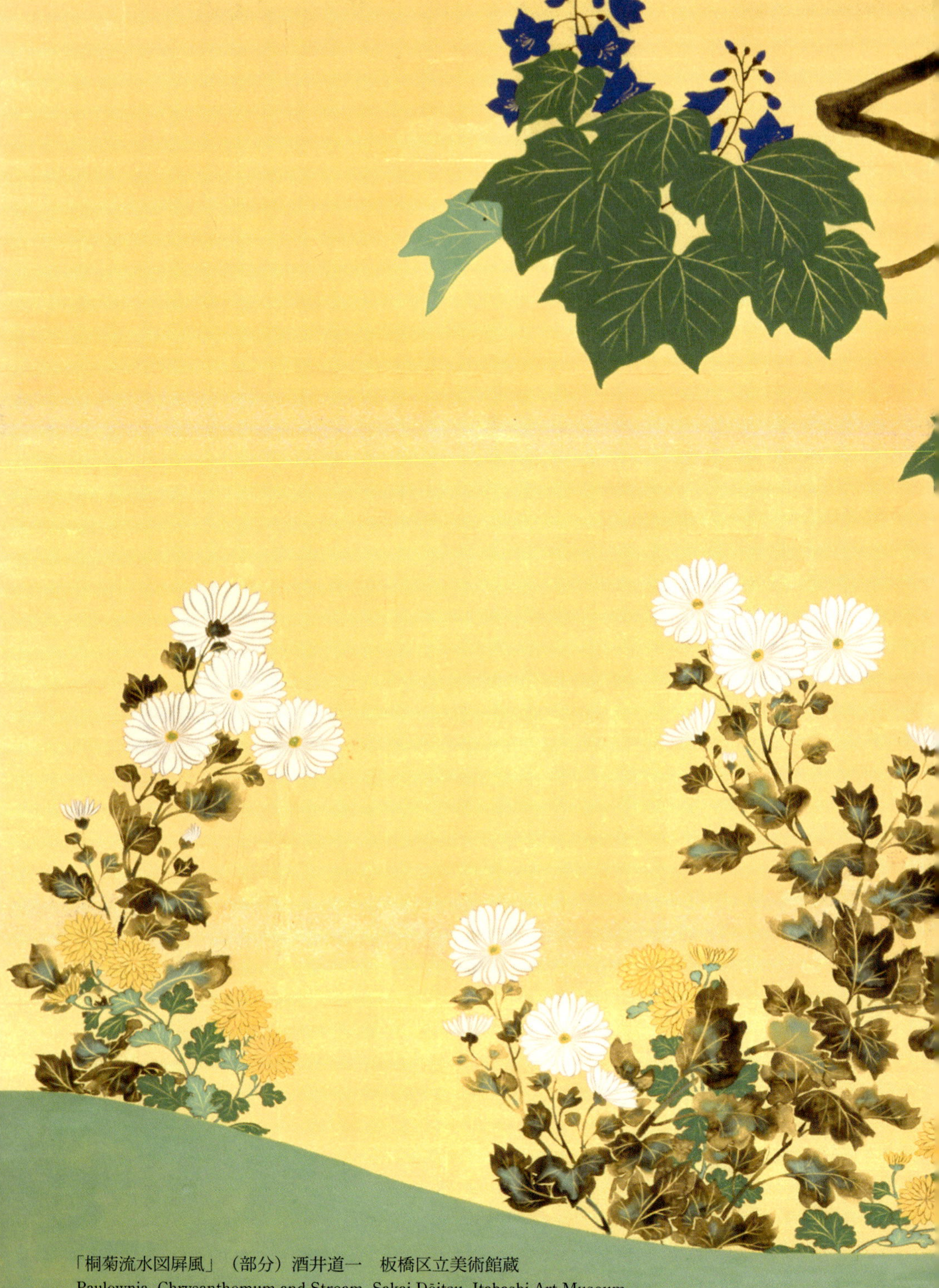

「桐菊流水図屏風」（部分）酒井道一　板橋区立美術館蔵
Paulownia, Chrysanthemum and Stream, Sakai Dōitsu, Itabashi Art Museum

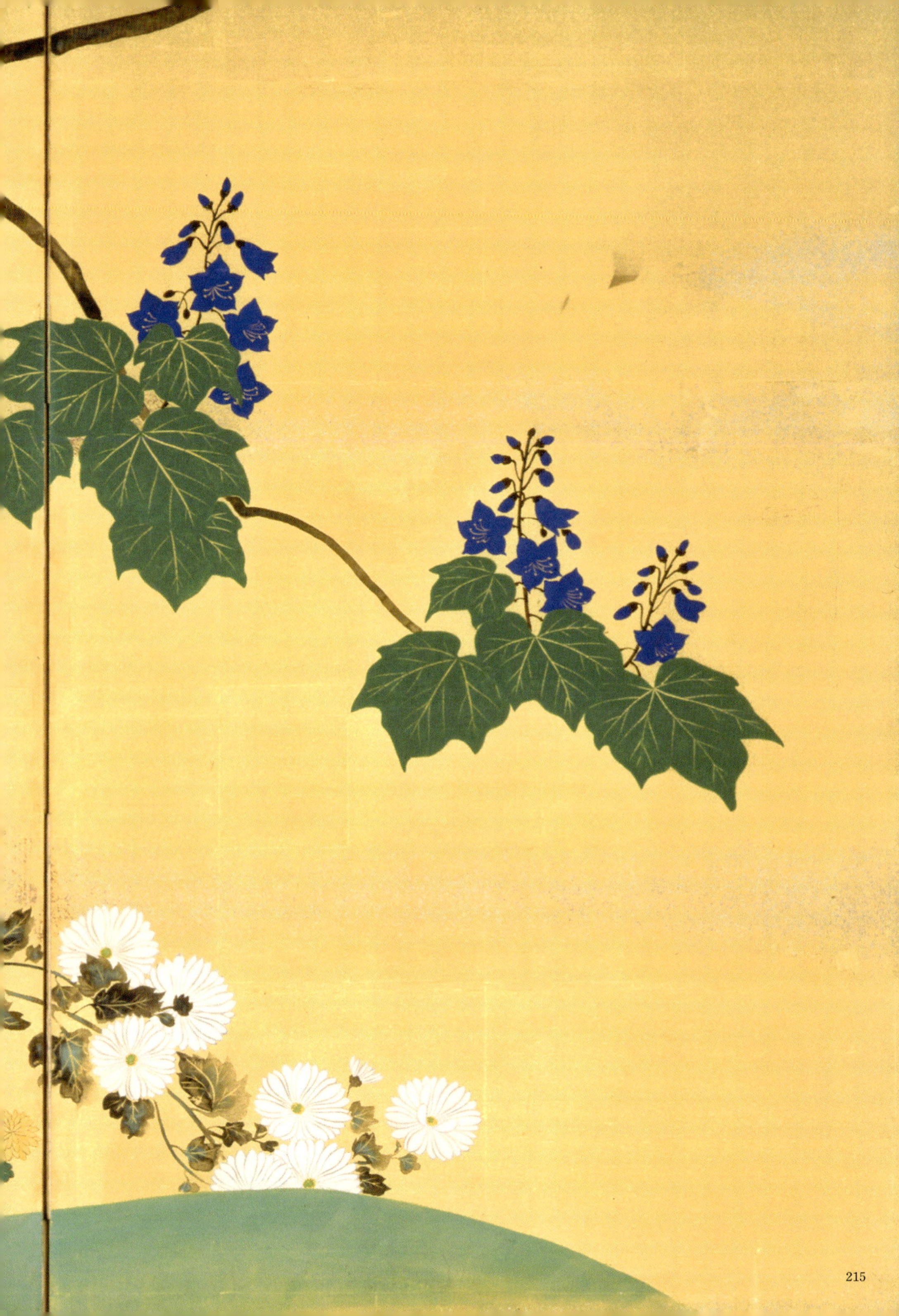

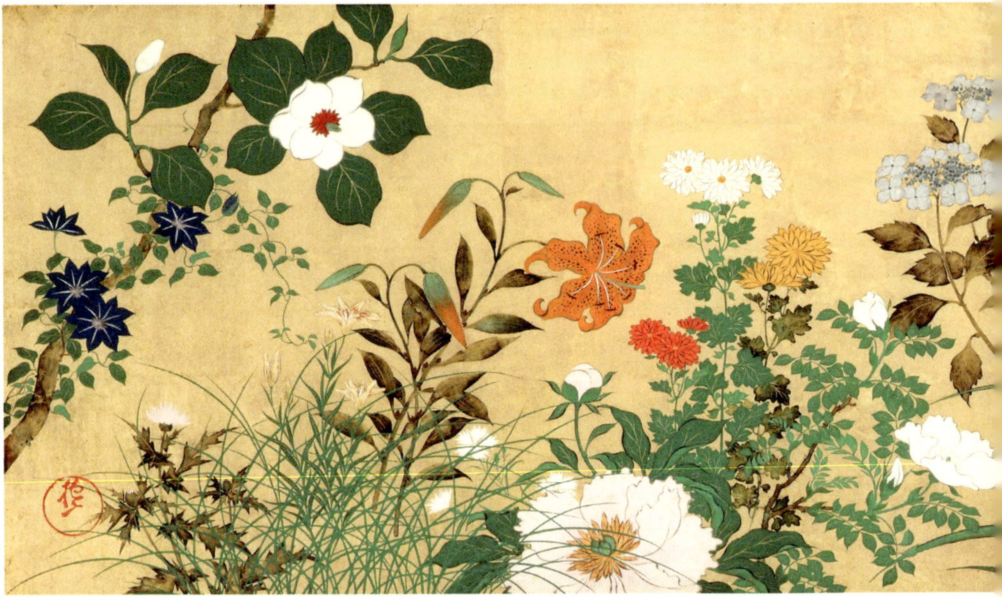

「夏草図屏風」　田中抱二　静嘉堂文庫美術館蔵
Summer Grass, Tanaka Hōji, Seikado Bunko Art Museum
画像提供：静嘉堂文庫イメージアーカイブ / DNPartcom

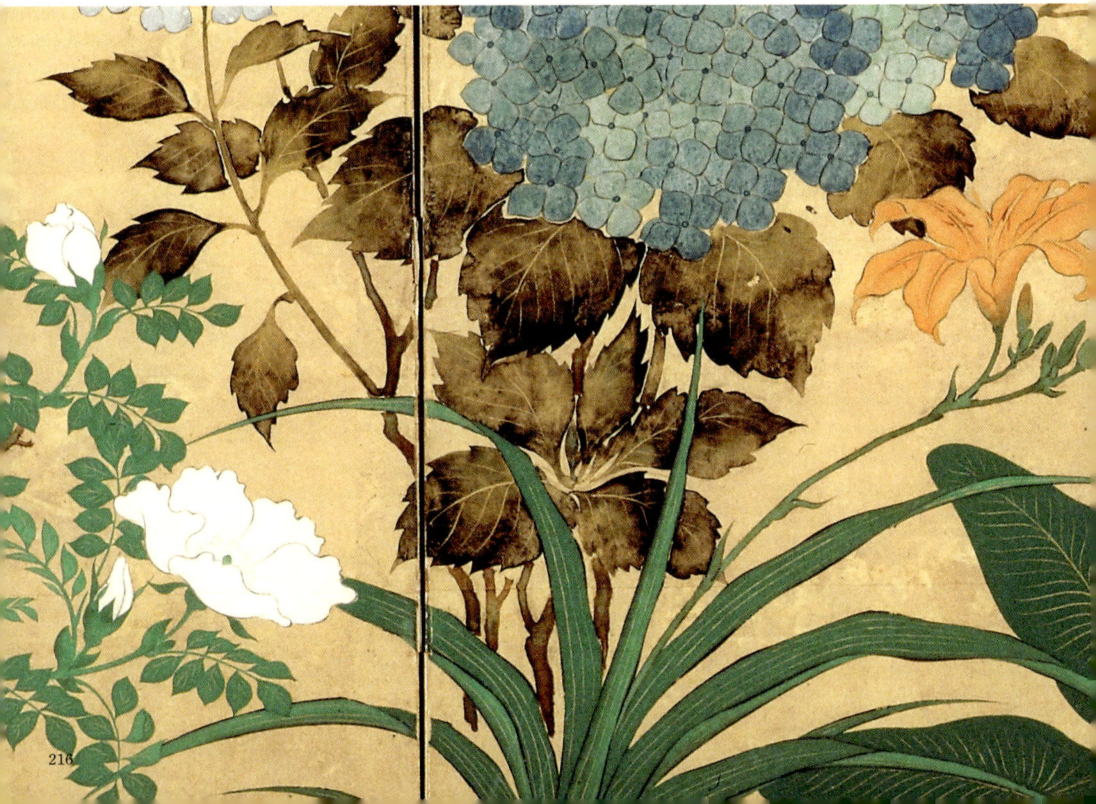

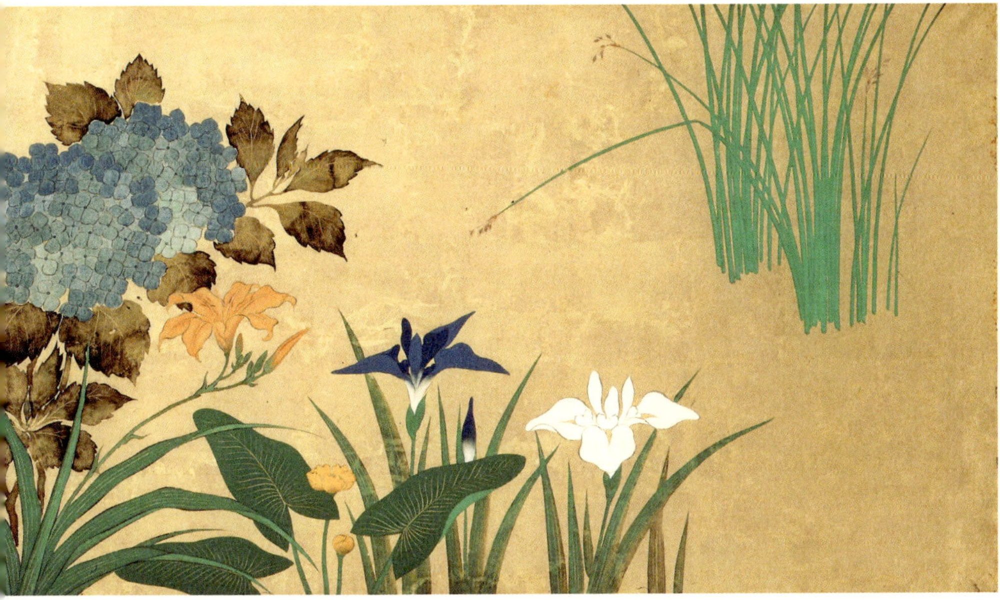

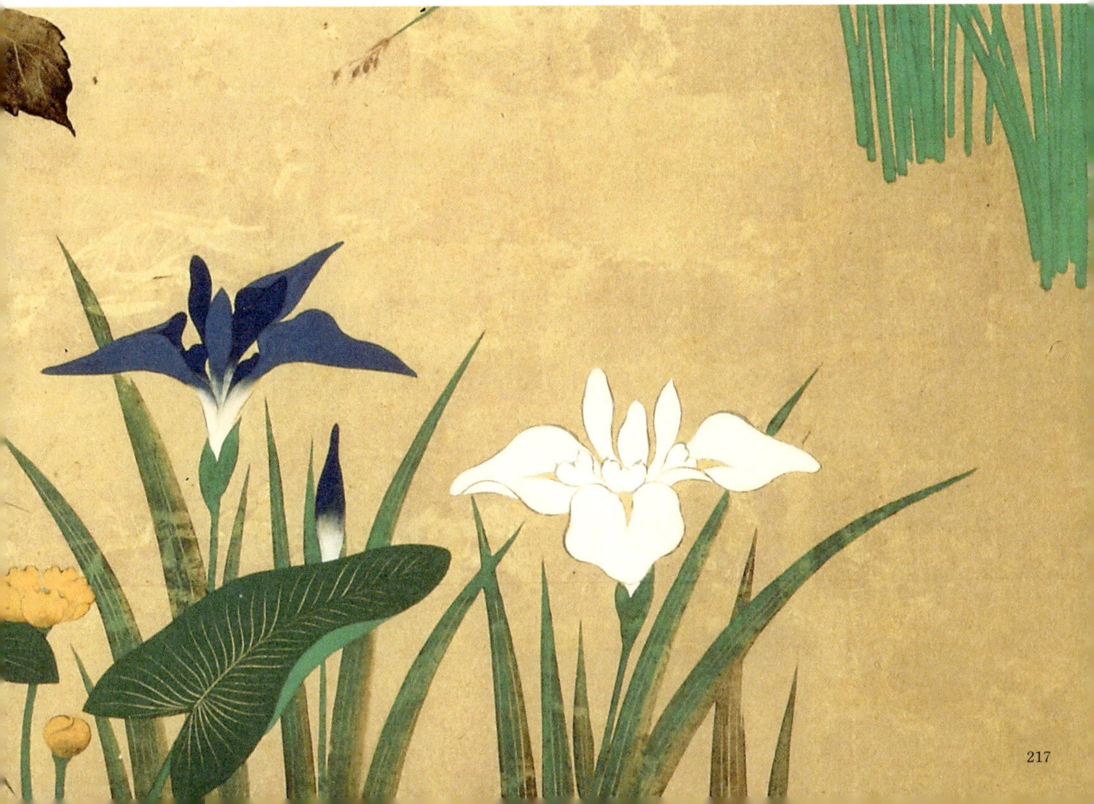

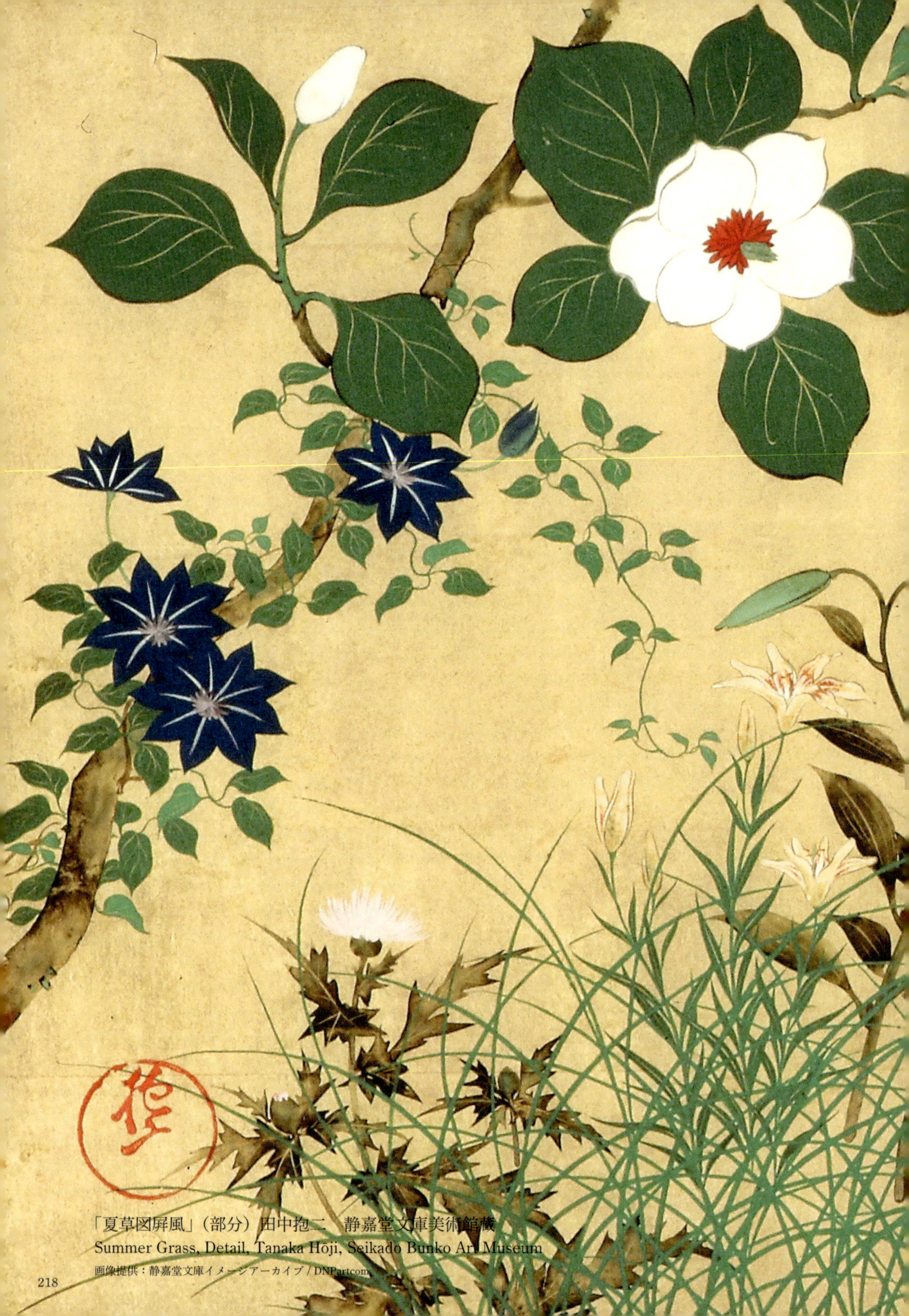

「夏草図屛風」（部分）田中抱二　静嘉堂文庫美術館蔵
Summer Grass, Detail, Tanaka Hoji, Seikado Bunko Art Museum
画像提供：静嘉堂文庫イメージアーカイブ／DNPartcom

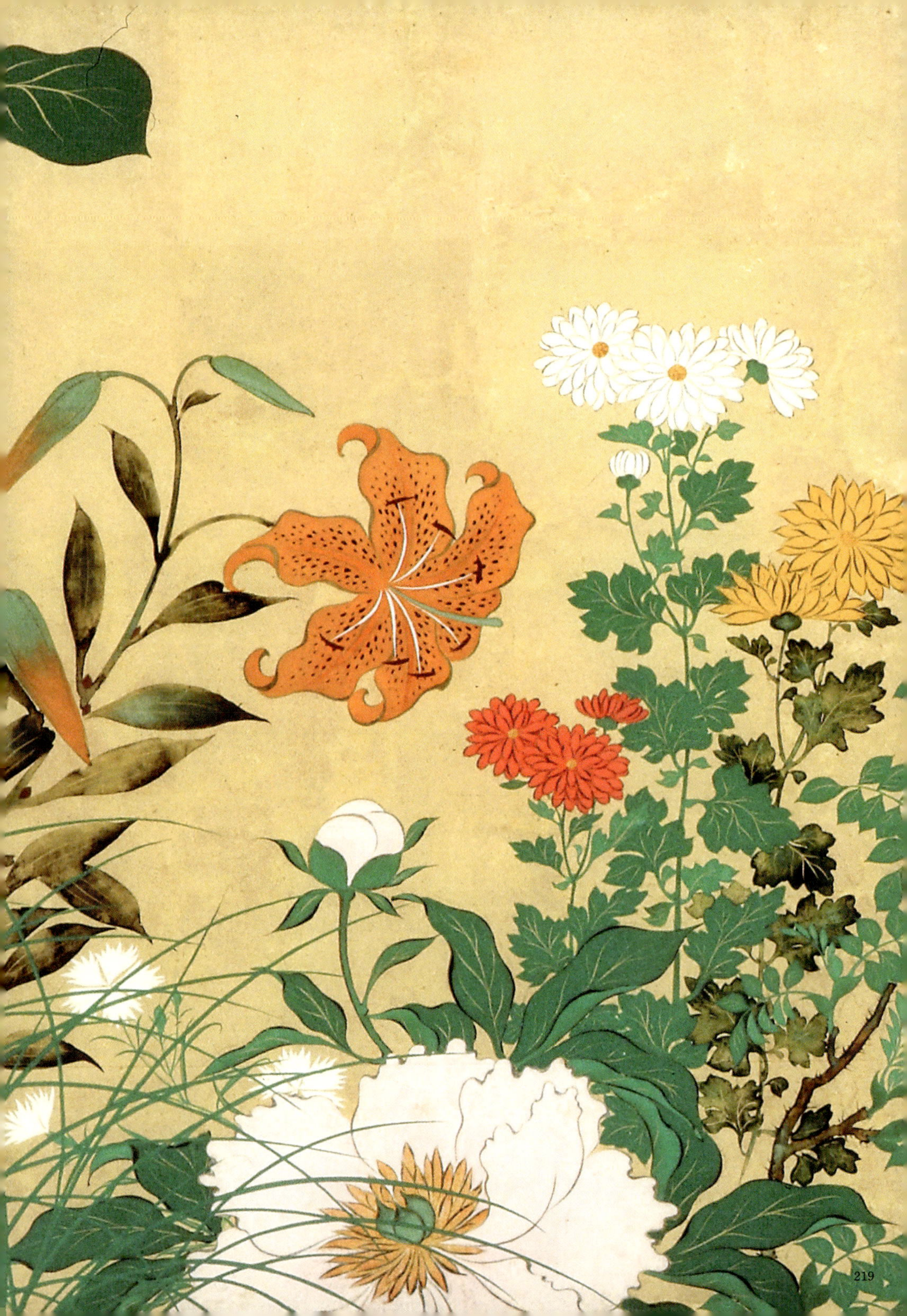

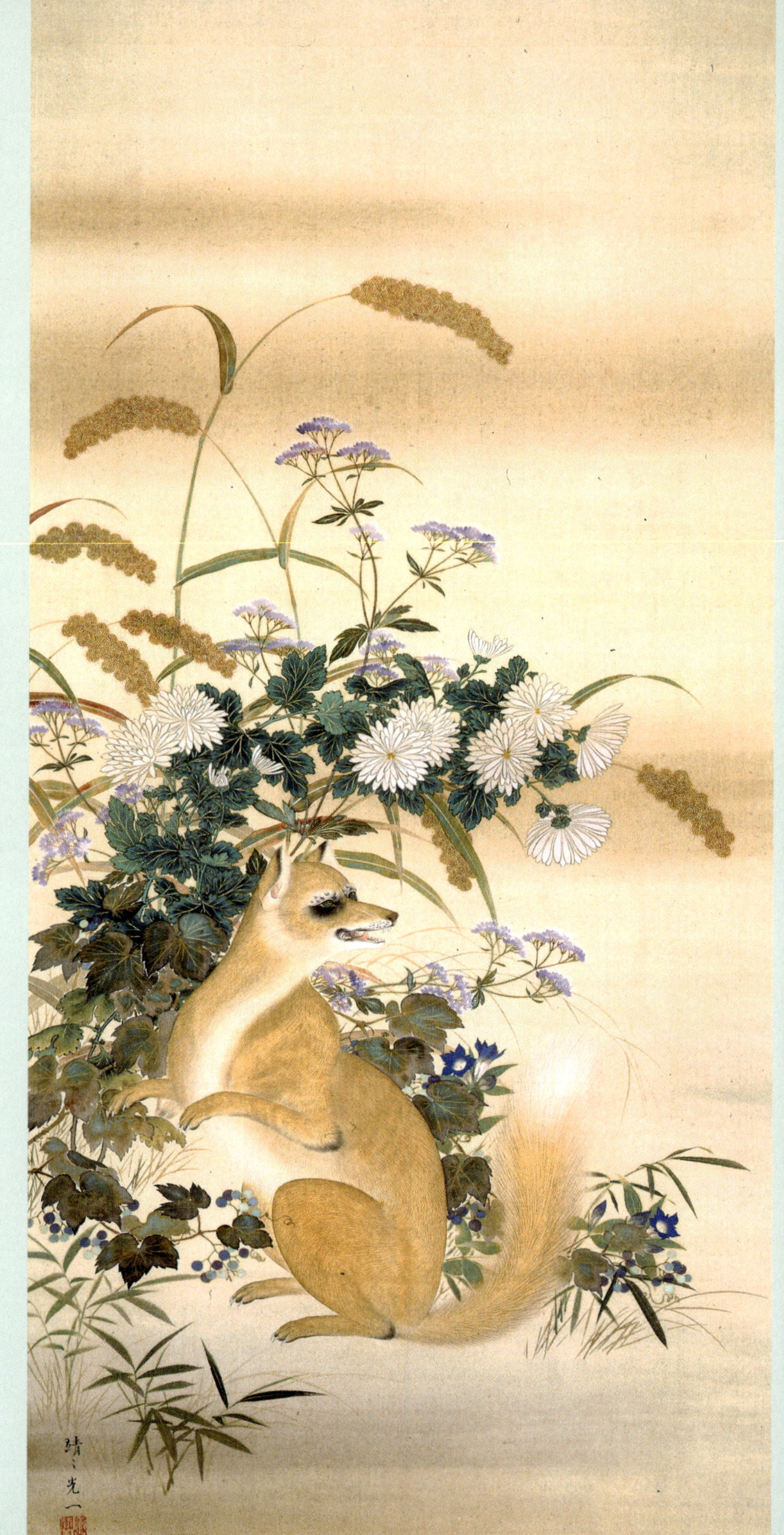

「孤狸図」 山本光一
板橋区立美術館蔵
Fox and Raccoon Dog,
Yamamoto Kōitsu,
Itabashi Art Museum

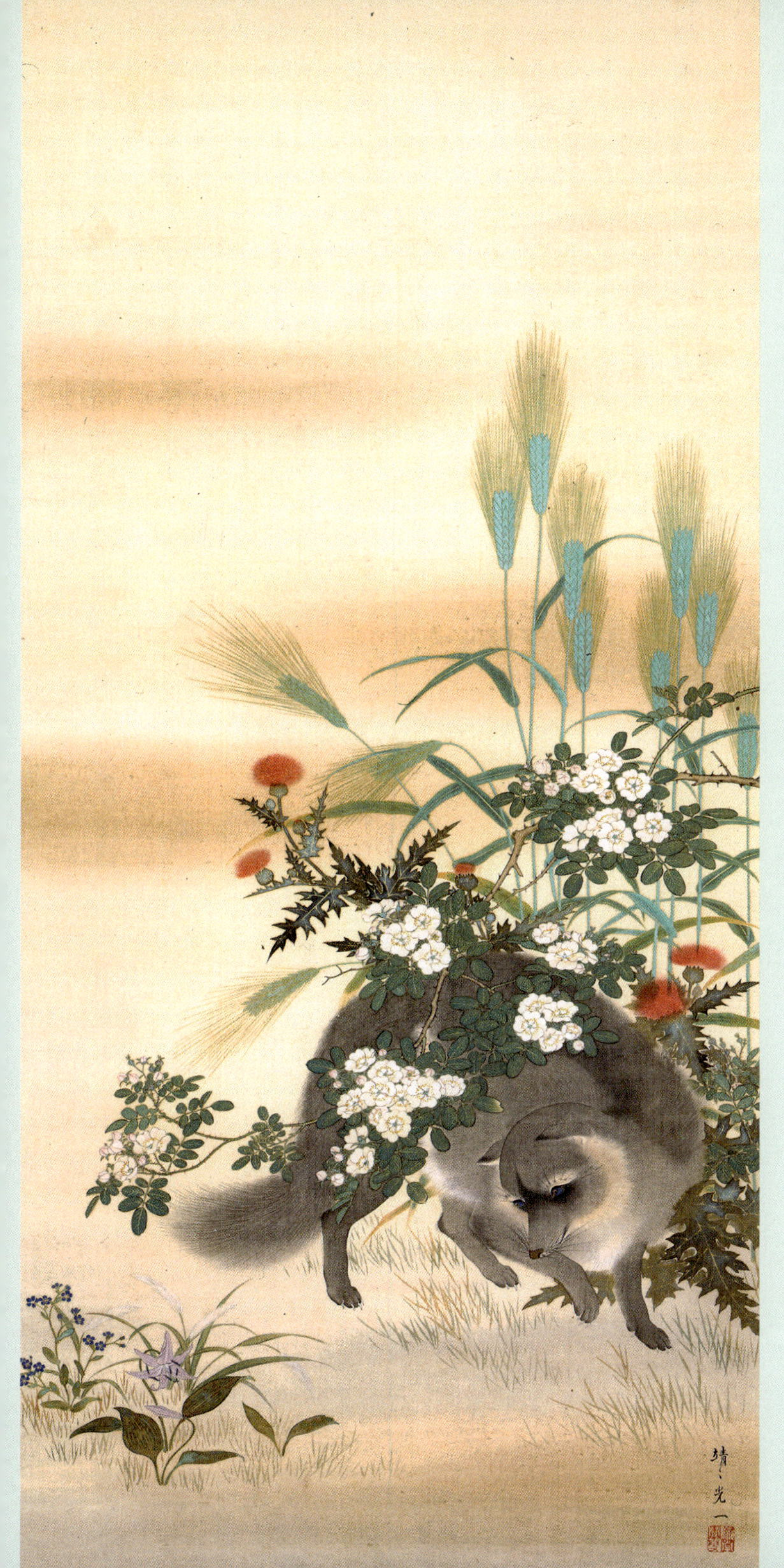

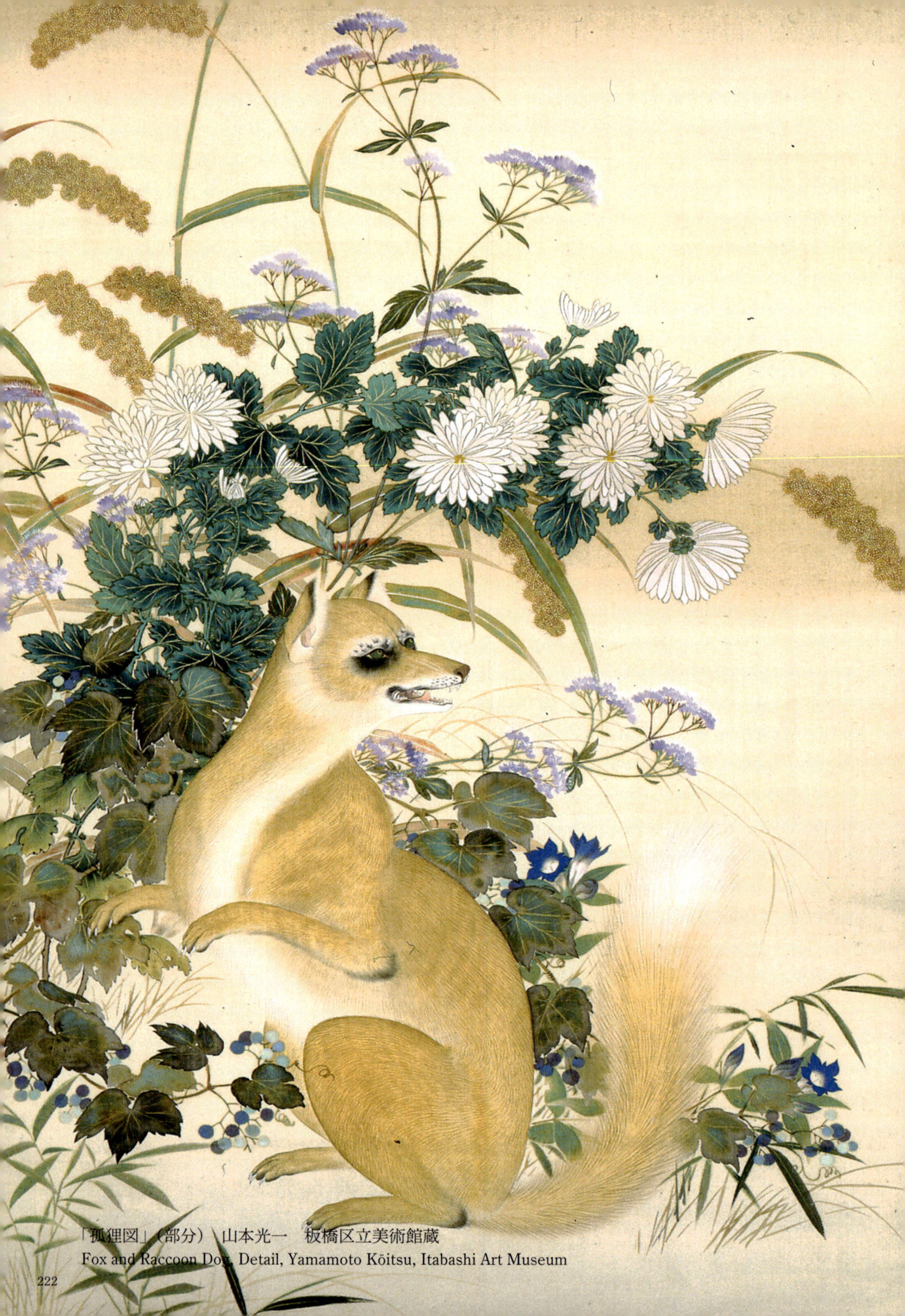

「孤狸図」（部分）山本光一　板橋区立美術館蔵
Fox and Raccoon Dog, Detail, Yamamoto Kōitsu, Itabashi Art Museum

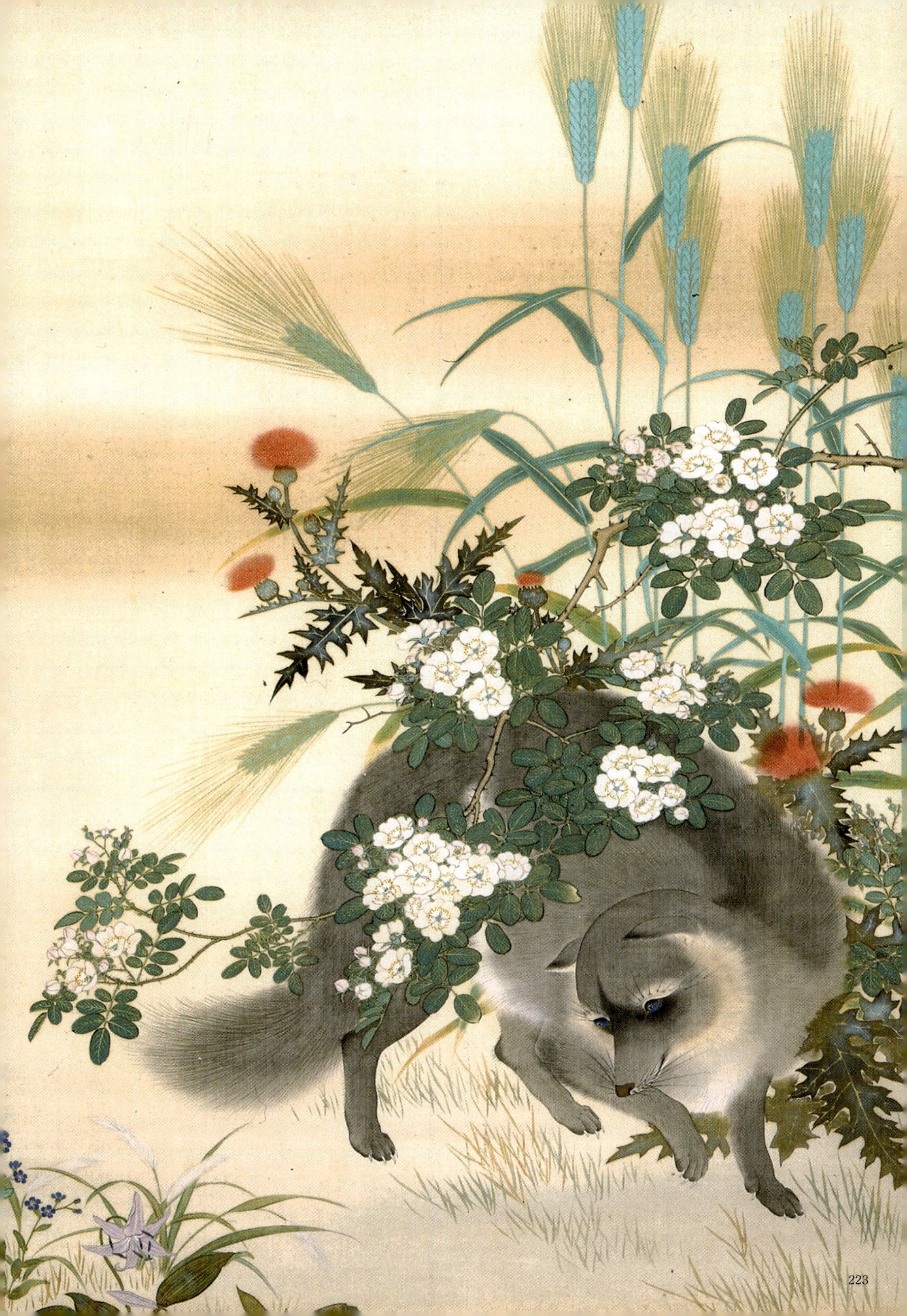

神坂雪佳

かみさか せっか　慶応 2 年〜昭和 17 年（1866 - 1942）

京都御所警護の武士、神坂吉重の長男に生まれる。初めに鈴木瑞彦に四条派の絵を、のち光琳画のコレクターでもあった図案家の岸光景に師事し、琳派や工芸意匠の図案を学んだ。漆器、陶器、染織品をはじめとする工芸品に精力的に図案を考案した。「光悦会」の設立や、光悦の伝記の編纂などの顕彰も行った。

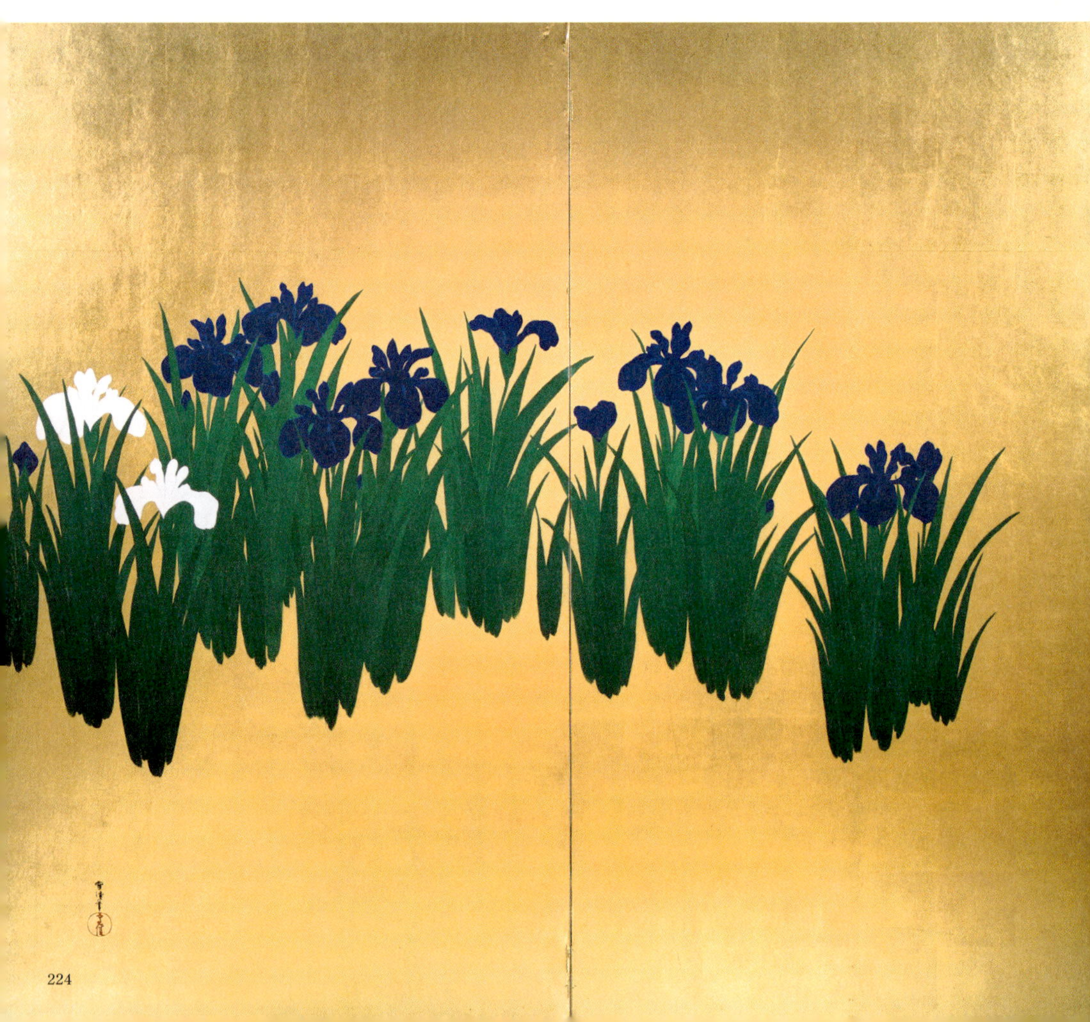

Kamisaka Sekka (1866 – 1942)
Born in Kyoto, Sekka studied the Shijo style with Suzuki Zuigen,
then Rinpa painting and design with Kishi Kokei, a designer
and collector of Rinpa paintings. Sekka tirelessly designed
lacquerware, ceramics, textiles, and other objects. He also
founded the Kōetsu-kai and compiled a biography of Kōetsu.

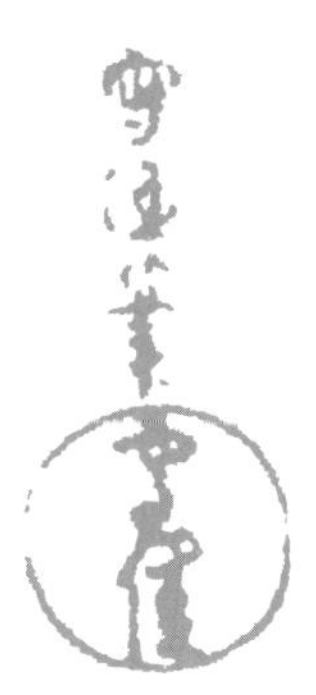

「杜若図屏風」　神坂雪佳　個人蔵
Folding Screens with Iris, Kamisaka Sekka, Private Collection

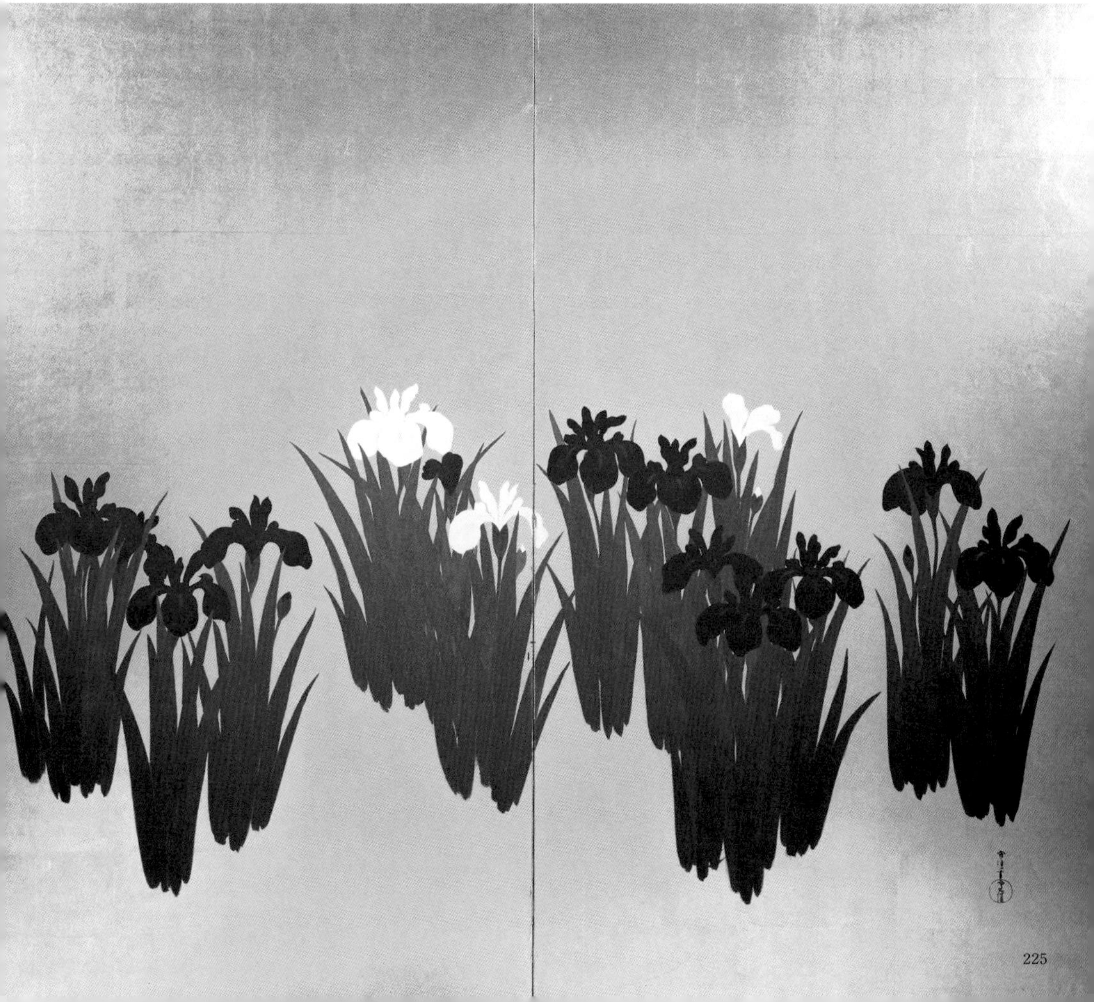

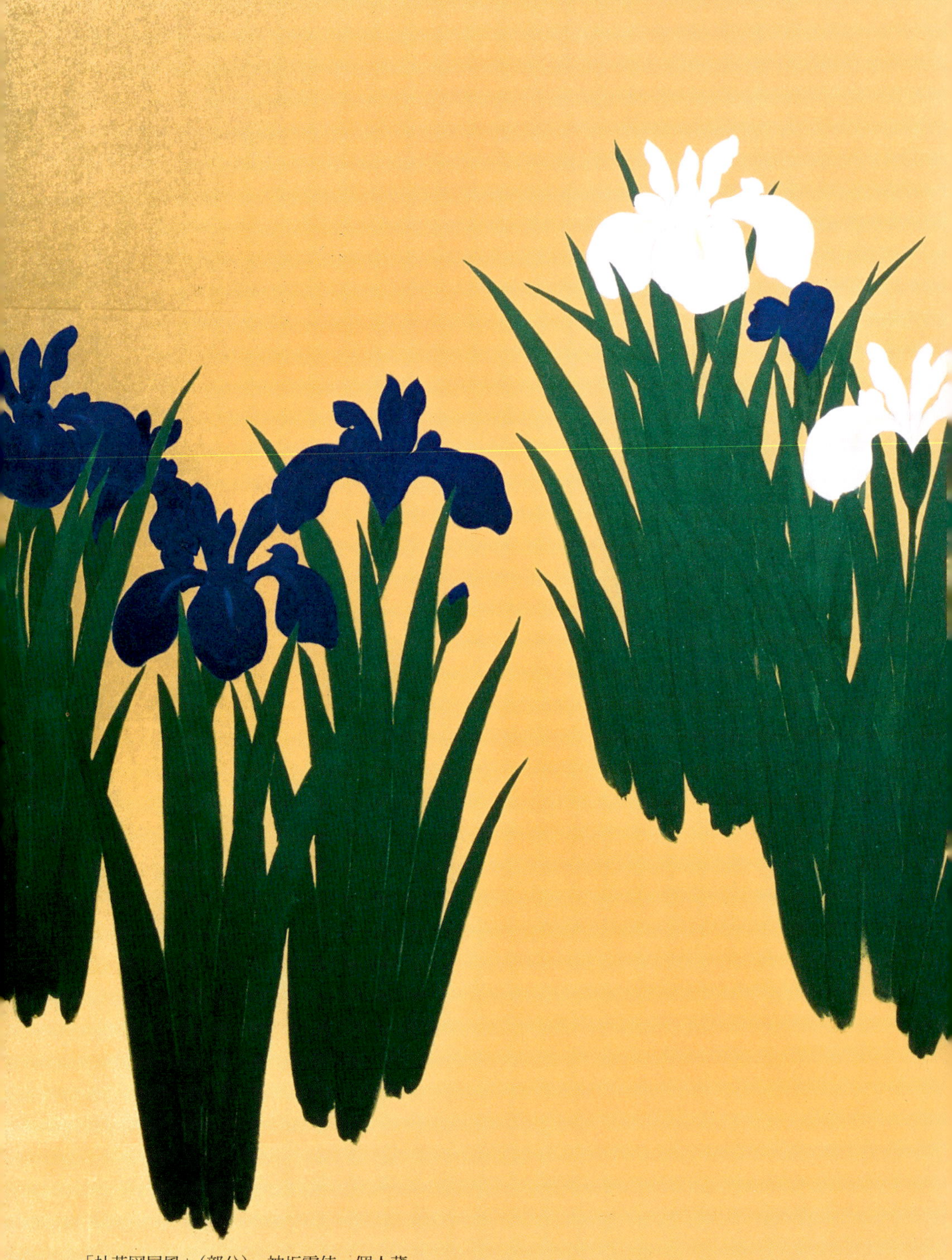

「杜若図屏風」（部分）　神坂雪佳　個人蔵
Folding Screens with Iris, Details, Kamisaka Sekka, Private Collection

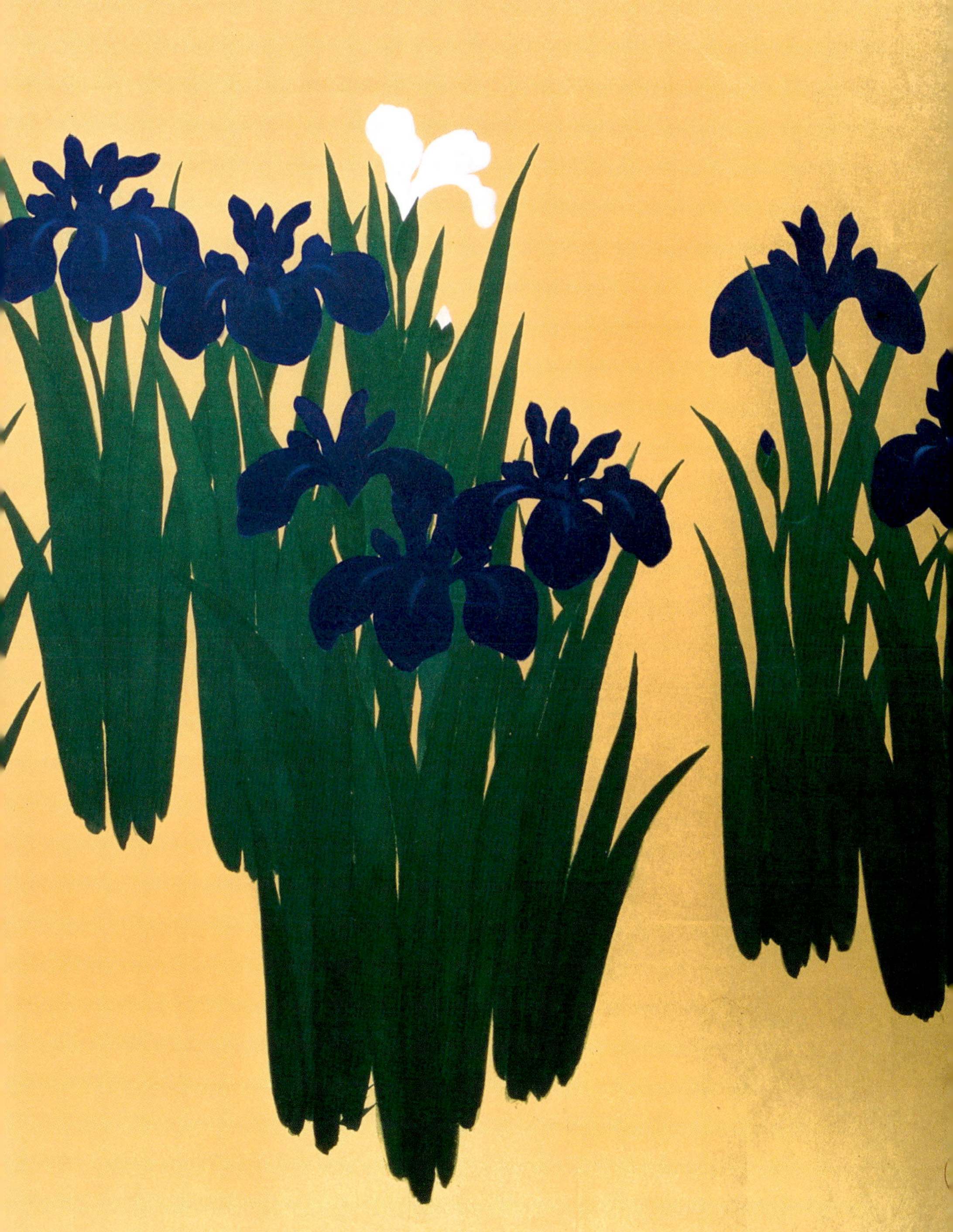

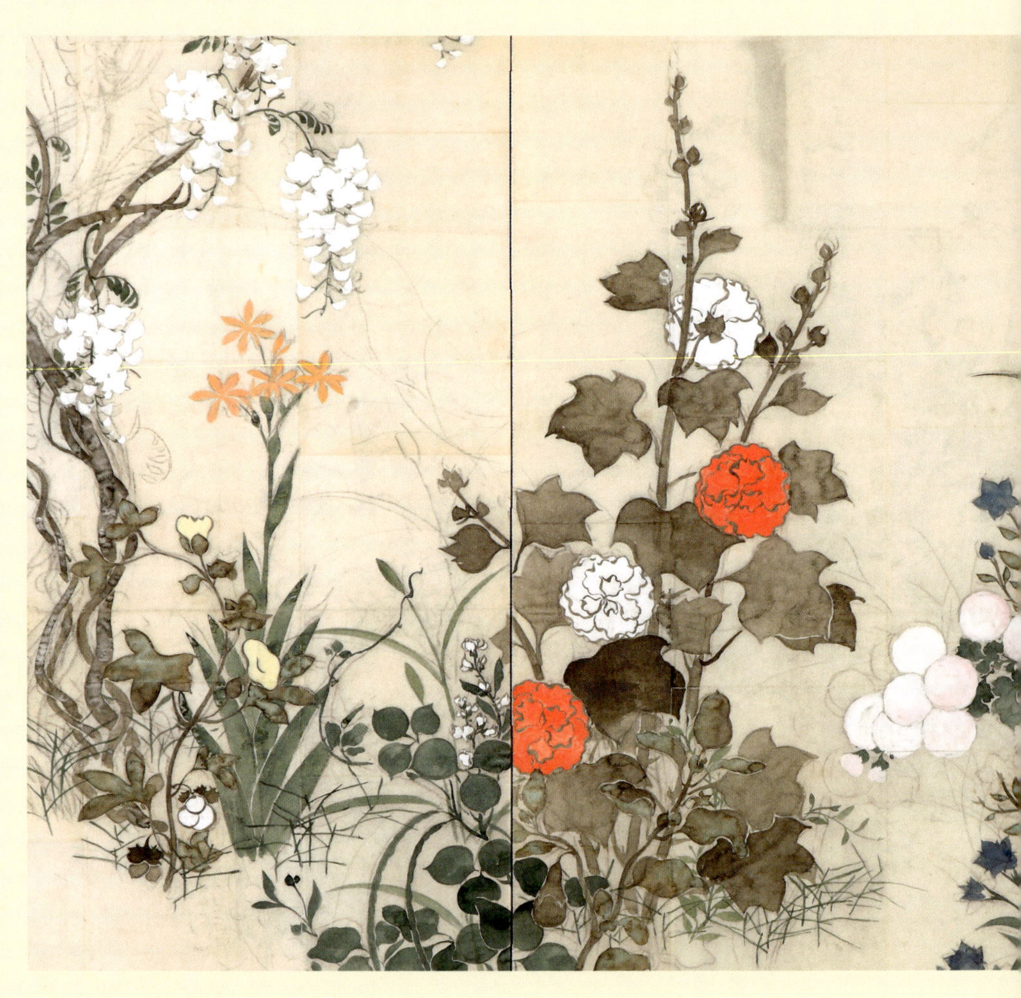

「光琳風草花」　神坂雪佳　髙島屋史料館蔵
Flowers, *Kōrin Style*, Kamisaka Sekka, Takashimaya Historical Museum, Osaka

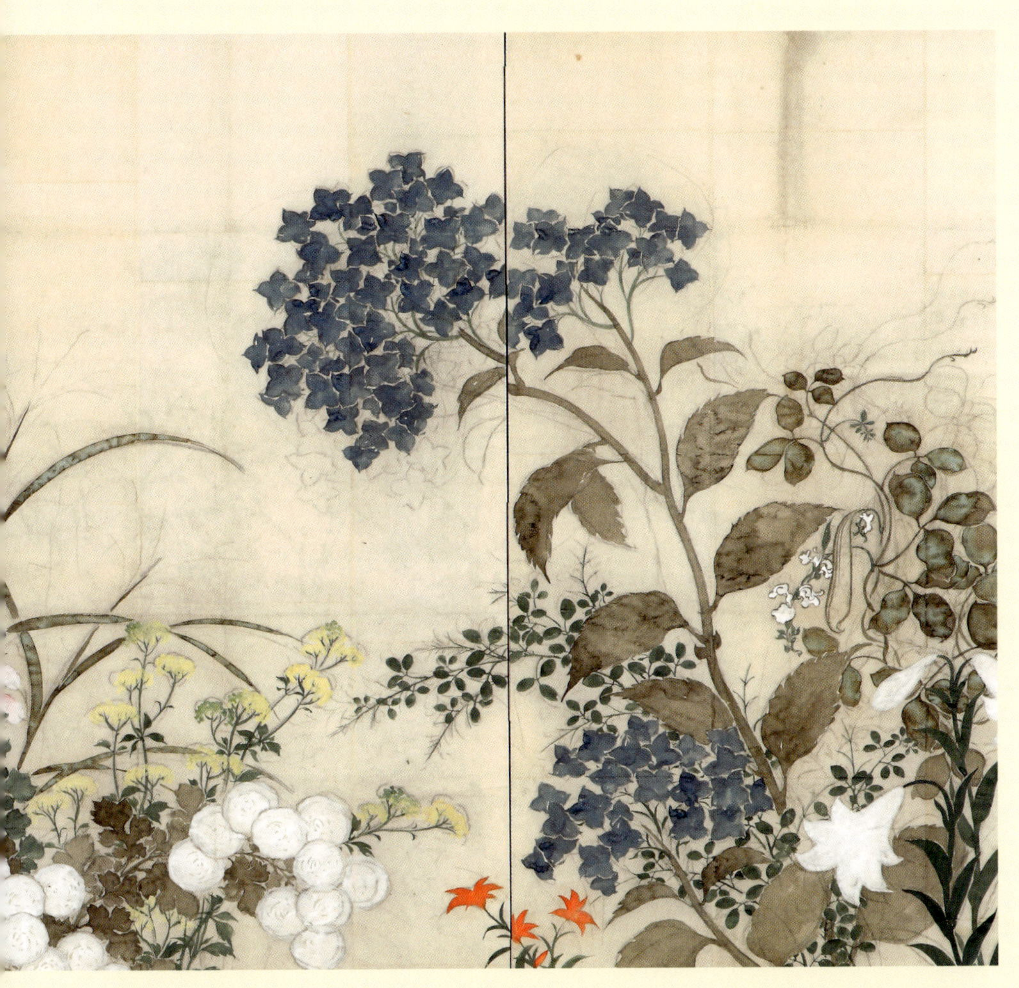

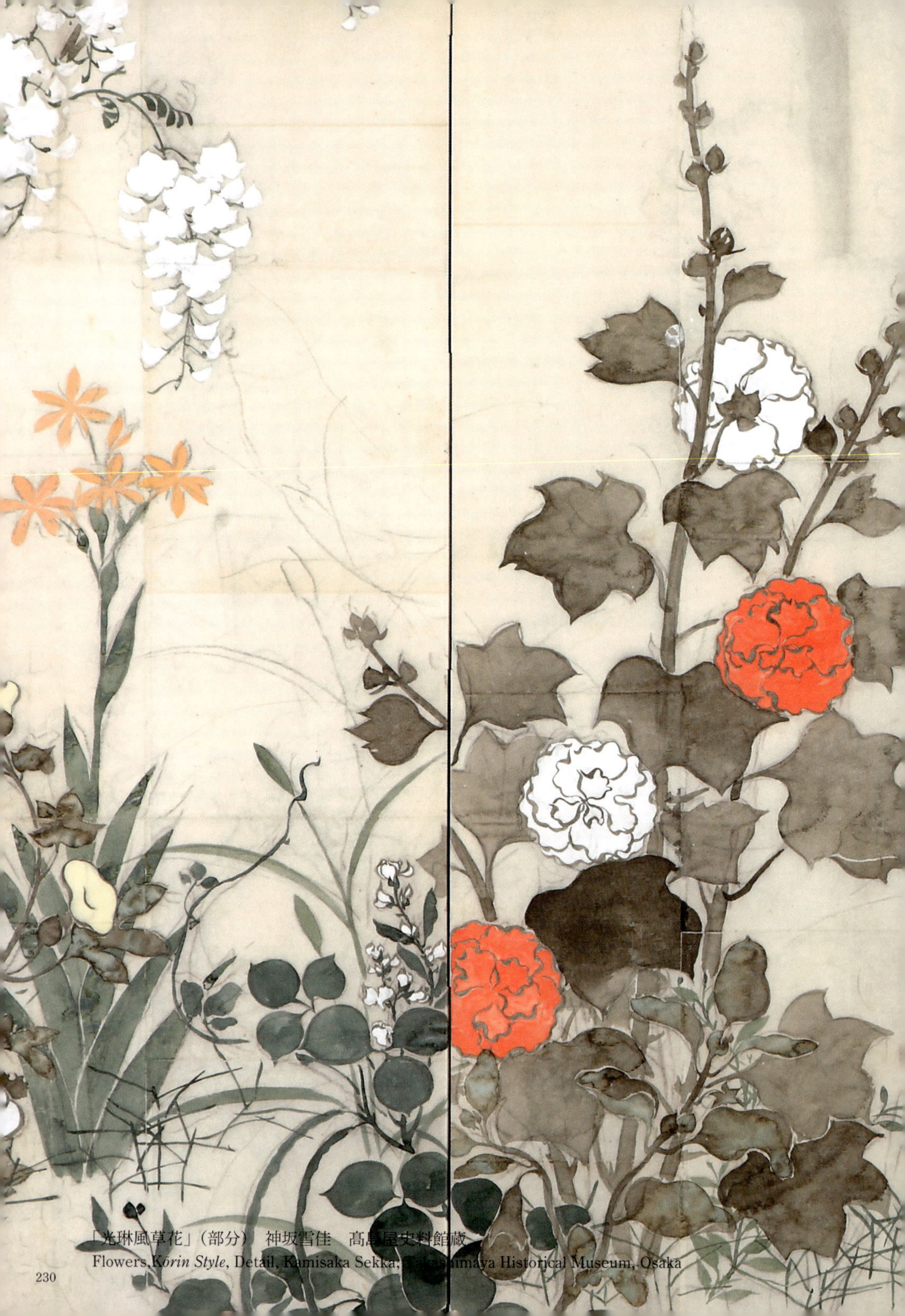

「光琳風草花」（部分）　神坂雪佳　高島屋史料館蔵
Flowers, *Korin Style*, Detail, Kamisaka Sekka, Takashimaya Historical Museum, Osaka

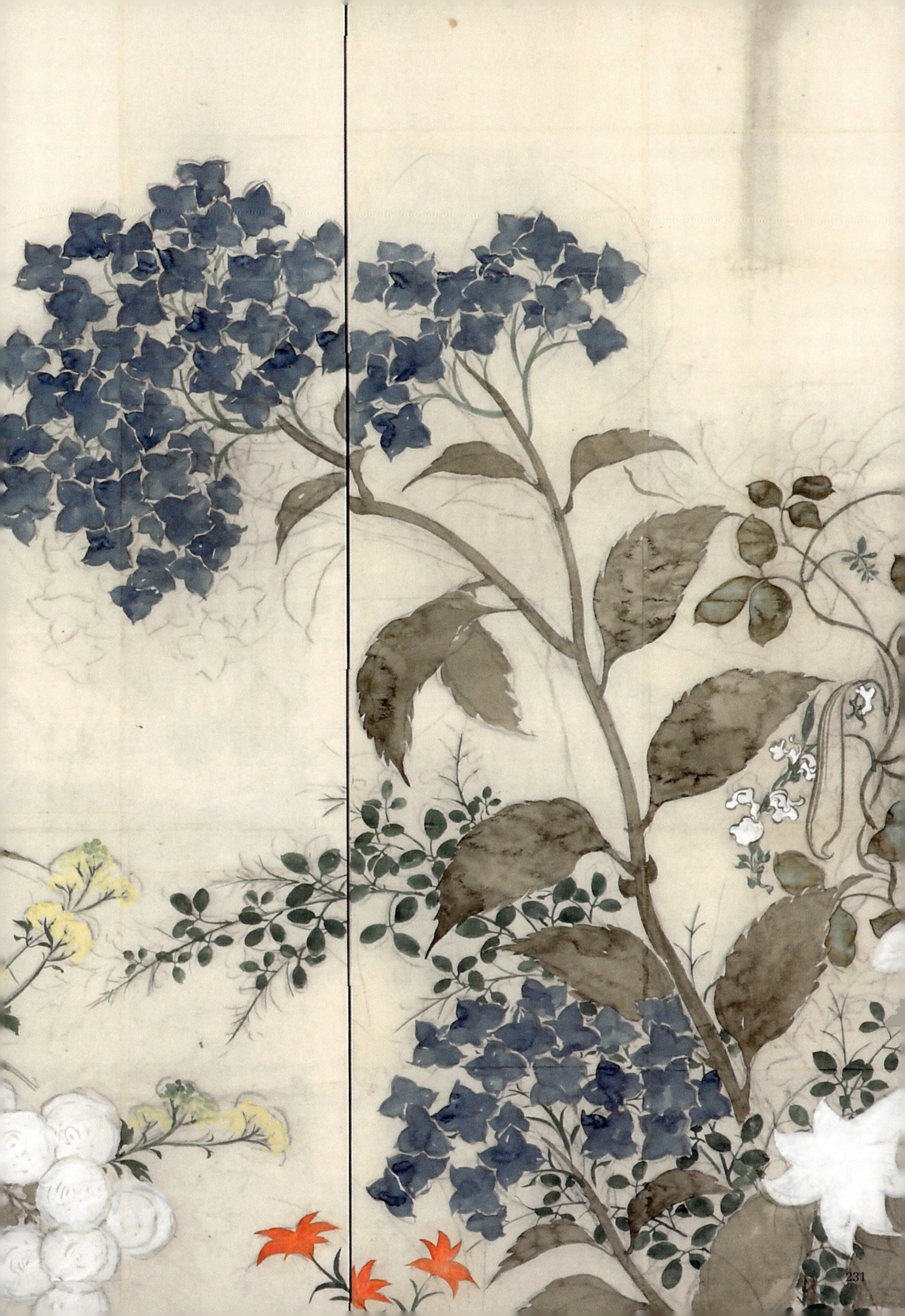

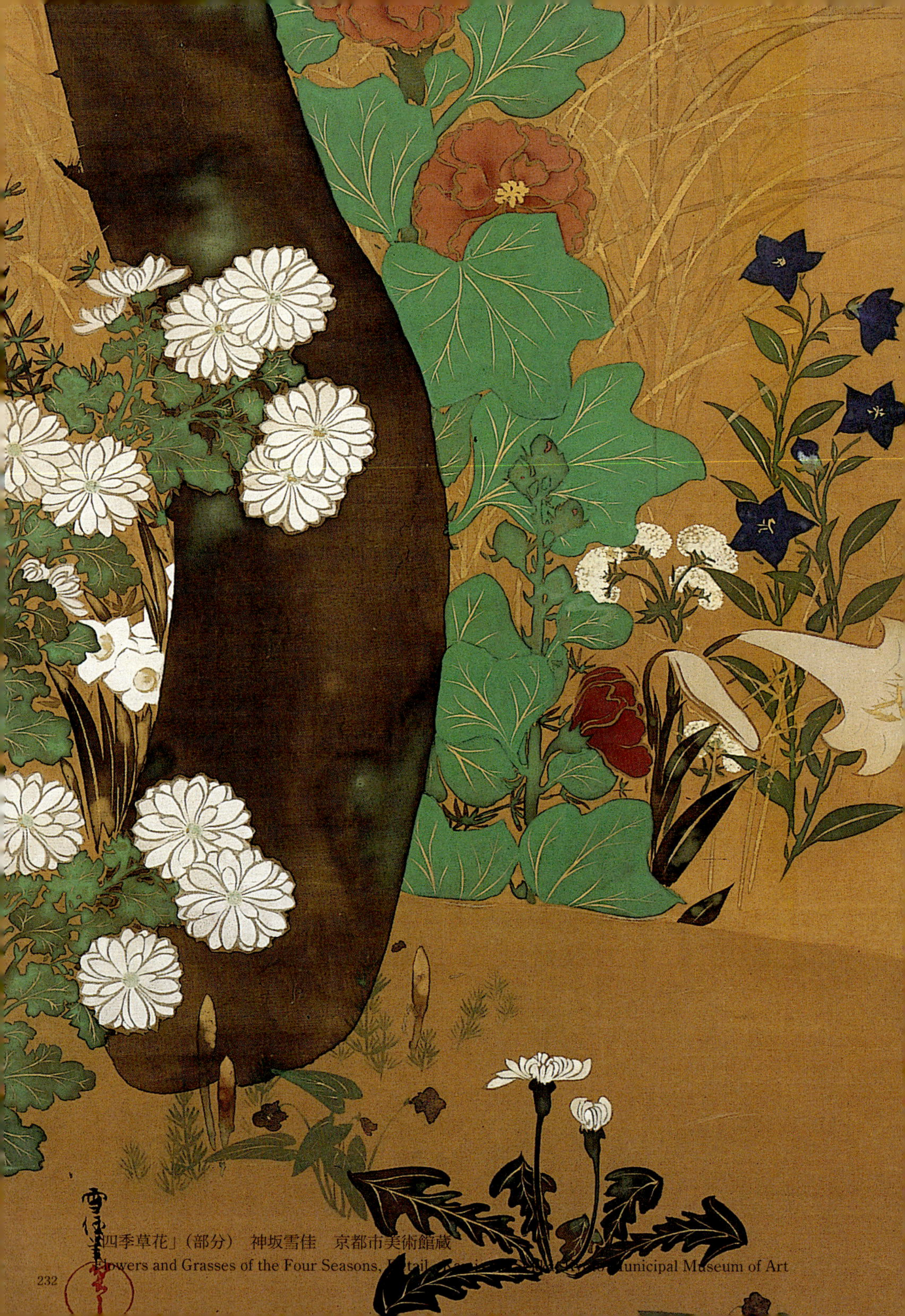

「四季草花」（部分）　神坂雪佳　京都市美術館蔵
Flowers and Grasses of the Four Seasons, Detail. Kamisaka Sekka. Kyoto Municipal Museum of Art

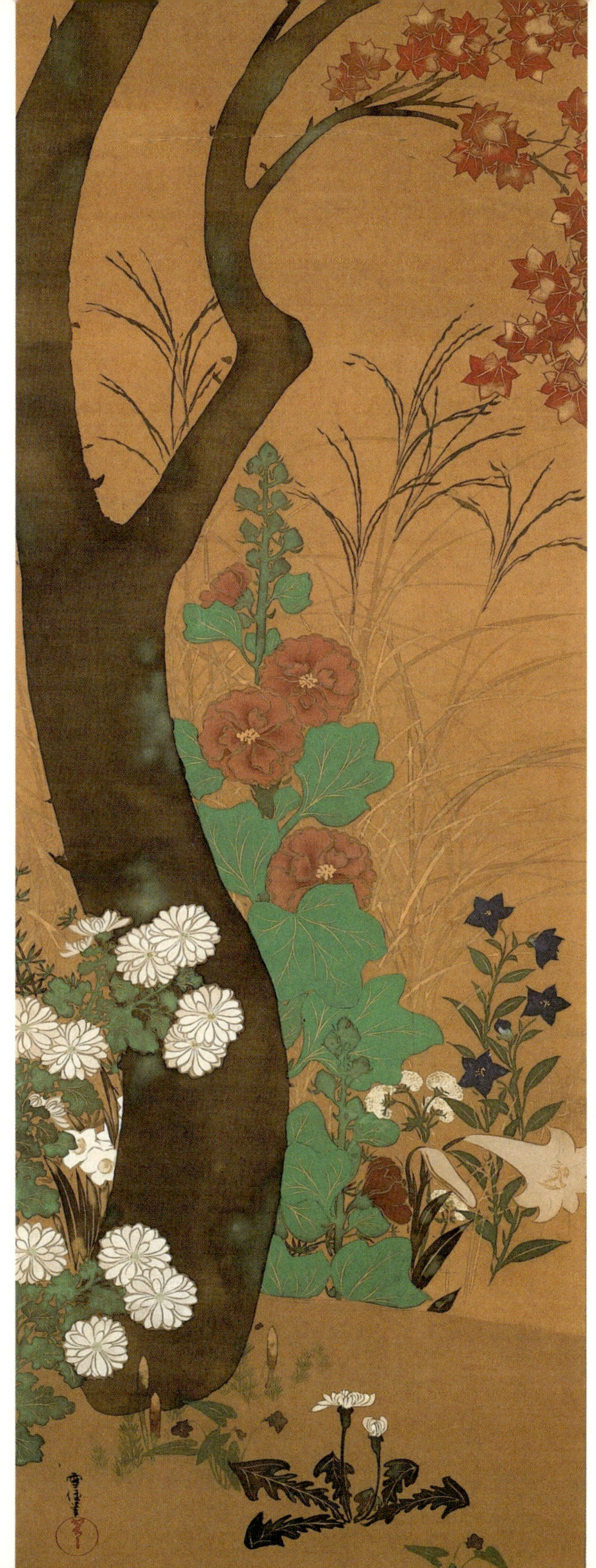

「四季草花」　神坂雪佳
京都市美術館蔵
Flowers and Grasses of the Four
Seasons, Kamisaka Sekka, Kyoto
Municipal Museum of Art

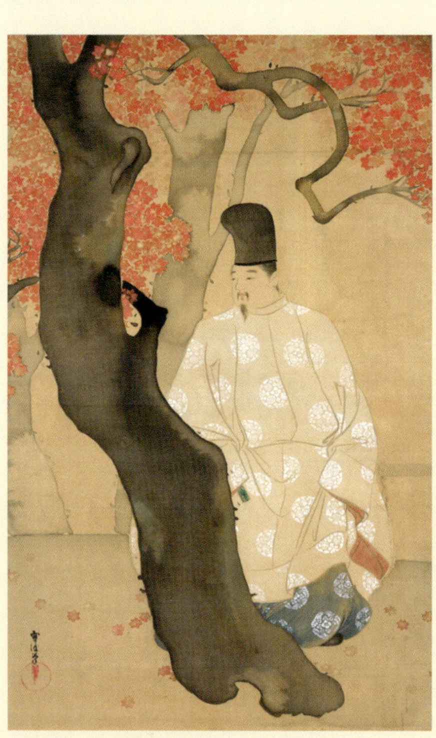

「観楓図」　神坂雪佳
京都市立芸術大学芸術資料館蔵
Autumn Maple Viewing, Kamisaka Sekka,
University Art Museum, Kyoto City
University of Arts

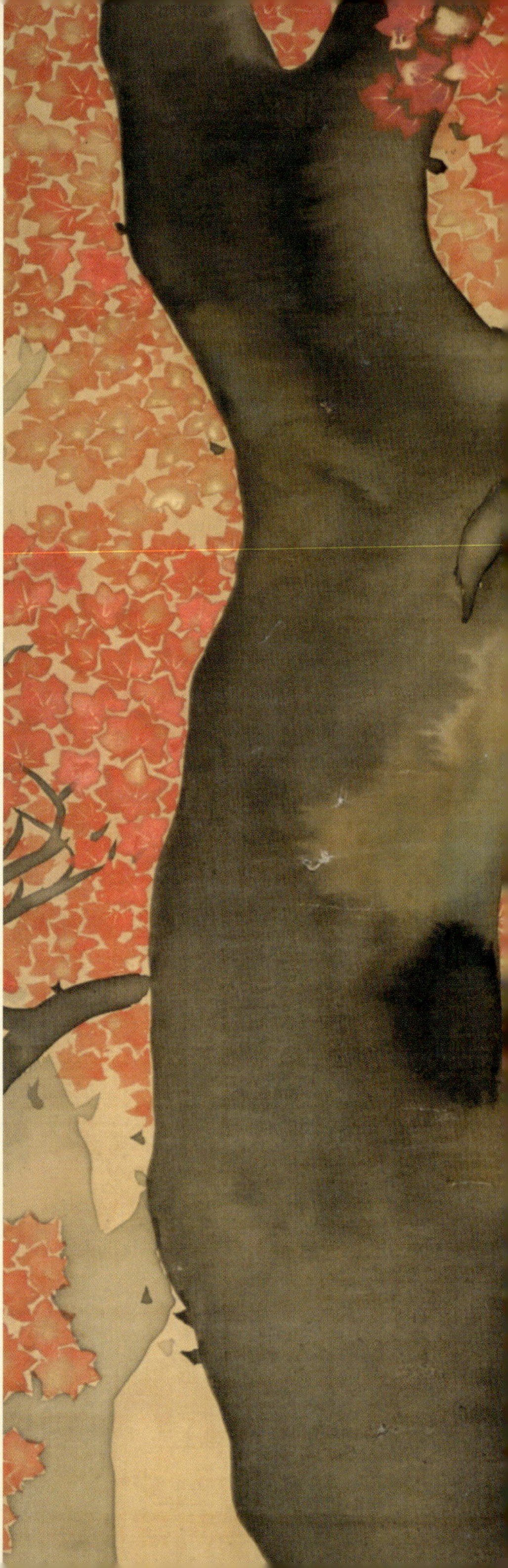

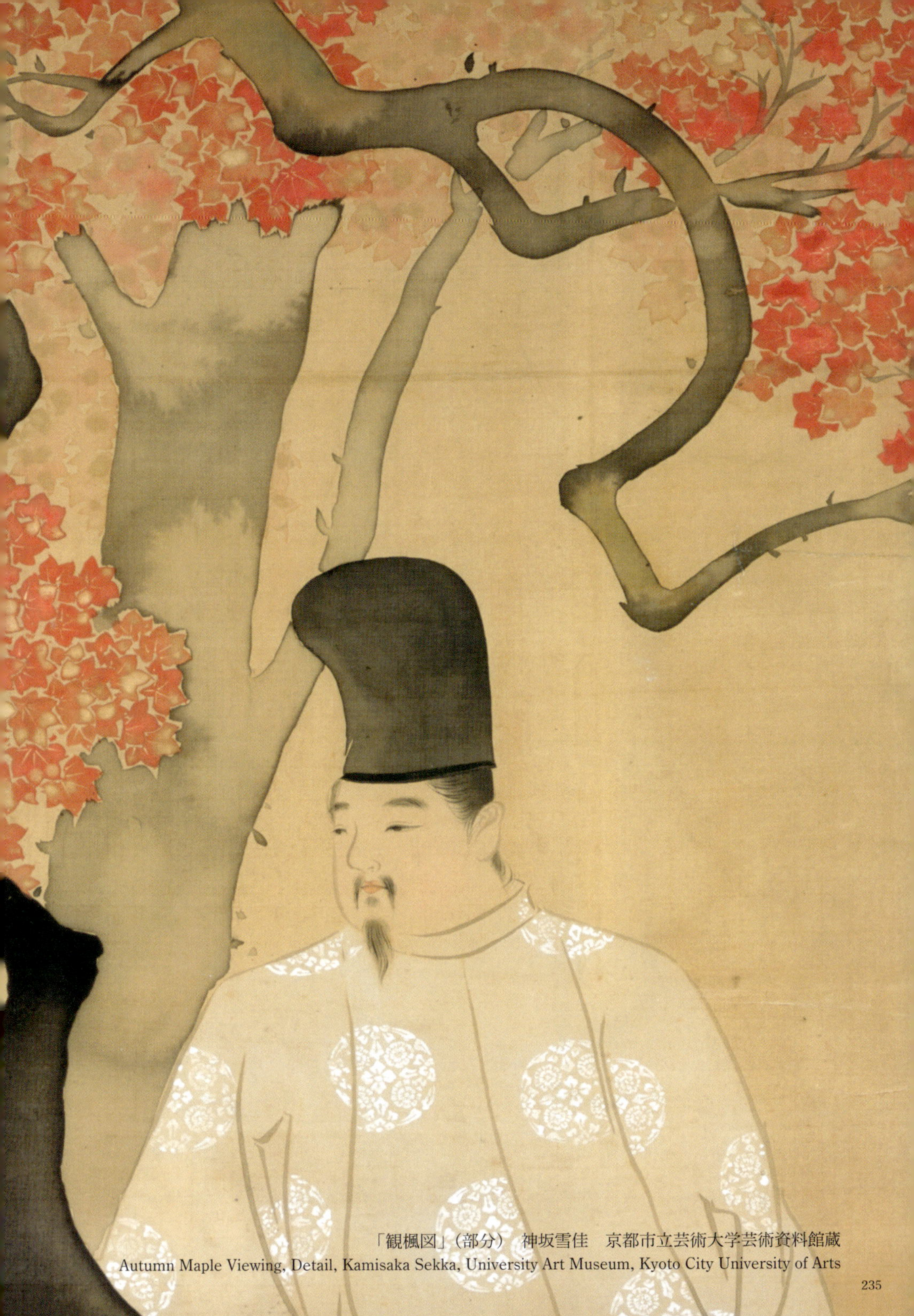

「観楓図」（部分）　神坂雪佳　京都市立芸術大学芸術資料館蔵
Autumn Maple Viewing, Detail, Kamisaka Sekka, University Art Museum, Kyoto City University of Arts

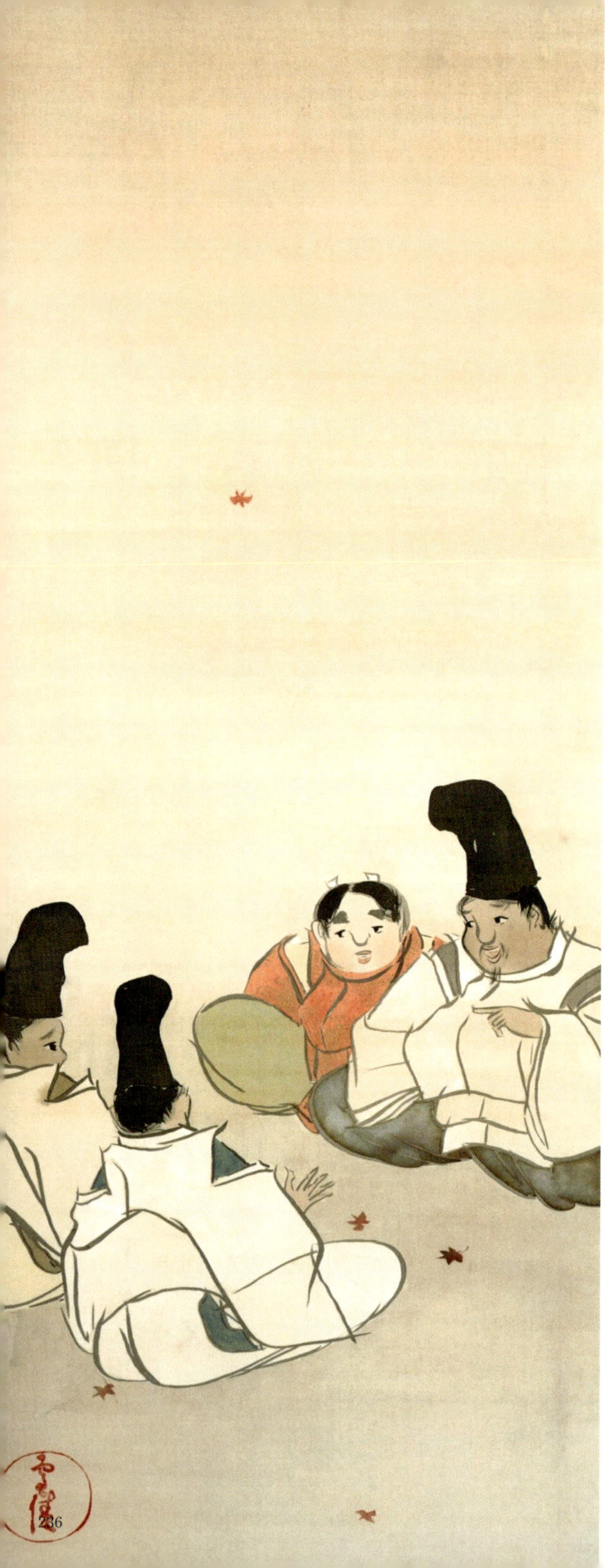

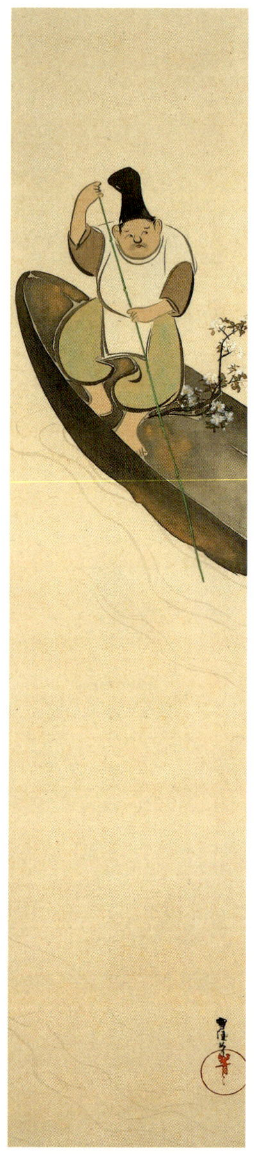

「軽舟図」神坂雪佳
京都市美術館蔵
Boatman, Kamisaka Sekka, Kyoto
Municipal Museum of Art

「供侍之図」 神坂雪佳
京都市美術館蔵
Samurai Attendant, Kamisaka Sekka, Kyoto
Municipal Museum of Art

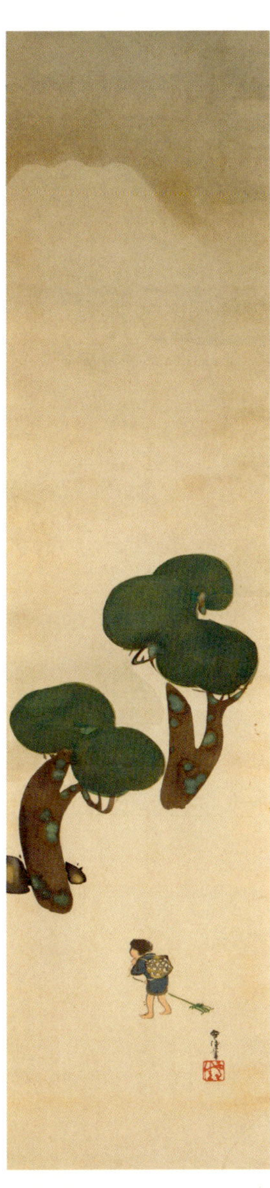

「松葉掻童子図」
神坂雪佳　今宮神社蔵
Boy Sweeping Pine Needles,
Imamiya-jinja, Kyoto

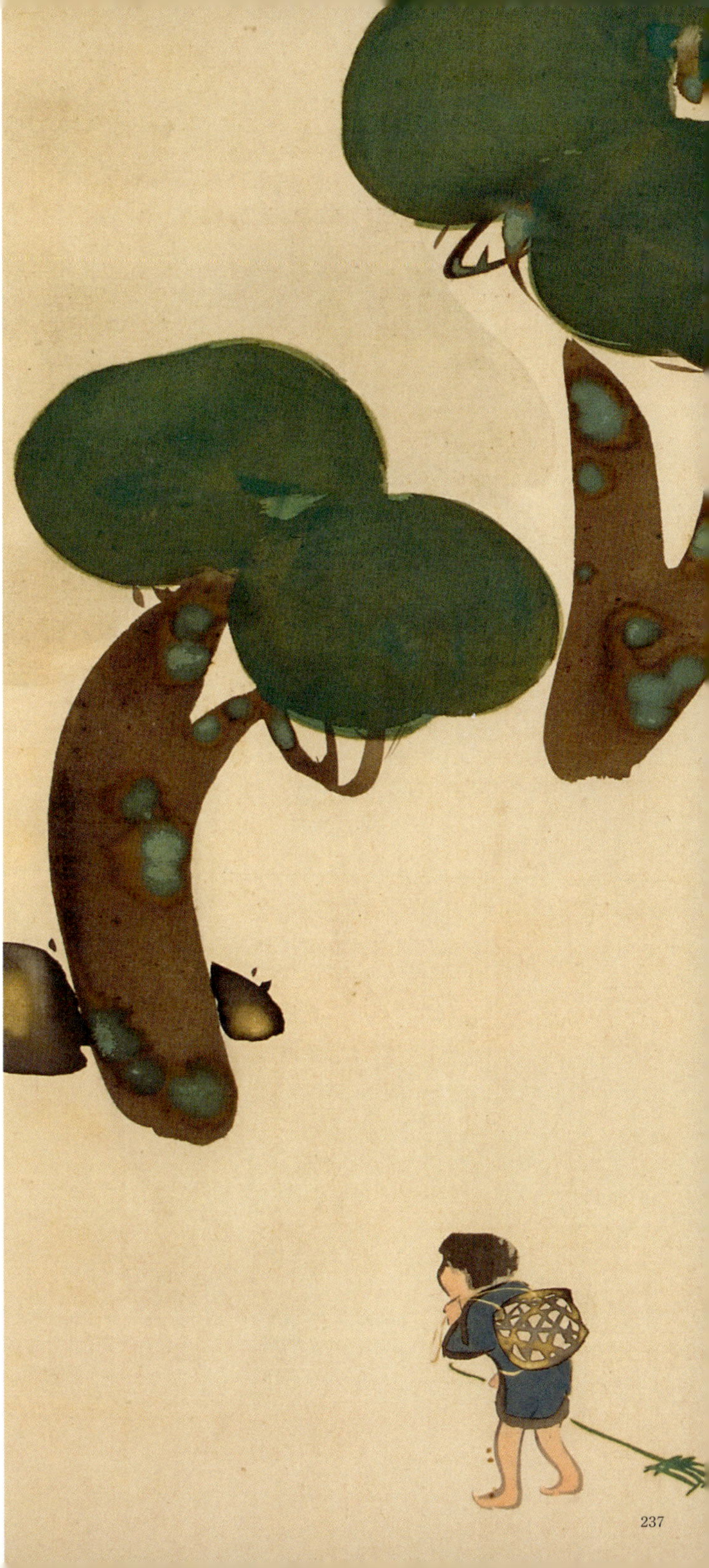

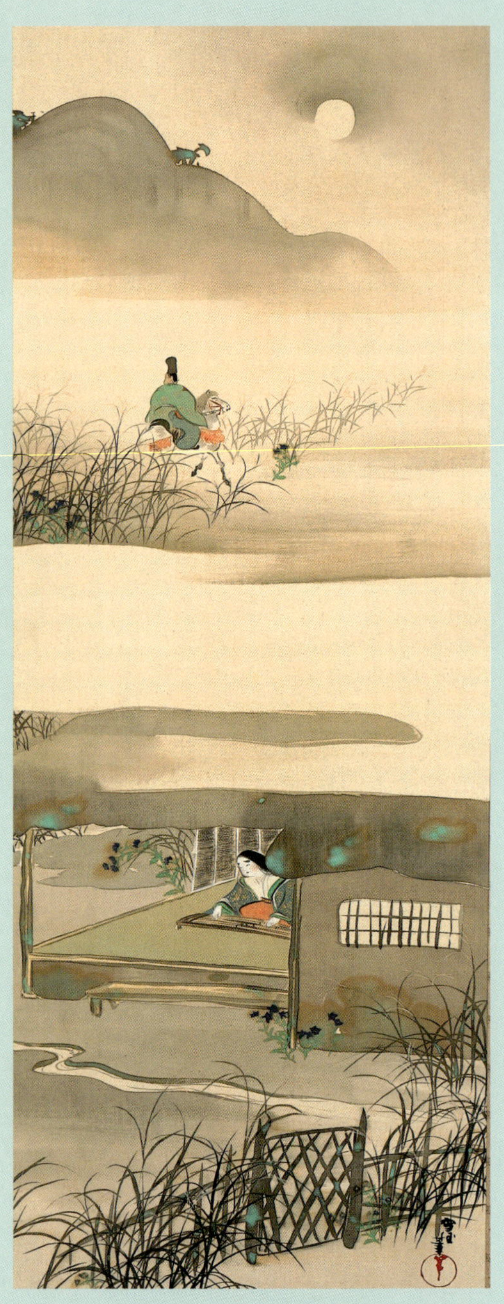

「小督」神坂雪佳　京都市美術館蔵
Kogō (Daughter of *Fujiwara-no Shigenori*), Kamisaka
Sekka, Kyoto Municipal Museum of Art

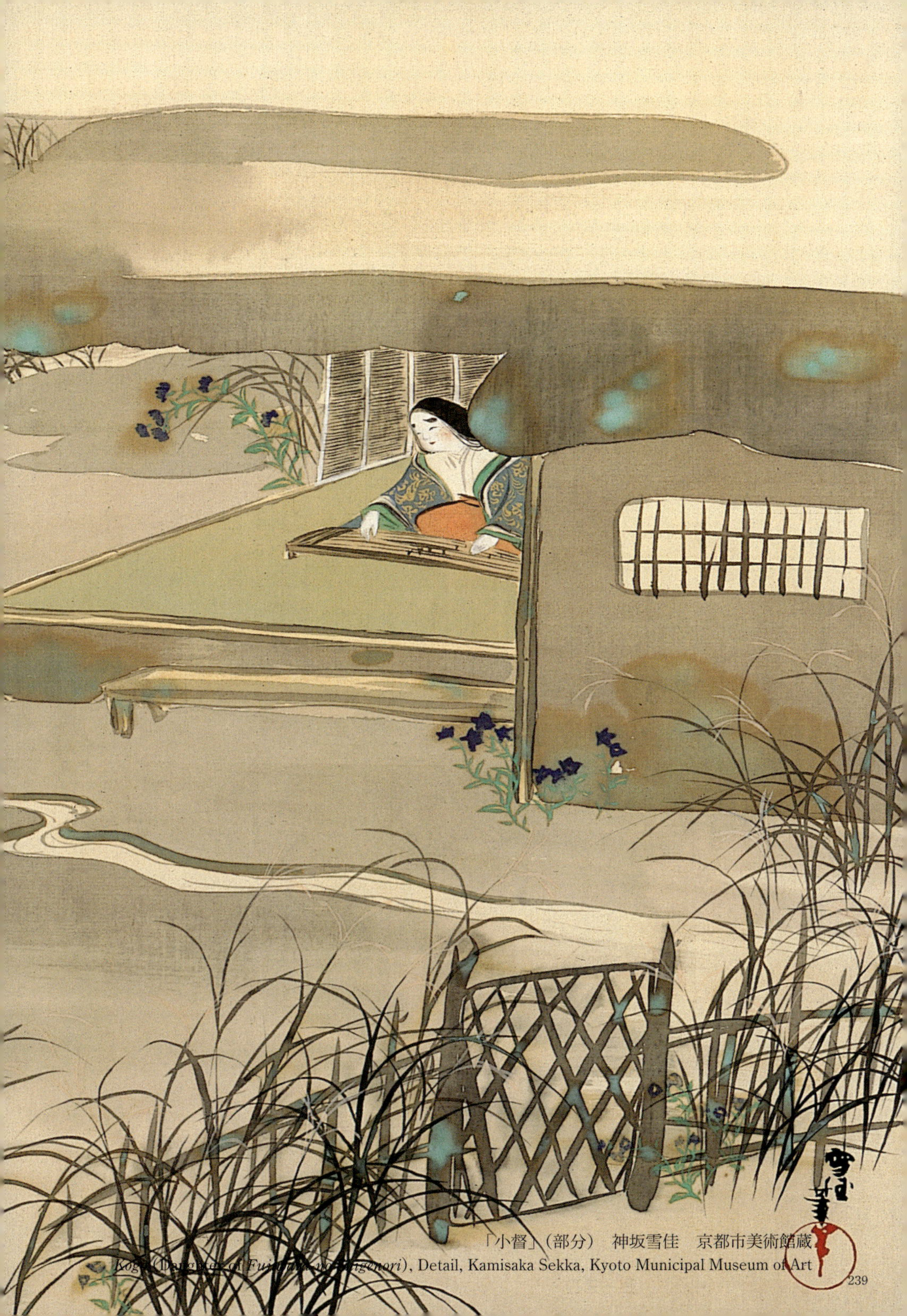

「小督」（部分）　神坂雪佳　京都市美術館蔵
Kogō (Daughter of Fujiwara no Shigenori), Detail, Kamisaka Sekka, Kyoto Municipal Museum of Art

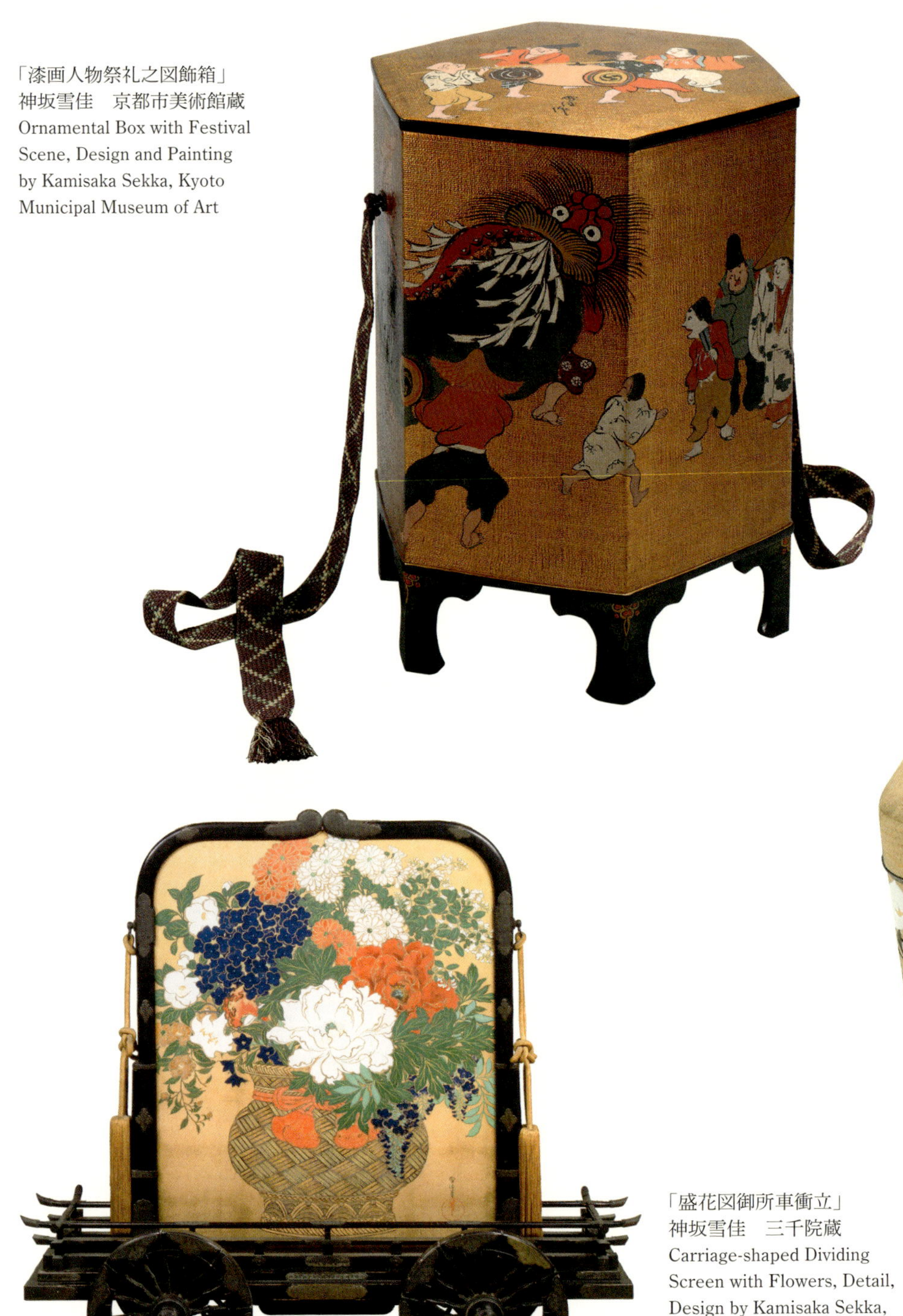

「漆画人物祭礼之図飾箱」
神坂雪佳　京都市美術館蔵
Ornamental Box with Festival
Scene, Design and Painting
by Kamisaka Sekka, Kyoto
Municipal Museum of Art

「盛花図御所車衝立」
神坂雪佳　三千院蔵
Carriage-shaped Dividing
Screen with Flowers, Detail,
Design by Kamisaka Sekka,
Sanzen-in, Kyoto

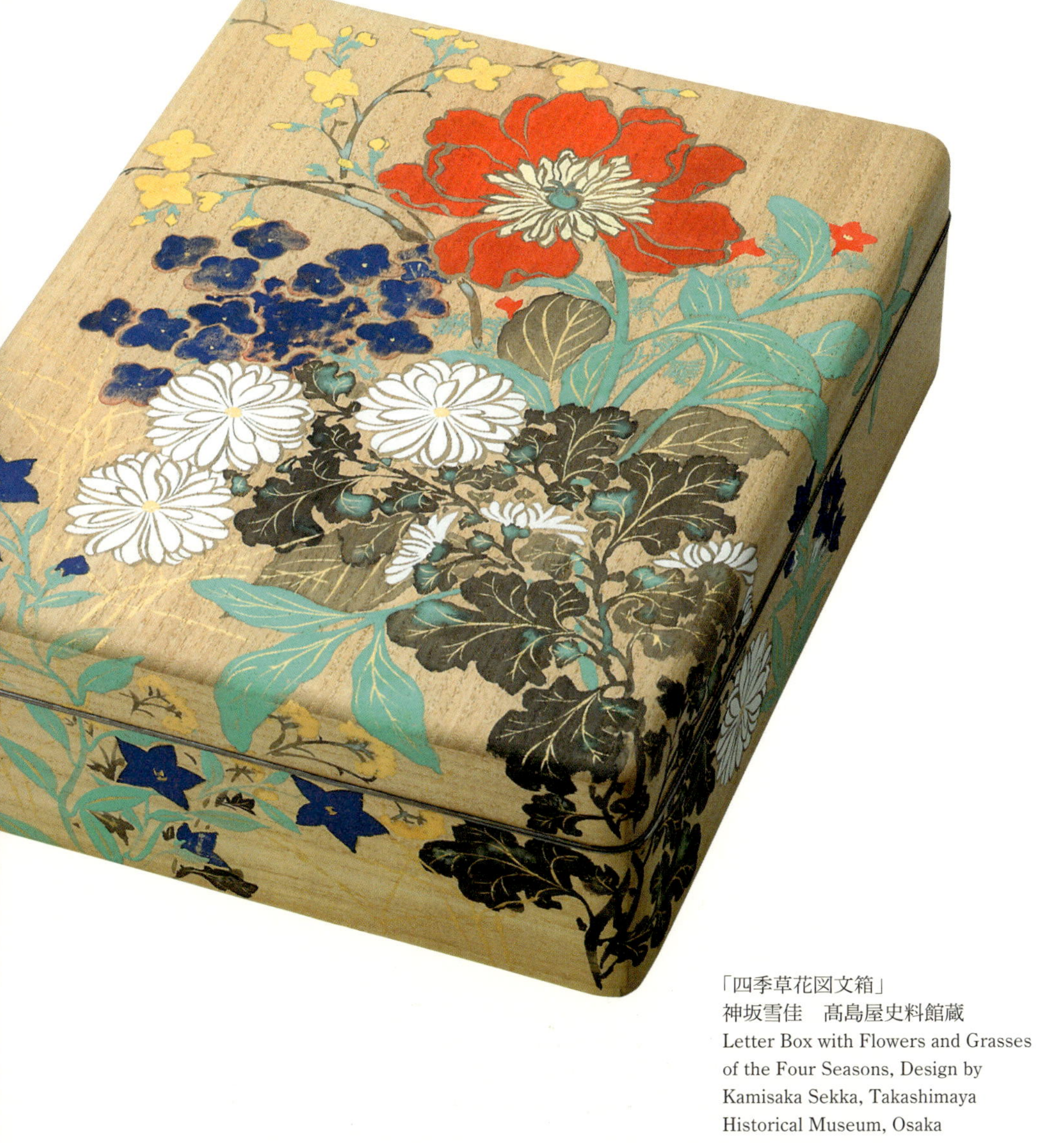

「四季草花図文箱」
神坂雪佳　髙島屋史料館蔵
Letter Box with Flowers and Grasses
of the Four Seasons, Design by
Kamisaka Sekka, Takashimaya
Historical Museum, Osaka

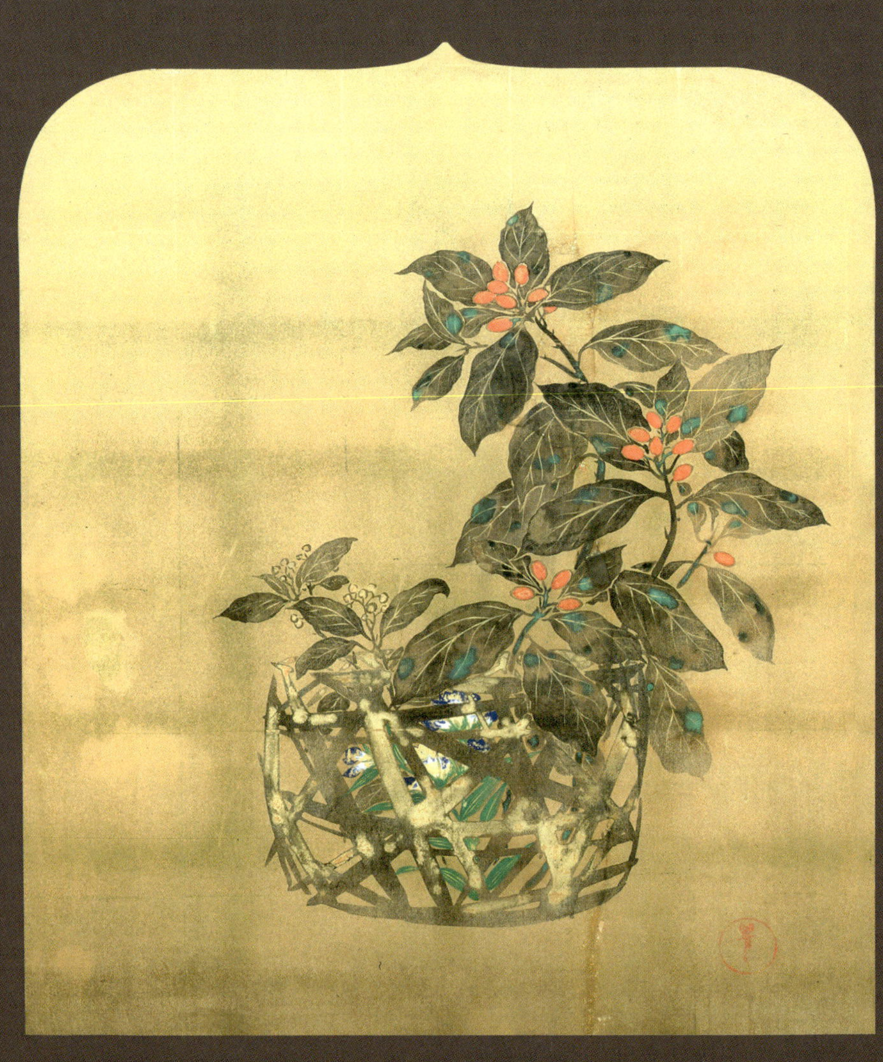

「盛花図御所車衝立」（部分・裏）　神坂雪佳　三千院蔵
Carriage-shaped Dividing Screen with Flowers, Detail,
Design by Kamisaka Sekka, Sanzen-in, Kyoto

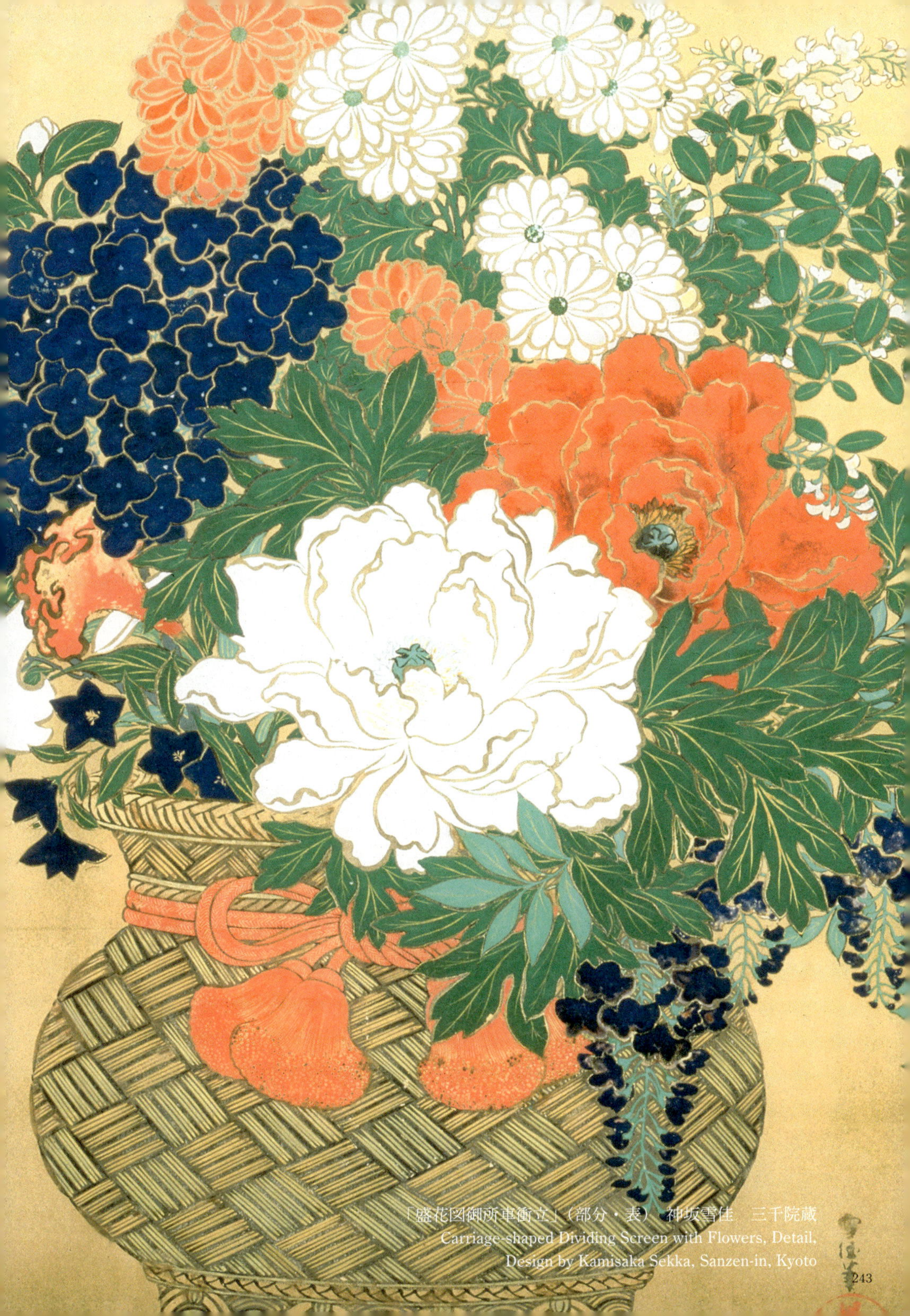

「盛花図御所車衝立」（部分・表）　神坂雪佳　三千院蔵
Carriage-shaped Dividing Screen with Flowers, Detail,
Design by Kamisaka Sekka, Sanzen-in, Kyoto

浅井忠

あさい ちゅう　安政 3 年〜明治 40 年（1856 - 1907）

江戸の佐倉藩邸内に生まれた浅井忠は、工部美術学校でイタリアの風景画家フォンタネージに洋画を学んだのち、明治美術会を結成した。明治 33 〜 35 年までパリに留学し、万国博覧会でアール・ヌーヴォーに触れ、その様式を反映させた図案を制作、また琳派の再発見にも繋がった。帰国後も絵画、工芸の両面で多くの作家に影響を与えた。

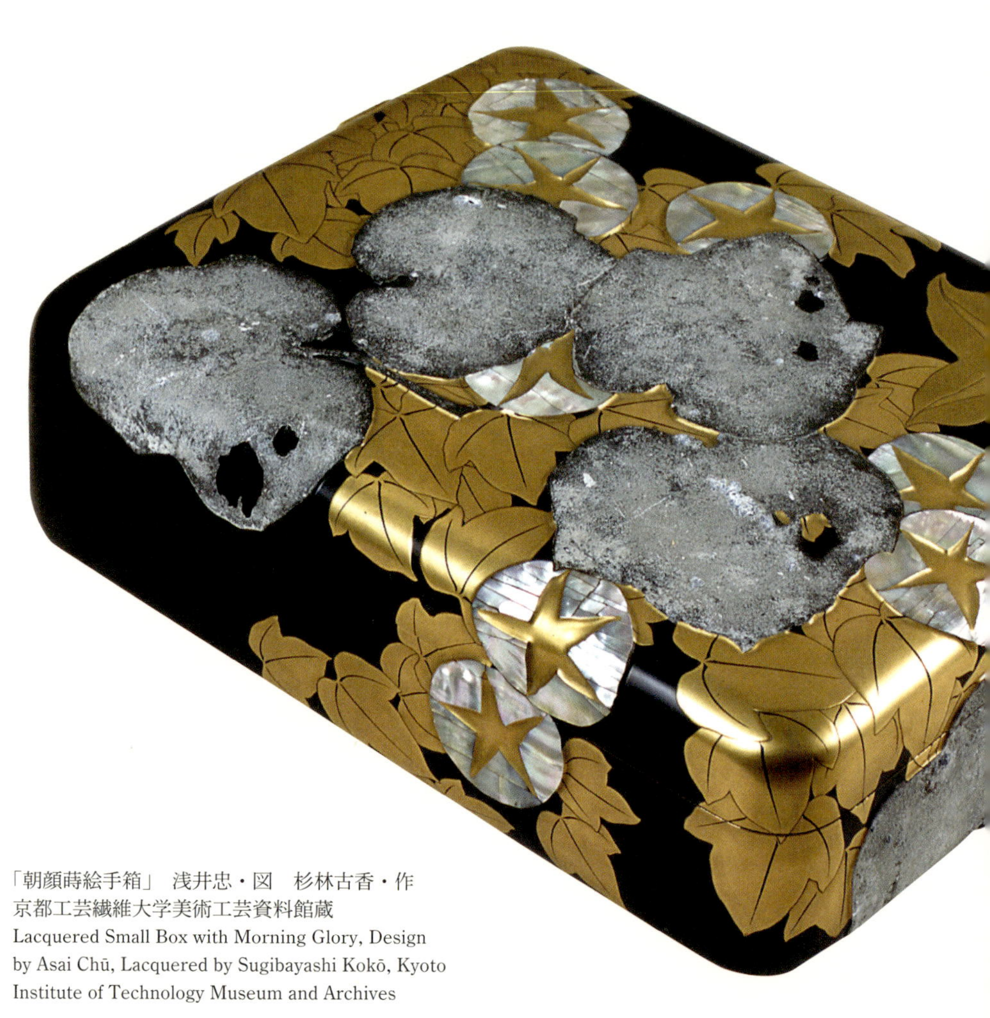

「朝顔蒔絵手箱」　浅井忠・図　杉林古香・作
京都工芸繊維大学美術工芸資料館蔵
Lacquered Small Box with Morning Glory, Design
by Asai Chū, Lacquered by Sugibayashi Kokō, Kyoto
Institute of Technology Museum and Archives

Asai Chū (1856 – 1907)

Asai, born in Edo, studied Western-style painting with Antonio Fontanesi at the Kobu Bijutsu Gakko, and founded the Meiji Art Society. Studying in Paris in 1900-1905, he encountered Art Nouveau at the Paris Exposition. While creating designs inspired by Art Nouveau, he rediscovered the Rinpa style. After returning to Japan, he influenced many other artists in both painting and the craft arts.

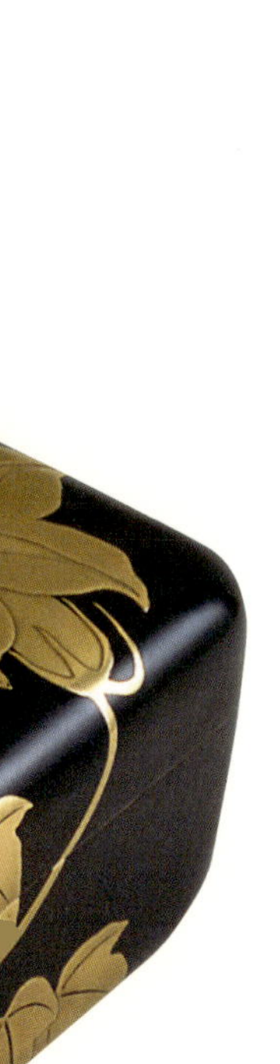

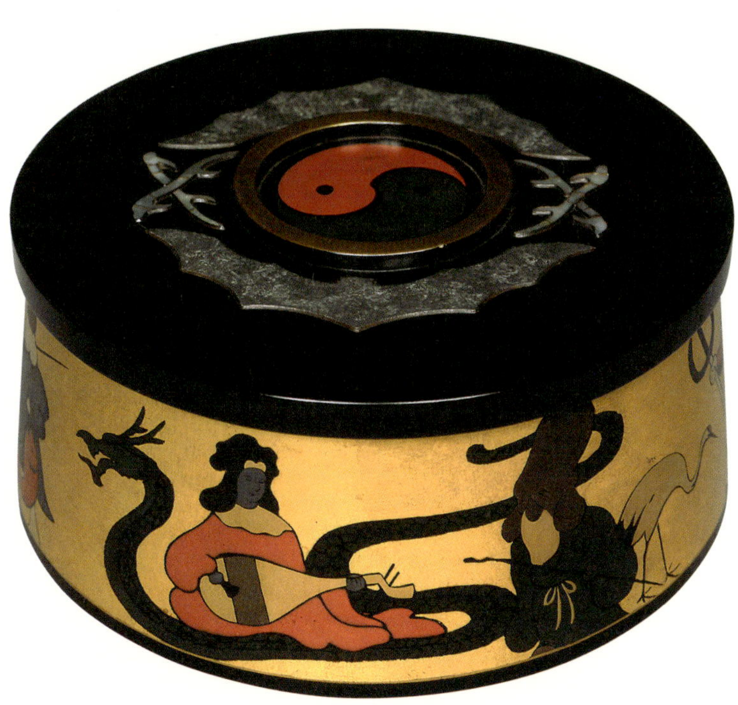

「七福神蒔絵蓋付菓子器」　浅井忠・図　迎田秋悦・作
京都工芸繊維大学美術工芸資料館蔵
Lacquered Sweets Box with the Seven Gods of Good Fortune, Design by Asai Chū, Lacquered by Kōda Shūetsu, Kyoto Institute of Technology Museum and Archives

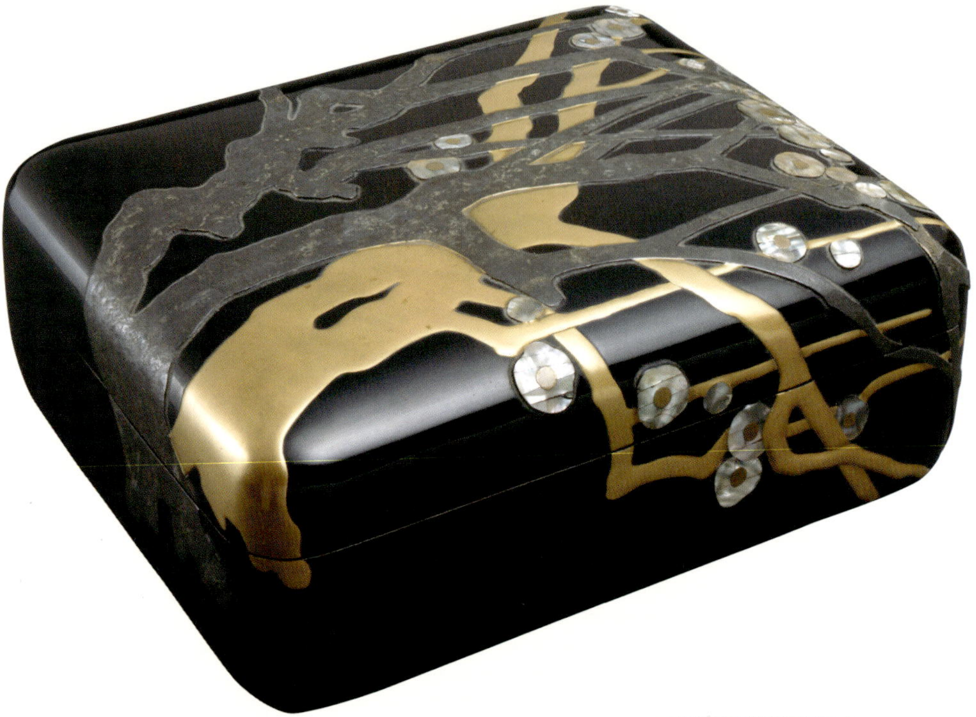

「梅文蒔絵文庫」　浅井忠・図
杉林古香・作　佐倉市立美術館蔵
Lacquered Stationery Box with
Plum Trees, Design by Asai Chū,
Lacquered by Sugibayashi Kokō,
Sakura City Museum of Art

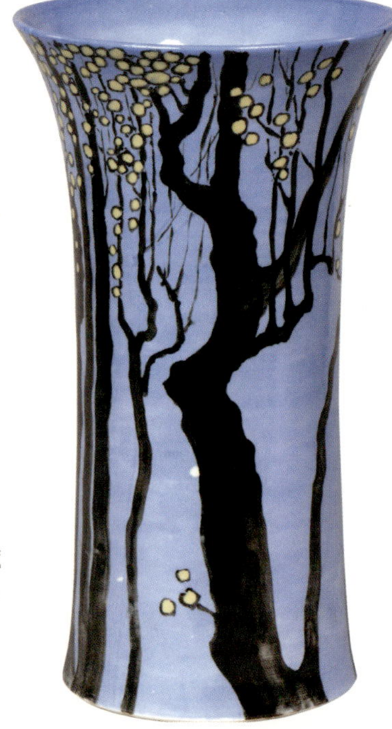

「梅図花生」　浅井忠・図
京都工芸繊維大学美術工芸資料館蔵
Vase with Plum Trees, Design by Asai
Chū, Kyoto Institute of Technology
Museum and Archives

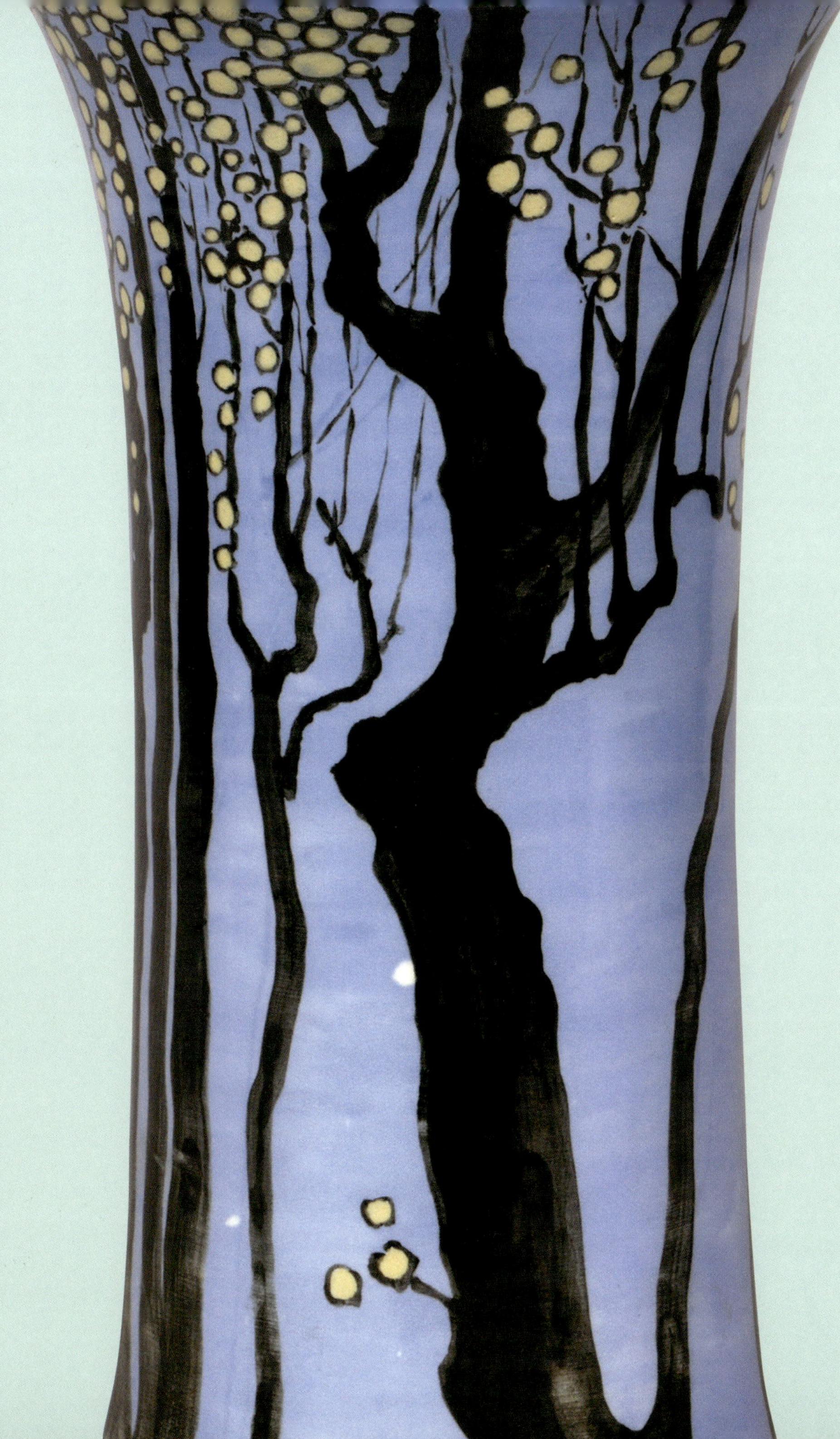

諸派の画家たち

琳派の特色は、画面構成が大胆で斬新、そして洒脱で軽快なことである。それはパターン化された配置やリズミカルな繰り返しで、眼に優しく伝わってくる。そしてその一方には金銀と極彩色の豪華さがある。この感覚が日本人の最も好む美的感覚であることに間違いはない。ここに紹介する作品は琳派の特徴である没骨、たらし込みなどの技法を用いずに独自の流儀で描かれているが、琳派風と眼に映るものが多い。装飾性に富んだ作品を制作すると自然と琳派的な作風をおびてくるのである。

Painters of Other Schools

The Rinpa style, perhaps the most distinctively Japanese of aesthetics, is epitomized by bold, fresh compositions that are deft and urbane, with attractive, rhythmic placement of stylized elements, and by an uninhibited gorgeousness, combining gold and silver pigments with vivid colors. The paintings introduced in this chapter seem, though without using Rinpa's signature mokkotsu (depiction of objects without outlines) and tarashikomi (application of pigments to a wet surface) techniques, to be in the Rinpa style, given their richly decorative quality.

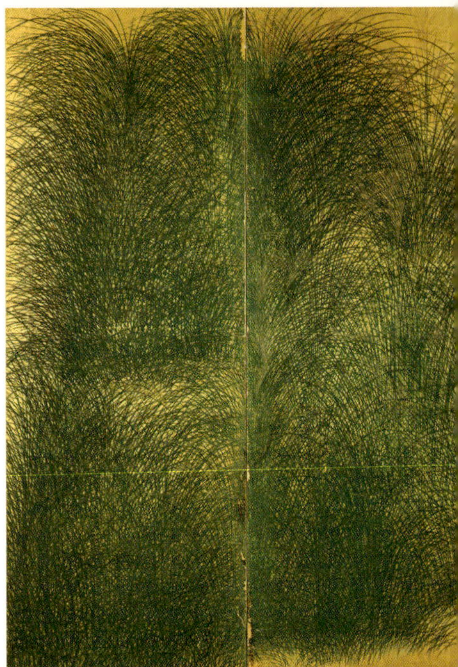

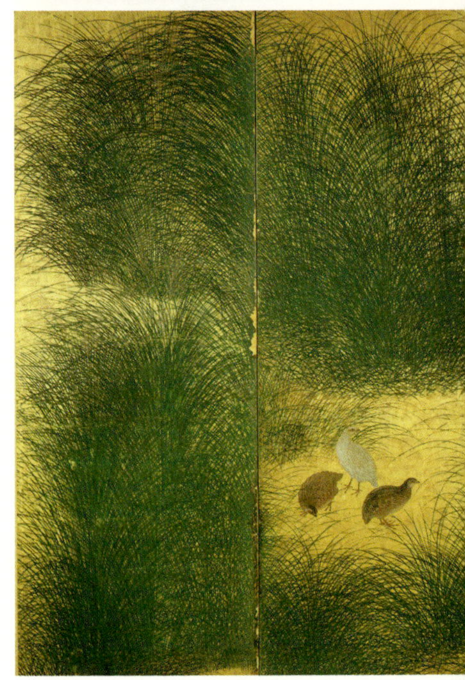

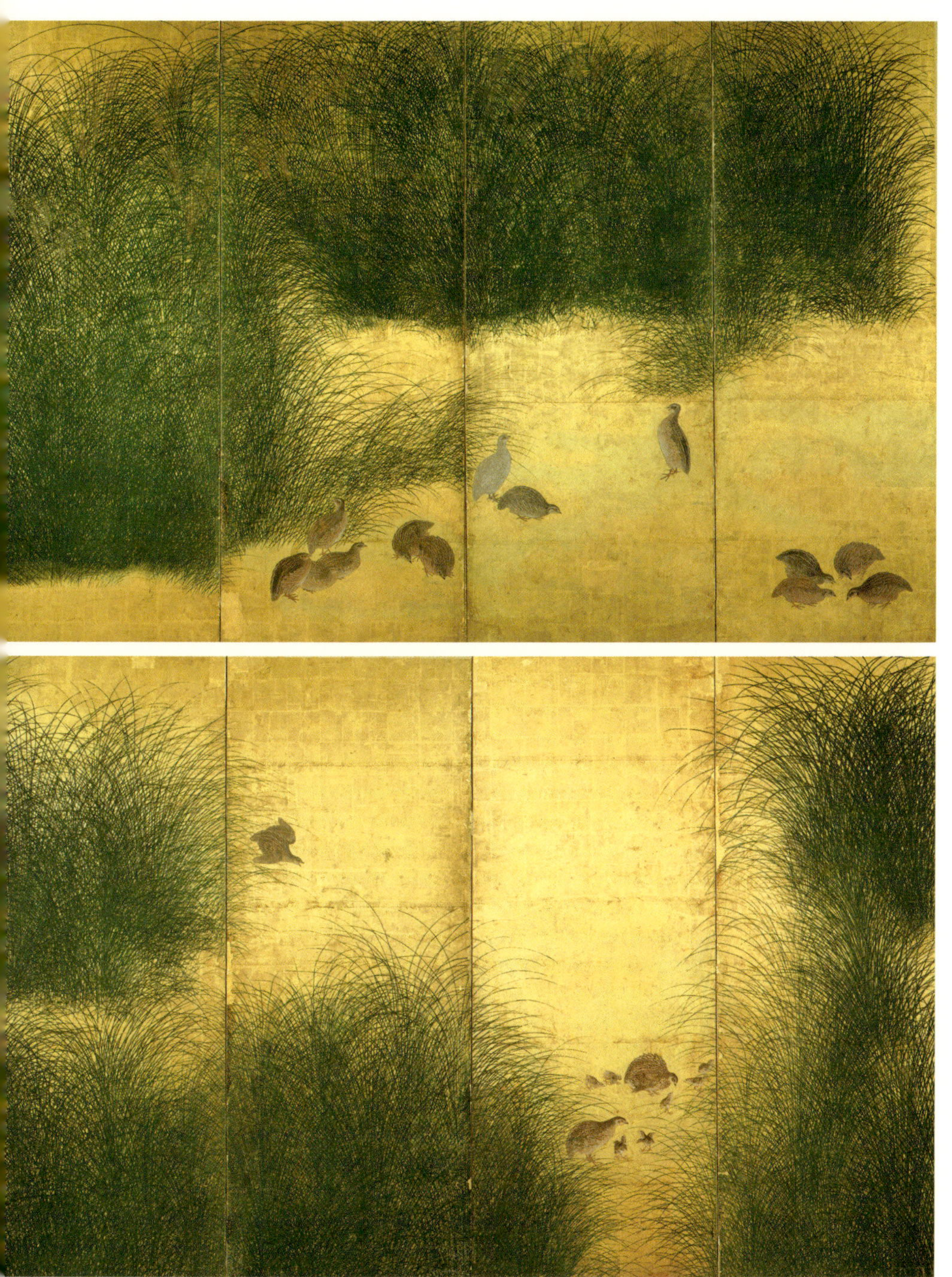

「秋草鶉図屏風」　重文　伝土佐光起　名古屋市博物館蔵
Flowering Plants of Autumn and Quail, Attributed to Tosa Mitsuoki,
Important Cultural Property, Nagoya City Museum

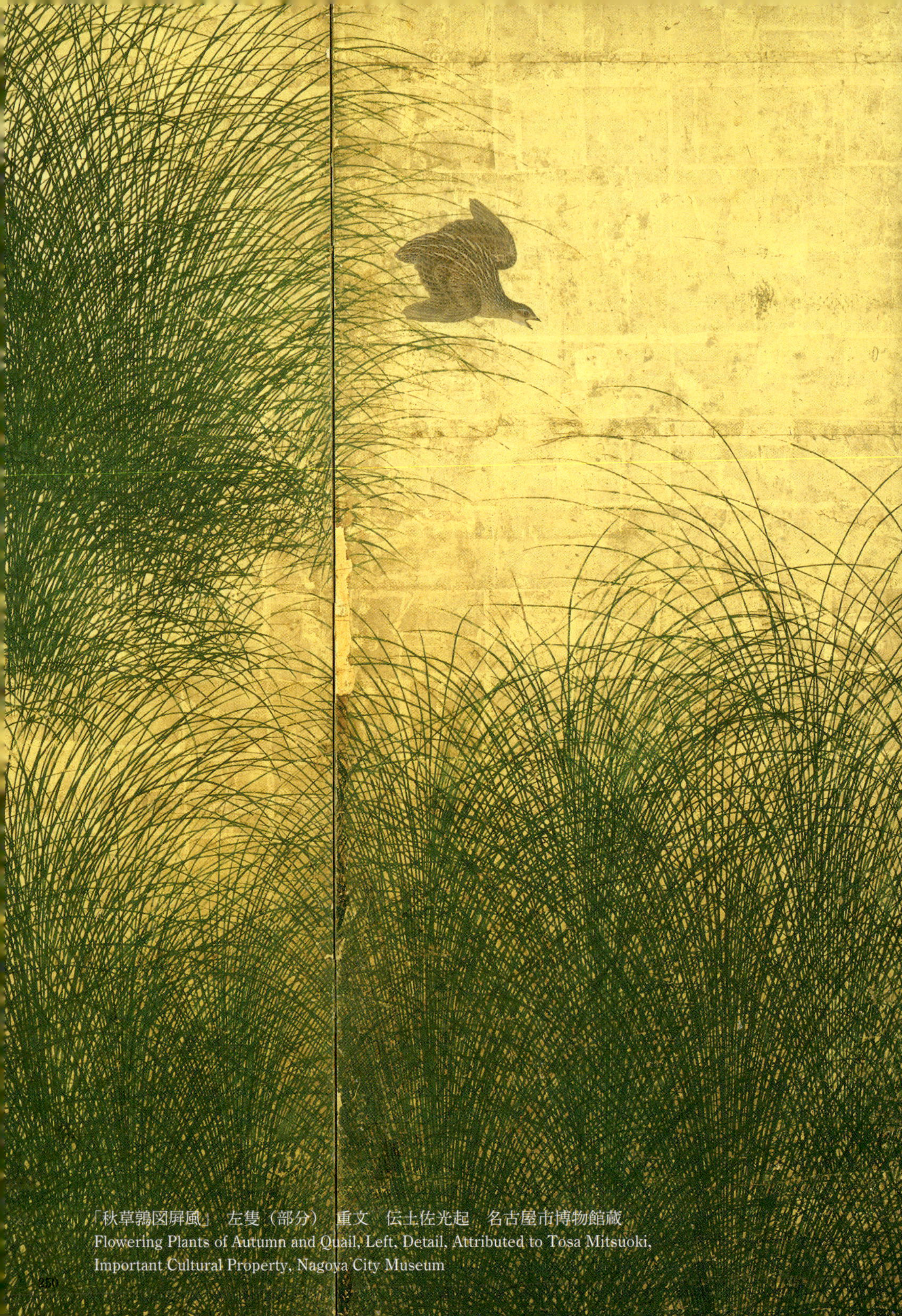

「秋草鶉図屏風」　左隻（部分）　重文　伝土佐光起　名古屋市博物館蔵
Flowering Plants of Autumn and Quail, Left, Detail, Attributed to Tosa Mitsuoki,
Important Cultural Property, Nagoya City Museum

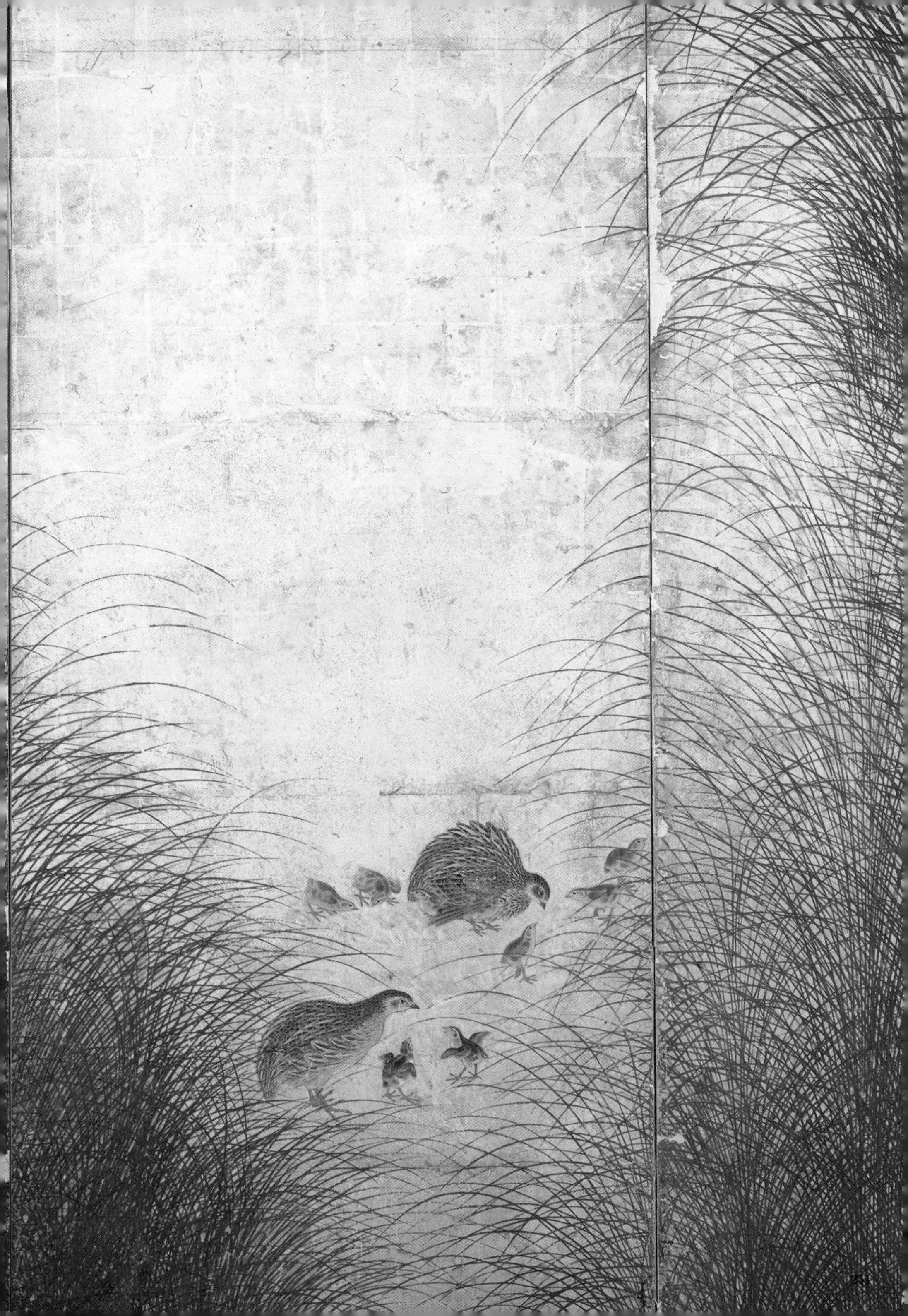

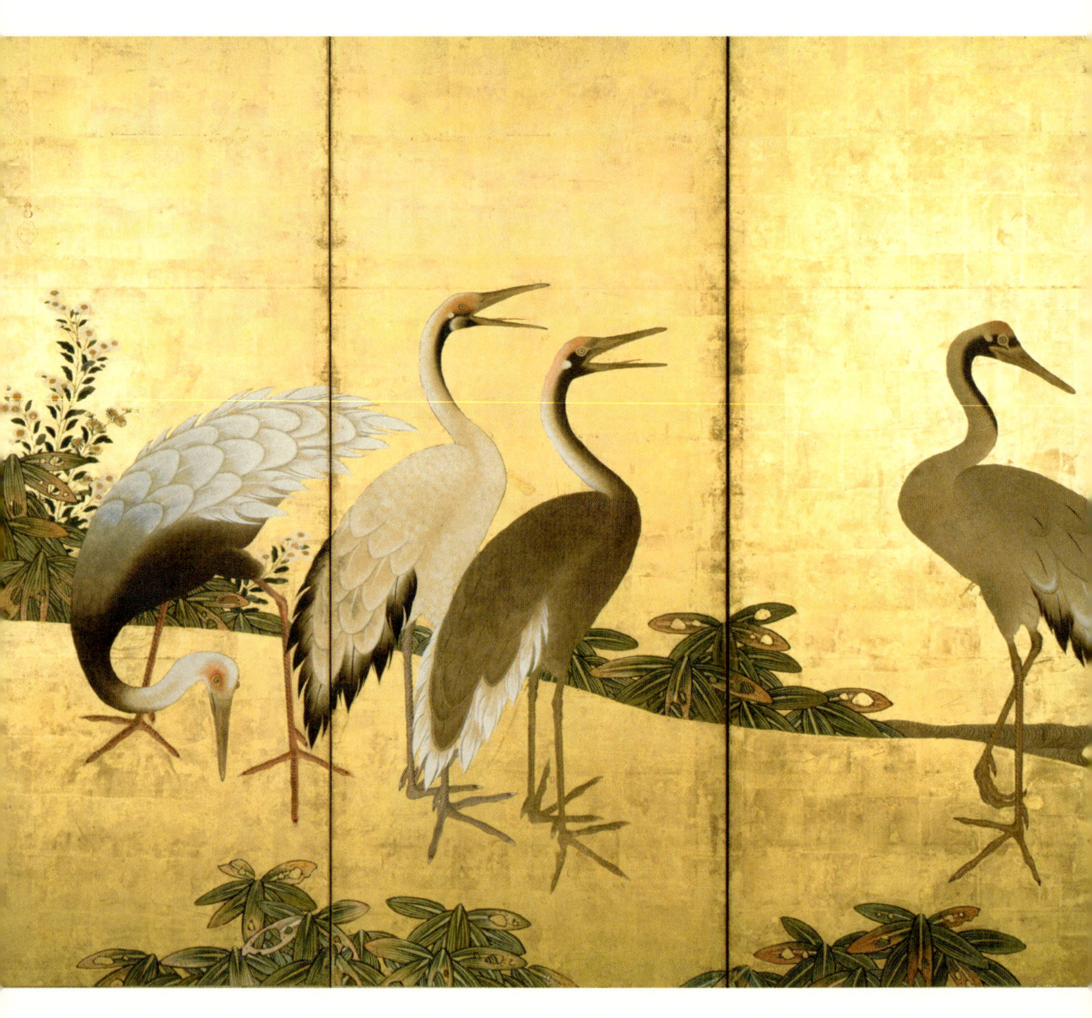

「群鶴図屏風」　左隻　雲谷等與　山口県立美術館蔵
Cranes, Left, Unkoku Tōyo, Yamaguchi Prefectural Art Museum

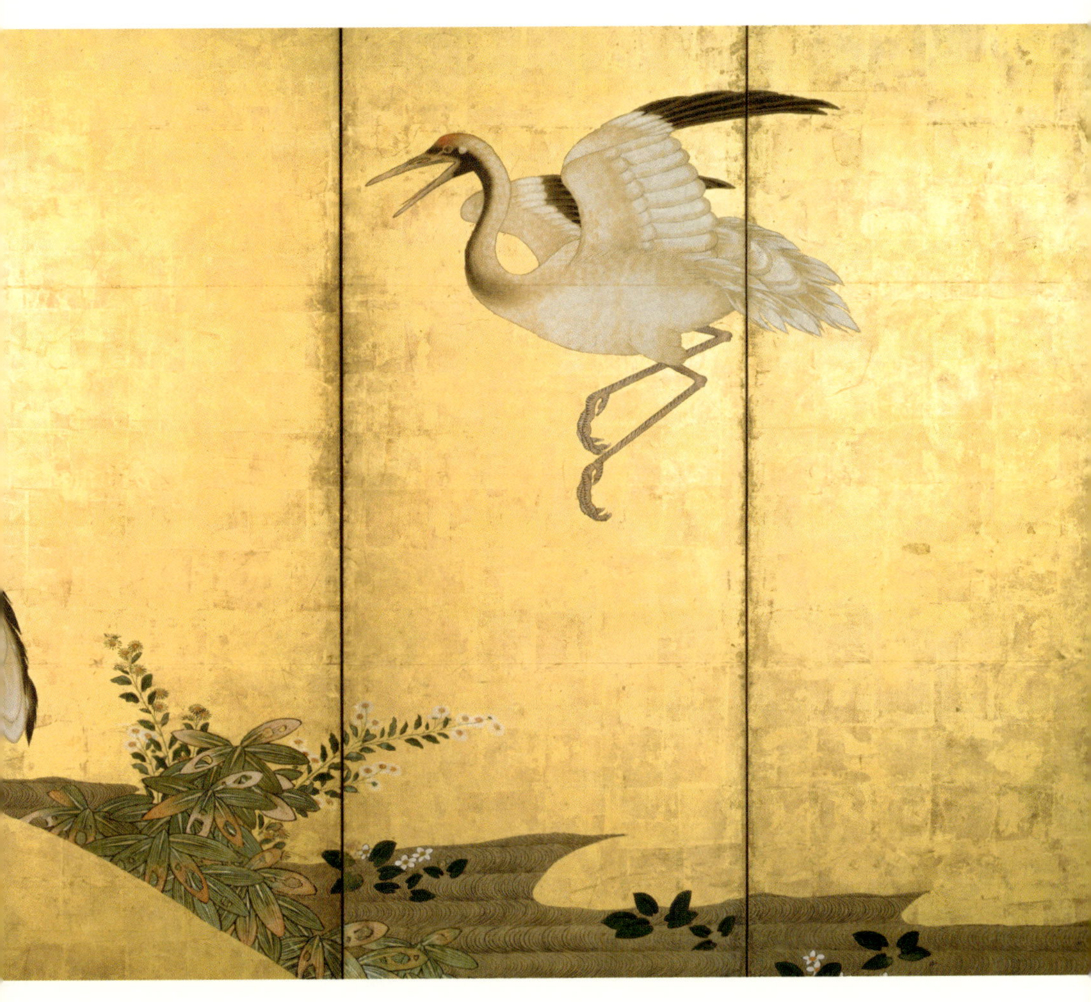

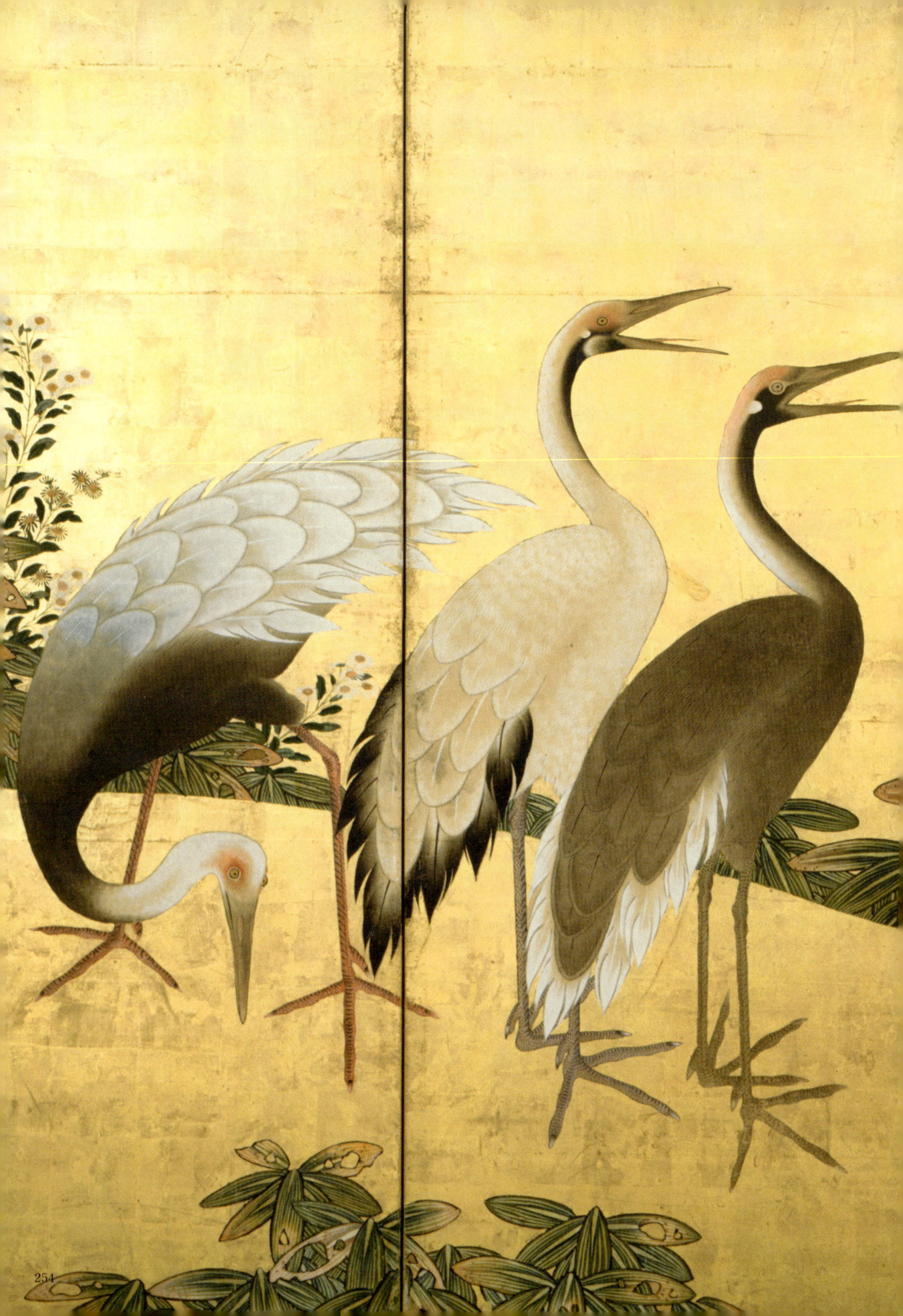

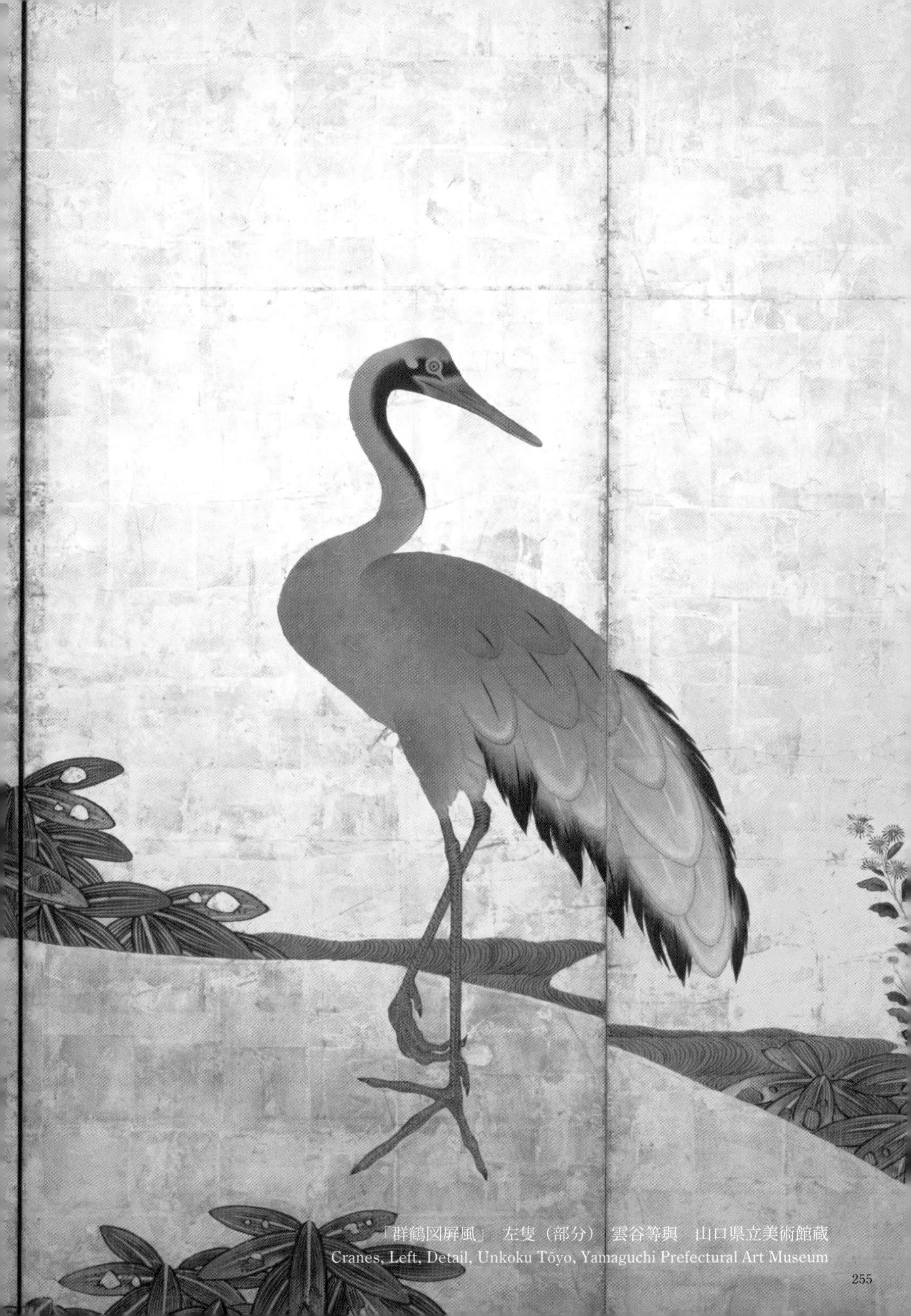

「群鶴図屛風」　左隻（部分）　雲谷等與　山口県立美術館蔵
Cranes, Left, Detail, Unkoku Tōyo, Yamaguchi Prefectural Art Museum

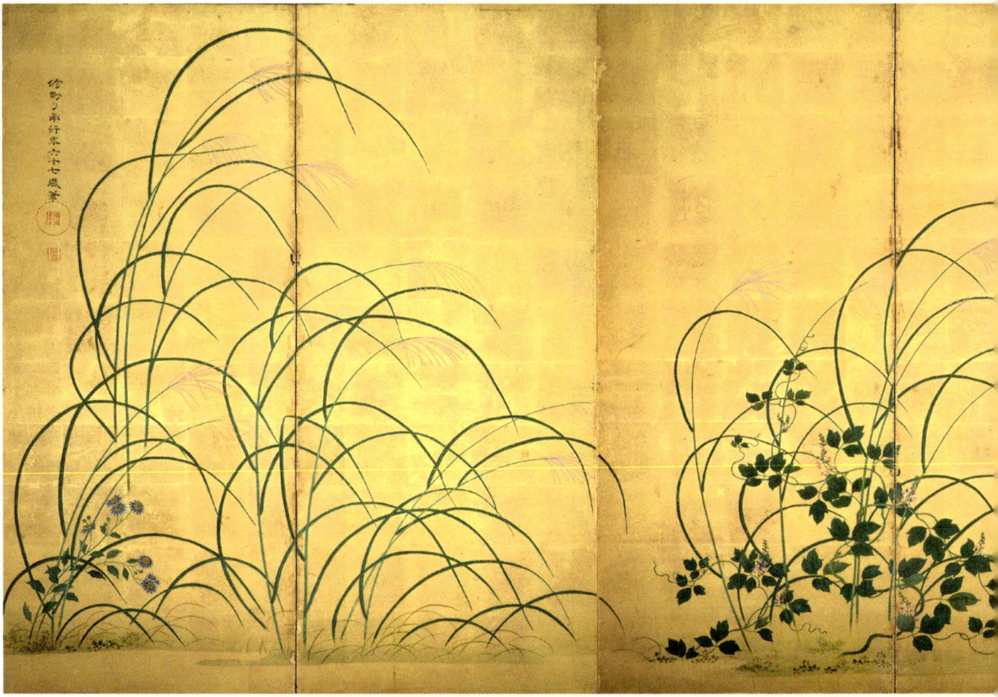

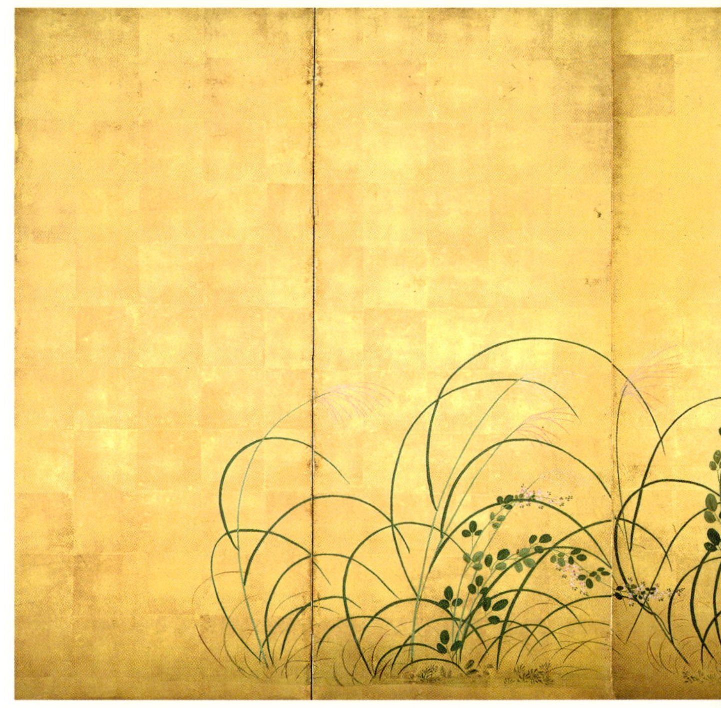

「秋草図屏風」　狩野了承
板橋区立美術館蔵
Autumn Flowers, Kanō Ryōshō,
Itabashi Art Museum

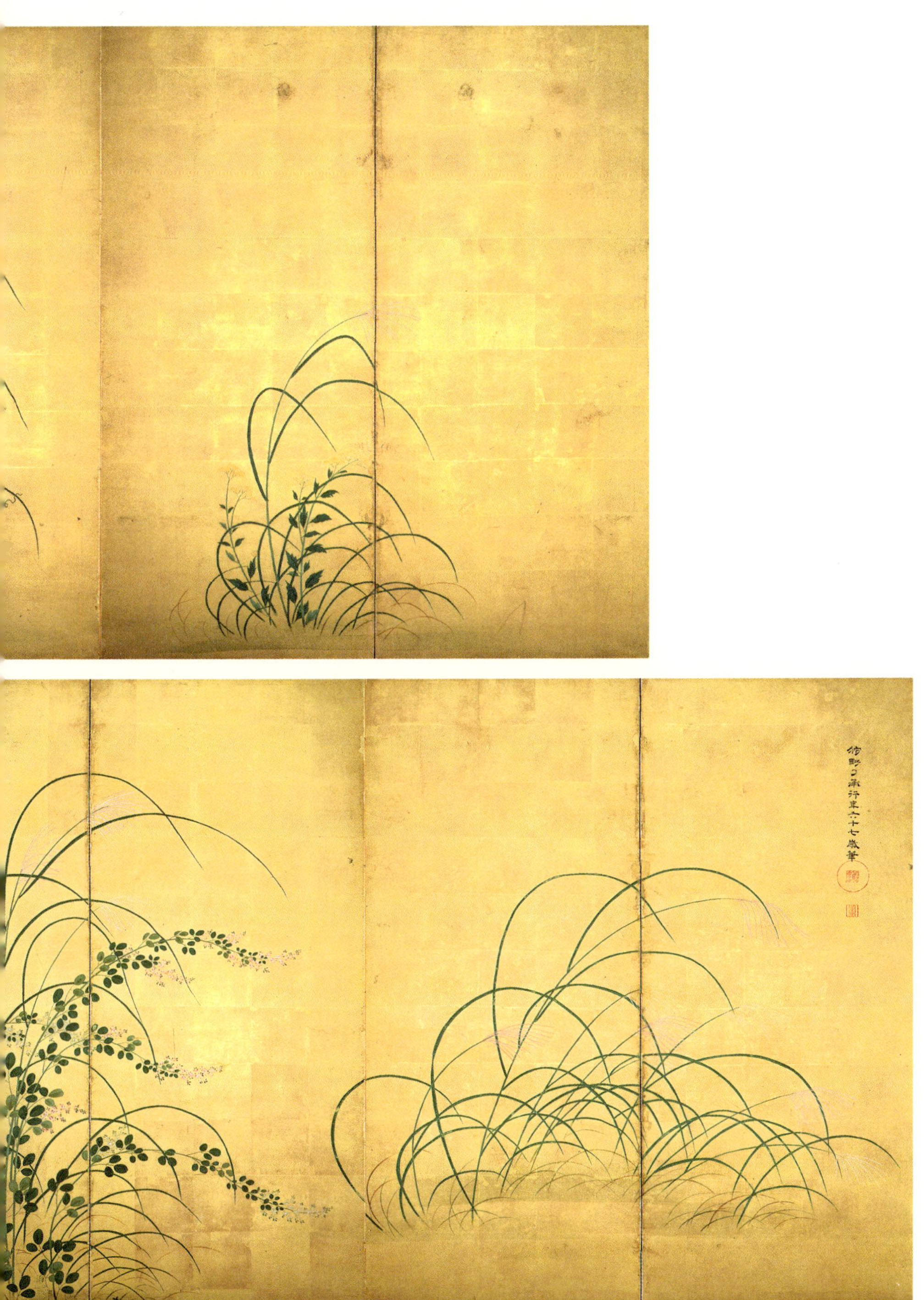
狩野□□行年六十七歳筆

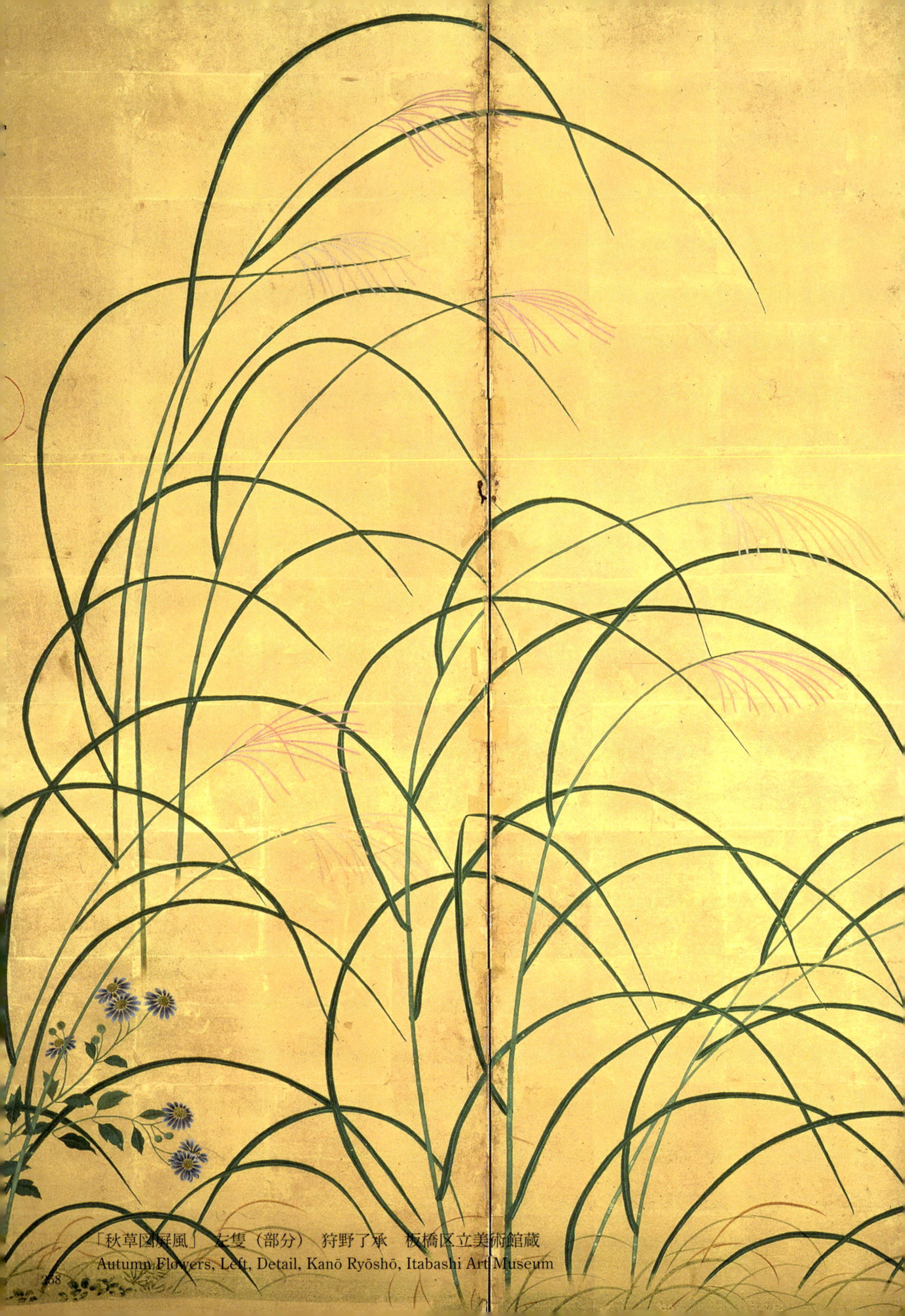

「秋草図屏風」　左隻（部分）　狩野了承　板橋区立美術館蔵
Autumn Flowers, Left, Detail, Kanō Ryōshō, Itabashi Art Museum

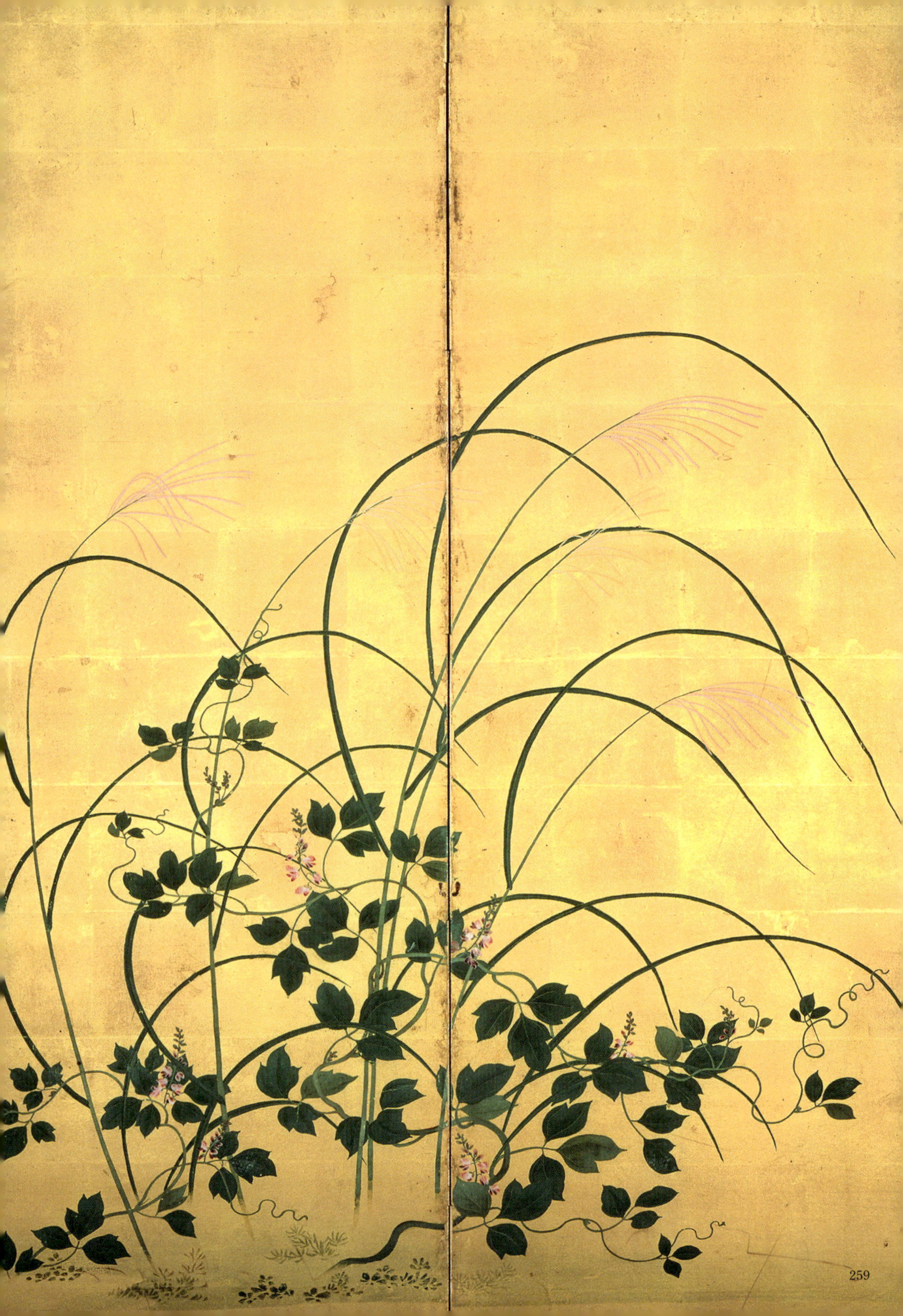

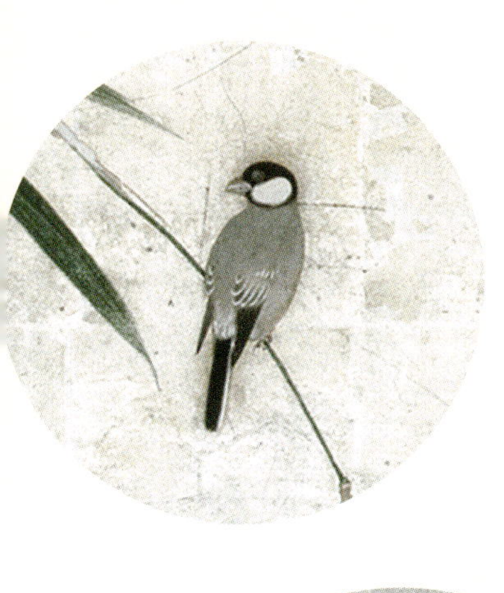

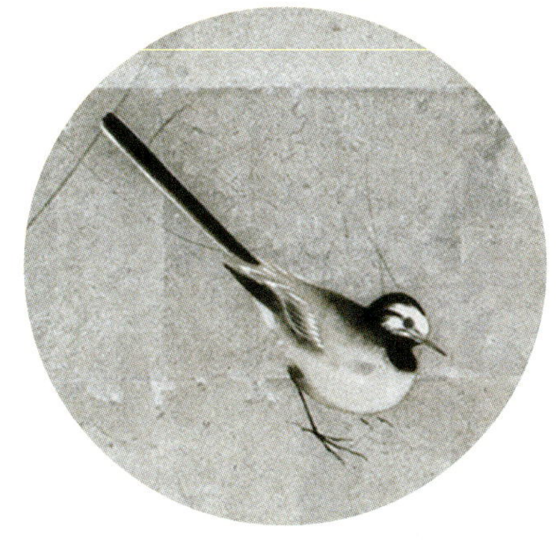

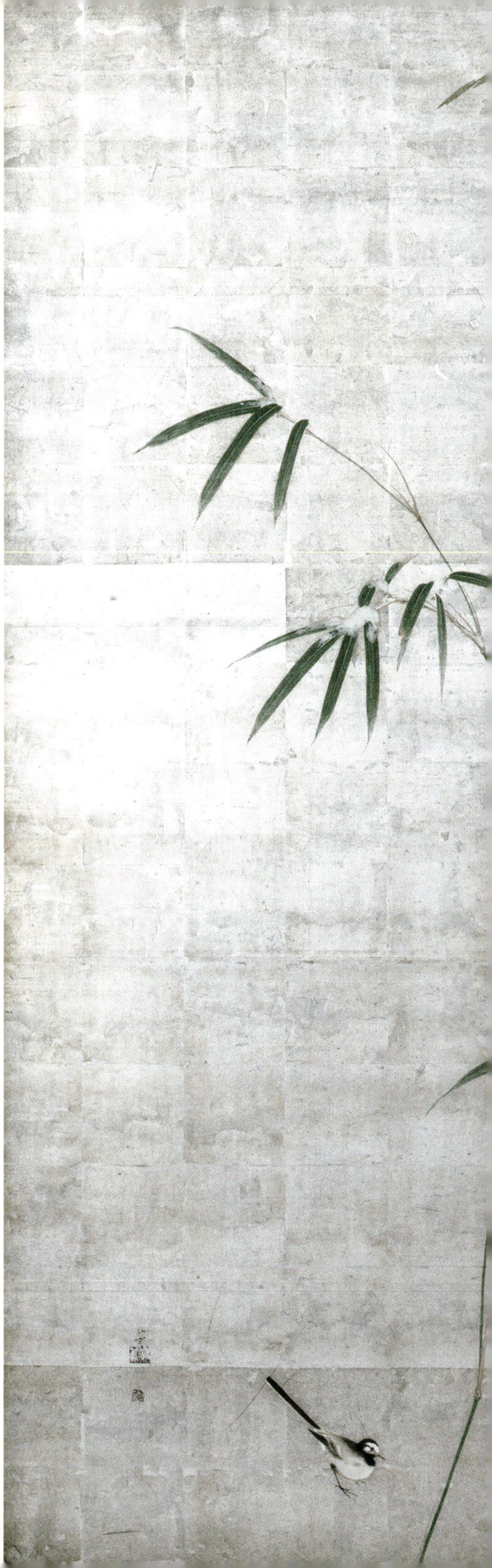

「若竹鶺鴒図屏風」
田中訥言
名古屋市博物館蔵
Young Bamboos and Wagtails,
Tanaka Totsugen,
Nagoya City Museum

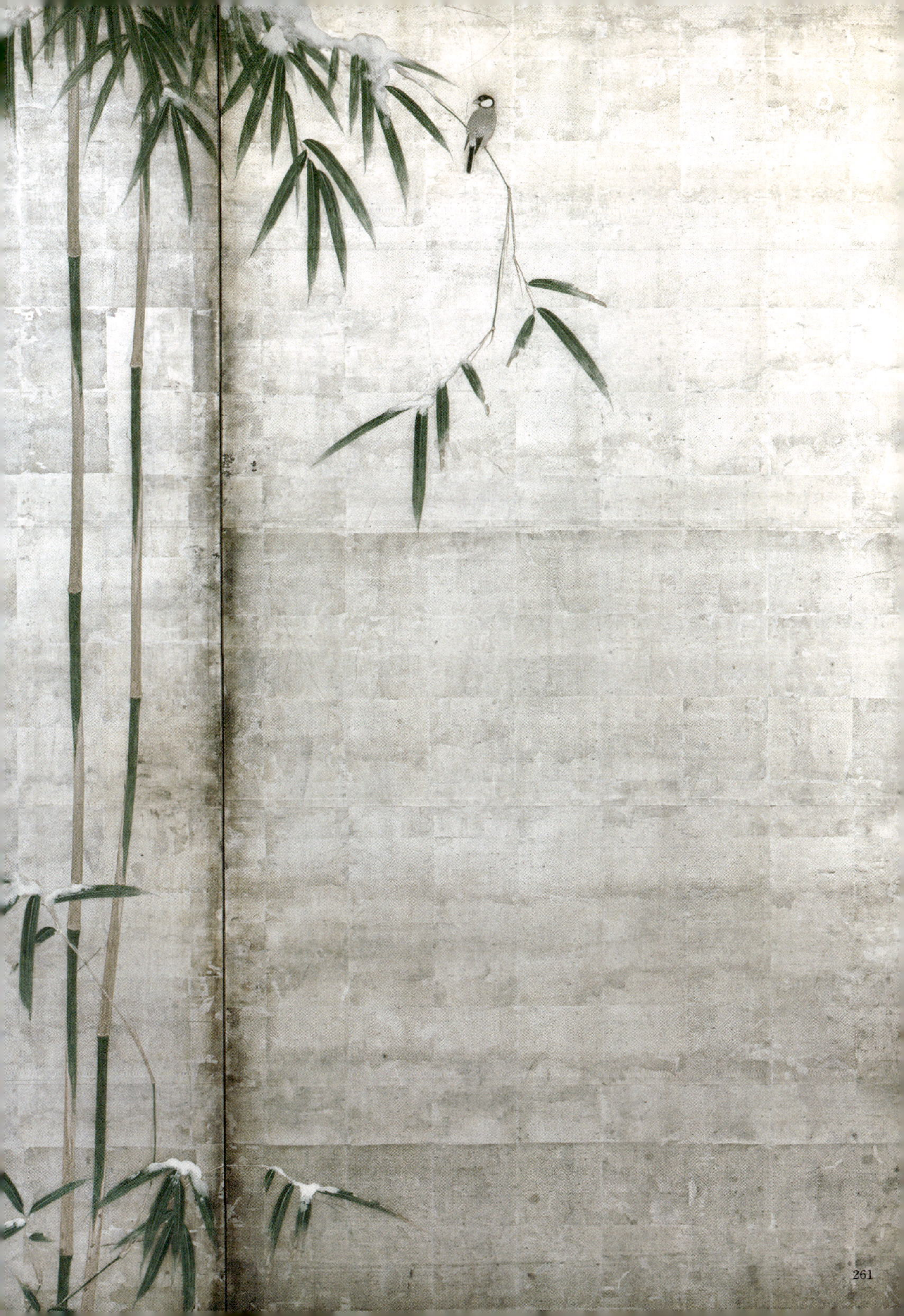

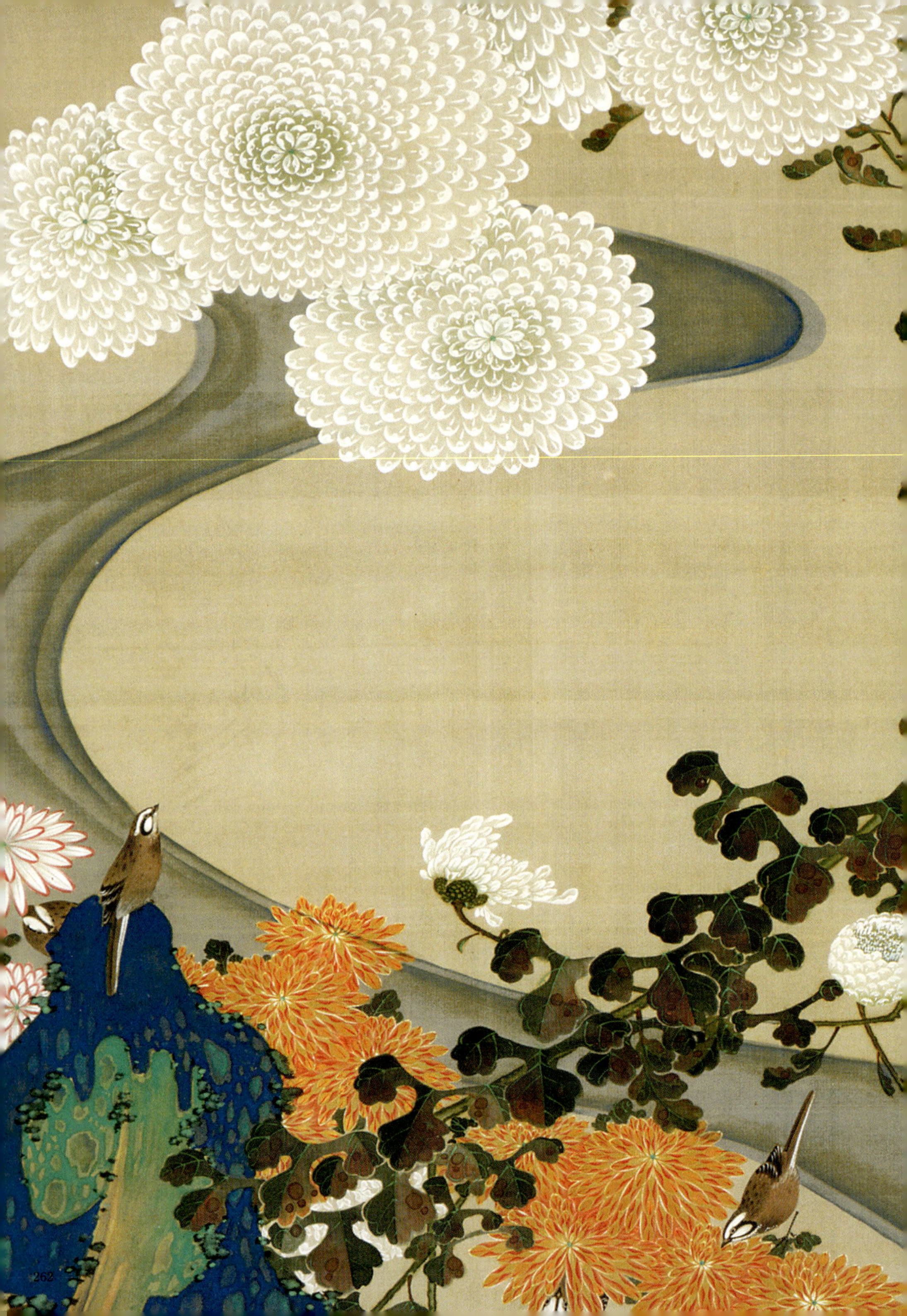

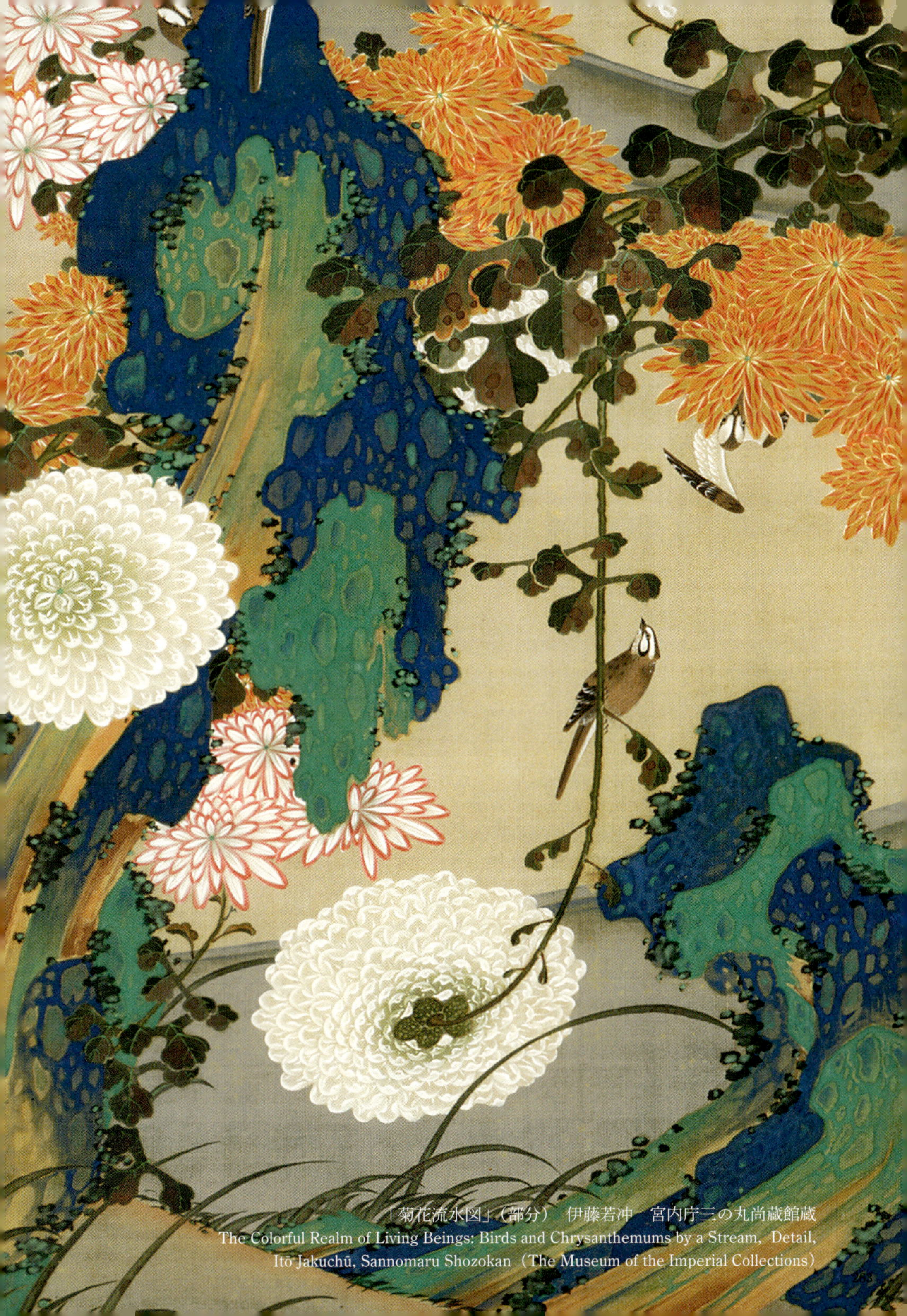

「菊花流水図」（部分）　伊藤若冲　宮内庁三の丸尚蔵館蔵
The Colorful Realm of Living Beings: Birds and Chrysanthemums by a Stream, Detail,
Itō Jakuchū, Sannomaru Shozokan（The Museum of the Imperial Collections）

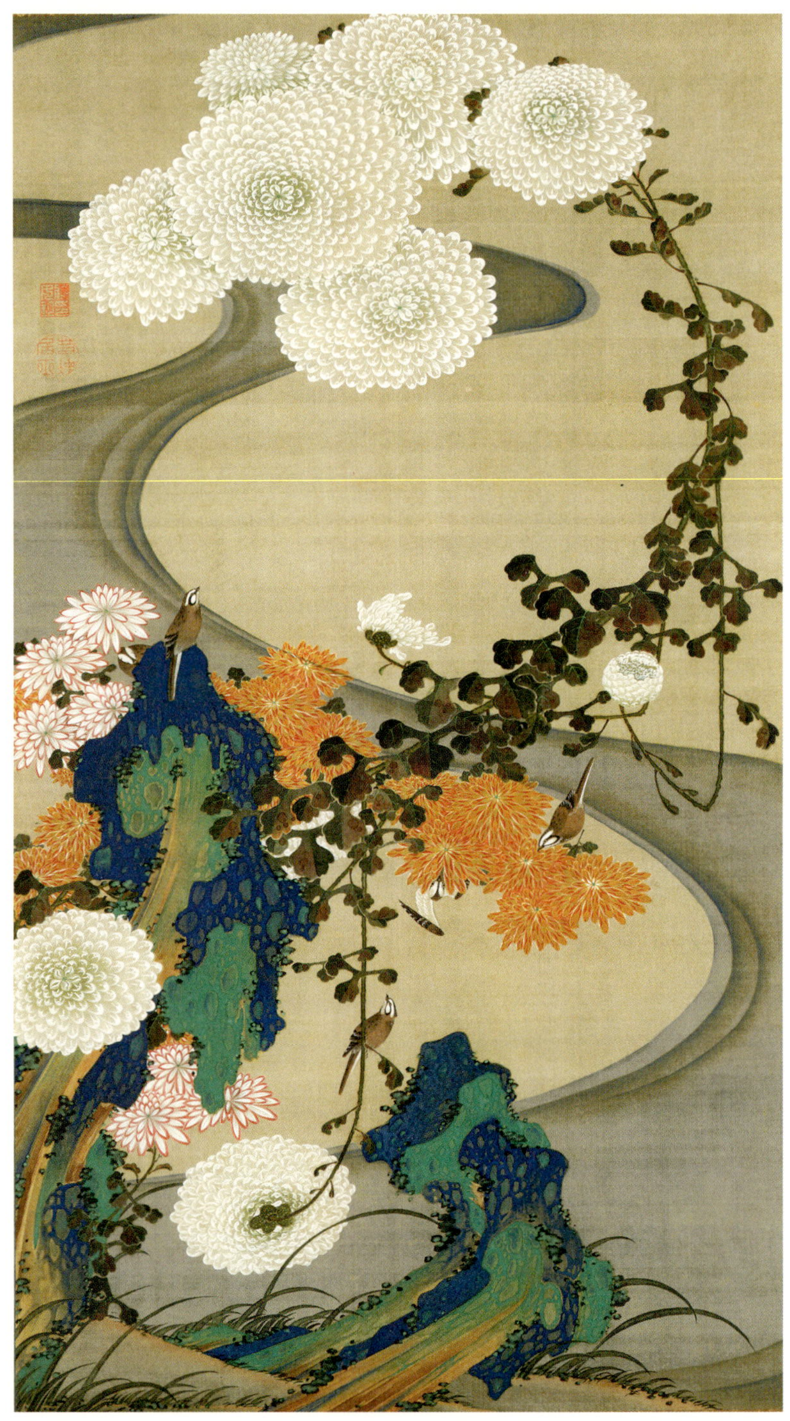

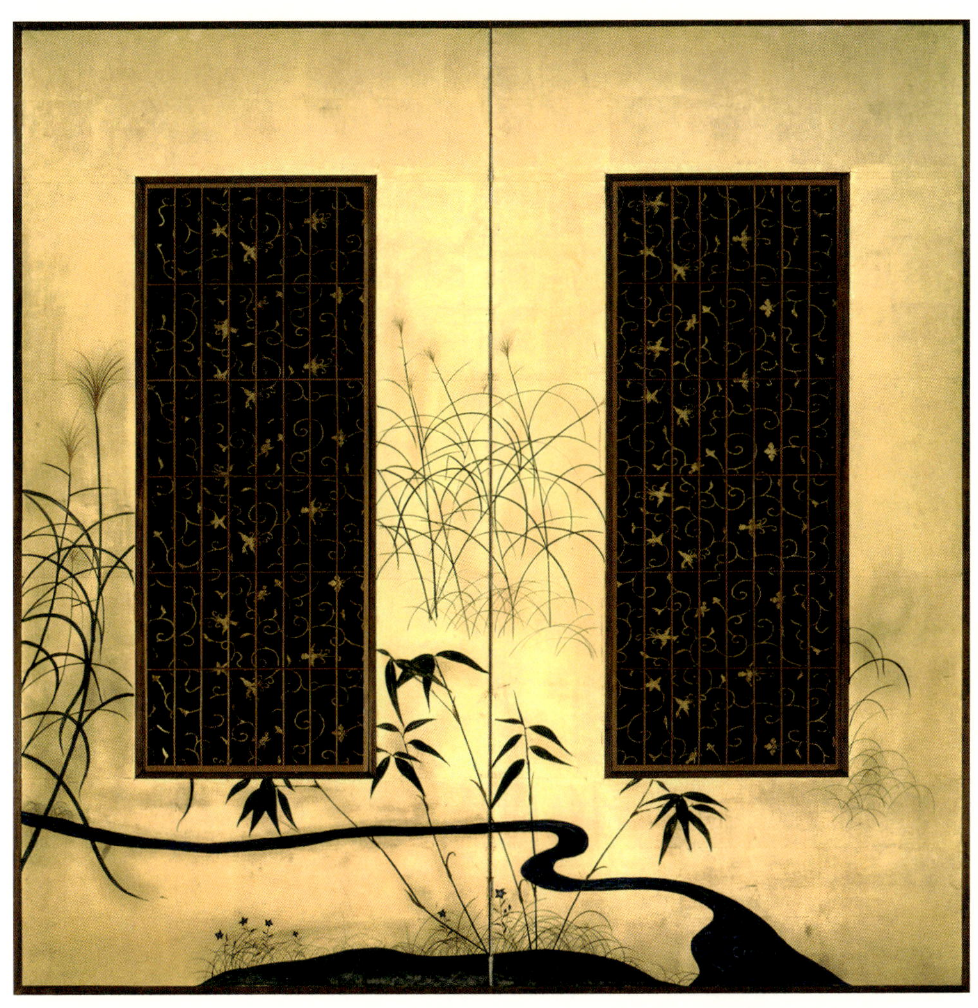

「秋草流水図屏風」　板橋区立美術館蔵
Autumn Plants and Stream, Itabashi Art Museum

「菊花流水図」　伊藤若冲　宮内庁三の丸尚蔵館蔵
The Colorful Realm of Living Beings: Birds and Chrysanthemums by a Stream,
Itō Jakuchū, Sannomaru Shozokan（The Museum of the Imperial Collections）

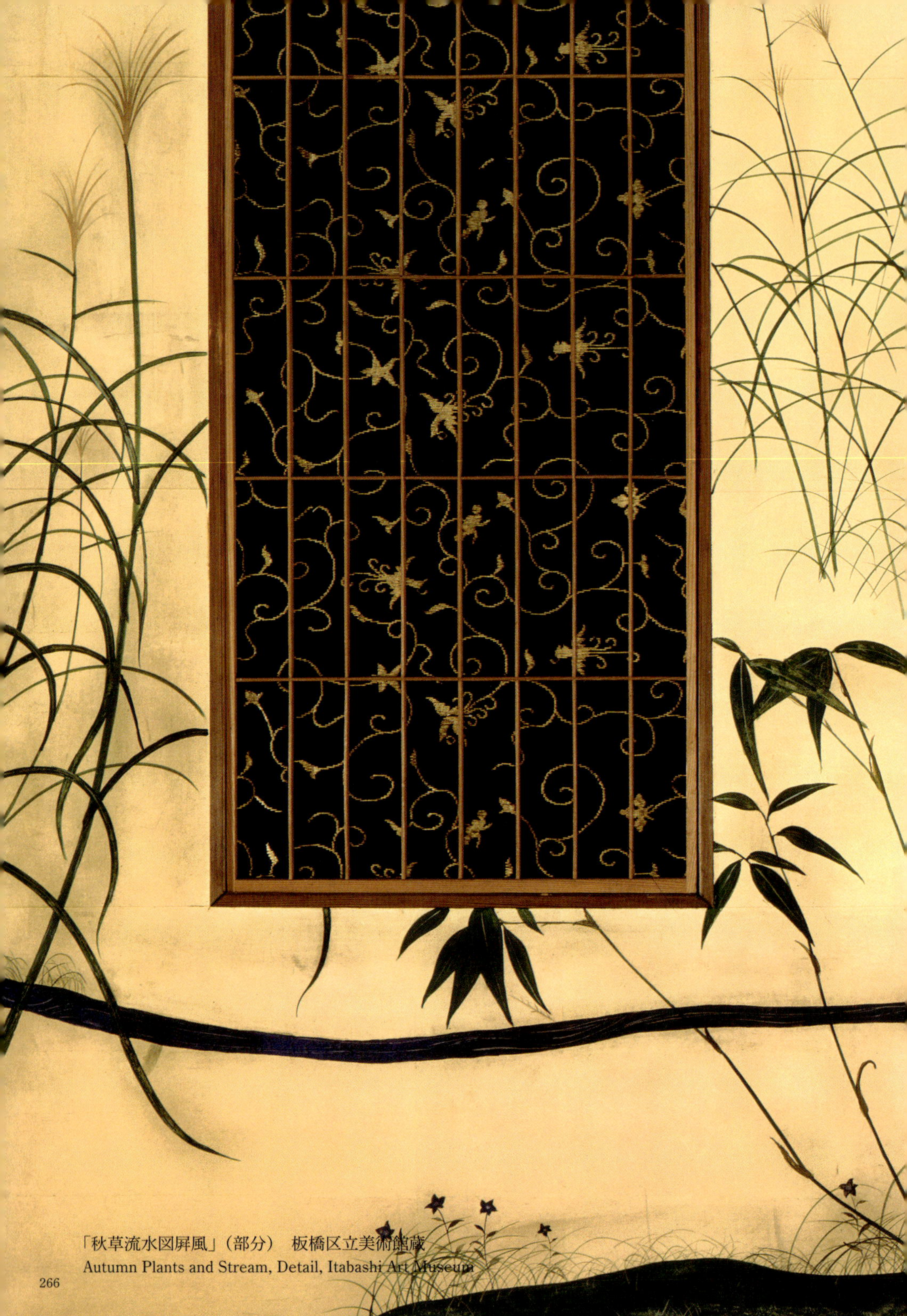

「秋草流水図屏風」（部分）　板橋区立美術館蔵
Autumn Plants and Stream, Detail, Itabashi Art Museum

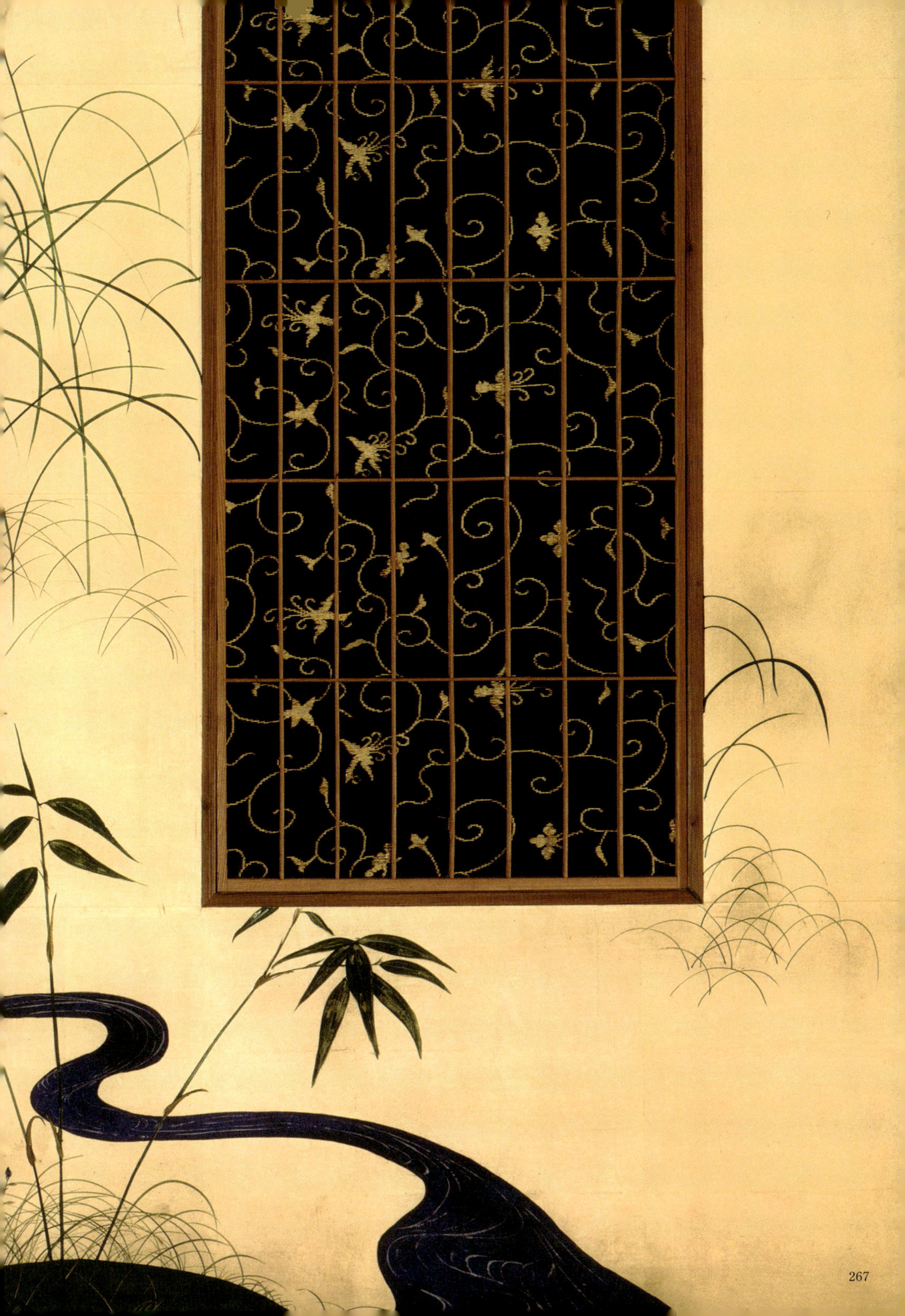

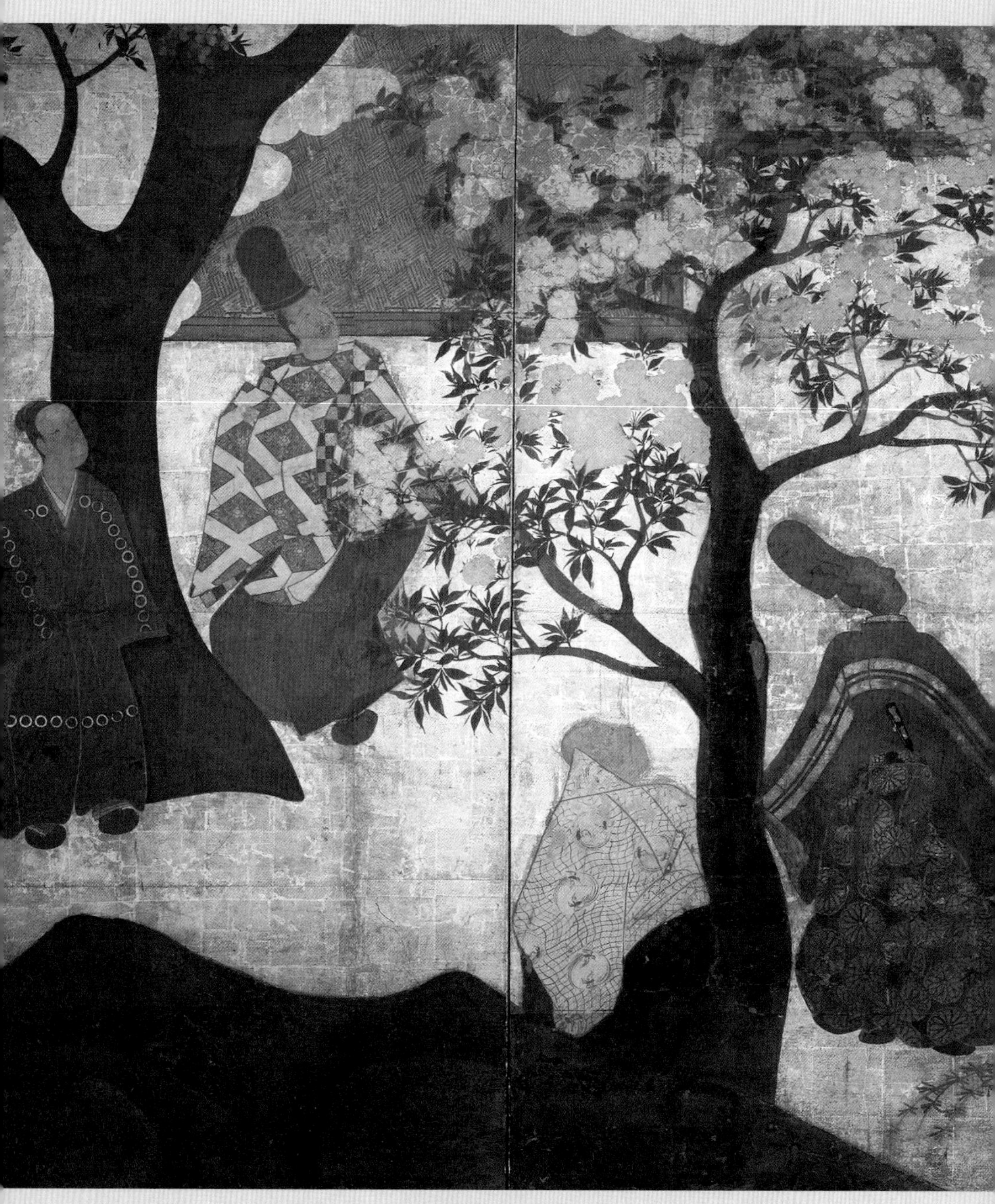

「蹴鞠図屏風」　堺市博物館蔵
Kemari (Traditional Kick-a-Ball Game), Sakai City Museum

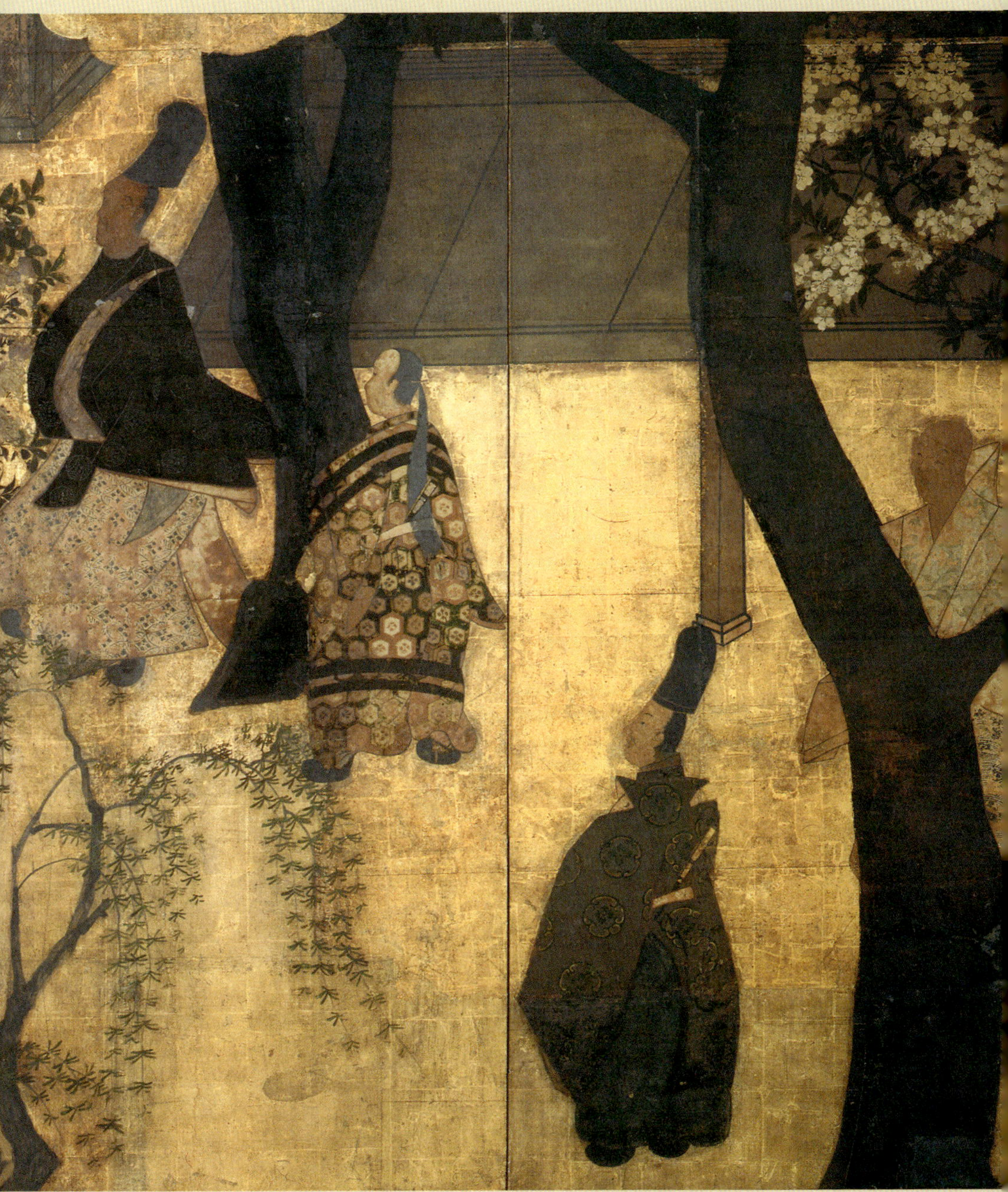

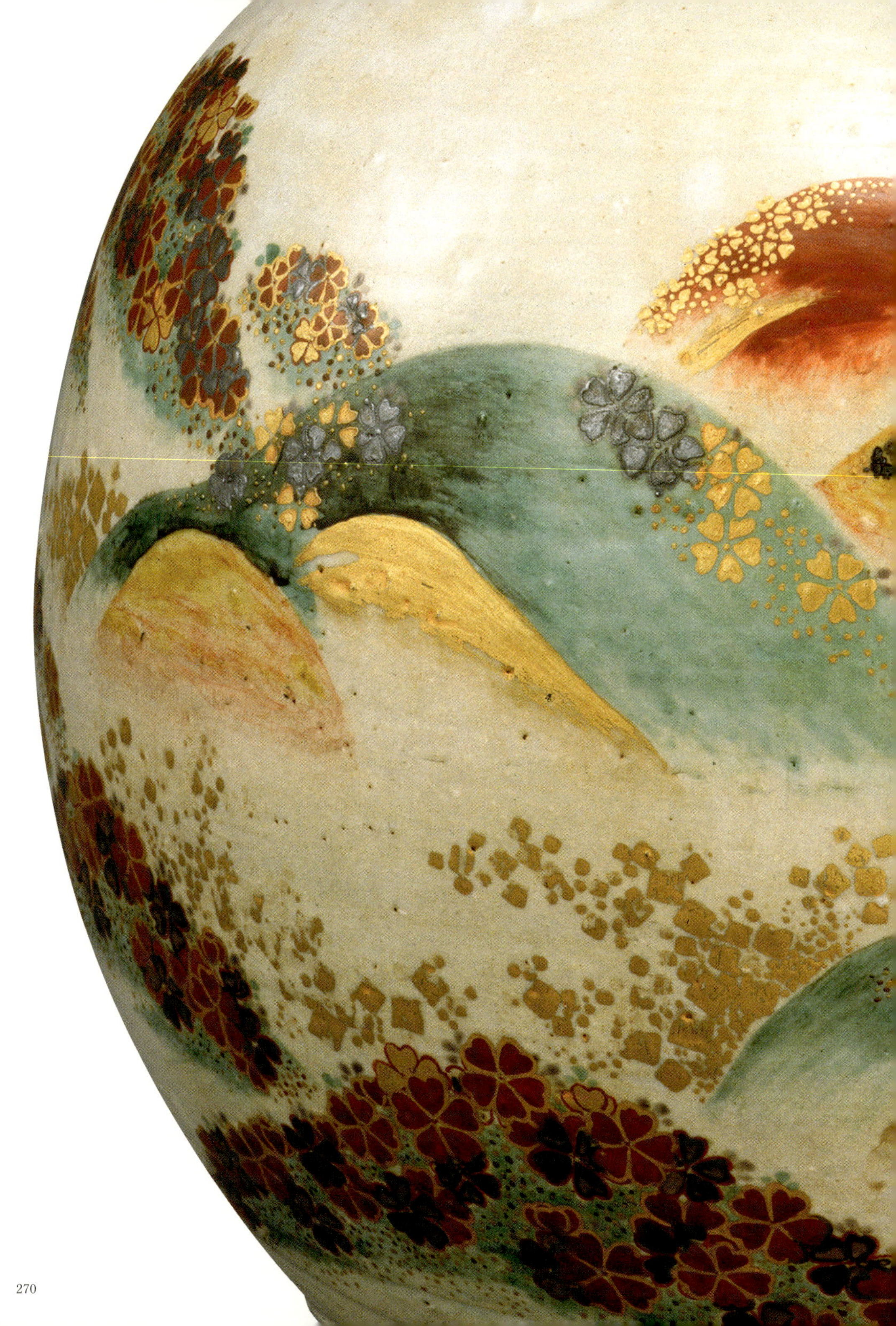

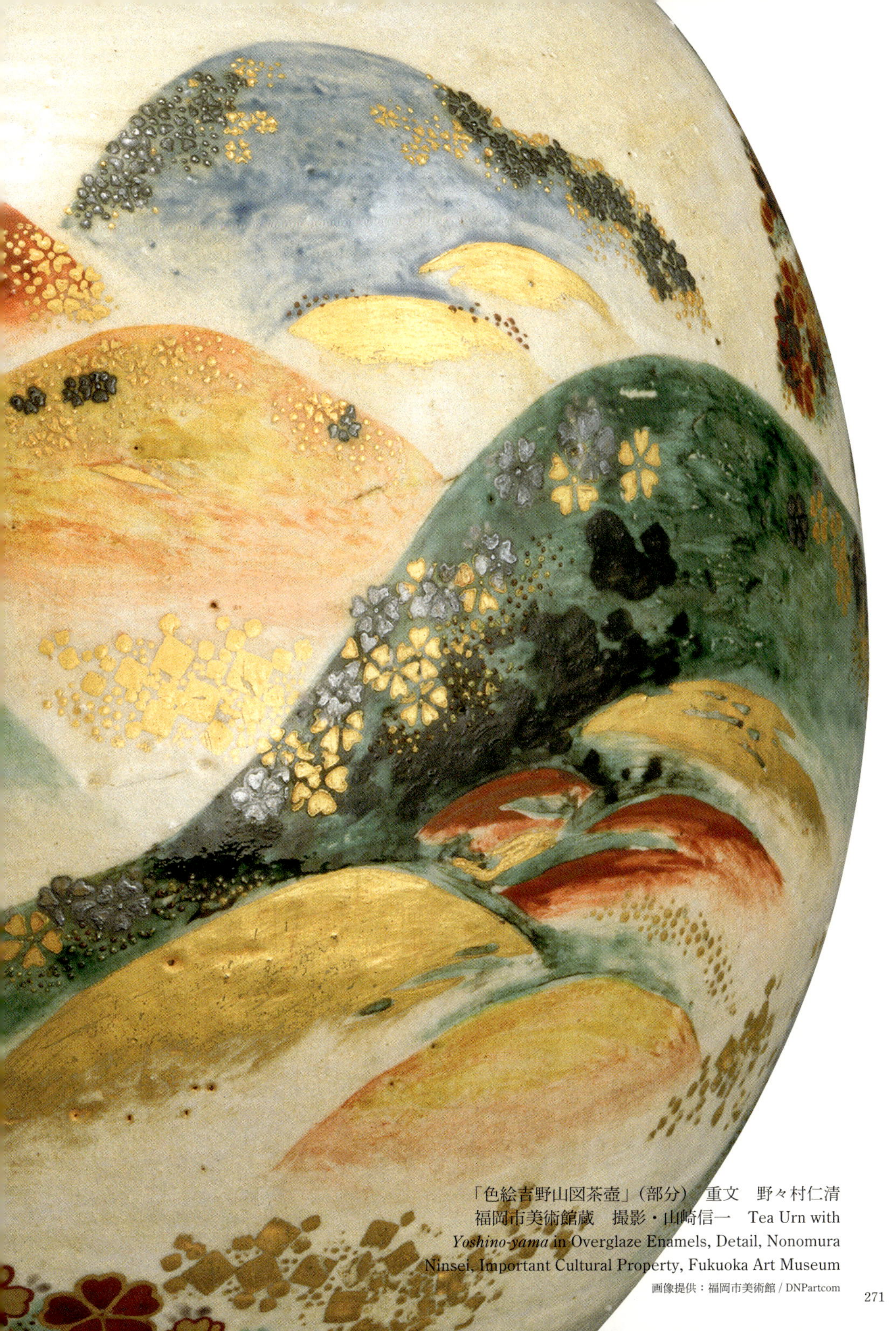

「色絵吉野山図茶壺」（部分）　重文　野々村仁清
福岡市美術館蔵　撮影・山崎信一　Tea Urn with
Yoshino-yama in Overglaze Enamels, Detail, Nonomura
Ninsei, Important Cultural Property, Fukuoka Art Museum

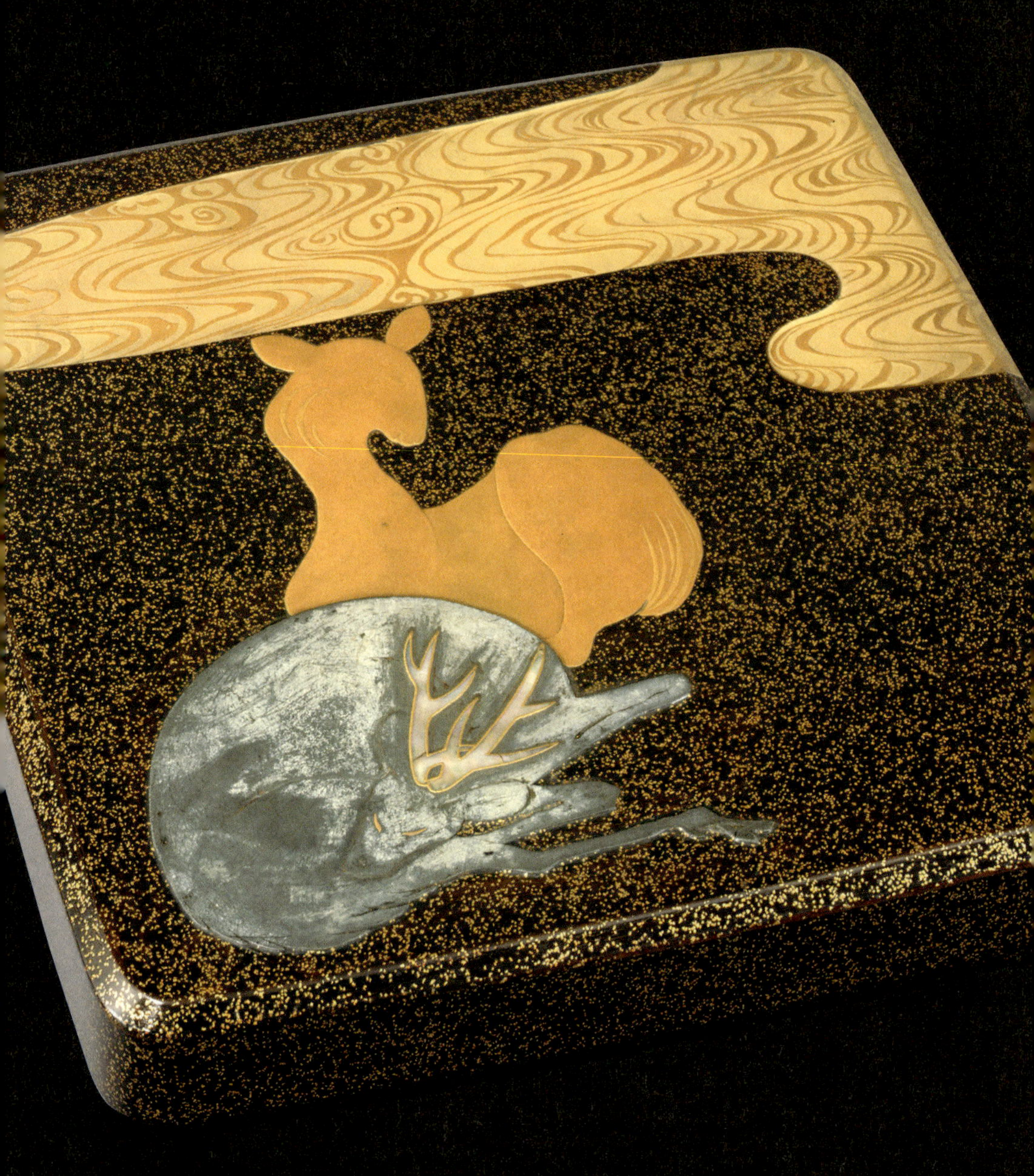

「槇鹿蒔絵螺鈿硯箱」　永田友治　京都国立博物館蔵
Stationery Set with Black Pines and Deer in Maki-e and Mother-of-Pearl Inlay,
Nagata Yūji, Kyoto National Museum

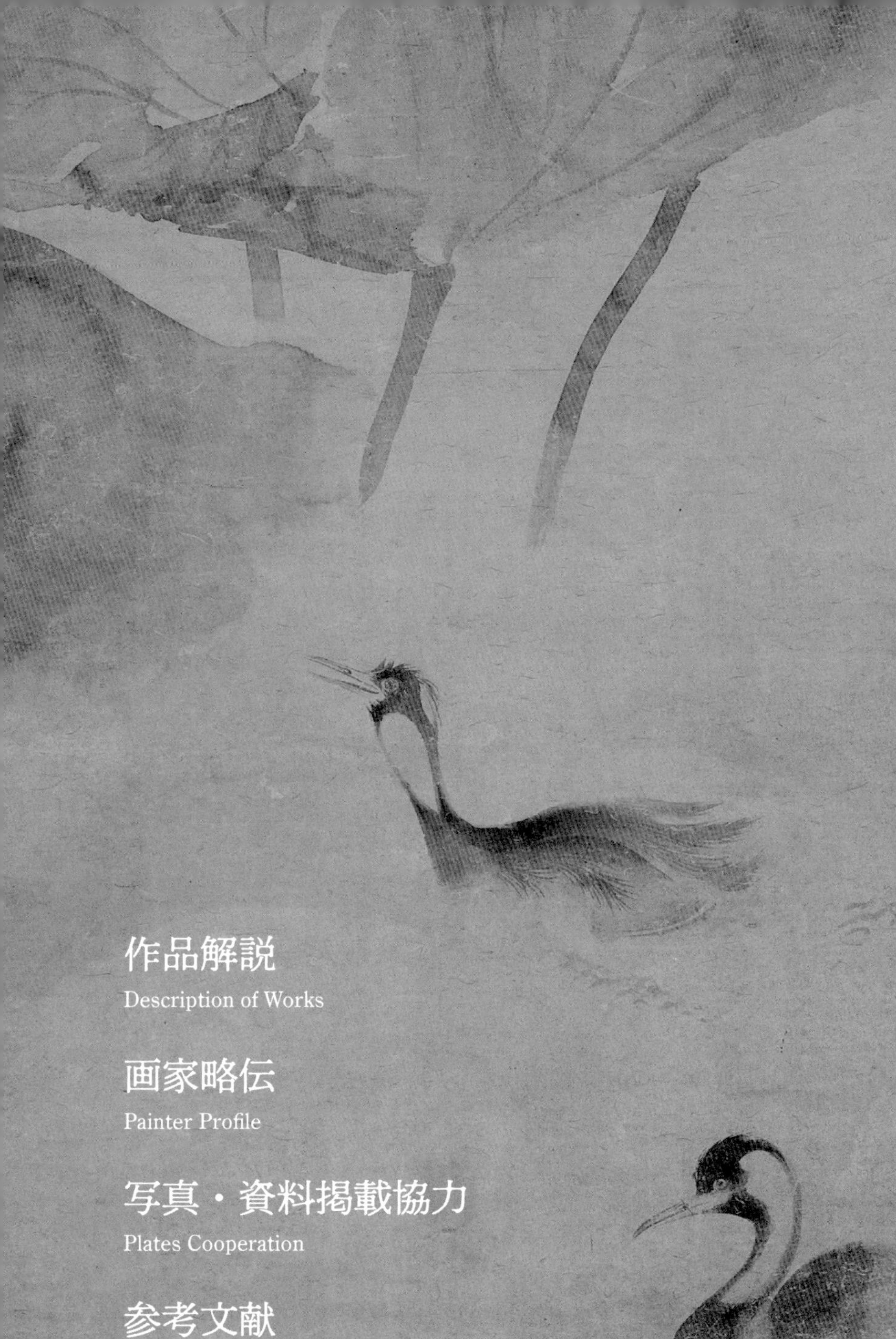

作品解説　Description of Works

凡例
○作品解説のデータは、掲載頁、作品名、作者名、員数、材質・技法、寸法、制作年代、所蔵の順に掲載している。
○法量の単位はセンチメートルで、特に表記のない場合はすべて縦 x 横である。
○一双屏風の場合、上段に右隻、下段に左隻を掲載している。

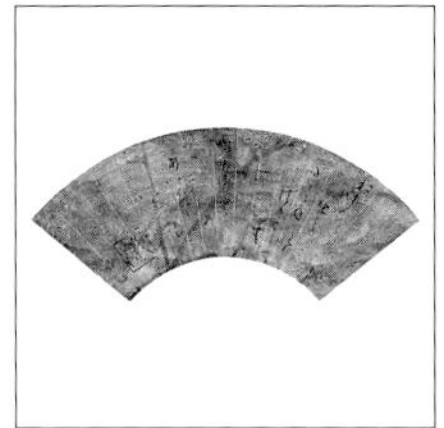

P26-27 「和歌扇面画賛」本阿弥光悦
軸一幅　紙本銀泥　36.2 x 57.9 cm　桃山時代（16 世紀）〜江戸時代（17 世紀）石川県立美術館蔵
Poem Anthology *Kokinshū* Over Painting of Plum Tree, Hon'ami Kōetsu, From Momoyama period, 16th century, to Edo period, 17th century, Hanging scroll, Color on silver ground on paper, 36.2x57.9 cm, Ishikawa Prefectural Museum of Art

扇面全体に銀泥を引き、下絵として墨で梅の枝を描いている。満開の花に白と緑青（ろくしょう）を点じ、『新古今和歌集』巻第十四恋歌中の藤原家隆（鎌倉時代初期の歌人）の歌を書いたものである。銀と墨の料紙装飾の美しさを求めたもので、その繊細さの裏に潜む美意識が伝わる作品である。

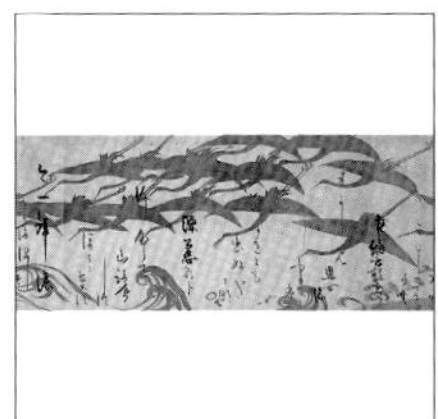

P26-31 「鶴図下絵和歌巻」重文　本阿弥光悦・書　俵屋宗達・下絵
一巻　紙本金銀泥　34.1 x 1356.0 cm　江戸時代（17 世紀）京都国立博物館蔵
Poem Scroll with Under Painting of Cranes, Painting by Tawaraya Sōtatsu, Calligraphy by Hon'ami Kōetsu, Edo period, 17th century, Handscroll, Ink on gold and silver ground on decorated paper, 34.1x1356.0cm, Important Cultural Property, Kyoto National Museum
胡粉（ごふん）下地に金銀泥で描かれた鶴の群れは、全長 13 メートルにおよぶ長大な巻物の冒頭から繰り広げられ、飛び立ち、舞い降り、水辺に集う。鶴の姿態は単純な筆遣いで捉えられているが、艶やかな光沢を放つシルエットの美しさは比類がない。この優美な下絵に「寛永の三筆」のひとり、本阿弥光悦が三十六歌仙の和歌を書いている。絵と書が競い合う素晴らしいコラボレーションである。

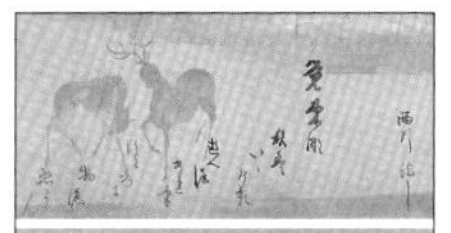
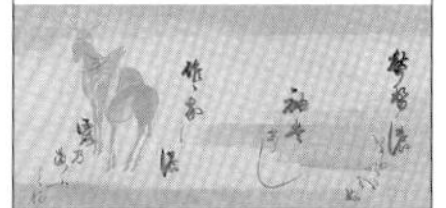

P32-33 「鹿下絵和歌」（新古今和歌集）本阿弥光悦
二巻三幅　紙本墨書　335.3 cmx34.1 cm　江戸時代（17 世紀）石川県立美術館蔵
Poem Scroll with Under Painting of Deer, *Shinkokin-wakashū* Anthology, Hon'ami Kōetsu, Edo period, 17th century, Handscroll, Ink on paper, 335.3 cmx34.1 cm, Ishikawa Prefectural Museum of Art

胡粉（ごふん）を引いた料紙に、鹿のさまざまな姿態や離合集散する動きをのびやかな線と金銀泥の濃淡で巧みに描いている。その上から光悦が『新古今和歌集』を書いた 2 巻 3 幅におよぶ大作である。光悦の流麗な筆致からは大らかな気風が感じられ、宗達工房の作と考えられる下絵は画面をいっそう華やかにし、美しいハーモニーを醸し出している。

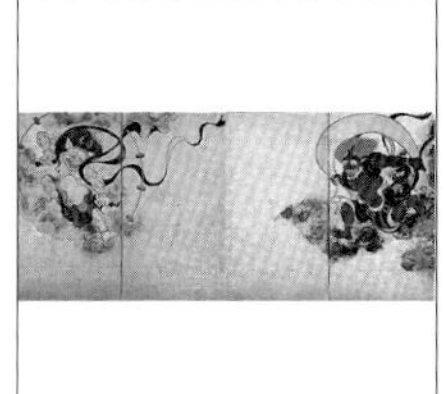

P6-7、34-37 「風神雷神図屏風」国宝　俵屋宗達
二曲一双屏風　紙本金地着色　各 154.5x169.8cm　江戸時代（17 世紀）建仁寺蔵
Wind and Thunder Gods, Tawaraya Sōtatsu, Edo period, 17th century, Pair of two-fold screens, Color on gold ground on paper, 154.5x169.8cm each, National Treasure, Kennin-ji, Kyoto

右隻に風袋を持って姿を見せた風神が緑青（ろくしょう）で描かれ、左隻には勢いよく舞い降りた雷神が胡粉（ごふん）の白で捉えられる。そしてその間に広い金地の空間をつくる。各隻の上端に配置された独特の構図が広がりを生み出し、風神雷神の躍動し、疾駆する体躯の力強さと、たらし込みによる雲の軽やかな表現の対比が絶妙である。

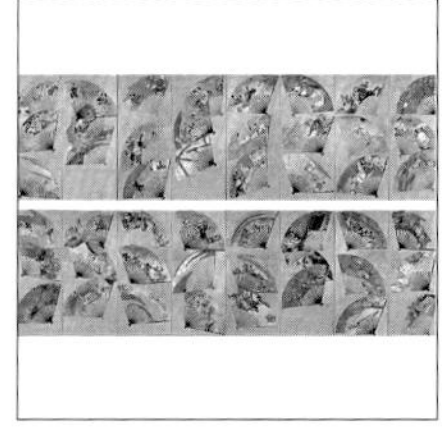

P38-41 「扇面散屏風」俵屋宗達
八曲一双屏風　紙本着色　各 111.8 x 376.0 cm　江戸時代（17 世紀）宮内庁三の丸尚蔵館蔵
Scattered Fans, Tawaraya Sōtatsu, Edo period, 17th century, Pair of eight-fold screens, Color on paper, 111.5 x 376.0 cm each, Sannomaru Shozokan（The Museum of the Imperial Collections）

この八曲一双の扇面貼交屏風には、一扇に三面ずつ合計 48 面の扇が散りばめられている。モチーフは『保元物語』『平治物語』の合戦絵をはじめ、『伊勢物語』『西行物語』、あるいは草花図などさまざまな主題が見られる。宗達は「扇」という特殊な画面形式を巧みに行かして構成するのが得意であった。

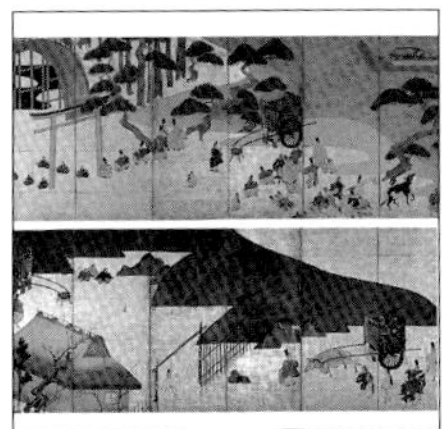

P42-47 「源氏物語関屋・澪標図屏風」国宝　俵屋宗達

六曲一双屏風　紙本金地着色　各 152.3 x 355.6 cm　江戸時代（17 世紀）静嘉堂文庫美術館蔵
Scenes from the Barrier Gate ("*Sekiya*") and Channel Buoys ("*Miotsukushi*") Chapters of the Tale of *Genji*, Tawaraya Sōtatsu, Edo period, 17th century, Pair of six-fold screens, Color on gold ground on paper, 152.3 x 355.6 cm each, National Treasure, Seikado Bunko Art Museum　画像提供：静嘉堂文庫イメージアーカイブ / DNPartcom

関屋（せきや）は『源氏物語』第十六帖の帖名で、光源氏 29 歳の秋、かつて一夜の契りを交わした空蟬の君と、偶然にも逢坂の関で行き会う話を右隻に描く。澪標（みおつくし）は第十四帖の帖名で、光源氏 28・29 歳の頃、妻のひとりである明石の君と住吉参詣の折に邂逅する場面が左隻に描かれている。いずれも光源氏が昔の恋人と偶然に出会う劇的な場面を扱っている。

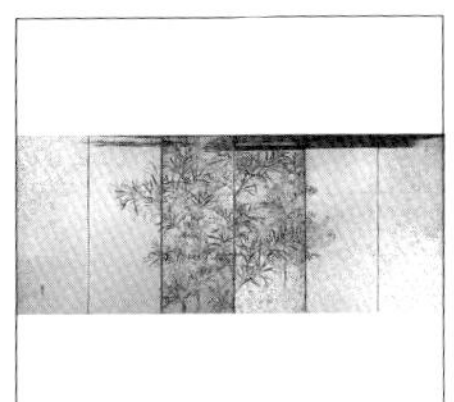

P48-49 「槙檜図屏風」俵屋宗達

六曲一隻屏風　紙本金砂子地着色　95.0 x 222.0 cm　江戸時代（17 世紀）石川県立美術館蔵
Chinese Black Pine and Cypress Trees, Tawaraya Sōtatsu, Edo period, 17th century, Six-fold screen, Ink, faint color on gold and silver on paper, 95.0 x 222.0 cm, Ishikawa Prefectural Museum of Art

屏風全体に金切箔を細かく蒔き、上部に銀の砂子と野毛（金銀箔を細長く切った切箔の一種）を交えて霞を引き、墨に藍を交えて槙と檜を没骨（もっこつ）法で描いている。金銀の複雑な装飾と水墨技法の調和を積極的に試みており、描写は左右を大きくあけて中央に集中し、明快なリズムを持って描かれた槙の葉は的確に空間を捉え、深い静寂感をたたえている。

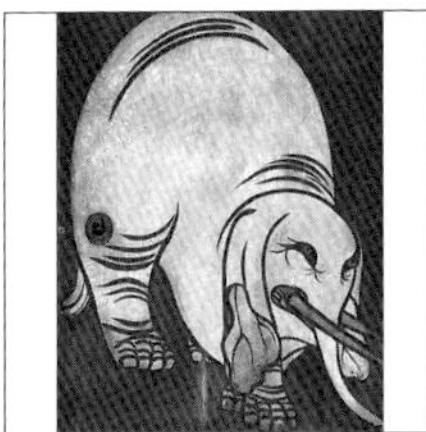

P50 「白象図」重文　俵屋宗達

杉戸絵一面（二面のうち）　板戸着色　182.0x125.0cm　江戸時代（17 世紀）養源院蔵
Cedar Doors with White Elephant, Tawaraya Sōtatsu, Edo period, 17th century, Two panels, Color on wooden board, 182.0x125.0cm, Important Cultural Property, Yōgen-in, Kyoto

宗達は、元和 7 年（1621）徳川秀忠夫人によって再建された養源院に、松図襖絵とともに四面の杉戸の表裏に八面の杉戸絵を描いている。白象図は、墨で引いた力強く豊かな輪郭線を残す彫り塗りの技法を用いて、象の身体は胡粉、眼と牙は金泥で描かれている。単純化されたフォルムと色彩の画面からは、今にも白象が飛び出してきそうな迫力がある。

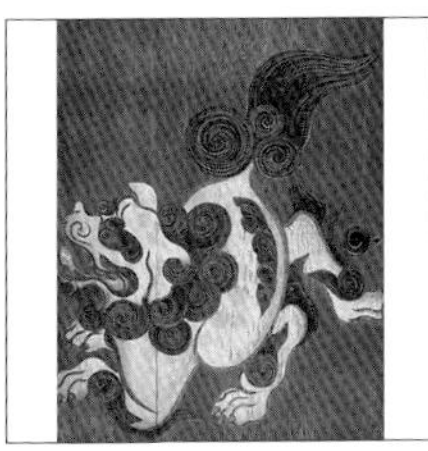

P51 「唐獅子図」重文　俵屋宗達

杉戸絵一面（二面のうち）　板戸着色　182.0 x 125.0 cm　江戸時代（17 世紀）養源院蔵
Cedar Doors with Chinese Lion, Tawaraya Sotatsu, Edo period, 17th century, Two panels, Color on wooden board, 182.0 x 125.0 cm, Important Cultural Property, Yōgen-in, Kyoto

唐獅子図は白象図と表裏をなすもので、養源院本堂廊下の両端にある杉戸絵に描かれている。弾力性のある太い描線による力強い表現は「風神雷神図」に通じるものを感じさせる。唐獅子の身体には金箔を貼り、尾や鬣の金泥の毛描きは美しく、新たな装飾的効果を見せている。このような霊獣は墓所を護り魔を退ける意味から描かれたのであろう。

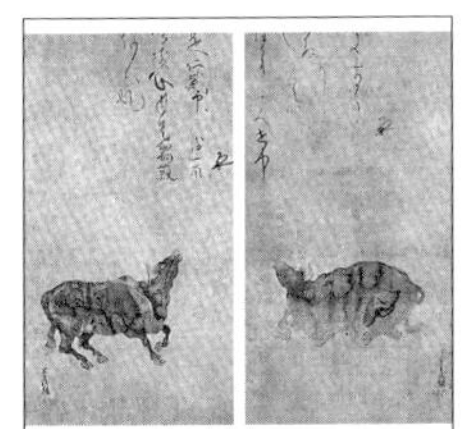

P52-53 「牛図」俵屋宗達・画　烏丸光広・賛

軸双幅　紙本墨画　各 94.8 x 43.6 cm　江戸時代（17 世紀）頂妙寺蔵
Oxen, Tawaraya Sōtatsu, Inscription by Karasumaru Mitsuhiro, Edo period, 17th century, Pair of hanging scrolls, Ink on paper, 94.8 x 43.6 cm each, Chōmyō-ji, Kyoto

宗達の水墨画の中でも傑作として知られるこの双幅は、重量感にあふれる牛の体軀を手慣れたたらし込みの技法によって実に躍動的に描き上げている。牛の形そのものは『北野天神縁起絵巻』に取材したものとされる。右幅の上部には、宗達とは縁の深い烏丸光広（からすまるみつひろ）の和歌の賛、左幅の上部には漢詩の賛がある。

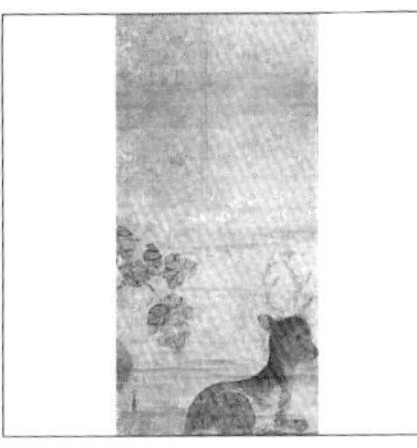

P54 「鹿図」俵屋宗達

軸一幅　紙本墨画　94.0 x 41.6 cm　江戸時代（17 世紀）宮内庁京都事務所
Deer, Tawaraya Sōtatsu, Edo period, 17th century, Hanging scroll, Ink on paper, 94.0 x 41.6 cm, Imperial Household Agency Kyoto Office

草花に寄り添うように足を曲げて坐る一頭の鹿を、柔らかい水墨の筆で軽妙に描いている。鹿の背には細やかな筆跡が見られ、生き生きとした眼と鼻の表情からは生暖かい鹿の体温すら伝わってきそうだ。鹿の体や草花にほどこされたたらし込みの技法が、それぞれの質感を見事に表現している。宗達の墨色の柔らかさは絶妙である。

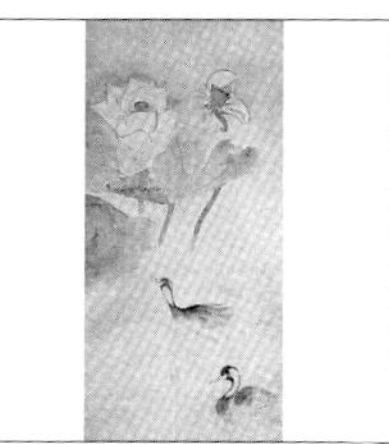

P54-55 「蓮池水禽図」国宝　俵屋宗達
軸一幅　紙本墨画　119 x 48.3 cm　江戸時代（17 世紀）京都国立博物館蔵
Water Birds in Lotus Pond, Tawaraya Sōtatsu, Edo period, 17th century, Hanging scroll, Ink on paper, 119 x 48.3 cm, National Treasure, Kyoto National Museum

湿潤な朝の大気に包まれた池に、今を盛りに花開く白蓮と番（つがい）で泳ぐカイツブリを水墨のみであっさりと描いている。水墨表現の可能性を極限まで求めた繊細きわまる作風である。宗達は日本や中国の水墨画法を学び、特に南宋の画僧牧谿（もっけい）の作品を始め、宋元水墨画を親しく見る機会があったのだろう、本図のような身近な自然を生き生きと描いている。

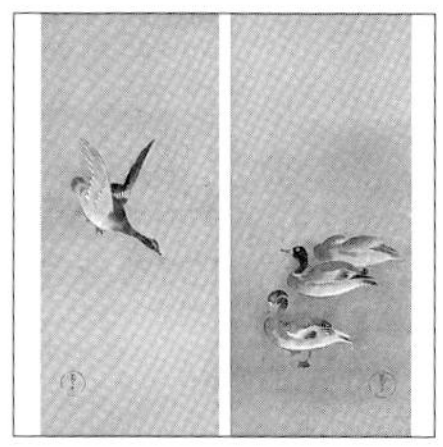

P56-57 「鴨図　山田近之助旧蔵」伝俵屋宗達
六曲一双屏風　132.7 x 52.2 cm（貼交部分）　桃山時代　京都国立博物館蔵
Wild Ducks, formerly belonged to Yamada Chikanosuke, Attributed to Tawaraya Sōtatsu, Momoyama period, Pair of six-fold screens, 132.7 x 52.2 cm each, Kyoto National Museum

六曲一双屏風に一扇ずつ貼られた十二図の鴨図はさまざまな鴨の姿勢を捉えている。水辺に佇む番の姿、頸をぐっと伸ばして羽根を搏（う）ち、今まさに飛び立とうとする姿など、さまざまなフォームを見せている。羽毛や脚に用いたたらし込みが簡略な画面の中で面白い味わいを見せている。鳥類を扱った宗達派の作品は多く遺っている。

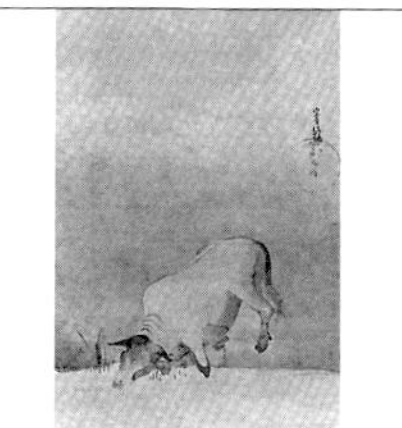

P58 「牛図」俵屋宗達
軸一幅　紙本墨画　64.6 x 43.5 cm　江戸時代（17 世紀）東京藝術大学大学美術館蔵
Ox, Tawaraya Sōtatsu, Edo period, 17th century, Hanging scroll, Ink on paper, 64.6 x 43.5 cm, The University Art Museum-Tokyo University of the Arts

よく肥えた牛の体軀や柔らかな体毛の感触までを捉えている。たらし込み技法による墨の滲みと広がりは、計算されたようにうまく形の枠に治まり、牛の存在感を際立てている。宗達派の作品の多くが古巻絵などから模写されていることが従来の研究で明らかになっているが、この作品の出所を考えるのも楽しいことである。

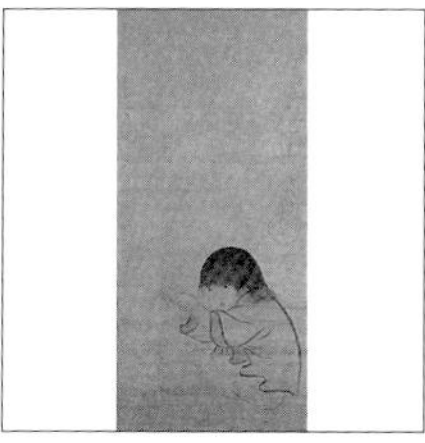

P59 「童子の図」伝俵屋宗達
軸一幅　紙本淡彩　72.5 x 30.5 cm　江戸時代（17 世紀）石川県立美術館蔵
A Child, Attributed to Tawaraya Sōtatsu, Edo period, 17th century, Hanging scroll, Ink and light color on paper, 72.5 x 30.5 cm, Ishikawa Prefectural Museum of Art

上着姿の童女が足を前に投げ出して座り、両手は眼の高さで差し出している。何を始めようとする姿なのかよくわからないが、童女のふっくらと柔らかな姿と、子供が見せる真剣な眼差しや力の入った両足の表現が巧みに表現されている。頭髪はたらし込みの技法でまるみをおび全体に流麗な描線で描かれている。襟や袖には薄く朱色がほどこされている。

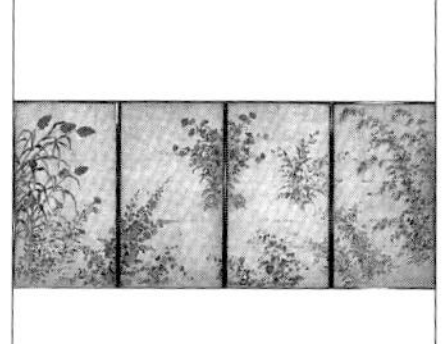

P60-63 「草花図」伊年印
襖四面　紙本金地着色　各 169.0 x 92.8 cm　江戸時代（17 世紀）京都国立博物館蔵
Flowering Plants, Seal of Inen, Edo period, 17th century, Four sliding wall panels, Color on gold ground on paper, 169.0 x 92.8 cm each, Kyoto National Museum

金地の落ち着いた色調の襖四面に、夏から秋にかけての草花が円環状の構図で配されている。右より竹に蔦（つた）、薔薇、薊（あざみ）、秋海棠（しゅうかいどう）、芥子、山帰来（さんきらい）、葵、鶏頭、黍（きび）が宗達風のつけたての技法で描かれている。右下に「伊年印」が捺されているが、宗達より写生が細やかで色調も異なることから寛永頃の周辺作家の手になると考えられる。

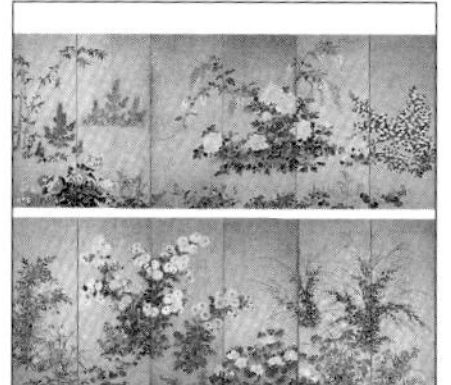

P60-61、64-65 「四季草花図屏風」伊年印
六曲一双屏風　紙本着色　各 141.0 x 335.6 cm　江戸時代（17 世紀）　石川県立美術館蔵
Flowers and Grasses of the Four Seasons, Seal of Inen, Edo period, 17th century, Pair of six-fold screens, Color on paper, 141.0 x 335.6 cm each, Ishikawa Prefectural Museum of Art

「伊年」の落款が捺された花草図屏風は数多く遺されているが、これはひとりの画家の印ではなく、宗達の工房で商標のように用いられていたと思われる。このような四季折々の草花を描いた屏風を部屋の中に飾ることは日本人の自然に対する願望であり生活の一部でもあった。本図は次の四季草花図に構成や描かれた草花がよく似通っている。

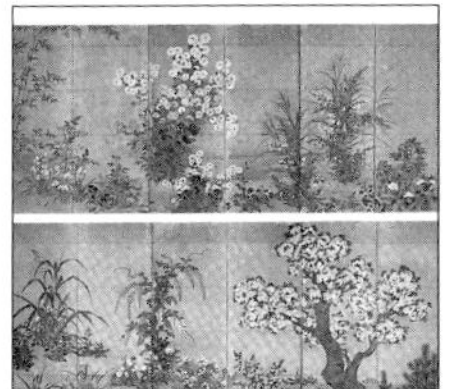

P66-69 「四季草花図屏風」伊年印

六曲一双屏風　紙本着色　各 152.3 x 345.6 cm　江戸時代（17 世紀）黒部市美術館蔵
Flowers and Grasses of the Four Seasons, Seal of Inen, Edo period, 17th century, Pair of six-fold screens, Color on paper, 152.3 x 345.6 cm each, Kurobe Art Museum

右隻には春から夏に咲く、桜、山吹、藤、玉蜀黍（とうもろこし）、左隻には芙蓉、萩、薄（すすき）、菊と画面下に切り取られたように描く方法でまとめられている。金沢地方では江戸時代から「たはらやの草花図屏風」といって嫁入り道具に持参することは家格をあらわすというほど好まれて多くの屏風が描かれた。

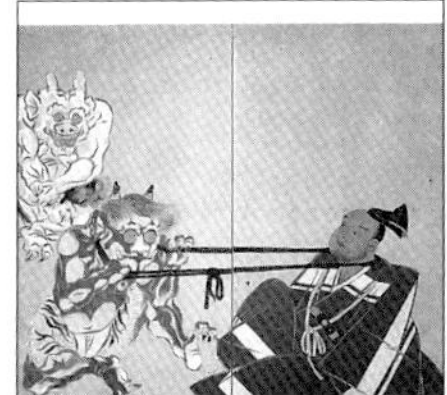

P70-71 「鬼との首引き」対青軒印

二曲一隻屏風　紙本着色　161.0 x 178.0 cm　福井県立美術館蔵
Watanabe-no Tsuna Playing a Neck-Pulling Game with Goblin, Seal of Taiseiken, Two-fold screen, Color on paper, 161.0 x 178.0 cm, Fukui Fine Arts Museum

鬼と人との首引き比べを描いている。描かれている人物は渡辺綱で、平安時代中期の武士である。京の鬼同丸（きどうまる）や大江山の酒呑童子（しゅてんどうじ）、羅生門の鬼を退治した伝説がある。赤鬼との首に綱を張り、力の入った表情でにらみ合っている。でもその表情はユーモラスで、後で白鬼がその様子を眺め笑っている。

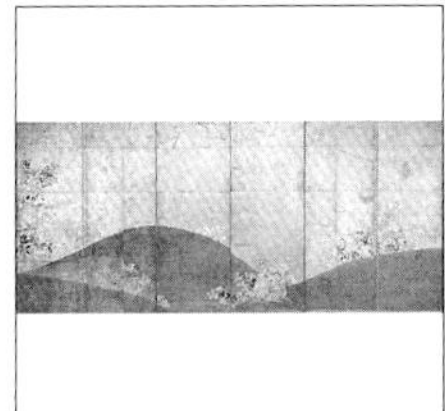

P72-75 「萩に兎図」俵屋宗雪

六曲一隻屏風　紙本金地着色　158.0x342.0cm　江戸時代（17 世紀）　石川県立美術館蔵
Bush Clover and Rabbits, Tawaraya Sōsetsu, Edo period, 17th century, Six-fold screen （Originally four sliding doors）, Color on gold ground on paper, 158.0x342.0cm, Ishikawa Prefectural Museum of Art

金地屏風に淡い緑青で小高く起伏した三つの土坡（どは）を描き、その陰から萩を覗かせている。画面中央にはかわいい二羽の兎が身を寄せあっている。一羽は身体をひねって正面を向き、もう一羽は首を伸ばして周囲に注意を向けている。兎は宗達工房で好んで描かれた画題である。

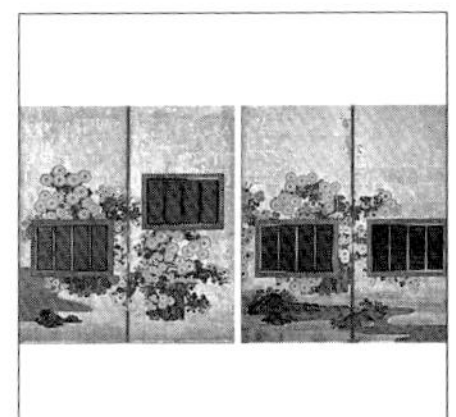

P76-77 「籬菊図」俵屋宗雪

六曲一双屏風　紙本金地着色　各 133.8 x 351.1 cm　江戸時代（17 世紀）京都国立博物館蔵
Chrysanthemums and Fences, Tawaraya Sōsetsu, Edo period, 17th century, Pair of six-fold screens, Color on gold ground on paper, 133.8 x 351.1 cm each, Kyoto National Museum

真物の簾（すだれ）を張った四角い窓を籬（まがき）に見立て、極端な盛り上げ技法で描かれた菊花を所々に配している。また小さな岩に流水を描くことによって庭園の趣を感じさせている。背景に貼りつめた金箔地を、菊花の胡粉（ごふん）や葉の緑青（ろくしょう）、流水の群青などが優美な装飾的効果を上げている

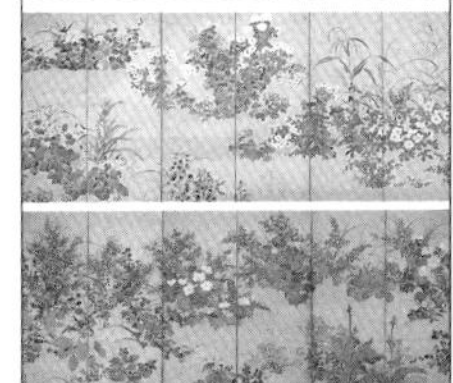

P78-81 「秋草図」喜多川相説

六曲一双屏風　紙本着色　各 160.0 x 410.0 cm　江戸時代（17 世紀）　石川県立美術館蔵
Flowering Plants of Autumn, Kitagawa Sōsetsu, Edo period, 17th century, Pair of six-fold screens, Color on paper, 160.0 x 410.0 cm each, Ishikawa Prefectural Museum of Art

萩、薄、芙蓉、菊などの秋を代表する草花が円弧を描くように配置され、その手前には女郎花（おみなえし）、秋海棠（しゅうかいどう）、擬宝珠（ぎぼうし）などを没骨の技法で並列的に描いている。相説の絵は紙本に墨彩や淡彩が多く、画面構成はおとなしく淡白な趣を持っている。各隻に「相説法橋」の落款と「宗雪」の朱白文小方印、「伊年」の朱文円印がある。

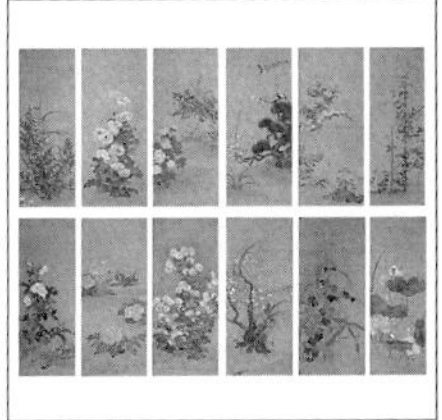

P82-87 「四季草花図押絵貼屏風」喜多川相説

六曲一双屏風　絹本着色　各 123.1 x 50.9 cm　黒部市美術館蔵
Flowering Plants of the Four Seasons, Kitagawa Sōsetsu, Paintings mounted on a pair of six-fold screens, Color on silk, 123.1 x 50.9 cm each, Kurobe City Art Museum

六曲一双の屏風に二扇ずつ貼られた 12 図の草花図は、モチーフの大胆さはなく全体にまとまりのあるおとなしい構図になっている。土坡や霞が効果的に用いられ、草花の葉脈も墨で描かれることで落ち着きのある画面構成に仕上がっている。右隻の鉄線図と左隻の黄蜀葵（おうしょっき）図に、「喜多川法橋相説七十二歳画之」の落款がある。

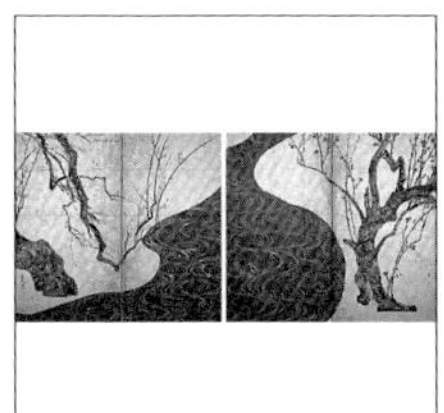

P10-11、88-91 「紅白梅図屏風」国宝　尾形光琳
二曲一双屏風　紙本金地着色　各 156.0 x 172.2 cm　MOA 美術館蔵
Red and White Plum Trees, Ogata Kōrin, Pair of two-fold screens, Color on gold ground on paper, 156.0 x 172.2 cm each, National Treasure, MOA Museum of Art, Shizuoka

最晩年に制作された光琳の代表作であり、日本絵画史上屈指の名作である。右隻には鮮やかな紅梅、左隻には低く枝を張った白梅を描き、その中央に意匠化した光琳波といわれる水流を配している。写実的な紅白梅とデザイン風の水流、人の意表をついたいかにも光琳らしい作品である。

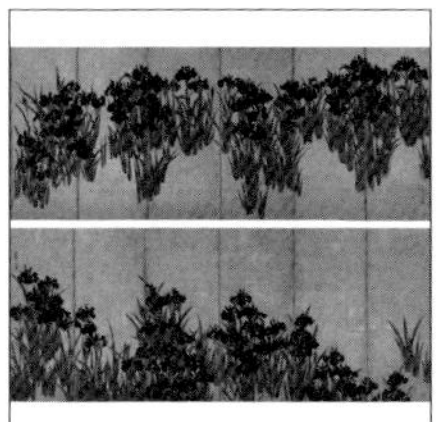

P14-15、92-95 「燕子花図」国宝　尾形光琳
六曲一双屏風　紙本金地着色　各 151.2 x 358.8 cm　江戸時代（18 世紀）　根津美術館蔵
Irises, Ogata Kōrin, Pair of six-fold screens, Color on gold ground on paper, 151.2 x 358.8 cm each, Edo period, 18th century, National Treasure, Nezu Museum

総金地屏風の大画面に満開の燕子花の群生をリズミカルに配置し、軽やかな画面構成と濃淡の群青、緑青の鮮やかな色彩で豪華絢爛に描き出している。燕子花は『伊勢物語』第九段の東下りのうち、三河の国八橋の場面にちなんだモチーフである。作品は光琳 40 歳代中頃に制作されたもので、もと西本願寺に伝来した。

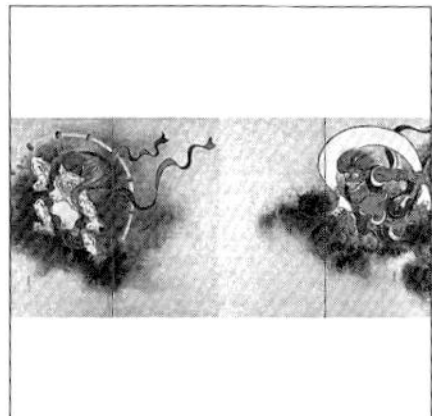

P96-99 「風神雷神図屏風」重文　尾形光琳
二曲一双屏風　紙本金地着色　各 164.5 x 181.8 cm　東京国立博物館蔵
Wind and Thunder Gods, Ogata Kōrin, Pair of two-fold screens, Color on gold ground on paper, 164.5 x 181.8 cm each, Important Cultural Property, Tokyo National Museum, Image : TNM Image Archives

宗達の「風神雷神図」を模したもので、形はほとんど忠実に写しているが、二神を少し下げて画面中心よりに配し、配色は光琳好みに変えている。画面は一回り大きく広げられ、宗達のように太鼓や天衣が画面からはみ出ることはない。後に酒井抱一はこの図を写し、そのときに本図の裏面に代表作「夏秋草図屏風」（東京国立博物館蔵）を描いた。

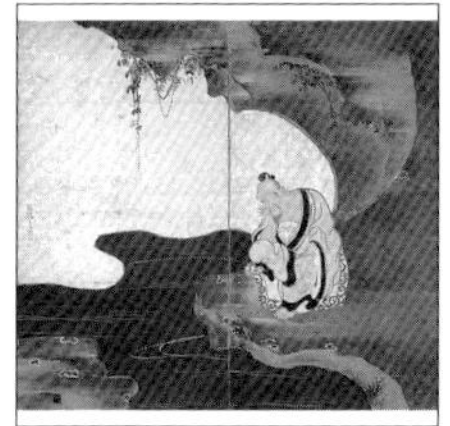

P100-101 「太公望図屏風」重文　尾形光琳
二曲一隻屏風　紙本金地着色　166.6 x 180.2 cm　江戸時代（18 世紀）　京都国立博物館蔵
General *Tai Gong Wang*, Ogata Kōrin, Edo period, 18th century, Two-fold screen, Color on gold ground on paper, 166.6 x 180.2 cm, Important Cultural Property, Kyoto National Museum

崖淵の岩場に男が膝を組み、頬杖をついて眠るように佇んでいる。釣りの異称ともなった太公望（たいこうぼう）とされる。体の衣紋線、背後の崖、水辺の輪郭線、金地の境界線など、画面にほどこされたすべての線が、太公望の腹のあたりから放射しているように描かれている。男の夢想が金地の画面に現れてきそうな構図である。

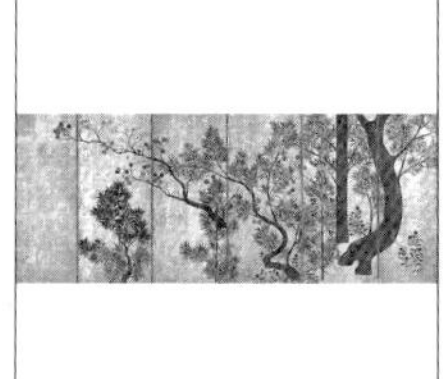

P102-105 「槇楓図屏風」重文　尾形光琳
六曲一隻屏風　紙本金地着色　145.0 x 351.0 cm　江戸時代（18 世紀）　東京藝術大学大学美術館蔵
Black Pine and Maple Tree, Ogata Kōrin, Edo period, 18th century, Six-fold screen, Color on gold ground on paper, 145.0 x 351.0 cm, Important Cultural Property, The University Art Museum-Tokyo University of the Arts
六曲一隻の金地画面に槇と楓を描き、下方に秋の草花を添えている。宗達派と伝えられる「槇楓図屏風」を模写した作品として有名なもので、光琳は槇の位置を左にずらせ、葉をすっきり整理し楓と重ならないようにしている。全体に金地の画面が広がり、重厚さはなくなったが華やかな調子の画面構成になっている。

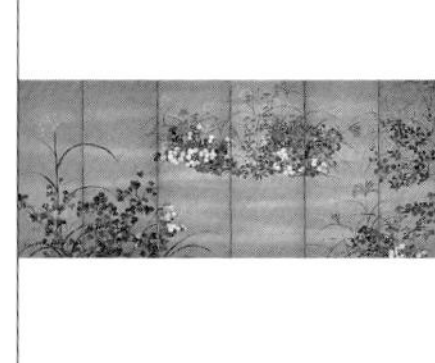

P106-109 「秋草図屏風」尾形光琳
六曲一隻屏風　紙本着色　151.5 x 355.2 cm　東京藝術大学大学美術館蔵
Flowering Plants of Autumn, Ogata Kōrin, Six-fold screen, Color on paper, 151.5 x 355.2 cm, The University Art Museum-Tokyo University of the Arts

菊・薄（すすき）・萩・桔梗（ききょう）・女郎花（おみなえし）など、秋の草花が六曲一隻の画面にバランスよく配されている。画面中央には豪華に咲き乱れた秋草の一叢を並列的に描き、左端には草花の上部のみ、右端には萩などが半分切れるように描き画面の奥行きをうまく表わしている。

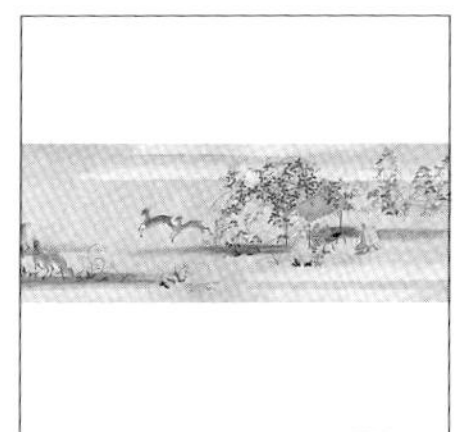

P106-107、110-111 「**西行物語絵巻　巻四第九段**」尾形光琳
一巻（四巻のうち）紙本着色　33.7 x 1684.6 cm　江戸時代（18 世紀）宮内庁三の丸尚蔵館蔵
Illustrated Scrolls of the Life of Priest *Saigyō*, Scroll 4, Chapter 9, Ogata Kōrin, Edo period, 18th century, Handscroll, Color on paper, 33.7 x 1684.6 cm, Sannomaru Shozokan (The Museum of the Imperial Collections)

宗達による采女本（うねめぼん）と称される西行法師行状絵を光琳が写したものである。各巻の奥付に「法橋光琳画」の落款と「方祝」印がある。歌人として著名な西行法師は 23 歳で出家し、生涯の大半を奥州から九州までをさすらいの旅で過ごした。その旅の行状は鎌倉時代から絵巻となっているが、その後いくつかのバリエーションが生まれた。

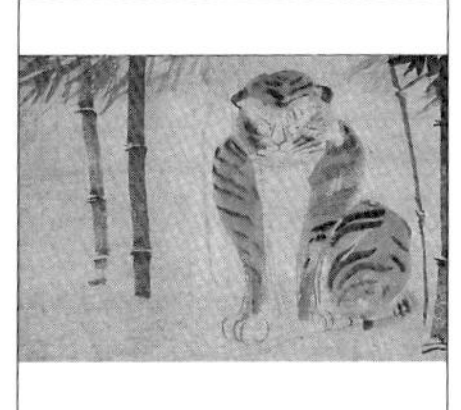

P112-113 「**竹虎図**」重文　尾形光琳
軸一幅　紙本墨画　28.0 x 38.7 cm　江戸時代（18 世紀）　京都国立博物館蔵
Bomboos and Tiger, Ogata Kōrin, Edo period, 18th century, Hanging scroll, Ink on paper, 28.0 x 38.7 cm, Important Cultural Property, Kyoto National Museum

竹林にちんまりと腰を下ろした虎は、少し腰をひねって前足で踏ん張っている。いかにも猛虎のポーズでいたずらっ子のようなやんちゃな眼をして横を睨んでいる。どこか肩の張らない軽妙で親しみやすい作品である。光琳の自由性とユーモア感覚が表れている。

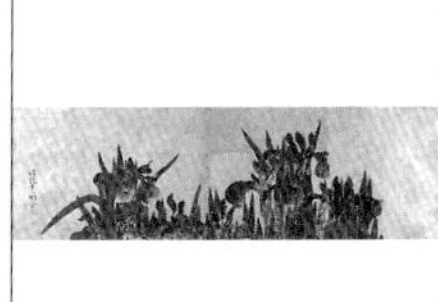

P114-115 「**燕子花図**」尾形光琳
軸一幅　紙本金地着色　江戸時代（18 世紀）　35.0 x 115.0 cm　大阪市立美術館蔵
Irises, Ogata Kōrin, Edo period, 18th century, Hanging scroll, Color on gold ground on paper, 35.0 x 115.0 cm, Osaka City Museum of Fine Arts

横長の金箔地に燕子花の花弁と葉先だけが切り取ったように描かれている。光琳の絶妙なトリミングは燕子花を熟知したモチーフであるからだろう。花弁や葉はのびやかにさまざまなかたちで捉えられ、リズミカルに配されている。群青と緑青だけの色彩でここまで清楚に描き出せるのは光琳だけであろう。左端の引手跡から当初は小襖として仕立てられたものと思われる。

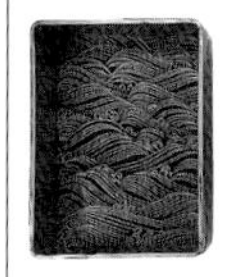

P116-119 「**八橋蒔絵螺鈿硯箱**」国宝　尾形光琳
一合　江戸時代（18 世紀）木製漆器　27.3 x19.7 x 11.2 cm　東京国立博物館蔵
Lacquered Writing Box, *Maki-e* design of *Yatsu-hashi* Bridge and Irises, Ogata Kōrin, Edo period, 18th century, Lacquered wood, 24.2 x 19.8 x 11.2 cm, National Treasure, Tokyo National Museum, Image: TNM Image Archives

蓋表から側面にかけて燕子花に板橋を渡した図は、『伊勢物語』の九段にちなんだ意匠である。上段を硯箱、下段をやや深い料紙箱とし、両側に手がけをえぐった被蓋をおいている。花に蛔（あわび）の厚貝を用い、貝の周縁には微妙な凹凸をつけている。葉は平蒔絵をほどこし、橋の鉛板もわずかな凹凸をつけて人の往来をあらわしている。

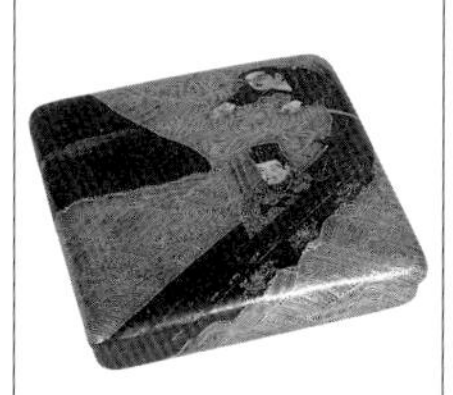

P120-121 「**蒔絵螺鈿白楽天図硯箱**」尾形光琳
一合　木製漆塗　22.5 x 23.5 x 5.5 cm　江戸時代（17 世紀）石川県立美術館蔵
Lacquered Writing Box with the Poet *Bo Juyi* Design, Ogata Kōrin, Edo period, 17th century, Lacquered wood, 22.5 x 23.5 x 5.5 cm, Ishikawa Prefectural Museum of Art

謡曲の「白楽天」を題材にした作品で、硯箱の蓋甲が盛り上がり、身部の左側に水滴と硯を嵌め、右に筆置きの空間を作り、右端に刀子入をえぐってある。唐の太子の宣旨を受け日本の知恵を探ろうと白楽天が海を渡ってきた。それに対し漁翁姿の住吉明神が和歌をもって対抗して船もろとも追い返すという物語である。

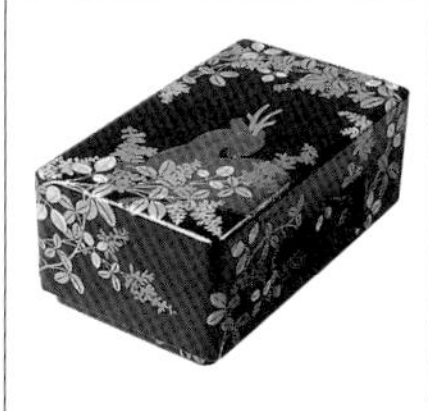

P122-123 「**蒔絵鹿に萩図硯箱**」尾形光琳
一合　木製漆塗　17.1 x 28.6 x 12.7 cm　江戸時代（17 世紀）　石川県立美術館蔵
Lacquered Writing Box with the Bush Clover and Deer Design, Ogata Kōrin, Edo period, 17th century, Lacquered wood, 17.1 x 28.6 x 12.7 cm, Ishikawa Prefectural Museum of Art

全体を萩や薄で包んだ意匠で、硯箱・色紙箱・被蓋で一具をなしている。縦長の画面の周囲に萩を散らし、葉を金蒔絵と蛔貝の螺鈿で表わし、穂状の花には銀を蒔き色に変化を付けている。咲き乱れる萩の叢の中から、振り向きざまの鹿が琳派特有の鉛板であしらわれている。しなやかな秋草の曲線は感傷的ではあるが格好の題材である。

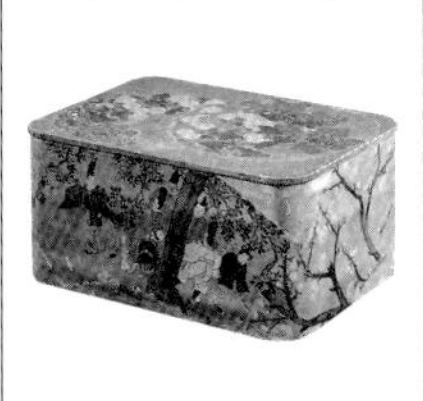

P124-125 「扇面貼交手筥」重文　尾形光琳
一合　木製金地・紙本着色・紙本墨画　27.3 x 38.2 x 18.8 cm　江戸時代（18 世紀）大和文華館蔵
Cosmetic Box with Fan-shaped Painting, Ogata Kōrin, Edo period, 18th century, Wood with gold ground, Color on paper, Ink on paper, 27.3 x 38.2 x 18.8cm, Important Cultural Property, The Museum Yamato Bunkakan, Nara
金箔を貼った木箱に懸子（かけご）を納め、箱の内外に団扇絵四枚と扇面絵八枚を貼った大変贅沢な手箱である。団扇や扇はいずれも実際に使用されたもので、箱の側面には「西行物語絵詞」の中から人物を描き出した「樹下人物図扇面」「西行物語図扇面」、謡曲を題材にした「白楽天図扇面」、「白梅図扇面」が貼られている。

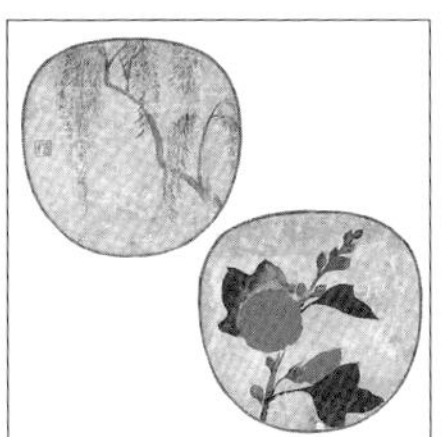

P126 「柳図団扇」方淑印　軸一幅　紙本金地着色　24.1 x 24.1 cm　大阪市立美術館蔵
Willows, Seal of Hōshuku, Hanging scroll, Color on gold ground on paper, 24.1 x 24.1 cm, Osaka City Museum of Fine Arts
P127 「立葵図団扇」方淑印　軸一幅　紙本金地着色　24.1 x 24.1c m　大阪市立美術館蔵
Hollyhock, Seal of Hōshuku, Hanging scroll, Color on gold ground on paper, 24.1 x 24.1 cm, Osaka City Museum of Fine Arts
金地の団扇の裏表に描かれた柳と立葵の図である。団扇という特殊なかたちからくるのであろうか、色彩、構図ともに対照的な作品に仕上がっている。このモチーフの組み合わせは、『光琳百図』に「金地団扇二枚柳葵彩色」として載っている。「方淑」印を使ったのは光琳の子である小西寿市郎とされている。

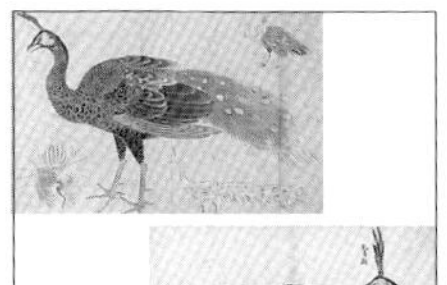

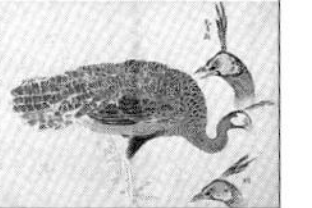

P128-129 「鳥獣写生図巻」（上巻）一巻（二巻のうち）重文　尾形光琳
二巻　紙本着色・墨画　縦 44.8 cm　江戸時代（18 世紀）　京都国立博物館蔵
Birds and Animals Sketches, (vol.1 of 2) Ogata Kōrin, Edo period, 18th century, Handscroll, Color on paper, 44.8 cm, Important Cultural Property, Kyoto National Museum

図巻には 66 種の鳥類と 3 種の動物が精緻に写されている。光琳の子の寿市郎の養子先である小西家に伝来した光琳関係の資料で、本来は冊子装であったが、現在は二巻の巻物に改装されている。大部分が狩野探幽の「写生帖」を引き写したものと思われる。写生帖や画稿の類は、光琳作品の制作過程がうかがえ大変興味深い資料である。

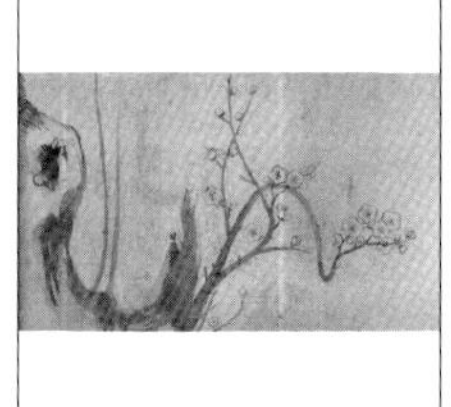

P128-129 「梅花図画稿」重文　尾形光琳
一巻　紙本墨画　34.9 x 56.9 cm　大阪市立美術館蔵
Sketch of a Plum Tree, Ogata Kōrin, Handscroll, Ink on paper, 34.9 x 56.9 cm, Important Cultural Property, Osaka City Museum of Fine Arts

梅の枝が修正されたあとや筆割れを生かして老梅の幹をガサガサと描いた筆遣い、また枝先に可愛くリズミカルに並んだ花弁など、味わい深い作品である。小西家文書の中の光琳画稿の一葉で、裏面には「六祖説法図」とされる人物画が描かれている。光琳の長男の養子先である小西家には、光琳および雁金屋の文書・史料が保管されていた。

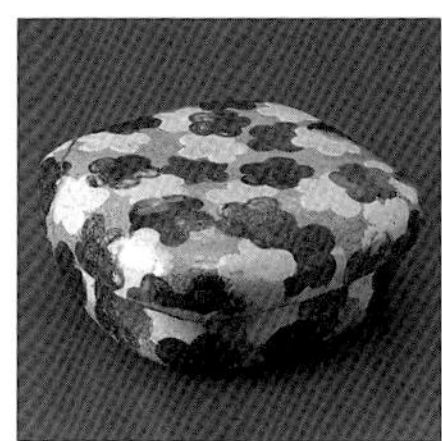

P130-131 「銹絵染付梅波文蓋物」　尾形乾山
一合　高 8.6 cm　縦 20.5 cm　横 20.5cm　江戸時代（18 世紀）　MIHO MUSEUM 蔵
Lidded dish with Design of Plum Blossoms and Waves in Iron Brown Underglaze, Ogata Kenzan, Edo period, 18th century, Miho Museum, Shiga

蓋表と身の外側に無数の梅花文を散りばめたモダンなデザインの蓋物である。身の側面の梅花は銹絵、白泥、染付で描き、蓋裏と身の内側には白化粧を施し、染付で梅花を浮き上がらせている。乾山は光琳を兄に持ち、野々村仁清（にんせい）の御室（おむろ）窯で陶芸を学んだ後、御室よりさらに北西にある鳴滝（なるたき）で開窯した。

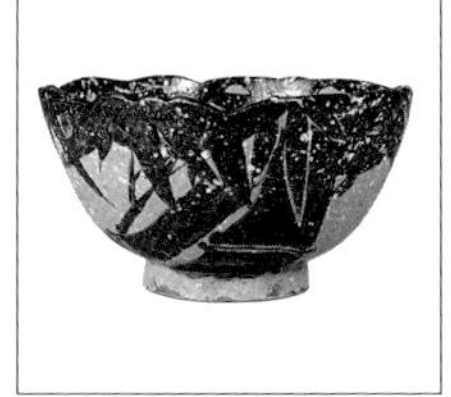

P132-133 「銹絵雪笹図鉢」尾形乾山
一口　高 9.6 cm　口径 18.0 cm　高台径 8.1 cm　江戸時代（18 世紀）　石川県立美術館蔵
Bowl with Design of Snow-covered Bamboo in Iron Brown Underglaze, Ogata Kenzan, Edo period, 18th century, 9.6 x 18.0 x 8.1 cm, Ishikawa Prefectural Museum of Art

薄鼠色をした胎土に、内外部とも吹雪で吹きよせられた竹笹を黒で、舞い散る粉雪を白で大胆に描いている。また口縁部には透かしや口造りを竹笹の形に合わせて切り込みを入れている。側面の竹笹には輪郭を釘彫りするなど装飾性の強い四方鉢に仕上がっている。高台内には「乾山」の銘が黒で書かれている。

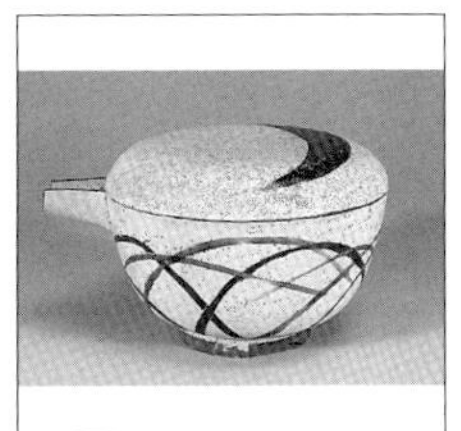

P132 「色絵武蔵野図片口水指」尾形乾山

一口　高 13.9 cm　口径 18.8 cm　幅 22.7 cm　江戸時代（18 世紀）　石川県立美術館蔵
Pitcher with Design of *Musashino* in Overglaze Enamels, Ogata Kenzan, Edo period, 18th century, 13.9 x 18.8 x 22.7 cm, Ishikawa Prefectural Museum of Art

茶褐色の胎土で蓋身とも薄作りに成形され、総体を白化粧し、蓋に三日月、身に薄をあしらって情趣豊かな武蔵野図を表している。武蔵野の意匠は、『続古今和歌集』に源通方が詠んだ「武蔵野は月の入るべき峰もなし　尾花が末にかかる白雲」とあるように、尾花と月が秋の風情を象徴し、古くから文学や絵画・工芸品に表現された。

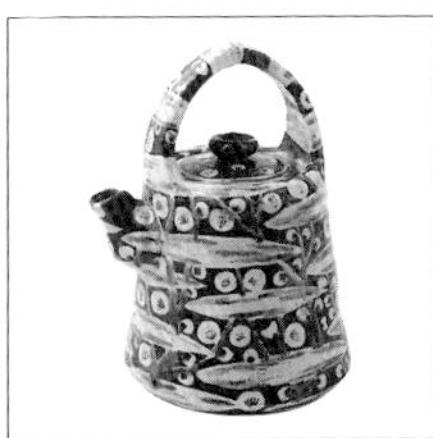

P133 「色絵槍梅文水指」尾形乾山

一口　高 24.6 cm　幅 24.6 cm　奥 17.0 cm　江戸時代（18 世紀）　京都市立芸術大学芸術資料館蔵
Pitcher with Design of Plum Blossoms in Overglaze Enamels, Ogata Kenzan, Edo period, 18th century, 24.6x24.6x17.0cm, University Art Museum, Kyoto City University of Arts

槍梅文は梅の枝を真っ直ぐに曲げないで幾本かを並べたものに、梅の花と蕾を添えた意匠である。陣屋などに槍を立てかけたように見えることからこの名前がついた。乾山の作品には槍梅文が多く、無造作に力強く表現された素朴な中に香り高い風格が備わっている。

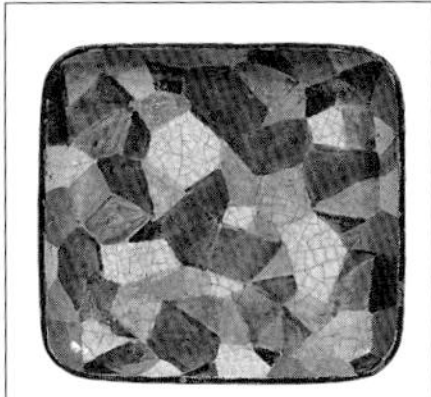

P134-135 「色絵石垣文角皿」尾形乾山

一枚　高 2.6 cm　縦 15.0 cm　横 15.8 cm　高台径 10.4 cm　江戸時代（18 世紀）　京都国立博物館蔵
Square Dish with Design of Stone Wall in Overglaze Enamels, Ogata Kenzan, Edo period, 18th century, 2.6 x 15.0 x 15.8 x 10.4 cm, Kyoto National Museum

五枚組の角皿で描かれた文様は石垣文、高台内に乾山自身が「石垣皿」と記している。この文様は中国の明時代後期に流行した「氷裂文」と考えられる。他の高台内に青の上絵付で「日本元禄年製乾山陶隠」と記されていて、現在知られている乾山焼の中で最も古いものの一つである。意匠はモダンで、乾山の並々ならぬデザインセンスが垣間見られる。

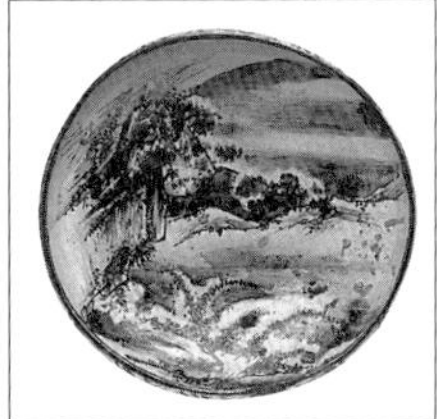

P136-137 「銹絵染付緑彩山水図鉢」尾形乾山

一口　高 7.0 cm　口径 27.5 cm　高台径 15.8 cm　江戸時代（18 世紀）　東京藝術大学大学美術館蔵
Flat Bowl with a Design of Landscape in Underglaze Blue and Iron Brown, Ogata Kenzan, Edo period, 18th century, 7.0 x 27.5 x 15.8 cm, The University Art Museum-Tokyo University of the Arts

轆轤（ろくろ）水挽きによるやや大ぶりの鉢で、表面には下絵である銹絵、染付、白彩により山水と草庵が描かれている。また樹木の部分には上絵で緑彩がほどこされており、手前の水の流れには白化粧が掛けられている。竹林や庵の情景から冬景色を捉えたものであろうか。裏面には染付による菱文が配されている。

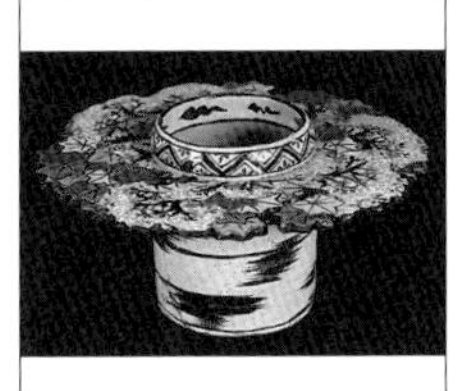

P138-139 「色絵雲錦手杯台」尾形乾山

一基　高 7.7 cm　径 5.5 cm　胴径 15.0 cm　江戸時代（18 世紀）　石川県立美術館蔵
Cup Stand with Design of Cherry Blossom and Maple in Overglaze Enamels, Ogata Kenzan, Edo period, 18th century, 7.7 x 5.5 x 15.0cm, Ishikawa Prefectural Museum of Art

杯を置く台として使われる杯台は円筒形の上部に鍔（つば）形のついたもので、杯を乗せたときの引き立て役である。図柄や技法の趣向が制作者の腕の見せ所となる。この作品は鍔形の部分に色絵で桜花や紅葉を華麗にデザインした雲錦手で、鍔縁は複雑な花形につくられ口銹がほどこされている。

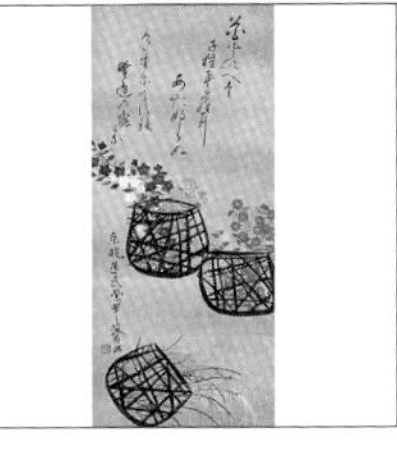

P140-141 「花籠図」重文　尾形乾山

軸一幅　紙本着色　112.5 x 49.2 cm　福岡市美術館蔵
Flowers in Baskets, Ogata Kenzan, Hanging scroll, Color on paper, 112.5 x 49.2 cm, Important Cultural Property, Fukuoka Art Museum　画像提供：福岡市美術館 / DNPartcom

太い墨の線で描かれた花籠に桔梗・女郎花・菊・薄などの秋草が投げ込まれている。図案的に描かれた籠のリズムと秋草の鮮やかな彩りが画面の調和を生んでいる。「花といへは千種なからにあたならぬ　色香にうつる野辺の露かな」の賛は、室町後期の歌人三条西実隆の『雪玉集』から引用したものである。

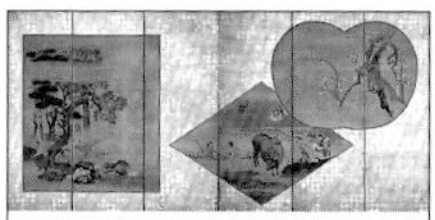

P142-145 「四季図屏風」 渡辺始興

六曲一双屏風　絹本着色　各 176.0 x 366.0 cm　宮内庁三の丸尚蔵館蔵
Landscapes of the Four Seasons, Wtanabe Shikō, Pair of six-fold screens, Color on silk, 176.0 x 366.0 cm each, Sannomaru Shozokan（The Museum of the Imperial Collections）

団扇型や色紙型、扇面型などの幾何学的な画面に狩野派風の筆致で描き、六曲一双の金箔地の屏風に貼付けている。右隻には白梅、田園風俗、樹下流水、左隻には枯芦に雁、唐子、雪中竹叢などの題材が描かれている。始興は初め山本素軒や鶴沢探山といった狩野派に学び、のちに光琳の影響を受けて琳派様式の作品を描いた。

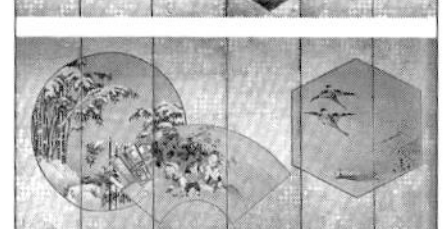

P146-147 「三十六歌仙図屏風」 渡辺始興

二曲一隻屏風　紙本墨画淡彩　135.0 x 58.1 cm　江戸時代（18 世紀）東京藝術大学大学美術館蔵
The Thirty-Six Immortal Poets, Watanabe Shikō, Edo period, 18th century, Two-fold screen, Ink and light color on paper, 135.0 x 58.1 cm, The University Art Museum-Tokyo University of the Arts

光琳の「三十六歌仙図屏風」（メナード美術館蔵）では時代の違う三十六人の歌人たちをあたかも同時代の人々のように一同に集め、楽しく語り合っている姿を描くという手法をとっている。この奇抜な発想から生まれたテーマは、その珍しさも手伝って始興をはじめ、江戸末期の抱一や其一の時代まで多くの作家に継承された。

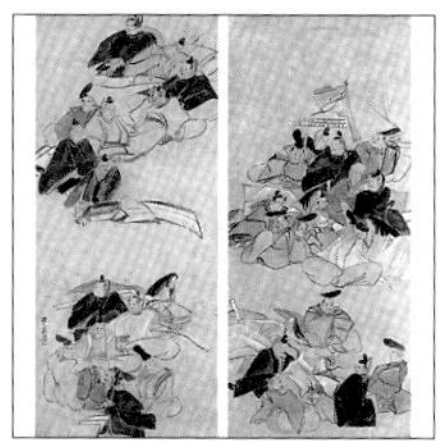

P148-149 「鶴図杉戸」 重文　渡辺始興

杉戸絵二面　板戸着色　各 166.0 x 86.0 cm　大覚寺蔵
Cranes, Watanabe Shikō, Two sliding doors, Color on wooden board, 166.0 x 86.0 cm each, Important Cultural Property, Daikaku-ji, Kyoto

杉戸二面には丹頂鶴の姿が描かれ、左面に空に向かって鳴く姿を、右面に毛繕いをする二羽の姿を捉えている。近衛家熙（いえひろ）の子息の律君がわずか 12 歳で大覚寺に入るのであるが（のち覚深門主となる）、これらはこのときに描かれたと考えられる。他に正寝殿狭屋（さや）の間の明障子の腰板に、愛くるしい野兎が 12 面描かれている。

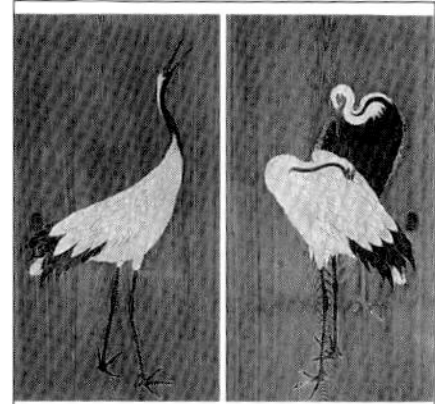

P150-153 「蔦の細道図屏風」 重文　深江蘆舟

六曲一隻屏風　紙本金地着色 132.4 x 264.4 cm　江戸時代（18 世紀）　東京国立博物館蔵
The Ivy Lane from The Tales of Ise, Fukae Roshū, Edo period, 18th century, Six-fold screen, Color on gold ground on paper, 132.4 x 264.4 cm, Important Cultural Property, Tokyo National Museum, Image: TNM Image Archives

在原業平の一行は東海道の難所として知られる宇津谷峠にさしかかる。蔦や楓が茂り、細く暗い山道は心細く不安をかき立てる。そんなところで都で知合いの修行者に出会った。そして「駿河なる宇津の山辺のうつつにも　夢にも人に逢わぬなりけり」の歌を都にいる人に届けてくれるように託したという『伊勢物語』九段東下りの場面を描いたものである。

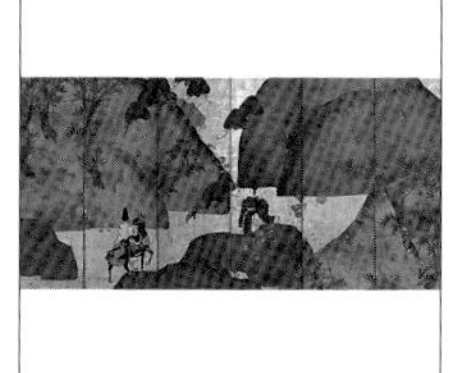

P154-157 「扇面貼交屏風」 立林何帠

二曲一双屏風　紙本着色　各 167.3 x 185.0 cm　江戸時代（18 世紀）　千葉市美術館蔵
Screens with Fan-shaped Paintings, Tatebayashi Kagei, Edo period, 18th century, Pair of two-fold screens, Color on paper, 167.3 x 185.0 cm each, Chiba City Museum of Art

二曲一双の屏風に署名と印文不明の円印のある 18 枚の扇面を貼付している。光琳落款の「扇面貼交屏風」（静嘉堂文庫美術館蔵）に共通する図様の扇面画 4 面を含み、乾山風の楓葉や芳中風の鹿などが描かれている。何帠は加賀前田家の侍医を努めたといわれており、江戸に出て乾山に師事した。

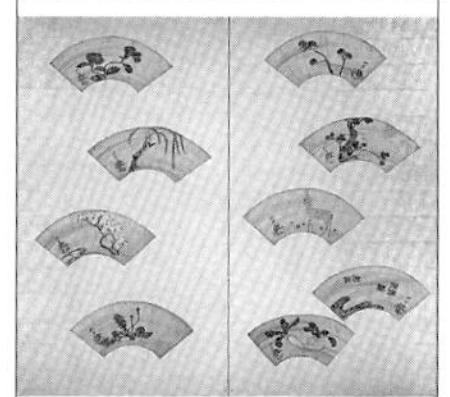

P18-19、158-161 「夏秋草図屏風」 酒井抱一

二曲一双屏風　紙本銀地着色　各 164.5 x 181.8 cm　江戸時代（18 〜 19 世紀）東京国立博物館蔵
Summer and Autumn Grasses, Sakai Hōitsu, Edo period, 18 〜 19th century, Pair of two-fold screens, Color on silver ground on paper, 164.5 x 181.8 cm each, Tokyo National Museum, Image: TNM Image Archives

この作品はもと光琳が宗達に私淑して描いた「風神雷神図屏風」の裏面に描かれていたもので、近年発見された下絵より文政 4 年(1821)一橋治済(はるさだ)の注文で雷神図の裏に「夏艸図」、風神図の裏に「秋草図」が描かれたことがわかる。雨を受けて円弧を描く夏草の叢、野風に吹かれる秋草を、静と動の表現で巧みに表わした抱一芸術の傑作である。

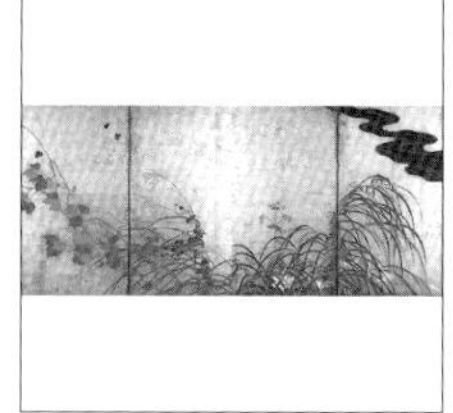

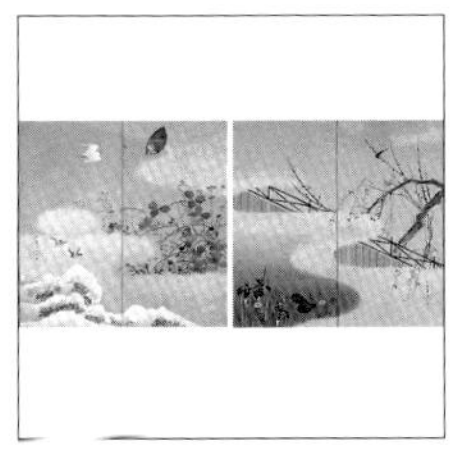

P162-165 「四季花鳥図屏風」酒井抱一
二曲一双屏風　紙本着色　各 156.0 x 161.8 cm　江戸時代（19 世紀）京都国立博物館蔵
Birds and Flowers of the Four Seasons, Sakai Hōitsu, Edo period, 19th century, Pair of two-fold screens, Color on paper, 156.0 x 161.8 cm each, Kyoto National Museum

二曲一双屏風の右隻には梅の小枝に小禽が佇み、水辺には燕子花が花開く春夏の景を描き、左隻には前景にうっすらと雪の綿帽子を被った万両と二羽の雀を描き、中景には薄・葛・桔梗・女郎花などの秋草を配し、空には月に向かって白鷺が飛ぶ秋冬の景を描いている。江戸琳派の総師らしく鮮やかな色彩を用いながらも瀟洒な作品に仕上げている。

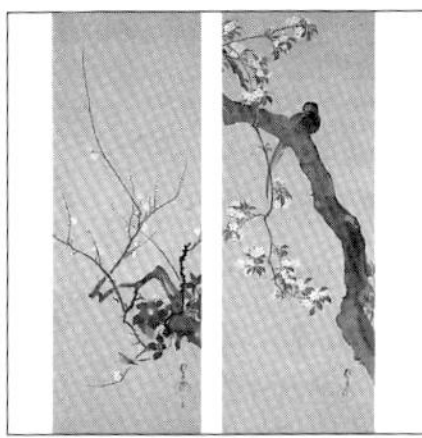

P166-167 「一月　梅椿に鶯図」（十二ヶ月花鳥図）酒井抱一
軸一幅　絹本着色　140.2 x 49.3 cm　文政 6 年（1823）　宮内庁三の丸尚蔵館蔵
Birds and Flowers of the Twelve Months: The First Month, Bush Warbler on a Plum Branch, Sakai Hōitsu, Edo period, Dated 1823（Bunsei 6）,Hanging scroll, Color on silk, 140.2 x 49.3 cm, Sannomaru Shozokan（The Museum of the Imperial Collections）
P166-167 「三月　桜に雉子図」（十二ヶ月花鳥図）酒井抱一
軸一幅　絹本着色　140.2 x 49.3 cm　文政 6 年（1823）　宮内庁三の丸尚蔵館蔵
Birds and Flowers of the Twelve Months: The Third Month, Pheasant on a Blooming Cherry Tree, Sakai Hōitsu, Edo period, Dated 1823（Bunsei 6）,Hanging scroll, Color on silk, 140.2 x 49.3 cm, Sannomaru Shozokan（The Museum of the Imperial Collections）

十二ヶ月花鳥図という画題は、「定家詠十二ヶ月花鳥歌絵」として古くからの伝統的な画題として、江戸時代には狩野派や住吉派、琳派でも光琳や乾山らもしばしば描いている。しかし抱一が得意とした十二ヶ月花鳥図はそれらの伝統にとらわれず、身近な花や鳥、虫などの珍しいチーフを取り混ぜて独自の世界を確立した。

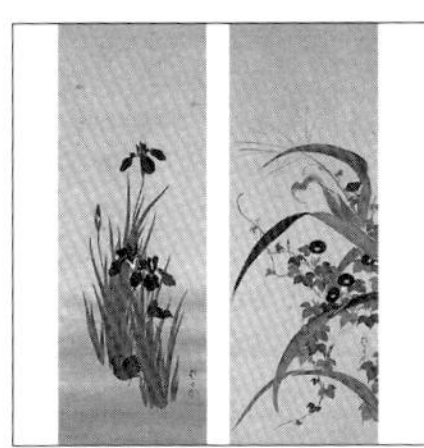

P168-169 「五月　燕子花に鶉図」（十二ヶ月花鳥図）酒井抱一
軸一幅　絹本着色　138.8 x 50.5cm　文政 6 年（1823）　宮内庁三の丸尚蔵館蔵
Birds and Flowers of the Twelve Months : The Fifth Month, Rail amid Sweet Flags, Sakai Hōitsu, Edo period, Dated 1823（Bunsei 6）, Hanging scroll, Color on silk, 138.8 x 50.5 cm, Sannomaru Shozokan（The Museum of the Imperial Collections）
P168-169 「七月　玉蜀黍朝顔に青蛙図」（十二ヶ月花鳥図）酒井抱一
軸一幅　絹本着色　138.8 x 50.5 cm　文政 6 年（1823）　宮内庁三の丸尚蔵館蔵
Birds and Flowers of the Twelve Months: The Seventh Month, Flog with Maize and Morning Glories, Sakai Hōitsu, Edo period, Dated 1823（Bunsei 6）, Hanging scroll, Color on silk, 138.8 x 50.5 cm, Sannomaru Shozokan（The Museum of the Imperial Collections）

十二ヶ月花鳥図の中でも、「五月　燕子花に鶉図」、「七月　玉蜀黍朝顔に青蛙図」はいずれも琳派の図様によく描かれるテーマである。ここには掲載していないが他に、「六月　立葵紫陽花に蜻蛉図」、「十一月　芦に白鷺図」がある。また円山四条派の影響が見られる、「二月　菜の花に雲雀図」、「八月　秋草に月図」も描いている。

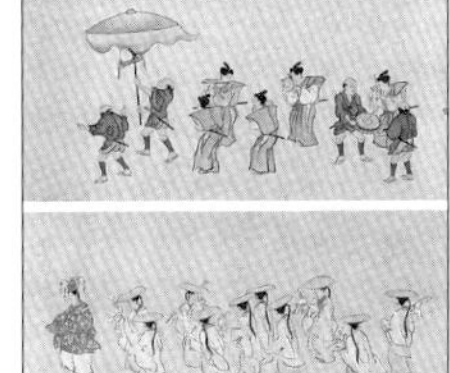

P170-171 「播州室明神神事　棹歌之遊女行列図」酒井抱一
絹本着色　26.8 x 101.2 cm　江戸時代（19 世紀）　姫路市立美術館蔵
Parade of Muromyojin Shrine in Banshu Area, Sakai Hōitsu, Edo period, Color on silk, 26.8 x 101.2 cm, Himeji City Museum of Art

室津（兵庫県南西部、たつの市）賀茂神社の祭礼「小五月祭」の中で行われる遊女行列の様子を描いたものである。現在は稚児行列に変わっているが、この行列で歌われる棹の歌は保存会によって歌い継がれている。抱一の代表作「夏秋草図屏風」と同じ頃制作されたと推定されている。

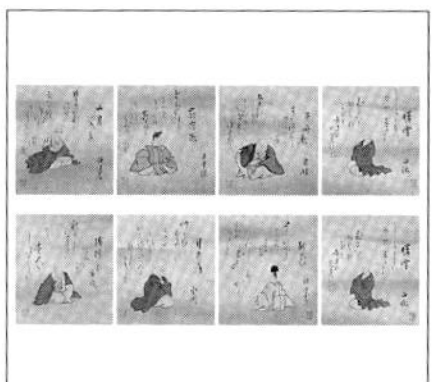

P172-173 「集外三十六歌仙」酒井抱一

絹本淡彩　各 23.7x21.4cm　江戸時代（19 世紀）姫路市立美術館蔵
Honorable Mention of 36 Master Poets, Sakai Hōitsu, Edo period, 19th century, Light color on silk,
23.7x21.4cm each, Himeji City Museum of Art

「集外三十六歌仙」は藤原公任撰の「三十六歌仙」にならって、室町時代中期から江戸時代初
期の歌人を選んだもので撰者は後水尾天皇といわれている。抱一のこの作品はそれぞれの歌人
の肖像に歌一首ずつを配した歌仙絵で、画帖に仕立て上げられている。

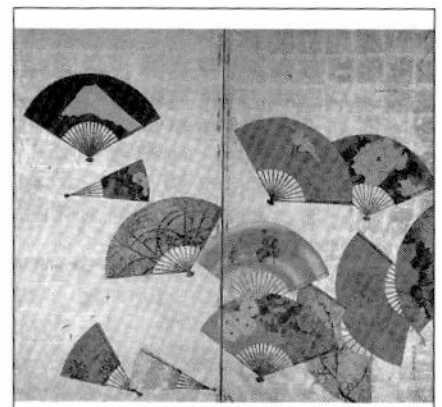

P174-177 「扇面散図屏風」酒井鶯蒲　他

二曲一隻屏風　紙本着色　163.6x151.5cm　江戸時代（19 世紀）　東京国立博物館蔵
Scattered Fans, Sakai Ōho and others, Edo period, 19th century, Two-fold screen, Color on paper,
163.6x151.5cm, Tokyo National Museum, Image: TNM Image Archives

金地の二曲屏風に扇面が配されている。扇面には、白梅、菫、蒲公英、紫陽花、牡丹、薄、菊
などの四季の草花、富士山、『伊勢物語』業平の東下り、波に白鷺などさまざまなテーマが描
かれている。扇面は開いたり半分閉じたり、また重ねたりとさまざまなかたちに変化させ画面
を華やかにしている。

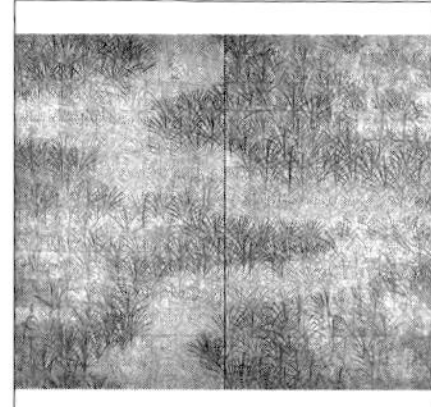

P178-181 「芒図」鈴木其一

二曲一隻屏風　紙本銀地銀泥墨画　144.2x165.6cm　江戸時代（19 世紀）　千葉市美術館蔵
Field of Pampas Grass, Suzuki Kiitsu, Edo period, 19th century, Two-fold screen, Ink on silver ground on
paper, 144.2x165.6cm, Chiba City Museum of Art

銀箔地の画面にびっしりと薄を配し、その叢を流れる霧は銀泥で、他の部分は墨線で微妙に使
い分けて描いている。江戸琳派の祖である抱一の高弟で、師風を忠実に継承したが、抱一が没
したのちはしだいに明快な色彩や構図による独自の世界を確立した。図柄や描法がほとんど同
じ別の作品がワシントンのフリーア美術館に所蔵されている。

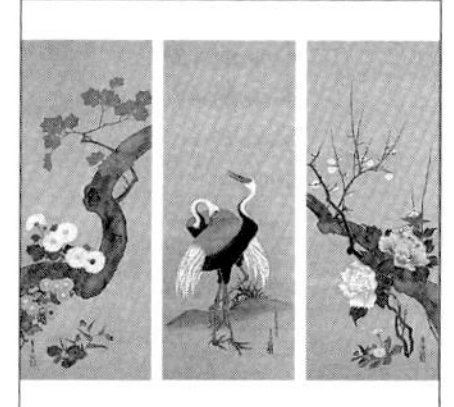

P182-185 「双鶴春秋花卉図」鈴木其一

三幅対　絹本着色　各 109.7x43.2cm　嘉永 5 年（1852）板橋区立美術館蔵
Cranes, Flowers of Spring and Autumn, Suzuki Kiitsu, Edo period, Dated 1852 (Kaei 5), Triptych of
hanging scrolls, Color on silk, 109.7x43.2cm each, Itabashi Art Museum

三幅対のこの作品は、中に土坡に立つ二羽の鶴を描き、右幅にはすくすく伸びた若枝に花をつ
けた白梅と牡丹、根元に蒲公英と菫を、左幅に楓の幹に紅白の菊を配し、その下に露草とオオ
バコを配している。春と秋のひとときを艶やかな草花で描き出している。

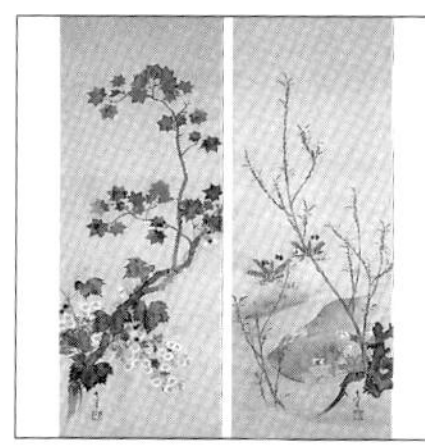

P186、188-189 「猫柳図・楓図」鈴木其一

軸二幅　絹本着色　各 94.5x36.1cm　群馬県立近代美術館蔵
Pussy Willow and Maple, Suzuki Kiitsu, Pair of hanging scrolls, Color on silk, 94.5x36.1cm each, The
Museum of Modern Art, Gunma

右幅には芽吹いたばかりの猫柳がすらりと伸び、水辺に菫（すみれ）と蓮華草（れんげそう）
が楚々と花をつけている。静かな早春の情景を捉えている。左幅には色づいた楓の幹に山葡萄
が絡みつき、根元に白菊の清楚な花を添えている。爽やかな風が流れる秋のひとときを描いて
いる。

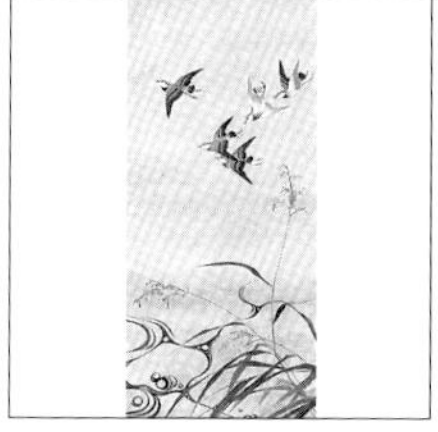

P187、190-191 「流水に千鳥図」鈴木其一

軸一幅　紙本着色　121.8x49.2cm　島根県立美術館蔵
Flowing Stream and Plovers, Suzuki Kiitsu, Hanging scroll, Color on paper, 121.8x49.2cm, Shimane Art
Museum

波に千鳥の意匠は、光琳と乾山の合作の角皿や光琳模様の小袖などにも見られる代表的な光琳
意匠である。千鳥や芦を墨の濃淡だけで描き、画面下方の水流の藍との対比が絶妙に映えてい
る。また千鳥の精緻な描写や抱一風の洒脱な水流の表現に、其一の画面構成の正確な力強さが
うかがえる。

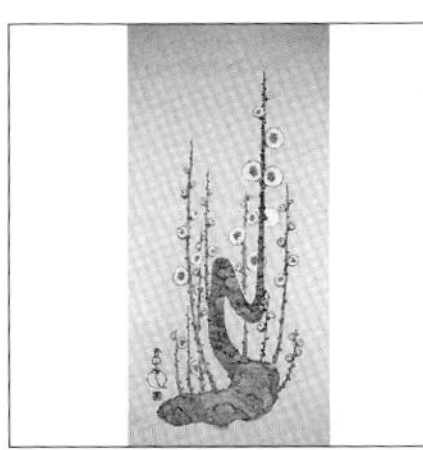

P192-193「白梅図」中村芳中
軸一幅　紙本着色　134.5 x 64.5 cm　文化期（1804 － 18）頃　千葉市美術館蔵
White Plum Tree, Nakamura Hōchū, Edo period, c.1804 -18, Hanging scroll, Color on paper, 134.5 x 64.5 cm, Chiba City Museum of Art

地に這う梅の古木から天に向かって勢いよく枝が伸び、馥郁（ふくいく）たる白梅が匂い立つようである。屈曲する太い幹と垂直に並ぶ細い若枝のバランスが小気味よく描かれ、芳中らしさを垣間見せている。幹や枝、そして花芯にもたらし込みの技法で金泥や緑青がほどこされ、琳派らしい特徴がよく出ている。

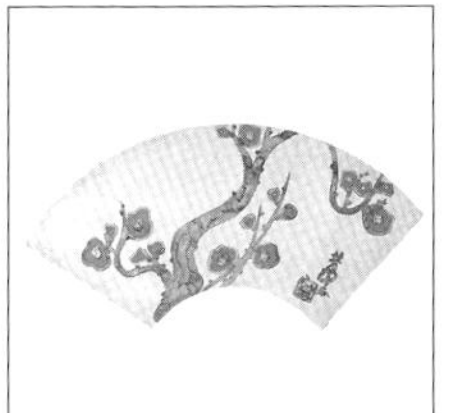

P194-195「梅図」中村芳中
軸一幅　紙本着色　20.3 x 52.0 cm　群馬県立近代美術館蔵
Plums, Nakamura Hōchū, Fan mounted on hanging scroll, Color on paper, 20.3 x 52.0 cm, The Museum of Modern Art, Gunma

樹幹は墨・緑青・金泥などをたらし込みで複雑に彩り、花弁はふっくらした線描で輪郭づけられている。宗達や光琳の用いた技法を用いながらも、芳中の扇面画は彼独特の素朴さが表現され、ユーモアがただよう作品である。

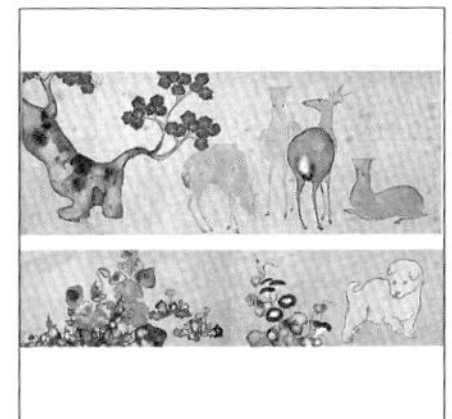

P196-197「人物花鳥図巻」中村芳中
一巻　絹本着色　28.4 x 520.7 cm　真田宝物館蔵
Scroll of Portrait, Flowers and Birds Pictures, Nakamura Hōchū, Handscroll, Color on silk, 28.4 x 520.7 cm, The Sanada Treasures Museum, Nagano

図巻には春から冬への四季の順に、正月初めの子（ね）の日に小松を引き若菜を採る子ノ日遊を描いた第一図に始まり、蒲公英（たんぽぽ）、菫（すみれ）、立葵、芥子（けし）の草花、蝦蟇（がま）、鉄拐仙人（てっかいせんにん・中国八仙のひとり）、丹頂鶴、住吉の松と高砂の松の精が姿を変えた翁と媼、群鹿と紅葉、犬と朝顔、奴と博打をして身ぐるみ剥がれた布袋、亀と藪柑子（やぶこうじ）の9図が描かれている。

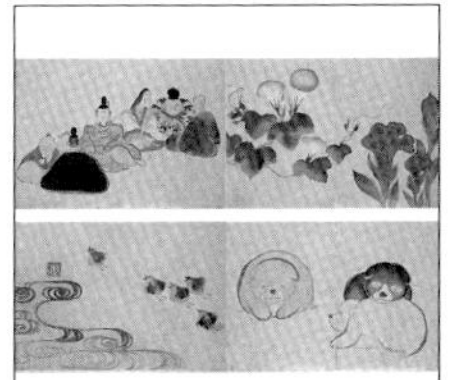

P198-199「光琳画譜」中村芳中
画譜二冊　彩色摺（一部手彩色）　各 27.1 x 19.4 cm　享和 2 年（1802）刊　千葉市美術館蔵　ラヴィッツコレクション
"Kōrin Gafu" (The Drawing Book of Kōrin), Nakamura Hōchū, Edo period, Dated 1802 (Kyōwa 2), Picture book, Two volumes, Color woodblock and hand-colored, 27.1 x 19.4 cm each, Chiba City Museum of Art, Ravicz Collection
芳中の『光琳画譜』は、鹿や鶴、梅や菊、そして翁と媼の吉祥モチーフ、波の表現を用いた波に千鳥など光琳を意識した図様が多く、乾・坤二冊、全25図からなる色摺絵本である。その他に六歌仙や竹林七賢をユーモラスに描いた人物画、仔犬や鳩、雀などの愛らしい動物も収められている。

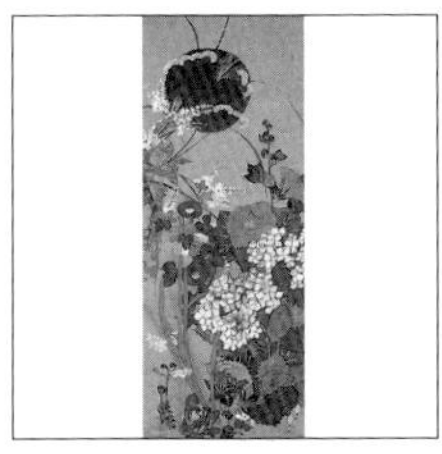

P200-202「四季草花図」池田孤邨
軸一幅　絹本着色　100.6 x 40.1 cm　江戸時代（19 世紀）　東京藝術大学大学美術館蔵
Flowers and Grasses of the Four Seasons, Ikeda Koson, Edo period, 19th century, Hanging scroll, Color on silk, 100.6 x 40.1 cm, The University Art Museum-Tokyo University of the Arts

大きく昇った月を背景に、土筆（つくし）、蒲公英（たんぽぽ）、蕨（わらび）、立葵、紫陽花、蕺草（どくだみ）、朝顔、薄（すすき）、萩、女郎花（おみなえし）、水仙、藪柑子（やぶこうじ）などの四季の草花が画面からあふれて描かれている。軸一幅にこれだけ盛りだくさんの草花が眺められる醍醐味を楽しみたい。

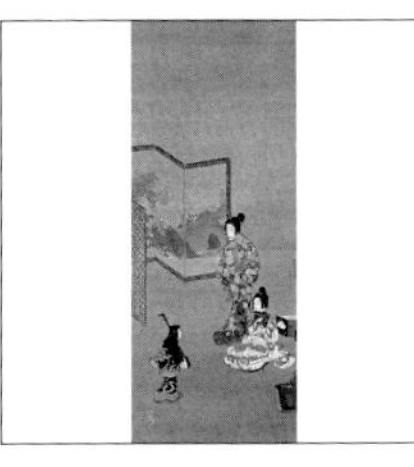

P203-204「浮世美人図」池田孤邨
軸一幅　絹本着色　122.1 x 49.2 cm　江戸時代（19 世紀）　板橋区立美術館蔵
Ukiyoe Beauties, Ikeda Koson, Edo period, 19th century, Hanging scroll, Color on silk, 122.1x49.2cm, Itabashi Art Museum

画面の中央に立てられた屏風にはたらし込みの技法を使った琳派風の草花図が描かれている。その前で二人の芸妓と禿（かむろ）が読書や双六、三味線に興じている。孤邨は越後の生まれで、江戸に出て抱一の弟子となり、江戸琳派の花鳥画を多く描いている。風俗画は珍しく、画中に浮世絵の祖とされる岩佐又兵衛の息子勝重に倣ったものと書かれている。

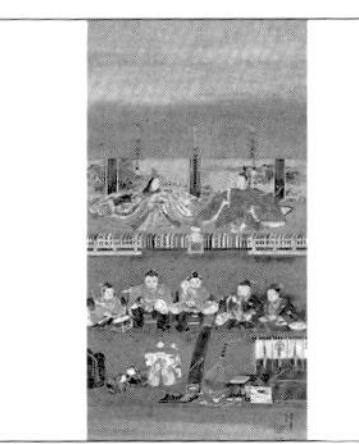

P204-205 「雛祭図」池田孤邨

江戸時代　111.6 x 56.5 cm　江戸時代（19 世紀）　板橋区立美術館蔵
The Doll's Festival, Ikeda Koson, Edo period, 19th century, Hanging scroll, Color on silk, 111.6 x 56.5 cm,
Itabashi Art Museum

「雛祭」は三月三日の上巳（じょうし）の節句に、女児のある家で雛人形を飾り、菱餅・白酒・
桃花などを供えて祝う行事である。孤邨が描いた三段の雛壇には、最上段に内裏雛を置き、男
雛は衣冠束帯、女雛は十二単（ひとえ）、中段には能のお囃子を奏でる五人の楽人を表わした
五人囃子、そして下段には琴や琵琶、紙雛が描かれている。

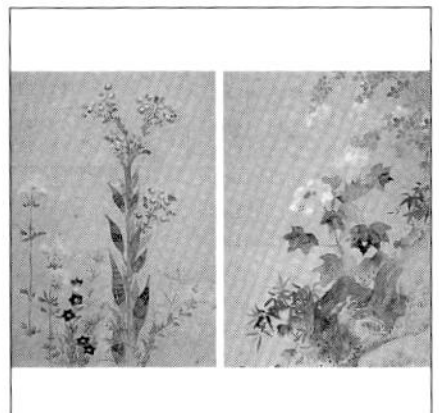

P206-207 「秋草図」俵屋宗理

軸二幅（旧押絵貼屏風　二曲一隻）紙本着色　各 150.0 x 62.6cm　大阪市立美術館蔵
Autumn Grasses, Tawaraya Sōri, Pair of hanging scrolls, formerly a two -fold screen, 150.0 x 62.6 cm
each, Osaka City Museum of Fine Arts

この「秋草図」二幅はもと二曲一隻の屏風に仕立てられていたが、画面の状態からさらに六曲
屏風の一部であった可能性もある。宗理は江戸人の洗練された趣味感覚をいち早く自分の作品
に盛り込んでいった画家で、19 世紀になって花開く抱一ら江戸琳派の先駆け的な画風も見せ
た画家でもある。

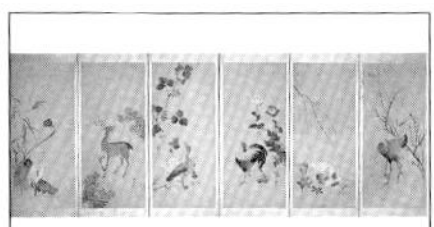

P208-211 「四季草花鳥獣図押絵貼屏風」市川其融

六曲一双屏風　紙本着色　各 142.5 x 47.5 cm　茨城県立歴史館蔵
Flowers, Birds and Animals of the Four Seasons, Ichikawa Kiyū, Twelve paintings mounted on a pair of
six-fold screens, Color on paper, 142.5 x 47.5 cm each, Ibaraki Prefectural Archives and Museum

片隻に季節の草花を、他隻に花鳥画 12 図を集めて押絵貼にした六曲一双の屏風である。花鳥
画には鹿や仔犬を草花と取り合わせたものも描かれている。軽快で鮮明な色彩とまとめられた
画面構成からは、其融のあか抜けし洗練された性格がうかがえる作品である。

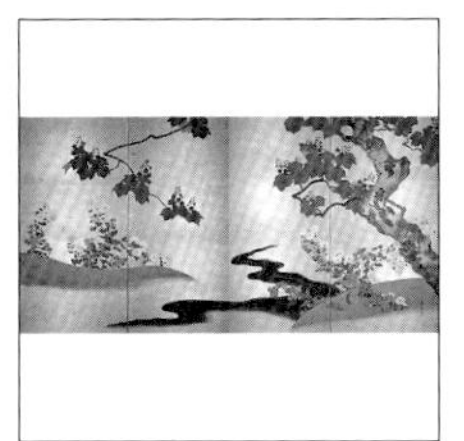

P22-23、212-215 「桐菊流水図屏風」酒井道一

二曲一双屏風　紙本金地着色　各 171.8 x 172.6 cm　江戸〜明治時代（19 世紀）板橋区立美術館蔵
Paulownia and Chrysanthemums, Sakai Dōitsu, From Edo to Meiji period, 19th century, Pair of two-fold
screens, Color on gold ground on paper, 171.8 x 172.6 cm each, Itabashi Art Museum

右隻から左隻にかけて桐の大木が枝振りもよく描かれている。樹幹はたらし込み技法で質感を
出し、初夏を思わせる青々とした葉と紫の花色の対比が鮮やかである。中央に流れる流水をは
さんで、白菊がこんもりとした土坡に咲いている。爽やかな夏秋草図に仕上がっている。

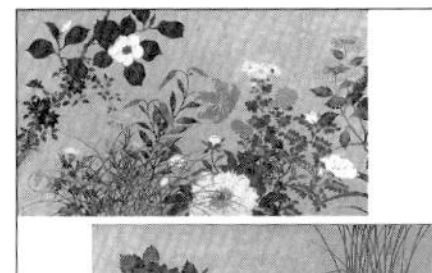

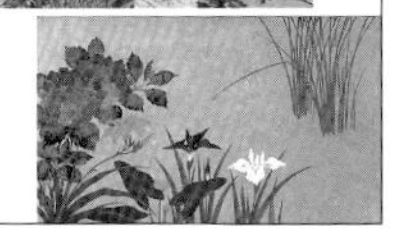

P216-219 「夏草図屏風」田中抱二

二曲一隻屏風　紙本金地着色　50.9 x 172.6 cm　静嘉堂文庫美術館蔵
Summer Grass, Tanaka Hōji, Two-fold screen, Color on gold ground on paper, 50.9 x 172.6 cm, Seikado
Bunko Art Museum　画像提供：静嘉堂文庫イメージアーカイブ / DNPartcom

二曲一隻の金地屏風に夏から秋にかけて咲く草花の姿を精緻な筆遣いで捉えている。中央に紫
陽花の大輪を置き、燕子花、菊、牡丹、山百合、薊、鉄線、泰山木と季節を違えて描かれている。
抱一の「四季花鳥図巻」（東京国立博物館蔵）や粉本を参照したことが想像される作品である。

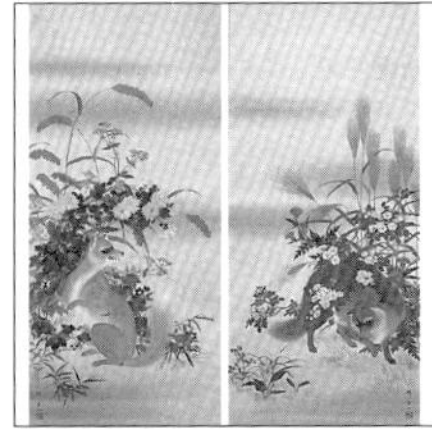

P220-223 「孤狸図」山本光一

軸二幅　各 111.6 x 50.7 cm　江戸〜明治時代　板橋区立美術館蔵
Fox and Raccoon Dog, Yamamoto Kōitsu, From Edo to Meiji period, Pair of hanging scrolls, 111.6 x 50.7
cm each, Itabashi Art Museum

右幅には麦や薊（あざみ）の咲く春の野辺でしきりに餌を探す愛らしい狸の姿を、左幅には菊
や桔梗、藤袴（ふじばかま）など秋草の咲く叢で前脚をあげて振り向く狐の姿を描いている。
柔らかそうな体毛や眼の細やかな表現と色彩の透明さが爽やかで心地よく伝わってくる。

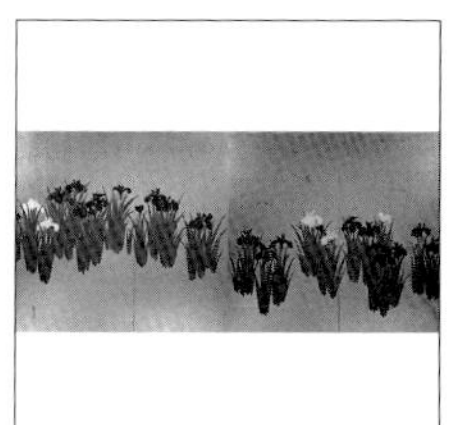

P224-227 「杜若図屏風」神坂雪佳

二曲一双屏風　紙本金地着色　各 167.5 x 183.0 cm　大正末～昭和初　個人蔵
Folding Screens with Iris, Kamisaka Sekka, c.1920-40, Pair of two-fold screens, Color on gold ground on paper, 167.5 x 183.0 cm, Private Collection

二曲一双の金地屏風に杜若がリズミカルに配されている。光琳の代表作である「燕子花図」（根津美術館蔵）の群青と緑青の単純な色調の反復とは異なり、アクセントのように白い杜若を描き込んでいる。光琳画のコレクターでもあった図案家の岸光景に学び工芸図案家として活躍した一方で、琳派の伝統を忠実に受け継いだ絵画作品を遺している。

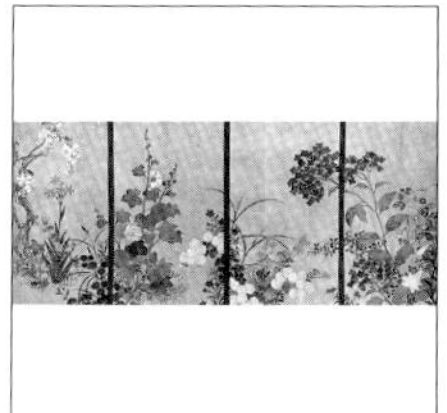

P228-231 「光琳風草花」神坂雪佳

四曲一隻屏風　紙本着色　117.0 x 253.0 cm　明治時代（19 世紀）　髙島屋史料館蔵
Flowers, *Kōrin Style*, Kamisaka Sekka, Meiji period, 19th century, Four-fold screen, Color on paper, 117.0 x 253.0 cm, Takashimaya Historical Museum, Osaka

四季折々の草花を光琳風に仕上げた四曲一隻の屏風である。四季の草花に墨や顔料のたらし込みで濃淡をつけ、大まかな花の輪郭の中を色でうめている。下描きの描線が残り、草花を曲線的で自由自在に捉えようとしている雪佳のデザイン性が見てとれる作品である。

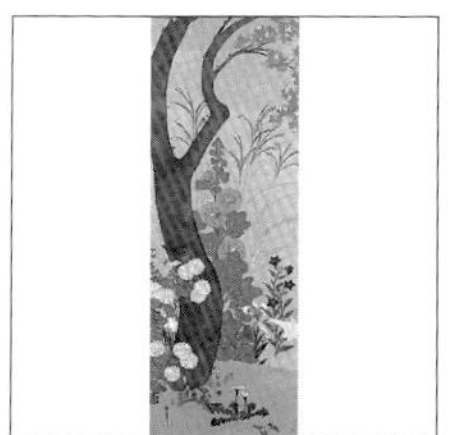

P232-233 「四季草花」神坂雪佳

軸一幅　絹本着色　120.0 x 42.0 cm　京都市美術館蔵
Flowers and Grasses of the Four Seasons, Kamisaka Sekka, Hanging scroll, Color on silk, 120.0 x 42.0 cm, Kyoto Municipal Museum of Art

樹幹にたらし込みをほどこした紅葉の楓を中心に、芙蓉、桔梗、菊などの四季の草花を描いている。鮮やかな色遣いや意匠化したモティーフはそのまま工芸デザインとして活用できる作品である。

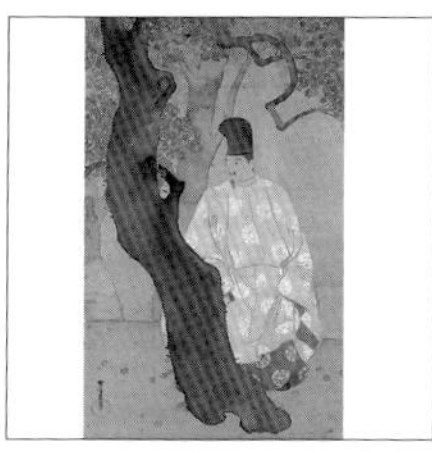

P234-235 「観楓図」神坂雪佳

額一面　紙本着色　127.1 x 77.0 cm　大正初頃　京都市立芸術大学芸術資料館蔵
Autumn Maple Viewing, Kamisaka Sekka, Taishō period, c.1910-20, Framed, Color on paper, 127.1 x 77.0 cm, University Art Museum, Kyoto City University of Arts

平安の殿上人の行楽として、北野の花見、嵯峨野の虫選、高雄の観楓などがよく知られている。楓の太い幹に墨の濃淡とたらし込みをほどこし、鮮やかな紅葉の中の静寂感を出している。烏帽子に狩衣姿の公家の表情から、過ぎ行く季節の名残りを惜しむ姿が読み取れる作品である。

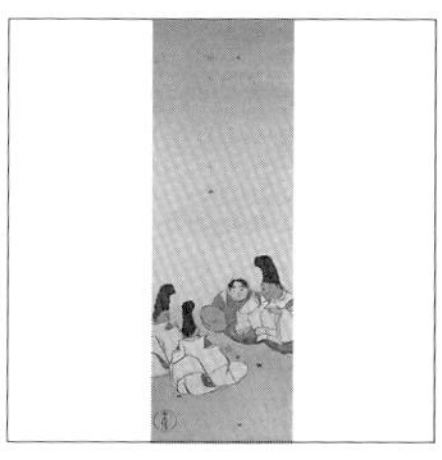

P236 「供侍之図」神坂雪佳

軸一幅　紙本着色　126.0 x 42.0 cm　京都市美術館蔵
Samurai Attendant, Kamisaka Sekka, Hanging scroll, Color on paper, 126.0 x 42.0 cm, Kyoto Municipal Museum of Art

供侍（ともざむらい）は供として従う侍のことで、車座になって談笑に夢中になる公家の会話に聞き耳を立てている。観楓に行った帰り道なのか、風に吹かれて紅葉が舞っている。人物の表現に余分な描線は用いず、的確な線と平面的な彩色によって姿態を表わしている。

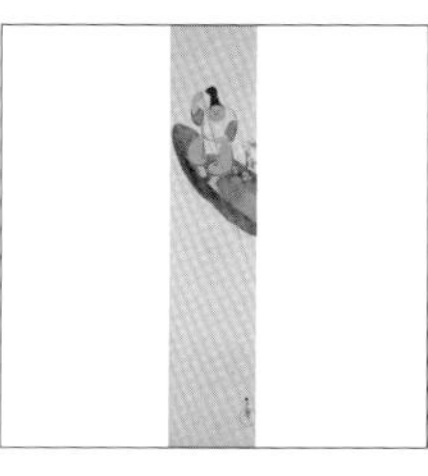

P236 「軽舟図」神坂雪佳

軸一幅　絹本着色　127.4 x 26.6 cm　大正 4 年（1915）頃　京都市美術館蔵
Boatman, Kamisaka Sekka, Taishō period, c.1915（Taishō 4）, Hanging scroll, Color on silk, 127.4 x 26.6 cm, Kyoto Municipal Museum of Art

船に竿をさす男のどこかとぼけたようなユーモラスな表情。その足下には手折ってきた桜の小枝が乗っている。嵐山の舟遊びに出掛けた帰り道であろうか。流れるような描線で男の姿を捉え、画面に微かに残る波紋から水の豊かさを感じさせてくれる作品である。

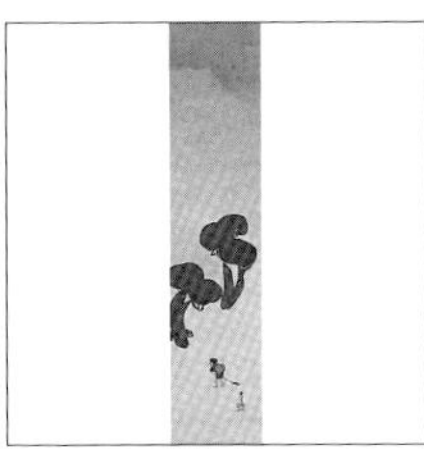

P237 「松葉掻童子図」神坂雪佳

軸一幅　絹本着色　113.0 x 27.0 cm　大正末～昭和初　今宮神社蔵
Boy Sweeping Pine Needles, Kamisaka Sekka, c.1920-40, Hanging scroll, Color on silk, 113.0 x 27.0 cm, Imamiya-jinja, Kyoto

雪佳の描く人物には、『伊勢物語』などの文学作品や能の登場人物が多い。その他には、吉祥、福寿を示す寿老人、節句の祝い用に描かれた桃太郎などが挙げられる。ここには箒をもち、浜辺の松葉を集める童子の姿が描かれている。遠く広がる背景の中に、デフォルメされた松は琳派風の表現を持ちのびやかである。

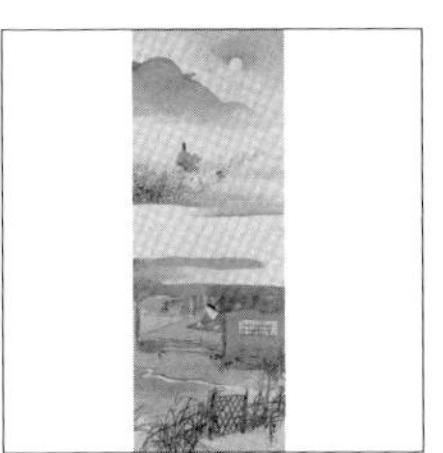

P238-239 「小督」神坂雪佳

軸一幅　絹本着色　114.0 x 42.0 cm　京都市美術館蔵
Kogō（Daughter of *Fujiwara-no Shigenori*), Kamisaka Sekka, Hanging scroll, Color on silk, 114.0 x 42.0 cm, Kyoto Municipal Museum of Art

小督（こごう）は中納言藤原成範（しげのり）の娘で、高倉天皇の寵愛を受けたため建礼門院の父・平清盛に憎まれ嵯峨野に身を隠したが、勅使の源仲国に捜し出され、23歳のとき尼にされ追放された。薄や桔梗の秋草が咲く簡素な庵で琴を爪弾く小督が描かれている。籬や屋根の庇に緑青のたらし込みがほどこされ静寂感が伝わってくる。

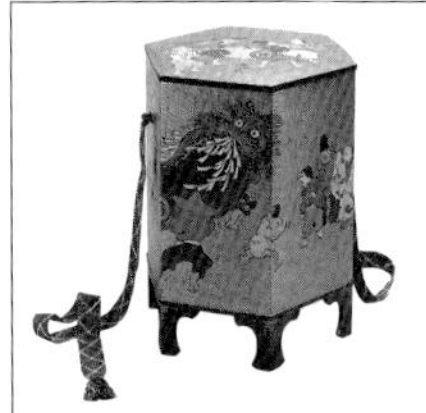

P240 「漆画人物祭礼之図飾箱」神坂雪佳

木、漆絵　30.0 x 27.0 x 39.0 cm　大正末頃　京都市美術館蔵
Ornamental Box with Festival Scene, Design and Painting by Kamisaka Sekka, Taishō period, c.1920-30, Lacquered wood, 30.0 x 27.0 x 39.0cm, Kyoto Municipal Museum of Art

行器（ほかい）は木製で蓋付きの容器で、食物の運搬用具である。木鉢や曲げ物製から精巧な漆蒔絵で反り足をつけたものまである。祭礼図が描かれた六角行器は全体に布目地に白檀塗り（箔の上に透漆〈すきうるし・透明度の高い精製漆〉を塗ったもの）の仕上げで、人物は色漆で描かれている。

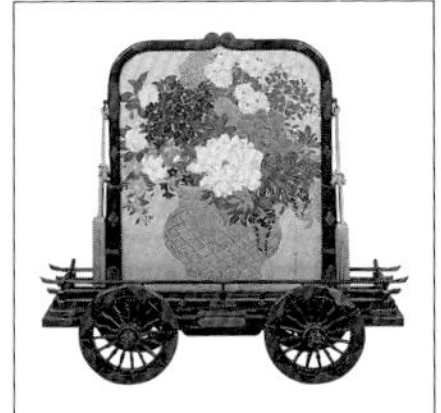

P240、242-243 「盛花図御所車衝立」神坂雪佳

紙本着色　各 79.0 x 99.8 cm　大正末頃（衝立部分・桃山～江戸初期）　三千院蔵
Carriage-shaped Dividing Screen with Flowers, Design by Kamisaka Sekka, Taishō period, c.1915-25, (dividing screen made from late 16 to early 17 century), Color on paper, 79.0 x 99.8 cm each, Sanzen-in, Kyoto

御所車にしつらえられた衝立の表面には、金地の画面に竹で編まれた大籠に藤、牡丹、菊、桔梗、萩など四季の草花が豪華にこぼれんばかりに生けられている。裏面は小さな竹籠に色づいた実をつけた千両と桔梗の花が清楚に描かれている。華やかさと静けさをうまく描き分けた作品である。

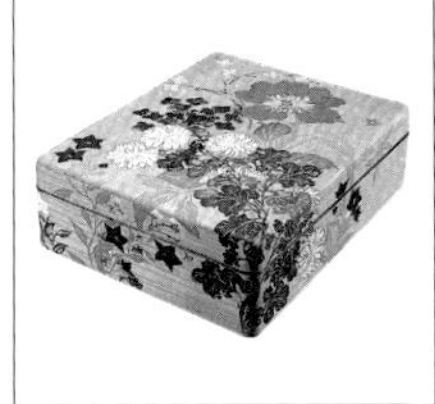

P241 「四季草花図文箱」神坂雪佳

一合　桐、金箔、着色　38.0 x 30.0 x 11.5 cm　大正末期頃　髙島屋史料館蔵
Letter Box with Flowers and Grasses of the Four Seasons, Design by Kamisaka Sekka, Taishō period, c.1920-30, Color on paulownia with gold, 38.0 x 30.0 x 11.5 cm, Takashimaya Historical Museum, Osaka

白木を用いた什器は古くより神事などに用いられることが多く、伝世品を見かけることは稀である。木地に鮮やかな色彩で山吹、牡丹、桔梗、菊などの季節の草花をほどこした文箱は近代の工芸品ならではの意匠で、写実的な絵画技法を駆使した作品である。

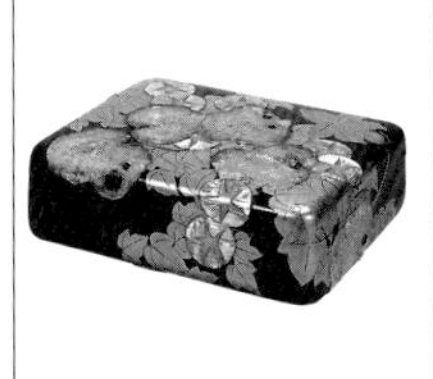

P244 「朝顔蒔絵手箱」浅井忠・図　杉林古香・作

一合　明治 42 年（1909）　28.0 x 22.0 x 8.5 cm　京都工芸繊維大学美術工芸資料館蔵　AN.1617
Lacquered Small Box with Morning Glory, Design by Asai Chū, Lacquered by Sugibayashi Kokō, Meiji period, Dated 1909（Meiji 42), Lacquered wood, 28.0 x 22.0 x 8.5 cm, Kyoto Institute of Technology Museum and Archives

漆芸家の杉林古香（ここう）は浅井忠の図案の多くを漆芸作品に仕上げ、浅井の図案を語る上で欠かせない作家である。また西洋のデザイン観がどのように受け入れられたか、明治時代末期の京都における図案と工芸の状況を伝えてくれる貴重な作品である。黒塗りの大きな手箱に大きく朝顔を高蒔絵と鉛貝で描いた手箱である。

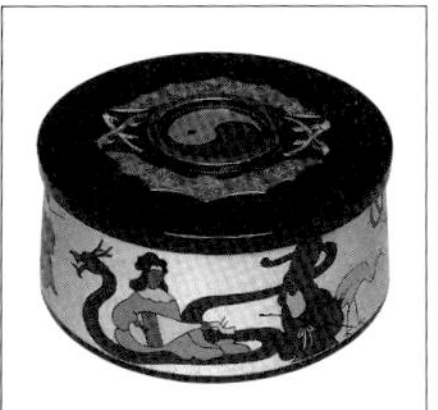

P245 「七福神蒔絵蓋付菓子器」浅井忠・図　迎田秋悦・作

一合　明治 42 年（1909）　径 20.3 cm　高 10.6 cm　京都工芸繊維大学美術工芸資料館蔵　AN.1620
Lacquered Sweets Box with the Seven Gods of Good Fortune, Design by Asai Chū, Lacquered by Kōda Shūetsu, Meiji period, dated 1909 (Meiji 42), Lacquered wood, 20.3 x 10.6 cm, Kyoto Institute of Technology Museum and Archives

七福神を意匠にした菓子器は、蓋を朱塗りと青漆で曲玉を描き、厚貝と鉛を貼っている。側面は金箔貼りに漆絵で七福神を描いている。作者の迎田秋悦は浅井について「浅井先生より親しく図案の事から、新しきものの事、万事お噺を聞く事が出来るようになった。そして色々聴くにつれて、成程自分等の作品の月並である事、陳腐である事を解するに至ったのであった」と述べている。

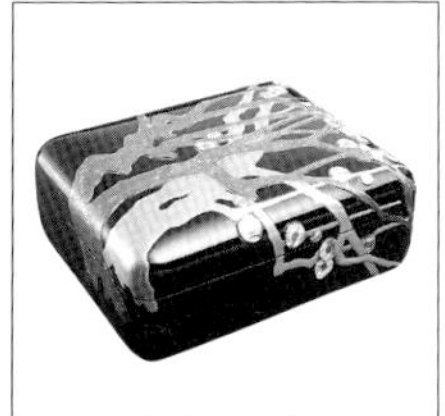

P246 「梅文蒔絵文庫」浅井忠・図　杉林古香・作

一合　11.0 x 27.5 x 33.5 cm　佐倉市立美術館蔵
Lacquered Stationery Box with Plum Trees, Design by Asai Chū, Lacquered by Sugibayashi Kokō, 11.0 x 27.5 x 33.5 cm, Sakura City Museum of Art

浅井忠の図案による文庫で、大胆な梅の意匠、黒塗りに鉛、蚫の割貝などの技法からも琳派漆器の特色を随所に生かした作品である。京都に生まれ、蒔絵師・二代浅野友七の四男であった杉林古香（ここう）は、浅井忠の知遇を得たことを契機に、漆器の図案研究団体「京漆園」に参加し、漆器意匠改良に意を注いだ。

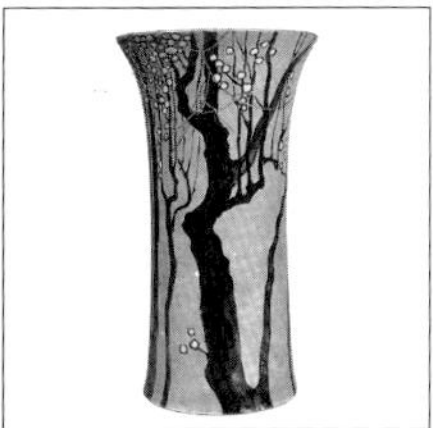

P246-247 「梅図花生」浅井忠・図

一個　高 37.6 cm　口径 21.6 cm　京都工芸繊維大学美術工芸資料館蔵　AN.3283
Vase with Plum Trees, Design by Asai Chū, 37.6 x 21.6 cm, Kyoto Institute of Technology Museum and Archives

浅井忠は明治 33 - 35 年（1900 -02）までパリに留学した。そのおりジャポニスムの影響をうけたアール・ヌーヴォーに万国博覧会の会場で触れ、琳派を再発見し図案の研究をしたといわれる。この花生も『琳派百図』からヒントを得たと思われるが、どちらかといえばアール・ヌーヴォーの感覚に近いものがある。浅井自身が絵付をして焼き上げたものといわれている。

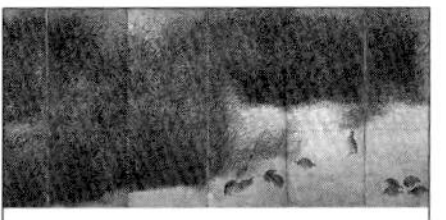
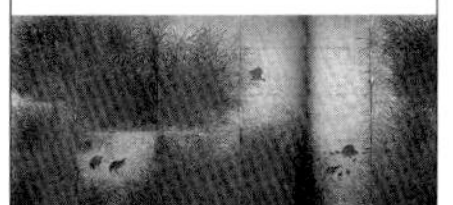

P248-251 「秋草鶉図屏風」重文　伝土佐光起

六曲一双屏風　紙本金地着色　各 151.5 x 354.5 cm　名古屋市博物館蔵
Flowering Plants of Autumn and Quail, Attributed to Tosa Mitsuoki, Pair of six-fold screens, 151.5 x 354.5 cm each, Important Cultural Property, Nagoya City Museum

六曲一双屏風の金地に錯綜する薄（すすき）の濃緑の描線が画面全体を引き締めている。土佐派得意の細く描かれた薄葉が金を透かして見せることで空間に遠近感を出している。叢（くさむら）で遊ぶ鶉は精緻な筆法で姿態を的確に捉えている。金と緑青の対比が鮮烈な印象を与える美しく見事な作品である。

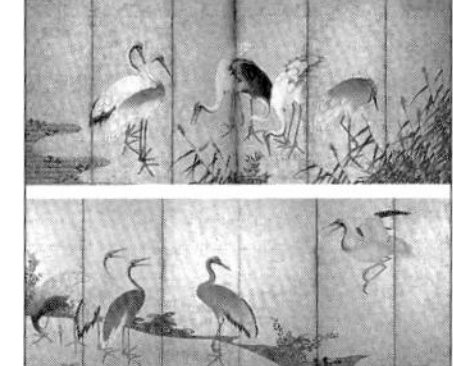

P252-255 「群鶴図屏風」雲谷等與

六曲一双屏風　紙本金地着色　右・154.0 x 364.6 cm　左・153.7x364.2cm　江戸時代（17 世紀）山口県立美術館蔵
Cranes, Unkoku Tōyo, Edo period, 17th century, Pair of six-fold screens, Color on gold ground on paper, right : 154.0 x 364.6 cm left: 153.7 x 364.2 cm, Yamaguchi Prefectural Art Museum

水辺に飛来する鶴、また岸辺で餌を啄む鶴の群れをさまざまな姿態で捉え金地の画面に配している。鶴の首の曲線がおなじかたちで繰り返し描かれる方法は、琳派をはじめとする作家たちの得意とした構図である。雲谷等與は等益（とうえき）の長男にあたり長門の萩藩に仕えた絵師である。

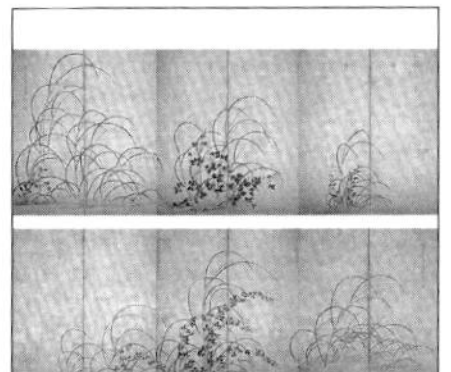

P256-259 「秋草図屏風」狩野了承

天保 5 年（1834）六曲一双屏風　紙本金地着色　各 125.0 x 313.6 cm　板橋区立美術館蔵
Autumn Flowers, Kanō Ryōshō, Edo period, Dated 1834 (Tenpō 5), Pair of six-fold screens, Color on gold ground on paper, 125.0 x 313.6 cm each, Itabashi Art Museum

秋の草花を代表する薄の叢を六曲一双の大画面に描いている。左から吹いてくる秋風を受けてか、薄葉は弧を描いてたなびき、その半弧のパターンがリズミカルに画面を構成している。薄の一叢ごとに、紫苑（しおん）、葛（くず）、女郎花（おみなえし）、萩が寄り添うように描かれている。狩野了承は江戸城障壁画にも腕を揮った御用絵師である。

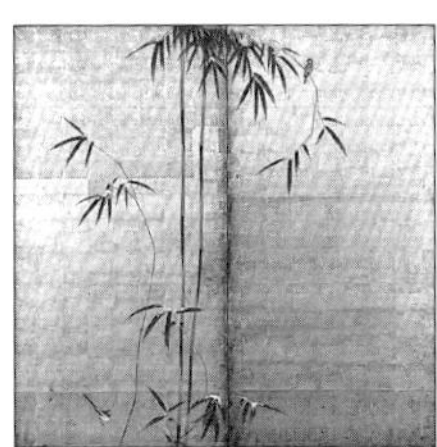

P260-261 「若竹鶺鴒図屏風」田中訥言
二曲一隻屏風　紙本銀地着色　170.1 x 175.0 cm　名古屋市博物館蔵
Young Bamboos and Wagtails, Tanaka Totsugen, Two-fold screen, Color on silver ground on paper,
170.1 x 175.0 cm, Nagoya City Museum

正方形に近い銀地の屏風に二本の若竹がすんなりと伸び、画面の上部と下部から覗かせる枝先
に雪が被っている。冬の早朝であろうか張りつめた空気の中で二羽の小鳥のさえずりだけが響
いている。訥言（とつげん）は名古屋の生まれで、古いやまと絵を模写することで古典の精髄
を学び、復古大和絵の祖とされている。

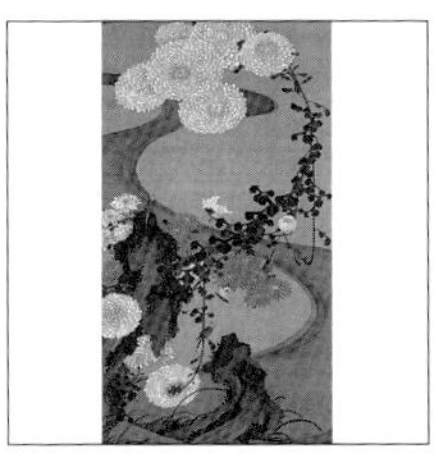

P262-264 「菊花流水図」伊藤若冲
軸一幅　絹本着色　142.0 x 72.9 cm　宮内庁三の丸尚蔵館蔵
The Colorful Realm of Living Beings: Birds and Chrysanthemums by a Stream, Itō Jakuchū, Hanging
scroll, Color on silk, 142.0 x 72.9 cm, Sannomaru Shozokan（The Museum of the Imperial Collections）

伊藤若冲の代表作である「動植綵絵」30 幅のうちの一幅で、水辺の岩上に咲く色とりどりの
菊花と、それに遊ぶ小禽が描かれている。そして背景の画面には光琳模様風な流水が大胆に蛇
行している。一見すると自然の描写に見えるが、若冲の筆にかかると画面上端に描かれた大輪
の白菊はあまりも幻想的な姿に変えられてしまう。

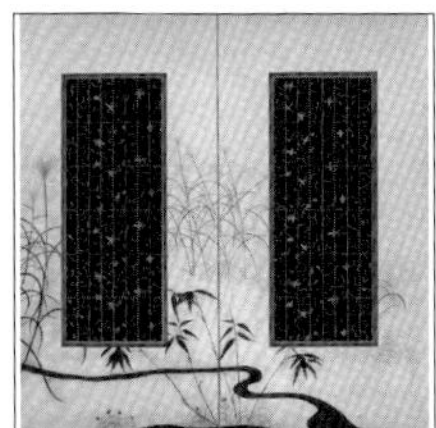

P265-267 「秋草流水図屏風」
二曲一隻屏風　紙本金地着色　154.0 x 148.0 cm　江戸時代　板橋区立美術館蔵
Autumn Plants and Stream, Edo period, Two-fold screen, Color on gold ground on paper, 154.0 x 148.0
cm, Itabashi Art Museum

この屏風は中央をくりぬいて障子のように桟をつくり、そこに竹屋町（たけやまち）と呼ばれ
る金紗の裂地を貼り込むという細工がある。そのため両方の窓からは紗を通して向こう側が透
けて見える趣向である。琳派風に描かれた繊細な薄は秋風に揺らぎ、デフォルメされた遣り水
を挟んで軽やかである。金地に濃緑、群青の色彩対比に趣がある。

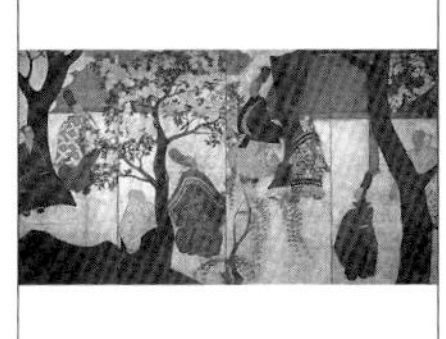

P268-269 「蹴鞠図屏風」
四曲一隻屏風　紙本金地着色　154.3 x 267.0 cm　堺市博物館蔵
Kemari (Traditional Kick-a-Ball Game), Four-fold screen, Color on gold ground on paper, 154.3 x 267.0
cm, Sakai City Museum

蹴鞠は古代以来、貴族の間で行われた遊戯で、革沓を履き鹿革製の鞠を落とさないように足の
甲で蹴って受け渡しする。鞠壺と呼ばれる四隅に、柳、桜、松、楓を植え、砂を敷き詰めた場
所で行う。宗達派が数多くの蹴鞠図を制作しているが、本図もユニークな顔や姿の人物表現な
どに宗達の影響が色濃く見られる作品である。

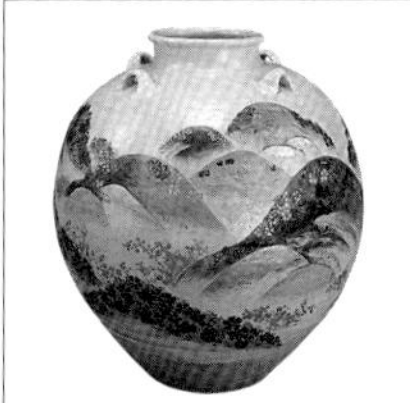

P270-271 「色絵吉野山図茶壺」重文　野々村仁清
一個　高・35.7 cm　福岡市美術館蔵
Tea Urn with *Yoshino-yama* in Overglaze Enamels, Nonomura Ninsei, 35.7 cm（Height）, Important
Cultural Property, Fukuoka Art Museum　画像提供：福岡市美術館 / DNPartcom　撮影：山崎信一

古来より桜の名所として知られる吉野山の満開の桜を描いた茶壺である。幾重にも連なる山肌
には今を盛りに桜が香り立っている。稜線にそって描かれた桜花を金彩で配し、丸い山並みは
色を変え優美でのびやかに表現している。仁清の茶壺に見られる金銀を使った彩画はまるで豪
奢な襖絵や屏風絵を見ているようで、桃山期の華やいだ気分が伝わってくる。

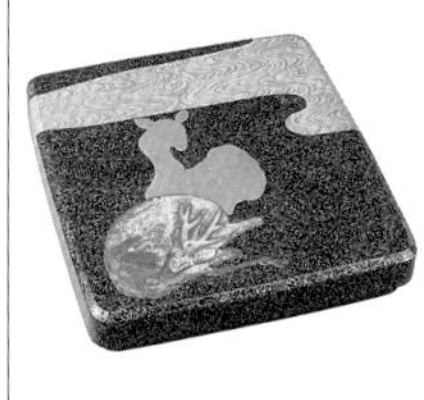

P272 「槇鹿蒔絵螺鈿硯箱」永田友治
一具　木製漆塗　41.2 x 31.2 x 14.1cm　江戸時代（18 世紀）京都国立博物館蔵
Stationery Set with Black Pines and Deer in Maki-e and Mother-of-Pearl Inlay, Nagata Yūji, Edo period,
18th century, Lacquer on wood, Stationery box: 41.2 x 31.2 x 14.1cm, Kyoto National Museum

梨地に平蒔絵、螺鈿、鉛板の象眼を使い、硯箱には水辺に憩う雌雄の鹿の姿を、料紙箱には土
坡に伸びる槇と鹿を描いている。蓋裏には鉛板製の文字で『新古今和歌集』の「秋の月山へさ
やかに照らせるは　おつるもみちのかすを見よとか」が散らし書きに配されている。鹿は小西
家文書の画稿などに見られる琳派好みの意匠である。

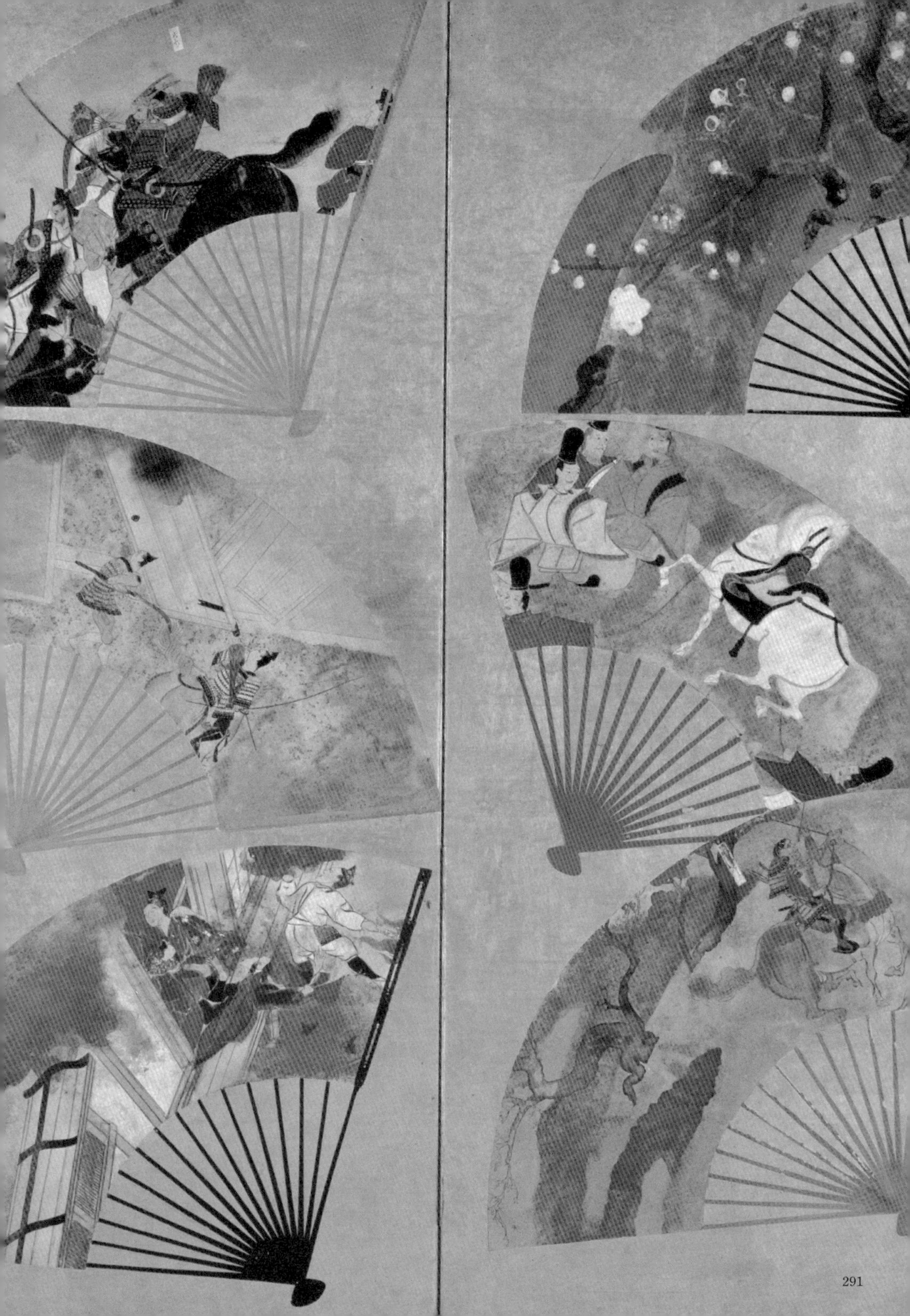

画家略伝　Painter Profile

◉**浅井忠**　**Asai Chū**　あさい ちゅう

安政 3 年〜明治 40 年（1856-1907）

　明治期の洋画家。幼名は忠之丞、のち常保。号は槐庭、木魚、黙語。江戸の佐倉藩邸内に生まれた。工部美術学校でイタリアの風景画家フォンタネージに洋画を学んでのち、明治美術会を結成した。明治 31 年（1911）東京美術学校西洋学科教授。明治 33 年〜 35 年までパリに留学し、当時万国博覧会で出会ったアール・ヌーヴォーに触れ、その様式を反映させた図案を制作、また琳派の再発見にも繋がった。帰国後は新設の京都高等工芸学校教授に就任して京都に移住する。安井曾太郎、梅原龍三郎らを指導し京都洋画壇の育成に尽くした。

［掲載頁 P244-247］

◉**池田孤邨**　**Ikeda Koson**　いけだ こそん

享和元年〜慶応 2 年（1810-66）

　江戸時代後期の画家。名は三信、字（あざな）は周二、別号は画戦軒、旧松軒など。越後の出身で、若い時に江戸に出て酒井抱一に師事し琳派様式を学ぶ。抱一の工房では鈴木其一と共に中核をなした一人である。書画の鑑定に優れ、茶や和歌も好んだと伝えられる。『光琳新撰百図』や『抱一上人真蹟鏡』を刊行して師の業績を守り伝えることに心血を注いだ。

［掲載頁 P200-205］

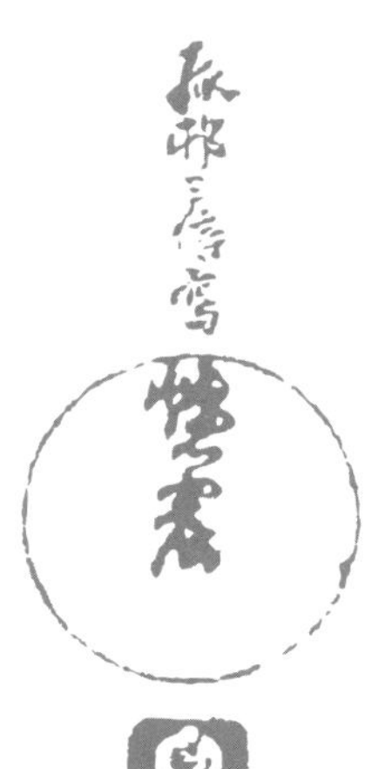

◉**市川其融**　**Ichikawa Kiyū**　いちかわ きゆう

生没年不詳

　江戸時代後期の画家。名は泰度、字（あざな）は子高、通称は其二で、端斎と号した。江戸詰の古河藩士で、嘉永・安政年間（1848-59）に活躍した。鈴木其一の門弟で鮮明な色彩と明確な構図には、其融のこざっぱりした性格がうかがえる。

［掲載頁 P208-211］

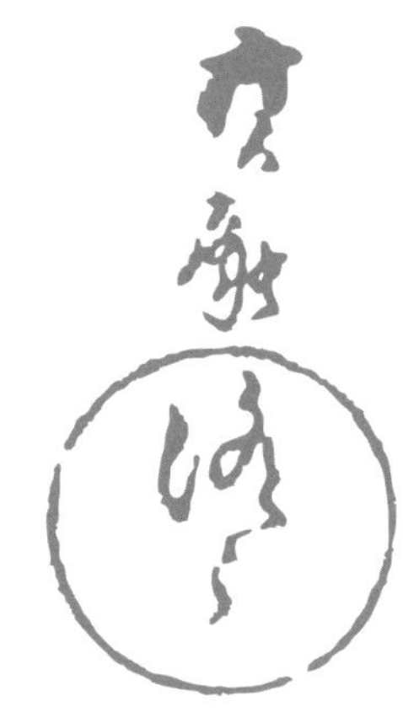

● **伊藤若冲**　Itō Jakuchū　いとうじゃくちゅう

正徳 6 年〜寛政 12 年（1716-1800）

　江戸時代中期の画家。京都高倉錦小路の青物問屋「枡源」の長男として生まれる。本名源左衛門、名は汝鈞、字は景和。また絵を依頼する人は必ず米一斗をもって謝礼としたことから斗米庵、そして心遠館と号した。初め狩野派を学び写生の重要性を認識し、さらにその後、中国の宋・元・明の花鳥画を模写した。また尾形光琳の画風を研究し独自の画風を開いた。特に鶏の絵を得意とし、写生を基礎にした装飾性のある作品を描いた。生涯独身で、晩年は京都深草の石峯寺の近くに隠棲し、五百羅漢を制作した。代表作に「動植 綵絵」30 幅（宮内庁三の丸尚蔵館）、「仙人掌群鶏図襖絵」（豊中市・西福寺）がある。

［掲載頁 P262-264］

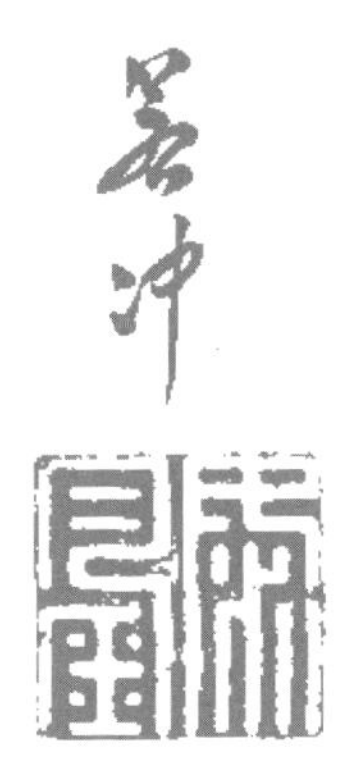

● **雲谷等與**　Unkoku Tōyo　うんこくとうよ

慶長 17 年〜寛文 8 年（1612-68）

　江戸時代前期の画家。名は就直、通称は図書。雲谷等益の長男。長門（山口県）萩藩につかえる。寛永 21 年（1644）雲谷派宗家を継ぎ、雪舟五代を称した。明暦元年（1655）弟の等爾らと御所の障壁画制作に加わった。

［掲載頁 P252-255］

● **尾形乾山**　Ogata Kenzan　おがたけんざん

寛文 3 年〜寛保 3 年（1663-1743）

　江戸時代中期の陶芸家、画師。京都の呉服商雁金屋宗謙の三男として生まれる。画家の尾形光琳は兄にあたる。学問、茶事を藤村庸軒に、絵を狩野安信に学んだといわれる。通称は権平、のち深省、別号は尚古斎、紫翠など。父の死後、元禄 2 年（1689）27 歳のとき御室に隠宅を構え文人生活に入る。野々村仁清に作陶の弟子入りし、元禄 12 年（1699）京都鳴滝に窯を開く。この窯が京都の乾の方角にあたるため「乾山」を窯の名につけ、雅号にもちいている。兄光琳が絵付けをした白地銹絵（銹漆を使った技法）陶器を多数つくり出したほか、釉下色絵の技法を生み出した。晩年は享保

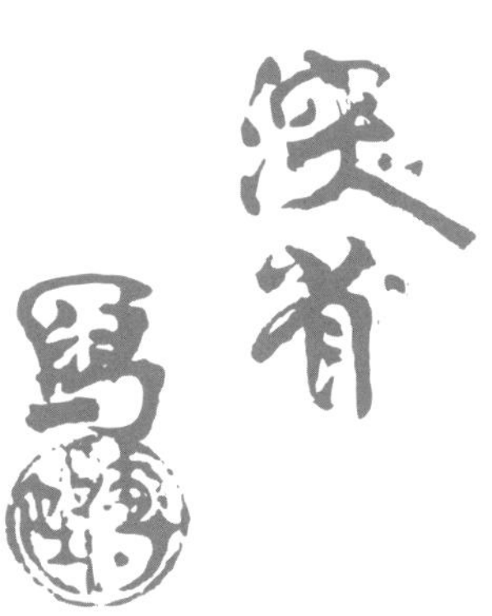

年間（1716-36）の中頃江戸入谷に移り住み、元文2年（1737）には下野（栃木県）佐野で作陶、江戸に没した。

［掲載頁 P130-141］

◉尾形光琳　Ogata Kōrin　おがた こうりん

万治元年〜享保元年（1658-1716）

　江戸時代前期の画家。京都有数の呉服商雁金屋に生まれ、幼少より能や絵に造詣の深かった父宗謙の影響を受けた。名は惟富、方祝、号は澗声、道崇、青々、寂明。初め山本素軒に狩野派を、のち生家に伝わる俵屋宗達画の美に出合いその画風を学んだ。元禄14年（1701）法橋となり「燕子花図屏風」（根津美術館）を描いて独自の世界を確立した。俵屋宗達の「風神雷神図」の模写を経て、「紅白梅図屏風」（MOA美術館）の代表作を完成させた。晩年は弟尾形乾山の陶器の絵付、蒔絵、小袖の下絵など、工芸意匠にも優れた作品を残した。

［掲載頁 P10-11、P14-15、P88-125、P128-129］

◉狩野了承　Kanō Ryōshō　かのう りょうしょう

明和5年〜弘化3年（1768-1846）

　江戸時代後期の画家。酒田（山形県）に生まれ、江戸に出て深川水場狩野家の梅笑師信の養子となり家督を継ぐ。名は賢信、初め信川と号したが、享和2年（1802）に了承と改名する。絵を狩野探幽を祖とする鍛冶橋狩野家の探信守道に学びやまと絵を得意とした。また同門の沖一蛾（1796-1855）の影響も受けた。江戸城障壁画にも腕を揮った御用絵師である。

［掲載頁 P256-259］

◉神坂雪佳　Kamisaka Sekka　かみさか せっか

慶応2年〜昭和17年（1866-1942）

　明治・昭和時代前期の図案家。本名は吉隆。京都御所警護の武士、神坂吉重の長男に生まれる。初めに鈴木瑞彦に四条派の絵を、のち光琳画のコレクターでもあった図案家の岸光景に師事し、琳派や工芸意匠の図案を学んだ。明治38年（1905）京都市美術工芸学校

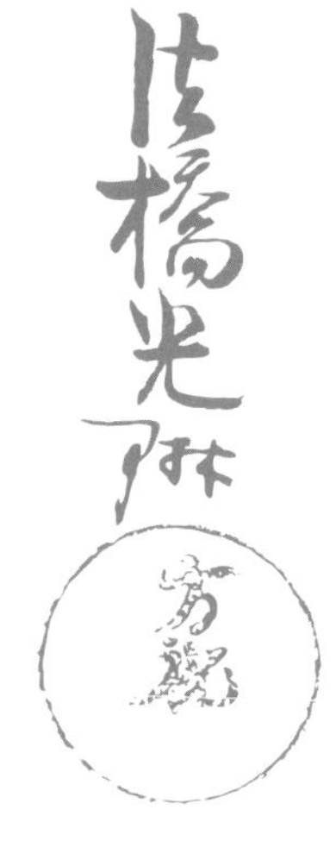
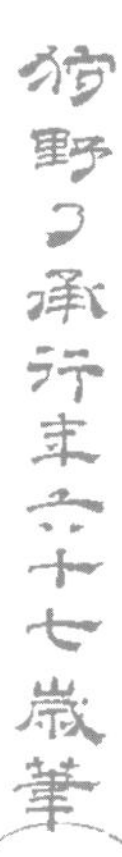
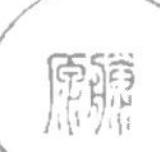

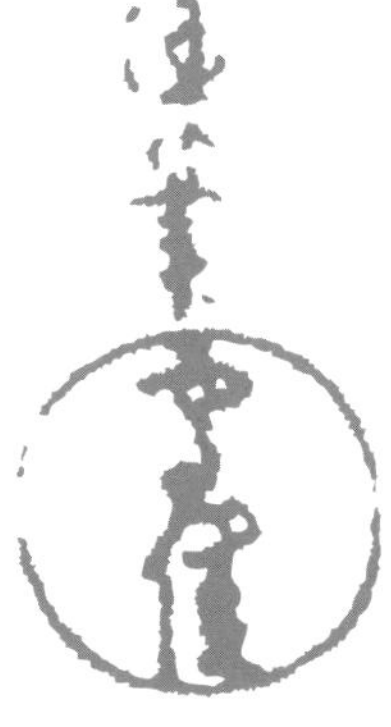

教諭となる。同 40 年佳都美会を創立して、漆器、陶器、染織品をはじめとする工芸図案界の発展につくした。著作に『百々世草』『海路』『蝶千種』などがある。
［掲載頁 P224-243］

●喜多川相説　Kitagawa Sōsetsu　きたがわ そうせつ
生没年不詳

　江戸時代前期の画家。伝記の詳細はわからないが金沢地方で活躍したと推定される。俵屋宗達、俵屋宗雪と同じ「伊年」印を用い、宗達の後継者と伝えられ、宗雪の没後はその工房の指導にあたったと思われる。草花図を得意とし、薄墨と淡彩を用いて繊細に描かれた押絵貼の屏風が多く残されている。
［掲載頁 P78-87］

●酒井鶯蒲　Sakai Ōho　さかい おうほ
文化 5 年〜天保 12 年（1808-41）

　江戸時代後期の画家。築地本願寺の末寺にあたる市ヶ谷浄栄寺の住職香阪雪仙の次男に生まれる。12歳の時、酒井抱一が吉原大文字楼から身請けして身の回りの世話をさせていた妙華の願いで迎えられ養子となり、抱一の門に学んだ。書物を学ぶ事が苦手であったが茶事を好んだといわれる。
［掲載頁 P174-177］

●酒井道一　Sakai Dōitsu　さかい どういつ
弘化 2 年〜大正 2 年（1845-1913）

　明治時代の日本画家。江戸の生まれで、名は顕真、号は光阿。酒井抱一の弟子である山本素堂の次男で、絵を父および鈴木其一に学んだ。酒井抱一の画風に傾倒し、酒井鶯一の養子となり、雨華庵四代を継いだ。明治の新しい気運にふれ、博覧会にも出品し活躍、琳派の画風を明治の画壇に伝えた。
［掲載頁 P22-23、P212-215］

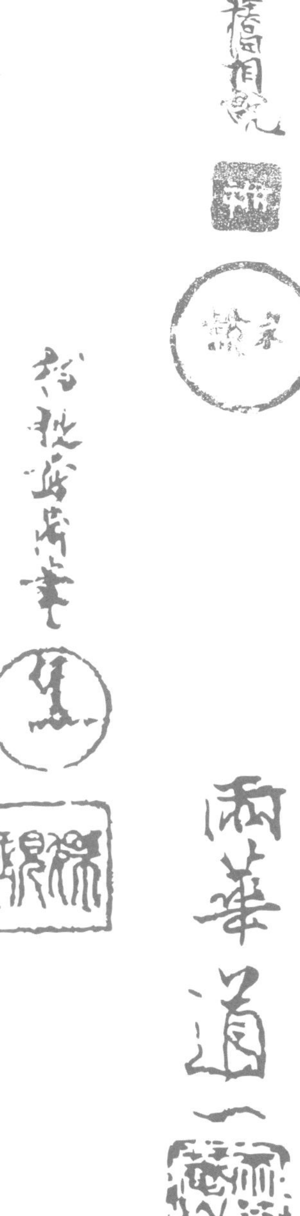

● **酒井抱一**　Sakai Hōitsu　さかい ほういつ

宝暦 11 年〜文政 11 年（1761-1828）

　江戸時代後期の画家。江戸に生まれる。酒井忠仰の次男。播磨（兵庫県）姫路藩主酒井忠以の弟。名は忠因、字は暉真。号は鶯村、軽挙道人、通称は栄八。37 歳で出家し、のち文化 6 年（1809）江戸根岸に雨華庵を結ぶ。絵は初め狩野高信から狩野風を学び、沈南蘋の花鳥画、浮世絵、円山派、土佐派など広く学び、のち尾形光琳（万治元〜享保元年・1658-1716）の作品に接し深く傾倒する。文化 12 年（1815）には光琳百年忌を催し、『光琳百図』、『尾形流略印譜』を刊行し、積極的に江戸での光琳・乾山の顕彰活動に努めた。代表作は光琳筆の「風神雷神図屏風」の裏面に描いた「夏秋草図屏風」（東京国立博物館）、「花鳥十二ヶ月図」（宮内庁三の丸尚蔵館）などがある。

[掲載頁 P18-19、P158-173]

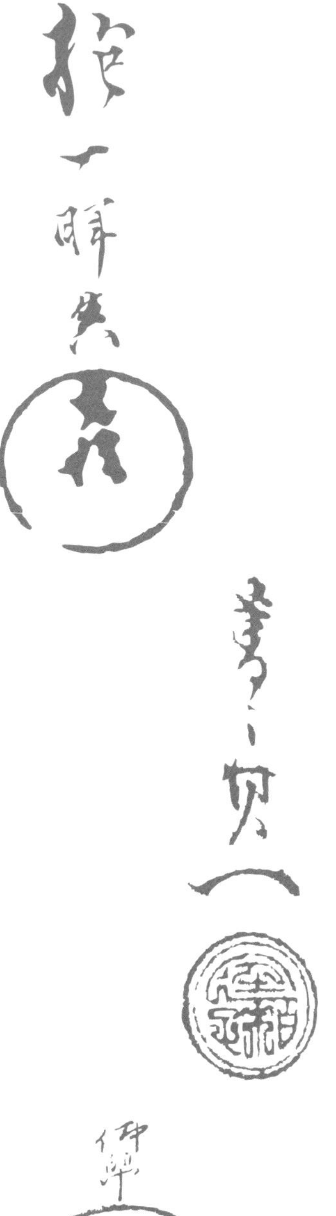

● **鈴木其一**　Suzuki Kiitsu　すずき きいつ

寛政 8 年〜安政 5 年（1796-1858）

　江戸時代後期の画家。近江（滋賀県）出身の染屋の子として江戸に生まれる。名は元長、字は子淵、号は噌々、菁々、庭柏子、祝琳斎など。文化 10 年（1813）、18 歳の時、酒井抱一の内弟子となり、のちに同門の鈴木蠣潭の養子となって酒井家に仕えた。蠣潭が没するとその跡目を継いで鈴木姓を名のる。抱一が没するまで師の画風を継承しつつ、新たな近代感覚を盛り込んだ独自の画風を築き上げ、琳派の流れに特異な存在を示した。代表作に「夏秋渓流図屏風」（根津美術館）、「椿・薄図屏風」（フリーア美術館）などがある。

[掲載頁 P178-191]

● **立林何帠**　Tatebayashi Kagei　たてばやし かげい

生没年不詳

　江戸時代中期の画家。名は立徳、別号は金牛山人、喜雨斎など。加賀前田家の侍医を努めたといわれており、のち江戸に出て白井宗謙と改めた。鎌倉に住んで鶴岡逸民とも称している。その伝記はよくわからないが江戸に移っていた尾形乾山に師事し、尾形光琳の宗

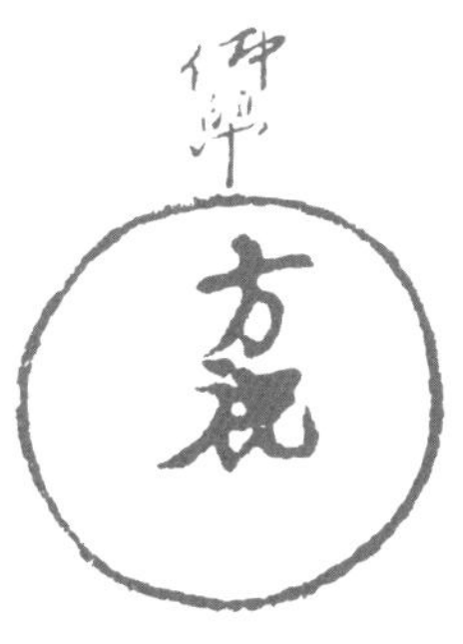

達写扇面画を与えられ、光琳画風の直系を託されたといわれる。また光琳の「方祝」印の使用も許され、光琳三世としてその画風の継承に努めた。酒井抱一、谷文晁ら江戸の文人の間でも、宗達・光琳・乾山の後継者として知られていた。

［掲載頁 P154-157］

◉田中訥言　Tanaka Totsugen　たなか とつげん

明和 4 年〜文政 6 年（1767-1823）

　江戸時代後期の画家。尾張（愛知県）に生まれる。名は痴、字は虎頭、号は大孝斎、痴翁、得中など。京都で土佐光貞に学んだが、のち平安・鎌倉時代の古画の模写を通してやまと絵を研究、その復興を志した。王朝的な主題を扱ったやまと絵風の作品や琳派の手法を取り入れた作品も描いている。

［掲載頁 P260-261］

◉田中抱二　Tanaka Hōji　たなか ほうじ

文化 11 年〜明治 17 年（1814-84）

　江戸後期・明治時代の日本画家。通称は金兵衛、別号は青々庵、鶯居など。江戸両替町の生まれで、酒井抱一に師事した。幕府の御用絵師となり、晩年は向島で隠遁生活を送った。

［掲載頁 P216-219］

◉俵屋宗雪　Tawaraya Sōsetsu　たわらや そうせつ

生没年不詳

　江戸時代前期の画家。俵屋宗達の子とも或は弟、弟子などとも伝えられ、宗達と同じ「伊年」印を用いている。寛永 19 年（1642）以前に法橋（僧侶、絵師などに与えられた称号）となる。加賀金沢藩の前田家の御用絵師になり、慶安 3 年（1650）前田利治の江戸屋敷の襖絵を描く。代表作に「秋草図屏風」（東京国立博物館）などがある。

［掲載頁 P72-77］

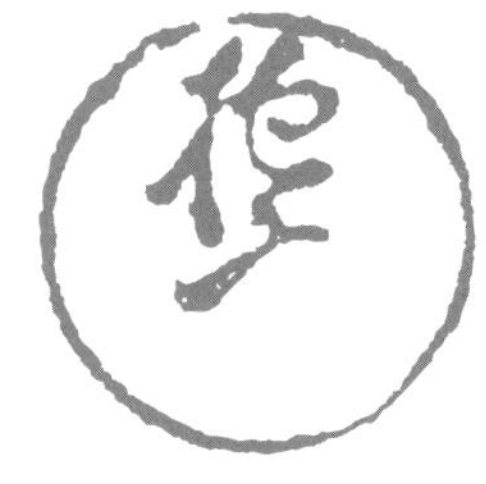

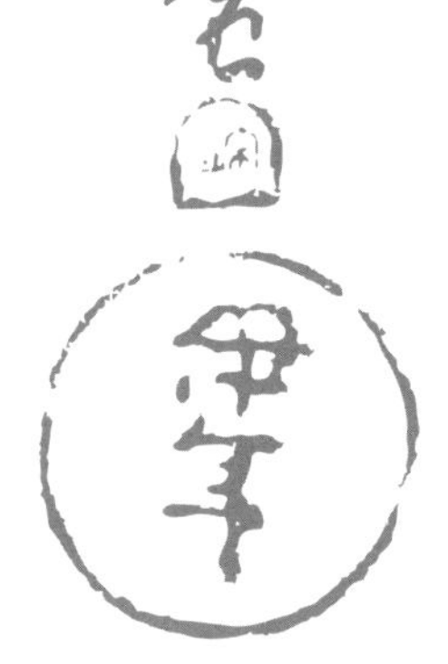

● **俵屋宗達**　Tawaraya Sōtatsu　たわらやそうたつ
生没年不詳

　桃山から江戸時代初期の画家。「伊年」印をもちい、号は対青軒。京都で活躍した町絵師で「俵屋」はその屋号である。宗達の伝記の詳細は不明であるが、絵師として活躍する一方、烏丸光広、千少庵ら当時の公卿や文化人との広い交際があった。扇面や色紙、短冊、巻子など、様々な形式の料紙装飾を手掛ける工房を主宰し、金銀泥を用いた雅で大胆な構図の金地屏風や華麗な料紙装飾に新しい画境を獲得した。また柔らかい筆致とたらし込みの技法で水墨画にも比類ない傑作を残した。元和7年（1621）再建の京都養源院の障壁画を制作した。代表作に「松島図屏風」（フリーア美術館）、「関屋・澪標屏風」（静嘉堂文庫美術館）、「風神雷神図屏風」（建仁寺）などがある。

［掲載頁 P6-7、P34-59］

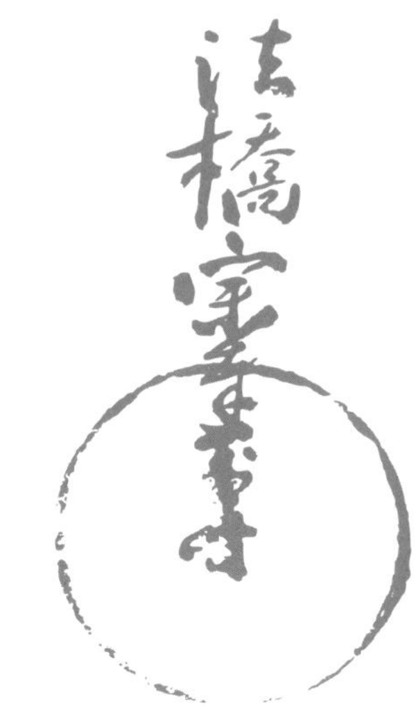

● **俵屋宗理**　Tawaraya Sōri　たわらやそうり
生没年不詳

　江戸時代中期の画家。元知と称し、号は柳々居、百琳。明和・安永年間（1764-81）江戸で活躍した。初め幕府御用絵師の住吉広守に学んだが、のち宗達、光琳の画風に私淑して俵屋宗理を名乗る。作風は光琳風であるが、19世紀になって開花する江戸琳派の先駆者で、代表作は「楓図屏風」など。弟子に葛飾北斎（1760-1849）がおり、一時「宗理」を襲名しているのは興味深い。

［掲載頁 P206-207］

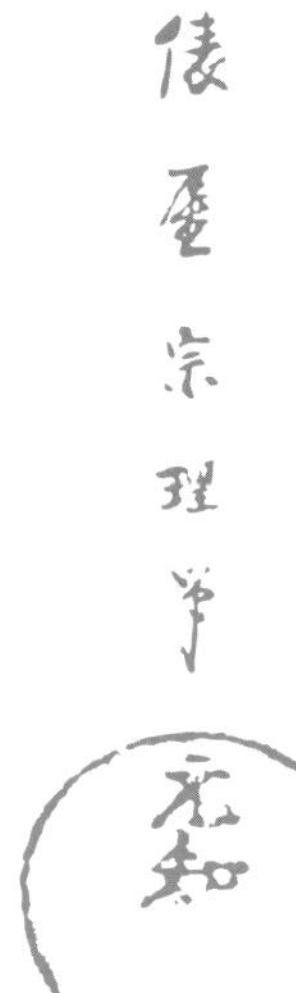

● **土佐光起**　Tosa Mitsuoki　とさみつおき
元和3年〜元禄4年（1617-91）

　江戸時代前期の画家。土佐光則の子。寛永11年（1634）生地の堺から父と共に上京する。承応3年（1654）土佐光元の代に途絶えた宮廷絵所預の職に就き、土佐家の再興を果たす。やまと絵の宗家にふさわしく源氏物語絵や歌仙絵が多く、また中国院体画を学んだことから、花鳥画では漢画とやまと絵を折衷した独自の画風を大成した。

［掲載頁 P248-251］

⦿永田友治　Nagata Yūji　ながた ゆうじ

生没年不詳

　江戸時代中期の蒔絵師。京都の人。号は金書子、青々子。一説に正徳・享保（1711-36）の頃京都で活躍。尾形光琳の作風にならった蒔絵をつくり、錫粉をもちいた高蒔絵の下あげ（下蒔き）を考案し、世に「友治あげ」といった。また色粉をもちいるなどいくつかの新技法を案出した。

［掲載頁 P272］

⦿中村芳中　Nakamura Hōchū　なかむら ほうちゅう

生年不詳〜文政 2 年（?-1819）

　江戸時代後期の画家。京都に生まれ、のちに大坂に移住し活躍した。初め方仲のちに芳仲、温知堂と号した。尾形光琳に私淑し、たらし込みの技法を用いた奈良絵風のユーモラスでほのぼのとした装飾的画風が特徴である。また草花を描いた琳派風作品も多く、特に扇面画を数多く制作している。寛政 11 年（1799）から享和初めにかけて江戸に下り、彩色板本『光琳百譜』を出版した。多くの狂歌本に挿絵を描き、俳諧も好んだと伝えられる。

［掲載頁 P192-199］

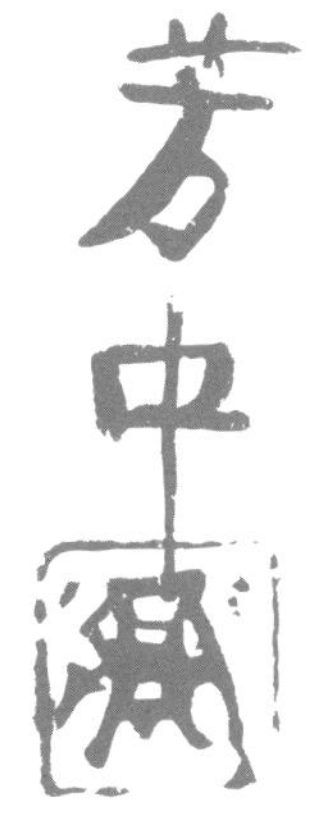

⦿野々村仁清　Nonomura Ninsei　ののむら にんせい

生没年不詳

　江戸時代前期の陶工。丹波国（京都府）野々村（現南丹市）の出身と伝えられ、本名は清右衛門。初め瀬戸に赴き陶業を学び、のち京都に上り作陶を始める。茶人の金森宗和の推挙で洛西の御室仁和寺門前に開窯する。門跡から仁和寺の「仁」と清右衛門の「清」をとった「仁清」の号を賜り、以後これを銘印とした。蒔絵の趣を応用した独特の色絵陶器を得意とし、梅月・藤・吉野山・若松・芥子などの茶壺、梅・牡丹・菊水などの水指、雉子や法螺貝の香炉などが著名で、国宝や重要文化財の指定も多い。寛文・延宝期（1661-81）が円熟期と推定される。作品に「色絵藤花文茶壺」（MOA美術館）などがある。元禄 8 年（1695）には、二代に家督を譲っていた。

［掲載頁 P270-271］

◉深江蘆舟　Fukae Roshū　ふかえ ろしゅう

元禄 12 年〜宝暦 7 年（1699-1757）

　江戸時代中期の画家。京都の銀座方役人、深江庄左衛門の長男。名は庄六、別号は青白堂。恵まれた幼年期を送ったが、正徳 4 年（1714）、16 歳の時父が銀座事件に連座して流罪に処され、蘆舟自身も追放の身となった。その後、父が尾形光琳のパトロン中村内蔵助の同僚であったところから、晩年の光琳に絵を学んだと思われる。のびやかな線描やたらし込みの筆致など光琳に直接師事した様子がうかがわれる。代表作に「蔦の細道図屏風」（東京国立博物館）などがある。

［掲載頁 P150-153］

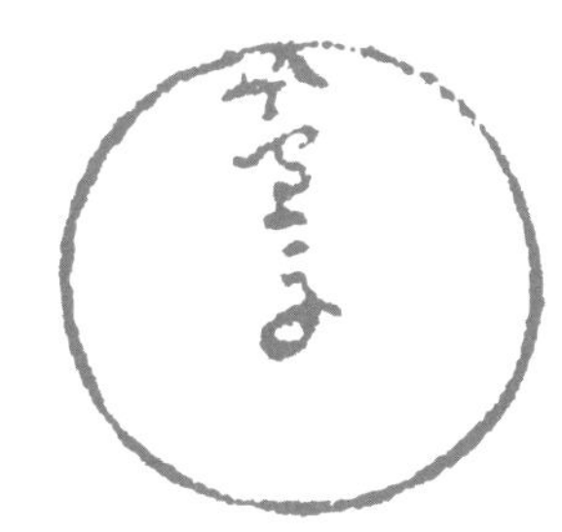

◉本阿弥光悦　Hon'ami Kōetsu　ほんあみ こうえつ

永禄元年〜寛永 14 年（1558-1637）

　桃山から江戸時代初期の芸術家。京都に生まれる。号は徳友斎、太虚庵。足利将軍家にも仕えた本阿弥家の分家筋に生まれ、刀剣の鑑定や研磨を家業とした。書、陶芸、漆工などに秀で、また古典や茶道などの諸芸に通じた幅広い教養を身につけた。特に書は近衛信尹、松花堂昭乗と共に「寛永の三筆」に数えられ、その書風は光悦流と呼ばれる様式をつくりあげた。俵屋宗達とは金銀泥下絵の色紙、和歌巻の共作を通して親しく交わっていたと思われる。元和元年（1615）徳川家康から洛北鷹峰を賜り、一族や工芸家と共に移り住み「光悦村」を開き、晩年は太虚庵を建てて芸術三昧の生涯を送った。

［掲載頁 P26-33］

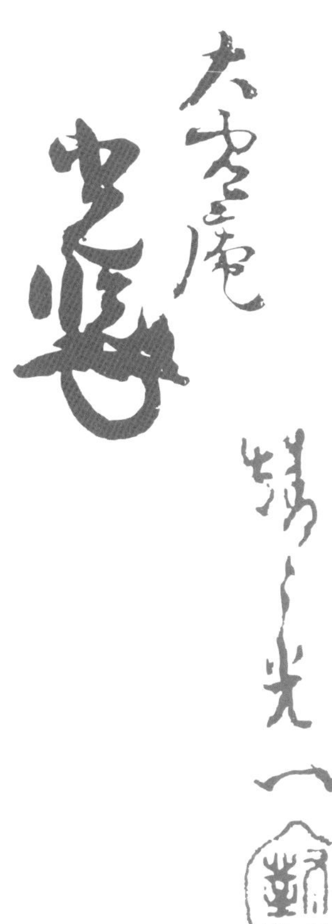

◉山本光一　Yamamoto Kōitsu　やまもと こういつ

天保 4 年〜明治 36 年（1833-1903）

　明治時代の日本画家。東京の生まれで、名を信敬、号は靖々、咬々、露聲、木石閑人などと称した。酒井抱一の弟子である山本素堂の長男で、酒井道一の兄。酒井鶯一の門下で明治年間に活躍した。

［掲載頁 P220-223］

● **渡辺始興**　Watanabe Shikō　わたなべ しこう

天和 3 年〜宝暦 5 年（1683 - 1755）

　江戸時代中期の画家。京都に生まれる。通称は求馬。
25 歳頃から近衛家熙に仕える。また東宮御所や光琳
にゆかりの深い二条家にも出入りしていた。初め山本
素軒や鶴沢探山といった狩野派に学ぶが、のちに光琳
の影響を受けて琳派様式の作品を描いた。また『春日
権現霊験記絵巻』を模写するなどしてやまと絵も学ん
でいる。18 世紀前半の京都にあって、特定の画派や
様式にとらわれず、様々な画風を巧みにこなして一家
をなした。

［掲載頁 P142-149］

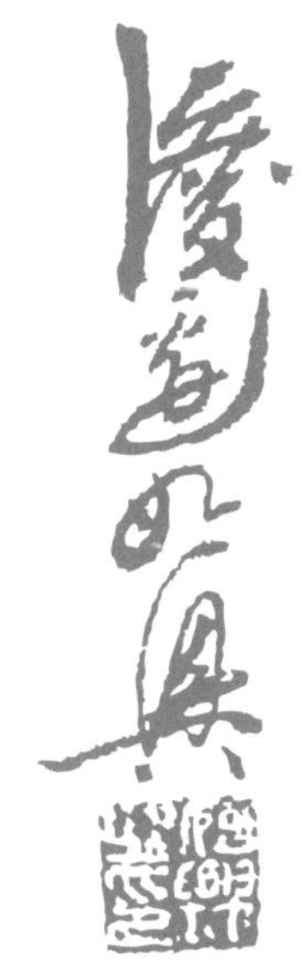

写真・資料掲載協力
（50 音順、敬称略）
Plates Cooperation

石川県立美術館
板橋区立美術館
茨城県立歴史館
MOA 美術館
大阪市立美術館
京都工芸繊維大学美術工芸資料館
京都国立博物館
京都市美術館
京都市立芸術大学芸術資料館
宮内庁京都事務所
宮内庁三の丸尚蔵館
黒部市美術館
群馬県立近代美術館
堺市博物館
佐倉市立美術館
真田宝物館
島根県立美術館
静嘉堂文庫美術館
髙島屋史料館
千葉市美術館
DNP アートコミュニケーションズ
東京藝術大学大学美術館
東京国立博物館
名古屋市博物館
根津美術館
姫路市立美術館
福井県立美術館
福岡市美術館
細見美術館
MIHO MUSEUM
山口県立美術館
大和文華館
今宮神社
建仁寺
三千院門跡
大覚寺
頂妙寺
養源院

参考文献
Bibliography

『宗達と光琳』（日本の美術 18）平凡社　1965
『光悦・宗達・光琳』（水墨美術大系 10）講談社　1975
『琳派』（日本美術全集 21）学習研究社　1979
『近代の琳派　神坂雪佳』京都書院　1981
『光琳百図』岩崎美術社　1981
『瀟洒な装飾美』（花鳥画の世界 5）学習研究社　1981
『幕末の百花譜』（花鳥画の世界 8）学習研究社　1982
『琳派の意匠』（アートジャパネスク日本の美と文化 14）
　　講談社　1982
『光琳鳥類写生帖』（双書美術の泉 56）岩崎美術社　1983
『琳派』紫紅社　1989
『宗達と光琳』江戸の絵画Ⅱ（日本美術全集 18）講談社　1990
『御物』皇室の至宝 2　毎日新聞社　1991
『琳派美術館』集英社　1993
『光琳デザイン』淡交社　2005
『琳派の愉しみ』ランダムハウス講談社　2008
『神坂雪佳の世界』（コロナ・ブックス 140）平凡社　2008
創立百年記念特別展「琳派」東京国立博物館 1972
特別展「烏丸光広と俵屋宗達」板橋区立美術館　1982
日本の美「琳派」宗達・光琳・抱一から現代まで
　　福岡市美術館　1989
日本の美「琳派」展　1996
没後 90 年記念「浅井忠展」京都新聞社　1998
「美し　乾山　四季彩菜」MIHO MUSEUM　2004
「京琳派　神坂雪佳展」宗達、光琳から雪佳へ　2006
「乾山の芸術と光琳」2007
尾形光琳生誕 350 周年記念「大琳派展　継承と変奏」東京
　　国立博物館　2008
「光琳」（日本の美術 53）至文堂　1970
「琳派百図」別冊太陽　平凡社　1974
「芸術新潮」2005 年 10 月号　新潮社
「琳派とデザイン」装飾・かざり（日本の美術 464）
　　至文堂　2005
「BRUTUS」2008 年 10 月 15 日号　マガジンハウス　2008
「琳派」美術手帖 2008 年 10 月号　美術出版社

Decorative Japanese Painting
The Rinpa Aesthetic in Japanese Art

Text by Seijinsha and Toshinobu Yasumura
Translated by The Word Works and Tamayo Samejima
Designed by Rieko Tanihira
Proofreading by Hakuhosha and Ouraido
English translation proofreading by Hironori Kadowaki

PIE International Inc.
2-32-4 Minami-Otsuka, Toshima-ku, Tokyo 170-0005 JAPAN
international@pie.co.jp
www.pie.co.jp/english

ISBN978-4-7562-5311-8 (Outside Japan)

Printed in Japan

日本の図像

琳派［新装版］

Decorative Japanese Painting
The Rinpa Aesthetic in Japanese Art

2020 年 2 月 16 日　初版第 1 刷発行

企画・編集・解説：濱田信義（編集室　青人社）
解説：安村敏信（北斎館館長）
翻訳：マクレリー　ルシー（ザ・ワード・ワークス）、鮫島圭代
デザイン：谷平理映子（SPICE design）
校閲：株式会社白鳳社、株式会社鷗来堂
英文校正：門脇弘典
制作進行：宮城鈴香（PIE International）

Text by Seijinsha and Toshinobu Yasumura
Translated by The Word Works and Tamayo Samejima
Designed by Rieko Tanihira
Proofreading by Hakuhosha and Ouraido
English translation proofreading by Hironori Kadowaki

発行人　三芳寛要
発行元　株式会社 パイ インターナショナル
〒 170-0005　東京都豊島区南大塚 2-32-4
TEL 03-3944-3981　FAX 03-5395-4830
sales@pie.co.jp

PIE International Inc.
2-32-4 Minami-Otsuka, Toshima-ku, Tokyo 170-0005 JAPAN
international@pie.co.jp

印刷・製本：アベイズム株式会社

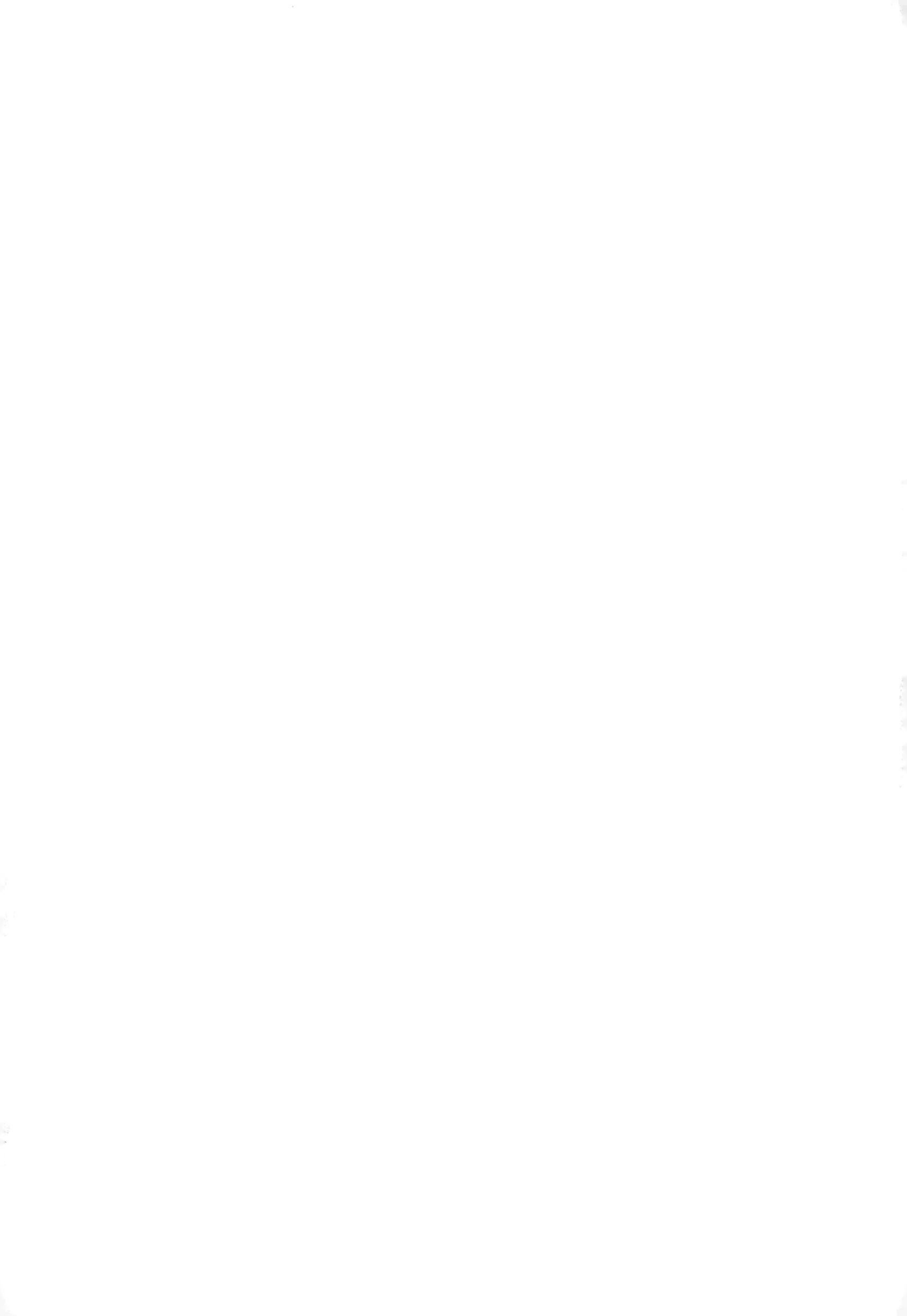

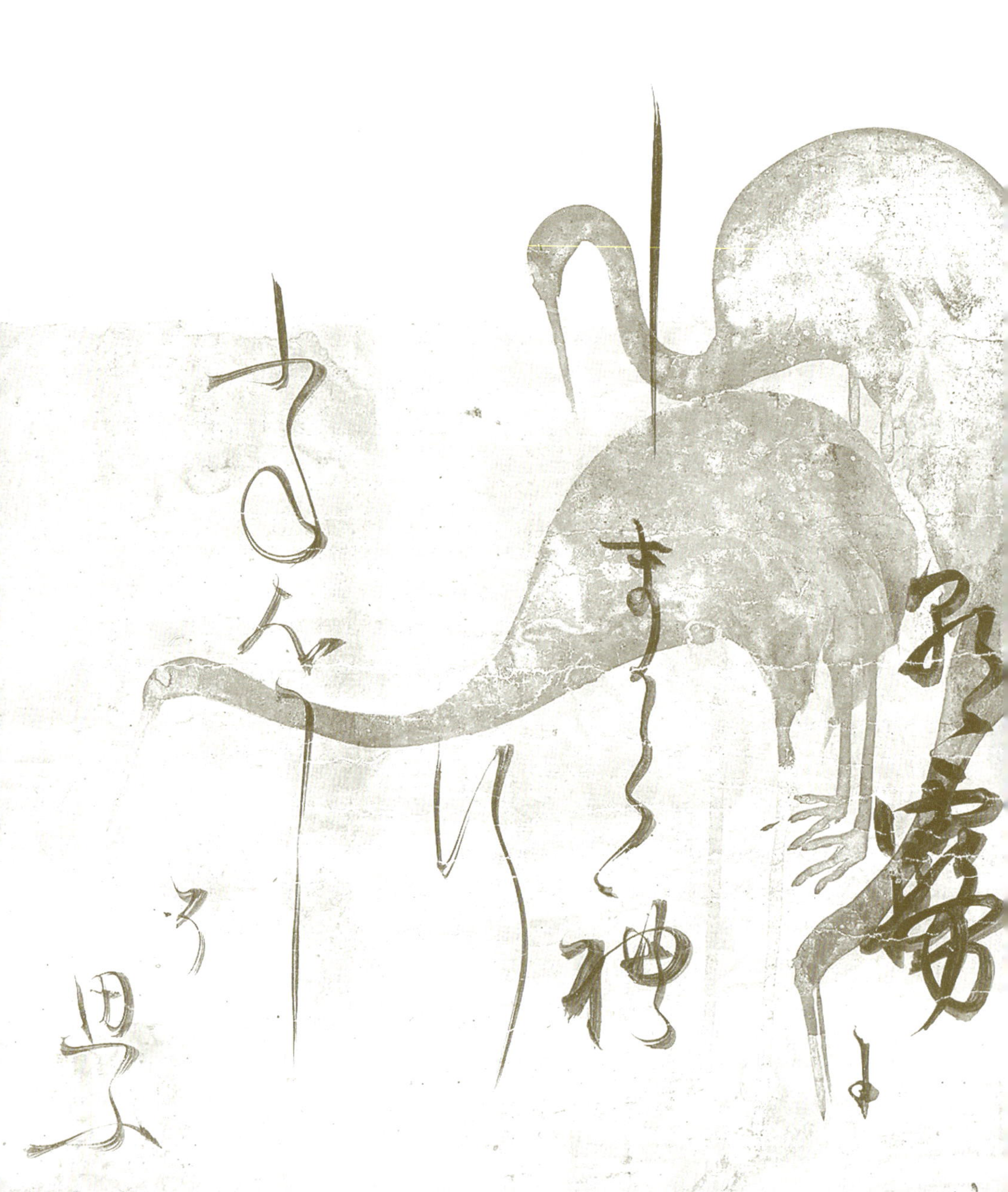